MEASUREMENT
and EVALUATION
IN EDUCATION AND PSYCHOLOGY

Second Edition

WILLIAM A. MEHRENS
Michigan State University

IRVIN J. LEHMANN
Michigan State University

HOLT, RINEHART AND WINSTON
*New York   Chicago   San Francisco   Dallas
Montreal   Toronto   London   Sydney*

Portions of this book appeared in *Standardized Tests in Education* by the same authors, ©
1969 by Holt, Rinehart and Winston, Inc.; © 1975 by Holt, Rinehart and Winston.

Library of Congress Cataloging in Publication Data

Mehrens, William A
  Measurement and evaluation in education and psychology.

  Bibliography: p. 705
  1. Educational Tests and measurements. 2. Mental
tests. I. Lehmann, Irvin J., joint author.
II. Title.
LB1131.M438 1978   371.2′6   77-25821
ISBN 0-03-089966-4

PREFACE

Educators have always been concerned with measuring and evaluating the progress of their students. As the goals of education have become more complex, and with the increasing demand by all parts of our citizenry—pupils, parents, taxpayers, and other decision makers—for accountability on the part of educators, these tasks of measurement and evaluation have become more difficult. Increased criticism of the quality of our educational product—students who are unable to read, students who are unable to write effectively, students who lack a knowledge of the fundamental arithmetical processes—as well as of the teaching-learning methods employed in our schools and colleges behooves us more than ever before to be concerned with valid and reliable measures of our educational product. The area of educational measurement and evaluation can, very broadly, be divided into two areas: the construction, evaluation, and use of teacher-made classroom tests and of standardized tests. This text covers both broad areas. In addition, it covers auxiliary topics related to the informed use of measurement.

Measurement and Evaluation in Education and Psychology can serve as the main text in the first course in measurement and evaluation at either the undergraduate or graduate level. The major focus of the text remains unchanged from the first edition. This is so, in part, because the original text has been well received by our students and colleagues. Just as important, however, is the fact that the basic principles involved in the construction, selection, evaluation, interpretation, and use of tests have not changed much since the first edition was published. Nevertheless, this revision should not be construed as only an updating of the first edition. Changes have been made both in organization and relative emphases of topics. And there have been, as one would expect, changes made with respect to those selections that hindsight reveals to be deserving of expansion, modification, or deletion. Among these are the following:

- An expansion of the discussion of validity;
- An expansion of the discussion of measurement in the affective domain;
- An expansion of the discussion of test bias;
- An expansion of the discussion of career awareness and development inventories;

- A modification and updating of the discussion of criterion-referenced measurement;
- A deletion of several formulas and theoretical concepts;
- A deletion of several brief test reviews.

The basic rationale behind this text is that educational decisions must be based on information, that this information should be accurate, and that the responsibility of gathering, using, and imparting that information belongs to educators. The contents of this book are based on the authors' conviction that there are certain knowledges, skills, and understandings for which classroom teachers, counselors, and school administrators should be held accountable in order to meet the responsibilities listed above. The selection of topics and the coverage given them have benefited from the advice of many colleagues. At all times the needs of educators have been kept foremost in mind.

No formal course work in either testing or statistics is necessary to understand the text. When we felt that the topic being presented could not be treated without some theoretical background, we attempted to present a simple but clear treatment of the theory. When we felt that the topic being discussed did not require a full theoretical treatment, we chose to omit the erudition.

The book is divided into five major parts. At the beginning of every chapter we present a set of 10 to 15 objectives stated as general outcomes. Some teachers may prefer to develop more specific behavioral objectives to aid in instructional planning. They are, of course, free to do so. In Unit I we have an introductory chapter in which we briefly discuss the relationship between information gathering and educational decision making and present a classification of purposes of measurement and evaluation. Chapter 2 is completely devoted to the role of objectives in educational evaluation. It covers the need for objectives and methods of determining and stating them. Chapter 3 covers Norm- and Criterion-Referenced Measurement.

Unit II covers some basic principles of measurement. It should be easier to read than Unit II of the first edition. We have deleted several formulas and extended some discussions. Chapter 4 covers methods of describing educational data. Chapter 5 covers reliability and validity. Chapter 6 discusses norms, types of scores, and profiles. Some readers of this text may wish to skip (or only skim) several sections of Chapter 5. The sections under reliability on "Estimating True Scores" and "Reliability of Difference Scores" are more technical than the rest of the chapter, and understanding of them is not necessary to comprehend the other material.

Unit III is on teacher-constructed measurement procedures. Chapter 7 is an overview of teacher-constructed tests. Chapter 8 is on essay test construction, Chapters 9 and 10 are on objective test construction. Chapter 11 discusses procedures for analyzing, evaluating, and revising teacher-constructed instruments. Chapter 12 covers other teacher-constructed devices such as rating scales, observational techniques, anecdotal records, and peer appraisal.

A new section has been added on measurement in the affective domain. Numerous examples of both poor and good test items have been provided in this unit to help illustrate the various test construction principles discussed.

Unit IV covers professionally constructed (standardized) measuring procedures. Chapter 13 presents an overview of standardized instruments. Chapters 14–16 cover aptitude, achievement, and noncognitive measures respectively. Some brief reviews of standardized tests and inventories are provided to familiarize the potential test user with the diversity of tests available. Critiques have also been provided to alert users of tests to the factors they must consider when selecting a test and using its results. At no time should it be considered that the tests reviewed are necessarily the best tests available—they are only exemplars. In addition, the reader is *not* expected to remember the many specifics discussed. Why then, one might ask, should we discuss them? To give the reader some acquaintance with the different kinds of standardized tests available to educators and how they should be evaluated. We have tried to evaluate the various tests critically, pointing out their strengths and weaknesses, so that the user will have some general notion as to what questions should be asked when he selects a test; how he should interpret the information presented in the test manual regarding the test's psychometric problems; and what this test has to offer, if anything, over other available tests. To derive maximum value from these brief test descriptions, we strongly urge the reader to have a copy of the test and manual available. Finally, examples are provided to illustrate how test results can be used in making educational decisions.

Instructors stressing teacher-made tests might wish to only skim Unit IV. Instructors stressing standardized tests could skip over Unit III.

Unit V includes three chapters: Chapter 17 on marking and reporting, Chapter 18 on accountability, program evaluation, and evaluation programs (local, state, and national), and Chapter 19 on some public concerns and future trends of educational evaluation.

We would like to thank all those who have assisted us in the revision of this book. Comments from students and instructors who used the first edition as well as comments from several anonymous reviewers of the revised manuscript were of considerable benefit. Dick Owen, Holt education editor, and Brian Heald, Holt project editor, assisted in many details and we thank them for their very competent and cordial professional help. Finally, we would like to thank our typists for their patient and conscientious typing job. Any errors of fact or awkward phrasings that remain are, however, the responsibility of the authors.

East Lansing, Michigan   W. A. M.
                                                                                                              I. J. L.

CONTENTS

EVALUATION IN EDUCATION

UNIT 1

CHAPTER ONE

Introduction to Measurement and Evaluation

Decisions, decisions, decisions! The world is full of decisions. And to make decisions, one needs information. The role of measurement is to provide accurate and relevant information to assist in wise decision making. Both educators and psychologists have been concerned with measurement as a necessary component in both research and practical decision making. The whole field of differential psychology is based on the fact that individuals differ, that these differences are important, and that we need to measure these differences and use this information in dealing with people. Educators particularly have been, are now, and will continue to be concerned with measuring and evaluating the progress of their students, the value and relevance of the curriculum, and the effectiveness of their teaching. As the goals of education have become more complex, and as the numbers of students have increased enormously, this task has become much more difficult.

As many writers have pointed out, we live in an age of crises. Education, along with other institutions in our society, has attempted to meet both the real and the perceived crises with revisions of existing programs and the innovation of other ones. Indeed, reconstruction of the total educational system has often been suggested and occasionally attempted.[1] Much of the responsibility for improving our society has been placed squarely on the shoulders of educators. Seemingly for every existing social ill there exists someone who strongly advocates that the responsibility for the solution lies with education. Thus it is exciting, yet awesome, to be an educator.

Education is the most important enterprise in our society. Every citizen is in some way directly involved with education. More than one-third of the nation's population attends school. Education is truly a giant and important enterprise, and therefore it is crucial that we evaluate its processes and products. In fact, evaluation is a major consideration in the schools of the 1970s. Why evaluate? For one reason, taxpayers are beginning to demand an accounting. If they expend all that money, they want to know the results. In 1973, the nation's longest teacher strike (in Detroit) centered primarily on the issue of accountability. (We will talk more about accountability in Chapter 18.) Another reason is that students, teachers, administrators, and parents all work hard toward achieving educational goals, and it is only natural that they should want to ascertain the degree to which those goals have been realized. Just the satisfaction of knowing, the removal of ignorance, is an important reason for evaluation. But these reasons must take second and third place to a far more important reason. *Measurement and evaluation are essential to sound educational decision making.*

We recognize that some educators and psychologists have somewhat negative feelings toward measurement and evaluation. While God evaluated His work and saw that it was "very good,"[2] the critics of evaluation may prefer another Biblical quote: "Do not criticize one another. . . . Who do you think you are, to judge your fellow man?" (James 4:11 and 12). Glass (1975) discusses the paradox that people may be opposed to evaluation, yet favor excellence where excellence is facilitated by evaluation. He has posed the following two questions to colleagues to point out the paradox:

"Would you show a judgmental-evaluative attitude toward a person whom you were counseling?"

"Would you show a judgmental-evaluative attitude toward a person if you sought to improve his performance as a professional or an employee?"

The typical answer to the first question is no and the second is yes. Yet counselors as well as other educators should be seeking to improve others'

---

[1] Unfortunately, many new or revised programs have not been evaluated. Educators tend toward hasty endorsement of a new procedure or program without attempting to determine its usefulness.

[2] Gen. 1: 1–31.

performances. When Glass asked his colleagues if they sensed an inconsistency, they admitted they did. One of our major goals is to assist you in recognizing that the purposes of measurement and evaluation are good—not bad. Again measurement and evaluation are essential to sound educational decision making.

In this chapter we will (1) define some terms, (2) discuss the role of information in educational decision making, and (3) present some classifications of purposes of measurement and evaluation.

After studying this chapter you should be able to—

1. Define and differentiate the terms "test," "measurement," and "evaluation."
2. Recognize that measurement and evaluation are essential to sound educational decision making.
3. Understand the components of a model of decision making.
4. Classify the purposes of measurement and evaluation.
5. Recognize the ways measurement and evalaution can assist in instructional, guidance, administrative, and research decisions.

DEFINITIONS: TEST, MEASUREMENT, AND EVALUATION

The terms *test*, *measurement*, and *evaluation* are sometimes used interchangeably, but some users make distinctions among them. The term *test* is usually considered the narrowest of the three items. *Test*, in the narrowest sense, connotes the presentation of a standard set of questions to be answered. As a result of a person's answers to such a series of questions, we obtain a measure (that is, a numerical value) of a characteristic of that person. *Measurement* often connotes a broader concept: We can measure characteristics in ways other than by giving tests. Using observations, rating scales, or any other device that allows us to obtain information in a quantitative form is measurement. Also, measurement can refer to both the score obtained and the process used.

Evaluation has recently been defined in a variety of ways. Stufflebeam et al. (1971, p. xxv) stated that evaluation is *"the process of delineating, obtaining, and providing useful information for judging decision alternatives."* This is perhaps one of the broader definitions currently in vogue. Used in this way, it encompasses but goes beyond the meaning of the terms test and measurement. A second popular concept of evaluation interprets it as the determination of the congruence between performance and objectives. Other definitions simply categorize evaluation as professional judgment or as a process that allows one to make a judgment about the desirability or value of a measure.

To evaluate, then, following approaches of the second or third definition, would require that we have a goal or objective in mind. In education we do occasionally gather data that are not measures of specific educational goals but are gathered instead to help us make decisions about what goals should be set or what instructional procedures should be employed to reach the goals. When we gather data regarding a person's interests or personality characteristics, for example, we may not be doing that for the purpose of placing a value judgment on the data. Yet we are evaluating in the Stufflebeam sense of the term. Thus, Stufflebeam's broader definition seems preferable. Even in the area of subject-matter achievement, measurement is not the same as evaluation. Two students may obtain the same measure (test score) but we might evaluate those measures differently. Suppose, at the end of fifth grade, we have two students who are both reading at the fifth-grade level. However, at the beginning of the year, one student was reading at the third-grade level, and one at the fourth-grade, fifth-month level. Our evaluations of those outcomes are not the same. One student progressed at an above-average rate, and the other at a below-average rate.

Also, it is important to point out that we *never* measure or evaluate *people*. We measure or evaluate *characteristics* or *properties* of people: their scholastic potential, knowledge of algebra, honesty, perseverance, ability to teach, and so forth. This is *not* to be confused with evaluating the worth of a person. Teachers, parents, and students do not always seem to keep this distinction clearly in mind.

INFORMATION GATHERING AND EDUCATIONAL DECISION MAKING

The direct involvement of everyone in education means that every person must at some time make *educational decisions.* Some educational decisions will affect many people (for example, federal decisions regarding funding of mammoth projects); others, only a single person (Johnny's decision not to review his spelling list). There are many decisions that educators must make, and many more that they must assist individual pupils, parents, and the general public in making. Should Susan be placed in an advanced reading group? Should Johnny take algebra or general mathematics next year? Should the school continue using the mathematics textbook adopted this year, revert back to the previous text, or try still another one? Is grammar being stressed at the expense of pronunciation in first-year German? Am I doing as well in my chemistry as I should? Have I been studying the right material? Should I go to college? These are just a few of the types of questions and decisions facing educators, parents, and students. Whoever makes a decision, and whether the decision be great or small, it should be based on as much and as accurate information as possible. The more, and the more accurate, the information on which a decision is based, the better that decision is likely to be. In fact, many scholars who study decision making define a good decision as one that is based on all *relevant* information.

Educators have the important responsibilities of (1) determining what information needs to be obtained, (2) obtaining accurate information, and (3) imparting that information in readily understood terms to the persons responsible for making the decisions—whether students, parents, teachers, college admissions officers, the Secretary of the Department of Health, Education and Welfare, or judges. The philosophy, knowledges, and skills that are covered in this book should assist the educator in fulfilling such responsibilities. This book, in general, deals with the development of information-gathering techniques and information that the teacher, counselor, administrator, student, parent, and all those concerned with the teaching–learning process need to make the soundest educational decisions possible. This brief introductory section is intended to focus the reader's attention on the basic notions that *educational decisions* must be made, that these decisions should be based on *information*, that this information should be *accurate*, and that the responsibility of gathering and imparting that information belongs to educators.

But, some people argue, shouldn't we be using test data to enhance learning instead of making decisions? Would not this be more humanistic? Such a reaction indicates a misunderstanding. Of course, the primary role of schools is to enhance learning. Tests should and do assist in this, but only by using the test data to make decisions—decisions about what and how to teach, decisions about what and how to study, and so on. Test data will not enhance learning unless we use the data to guide us in subsequent actions, in other words, in using the data for decision making. In the remainder of this chapter we will discuss the basics of decision theory, and some specific purposes of measurement and evaluation.

DECISION THEORY

We have stated that accurate, relevant information is necessary for good decision making. Physiologists, economists, political scientists, educational administrative theorists, and others have been studying the whole process of decision making and have built various models describing how people should make decisions. Although these models vary somewhat in detail, they have several things in common: A person making a decision should be aware of (1) all the alternatives, (2) the possible outcomes of every alternative, and (3) the probabilities and utilities of those outcomes. The more information one has about these variables, the better the decision is likely to be. The decision-making process portrayed by the model is time consuming, but is less expensive in the long run than the result of making poor decisions. Actually, most decision theorists would not suggest that people follow consciously the steps proposed in a decision-making model. But the underlying principles of good decision making would incorporate gathering information on alternatives, outcomes, and the probabilities and utilities of these outcomes.

Certainly, no single course in educational measurement can teach you how to obtain all the information needed to make all the decisions with which you will be confronted as educators, but it can be of considerable help. It can suggest principles and methods of deciding what information would be useful for various decisions and how this information should be gathered. If these principles and methods are applied, it is more likely that the information gathered will be accurate and useful. Numerous existing tests and inventories can be used to gather important data, particularly with regard to the probabilities of alternative courses of action, and there are limitations of measurement data that users should know about.

A CLASSIFICATION OF PURPOSES
OF MEASUREMENT AND EVALUATION

Schutz (1971) has written an entertaining but very thought-provoking article on whether the role of measurement in education is that of servant, soul mate, stool pigeon, statesman, or scapegoat—all of these or none of them. One could build a case for any of the roles as being the "correct answer." Merwin (1973) presented a classification scheme based on measurement of *what* of *who* by *whom* to *what*. Examples of purposes of educational measurement following his approach are presented in Table 1–1. This list could be expanded almost indefinitely. His categorization scheme certainly helps one realize that the purposes of measurement are quite diverse.

We find it useful to consider the purposes of measurement in terms of decisions that must be made. It is helpful in conceptualizing these decisions to classify them in some fashion. One way is to classify decisions as either *institutional* or *individual* decisions. *Institutional decisions are ones in which a large number of comparable decisions are made. Individual decisions are ones where the choice confronting the decision maker will rarely or never recur.* In education, institutional decisions are typically those made by school personnel concerning students (for example, grouping and college admissions). Individual decisions are typically those the individual makes about himself[3] (for example, vocational choice). At times, institutional decision making will restrict individual decision making. (For example, when a college does not admit a student who would like to attend.)

Another way to classify educational decisions is by kind: *instructional*, *guidance*, *administrative*, or *research*. These categories are, of course, somewhat arbitrary and overlapping. If a decision is made that programmed texts are to be used in all ninth-grade algebra classes, it might be considered either an instructional or an administrative decision. Ordinarily, instructional decisions are thought of as decisions that affect activities that occur in a particular classroom, and administrative decisions as those that affect activities in the total school building.

[3] For clarity and economy, we use the masculine form of pronouns throughout this text when no specific gender is implied. We hope the reader will impute no sexist motives; none is intended.

TABLE 1-1   Educational Measurement

EDUCATIONAL MEASUREMENT OF ____ OF ____ BY ____ TO ____.

1. Educational measurement of *academic achievement* of *a student* by *a teacher to aid in selecting a learning experience.*
2. Educational measurement of *individual differences* of *students* by *a teacher to aid in selecting the most effective of alternative learning experiences for each.*
3. Educational measurement of *vocational interests* of *a student* by *that student to help in planning an academic program.*
4. Educational measurement of *the gain in level of achievement* of *a group of students* by *a teacher to determine the effectiveness of a learning experience.*
5. Educational measurement of *the efficiency* of *a curriculum* by *a curriculum team to help determine whether it is preferable to alternative curricula.*
6. Educational measurement of *the potential value* of *a course* by *a student to assist in arriving at a decision as to whether or not to enroll.*
7. Educational measurement of *levels of achievement* of *groups of students* by *a legislative body to aid in allocation of funds.*
8. Educational measurement of *accomplishment* of *a teacher* by *an administrator to assist in arriving at a recommendation regarding continued employment.*
9. Educational measurement of *the needs* of *a school system* by *taxpayers to aid in marking a ballot on a bond issue.*
10. Educational measurement of *attitudes* of *teachers* by *a student to aid in selecting among sections of a course.*
11. Educational measurement of *the potential effectiveness* of *schools* by *parents to aid them in selecting a school in which to enroll their child.*
12. Educational measurement of *parents' perceptions* of *school programs* by *an administrator to aid in planning information dissemination activities.*

Source: From Jack C. Merwin, "Educational Measurement of What Characteristic of Whom (or What), by Whom and Why?" Presidential address to the 1972 National Council on Measurement in Education. *Journal of Educational Measurement*, Volume 10 No. 1, Spring 1973, p. 4. Copyright 1973, National Council on Measurement in Education, Inc., East Lansing, Michigan. Reprinted by special permission.

Instructional Decisions

The major role of the school and the individual classroom teacher is to facilitate certain types of student learning. The teacher should *encourage* those activities that promote desirable student learning and *discourage* those that do not. Sometimes teachers feel that evaluation is the antithesis of instruction—that somehow the role of evaluator is at odds with the role of a stimulator and promoter of learning (Lindgren, 1967, p. 426). That is not necessarily true, even if evaluation is defined narrowly as judging. It certainly is never true under the broader definition of evaluation. Evaluation incorrectly done is at odds with the promotion of learning. Evaluation correctly done should enhance learning because it aids both the teacher in teaching and the student in learning. Dressel (1954), a leading evaluator, depicts the relation-

TABLE 1–2   Relationship between Instruction and Evaluation

INSTRUCTION	EVALUATION
1. Instruction is effective when it leads to desired changes in students.	1. Evaluation is effective when it provides evidence of the extent of the changes in students.
2. New behavioral patterns are best learned by students when the inadequacy of present behavior is understood and the significance of the new behavioral patterns thereby made clear.	2. Evaluation is most conducive to learning when it provides for and encourages self-evaluation.
3. New behavioral patterns can be more efficiently developed by teachers who know the existing behavioral patterns of individual students and the reasons for them.	3. Evaluation is conducive to good instruction when it reveals major types of inadequate behavior and the contributory causes.
4. Learning is encouraged by problems and activities that require thought and/or action by each individual student.	4. Evaluation is most significant in learning when it permits and encourages the exercise of individual initiative.
5. Activities that provide the basis for the teaching and learning of specified behavior are also the most suitable activities for evoking and evaluating the adequacy of that behavior.	5. Activities or exercises developed for the purpose of evaluating specified behavior are also useful for the teaching and learning of that behavior.

SOURCE: From "Evaluation as Instruction" by Paul L. Dressel. *Proceedings of the 1953 Invitational Conference on Testing Problems.* Copyright 1954 by Educational Testing Service. Adapted and reproduced by permission.

ship between instruction and evaluation presented in Table 1–2. The Joint Committee of the American Association of School Administrators stated that "to teach without testing is unthinkable" (1962, p. 9). Parnell (1973, p. 2698) states it well:

> Measurement is the hand-maiden of instruction. Without measurement, there cannot be evaluation. Without evaluation, there cannot be feedback. Without feedback, there cannot be good knowledge of results. Without knowledge of results, there cannot be systematic improvement in learning.

Measurement and evaluation can help both the teacher and the student. Let us look at both aspects more carefully.

MEASUREMENT AND EVALUATION HELP THE TEACHER

As stated above, the major role of the school is to facilitate learning. The kinds of changes we wish to obtain in pupils are commonly referred to as *objectives*, or goals. The means we employ to help pupils realize the objectives constitute *instruction*. The *evaluation procedures* are the means of determining the extent to which the instruction has been effective. There is a definite relationship among instruction, objectives, and evaluation. Schematically, we can represent this relationship as follows (Furst, 1958, p. 3):

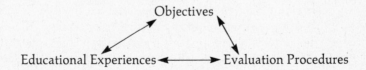

Tentative, preliminary objectives determine the instructional procedures to be used and the method to be used to evaluate both educational experiences and objectives. At the same time, evaluation and educational experiences help clarify the objectives, and the learning experiences help determine the evaluative procedure to be used. Moreover, the results of our evaluation provide feedback on the effectiveness of the teaching experience and ultimately on the attainability of the objectives for each student.

There are several ways, then, in which evaluation procedures aid the teacher: (1) they help in providing knowledge concerning the students' entry behaviors; (2) they help in setting, refining, and clarifying realistic goals for each student; (3) they help in evaluating the degree to which the objectives have been achieved; and (4) they help in determining, evaluating, and refining his instructional techniques.

The importance of readiness for learning is a well-accepted fact. To teach effectively we must find out where a student is, and start from there. We should have estimates of the student's capacity for learning, as well as estimates of what he currently knows. We cannot, for example, teach long division to a student who cannot subtract. To be effective teachers, we must be aware of what our students already know.

There are many ways we can obtain data about entry behavior. Aptitude tests provide general information concerning the speed and ease with which a student can be expected to learn. Achievement tests provide information as to whether a student is weak or strong in a subject-matter area. For more specific information regarding the deficiency, diagnostic instruments are needed. Knowledge obtained from previous teachers also assists in determining entry behavior. These various instruments and techniques will be discussed more in later chapters. The major point we wish to make here is that good instruction does take into account what an individual knows or does not know at the beginning of instruction. It is inefficient—and perhaps even damaging to the individual—to place him at too high or low a step in an instructional sequence. This determination of entry skills should occur every time one is considering a new unit of instruction.

Measurement and evaluation also aid the teacher in setting, refining, and clarifying realistic goals for each student. Knowledge of the entry behavior discussed in the preceding paragraph obviously helps in the setting of realistic goals. The very act of building a measurement–evaluation device and carefully looking at the outcomes should help in refining and clarifying these goals. Nothing is quite so helpful in forcing a teacher to think through his goals carefully as is the act of constructing or choosing measuring devices. To determine what behaviors will be observed in order to ascertain whether goals have been reached requires careful consideration of these goals.

After administering an instrument following an instructional unit, one can make some judgment about how realistic the goals were, and can also make some judgments about the degree to which the instructional objectives had been achieved and the effectiveness of the instructional procedure. For example, if a third-grade teacher used the Cuisenaire method for teaching arithmetic, knowledge about the degree of student success would be necessary to evaluate the efficacy of that method. Program evaluation is a complicated topic. It relates to instructional, administrative, and research uses of measurement and evaluation. We will discuss this topic further in Chapter 18. However, we would like to point out here that teachers can use the results of evaluation to improve their classroom procedures. Such techniques as preparing an analysis of the errors on classroom tests (described in Chapter 11) and looking carefully at the results of standardized achievement tests (Chapter 15) can give good clues to the teacher regarding strengths and weaknesses in his instruction.

MEASUREMENT AND EVALUATION HELP THE STUDENT

Measurement and evaluation aid the student by (1) communicating the teacher's goals, (2) increasing motivation, (3) encouraging good study habits, and (4) providing feedback that identifies strengths and weaknesses.

Of course, the goals of instruction should be communicated to students well in advance of any evaluation. Students are much more apt to learn what we deem important if they know our thinking. But if we never evaluated to find out whether our objectives were being achieved, the students might well become cynical about what our goals really are, or indeed whether we have set any. Valid examinations during and at the end of a course are very effective ways of convincing the students as to our objectives. Occasionally, people will criticize testing because the student tries to "psych out the teacher" and learn what the teacher thinks is important. This criticism seems to assume that it is better if students do not bother trying to ascertain the teacher's objectives! Also, when the teacher's goals are communicated, this gives the students an opportunity to have input into the instructional goals. Once these goals are stated and understood, they become the "property" of the students, and this serves to increase their motivation.

Knowing that one's performance is to be evaluated also increases motivation, which facilitates learning. Some have argued that we should not have to resort to measurement techniques (such as testing) in order to motivate students. They argue that learning should be fun and that the intrinsic joy of learning is more desirable than extrinsic motivation. However, as Ebel (1972, p. 42) pointed out, "no choice need be made between extrinsic and intrinsic motivation." Learning should be fun, but this does not mean that measurement and evaluation are bad. In fact, learning is apt to be made even more fun and intrinsic motivation (as well as extrinsic motivation) should increase if students realize that their efforts and achievements are being recognized. Realists, though, are aware that striving toward excellence in any endeavor is not all fun. The professional baseball player does not play ball just for fun. The extrinsic factors of money, fame, and fear of losing a job exist in real life. Without extrinsic motivation many people would not work so hard or accomplish so much. The same is true of students. This may not be an ideal aspect of the world, but it is a realistic one.

One aspect of good study habits is frequent review. Frequent evaluation encourages this study habit. Another important aspect of learning is that the student must be aware of his strengths and weaknesses. Evaluation, and subsequent feedback to the student regarding the evaluation, can play a big role in guiding the student's future efforts. In recent years there has been an increasing awareness of the importance of feedback to students as well as teaching students self-evaluation (see Wilhelms, 1967, chap. 1). Of course, there are always a few educators who argue that we should not evaluate—or at least not communicate the results of the evaluation—because it might harm a pupil's self-concept. This is faulty reasoning. There is no good evidence that accurate feedback damages students' self-concepts, but there is much evidence that such feedback improves subsequent performance. Going over tests constructed by the classroom teacher is an extremely good technique for providing for both feedback and a learning experience. Even the experience of taking a test facilitates learning. Stroud stated:

> It is probably not extravagant to say that the contribution made to a student's store of knowledge by the taking of an examination is as great, minute for minute, as any other enterprise he engages in (Stroud, 1946, p. 476).

This may be particularly true if a student is using an answer sheet that provides immediate feedback as to the correctness of the answer. In summary, then, students learn while studying for the test, while taking the test, and while going over the test after it is completed.

Guidance Decisions

Students need to be guided in their vocational choice, in their educational program, and in their personal problems. What course should Sharon take in tenth grade? Should she improve her study skills? In what should she major in college? What should she do after graduation from college? Should she try to become less aggressive, more orderly, more independent, and more nurturant? For students to make sound decisions in these areas it is crucial that they have accurate self-concepts. Students depend, in part, upon the school to help them form those self-concepts. Tests of aptitude and achievement, and interest and personality inventories, provide students with data about significant characteristics, which can help them develop realistic self-concepts. The classroom teacher can help also, particularly in providing the student with information concerning his mastery of subject matter.

Flanagan and Russ-Eft (1975) have done a study on what educational experiences contribute toward overall well-being or quality of life. From interviews of 30-year-olds they concluded among other things that

> . . . by far *the most important factor* inhibiting the personal and educational development of these young people was the failure to assist them in developing goals and plans. *Lack of knowledge of their own interest, abilities and values and the relations of these to the requirements for various types of educational programs and career activities resulted in much wasted time, lack of motivation, and personal frustration* (Flanagan & Russ-Eft, 1975, p. 62).

Administrative Decisions

Administrative decisions include *selection, classification*, and *placement* decisions. In selection decisions one decides whether to accept or reject a person for a particular program or treatment. In classification one decides the type of program or treatment (for example, enrolling in the college of education, engineering, or liberal arts), and in placement one decides the level of treatment (for example, no-credit English, the regular program, or the honors program). Administrative decisions are also involved in such things as curriculum planning and hiring and/or firing teachers.

Knowledge of various characteristics of the student body in general is required for some questions to be answered properly. What should be the ratio of algebra to general math sections in ninth grade? Does the school system need another remedial reading teacher? Should the school district be offering more college prep courses, or should it be emphasizing vocational education? Should the work study program be expanded? Other decisions depend upon knowledge concerning specific students. Should Billy be admitted to kindergarten this year, or should he wait until he is one year older? Will Susan profit from a remedial reading program? Whatever the question, the administrator often depends upon the teacher to obtain the necessary data, and at times to make the actual decision.

There is a trend to move away from the use of measurement for educational selection decisions and toward measurement for aid in the instructional decisions mentioned earlier (Bloom, Hastings, & Madaus, 1971, p. 6). This development does not mean that measurement has not been a successful aid in selection decisions but rather that there is a general disenchantment with the notion that educators should be engaged in any selection processes. Bloom et al. said:

> . . . education, at least through secondary school, will be provided for the large majority of young people. Selection procedures, prediction, and other judgments to determine who is to be given educational opportunities are quite irrelevant when most young people complete secondary school (or, in the more distant future, two or four years of college) (Bloom et al., 1971).

This is certainly true, especially at the precollege level, if by selection one means that one accepts or rejects a person for educational opportunities. If one calls every decision made, once a child has been accepted for schooling, a classification or placement decision, there certainly is little reason for selection decisions. However, decisions such as who makes the traveling squad in any sport, music, or dramatic activity, and who gets to represent the school in a state math contest or science fair are probably more reasonably called selection rather than classification or placement decisions. There will continue to be activities in educational institutions that, by their very nature, must restrict the number of those who participate. Although we agree with those who say measurement's most important role in education is to aid in decision making designed to improve the development of all individuals, we also feel that selection decisions are necessary in education and that measurement should play an important role in making these decisions. The humanitarian notion that no one should ever be rejected from any publicly funded activity he wishes to engage in is idealistic, not realistic. Martin Mayer proposes the following curse for extreme egalitarians who do not wish to make any selection decisions based on merit.

> That they should cross the river on a bridge designed by an engineering school where students were admitted by lottery; and that their injuries should be treated by a doctor from a medical school where students were admitted by lottery; and that their heirs' malpractice suit should be tried by a lawyer from a law school where students were admitted by lottery (Mayer, 1973, p. 47).

Research Decisions

Research decisions cut across the three preceding types of decisions. Instructional, guidance, and administrative decisions may all be based on research.

In fact, under a broad definition of research, one could say research decisions are being made whenever information is gathered as a prelude to the decision making. In research, however, the experimenter may not necessarily wish to make any decisions with regard to the particular people who participate in his research project. He may instead be trying to verify some particular scientific hypothesis.

SUMMARY

The following statements summarize the major points of this chapter.

1. Measurement and evaluation are essential to sound educational decision making.
2. The term *test* often suggests presenting a standard set of questions to be answered.
3. The concept of measurement is broader than that of testing. We can measure characteristics in ways other than by giving tests.
4. Evaluation is the process of delineating, obtaining, and providing useful information for judging decision alternatives.
5. Every person must at some time make educational decisions.
6. A good decision is one that is based on relevant and accurate information. The responsibility of gathering and imparting that information belongs to the educator.
7. Decision theorists suggest that good decision making is dependent upon awareness of (a) all the alternatives, (b) the possible outcomes of every alternative, and (c) the probabilities and utilities of those outcomes.
8. Educational decisions are classified as instructional, guidance, administrative, and research decisions.
9. Evaluation procedures aid the teacher by (a) helping to provide knowledge concerning the students' entry behaviors; (b) helping to set, refine, and clarify realistic goals for each student; (c) helping to determine the degree to which objectives have been achieved; and (d) helping to determine, evaluate, and refine his instructional techniques.
10. Evaluation aids the student by (a) communicating the goals of the teacher, (b) increasing motivation, (c) encouraging good study habits, and (d) providing feedback that identifies his strengths and weaknesses.
11. Evaluation aids in the administrative decisions of selection, classification and placement.

CHAPTER TWO

The Role of Objectives in Educational Evaluation

"Would you tell me, please, which way
I ought to go from here?"
"That depends a good deal on where
you want to get to," said the Cat.
"I don't much care where—" said Alice.
"Then it doesn't matter which way you
go," said the Cat.
"—so long as I get somewhere," Alice
added as an explanation.
"Oh, you're sure to do that," said the
Cat, "if you only walk long enough."
(Carroll, 1916, p. 60)

The role of objectives in education has been a reasonably controversial topic. In this chapter we define some terms, discuss the importance of objectives, cover approaches to determining and communicating educational objectives, explain how objectives can be made amenable to evaluation, and cover the topic of unanticipated and/or unmeasurable outcomes.

After studying this chapter you should be able[1] to—

1. Understand the basic terms used in discussing obejctives.
2. Recognize several purposes of objectives.
3. Recognize some factors that must be considered in determining objectives.
4. Know some sources of information about objectives.
5. Appreciate the necessity for communicating objectives to different groups of people.
6. Comprehend that objectives are stated differently, depending on the purpose of the communication.
7. Recognize the advantages and disadvantages of different ways of stating objectives.
8. Judge whether an objective has been written in behavioral terms.
9. Appreciate the value (and potential dangers) of making objectives behavioral.
10. Apply the material in this chapter so that you can effectively determine, communicate, and evaluate objectives in your own areas of teaching.

DEFINITION OF TERMS

Part of the controversy concerning objectives is due to differences in philosophy among educators, but certainly another part of the controversy is due to semantic problems. Terms such as *needs, goals, behavioral goals, aims, outcomes, objectives,* and *behavioral objectives* have been used almost synonymously by some writers but with sharply different meanings by others. We do not wish to suggest that each of these terms must be defined by everyone in the same fashion—but it would be beneficial to the readers trying to formulate their own opinions as to, say, the importance of behavioral objectives if they could be certain as to how writers were using the term. The definitions we are using are stated below:

Outcome. What occurs as a result of an educational experience.
Objective. A stated desirable outcome of education.
Goal. In our writing we are somewhat more apt to use "goal" in a general sense and "objective" in a more explicit sense.
Need. The discrepancy between an objective and the present level of performance.

[1] We recognize that the objectives stated here and at the beginning of each chapter are *not* behavioral. They are similar in format to Gronlund's (1970) general learning outcomes. Behavioral objectives are *essential* in evaluation and may well be useful in planning instructional strategies. It may not *always* be best to *communicate* specific behavioral objectives to the student. You will understand why as you read this chapter.

Behavioral objective (goal). A statement that specifies what observable performance the learner will be engaged in when we evaluate whether or not he has achieved the objective. Behavioral objectives require action verbs such as *discuss, write,* and *read.* Verbs such as *understand* or *appreciate* are not considered behavioral because one cannot observe a person "understanding" or "appreciating."

WHY HAVE GOALS OR OBJECTIVES?

A fanatic has been defined as one who, having lost sight of his goals, redoubles his efforts. The occasionally heard statement that there are too many fanatics in education is not without some truth. It is absolutely necessary to establish goals in education, for without them we have no way of knowing in which direction to head.

Educational goals are many and varied. They are not easy to specify or agree upon. Indeed, educators have long been faced with choosing between competing, if not conflicting, goals. All worthwhile goals will not be attained, nor should they all be striven for with equal fervor. Some are more important than others. Priorities must be established. What and how much should students learn? Should schools strive for excellence or equality, diversity or conformity? Are schools to be more concerned with teaching the three R's, developing character, or instilling good self-concepts in their pupils? Should schools be a vital force in promoting social change? If so, can they also completely accept all the various value systems held by different American subcultures? Is it democratic to expend more or less time, money, and energy on those who come to school from impoverished environments? Ordering, or attaching values to goals or objectives, is a decision that must precede many other educational decisions, such as which of several alternate instructional strategies should be employed.

Traditionally, educational measurement has been more helpful in determining the degree to which certain outcomes have been achieved than in determining the goals of education and setting priorities. But as we pointed out in Chapter 1, there is a circular relationship among objectives, instruction, and evaluation, and the field of measurement has played at least several minor roles in the determination of objectives. In the first place the importance of stating educational objectives and determining their priorities has been stressed by those responsible for measurement, and this stress has provided the impetus for others to consider objectives.

Why state objectives? As we have already suggested, objectives give direction to education: They tell us in which way to head, a decision that is necessary before taking the first step on an educational journey. Specifically, objectives help a teacher plan instruction, guide student learning, and provide criteria for evaluating student outcomes. Further, once stated they provide a public record of intent and therefore facilitate open discussions regarding their appropriateness and adequacy. Objectives are considered so important to quality education that the academic council of at least one large university (Michigan State University) adopted a Code of Teaching Responsibilities (Academic Council, 1969) that states:

> Instructional staff members are responsible for:
> 1. Stating clearly the instructional objectives of each course they teach;
> 2. Directing their instruction toward the fulfillment of those objectives; and
> 3. Designing their examinations to be consistent with these objectives.

Not only do objectives aid in evaluation, but evaluation assists in examining objectives as well. Measurement specialists have pointed out that the measurement of what education *has* achieved may be useful for determining what education *should* achieve. "People are more likely to get clear in their minds what the outcomes of education *ought* to be if they first get clear in their minds what the outcomes actually *are*" (Dyer, 1967, p. 20). Thus, the specification and measurement of objectives are cyclical. One needs to set tentative objectives, employ an educational strategy to reach those objectives, measure the degree of attainment, and then reevaluate both objectives and strategy.

In addition to stressing the importance of objectives and how objective specification and evaluation are cyclical, educational psychologists have suggested certain approaches to the objective-setting decisions and methods of wording educational objectives.

APPROACHES TO DETERMINING (SELECTING) OBJECTIVES

Two considerations in setting objectives are the *relevance* of the goals and their *feasibility*. We will also discuss assigning priorities to goals and some sources of information about them, giving particular attention to the various existing taxonomies.

Relevance of Goals

Goal relevance is dependent upon both the needs of society and the needs of the learner (Tyler, 1950). In the satirical story of *The Saber-Tooth Curriculum* (Peddiwell, 1939) a society was described in which the major tasks necessary for survival were catching fish to eat, clubbing horses, and scaring away the saber-tooth tigers. The school in this society set up a curriculum ideal for the society's needs, that is, teaching a course in each of those three areas. But the environment changed; the stream dried up, and the horses and tigers went away. The new society was faced with different tasks necessary for survival, but strangely enough the school curriculum did not change!

Teachers, school districts, and the entire "educational establishment" must continually reexamine the goals of education in view of society's needs. For example, the perceived needs of society are different now from what they were immediately following Sputnik. What kinds of marketable skills do present-day students need to be taught? Should education be job-oriented or more general in nature? Do we need to teach individuals what to do with their "leisure" time? Should we be stressing the achievement ethic or the affiliation ethic? Questions such as these can be answered on both philosophical and empirical bases (Flanagan & Russ-Eft, 1975).

The psychological needs of the learner must also be considered when specifying relevant goals. The need to achieve, for example, is related to the probability of success. Students' aspirations will vary, depending upon how they perceive their chances of success and whether or not they were successful on a previous task. (A series of successes or failures will have a cumulative effect on level of aspiration.) Needs such as affiliation, self-worth, and nurturance should all help determine the goals of education.

Realism of Goals

As Dyer (1967, p. 20) suggested, the knowledge of present outcomes should help in setting realistic objectives.

Setting unrealistic goals is a sure way to discourage both students and teachers. The psychological nature of individuals delimits to a large extent what teachers should and should not expect. If kindergarten teachers had the goal of having their 5-year-old students sit quietly and attentively during the school day, they would be sure to be disappointed. They would have set unrealistic goals because the psychological nature of children precludes such physical restraint.

Other delimiting factors in goal attainment include the facilities of the school. Given a set of teachers with certain qualifications, a certain number of hours available to devote to a given objective, certain constraints due to lack of equipment, and similar conditions, certain goals may be quite unrealistic. In short, we should strive for goals that are in harmony with what educational psychologists know about how children develop, how they learn, and how they differ from one another in these two respects, as well as the availability of resources necessary to reach those goals successfully.

Priorities of Goals

The term *needs assessment* is currently popular among those who advocate the systems approach to education (see Sweigert, 1968a, b). It is based on the notion that the relevancy of education must be empirically determined and should identify the discrepancy between "what is" and "what should be" (Kaufman, 1971). Klein (1971) suggested that needs assessments should include four basic activities:

1. Listing the full range of possible goals (or objectives) that might be involved in the needs assessment
2. Determining the relative importance of the goals (or objectives)
3. Assessing the degree to which the important goals (or objectives) are being achieved by the program (that is, identifying discrepancies between desired and actual performance)
4. Determining which of the discrepancies between present and desired performance are the ones most important to correct

In preparing sets of goals we should, of course, consult with teachers, students, parents, and the general public. However, if such groups are included from the very beginning, the process of building goals can be very frustrating. Klein (1971) suggested that it is most efficient to have, as a first step, a team of experts construct a *full set* of objectives that might be included in a needs assessment. These experts should not, at this stage, be concerned with what should be accomplished but rather with what might be. After a full set of potential objectives is drawn up, this total list could be presented to teachers, students, parents, and others for the process of selecting and ordering a subset of the objectives most relevant for that particular school district.

One program that could assist in this task is the *Elementary School Evaluation Kit: Needs Assessment* (published by Allyn and Bacon). This kit contains 106 goals of elementary education determined through national field testing. It describes three methods for setting local priorities for these goals and contains the necessary rating forms and so on to conduct the evaluation. Another program designed to facilitate the development and priority listing of goals and objectives is the *Educational Goals and Objectives: A Model Program for Community and Professional Involvement* (distributed by the Commission on Educational Planning, Phi Delta Kappa). This program provides for the involvement of the community, the professional staff, and students in (1) ranking educational goals, (2) determining how well the school's current programs meet the ranked goals, and (3) developing performance objectives. Page (1974) has proposed two techniques for rendering judgments about goals under a general approach called the Top-Down Trees of Educational Values. In essence his technique starts by first considering the value of the very broadest goals, and then within each of those goals attaching values to the subgoals until through several such processes one eventually establishes values for some fairly specific objectives.

Sources of Information about Goals

Although establishing objectives for a school, a class, or even a single student is certainly not an easy task, one does not have to start from scratch. Many published statements of educational goals can serve as guidelines. Some of these, such as the *Seven Cardinal Principles of Secondary Education* (Commission, 1918), while helpful in spelling out why schools exist in a very general or philosophical sense, are somewhat too vague to be of much help for the specific purpose of guiding instruction. The principle of "good citizenship" does not really present an adequate guideline for classroom instructional practices. However, other published objectives are more detailed and therefore more useful for this purpose. Two such examples are the *Elementary School Objectives* (Kearney, 1953) and *Behavioral Goals of General Education in High School* (French et al., 1957). In both volumes an effort is made to state the objectives in at least semibehavioral terms. The Kearney volume, for example, considers nine curriculum areas, with each area subdivided into four types of behavioral patterns.

The curriculum areas are:

Physical development, health, and body care
Individual social and emotional development
Ethical behavior, standards, and values
Social relations
The social world
The physical world
Esthetic development
Communication
Quantitative relationships

The four types of behavioral patterns are:

Knowledge and understandings
Skills and competences
Attitudes and interests
Action patterns

Another source of objectives is the National Assessment of Educational Progress (1972b), which has published separate booklets of objectives for ten subject-matter areas: art, career and occupational development, citizenship, literature, mathematics, music, reading, science, social studies, and writing. The objectives in each of these areas had to meet three criteria: They had to be ones that (1) the schools were currently seeking to attain, (2) scholars in the field considered authentic to their discipline, and (3) thoughtful laymen considered important. The third criterion was the unique aspect of the National Assessment approach to developing objectives. Most published lists of objectives meet the first two criteria, but few, if any, other lists received so much scrutiny by laymen prior to publication. Eleven different lay panels reviewed the objectives in each of the subject-matter areas and, following these panel meetings, the eleven panel chairmen met and pooled their recommendations. In revision of these published objectives the National Assessment

TABLE 2–1 The Educational Goals for Elementary and Secondary
Education as Adopted by the Various State Governments[a]

PHYSICAL AND MATERIAL WELL-BEING		PERSONAL DEVELOPMENT AND FULFILLMENT	
22	A. Each individual must *develop an understanding* of the principles involved in the product of goods and services and *of the skills relating to the management of personal resources.*	47	H. Each individual must *master the basic skills of* reading, writing, speaking, listening, computation, and problem solving.
41	B. Each individual must *acquire* good health and safety habits and an *understanding of the conditions necessary for physical and mental well-being.*	38	I. Each individual must *master the skills of constructive and critical thinking and decision-making* so that he can deal effectively with problems in an open-minded and adaptable manner.
29	C. Each individual must *develop the knowledge and respect necessary for the maintenance, appreciation, protection and improvement of the physical environment.*	36	J. Each individual must *gain knowledge* of the human achievement and experience in the areas of *natural sciences, social sciences, humanities, and creative and fine arts.*
	RELATIONS WITH OTHER PEOPLE	41	K. Each individual must *gain an eagerness for learning* and self-development beyond the formal schooling process.
24	D. Each individual must learn the rights and responsibilities of family members and *prepare for family life.*	40	L. Each individual must *develop a positive self-image* and an un-

organization is actively soliciting student opinions of the legitimacy of the objectives.

At the time of this writing, 47 states have published lists of educational goals. Flanagan and Russ-Eft (1975) have combined those lists into a final set of 16 goal categories. Table 2–1 lists those final 16 goals and indicates the number of states that have adopted each goal. Some states, such as Michigan and Florida, have translated some of their general goals to performance objectives.

Other sources for more specific objectives include the Instructional Objectives Exchange (see Popham, 1970) and the Westinghouse collection (Flanagan, Shanner, & Mayer, 1971). At the time of this writing, the Instructional Objectives Exchange had 53 different collections of behavioral objectives covering a range of subject matter. Most objectives are accompanied by six test items, which may be used to assess whether or not the objective has

TABLE 2–1 (Continued)

PHYSICAL AND MATERIAL WELL-BEING		PERSONAL DEVELOPMENT AND FULFILLMENT	
36	E. Each individual must learn to *develop and maintain interpersonal relationships* and have command of social skills.		derstanding and appreciation of his unique capacities, interests, and goals.
SOCIAL, COMMUNITY. AND CIVIC ACTIVITIES		45	M. Each individual must select and *prepare for a career* of his choice consistent with his capabilities, aptitudes, desires, and the needs of society.
39	F. Each individual must come to *understand and appreciate different cultures*, governments, races, generations and life-styles.	35	N. Each individual must *develop* a personal philosophy and a *basic set of values, morals, and ethics* acceptable to society.
43	G. Each individual must *learn the rights and responsibilities of citizens* of the community, state and nation.	29	O. Each individual must *acquire the desire and ability to express himself creatively* and to appreciate creativity in others.
		RECREATION	
		27	P. Each individual must have knowledge of and *skills in recreation and leisure-time activities* for nonvocational use of time.

a Includes all 50 state governments except Arkansas, Indiana, and Minnesota. The figure at the left of each goal indicates the number of states that have adopted it as one of their educational goals.

Source: J. C. Flanagan and D. Russ-Eft, *An Empirical Study to Aid in Formulating Educational Goals.* Palo Alto, Calif.: American Institute for Research, 1975. With permission of the publisher.

been achieved.[2] The Westinghouse collection contains more than 4000 behavioral objectives covering language arts, social sciences, mathematics, and sciences for grades 1–12. In addition, Westinghouse has published four volumes containing over 5000 learning objectives for individualized instruction in the same four areas for what they describe as basic college and precollege courses.

One of the limitations of many national sources of objectives is that they have no provisions for accommodating local options. There are obviously objectives not listed in these sources toward which school districts, class-

[2] A current description of available objectives can be obtained from the Instructional Objectives Exchange, Box 24095, Los Angeles, Calif. 90024.

rooms, and individual pupils should strive. We wish to stress, however, that this limitation is not an argument for not using the aforementioned publications, for they can be very useful. But educators in various localities should not accept them as definitive guides. Local educators still have the obligation of stating, teaching toward, and evaluating objectives that may be unique to their communities. As Popham (1970a, p. 175) pointed out: "Objectives should increase the educator's range of alternatives, never decrease his self-direction."

Major textbooks can be quite useful in determining objectives for specific courses. However, it is possible to be too dependent upon a textbook when developing objectives. Such a source is often an inadequate guide for developing affective objectives (those related to the development of attitudes and appreciations). Other specific aids would be publications (if they exist) of the local curriculum and previously developed course syllabi.

Taxonomies of Educational Objectives

Educational psychologists have advocated various techniques of stating objectives, but before we delve into that topic we should discuss one more general source of ideas concerning objectives—the taxonomies. Educational psychologists also have assisted in specifying (as well as communicating and evaluating) goals by constructing taxonomies of educational objectives. These taxonomies have classified the goals of education and are useful as a means both of communicating goals and of understanding some relationships among them. Original plans for one classification system called for the development of taxonomies in three domains—cognitive, affective, and psychomotor. *The Cognitive Domain, Handbook I*, was published in 1956 (Bloom, 1956) and *Handbook II, The Affective Domain* in 1964 (Krathwohl, Bloom, & Masia, 1964). Simpson (1966); Kibler, Barker, and Miles (1970), and Harrow (1972) have all published taxonomies in the psychomotor domain. Derr (1973) published a taxonomy of social purposes of public schools. He feels that such a taxonomy will serve the purpose of identifying various options and pointing out their possible advantages and disadvantages. This should facilitate efforts in judging the social role of the schools.

The *cognitive domain* "includes those objectives which deal with the recall or recognition of knowledge and the development of intellectual abilities and skills" (Bloom, 1956, p. 7). The cognitive taxonomy contains six major classes of objectives arranged in hierarchical order on the basis of complexity of task (knowledge, comprehension, application, analysis, synthesis, and evaluation). Each of these six classes is subdivided further. The *affective domain* is concerned with changes in interest, attitudes, and values and the development of appreciations and adjustment. It is divided into five major classes arranged in hierarchical order on the basis of level of involvement (receiving, responding, valuing, organization, and characterization by a value). The psychomotor domain includes objectives related to muscular or motor skill, manipulation of material and objects, and neuromuscular coordination.

The taxonomies have provided a common basis or "jargon" for communicating about objectives and have been of assistance in helping educators think about goals for their students, the relationships among these goals, and how different assessment procedures need to be established to evaluate these various goals. Educators have a tendency to spend an inordinate amount of time teaching—and testing for—the lower-level objectives in the cognitive domain, such as knowledge, comprehension, and application. The taxonomies call attention to the higher-level cognitive objectives and the affective objectives and thereby assist teachers in setting a better balance of objectives.

Another hierarchical classification of behavior that can be helpful to educators in selecting goals is one developed by Gagné (1965), who discussed the following six classes[3] of behavior going from the simplest to most complex:

1. Connections or response learning
2. Chaining or sequencing
3. Identification
4. Concepts
5. Principles
6. Higher-order or general principles

These categories constitute a helpful framework for selecting goals, and each of them carries some definite implications for procedures in education. Each class requires a different set of conditions of learning and uses different methods of instruction. Also, these classes imply a certain sequencing of instruction within a topic, since each specifies prerequisite behaviors for the more complex categories listed below it. Consideration of this hierarchy may be useful when constructing diagnostic assessments of student progress.

Admittedly, we have not discussed any of the taxonomies in so great a detail as to obviate the need for a serious student to turn to the sources cited. To condense and incorporate in this book all the useful material in those sources would be impossible. In the last few pages we have tried to alert the readers first to different general sources of information that would be useful in formulating objectives and secondly to several taxonomies that are useful in formulating and communicating objectives as well as helpful in determining instructional and diagnostic procedures. In Unit III we will discuss some uses of the taxonomies in test construction procedures.

[3] Gagné classified eight types of learning in his book *The Conditions of Learning* (1970). This expansion from six to eight classes is more confusing than illuminating to readers not familiar with learning theory.

APPROACHES TO STATING (COMMUNICATING) GOALS

Not all ways of wording goals aid much in communication. For example, in 1947 the report of the President's Commission on Higher Education (1947, p. 9) contained the following paragraph:

> The first goal in education for democracy is the full, rounded, and continuing development of the person. The discovery, training, and utilization of individual talents is of fundamental importance in a free society. To liberate and perfect the intrinsic powers of every citizen is the central purpose of democracy, and its furtherance of individual self-realization is its greatest glory.

As Dyer (1967) pointed out, this is an example of word magic—an ideal that many Americans would enthusiastically support without knowing what the words are saying. Educational goals, no matter how appropriate, that are worded in such a way that they do not communicate clearly are relatively worthless. Many such goal statements serve more as political documents designed to placate the public rather than to serve as guides in directing and guiding the work of the schools.

To Whom Must Educators Communicate Goals?

Many individuals and groups need to be told the goals of education in words they can understand. Consider the goals that Mr. Howe, a ninth-grade social studies teacher, has projected for his students. Students, other teachers, the principal, the school board, parents, and indeed the whole taxpaying public have both a need and a right to know what goals Mr. Howe has set for his students. If he cannot articulate them, we may doubt if he even has any!

Logic and research studies (for example, Dallis, 1970; Harrison, 1967; Huck & Long, 1972; Morse & Tillman, 1972) tell us that students are more apt to learn what the teacher expects them to learn if they are told just what those things are. Other teachers should know what Mr. Howe expects the students to learn so that they will not duplicate that material in their classes or skip some important complementary material; in turn, Mr. Howe needs to be aware of their objectives. If curricula are to be coordinated, it is obvious that the tenth-grade history teacher needs to know the goals of the ninth-grade social studies teacher. The principal and school board members need to know goals so that they can evaluate both the goals and the degree to which they are being reached. They also have responsibility for curriculum coordination and need to know goals for that reason. Parents, and the public in general, also have a right to know what the schools are attempting to accomplish so they so they can understand and evaluate the objectives and judge how well they are being accomplished.

While it may seem ridiculous to say so, Mr. Howe also needs to communicate his goals to himself. Most teachers have an affective feeling that they know what their goals are. But only if they can *articulate* them clearly will they find them useful in planning curriculum and instructional strategies.

How Should Goals Be Communicated?

There are different points of view concerning the best way to communicate educational goals. Whether the goals should focus on the teaching activities of the learner, whether or not one states immediate or ultimate goals, what the level of specificity should be, and whether they should be behavioral or nonbehavioral are some of the dimensions subject to disagreement among educators. The truth is that there is no single, best way to state goals; it depends upon whom you are communicating with and the purpose of the communication. For example, goals should be stated one way for helping plan instructional strategies and another for informing taxpayers. They have to be stated differently to aid in evaluation from when they are used to explain the school's objectives at a PTA meeting.

In this book we are primarily interested in discussing how objectives should be stated for evaluation purposes. However, we wish to stress that stating objectives in a form functional for evaluation is not necessarily the best procedure to follow for the purposes of communicating objectives.

In this section we will discuss some of the general considerations in stating objectives for communication purposes. In the next section we will discuss specifically how one states objectives so that they serve as adjuncts to the evaluation process.

TEACHER OR LEARNER FOCUSED

Goals can be stated either in terms of what teachers are going to do or in terms of the outcomes they expect from their students. When goals are stated in terms of teacher activity they are more likely to be referred to as aims or directions; when stated in terms of student outcome, they are more likely to be called objectives. Most educational psychologists feel it is more fruitful to state the goals in terms of expected student outcomes of the instruction rather than the teaching activity or process. This is in keeping with the generally accepted definition of teaching as an activity for which the goal is to induce learning or change behavior.

Eisner is the leading spokesman for those who do not feel *all* goals need to be stated in terms of student outcomes. He feels that there is a distinction between establishing a direction and formulating an objective and that "much in school practice which is educational is a consequence of establishing directions rather than formulating objectives" (Eisner, 1969, p. 13). Eisner thus argues for two kinds of objectives. He agrees that some objectives should be stated in terms of student outcomes. (He labels these instructional objectives.)

He also believes there is a place in education for what he calls expressive objectives. These are objectives that describe educational encounters. Such an objective

> . . . identifies a situation in which children are to work, a problem with which they are to cope, a task in which they are to engage; but it does not specify what from that encounter, situation, problem, or task they are to learn. An expressive objective provides both the teacher and the student with an invitation to explore, defer, or focus on issues that are of peculiar interest or import to the inquirer (Eisner, 1969, pp. 15, 16).

Eisner contended that "instructional objectives emphasize the acquisition of the known; while expressive objectives its elaboration, modification, and, at times, the production of the utterly new" (Eisner, 1969, p. 17). He used an example of appropriate expressive objectives: A teacher may wish his suburban class to visit the slums, but may be either unable or unwilling to formulate specific outcomes for the multiplicity of potential learning experiences the students will undergo. Strong believers in the value of stating all objectives in terms of student outcomes might argue that the teacher should not provide the students with that experience unless he is willing to specify anticipated, desirable behavioral changes in the students.

We believe that teachers should strive to express as many goals as possible in terms of student outcomes, but that, *on occasion*, the wish to expose students to an experience may in and of itself constitute an objective even though specific outcomes of the exposure may not be identifiable. Thus, we are, in general, arguing *against* wording objectives like the following:

> The teacher will lead a discussion on ecology.

A better wording would be:

> The students will be able to accurately describe the U.S. conditions with respect to air and water pollution.

IMMEDIATE VERSUS ULTIMATE GOALS

The welfare of our nation depends upon what people can and will do in their life. The only reason we have for teaching anything in school is that the subject matter is intended to have a permanent effect on the learner. We, as educators, are interested in the ultimate behavior of our students. In our society, they should be—among other things—informed voters, able to handle their own finances, and capable of holding jobs.

It is certainly appropriate to communicate these ultimate goals, but a generalized statement is insufficient communication for several reasons. Generalizations of ultimate goals are not adaptable to the processes of meaningful evaluation. Certainly, education of the past can be evaluated in a very general sense by looking at today's society, and we will be able to evaluate today's education sometime in the future. But this evaluation is far too broad—it cannot be specifically applied to a particular teacher's instructional procedure or even to a general curriculum. These ultimate goals are not in themselves sufficient guidelines for the administrator, teacher, or student.

In communicating goals, then, we should also talk about *immediate* goals. When setting these immediate goals, we should consider how their achievement will relate to the ultimate goals, and we should communicate this relationship. More than 25 years ago Lindquist (1951) spelled out the ideal relationship between immediate and ultimate objectives.

> Ideally . . . immediate objectives should in every instance have been clearly and logically derived from accepted ultimate objectives, in full consideration of all relevant characteristics of the pupils who are to receive the instruction. Ideally, also, the immediate objectives should be supported by dependable empirical evidence that their attainment will eventually lead to or make possible the realization of the ultimate objectives. Finally, the content and methods of instruction should, ideally, be logically selected, devised, and used with specific reference to these immediate and ultimate objectives, and should likewise be supported by convincing experimental evidence of their validity (Lindquist, 1951, p. 121).

As Lindquist pointed out, "Unfortunately this ideal relationship among ultimate objectives, immediate objectives, and the content and methods of instruction has only rarely been approximated in actual practice" (1951, p. 121). The same unfortunate circumstance exists today, but educators should continue to push hard for such relationships. Although the empirical support for all such relationships is admittedly difficult to build, the logical relationships should at least exist. (This is obviously related to the relevance issue discussed earlier.) For example, we could probably successfully argue that some basic knowledge of our governmental structure is necessary (although not sufficient) for a person to be an informed voter. Also, some basic knowledge about arithmetic processes is necessary for a person to make purchases, to balance a checkbook and, generally, to function as a consumer in our society.

GENERAL OR SPECIFIC

Educational goals can be written at very general or very specific levels. The earlier quote by the President's Commission would be an example of an extremely general goal, one so general as to be vague and therefore meaningless. A goal that Johnny will answer "two" when asked "What is $1+1$?" is a very specific goal. That goal is certainly not vague, but the degree of meaning is limited. Certainly, it would be inefficient to *communicate* goals to anyone—student, parent, or other teacher—at that level of specificity. It would be much better to state that Johnny should be able to add all combinations of single-digit numbers, or two-digit numbers, or whatever.

Popham, an early advocate of using very specific objectives in the same way as Meger (1962), has recently recognized the *inappropriateness* of such a process.

> There was a belief in the early sixties that the more specific an objective was, the more useful it would be. Yet, as educators went about devising superspecific objectives they ended up with encyclopedic lists of those detailed statements. Those who generated such elongated lists of instructional goals soon discovered another instance where *more is less* (Popham, 1975, p. 51).

Of course, when *evaluating* Johnny's ability to add, we will ask him to add several specific combinations. These tasks we ask Johnny to perform in a test are objectives stated in a most specific fashion, so we are not denying that specific objectives are relevant. But what we wish to do is to generalize from observing Johnny's performance on a limited number of combinations to his ability to add other combinations. If we had *communicated* to Johnny on which specific combinations we were going to test him, we would be unable to infer or generalize about his ability to add other combinations.

This is not always a well-understood point by educators. The philosophy of stating goals, teaching toward them, and then assessing their attainment has confused some people. They argue as follows: "If we really want students to know certain things, we should tell them which specific things we wish them to learn, teach those things, and then test over those same things." This is an accurate way of looking at the teaching-learning process, and an accurate way to communicate objectives only if those objectives communicated are all-inclusive. Otherwise, students will concentrate on the objectives communicated and exclude those uncommunicated. This is one concern of educators who contemplate using performance contracting. If teachers or students know which specific performances are to be required, they can concentrate on those particular ones and learn them. But in such a situation we cannot *generalize* from the achievement of those specifics to what the students know about the subject matter as a whole.

Very specific objectives (for example, test questions) should be communicated only when those specifics are indeed absolutely essential or when we have such a small set of goals that all specifics can be communicated. Otherwise, we should talk in more general terms. An example of a task where communicating specific objects would be appropriate would be learning the letters in the alphabet. In such a training process it may be quite beneficial to tell a student, or his parents, that by a certain day you expect him to be able to recognize the first five letters in the alphabet. Actually, communicating specific objectives may be appropriate for almost any training program of limited duration. The goals are hopefully essential and probably few enough in number so that they can all be specified. However, when education—as opposed to training—is taking place, the number of specific kinds of goals that may be appropriate is too large. *All specific objectives cannot be communicated.* In a course like ninth-grade social studies or an introductory course in educational psychology one has to communicate at a more general level. Giving examples or samples of specific goals is appropriate, but the student must be told that these objectives are only sample ones and that his learning is not to be restricted to those specifics. That the student should be able "to add fractions correctly" is a better way of communicating than to say the student should be able to add ½ + ½, ½ + ⅓, ½ + ¼, ½ + ⅕, and so on. "To read music symbols" is a better way of communicating than to say that the student will recognize A, B, C, D, E, F, G, A-flat, or A-sharp.

A further difficulty with very specifically worded objectives is that they may actually complicate the measurement problems. If followed precisely they may dictate the form of the test item. Now this *may* be appropriate, but often it is the *wording* of the objective, and not the *intent* of the objective that dictates the form of the test items. This type of objective wording is counterproductive.

Of course, it is easy to be too general in the communication of goals. To say that a student should "understand mathematics" or "understand music" is not adequate. More detail than that is necessary. Many measurement specialists thus prepare different levels of objectives. For example, Krathwohl and Payne (1971) advocate three levels of objectives. The first level contains very broad objectives, the second level more specific, and the third level quite specific objectives. A fourth level would be the test items themselves: very specific objectives usually *not* communicated in advance of instruction.

An example of first- and second-level objectives in the Citizenship area in the National Assessment of Educational Progress (1972) follows:

Citizenship
First level:
    Show concern for the well-being and dignity of others.
Second level:
    1. Treat others with respect.
    2. Consider the consequences for others of their own actions.
    3. Guard safety and health of others.
    4. Offer to help others in need.

Many third-level objectives could be derived from each second-level objective, and many test questions could be written for each third-level objective. One could communicate all the objectives at the first or second level. At times, *samples* of third-level objectives and test questions would be useful for communication purposes.

BEHAVIORAL VERSUS NONBEHAVIORAL OBJECTIVES

Perhaps one of the bigger controversies in recent years with respect to the communication of goals is whether or not they need to be stated in behavioral terms. A behavioral goal (usually called an objective) is one that specifies what the learner will be *doing* when we evaluate whether or not he has attained the goal. (Thus, one would state a behavioral goal by saying "the student will add" instead of "the student will understand how to add.") The difference in the wording of the goals is that behavioral objectives use action verbs, whereas nonbehavioral objectives do not. There is no disagreement that when we evaluate whether or not students have met certain goals, we must also evaluate the students' behaviors. There is some disagreement about whether we should, prior to the evaluation, specify our goals in behavioral terms or, indeed, whether all goals specified are required to be adaptable to evaluation processes.

Some of the controversy in this area cuts across two other dimensions we have discussed: degree of specificity and whether the goals focus on the teacher or the learner. Behavioral objectives focus on learner outcomes; nonbehavioral objectives may focus on learner outcomes or teacher activities. Behavioral objectives tend to be more specific than nonbehavioral objectives. This last point has contributed to the controversy on behavioral objectives. Advocates of behavioral objectives often wish the objectives to be stated very specifically, even to the point of detailing what *conditions* must exist while the behavior is being performed and of specifying the *criteria* that must be met in order to conclude that the objective has been attained satisfactorily. For example, a nonbehaviorally worded objective might be as follows:

1. The students will understand how to take the square root of 69.

The behavioral counterpart would be as follows:

2. The students will compute the square root of 69.

Many advocates of behavioral objectives might argue that this statement is *not specific* enough. They would prefer even more detail such as

3. The students will compute the square root of 69 without the use of tables, slide rules, or any mechanical device. They will use paper and pencil, show all work, finish within 60 seconds, and be accurate to the nearest hundredth.

Again, conditions and criteria must be specified for evaluation, but many educators do not feel it necessary to communicate specific behavioral objectives prior to instruction. Few would feel it necessary to specify as much detail as is presented in the third statement in order to plan instruction. We should keep in mind, however, that the debate about whether or not one communicates in behavioral terms is often intertwined with the debate about how specific our communication of goals needs to be.

Advocates of behavioral objectives state that they are clearer and less ambiguous than nonbehaviorably stated objectives. Behavioral objectives are supposedly a better aid in curriculum planning, promoting student achievement, and improving evaluation (Dallis, 1970; Huck & Long, 1972). Supposedly, teachers better "understand" behaviorally stated objectives and therefore "know" more about how to teach.

It is certainly true that statements of objectives are ambiguous when they are expressed as: "a student will *understand* how to add, subtract, multiply, and divide; or, *appreciate* classical music; or *enjoy* physical activity; or *comprehend* the workings of an internal combustion engine." What do we mean by understand, appreciate, enjoy, comprehend, or relish? "It is difficult to tell when a child is relishing great literature. Although we can discern whether a child relishes a hamburger, as opposed to mustarding it, the detection of literature-relishing is far trickier" (Popham, 1975, p. 46). One way we can explain what we mean by "understand" is to describe how a person who understands behaves differently from one who does not understand. If a person who "appreciates" classical music does not behave any differently from one who does not appreciate classical music, then the goal of classical music appreciation is not worth working for.

Thus we argue that every worthwhile goal of education is, *in principle*, capable of being stated in behavioral terms. But it does not necessarily follow that behavioral statements are the best way to communicate goals to all people. We in education often do have what Waks (1969) called mentalistic aims. We actually want students to appreciate, comprehend, understand, and think creatively. The fact that we can evaluate these goals only through the observation of behaviors does not mean that the behaviors per se are our goals. And, as a matter of fact, if we specify to our students what behaviors we are going to observe to infer "appreciation," the inference may no longer be correct. (This seems to be more of a problem if our goal is affective rather than cognitive.)

We could specify, for example, that a person who appreciates classical music, in contrast to one who does not appreciate such music, will (1) spend more time listening to classical music on the radio, (2) be more attentive while listening, and (3) buy more classical records. We could make a long, but not exhaustive, list of such behaviors. These would be the behaviors from which we would infer appreciation. But if we *told* our students that our goals were the behaviors listed, they might engage in those behaviors (only during the time period in which the teacher was doing the evaluation) without ever appreciating classical music at all! The students would not be performing the behaviors under natural conditions. As Waks pointed out:

> If it is not possible to state exhaustive behavioral conditions, then there is a logical gap between bringing about the criterial behavior and satisfying

the original "mentalistic" aim, a gap caused by the "normal conditions" qualification. This gap is of great practical significance, for aiming at ordinary criterial behavior will generally make conditions abnormal, in the respect that under those conditions the behavior is no longer indicative of original aim satisfaction. . . . Once criterial behavior becomes aim, short cuts skirting the original aim become available (Waks, 1969, p. 618).

Perhaps we need to state clearly at this point that the foregoing is not an argument against behavioral objectives. Stating objectives in behavioral terms is absolutely mandatory if we are to *evaluate* those objectives. Behavioral objectives may well be desirable in planning instructional strategies. Stating objectives in behavioral terms forces teachers to think clearly, and in some detail, about just what they are trying to accomplish. Thus, behavioral objectives serve valuable functions. But we are suggesting that there are potential problems of communication if we use behavioral objectives. One of these problems is to mistake the product or behavior as an end in itself rather than as a specific behavior from which we can infer the mentalistic aim. A second related problem is that one may mistake a set of stated behavioral objectives as exhaustive when, in fact, they are only a sample of the behaviors we wish the student to be able to exhibit. The definition Gideonse gave to behavioral objectives helps avoid these problems:

What we *should* mean by behavioral objectives is not so much the *ends* that we are trying to achieve through schooling as the performance indices that *we would accept as evidence* that we have achieved, or had a reasonable hope of achieving over time, the objectives . . . The behaviors may be ends in themselves, or they may be simply indicators. . . . (Gideonse, 1969).

By suggesting that there are problems in communicating via behavioral objectives we are not suggesting that adequate communication can always take place without them. If your instructor tells you that you are to "understand" the concept of reliability in measurement, what does he mean? Does he want you to be able to define it, compute it, or list factors that affect reliability? If he wants you to understand correlation, does he wish you to be able to compute a correlation coefficient, interpret one, determine its statistical significance, derive the formula, or list common errors of interpretation? If the teacher means all of these by "understand," he should say so. If he means only certain ones he should so state. A student has a right to know, in general, what types of behaviors the teacher expects him to exhibit when he is being evaluated. But if we expect a student to derive an equation, it is not likely that the derivation per se is our goal. Rather, we wish to infer some mental process such as understanding from that act. If we teach a particular derivation and the student memorizes it, we may end up making an incorrect inference of understanding rather than memory.

The problems that result from confusion as to whether a behavioral objective is really our main objective or only an indicant of our objective can usually be minimized by employing the levels approach discussed in the previous section. If we *start* with the broader goal statements and develop our behavioral objectives (usually third-level objectives) from them, it will typically be clear whether they are main intents or only indicants. Further, we wish to emphasize that it is preferable to *start* with the broader goals. Although it occasionally may help clarify goals by first attempting to list all the possible specific behaviors, it is likely to be more beneficial to work the other way around (McAshon, 1974, pp. 47–48). And thinking of behaviors first does put the cart before the horse. As important as evaluation is, it should not *determine* the goals of education.

A GENERAL APPROACH TO GOAL COMMUNICATION: A SUMMARY

Ordinarily goals should be stated in terms of learner outcomes, not teacher processes. We should communicate both immediate and ultimate goals. Goals should be specific enough that they are not vague, yet general enough to communicate efficiently. Very specific goals are almost always only samples of what we want students to have learned. When listing specific goals, we should make clear that these are samples only. Neither teacher nor students should concentrate on these specifics to the exclusion of other material. We can infer the accomplishment of goals only through observing behavior. Specifying the type of behavior we will accept, as evidence that the student has reached the goal, is helpful. Sometimes the behavior itself is the goal. At other times it is only an indicant of the goal. This is an important distinction. Behavior is an indicant of the accomplishment of a mentalistic aim only when performed under natural conditions. If a teacher or student concentrates on the specific behavior as the goal, it can no longer be interpreted as an indicant that the desired goal has been attained. By listing objectives by levels and by listing only samples on third-level objectives and fourth-level test items it should be clear when specific behaviors are our objectives and when they are only indicants.

AN ANECDOTE

By way of summarizing the importance of communicating goals, we present the following anecdote:

> At a parent-teachers conference the teacher complained to Mr. Bird about the foul language of his children. Mr. Bird decided to correct this behavior. At breakfast he asked his oldest son, "What will you have for breakfast?" The boy replied, "Gimme some of those damn cornflakes." Immediately Mr. Bird smashed the boy on the mouth. The boy's chair tumbled over and the boy rolled up against the wall. The father then turned to his second son and politely inquired, "What would you like for breakfast?" The boy hesitated, then said, "I don't know, but I sure as hell don't want any of those damn cornflakes!"

Moral: If you want someone to change his behavior, tell him your goals.

MAKING OBJECTIVES AMENABLE TO EVALUATION

The key to making an objective behavioral lies in the verb used. Such statements as to "become cognizant of," "familiar with," "knowledgeable about," "mature," or "self-confident" are *not* behavioral. They do not tell us what the learner will be *doing* when *demonstrating* his achievement of the objective. Action verbs are needed. Claus (1968) suggested that one use only imperative sentences in stating educational objectives. These sentences begin with a verb and are a call to action. Whether or not one follows the Claus suggestion, the verbs used in the objective are important. Claus compiled a list of 445 "permissible" verbs and placed them in various categories. Examples from the list are presented in Table 2–2. These may assist teachers who are trying to decide what student behaviors are required for one to infer understanding, cognizance, or maturity. Table 2–3 presents some examples of infinitives that relate to Bloom's taxonomic classification of cognitive objectives.

Besides specifying the *performance* or behavior of the learner, it is often helpful to specify the *conditions* that will be imposed upon the learner while demonstrating ability to perform the objective. It is one thing to compute a

TABLE 2–2   Index Verborum Permissorum

"CREATIVE" BEHAVIORS

Alter	Paraphrase	Rephrase
Change	Question	Restructure
Design	Reconstruct	Synthesize
Generalize	Reorganize	Vary

GENERAL DISCRIMINATIVE BEHAVIORS

Collect	Discriminate	Match
Define	Identify	Order
Describe	Isolate	Select
Differentiate	List	Separate

LANGUAGE BEHAVIORS

Abbreviate	Outline	Spell
Alphabetize	Punctuate	Syllabicate
Capitalize	Recite	Translate
Edit	Speak	Write

MUSIC BEHAVIORS

Blow	Harmonize	Practice
Clap	Hum	Sing
Compose	Play	Strum
Finger	Plunk	Whistle

ART BEHAVIORS

Assemble	Draw	Paint
Brush	Form	Sculpt
Carve	Illustrate	Sketch
Cut	Mold	Varnish

MATHEMATICAL BEHAVIORS

Bisect	Extract	Plot
Calculate	Graph	Solve
Derive	Interpolate	Tabulate
Estimate	Measure	Verify

COMPLEX, LOGICAL, JUDGMENTAL BEHAVIORS

Analyze	Criticize	Formulate
Combine	Deduce	Generate
Conclude	Defend	Infer
Contrast	Evaluate	Plan

SOCIAL BEHAVIORS

Agree	Discuss	Participate
Aid	Forgive	Praise
Contribute	Interact	React
Cooperate	Invite	Volunteer

"STUDY" BEHAVIORS

Arrange	Diagram	Organize
Categorize	Itemize	Quote
Compile	Mark	Reproduce
Copy	Name	Underline

PHYSICAL BEHAVIORS

Arch	Hit	Ski
Bat	Hop	Skip
Climb	March	Swim
Face	Run	Swing

DRAMA BEHAVIORS

Act	Enter	Respond
Direct	Express	Show
Display	Pantomime	Start
Emit	Perform	Turn

LABORATORY SCIENCE BEHAVIORS

Apply	Dissect	Reset
Calibrate	Manipulate	Set
Convert	Operate	Transfer
Demonstrate	Report	Weight

GENERAL APPEARANCE, HEALTH, AND SAFETY BEHAVIORS

Button	Dress	Tie
Clean	Empty	Wash
Comb	Fasten	Wear
Cover	Lace	Zip

SOURCE: C. K. Claus, "Verbs and Imperative Sentences as a Basis for Stating Educational Objectives." Paper given at a meeting of the National Council on Measurement in Education, Chicago, 1968.

**TABLE 2–3   Instrumentation of the Taxonomy of Educational
Objectives: Cognitive Domain**

	KEY WORDS	
Taxonomy Classification	Examples of Infinitives	Examples of Direct Objects
1.00 Knowledge		
1.10 Knowledge of specifics		
1.11 Knowledge of terminology	To define, to distinguish, to acquire, to identify, to recall, to recognize	Vocabulary, terms, terminology, meaning(s), definitions, referents, elements
1.12 Knowledge of specific facts	To recall, to recognize, to acquire, to identify	Facts, factual information, (sources), (names), dates), (events), (persons), (places), (time periods), properties, examples, phenomena
1.20 Knowledge of ways and means of dealing with specifics		
1.21 Knowledge of conventions	To recall, to identify, to recognize, to acquire	Forms(s), conventions, uses, usage, rules, ways, devices, symbols, representations, style(s), format(s)
1.22 Knowledge of trends, sequences	To recall, to recognize, to acquire, to identify	Action(s), processes, movement(s), continuity, development(s), trend(s), sequence(s), causes, relationship(s), forces, influences
1.23 Knowledge of classifications and categories	To recall, to recognize, to acquire, to identify	Area(s), type(s), feature(s), class(es), set (s), division(s), arrangement(s), classification(s), category/categories
1.24 Knowledge of criteria	To recall, to recognize, to acquire, to identify	Criteria, basics, elements
1.25 Knowledge of methodology	To recall, to recognize, to acquire, to identify	Methods, techniques, approaches, uses, procedures, treatments

TABLE 2–3 (*Continued*)

KEY WORDS

Taxonomy Classification	Examples of Infinitives	Examples of Direct Objects
1.30 Knowledge of universals and abstractions in a field		
1.31 Knowledge of principles, generalizations	To recall, to recognize, to acquire, to identify	Principle(s), generalization(s), proposition(s), fundamentals, laws, principal elements, implication(s)
1.32 Knowledge of theories and structures	To recall, to recognize, to acquire, to identify	Theories, bases, interrelations, structure(s), organization(s), formulation(s)
2.00 Comprehension		
2.10 Translation	To translate, to transform, to give in words, to illustrate, to prepare, to read, to represent, to change, to rephrase, to restate	Meaning(s), sample(s), definitions, abstractions, representations, words, phrases
2.20 Interpretation	To interpret, to reorder, to rearrange, to differentiate, to distinguish, to make, to draw, to explain, to demonstrate	Relevancies, relationships, essentials, aspects, new view(s), qualifications, conclusions, methods, theories, abstractions
2.30 Extrapolation	To estimate, to infer, to conclude, to predict, to differentiate, to determine, to extend, to interpolate, to extrapolate, to fill in, to draw	Consequences, implications, conclusions, factors, ramifications, meanings, corollaries, effects, probabilities
3.00 Application	To apply, to generalize, to relate, to choose, to develop, to organize, to use, to employ, to transfer, to restructure, to classify	Principles, laws, conclusions, effects, methods, theories, abstractions, situations, generalizations, processes, phenomena, procedures
4.00 Analysis		

TABLE 2–3 *(Continued)*

KEY WORDS

Taxonomy Classification	Examples of Infinitives	Examples of Direct Objects
4.10 Analysis of elements	To distinguish, to detect, to identify, to classify, to discriminate, to recognize, to categorize, to deduce	Elements, hypothesis/hypotheses, conclusions, assumptions, statements (of fact), statements (of of intent), arguments, particulars
4.20 Analysis of relationships	To analyze, to contrast, to compare, to distinguish, to deduce	Relationships, interrelations, relevance/relevancies, themes, evidence, fallacies, arguments, cause-effect(s), consistency/consistencies, parts, ideas, assumptions
4.30 Analysis of organizational principles	To analyze, to distinguish, to detect, to deduce	Form(s), pattern(s), purpose(s), point(s) of view(s), techniques, bias(es), structure(s), theme(s), arrangement(s), organization(s)
5.00 Synthesis		
5.10 Production of a unique communication	To write, to tell, to relate, to produce, to constitute, to transmit, to originate, to modify, to document	Structure(s), pattern(s), product(s), performance(s), design(s), work(s), communications, effort(s), specifics, composition(s)
5.20 Production of a plan, or proposed set of operations	To propose, to plan, to produce, to design, to modify, to specify	Plan(s), objectives, specification(s), schematic(s), operations, way(s), solution(s), means
5.30 Derivation of a set of abstract relations	To produce, to derive, to develop, to combine, to organize, to synthesize, to classify, to deduce, to develop, to formulate, to modify	Phenomena, taxonomies, concept(s), scheme(s), theories, relationships, abstractions, generalizations, hypothesis/hypotheses, perceptions, ways, discoveries
6.00 Evaluation		
6.10 Judgments in terms of internal evidence	To judge, to argue, to validate, to assess, to decide	Accuracy/accuracies, consistency/consistencies, fallacies, reliability, flaws, errors, precision, exactness

TABLE 2–3 *(Continued)*

KEY WORDS

Taxonomy Classification	Examples of Infinitives	Examples of Direct Objects
6.20 Judgments in terms of external criteria	To judge, to argue, to consider, to compare, to contrast, to standardize, to appraise	Ends, means, efficiency, economy/economies, utility, alternatives, courses of action, standards, theories, generalizations

SOURCE: Reprinted from N. Metfessel, W. B. Michael, and D. A. Kirsner, "Instrumentation of Bloom's and Krathwohl's Taxonomies for the Writing of Behavioral Objectives," *Psychology in the Schools*, 1969, **6**, 227–231. With permission of the publisher.

square root on an electronic calculator and quite another to do it by hand. Computing the volume of a sphere requires different skills if one needs to know the formula from those needed if the formula is available.

Some advocates of behavioral objectives also suggest specifying the criterion, or standard, by which the behavior is evaluated. This is clearly necessary if by "standard" one means advance preparation of the answer to a test question or the criterion that will be used in evaluating, for example, the goodness of a bead in welding or the quality of a vocal solo. One cannot evaluate unless there are criteria that can be used to differentiate quality of behavior. However, if by "standard" one means setting an arbitrary cutoff determination of whether one can weld or sing, the advisability of setting a criterion becomes more debatable. Usually, there are *degrees* of performance. It is not particularly wise to think of an objective as being either met or not met. More often the degree to which the objective has been achieved is the information desired. (More will be said on this topic in Chapter 3.)

Although there are certain techniques of wording objectives in order to make them behavioral, the major problem in writing them is that probably teachers have not really thought through what behaviors are reasonable indicants of their nonbehaviorally stated objectives. They do not "really understand" their objectives![4] Tables 2–2 and 2–3 are hopefully helpful, but to write objectives that are amenable to evaluation requires considerable knowledge about the subject matter being taught and about the change in behavior one hopes to elicit from the students as a result of an instructional sequence.

[4] We hope the reader recognizes this statement as nonbehavioral. In behavioral terminology we are saying that if they cannot write behavioral objectives, we can infer from this lack of behavior that they have not adequately "thought through" or "understood" their objectives.

Certainly, it is more difficult to word objectives behaviorally in some areas than in others. Whenever the objective is one from the affective domain, it is particularly hard to specify behaviorally. As we stated before, the reason for this is that the behaviors themselves are often *not* our objectives, but are the indicants of the particular affect that we are trying to instill.

One more point should be mentioned. Writing educational objectives behaviorally is a difficult task. It is obvious that most educators do not do this task nearly so well as the theorists suggest. (See Ammons, 1964.) As a partial help for teachers who recognize the need for behavioral objectives, but who have neither the time nor talent to develop a comprehensive list of their own, the sources listed earlier (e.g., Flanagan et al., 1971; Popham, 1970) may be helpful. Also, several small books have been written by educational psychologists to teach educators how to write objectives (see Burns, 1972; Gronlund, 1970; Kibler et al., 1970; Lee & Merrill, 1972; Lindvall, 1964; Mager, 1962; McAshan, 1974; Vargus, 1972; Yelon & Scott, 1970).

An Example of Stating Objectives for Instruction and Evaluation

In writing behavioral objectives, one begins by stating a general learning outcome. For this statement such nonaction verbs as "applies," "comprehends," "knows," and "understands" are permissible. (These are probably second-level objectives.) Examples of objectives for this chapter, stated as general learning outcomes, would be as follows:

1. Knows sources of information about objectives
2. Comprehends that objectives are stated differently, depending on the purpose of the communication
3. Appreciates the value of making objectives behavioral

Once all general outcomes are stated, the next task is to make a representative list of explicit student behaviors which can be used as evidence that the general objective has been achieved. Since making affective objectives behavioral is the most challenging, let us try to specify some behavorial objectives for the general statement 3 listed above.

a. Completes a nonrequired assignment on writing behavorial objectives
b. Gives a report on one of the texts mentioned on behavorial objectives
c. Enrolls in a one-hour seminar devoted solely to writing behavorial objectives
d. Proselytizes the need for behavorial objectives with other students
e. Completes favorably a confidential rating scale on the importance of behavioral objectives
f. Asks for further information about affective behavorial objectives

This sample of specific learning outcomes could be made much more complete. Only time, divergent thinking, an understanding of the word "appreciates," and an awareness of the multiple ways to measure are necessary. These behaviors, if performed under natural conditions, are ones from which we can reasonably infer positive affect. Of course, it is always possible to *fake* affect. This is one reason we argue for not considering a student's affect in a course when reporting his level of achievement. See Chapter 17, "Marking and Reporting the Results of Measurement," for a fuller discussion of this issue.)

UNANTICIPATED AND/OR UNMEASURABLE OUTCOMES

Most educators will admit that stating objectives behaviorally is not a panacea for existing weaknesses and limitations of educational evaluation. Lists of objectives will always be incomplete. There will be unanticipated outcomes and these too should be evaluated. Also, while in principle every objective is measurable, we must admit that in practice it is not so.[5] Eisner's example of a teacher taking her suburban children to visit the slums is a good illustration of an educational procedure that will have both unanticipated and unmeasurable outcomes. The same holds true of *any encounter* with students. There will always be unanticipated and unmeasurable outcomes. With regard to the unanticipated outcomes, educators should be alert to recognize them and should try to evaluate as many as possible. But to do this, one has to seek clues as to what they might be, so that they can be evaluated. These clues may be obtained in many ways, such as by interviewing students or parents and by carefully observing classroom, lunchroom, and recess situations. There are probably not so many "unmeasurable outcomes" as many educators suppose. By employing a variety of measurement techniques, many of the outcomes considered unmeasurable can be measured. Certainly, a fair number of outcomes cannot be measured via the traditional paper-pencil achievement test, but such procedures as observations, anecdotal records, sociometric devices, and attitude inventories can be used to obtain evidence for many of these outcomes.

The situation is schematically represented by Figure 2–1. Cell A contains intended, measurable results. These are the ones we state behaviorally and for which we develop appropriate measuring instruments. In cell B are the unanticipated outcomes. If educators carefully consider possible outcomes to instructional procedures, there should *not* be a great many unanticipated outcomes. If there are, insufficient thought went into the instructional planning. The intended, unmeasurable outcomes in cell C should also be few in

[5] This can be seen if learning is defined as the predisposition to respond in a certain way under certain environmental conditions. The evaluator may simply not have the environmental conditions sufficiently under control to make an evaluation of whether learning has occurred.

	INTENDED OUTCOMES	UNANTICIPATED OUTCOMES
MEASURABLE OUTCOMES	A	B
UNMEASURABLE OUTCOMES	C	D

FIGURE 2–1 A two-way categorization of outcomes.

number. If an educator has expected outcomes, he should want to find out whether or not they are being realized. Careful and creative consideration of his objectives should ordinarily lead him to the realization that there are measurable behaviors from which he can reasonably infer whether the intended outcome has been achieved. This is true regardless of the subject matter or age level taught. If you have many objectives in cell C, it is probably because you have not thought about what behaviors may indicate that objective, or perhaps you are not knowledgeable enough about measurement techniques to be aware of the variety of behaviors that can be measured. For every objective in cell C, you are admitting that you have an important goal but that you have no way of knowing the degree to which it is being realized. While one should not discard goals that cannot be evaluated, it would certainly be disquieting to teach for 30 years if very many of one's objectives were in that category!

SUMMARY

The principal ideas, conclusions, and implications of this chapter are summarized in the following statements:

1. One of the important tasks of educators is to determine the goals of education.
2. Goals (objectives) help an instructor in instructional planning, guide

student learning, and provide a criterion for evaluating student outcomes.

3. Two considerations in selecting goals are their relevance and the feasibility of attaining them. After they are selected, their priorities must be determined.

4. Many published statements can serve as guidelines for the teacher involved in determining goals. Such published statements as those of Kearney (1953) and French et al. (1957), the National Assessment of Educational Progress booklets (no date), the Instructional Objectives Exchange Center (Popham, 1970), and the Westinghouse collection (Flanagan, 1971) are all helpful guidelines.

5. The taxonomies have also been of assistance in helping educators determine and communicate about goals. They are also helpful in preparing assessment devices.

6. Once goals are selected, they need to be communicated to a variety of people. There is no one best way to communicate educational goals; it depends upon whom you are communicating with and the purpose of the communication.

7. It is generally better to state goals in terms of the student outcomes than of the teaching processes.

8. We should communicate both immediate and ultimate goals and the relationships between them.

9. Most educational goals can be more efficiently communicated in somewhat general terms. At times, however (for example, in specific training programs within an educational setting), it is appropriate and expedient to communicate very specific objectives.

10. A behavioral objective is one that specifies what the learner will be *doing* when we evaluate whether or not he has attained the goal. Thus, statements of behavioral objectives make use of action verbs.

11. Stating objectives in behavioral terms is mandatory if we are to evaluate those objectives. Such behavioral statements are also typically helpful in planning instructional strategies.

12. One potential problem of stating behavioral objectives is that one can confuse the behavior with the objective. At times, the behavior is the objective. At other times, it is only an indicant of an objective.

13. Stating objectives via a levels approach has much to recommend it. First one states general learning outcomes, often in nonbehavioral terms. Then one lists under each of those outcomes a representative sample of the specific types of behavior that indicates attainment of the objective.

14. Unanticipated and/or unmeasureable outcomes do occur as a result of education. If there are too many of these, it may well indicate that insufficient thought went into specifying the original objectives and planning the instruction and evaluation procedures.

CHAPTER THREE
Norm- and Criterion- Referenced Measurement

One current issue in measurement is with regard to the distinctions between, and relative advantages and disadvantages of, norm-referenced and criterion-referenced measurement (NRM and CRM). What do those two terms mean? What are the advantages and disadvantages of each? Which is the more useful for various purposes? We believe a brief discussion of this topic early in the book will benefit our readers. Further elaborations of this same topic will occur at subsequent places in the book. After completing this chapter, the student should be able to—

1. Recognize the distinctions and similarities between norm- and criterion-referenced measurement.
2. Recognize the need for both norm- and criterion-referenced measurement.
3. Determine, for a given decision, which types of data are likely to prove most useful.

DISTINCTIONS BETWEEN NORM- AND CRITERION-REFERENCED MEASUREMENT

Although there is confusion with respect to how the terms NRM and CRM are used, the distinction between the two types of *scores* seems clear enough. If we interpret a score of an individual by comparing that score with those of other individuals (called a norm group) this would be norm referencing. If we interpret a person's performance by comparing it with some specified behavioral criterion of proficiency, this would be criterion referencing. To polarize the distinction, we could say that the focus of a normative score is on how many of Johnny's peers do not perform (score) as well as he does; the focus of a criterion-referenced score is on what it is that Johnny can do. Of course we can, and often do, interpret a single test score both ways. In norm referencing we might make a statement that "John did better than 80 percent of the students in a test on addition of whole numbers." In criterion referencing we might say that "John got 70 percent of the items correct in a test on addition of whole numbers." Usually we would add further "meaning" to this statement by stating whether or not we thought 70 percent was inadequate, minimally adequate, excellent, or whatever.

Although measurement experts generally agree on the distinction between norm-referenced and criterion-referenced score interpretation, some misunderstanding exists about the norm-referenced interpretation. Some individuals seem to think that norm-referenced measurement tells us nothing about what a person can do, but only how the person compares with others, period—as if the comparison were not on some specified *content!*

Ebel (1962, p. 19) correctly pointed out that "to be meaningful any test scores must be related to test content *as well as* to the scores of other examinees." Jackson (1970, p. 2) agreed and stated that any test will sample the content of some specified domain and that there is always an implicit behavioral element. Careful reading of the content validity section of Chapter 5 should convince you that experts in achievement test construction have always stressed the importance of defining the specified content domain and sampling from it in some appropriate fashion. Thus, all good achievement test items, be they norm or criterion referenced, should be keyed to a set of objectives.

Whether this keying to objectives is sufficient to allow a criterion-referenced interpretation depends on how restrictive a definition one holds for a criterion-referenced test. Ivens (1970, p. 2) simply defines a criterion-referenced test as one "comprised of items keyed to a set of behavioral objectives." Harris and Stewart (1971, p. 1) give a much more restrictive definition: "A pure criterion-referenced test is one consisting of a sample of production tasks drawn from a well-defined population of performances, a sample that may be used to estimate the proportion of performances in that population at which the student can succeed." Glaser and Nitko (1971) define criterion-referenced tests as those deliberately constructed so as to yield scores directly interpretable in terms of specified performance standards. Millman (1974) would use the term domain-referenced test for the Harris-Stewart definition of CRTs, and the term objective-based test for Ivens' definition. All good achievement tests (those with high content validity) are objective based, very few can truly be called domain-referenced (or fit the Harris-Stewart definition of a pure criterion-referenced test). Most existing achievement tests probably fit in the general category of what Millman (1974) calls a criterion-referenced differential assessment device (CRDAD). In constructing such tests, one defines a content domain (but generally not with *complete* specificity) and writes items measuring this domain. But if one uses statistical procedures to judge the quality of the items with respect to their ability to differentiate groups and/or individuals on the degree to which they have achieved the attribute, then one can no longer make an inference that a student "knows" 75 percent of the domain because he/she answered 75 percent of the items correctly. The inability to make this particular inference is due to the use of empirical data in choosing items, whether those empirical data are pretest-posttest differences in item difficulty or the capabilities of the items to discriminate between good and poor students at a single point in time. Actually there are probably few situations where we need to make the pure criterion-referenced interpretation. To know that an individual can type 60 words per minute on an IBM Selectric is useful data whether or not the words on the test were randomly chosen from some totally specified domain of words. To know that an individual can correctly add 80 percent of the items on paired three-digit whole numbers asked on a test is useful whether or not those items were randomly pulled from the total set of permutations possible.

Our definition of "criterion-referenced interpretation" does not take on the narrow, pure meaning specified by Harris and Stewart. Rather, the distinction between the two terms is whether the *comparison* of the score is made to other individuals' scores (norm referencing) or to some specified standard, or set of standards (criterion referencing).

Depending on the decision we wish to make, one of these two ways of interpreting the score will likely be more useful than the other, and it has been suggested by many that for those situations where criterion referencing is likely to be the most useful, a measuring instrument should be constructed and analyzed somewhat differently from what "classical measurement theory" suggests.

Classical measurement theory originated and developed from an interest in measuring the aptitudes of individuals. Thus, the emphasis has been on devising measures that differentiate or discriminate among individuals at all points along the continuum. That is, a test is devised so that individuals who have more aptitude will score higher on the test than those who possess less. The interpretation here of "how much" aptitude a person possesses is a normative one. The same test theory, and this tendency to construct tests that discriminate among individuals, has carried over to achievement testing. There are times, however, when it is not necessary, and perhaps not even advisable, to differentiate individuals at all degrees of achievement. We may simply want to find out whether individuals have achieved a specific set of objectives. In other words, we reference a person's score against a criterion. Thus, there are really two different goals or objectives in *achievement testing*: (1) to discriminate among all individuals according to their degrees of achievement and (2) to discriminate among those who have and have not reached set standards (or to determine whether each person has or has not achieved a specific set of objectives). Textbooks on constructing achievement tests have typically discussed testing techniques that lead to the first goal. Some educators feel that this is somewhat deplorable, and suggest that more emphasis be placed on achieving the second goal.

CONSTRUCTING CRITERION- AND NORM-REFERENCED ACHIEVEMENT TESTS

As mentioned, traditional test theory and techniques of test construction have been developed on the assumption that the purpose of a test is to discriminate among individuals. If the purpose of a test is to compare each individual to a standard, then it is irrelevant whether or not the individuals differ from each other. Thus, some of the criteria of a measuring instrument considered essential for a norm-referenced measure are not important for criterion-referenced measures (see Popham & Husek, 1969). What one looks for in item analysis, reliability, and some types of validity are different in a criterion-referenced measure.

However, for many aspects of test construction, such as considering the objectives, preparing test blueprints, and actually wording the items, there are more similarities than differences in the preparation of norm- and criterion-referenced tests. There is a healthy emphasis, for example, on making sure that items measure certain specified objectives in criterion-referenced tests. But this same characteristic should hold for a norm-referenced instrument.

However, often when one is constructing a test that is intended for a criterion-referenced *interpretation*, the objectives sampled are more limited in number. When one is constructing a test that is intended for norm-referenced interpretation, the objectives are typically broader in focus.

Differences and similarities between the two approaches—as they pertain to reliability, validity, test blueprints, item writing, and item analysis—will all be discussed in later sections of the text.

USES FOR CRITERION-REFERENCED MEASUREMENT

The recent support for criterion-referenced measurement seems to have originated in large part from the emphases on behavioral objectives, the sequencing and individualization of instruction, the development of programmed materials, a learning theory that *suggests* that most anybody can learn most anything if given enough time, the increased interest in certification, and a belief that norm referencing promotes unhealthy competition and is injurious to low-scoring-students' self-concepts.

If we can specify important objectives in behavioral terms, then, many would argue, the important consideration is to ascertain whether a student obtained those objectives rather than his position relative to other students. Traditionally, the principal use of criterion-referenced measurement has been in "mastery tests." A mastery test is a particular type of criterion-referenced test. Mastery, as the word is typically used, connotes an either/or situation. The person has either achieved (mastered) the objective(s) satisfactorily or has not. Criterion-referenced testing in general could also apply to degrees of performance. Mastery tests are used in programs of individualized instruction, such as the Individually Prescribed Instruction (IPI) program (Lindvall & Bolvin, 1967), or in the mastery learning model devised by Bloom (1968). Such instructional programs are composed of units or modules, usually considered hierarchical, each based on one or more instructional objectives. Each individual is required to work on the unit until he has achieved a specified minimum level of achievement. Thus he is considered to have "mastered" the unit. In such programs the instructional decision of what to do with a student is *not* dependent on how his performance compares to others. If he has performed adequately on the objectives, then the decision is to move on to the next unit of study. If he has not, then he is required to restudy the material (although perhaps using a different procedure) covered in the test until he performs adequately, that is, "masters" the material. If instructional procedures are organized so that time is the dimension that varies and degree of mastery is held constant, then mastery tests should be used in greater proportion than they are now.

Employing the individually prescribed instruction or mastery model of learning is not the only use for criterion-referenced measures. One may also use such data to help evaluate (make decisions about) instructional programs. In order to determine whether specific instructional treatments or procedures have been successful, it is necessary to have data about the outcomes on the specific objectives the program was designed to teach. A measure comparing students to each other (norm referencing) may not give so effective data as a measure comparing each student's performance to the objectives.

Also, criterion-referenced measures offer certain benefits for instructional decision making within the classroom. The diagnosis of specific difficulties, accompanied by a prescription of certain instructional treatments, is necessary in instruction whether or not one uses a mastery approach to learning.

Finally, criterion-referenced tests can be useful in broad surveys of educational accomplishment such as the National Assessment of Educational Progress or state assessment programs (see Chapter 18).

Mastery Testing

Since in education mastery testing is apparently the most frequently used criterion-referenced approach and has been strongly advocated as "one of the most powerful ideas beginning to shape educational views and practices" (Block, 1971, iii), we will discuss the rationale behind it a bit more thoroughly. The idea of mastery learning and mastery testing is certainly not new (see Morrison, 1926; Washburne, 1922), and as Baker (1971b, p. 65) suggested, "A considerable literature relating to the evils of mastery tests exists, and much of the work of early educational psychologists was in reaction to the unreal requirement that all pupils achieve criterion performance." The basic idea of mastery learning, however, was revitalized with the publication of a paper by Carroll (1963) entitled "A Model of School Learning." Essentially, the model suggests that the degree of learning is a function of the time the student spends on the material, divided by the time needed. More precisely, Carroll suggested that the degree of learning is some function of the time allowed and the perseverance of the student, divided by the student's aptitude for the task, his ability to understand the instruction, and the quality of instruction.

Bloom (1968) agreed with the basics of the model and suggested that the degree of learning required should be fixed at some "mastery" level and that the instructional variables should be manipulated so that all (or almost all) students achieve mastery. Bloom stated that "Most students (perhaps over 90 percent) can master what we have to teach them" (Bloom, 1968, p. 1). (Interestingly enough, this bold statement was made prior to defining mastery, for later in the same paragraph Bloom stated that "Our basic task is to determine what we mean by mastery. . . ." How do we know that 90 percent can master what we have to teach them if we haven't defined what mastery is?) If the model is correct and if people should all persevere until they have "mastered" the material, then the mastery learning model of instruction should be employed—and mastery testing needs to be used to determine whether mastery has occurred.

Tentative evidence (Block, 1971; 1974) suggests that in many subject-matter areas all students can achieve some (often arbitrarily) defined level of mastery, although—as Carroll (1971, p. 31) pointed out—if the task is very difficult or depends upon special aptitudes, there may be a number of students who never make it. Becoming a 4-minute miler or a concert pianist are examples.

Excluding the extreme 5 percent of the students, the time ratio between slower and faster students to master a set of objections is about 6 to 1, although Bloom, Hastings and Madaus (1971, p. 51) and Bloom (1974, p. 685) have suggested that this may be reduced to about 3 to 1. This 3-to-1 ratio is elapsed time. Bloom suggests that a more precise measure is the amount of time a student is actively working on a project. He feels the differences on this variable may be reducible to a ratio of 1.5 to 1 (Bloom, 1974, p. 688). Glaser (1968, p. 28) reported that in three years of Individually Prescribed Instruction in mathematics, one student had covered 73 units, one only 13. Whether or not it is worthwhile educationally to have a student persist for three to six days, weeks, or years on a task others can complete in one day, week, or year is debatable. They probably should for those few basic skills that indeed are essential for survival and must be achieved before further hierarchical skills can be acquired. For other things we attempt to teach in school—like understanding of modern literature—a mastery model should probably not be employed. There is even some doubt if it would work for such a subject. As both Block (1971, p. 66) and Bloom (1971b, p. 33) pointed out, mastery learning strategies are more effective for *closed* subjects (those whose content has not changed for some time) and those that emphasize convergent rather than divergent thinking. The implications for education of this admission by mastery advocates are not always fully appreciated. However, Cronbach, in a reaction to one of Bloom's mastery learning papers, brought the issue into sharp focus:

> I find the concept of mastery severely limiting, and in trying to find out where my distress lies, I finally focused on one word in the Bloom paper: he states that mastery learning is *closed*. Training is closed. In education the problems are open. . . .
> I see educational development as continuous and open-ended. "Mastery" seems to imply that at some point we get to the end of what is to be taught (Cronbach, 1971, pp. 52, 53).

Anastasi (1976, p. 99) states flatly that "beyond basic skills, mastery testing is inapplicable or insufficient."

MASTERY TESTING AND GRADES

Bloom began his 1968 paper with the statement: "Each teacher begins a new term with the expectation that about a third of his students will adequately learn what he has to teach." As his paper proceeded, it is apparent that he based this statement on the fact that if a teacher graded on a normative basis about 33 percent would receive A's or B's. He suggested that "we proceed in our teaching as though only the minority of our students should be able to learn what we have to teach." What Bloom did, of course, was to attach his own absolute standards of interpretation to a normative reporting system. If a teacher gives a student a C because the teacher is using a normative system and because the student is average (that is, in comparison to others, he was close to the middle), the grade of C in no way indicates inadequate performance. The symbols A through F can obviously take on any meaning a person assigns to them. But if a teacher assigns them on a relative basis, it is hardly appropriate for someone else to interpret them on an absolute basis. We do not doubt that if those who score below a normative-based A were to continue studying the course material, many of them could in time achieve as well as the A students did originally. But we wonder why average performance should be interpreted as inadequate by a student, teacher, or educational psychologist, or why mastery should, as Bloom suggested, be considered identical to an A grade. One may well want students to "master" a certain amount of material before being allowed to advance to a higher unit or course. Whether one labels this mastery as an A or a D is irrelevant as long as the meaning is made clear. We will talk more about this point in Chapter 17.

MASTERY LEARNING AND SELF-CONCEPT

Bloom et al. felt that:

> Mastery learning can be one of the more powerful sources of mental health. We are convinced that many of the neurotic symptoms displayed by high school and college students are exacerbated by painful and frustrating experiences in school learning. If 90 percent of the students are given positive indications of adequacy in learning, one might expect them to need less and less in the way of emotional therapy and psychological help. Conversely, frequent indications of failure and learning inadequacy are bound to be accompanied by increased self-doubt in the student (Bloom et al., 1971, p. 56).

With the exception of the first sentence in the preceding statement, we are inclined to agree (although no good evidence exists). The question remains, however, whether the mastery learning approach will decrease a student's painful and frustrating experiences in school learning, or whether it will increase the positive indications of adequacy in learning. We are inclined to think that the student who is forced to spend ten weeks on a unit that another student finished in two weeks will perceive that experience to be more painful and that he will have experienced more indications of failure and inadequacy than if we had assigned him a grade of C or D after the first two weeks. Contrary to Bloom's impression, many students perceive C's and D's to be quite adequate. Of course Bloom's hope is that the time ratio may be reduced to a vanishing point (Bloom, 1971a, p. 8), but he admits such a point has never been reached, and it is indeed very doubtful that individual differences in school will or should reach a vanishing point.

These last few paragraphs have not been written to denigrate the mastery learning approach. The mastery learning-testing model is useful for some situations. But it is probably not the pervasive good that some of its proselytizers would suggest.

CAUTIONS IN CRITERION-REFERENCED MEASUREMENT

The 1970s saw criterion-referenced measurement revitalized from the 1920 era. Many recent writers (particularly in the more popularized, nontechnical professional journals) have been singing the praises of CRM and ignoring some cautions, dangers, and limitations. Although CRM can serve some important functions it is useful to keep in mind the following points:

1. Criterion-referenced measurement gets defined in a myriad of ways. The narrow, specific definition by Harris and Stewart, which states that a CRM is one which allows us to estimate the proportion of performances in a domain at which a student can succeed, is one perfectly legitimate definition. However, extremely few tests fit this definition, and we should recognize the limitations of making the strong inference from proportion correct in a sample of items to proportion correct in a population of items for most tests that are called criterion referenced.

2. Many so-called CRTs have no more content validity than many NRTs.

3. If we choose items based on sensitivity to instruction (postinstruction minus preinstruction gain scores), then the resultant test is just as content "biased" as if we choose items based on their ability to differentiate between good and poor students.

4. Typically, in mastery testing we would not use items that tap the depth of learning of the few very best students. The next step might be to inappropriately exclude from the curriculum the ideas with which only a few students can cope (Gladstone, 1975). One should not reduce all teaching and testing to the minimal mastery level.

5. Many criterion-referenced tests are shorter and therefore are not as reliable as norm-referenced tests.

6. The questions of how long to make the test and how high to set the cutting score can be answered only by reasonably complicated psychometric procedures that require some fairly specific assumptions about the costs of making errors (Hambleton & Novick, 1973; Millman, 1974; Swaminathan, Hambleton, & Algina, 1975).

7. Criterion-referenced test results do not inform decision makers whether children achieve what they should when they should (Grosswald, 1973).

8. Criterion-referenced test prescriptions can be ignored by teachers as readily as they ignore item analyses of norm-referenced tests (Grosswald, 1973).

9. One must interpret criterion-referenced tests cautiously. If students fail to master an objective, the fault may be in the instruction, the test items, the standard of mastery and/or the objective itself (Gronlund, 1973, p. 40).

USES FOR NORM-REFERENCED MEASUREMENT

As stated earlier in this chapter, most testing and the theory of testing have been based on the norm-referenced approach. There is little argument that such an approach is useful in aptitude testing where we wish to make differential predictions. It is also often very useful to achievement testing. Many educators would agree with Gronlund's (1971, p. 139) statement: "In measuring the extent to which pupils are achieving our course objectives, we have no absolute standard by which to determine their progress. A pupil's achievement can be regarded as high or low only by comparing it with the achievement of other pupils."

Accepting this view, the role of a measuring device is to give us as reliable a rank ordering of the pupils as possible with respect to the achievement we are measuring. Knowing what we do about individual differences, it is obvious that students will learn differing amounts of subject matter even under a mastery learning approach. It may be that all students, or at least a high percentage of them, have learned a significant enough portion of a teacher's objectives to be categorized as having "mastered" the essentials of the course or unit. But some of these students have learned more than others, and it seems worthwhile to employ measurement techniques that identify these pupils. In the first place, students want and deserve recognition for accomplishment that goes beyond the minimum. If we continually gave only mastery tests, those students who accomplish at a higher level would lose one of the important extrinsic rewards of learning, that is, recognition for such accomplishments.

Perhaps a more important reason for discrimination testing than student recognition is in its benefits for decision making. If two physicians have mastered surgery, but one has mastered it better, which one do you wish to have operate on you? (For that matter, even if two physicians had equally mastered their training program, one would probably want some norm-referencing information about time to completion. If one physician is such a slow learner that it takes him five times as long to learn the material as the other one, it is probably safe to assume that after he has been on the job ten years, he will not be so up to date on current medical practices as the fast learner.) If two teachers have mastered the basics of teaching, but one is a much better teacher, which do we want to hire? If two students have mastered first-semester algebra, but one has learned it much better (or faster, time being norm-referenced), which should receive the most encouragement to continue in mathematics? We probably all agree on the answers to these questions. However, if we have not employed evaluation techniques that allow us to differentiate between the individuals, we cannot make these types of decisions. Certainly, norm-referenced measures are the most helpful in fixed-quota selection decisions. For example, if there are a limited number of openings in a pilot training school, the school would want to select the best of the applicants—even though all may be above some "mastery level."

Norm-referenced testing is often considered a necessary component of program evaluation. We have mentioned earlier that CRTs are often more narrow in focus than NRTs. Some view this more narrow focus as an advantage in program evaluation. You can construct a CRT over the particular program objectives and see if they have been achieved. However, in evaluating a program we also would wish to know how effective it is in comparison to other possible programs. Without random assignment of students to programs (which we seldom have in the public schools) the comparison needs to be through some norm-referenced procedure that compares the performance of the pupils in the program with that norm group.

Also, the more narrow focus of a CRT may not be an unmitigated blessing. At times one would wish to evaluate broader outcomes. Consider the following quote by Cronbach (1963, p. 680).

> In course evaluation, we need not be much concerned about making measuring instruments fit the curriculum. However startling this declaration may seem, and however contrary to the principles of evaluation for other purposes, this must be our position if we want to know what changes a course produces in the pupil. An ideal evaluation would include measures of all the types of proficiency that might reasonably be desired in the area in question, not just the selected outcomes to which this curriculum directs substantial attention. If you wish only to know how well a curriculum is achieving its objectives, you fit the test to the curriculum; but if you wish to know how well the curriculum is serving the national interest, you measure all outcomes that might be worth striving for. One of the new mathematics courses might disavow any attempt to teach numerical trigonometry, and indeed, might discard nearly all computational work. It is still perfectly reasonable to ask how well graduates of the course can compute and can solve right triangles. Even if the course developers went so far as to contend that computational skill is no proper objective of secondary instruction, they will encounter educators and laymen who do not share their view. If it can be shown that students who come through the new course are fairly proficient in computation despite the lack of direct teaching, the doubters will be reassured. If not, the evidence makes clear how much is being sacrificed.

COMPARING THE TWO MEASURES

The decision concerning when to use norm-referenced and when to use criterion-referenced interpretations depends upon the kind of decision one wishes to make. For guidance decisions we should employ both NR and CR interpretations. CRTs are promoted mostly in achievement testing. Aptitude, interest, and most personality inventories are norm referenced. This seems appropriate. In general it is probably more useful for a person to know how his aptitudes or interests compare with those of others than to obtain some kind of CR score. For selection decisions, NRT is preferred. For classification decisions one might use both. For placement and certification decisions, one might well use primarily CRT. For instructional decisions, it depends mostly upon the instructional procedures employed. If instruction is structured so that time is the variable, and a student keeps at a task until he has mastered it, then we should use mastery testing. This type of instruction is often employed in individualized instruction. If instruction is structured so that time of exposure is constant, then students will achieve at different levels, and we should attempt to discern this differential achievement with a test that discriminates, although we might well want to attach both normative and criterion-referenced meaning to the score. Which instructional procedure should be used depends upon the structure and importance of the subject matter being taught.

There surely are some subjects so structured that it is futile to teach higher concepts until basic ones have been mastered. For example, students cannot do long division until they can subtract and multiply at some basic level (although precisely at *what* level is unknown). This is certainly not true of all subjects, however. We do not really need to have mastered (or even have read) *A Tale of Two Cities* before reading *Catcher in the Rye*, or vice versa.

Likewise, as mentioned earlier, there may well be some skills or knowledges so important that all students should master them, regardless of how long it takes. Knowing how to spell one's name probably fits in this category. But, again, this is not true of all subjects. With regard to this point, Ebel stated:

> We might be willing to allow one student a week to learn what another can learn in a day. But sum these differences over the myriads of things to be learned. Does anyone, student, teacher, or society, want to see one person spend 16 or 24 years getting the same elementary education another can get in eight? Should it be those least able to learn quickly who spend the largest portion of their lives in trying to learn? Our present practice is quite the reverse. Those who are facile in learning make a career of it. Those who are not find other avenues of service, fulfillment and success (Ebel, 1969, p. 12).

Gronlund (1970, p. 32) made a distinction between objectives that are considered as *minimum essentials* and those that encourage *maximum development*. For the former, one would want to employ mastery testing; for the latter, discrimination testing. Thus for instructional decision making we are suggesting that there is a place for both mastery (criterion-referenced) and discrimination (norm-referenced) testing. The way most schools are currently organized, with time of instruction constant for all individuals and degree of learning the variable, discrimination testing should be prevalent. However, as more individualized instructional processes are used and as more is learned about how various subject matters should be sequenced, mastery testing may

TABLE 3–1   **Summary Position Statements on the Mastery-Discrimination Controversy**

Advcoates of discrimination testing believe that—	Advocates of mastery testing believe that—
1. Mastery can be only arbitrarily defined and that there are important decisions to be reached from knowledge of degrees of achievement.	1. Mastery is definable in a meaningful, useful way, and degrees of mastery for many subjects either do not exist or are unimportant.
2. Most subject matter is not so structured that understanding one concept requires "complete mastery" of a previous concept.	2. Most subject matter is hierarchically structured.
3. Varying time rather than amount learned is not the most beneficial or efficient instructional strategy.	3. For hierarchically structured subjects it is an unwise pedagogical decision to attempt to teach higher concepts if the basics have not been mastered.
4. All students need not, and probably should not, learn many (if any) things to the same degree of proficiency.	4. Therefore, it is better to allow variations in the time spent in learning than in the amount learned (that is, it is better for a student to learn fewer things more thoroughly).
5. Even if item 4 were a reasonable goal, what we know about individual differences suggests that even by making time a variable, student proficiencies are not likely to be very homogeneous.	5. All pupils enrolled in a course should learn the same things from that course.
6. If differential learning exists, it is wasteful not to measure it, since it is a potential aid in decision making.	

increase in importance. Mastery testing is probably more important in the early elementary grades than later in school. Table 3–1 is an oversimplification, but it summarizes the polar positions for instructional purposes.

Finally, we should mention again that many tests are amenable to both norm- and criterion-referenced interpretation. Publishers of some standardized achievement tests, for example, report a norm-referenced score on each subtest and within each subtest report whether a pupil answered each item correctly as well as the percent of pupils in the classroom, building, district, and national norm group who got the item correct. These item statistics are also frequently collated over items for each objective and the data reported for each objective.[2]

---

[2] Remember, we are not using the precise Harris-Stewart definition of CRM. Standardized achievement tests are seldom, if ever, CR under this definition.

SUMMARY

The principal ideas, conclusions, and implications of this chapter are summarized in the following statements:

1. Norm referencing is used to interpret a score of an individual by comparing it with those of other individuals.
2. Criterion referencing is used to interpret a person's performance by comparing it to some specified behavioral criterion.
3. A test score, to be most meaningful, should be related to both norms and criteria.
4. A test should have content validity whether one employs norm or criterion referencing.
5. A *pure* criterion-referenced *test* (also called a domain-referenced test) is one consisting of a sample of questions drawn from a domain in such a fashion that one may estimate the proportion of questions from the total domain a student knows based on the proportion correct in the test. Few tests fit this narrow definition.
6. Typically, the objectives sampled in a criterion-referenced test are more narrow in focus than the objectives sampled in a norm-referenced test.
7. The principal use of criterion-referenced measurement is in mastery testing.
8. In mastery testing, one is concerned with making an either/or decision. The person has either achieved (mastered) the objective(s) satisfactorily or has not.
9. Mastery tests are used in programs of individualized instruction where a mastery learning model is employed.
10. The mastery learning model suggests that the degree of learning is a function of the time spent on the material.
11. If degree of learning is fixed at some mastery level, then the amount of time individuals must spend to reach this level will vary. The most rapid learners learn about six times as fast as the slowest learners.
12. Mastery tests are probably most useful for closed subjects at the early elementary school level.
13. Some educators feel that the mastery learning model is a powerful source of mental health, but evidence is lacking and there are reasons to doubt this.
14. There are limitations to criterion-referenced tests just as there are to norm-referenced tests.
15. Norm-referenced measurement is necessary if we wish to make differential predictions.
16. If students differ in achievement levels, this normative information can often assist in decision making.
17. Norm-referenced testing is often considered a necessary component of program evaluation.
18. Whether one uses norm- or criterion-referenced measurement depends upon the kind of decision one wishes to make.

BASIC PRINCIPLES
OF MEASUREMENT

UNIT 2

CHAPTER FOUR
Describing Educational Data

Often when teachers are given a set of scores for their pupils, they have difficulty in determining the meaning of the scores. If educators are going to use data successfully in decision making, they must have some knowledge of how to describe and synthesize data. In this chapter we present some basic ideas about various types of data and the properties of these types; suggest some methods of tabulating and graphing data; discuss various kinds of data distributions; and discuss some of the concepts of basic descriptive statistics, such as measures of central tendency, variability, and relationship.

After completing this chapter the student should be able to—

1. Comprehend the differences between nominal, ordinal, interval, and ratio data.
2. Interpret correctly data presented in a tabular or graphic format.
3. Arrange data in tables and graphs in a correct fashion.
4. Determine the mean, median, and mode of a set of test scores.

5. Recognize the relationship between the shape of the data distribution and the relative positions of measures of central tendency.

6. Understand how the measures of central tendency differ and the significance of those differences.

7. Determine the variance and standard deviation of a set of test scores.

8. Know the relationship between standard deviation units and the area under a normal curve.

9. Interpret the Pearson r and the Spearman ρ as measures of relationship.

10. Appreciate the value of the information presented in this chapter to an educator who wishes to describe or interpret data.

KINDS OF SCORES

Data differ in terms of what properties of the real number series (order, distance, or origin) we can attribute to the scores. The most common—though not the most refined—classification of scores is one suggested by Stevens (1946), who classified scales as *nominal, ordinal, interval,* and *ratio* scales.

Nominal Scales

A nominal scale is the simplest scale of measurement. It involves the assignment of different numerals to categories that are qualitatively different. For example, for purposes of storing data on IBM cards, we might use the symbol "0" to represent a female and the symbol "1" to represent a male. These symbols (or numerals) do not have any of the three characteristics (order, distance, or origin) we attribute to the real number series. The 1 does not indicate more of something than the 0. Some psychologists do not wish to consider the nominal scale as a scale of measurement, but others do. It depends on how one defines measurement. If measurement is defined as "the assignment of numerals to objects or events according to rules" (Stevens, 1946), then nominal data indicate measurement. If, on the other hand, measurement implies a *quantitative* difference, then nominal data do not indicate measurement.

Regardless of how we define measurement, nominal data have some uses. Whether or not categories (such as sex) are ordered, it is often helpful to know to which category an individual belongs.

Ordinal Scales

An ordinal scale has the order property of a real number series and gives an indication of rank order. Thus, magnitude is indicated, if only in a very gross fashion. Rankings in a music contest or in an athletic event would be examples of ordinal data. We know who is best, second best, third best, and so on, but the ranks provide no information with regard to the differences between the scores. Ranking is obviously sufficient if our decision involves selecting the top pupils for some task. It is insufficient if we wish to obtain any idea of the magnitude of differences or use it to perform certain kinds of statistical manipulations.

Interval Scales

With interval data we can interpret the distances between scores. If, on a test with interval data, Shelly has a score of 60, Susan a score of 50, and Sally a score of 30, we could say that the distance between Susan's and Sally's scores (50–30) is twice the distance between Shelly's and Susan's scores (60–50). This additional information is obviously of potentially greater use than just knowing the rank order of the three students. It has been hotly debated whether or not most psychological data really have the properties of an interval scale. (See, for example, Coombs, 1964.) In general, however, educators and psychologists have treated (interpreted) most test data as being interval measurement.

Ratio Scales

If one has measured with a ratio scale, the ratio of the scores has meaning. Thus, a person who is 7'2" is twice as tall as another person who is 3'7". We can make this statement because a measurement of "0" actually indicates no height. That is, there is a meaningful zero point. Very few (if any) psychological measures provide ratio data. (Occasionally a psychologist will suggest that something like attitude can be measured on a ratio scale, since a neutral attitude could be considered a meaningful zero.) Note that in the interval-data example of Shelly's, Susan's, and Sally's scores, we could not say that Shelly had twice as much of the characteristic being measured as Sally. To make such a statement would require that one assume a score of "0" to actually represent *no amount* of the characteristic. In general, if a person received a score of zero on a spelling test, we would not interpret the score to mean that the person had *no* spelling ability. The same is true of any other test.

Educators, then, usually interpret (treat) test data as representing interval but not ratio scales, although when using percentiles only ordinality need be assumed. Assuming we obtain a set of scores having properties of interval data, what can we do to aid us in interpreting these scores?

PRESENTING DATA SUCCINCTLY: TABULATING AND GRAPHING

Suppose a teacher has just given a final examination to a class of 50 pupils (large class!) and has obtained the results shown in the first two columns of Table 4–1. How can the data be arranged to make them easier to interpret?

TABLE 4-1 Scores of 50 Students on a Classroom Mathematics Exam and Their Previous Grade Point Average (GPA) and IQ Scores

STU-DENT	SCORES (X)	GPA (Y)	IQ SCORE (Z)	STU-DENT	SCORES (X)	GPA (Y)	IQ SCORE (Z)
1	83	3.6	120	26	71	2.6	111
2	72	3.5	121	27	29	2.7	109
3	53	2.5	105	28	93	3.5	118
4	35	2.4	104	29	45	3.1	120
5	39	2.9	106	30	88	3.0	115
6	53	2.8	110	31	82	2.9	113
7	17	1.9	85	32	75	2.9	112
8	19	2.1	93	33	40	2.1	103
9	64	2.4	112	34	31	2.0	100
10	24	2.5	107	35	59	2.6	111
11	42	2.5	111	36	61	2.7	110
12	31	2.5	108	37	34	2.8	103
13	45	2.8	109	38	66	2.8	109
14	77	2.7	106	39	95	3.7	119
15	76	3.3	115	40	49	2.2	105
16	80	3.1	114	41	54	3.1	113
17	70	3.0	117	42	93	3.3	111
18	58	2.9	116	43	36	2.6	103
19	68	3.2	118	44	55	2.3	103
20	86	3.2	117	45	49	2.9	112
21	50	2.6	113	46	63	3.0	115
22	34	2.2	110	47	83	3.4	118
23	64	3.4	111	48	55	3.3	110
24	42	2.7	109	49	47	2.4	100
25	21	2.3	100	50	92	3.1	118
				Totals	2848	140.0	5498

One way, of course, is to *order the test scores*, as shown in Table 4-2. By looking at this table one can immediately see that the scores ranged from a high of 95 for student 39 to a low of 17 for student 7. Note that several students had identical scores. For these students, it does not matter which one is listed first. For example, student 28 could have been listed before student 42.

At times, teachers will want to present these data in other tabular or graphic forms. Table 4-2 gives one a fairly clear picture of how the students performed, but a *frequency* distribution, a *histogram*, a *frequency polygon*, or a *cumulative frequency* or *percent curve* would make the data even more

**TABLE 4–2 Mathematics Test Scores in Table 4–1
Ordered from Highest to Lowest**

STUDENT	TEST SCORE	STUDENT	TEST SCORE	STUDENT	TEST SCORE
39	95	38	66	13	45
42	93	23	64	24	42
28	93	9	64	11	42
50	92	46	63	33	40
30	88	36	61	5	39
20	86	35	59	43	36
47	83	18	58	4	35
1	83	48	55	37	34
31	82	44	55	22	34
16	80	41	54	34	31
14	77	6	53	12	31
15	76	3	53	27	29
32	75	21	50	10	24
2	72	45	49	25	21
26	71	40	49	8	19
17	70	49	47	7	17
19	68	29	45		

interpretable. Even if teachers think it is unnecessary to prepare one of these graphic forms for their own ease of interpretation, they may well want to prepare such an aid for their students or for occasional presentation at a teachers' meeting or to the PTA. A frequency distribution, frequency polygon, or bar graph would be particularly beneficial if there were many more scores, as might be the case if teachers gave the same exam to, say, five different sections of the same course. Whether or not a teacher ever tabulates data by any of the methods to be discussed, every teacher will read literature where such tabulation is presented, so it is vital that one understand the procedures.

Frequency Distributions

One way to reduce the size of Table 4–2 (and thereby make it easier to interpret and/or graph) would be to list every different score and then, to the right of each score, list the number (or frequency) of times that score occurred in the distribution. Since there are 40 different math scores in Table 4–2, that would reduce the number of entries in the test score column from 50 to 40. To reduce the number in the column still further, one could *group* the data or combine different scores into *class intervals*. Table 4–3 shows a frequency distribution using a class interval of five. There are some general guidelines for preparing class intervals:

1. The size of the class interval should be selected so that between 10 and 18 such intervals will cover the total range of observed scores.

2. The size of the class interval should be an odd number so that the midpoint of the interval is a whole number (see Table 4–3, column 6). This makes some types of computation easier and facilitates graphing.

3. It is generally considered good style to start the class interval at a value that is a multiple of that interval. For example, the interval in Table 4–3 is 5, so the lowest class interval started with a value (15) that was a multiple of 5.

Notice the cumulative frequency column in Table 4–3. It is obtained by summing the entries in the frequency column, starting with the *lowest* class interval (15–19). The cumulative % column is obtained by dividing the values in the cumulative frequency column by 50 (the number of pupils in the class) and changing the decimal fraction to a percent. It should also be pointed out that the class intervals shown in column 1 are not *theoretical intervals*. The

TABLE 4–3   Frequency Distribution of the Mathematics Test Scores of Table 4–1

CLASS INTER-VAL	THEO-RETICAL LIMITS	FRE-QUENCY f	CUMU-LATIVE f	CUMU-LATIVE %	MID-POINTS
95–99	94.5–99.5	1	50	100	97
90–94	89.5–94.5	3	49	98	92
85–89	84.5–89.5	2	46	92	87
80–84	79.5–84.5	4	44	88	82
75–79	74.5–79.5	3	40	80	77
70–74	69.5–74.5	3	37	74	72
65–69	64.5–69.5	2	34	68	67
60–64	59.5–64.5	4	32	64	62
55–59	54.5–59.5	4	28	56	57
50–54	49.5–54.5	4	24	48	52
45–49	44.5–49.5	5	20	40	47
40–44	39.5–44.5	3	15	30	42
35–39	34.5–39.5	3	12	24	37
30–34	29.5–34.5	4	9	18	32
25–29	24.5–29.5	1	5	10	27
20–24	19.5–24.5	2	4	8	22
15–19	14.5–19.5	2	2	4	17

characteristic we have measured (in this case, mathematics achievement) is actually a continuous characteristic. By this we mean that, theoretically, there are levels of achievement between, say 79 and 80, but our measuring instrument has not been precise enough to obtain such values. (This is analogous to measuring height to the nearest inch so that we obtain values like 62, 66, 67, and so forth. We know there are heights such as 62.25 and 66.58 inches, but they are recorded as 62 and 67 inches, respectively.) The *theoretical limits* of the frequency distribution are shown in column 2 of Table 4–3. You will notice that the intervals are extended a half-unit in both directions from those in column 1.

Of course, it should be recognized that when grouping occurs, some information is lost. For example, the scores of 61, 63, 64, and 64 have all been put in the interval 60–64 (theoretical limits interval 59.5–64.5). When one computes certain statistics or prepares graphs from frequency distributions, it is necessary to make an assumption regarding the values within the intervals. One typically assumes that either (1) the observations are uniformly distributed over the theoretical limits of the interval, or (2) all scores fall on the midpoint of the interval. The degree to which such assumptions affect the accuracy of the graphs and statistics computed from the class intervals depends upon the size and number of class intervals and the total frequency of scores.

Histograms

The data displayed in Table 4–3 may also be graphed. Graphic representation helps greatly in enabling us to understand the data of frequency distributions and in comparing different frequency distributions to each other. A histogram (sometimes referred to as a bar graph) is a graph in which the frequencies are represented by bars. Figure 4–1 displays the data of Table 4–3 in the form of a histogram. Notice that frequencies are along the vertical axis and the scores are along the horizontal axis. This arrangement is not mandatory, but it is by far the most usual procedure. In making a histogram from grouped data, one assumes that the scores are evenly distributed within the class interval, thus giving rectangular bars. It is difficult to superimpose more than one histogram on the same figure. Thus, comparisons of several frequency distributions cannot readily be made via histograms. Frequency polygons are much better suited to that purpose.

Frequency Polygons

A frequency polygon (or graphed frequency distribution) is shown in Figure 4–2. As with the histogram, one could construct such a polygon either from original data or from grouped data. Figure 4–2 was constructed from the grouped data of Table 4–3. In constructing a frequency polygon for

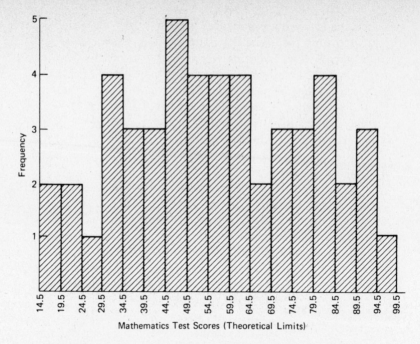

FIGURE 4-1   Histogram of the mathematics test scores.

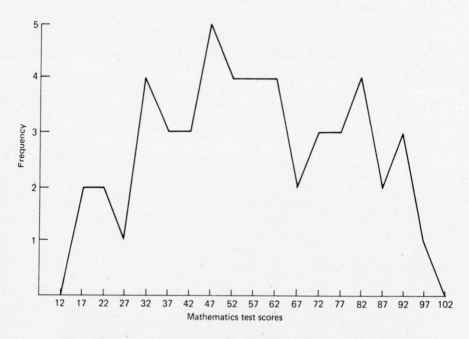

FIGURE 4-2   Frequency polygon of the mathematics test scores.

grouped data, one assumes that all scores within a class interval fall at the midpoint of that interval. Notice that the midpoint of the class intervals just above and below the highest and lowest intervals that contain actual scores are also marked on the horizontal axis and given a frequency of zero. This is typically done. For example, in Table 4–3 the midpoints of the lowest and highest class intervals with actual scores are 17 (15–19) and 97 (95–99), respectively. The next lowest and highest interval midpoints (12 and 102, respectively) are plotted as having a frequency of zero. If a teacher had frequency distributions for other classes that he wished to compare with this one, he could plot them on the same graph by using colored lines, broken lines, dotted lines, or some other differentiating procedure, and labeling the lines appropriately. Of course, if class sizes differed, it would be better to change all frequencies to percentages and plot percentile polygons.

Cumulative Frequency and Percentile Polygons

Columns 4 and 5 of Table 4–3 give the data necessary to construct a cumulative frequency polygon and a cumulative percentile polygon (ogive). Both curves can be represented on the same graph, as shown in Figure 4–3,

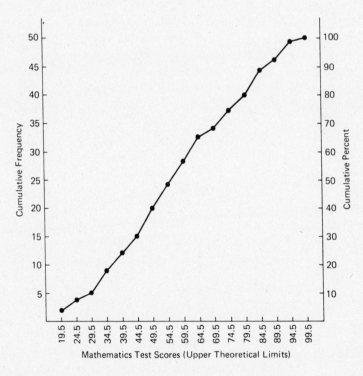

FIGURE 4–3   Cumulative polygon of the mathematics test scores.

or a separate graph could be constructed for each. When plotting the cumulative polygons, we use the *upper theoretical limits* of each of the class intervals on the horizontal axis. The cumulative percentile polygon (ogive) is frequently used to display percentiles (see the section on measures of relative position, "Percentiles and Percentile Ranks," in Chapter 6).

SHAPES OF DATA DISTRIBUTIONS

Distributions of scores such as that shown in Figure 4–2 could assume many different shapes. When a frequency distribution is plotted with only a small number of scores, the shape of the curve will be very uneven or irregular. With a large number of scores, the curve would ordinarily be expected to take on a more smoothed or regular appearance. The shape of this smooth curve will depend both upon the properties of the measuring instrument and the distribution of the underlying characteristic we are attempting to measure. Four types of distributions most frequently discussed in educational measurement are *normal distributions, positively skewed distributions, negatively skewed distributions*, and *rectangular distributions*.

A. *normal distribution* (curve) is a bell-shaped curve, as shown in Figure 4–4. There has been considerable discussion in the past about whether human characteristics are normally distributed. Evidence of physical characteristics such as height and weight lend some support to those who take the position that these characteristics are normally distributed. Whether one can infer anything about the distribution of psychological characteristics from this observation is debatable. The distributions obtained from tests cannot be used as evidence of the distribution of the characteristic itself because the test-score distributions may be influenced greatly by the characteristics of a test. For

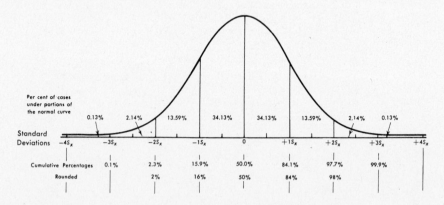

FIGURE 4–4 Chart showing the normal curve and the percent of cases under various portions of the normal curve. (Reproduced by permission. All rights reserved. Copyright 1953, © 1964, 1967 by The Psychological Corporation, New York, N.Y.)

example, tests that are difficult will result in a positively skewed distribution, and tests that are easy will result in a negatively skewed distribution of scores. Whatever the truth about the underlying distribution of a characteristic for humans in general, classes of 20 to 50 students are *not* likely to be distributed normally with respect to any characteristic. The test results from the large norm groups used for standardized tests are likely to be more normal in appearance. (We will not concern ourselves about whether this is due to the normal distribution of the characteristic we are measuring or is an artifact of the properties of the measuring instrument.) We will discuss further some properties of the normal curve when discussing measures of central tendency and variability.

In a positively skewed distribution (see Figure 4–5) most of the scores pile up at the low end of the distribution. This might occur, for example, if we gave a test that was extremely difficult for the students. Or, if we were plotting teachers' salaries and most of the teachers had very little experience (thus having relatively low salaries), we might obtain a postively skewed distribution.

A negatively skewed distribution is shown in Figure 4–6. In this case the majority of scores are toward the high end of the distribution. This could occur if we gave a test that was easy for most of the students, such as a mastery

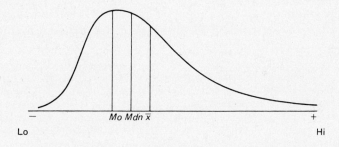

FIGURE 4–5   A positively skewed distribution.

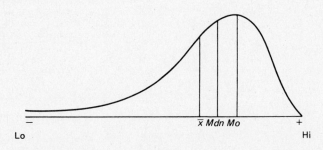

FIGURE 4–6   A negatively skewed distribution.

test. Or, if we were plotting teachers' salaries in a school district where most of the teachers were experienced and were close to the maximum on the salary schdule, we would expect such a distribution.

A rectangular distribution will result if the same number of people obtain each of the possible scores (see Figure 4–7). This would occur, for example, if one were plotting percentiles (see Chapter 6).

In the next section we will relate measures of central tendency to score distributions.

MEASURES OF CENTRAL TENDENCY

It is often of value to summarize certain characteristics of a distribution of test scores. One characteristic that is of particular interest is a measure of central tendency, which gives some idea of the average or typical score in the distribution. We are sure that you as a student would wish to know not only how you performed on an examination, but also how well, in general, the other students performed. When you teach, of course, your students may want the same information. Three measures of central tendency—the *mean, median,* and *mode*—all present this type of information.

Mean

The mean (X) is the arithmetic average of a set of scores. It is found by adding all the scores in the distribution and dividing by the total number of scores (N).[1] The formula is

[1] The mean, median, variance, and standard deviation can also be obtained for grouped data such as that displayed in Table 4–3. However, the grouped-data methods are somewhat more difficult to understand, and for the number of scores teachers are ordinarily dealing with—if a person has access to a desk calculator or even an adding machine—it is easier to use the methods given in this book. Also, as mentioned earlier, statistics computed from class-interval data are not quite so precise, owing to the assumptions that have to be made. For a reference showing the computational procedures for grouped data see Downie and Heath (1970).

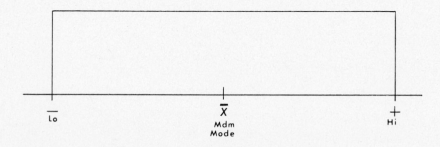

FIGURE 4–7   A rectangular distribution.

$$\bar{X} = \frac{\Sigma X}{N} \qquad\qquad \textbf{(4-1)}$$

where $\bar{X}$ = mean
$\quad\quad X$ = raw score for a person
$\quad\quad N$ = number of scores
$\quad\quad \Sigma$ = summation sign indicating that all Xs in the distribution are added

The mean for the test scores given in Table 4–1 is

$$\bar{X} = \frac{\Sigma X}{N} = \frac{2848}{50} = 56.96$$

which would, for most practical purposes, be rounded to 57.0. Another example of computing the mean is given in Table 4–4.

**TABLE 4–4   Hypothetical Distribution of IQ Scores
for a Class of 20 Students**

IQ SCORES
185
185
83
83
82          $N = 20$
81
81          $\Sigma X = 1780$
80
80          $\bar{X} = \dfrac{\Sigma X}{N} = \dfrac{1780}{20} = 89$
80
78
78      $\text{Mdn} = 79$
78
77      $\text{Mode} = 74$
77
76
74
74
74
74

Median

The median (Mdn) is the point below which 50 percent of the scores lie. While not completely precise mathematically, an approximation to that point is obtained from *ordered* data by simply finding the score in the middle of the distribution. For an odd number of scores, such as 25, the approximation to the median would be the middlemost score, or the score below which and above which 12 scores lie (actually 12½ if one splits the middle score and considers half of it to be above the midpoint and half below). That is, the median is considered to be the 13th score. For an even number of scores the median would be the point that lies halfway between the two middlemost scores. For the data in Table 4–2, the median would be 55, since both the 25th and 26th scores are 55. The median for the data in Table 4–4 is 79, halfway between the 10th and 11th scores.

Mode

The mode is the most frequently occurring score in the distribution. It, however, can be greatly influenced by chance fluctuations or sampling error and is seldom used. For the data in Table 4–4, the mode is 74 (it occurred four times).

Comparisons of Mean, Median, and Mode

The mean is generally the preferred measure of central tendency by statisticians. It takes into account the actual numerical value of every score in the distribution and therefore tends to fluctuate less from sample to sample from the same population than would the median or mode. The median is preferred if one wants a measure of central tendency that is not affected by a few very high or very low scores. It is also sometimes preferred by classroom teachers because it is easier to determine. Table 4–4 presents a *hypothetical* distribution of IQ scores where the median rather than the mean would be considered a better indicator of central tendency. The mean of 89 is a misleading figure, greatly influenced by two students with very high scores. Note that in this case the mean is actually six points above the third highest score! The median of 79 is a much more representative figure. (In this case the mode of 74 is a very nonrepresentative measure of central tendency. It is the lowest score in the distribution!)

If you will reexamine the distributions presented in Figures 4–4 through 4–7, you will note that there is a relationship between the shape of the distribution and the relative placement of the mean, median, and mode. For normal and rectangular distributions (or for any distribution that is symmetrically shaped about the mode), the mean, median, and mode all coincide. In a positively skewed distribution the mean will give the highest measure of central tendency and the mode the lowest. In a negatively skewed distribution, just the opposite occurs. Thus, for classroom tests or teacher salary distributions, one could present a different image by presenting a median rather than a mean (modes should probably not be used). But for test results with fairly normal distributions, it would matter little which measure of central tendency was used.

MEASURES OF VARIABILITY

To know only a person's raw score is of little value. To know that a person's score is so much above or below the mean is of some value. If one has an indication of the variability of a distribution of scores as well, much more information is obtained.

The measures of variability most often used in testing are the *standard deviation* (S), and the *variance* (S²).[2] These two have a very precise mathematical relationship to each other: The standard deviation is the square root of the variance. This relationship is indicated in the symbols by use of the exponent 2 when indicating variance. The variance can be computed by

$$S_x{}^2 = \frac{\Sigma(X - \bar{X})^2}{N} \tag{4-2}$$

where all symbols on the right-hand side have been previously defined and the subscript x identifies the score distribution (here the X scores) whose variance is being computed.

Equation (4–2) is sometimes called a definitional formula. Expressed in words, it states that the variance is the arithmetic average (notice that we are summing several values and dividing by the number we sum, just as when computing the mean) of the squares of the deviation scores from their mean. The $X - \bar{X}$, then, is known as a deviation value showing the distance between a person's score (X) and the mean ($\bar{X}$). Equation (4–2) is easy to use if one is doing the computing by hand. (Rounding $\bar{X}$ to the nearest whole number, while destroying accuracy somewhat, makes hand computation quite easy.)

The standard deviation (S_x) is obtained by taking the square root of the variance. The standard deviation, then, is

$$S_x = \sqrt{\frac{\Sigma(X - \bar{X})^2}{N}} \tag{4-3}$$

Two examples of computing the variance and standard deviation are illustrated in Table 4–5. If a new student with an IQ score of 120 (assume

[2] Occasionally the range (high score − low score + 1) is used, but this measure, like the mode, is very unstable.

all IQ scores were obtained from the same test) were to join a class of pupils with IQ scores as shown in Example A in Table 4–5, he would be 20 points above the mean and 11 points above the second pupil in his class in measured aptitude. If he were to join a class with scores as shown in Example B, he would still be 20 points above the mean, but there would be three pupils who would have higher measured academic aptitude. The class depicted in Example B would be much harder to teach than the class depicted in Example A because of the extreme variability in academic aptitude of the students.

The standard deviation is used to describe the amount of variability in a distribution. Although it can be computed for any size distribution, it is

TABLE 4–5   Two Distributions of IQ Scores
with Equal Means but Unequal Variances

| | EXAMPLE A | | | EXAMPLE B | |
X	$(X-\overline{X})$	$(X-\overline{X})^2$	X	$(X-\overline{X})$	$(X-\overline{X})^2$
109	9	81	185	85	7225
108	8	64	147	47	2209
107	7	49	121	21	441
105	5	25	108	8	64
105	5	25	106	6	36
103	3	9	104	4	16
102	2	4	103	3	9
101	1	1	103	3	9
101	1	1	102	2	4
101	1	1	101	1	1
99	−1	1	99	−1	1
99	−1	1	96	−4	16
97	−3	9	91	−9	81
97	−3	9	83	−17	289
96	−4	16	82	−18	324
95	−5	25	80	−20	400
95	−5	25	74	−26	676
94	−6	36	74	−26	676
93	−7	49	71	−29	841
93	−7	49	70	−30	900
$\Sigma X = 2000$		$\Sigma(X-\overline{X})^2 = 480$	$\Sigma X = 2000$		$\Sigma(X-\overline{X})^2 = 14{,}218$

$$N=20 \quad \overline{X}=\frac{\Sigma X}{N}=\frac{2000}{20}=100$$

$$S_x{}^2 = \frac{480}{20} = 24$$

$$S_x = \sqrt{24} = 4.9$$

$$N=20 \quad \overline{X}=\frac{\Sigma X}{N}=\frac{2000}{20}=100$$

$$S_x{}^2 = \frac{14{,}218}{20} = 710.9$$

$$S_x = \sqrt{710.9} = 26.66$$

particularly useful for reporting the variability of large sets of scores, such as the norms on standardized tests, because of the relationship between the standard deviation and a normal distribution. In a normal distribution a specified percentage of scores fall within each standard deviation from the mean. As can be seen from Figure 4–4, about 68 percent of the area under a normal curve (or 68 percent of the scores if the normal curve depicts a distribution of scores) falls between $\pm 1S_x$ (that is, plus or minus one standard deviation from the mean), 95 percent between $\pm 2S_x$ (the 95 percent interval is actually $\pm 1.96S_x$, but for practical work it is often computed as $\pm 2S_x$), and 99.7 percent between $\pm 3S_x$. More will be said about this relationship between a normal curve and the standard deviation when we discuss reliability and validity in Chapter 5 and type of scores in Chapter 6.

MEASURES OF RELATIONSHIP

If we have two sets of scores from the same group of people, it is often desirable to know the degree to which the scores are related. For example, we may be interested in the relationship between the mathematics test scores and GPA for the individuals whose scores are given in Table 4–1. (Do people who do well in mathematics also, in general, do well in other areas in school?) Or we may be interested in both or either of the other relationships: test score and IQ score, or GPA and IQ score. We are also interested in relationships between two sets of scores when we are studying the reliability or validity of a test (see Chapter 5 for a discussion on reliability and validity). The Pearson product moment correlation coefficient (r) is the statistic most often used to give us an indication of this relationship. It can be calculated from the formula:

$$r = \frac{\Sigma[\,(X - \bar{X})\,(Y - \bar{Y})\,]}{NS_x S_y} \tag{4-4}$$

where
X = score of a person on one variable
Y = score of same person on the other variable
$\bar{X}$ = mean of the X distribution
$\bar{Y}$ = mean of the Y distribution
S_x = standard deviation of the X scores
S_y = standard deviation of the Y scores
N = number of scores within each distribution

If the data exist only in ranked (ordinal) form, it is easier to use the Spearman rank-order correlation coefficient rho (ρ). Interval data can, of course, be converted into ordinal data, and this is occasionally done to make computation easier. However, information would be lost in such a conversion, and for some particular data distributions ρ may be considerably different from the r that would have been obtained from the original data. The formula for rho is

$$\rho = 1 - \frac{6\Sigma D^2}{N(N^2 - 1)} \tag{4-5}$$

where D is the difference *in ranks* for a pair of scores and Σ and N have been previously defined.

Table 4–6 illustrates the computation of r using Formula (4–4); Table 4–7, the computation of ρ for the same data after it had been ranked. Notice that the two values are quite different. This is true because when one rank-orders data information is lost about the size of the score differences. If one had only the ranked data to begin with, ρ and r would give the same value and ρ is easier to compute.

The value of r (or ρ) may range from +1.00 to −1.00. When an increase in one variable tends to be accompanied by an increase in the other variable (such as aptitude and achievement), the correlation is positive. When an increase in either one tends to be accompanied by a decrease in the other (such as age and value of a car), then the correlation is negative. A perfect positive correlation (1.00) or a perfect negative correlation (−1.00) occurs when a change in the one variable is *always* accompanied by a commensurate change in the other variable. A zero (.00) correlation occurs when there is no relationship between the two variables.

TABLE 4–6   The Calculation of r Using Formula (4–4)

X	Y	$X-\bar{X}$	$(X-\bar{X})^2$	$Y-\bar{Y}$	$(Y-\bar{Y})^2$	$(X-\bar{X})(Y-\bar{Y})$
50	45	20	400	16	256	320
49	50	19	361	21	441	399
30	25	0	0	−4	16	0
11	10	−19	361	−19	361	361
10	15	−20	400	−14	196	280
			1522		1270	1360

$$\Sigma X = 150 \qquad 145 = \Sigma Y$$
$$\bar{X} = 30 \qquad 29 = \bar{Y}$$
$$\Sigma(X-\bar{X})^2 = 1522 \qquad \Sigma(Y-\bar{Y})^2 = 1270$$

$$S_x = \sqrt{\frac{\Sigma(X-X)^2}{N}} = \sqrt{\frac{1522}{5}} = \sqrt{304.4}$$

$$S_y = \sqrt{\frac{1270}{5}} = \sqrt{254}$$

$$r = \frac{\Sigma(X-\bar{X})(Y-\bar{Y})}{NS_xS_y} = \frac{1360}{5\sqrt{304.4}\ \sqrt{254}} \pm .98$$

TABLE 4–7   The Calculation of ρ

X	Y	RANK X	RANK Y	D	D²
50	45	5	4	1	1
49	50	4	5	−1	1
30	25	3	3	0	0
11	10	2	1	1	1
10	15	1	2	−1	1

$$\rho = 1 - \frac{6\Sigma D^2}{N(N^2 - 1)} = 1 - \frac{6(4)}{5(5^2 - 1)} = 1 - \frac{24}{5(24)} = 1 - \frac{24}{120} \qquad 4 = \Sigma D^2$$

$$1 - 1/5 = .80$$

How close to 1 (positively or negatively) an r must be in order to indicate that a significant relationship exists is difficult to specify. It is dependent upon how one defines significance. Significance may be considered in either a statistical or practical sense. For example, a correlation coefficient of .08 (say, between teaching method and grades) will be statistically significant if the number of cases used to compute the correlation is sufficiently large. But this correlation is so low that it has no practical significance in educational decision making.[3] The scattergrams in Figure 4–8 depict the amount of relationship for various correlation coefficients. (A scattergram is a plot showing each individual's scores on both X and Y.)

Obviously, we do not expect all different sets of variables to have equal degrees of relationship. Correlations vary considerably in size, and the value of a given correlation must be interpreted in part by comparing it to other correlations obtained for similar variables. For example, a correlation of .85 would be considered somewhat low if one were correlating two equivalent forms of an aptitude test. However, a correlation of .70 between scholastic aptitude test scores and college grade point averages would be interpreted as quite high. Table 4–8 gives some typical correlation coefficients for selected variables. The more experience you obtain, *the more you will know* what degree of relationship is expected between different variables.

Two cautions should be mentioned concerning the interpretation of correlation coefficients:

1. They are *not* an indication of cause and effect. One can find all sorts of variables that are related but have no causal relationship. For example, for children the size of the big toe is slightly correlated with mental age—yet

---

[3] However, low but statistically significant correlations could be of practical significance if a decision vital to life, such as in medical research, were pending.

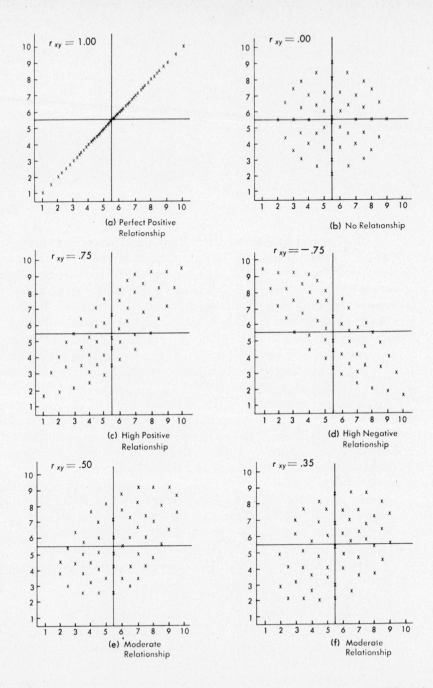

FIGURE 4–8 Scattergrams indicating correlations of various sizes ($N = 50$).

TABLE 4–8   Typical Correlation Coefficients for Selected Variables

VARIABLES	r
Two equivalent forms of a test	.95
Intelligence of identical twins	.90
Height and weight of adults	.60
High school and college GPA	.50
Intelligence of pairs of siblings	.50
Height and intelligence	.05

one does not cause the other. They are correlated simply because they are both related to a third variable: chronological age.

2. The Pearson product moment correlation is a measure of linear relationship. In Figure 4–9 there is a perfect relationship between variables X and Y. The Pearson r, however, is zero. If one suspects that two variables have a relationship other than linear, a different index of correlation should be computed.[4] One might find a relationship somewhat like that in Figure 4–9 if X were stress and Y were performance on some task (although it would not be perfect).

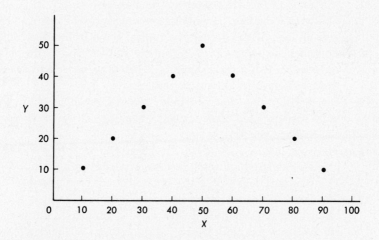

FIGURE 4–9   A scattergram showing two variables that are perfectly selected but with a zero Pearson product moment r.

[4] An explanation of curvilinear relationships is found in William A. Hays, *Statistics for Psychologists* (2d ed.). New York: Holt, Rinehart and Winston, 1973.

SUMMARY

The following statements summarize the major points of this chapter.

1. Data can be classified as nominal, ordinal, interval, and ratio scales.
2. A nominal scale involves the assignment of numerals to categories that are qualitively different.
3. An ordinal scale gives an indication of rank order.
4. With interval data we can interpret the distance between scores. In general, educators and psychologists have treated most test data as being interval measurement.
5. With ratio scales the ratio of the scores has meaning because there is a meaningful zero point. True ratio scales probably do not exist in educational and psychological measurement.
6. Tabulating and/or graphing data aids in ease of interpretation.
7. The shape of a distribution of scores will depend both upon the properties of the measuring instrument and the distribution of the underlying characteristic we are attempting to measure.
8. The mean, median, and mode are measures of central tendency. They give an idea of the average or typical score in the distribution.
9. The mean is generally preferred by statisticians as the measure of central tendency, but the median is easier to compute and therefore is sometimes preferred by classroom teachers.
10. For distributions that are fairly normal (such as those obtained from most standardized tests results), it matters little which measure of central tendency is used.
11. The variance and standard deviation are measures of variability. They give an indication of the spread of scores in a distribution.
12. The standard deviation is the square root of the variance.
13. The Pearson product moment correlation coefficient is the statistic most often used to provide a measure of relationship. The values of the coefficient may range between -1.00 and $+1.00$, indicating perfect negative and perfect positive relationships, respectively. A value of 0 (zero) indicates no relationship.
14. There are two major cautions in interpreting correlation coefficients:
    a. They are not an indication of cause and effect.
    b. The ones we have studied in this chapter are only measures of linear relationship.

CHAPTER FIVE
Reliability and Validity

There are certain qualities that every measurement device should possess. Perhaps the two most important technical concepts in measurement are reliability and validity. These concepts are presented in this chapter. Although validity is the more important concept, we discuss reliability first, since validity involves reliability to some extent and therefore the structure of the subject matter makes that order of presentation a little more straightforward.

The only statistics one will need as a background for understanding this chapter have been presented in Chapter 4. For those readers who have the necessary statistical background and would prefer a more sophisticated treatment of the topics, we highly recommend Cronbach (1971); Cronbach, Gleser, Nanda, and Rajaratnam (1972); and Stanley (1971). Some readers of this text may wish to skip (or only skim) several sections of this chapter. The sections under reliability on "Estimating True Scores" and "Reliability of Difference Scores" are more technical than the rest of the chapter, and understanding them is not necessary to comprehending the other material.

After studying this chapter the reader should be able to—

1. Recognize some sources of error variance in educational and psychological measurement.
2. Understand the theoretical concept of reliability as the ratio of true-to-observed score variance.
3. Recognize that the standard error of measurement can be derived from the theoretical reliability formula.
4. Compute the standard error of measurement and interpret score bands.
5. Estimate a person's true score.
6. Obtain various estimates of reliability and understand how these estimates differ.
7. Recognize several factors that influence reliability estimates, and understand the nature of the influence.
8. Understand the computational procedures and interpretation of the reliability of difference scores.
9. Appreciate the importance of reliability in data used for decision making.
10. Understand the relationship between reliability and validity.
11. Understand the basic kinds of validity.
12. Interpret various expressions of validity.
13. Recognize what factors affect validity and how they affect it.
14. Recognize the relationships between test validity and decision making.

RELIABILITY

Reliability can be defined as the degree of consistency between two measures of the same thing. This is neither a theoretical nor an operational definition, but is more of a conceptual (or layman's) definition. Any measurement device provides only very limited data. What we would hope is that a person's score would be similar under slightly different conditions. For example, if we measure a person's weight, we would hope that we would have gotten almost the same measure had we used a different scale or weighed him one day later. If we were to measure a person's level of achievement, we would hope that his score would be similar under different administrators, using different scorers, with similar but not identical items, or during different times in a day. In other words, we wish to *generalize* from the particular score obtained to the score we might have received had conditions been slightly different.

In physical measurement we can ordinarily obtain very reliable measures. This is true primarily for three basic reasons:

1. Physical characteristics can be usually measured directly rather than indirectly.[1]
2. The instruments used to obtain the measures are quite precise.
3. The traits or characteristics being measured are relatively stable.

However, even in physical measurement, there is some unreliability or inconsistency. If we are interested in determining the reliability with which we can measure a person's weight, we may proceed in a variety of ways. We may, for example, have a person get on and off a scale several times, and we may record his weight each time. These recorded weights may differ. The person may stand somewhat differently on the scale from one time to the next, which would influence the reading, or the individual doing the measuring may not read or record the numbers correctly.

Another method of checking the consistency with which we can measure weight would be to record the weight of a person as obtained on ten different scales and to compare these values. These values may vary for the reasons just given. In addition, they may vary due to whatever differences exist in the scales. Thus, one would expect to obtain a somewhat more variable (less consistent) set of values.

Still different methods of checking the consistency of weight measures would be to weigh a person on ten successive Saturday mornings on (1) the same scale each time or (2) ten different scales. With these two procedures one would have an additional source of variance from those already mentioned: the stability of the person's weight from one week to the next.

In all methods mentioned so far we would be obtaining information about consistency by determining how much variation exists in a specific individual's score (intraindividual variability). This variability is expressed as a *standard error of measurement* and will be explained in a forthcoming section.

Another approach to studying consistency would be to have a whole group of people weigh themselves twice (changing scales and/or times and/or the reader and recorder of the measure) and determine whether the relative standing of the persons remained about the same. This would give us an estimate of the *reliability* (or interindividual variability) of the measure. In educational or psychological[2] measurement it is often unrealistic, or indeed impossible, to measure a single person repeatedly, so no direct measure of intraindividual variability can be obtained. Reliability theory, however, gives

---

[1] For many physical characteristics the characteristic itself is observable (for example, height) and we can measure that directly. For psychological (or educational or sociological) characteristics (for example, motivation or scholastic aptitude) we must measure behavior and, indirectly, make an inference about the amount of the characteristic an individual possesses.

[2] The terms *psychological* and *educational* measurement are used almost synonymously in this book. For flow in reading we will often use only one term or the other when both are applicable.

us ways to estimate this intraindividual variability through interindividual variability data, as we will see in the subsequent two sections. Thus there are many different procedures for estimating the consistency or reliability of measurement. Each procedure allows a slightly different source of variation to affect the values obtained.

Psychological and educational measurement are typically much less reliable than physical measurement. Psychological measurement is indirect and is conducted with less precise instruments on traits that are not always stable or well defined. As with the physical example mentioned, there are many reasons a pupil's test score may vary. The amount of the characteristic we are measuring may change across time (trait instability); the particular questions we ask in order to infer a person's knowledge could affect his score (sampling error); any change in directions, timing, or amount of rapport with the test administrator could cause score variability (administrator error); inaccuracies in scoring a test paper will affect the scores (scoring error); and finally such things as health, motivation, degree of fatigue of the person, and good or bad luck in guessing could cause score variability.

The variation in a person's scores is typically called *error variance*, and the sources of the variation are known as *sources of error*. The fewer and smaller the errors, the more consistent (reliable) the measurement. With this general background, let us turn to a brief discussion of the theory of reliability.

Theory of Reliability

The theory of reliability can best be explained by starting with observed scores (X). These observed scores may be conceptualized as containing various component parts. In the simplest case we think of each observed score as being made up of a "true score" and an "error score" such that

$$X = T + E \tag{5-1}$$

where X = observed score
   T = true score
   E = error score

The true score is similar to what some psychologists refer to as the "universe score" (see Cronbach et al., 1972). The term *true score* can be a bit misleading. "As used true score is not the ultimate fact in the book of the recording angel" (Stanley, 1971, p. 361). It is, rather, that portion of the observed score not affected by random error. Any systematic error (such as a scale always weighing everyone 2 pounds too heavy) does not affect reliability or consistency, and so, in reliability theory, it is considered as part of the "true," stable, or unchanging part of a person's observed score.

People, of course, differ from each other with regard to both their true scores and their observed scores. Since the errors are assumed to be random, theoretically the positive and negative errors will cancel each other, and the mean error will be zero. Also, if the errors are random, they will not correlate with the true scores or with each other. By making these assumptions, we can write the variance of a test as

$$S_x{}^2 = S_t{}^2 + S_e{}^2 \tag{5-2}$$

where $S_x{}^2$ = variance of a group of individuals' observed scores

$S_t{}^2$ = variance of a group of individuals' true scores

$S_e{}^2$ = error variance in a group of individuals' scores

Theoretically, reliability (r_{xx}) is defined as the ratio of the true score and observed score variances:

$$r_{xx} = \frac{S_t{}^2}{S_x{}^2} \tag{5-3}$$

Reliability, then, tells us to what extent the observed variance is due to true score variance. The symbol r_{xx} is used for reliability because so many of the reliability estimates are computed by the Pearson product correlation coefficient (r) procedure. The double x subscript is used to indicate measurement of the same trait. Formulas (5–2) and (5–3) are basic formulas from which most of the commonly written expressions concerning reliability and the standard error of measurement (see next section) are derived. Rewriting (5–2) as $S_t{}^2 = S_x{}^2 - S_e{}^2$ and substituting into (5–3), we get

$$r_{xx} = 1 - \frac{S_e{}^2}{S_x{}^2} \tag{5-4}$$

Reliability is often expressed in this fashion.

Standard Error of Measurement of Observed Scores

From either (5–3) or (5–4) it can be seen that reliability increases as error variance decreases, if $S_x{}^2$ remains constant. Or, if error variance remains constant and we increase $S_x{}^2$, reliability also increases.

Solving Equation (5–4) for S_e, we get

$$S_e = S_x\sqrt{1 - r_{xx}} \tag{5-5}$$

which is called a *standard error of measurement*. This is the measure of intra-individual variability mentioned earlier. Since we often cannot test a person repeatedly, this statistic is typically estimated from group data, using Equation

(5–5). It is frequently conceptualized, however, as the standard deviation of a person's observed scores (from many administrations of the same test) about his true score on that test. Theoretically, the true score (T) of an individual does not vary. If we retested the same person many times, there would be some inconsistency (error), and therefore the observed scores (X) of this single person would vary, sometimes being greater than T and sometimes less. Making the assumption that the errors within a person's score, across testing sessions, are random, the positive and negative errors will cancel each other, and the mean error will be zero. Thus, the mean of the observed scores over repeated testings is the individual's true score ($X_i = T_i$) where the subscript i refers to the individual.

It is assumed that these observed scores for an individual will fall in a normal distribution about his true score. The standard deviation of the observed scores across repeated testings should become clear if we look at (5–2):

$$S_x{}^2 = S_t{}^2 + S_e{}^2$$

If we think of these values as being obtained from the data for a single individual over many testings, then the true score does not change and hence $S_t{}^2 = 0$. Changing the notation of $S_x{}^2$ to $S_{xi}{}^2$ to indicate the variance of a single person's observed scores over repeated testings, we get

$$S_{xi}{}^2 = 0 + S_e{}^2$$
$$S_{xi} = S_e$$

Note that this holds only for the case where S_{xi} represents the standard deviation of a person's observed scores over repeated testing. If a test has any reliability at all, S_e will be smaller than the S_x for a *group* of individuals, each tested once, because as a group their true scores will vary, even though for each *individual* $S_t{}^2 = 0$.

To reiterate: The standard error of measurement is conceptualized as providing information about the variability of a person's scores on repeated testings. Ordinarily, we do not give a person the same test many times because it is uneconomical and because these repeated testings could result in changes in the individual (fatigue, learning effects). Thus, the standard error of measurement is usually estimated from group data. Using group data and Equation (5–5), we obtain only one standard error and interpret every individual's score using this same standard error. This could lead to slight misinterpretations, particularly if the group is fairly heterogeneous. The better commercially published tests report different standard errors of measurement for different homogeneous subgroups along the continuum of the trait being measured.

Another approach to estimating the standard error, developed by Lord

(1957), is used by some commercial test builders but very infrequently by classroom teachers.

The standard error of measurement has an interpretative advantage over the reliability coefficient in that it allows us to state how much we think an individual's score might vary. The standard error of measurement is often used for what is called *band interpretation*. Band interpretation helps convey the idea of imprecision of measurement. Because it is assumed that the errors are random, an individual's observed scores are normally distributed about his true score. Thus, one can say that a person's observed score will lie between $\pm 1 S_e$ of his true score approximately 68 percent of the time, or $\pm 2 S_e$ of his true score about 95 percent of the time. (See Figure 4–4 and the discussion in Chapter 4 on the normal curve.) Although it is not precise mathematically, one usually interprets with about 68 percent (or 95 percent) *certainty* a person's true score to be within $\pm 1 S_e$ (or $\pm 2 S_e$) of his observed score. (Note that this is *not* the same as saying a person's true score is within those limits 68 (or 95) percent of the time. The true score is fixed and either is or is not within the given interval. But we can talk about how certain we are that the true score is within a given interval.) The interval $X \pm 1 S_e$ is ordinarily the band used when interpreting scores to others.

Suppose, for example, that a scholastic aptitude test as an r_{xx} of .91 and an S_x of 15. Thus, using Equation (5–5),

$$S_e = S_x \sqrt{1 - r_{xx}}$$

$$= 15\sqrt{1 - .91} = 15\sqrt{.09} = 15(.3) = 4.5$$

An example of using the traditional interpretation of the standard error of measurement of the observed score would be as follows: If an individual obtained a score of 112, we could be about 68 percent confident that his true score would lie between 112 ± 4.5, or 107.5 to 116.5. We would be about 95 percent confident that his true score would lie between $112 \pm 2(4.5)$, or between 103 and 121.

Estimating True Scores

Reliability theory gives us a way of estimating a person's true score. If we know the reliability of a measuring instrument, a person's observed score, and the mean score for people in the group to which the individual belongs, we can estimate his true score. This estimate will be closer to the mean score than was his obtained score. In other words, we predict a *regression (movement) toward the mean*. We do this because if we know nothing about an individual except his score and the group mean, and if his score is above the mean, our best guess is that his obtained score contains positive errors of measurement. If his score is below the mean, our best guess is that his observed score contains negative errors of measurement. The formula for obtaining the predicted true score $(\hat{T})$ is given below. The derivation can be found in most test theory or statistics texts.

$$\hat{T} = r_{xx}(X - \bar{X}) + \bar{X} \qquad (5\text{-}6)$$

For the individual (in the example given in the preceding section) who had an observed score of 112 (and assuming an $\bar{X}$ of 100 and an r_{xx} of .91), his $\hat{T}$ would be $\hat{T} = .91(112 - 100) + 100 = 110.92 \doteq 111$.[3]

Estimates of Reliability

Now that reliability has been defined and discussed conceptually and theoretically, let us consider the operational definitions of reliability. How do we obtain estimates of the theoretically defined reliability? Given one set of observed scores for a group of people, we can obtain $S_x{}^2$. From Equation (5–4) we can see that one must get an estimate of either r_{xx} or $S_e{}^2$ in order to solve the equation. Ordinarily, one estimates r_{xx} first and then uses Equation (5–5) to estimate S_e.

The methods used to estimate reliability differ in that they allow different sources of error to show up. Many different approaches can be used to estimate reliability, but the more common ones reported in test manuals are as follows:[4]

1. Measures of stability
2. Measures of equivalence
3. Measures of equivalence and stability
4. Measures of internal consistency
   a. Split-half
   b. Kuder-Richardson estimates
   c. Coefficient alpha
   d. Hoyt's analysis of variance procedure
5. Score (judge) reliability

MEASURES OF STABILITY

A measure of stability, often called a test-retest estimate of reliability, is obtained by administering a test to a group of individuals, readministering

---

[3] The standard error of measurement of the predicted true scores is $r_{xx}S_e$ (see Stanley, 1971, p. 381).

[4] Methods 1, 2, 3 and 4(a) all use the Pearson product moment correlation coefficient r. It is not obvious why this should be a reasonable estimate of reliability as defined in Formula (5–3). Space does not allow us to present all algebraic derivations. However, given the assumption that the error is random error and that the two distributions have equal means and variances, it can be shown that Formula (5–3) is equal to Formula (4–4) for the Pearson product moment coefficient. Thus, a correlation is a good estimate of reliability to the extent that the assumptions are met.

the same test to the same individuals at a later date, and correlating the two sets of scores.

With this type of reliability estimate we can determine how confidently we can generalize from the score a person receives at one time to what he would receive if the test had been given at a different time. There are various possible time intervals. The estimate of reliability will vary with the length of the interval, and thus this interval length must be considered in interpreting reliability coefficients. Therefore, when stability reliability is reported in a test manual, the time interval between testings should always be specified as well as some indication of the relevant intervening experiences. Any change in score from one setting to the other is treated as error (it is assumed that the trait is stable). This is analogous to weighing a person at two different times and ascribing the difference in the two recorded measures to error. The difference may be due to standing on the scale somewhat differently, it may be due to the scale breaking (becoming inaccurate) between measures, it may be due to a mistake in reading or recording the numbers, or it may be due to an actual weight change (trait instability) over time. In this type of estimate we cannot isolate which of the sources of error contribute to the difference in performance (weight). What is really being measured is the consistency over time of the examinees' performances on the test.

The stability estimate is often difficult to obtain and interpret in psychological measurement. Many psychological tests are reactive measures (Webb et al., 1966). That is, the very act of measurement causes the person to change on the variable being measured. The practice effects from the first testing, for example, will likely be different across students, thus lowering the reliability estimate. On the other hand, if the interval is short, there may be a strong recall or memory effect. That is, students may mark a question the same as before, not because they decide again that that is the correct answer but just because they remember marking it that way before. This memory effect would tend to make the retest reliability estimate spuriously high. Problems such as memory are usually of less concern for tests in the psychomotor domain, but could be troublesome in tests in the cognitive and affective domains.

MEASURES OF EQUIVALENCE

In contrast to the test-retest procedure, the equivalent forms estimate of reliability is obtained by giving two forms (with equal content, means, and variances) of a test to the same group of individuals on the same day and correlating these results. With this procedure we are determining how confidently we can generalize a person's score to what he would receive if he took a test composed of similar but different questions. Here, also, any change in performance is considered error, but instead of measuring changes from one time to another, we measure changes due to the specificity of knowledge. That is, a person may know the answer to a question on form A and not know the answer to the equivalent question on form B. The difference in the scores would be treated as error. This procedure is somewhat analogous to weighing a person on two different scales on the same day. Here, we are unlikely to have much of a difference score (if any) due to weight change, but a difference could exist because two different scales are being used.

In constructing equivalent tests, care must be taken that the two measures are equivalent in a statistical sense with equal means, variances, and item intercorrelations. But the equality of content is also important. (Sometimes the term *parallel* is used rather than *equivalent* to connote the similarity of content.) The same table of specifications in building the test (see Chapter 7) should be followed for both forms. The items should be of similar difficulty and of the same format (for example, multiple-choice), and administrative instructions should be the same for both tests.

Equivalent forms of a test are, of course, useful for reasons other than estimating reliability. For curriculum and/or student evaluation one might want to administer a posttest over the same type of material as was presented in a pretest. Using an equivalent form rather than repeating the same test helps reduce teaching for the test (in a specific pejorative sense), as well as reduce the memory effects noted earlier.

The two methods of estimating reliability discussed above are quite different and may give different results. Which, then, should be used? It depends on the purposes for which the test is administered. If one wishes to use the test results for long-range predictions, then he would want to use a coefficient of stability. For example, in order for a scholastic aptitude test in grade 9 to predict college GPA (grade-point average), the scores must be fairly stable. If not, we would fail in long-term predictions. Thus, we would want a reliability estimate to reflect any trait change as error so that our confidence in any prediction would be appropriately tempered by a lower reliability coefficient.

If the purpose of giving a test is not for long-range prediction but rather, say, for the purpose of making inferences about the knowledge one has in a subject-matter area, then one would be primarily interested in a coefficient of equivalence. In this case we are less interested in how stable the knowledge is over time and are more interested in whether we can infer or generalize to a larger domain of knowledge from a sample. If there were a considerable change in score from one equivalent form to another, then the score on either or both forms is due, in large part, to specificity of knowledge. Inferences to the domain of knowledge from a score so influenced by the properties of a specific sample are hazardous. This fact would be reflected by a low equivalent-forms reliability estimate.

MEASURES OF EQUIVALENCE AND STABILITY

At times people are concerned with both long-range prediction and inferences to a domain of knowledge. This is actually more likely to occur than a concern for just stability. For example, the measurement of constructs[5] such as intelligence, creativity, aggressiveness, or musical interest are probably not dependent upon a specific set of questions. If it is, the construct is not of very much interest. We would like to know whether a different, but similar, set of questions asked at a different point in time would give similar results. In that case a coefficient of equivalence and stability could be obtained by giving one form of the test and, after a period of time, administering the other form and correlating the results. This procedure allows for both changes in scores due to trait instability and changes in scores due to item specificity. This estimate of reliability is thus usually lower than either of the other two procedures.

MEASURES OF INTERNAL CONSISTENCY

The three estimates of reliability previously discussed require data from two testing sessions. At times it is not feasible to obtain these kinds of data. Using the methods to be described, it is possible to obtain reliability estimates from only one set of test data. With the exception of the split-half method, these estimates are really indices of the homogeneity of the items in the test, or the degree to which the item responses correlate with the total test score.

SPLIT-HALF   The split-half method of estimating reliability is theoretically the same as the equivalent-forms method. Nevertheless, the split-half method is ordinarily considered as a measure of internal consistency because the two equivalent forms are contained within a single test. That is, instead of administering an alternate form of the test, only one test is administered; in estimating reliability, one obtains a subscore for each of two halves, and these two subscores are correlated. In most cases the Pearson product moment correlation coefficient (described in Chapter 4) is used. This correlation coefficient ($r_{\frac{1}{2}\frac{1}{2}}$) is an estimate of the reliability of a test only half as long as the original. To estimate what the reliability of the whole test would be, a correction factor needs to be applied. The appropriate formula is a special case of the Spearman-Brown prophecy formula and is as follows:

$$r_{XX} = \frac{2r_{\frac{1}{2}\frac{1}{2}}}{1 + r_{\frac{1}{2}\frac{1}{2}}} \tag{5-7}$$

where r_{XX} = estimated reliability of the whole test

$r_{\frac{1}{2}\frac{1}{2}}$ = reliability of the half-test

Thus, if two halves of a test correlated .60 ($r_{\frac{1}{2}\frac{1}{2}} = .60$), the estimated reliability of the whole test would be

[5] Constructs are unobservable phenomena, both inferred from and used to help explain an individual's behavior.

$$r_{xx} = \frac{2(.60)}{1+.60} = \frac{1.20}{1.60} = .75$$

The advantage of the split-half method is that there need be only one form of the test and one administration to estimate reliability.

The Spearman-Brown prophecy formula assumes that the variances of the two halves are equal. If they are not, the estimated reliability of the whole test will be greater than that obtained by other methods of internal consistency. Thus, one of the problems that exists in the split-half method is how to make the split. This problem can be approached in a variety of ways. But if one really attempts to make the two halves equivalent (and parallel), it requires all of the same efforts necessary to construct two equivalent forms (except that only half as many items are needed). Ordinarily, the test is just split into two parts by a preconceived plan (for example, odd items versus even items) without statistically attempting to make the two parts equivalent.[6]

KUDER-RICHARDSON ESTIMATES   If items are scored dichotomously (right or wrong), one way to avoid the problems of how to split the test is to use one of the Kuder-Richardson formulas. One can think of the formulas as representing the average correlation obtained from all possible split-half reliability estimates. K-R 20 and K-R 21 are two formulas that are used extensively. They are as follows:

K-R 20: $$r_{xx} = \frac{n}{n-1}\left[1 - \frac{\Sigma pq}{S_x^2}\right]$$ (5-8)

K-R 21: $$r_{xx} = \frac{n}{n-1}\left[1 - \frac{\bar{X}(n-\bar{X})}{nS_x^2}\right]$$ (5-9)

where n = number of items in test
p = proportion of people who answered item correctly. (If, for example, on Item 1, 6 of 30 people answered the item correctly, p for this item would be $6/30 = .20$)
q = proportion of people who answered item incorrectly $(q = 1 - p)$
pq = variance of a single item scored dichotomously (right or wrong)
Σ = summation sign indicating that pq is summed over all items
S_x^2 = variance of the total test
$\bar{X}$ = mean of the total test

[6] In reading other materials, such as test manuals for standardized tests, you may see references made to Rulon's, Guttman's, or Flanagan's split-half procedures. If the two halves of the test have equal variances, the results will be the same by using their methods as by using the procedure discussed here. If not, they will give slightly lower reliability estimates.

The distinction between K-R 20 and K-R 21 is that the latter assumes all items to be of equal difficulty; that is, p is constant for all items. Given this assumption, K-R 21 is simply an algebraic derivation of K-R 20. If the assumption is not met, K-R 21 will give a slightly lower estimate of reliability. Both formulas are frequently used by test publishers.

K-R 21 is a particularly useful formula for teachers. It requires much less computation than K-R 20. Given the number of items in the test, one needs only to compute the mean and variance of the test, substitute these three values into Equation (5–9), and do the arithmetic. Using this formula teachers can, with very little effort, obtain estimates of the reliability of their classroom tests.

COEFFICIENT ALPHA (α)   Developed by Cronbach (1951), the coefficient alpha method is a generalization of the K-R 20 formula when the items are *not* scored dichotomously. The formula for coefficient alpha is the same as the K-R 20 formula except that the Σpq is relaced by $\Sigma S_i{}^2$, where $S_i{}^2$ is the variance of a single item. It is a useful formula to use for a test composed of essay questions where a student's score on each question could take on a range of values. The formula is

$$\alpha = \frac{n}{n-1}\left[1 - \frac{\Sigma S_i{}^2}{S_x{}^2}\right] \qquad\qquad \textbf{(5–10)}$$

where $S_i{}^2$ is the variance of a single item. All other terms have been defined previously.

HOYT'S ANALYSIS OF VARIANCE PROCEDURE   The important point to remember about Hoyt's (1941) analysis of variance procedure is that it yields exactly the same results as K-R 20 or coefficient alpha. Although his method has certain theoretical and conceptual advantages, they will not be discussed because understanding analysis of variance is prerequisite to understanding Hoyt's procedure. This method has been mentioned here only because you will probably see references made to it in the literature. Stanley (1971) discusses both coefficient alpha and the analysis-of-variance procedures in more detail.

SCORER (JUDGE) RELIABILITY

In the introduction to this section we mentioned various sources of random error. We have just studied some methods of estimating reliability that have allowed or disallowed various sources of error to occur. Thus trait instability can occur and is counted as random error if we use stability estimates; sampling error can occur if we use equivalent (or split-half) estimates;

administrator error can occur if two different administrations of the same test, or equivalent tests, are given.

For most objective tests we need not concern ourselves with scorer reliability. However, for such measures as essay tests of achievement, projective personality tests, and various rating scales, one should attempt to determine how much error may occur in a score due to the person(s) who did the scoring or rating.

If a sample of papers has been scored independently by two different readers, the traditional Pearson product moment correlation coefficient (r) can be used to estimate the reliability of a single reader's scores. If one wished to know the reliability of the sum (or average) of the two readers' scores, he could use the Spearman-Brown prophecy formula given in Equation (5–7). In this case, the $r_{\frac{1}{2}\frac{1}{2}}$ would be the correlation between the two sets of scores, and r_{xx} would be the estimated reliability of the summed (or averaged) scores. At times, one or even two judges will not provide data that are reliable enough. If more than two judges are used, there are various intraclass correlation formulas that one can use to obtain estimates of the scorer reliability of the summed scores. Since these require analysis-of-variance procedures, we will not discuss them here but will refer interested readers to Cronbach et al. (1972). An estimate of what the reliability would be for the summed (or average) score using three or more judges could be obtained by substituting the obtained correlation for scores of two judges into the general expression of the Spearman-Brown prophecy formula given in Equation (5–11) and letting K equal the total number of judges who will be used to determine the summed score.

COMPARISON OF METHODS

Table 5–1 presents a comparison of the different methods of estimating reliability. As can be seen, more sources of error can occur when using a coefficient of equivalence and stability procedure than with any other method. Thus, reliability estimated by this procedure is likely to be lower (excluding scorer reliability which, in subjective measures, could be very low). When one is choosing a standardized test or interpreting its results, it is not sufficient to just look at the numerical value of a reliability estimate. One must also take into account how that estimate was obtained.

Factors Influencing Reliability

As has been pointed out, the specific procedure (equivalent forms, test-retest, and so on) used will affect the reliability estimate obtained. Other factors will also affect the reliability estimates. Five of these will now be discussed: test length, speed, group homogeneity, item difficulty, and objectivity.

TABLE 5–1 **Sources of Error Represented in Different Methods of Estimating Reliabilty**

| | METHOD OF ESTIMATING RELIABILITY | | | | |
SOURCE OF ERROR	Sta-bility	Equiva-lence	Equiv. and Stab.	Internal Consist-ency	Scorer Relia-bility
Trait instability	X		X		
Sampling error		X	X	X	
Administrator error	X	X	X		
Random error within the test	X	X	X	X	X
Scoring error					X

TEST LENGTH

When discussing the split-half method of estimating reliability, a specific case of the Spearman-Brown prophecy, Formula (5–7), was illustrated. The more general expression of this formula is

$$r_{xx} = \frac{Kr}{1+(K-1)r}$$ (5–11)

where r_{xx} = predicted reliability of a test K times as long as original test
. r = reliability of original test
K = ratio of number of items in new test to number of items in original one

Thus, if a test has an original reliability of .60 and if the test were made three times as long ($K = 3$), we would predict the reliability of the lengthened test to be

$$r_{xx} = \frac{3(.60)}{1+2(+.60)} = .818$$

As previously stated, when $K = 2$ (as in the case of split-half reliability) the Spearman-Brown prophecy formula makes the assumption that the two subtests are equivalent. A more general way of stating this assumption is that the items added to a test must be equivalent to the items already in the test.

Just as adding equivalent items makes a test more reliable, so deleting equivalent items makes a test less reliable. A test may have very high reliability but be simply too lengthy to be usable. One can also use Formula (5–11) to estimate the reliability of a test shorter than the original. For example, if one wanted to know what the estimated reliability of a test half as long as the original would be, $K = \frac{1}{2}$ could be used in the formula.

SPEED

A test is considered a pure speed test if everyone who reaches an item gets it right but no one has time to finish all the items. Thus, score differences depend upon the number of items attempted. The opposite of a speed test is a power test. A pure power test is one in which everyone has time to try all items but, because of the difficulty level, ordinarily no one obtains a perfect score. (Items in a power test are usually arranged in order of difficulty.) Few tests are either pure speed or pure power tests. However, to the extent that a test is speeded, it is inappropriate to estimate reliability through the methods of internal consistency, and the measures of stability or equivalence should be used.

It is easy to see that, in a pure speed test, if the items were split into odd and even, then a person who got n odd items right would get either n or $n - 1$ even items right. (For example, if a person answered the first 30 items correctly, he would get 15 odd and 15 even items right. If he answered the first 31 items correctly, he would get 16 odd and 15 even items right.) If all examinees marked an even number of items, the correlation between the two split-halves would be 1. It would be slightly less than 1 if some examinees marked an odd number of items. Thus, odd-even reliabilities of speeded tests are spuriously high. Typically, other internal consistency estimates also are too high, since some items are reached by some pupils but not by others, which tends to increase the mean interitem correlation. If a test is speeded, reliability should be computed by one of the methods that requires two administrations of the test.

GROUP HOMOGENEITY

A third factor influencing the estimated reliability of a test is group homogeneity. Other things being equal, the more heterogeneous the group, the higher the reliability. The reason for this can be best explained by looking at a definitional formula for reliability, such as Formula (5–4):

$$r_{xx} = 1 - \frac{S_e^2}{S_x^2}$$

There is no reason to expect the precision of an individual's observed score to vary as a result of group characteristics. Because S_e^2 is the variance of a person's observed score about his true score, S_e^2 should remain constant with changes in group heterogeneity. But S_x^2 increases with group heterogeneity. If S_e^2 remains constant and S_x^2 increases, r_{xx} increases. Thus, when evaluating tests for selection purposes, it is important to note the heterogeneity of the group from which the reliability was estimated. If the reported reliability were estimated on a group of sixth- through ninth-graders and if the test were then administered to only seventh-graders, it would be safe to conclude that because the students in the seventh grade are more homogeneous, the reliability of the test for those seventh-graders would be considerably lower than the reported reliability.

DIFFICULTY OF THE ITEMS

The difficulty of the test, and of the individual items, also affects the reliability of the test. Since traditional reliability estimates are dependent upon score variability, tests in which there is little variability among the scores give lower reliability estimates than tests in which the variability is large. Tests that are so easy that almost everyone gets all items correct or, conversely, so hard that almost everyone gets all the items wrong (or a chance score if guessing is involved) will have little variability among the scores and will tend to have lower reliability.

OBJECTIVITY

As already discussed under scorer reliability, the more subjectively a measure is scored, the lower the reliability of the measure.

Reliability of Difference Scores

When we are interested in difference scores, we ask (and answer) questions like the following: Is John really better in numerical or verbal ability? Did Susan gain significantly in reading ability this year? Whose arithmetic skill is better, Irv's or Bill's? To answer each of these questions, we need to consider whether there are reliable differences between two observed scores. We wish to know how appropriate it is to generalize from an observed difference to a "true" difference.

Unfortunately, difference scores are considerably less reliable than single scores. The errors of measurement on each test contribute to error variance in the difference scores, and the true variance that the two tests measure in common reduces the variability of the difference scores. (See Thorndike and Hagen, 1977, pp. 98–100.) Theoretically the reliability of difference scores (like reliability of single sets of observed scores) is the ratio of two variances. In this case, reliability is equal to the true variance of the difference scores divided by the observed variance of the difference scores. If two tests have equal variances,[7] the reliability of a difference score can be computed as follows:

$$r_{\text{diff}} = \frac{\dfrac{r_{xx}+r_{yy}}{2}-r_{xy}}{1-r_{xy}} \qquad (5\text{–}12)$$

where r_{diff} = reliability of the difference scores
  r_{xx} = reliability of one measure
  r_{yy} = reliability of other measure
  r_{xy} = correlation between the two measures

From this equation it can be seen that three variables affect the reliability of the difference scores: the reliability of each of the two measures and their intercorrelation. To obtain reliable difference scores, we would need tests that have high initial reliabilities and low intercorrelation. This can be seen by studying Table 5–2. Blanks are left in the table where the computation would result in a negative value. Theoretically such values cannot occur. One could, but seldom would, have such numbers occur in actual practice. If so, they would be interpreted as indicating zero reliability.

TABLE 5–2   Reliability of Difference Scores

CORRELATION BETWEEN THE TWO TESTS (r_{xy})	AVERAGE RELIABILITY OF THE TWO TESTS $\dfrac{r_{xx}+r_{yy}}{2}$						
	.50	.60	.70	.80	.90	.95	1.00
.00	.50	.60	.70	.80	.90	.95	1.00
.20	.38	.50	.63	.75	.88	.94	1.00
.40	.17	.33	.50	.67	.83	.92	1.00
.50	.00	.20	.40	.60	.80	.90	1.00
.60		.00	.25	.50	.75	.88	1.00
.70			.00	.33	.67	.83	1.00
.80				.00	.50	.75	1.00
.90					.00	.50	1.00
.95						.00	1.00

SOURCE: Adapted from R. L. Thorndike and E. Hagen, *Measurement and Evaluation in Psychology and Education,* © 1967, p. 197. By permission of John Wiley & Sons, Inc.

[7] The assumption of equal variances is not unduly restrictive. As we explain in Chapter 6, score distributions can be transformed so that the variances can be made equal.

SIGNIFICANCE OF DIFFERENCE SCORES

A commonly suggested caution in standardized test manuals is that one should not interpret a difference between two scores as significant unless the lowest score plus one standard error of measurement of that score is less than the highest score minus one standard error of measurement of that score. In other words, if one uses the band interpretation of scores discussed in the earlier section "Standard Error of Measurement of Observed Scores," it is only when the two bands do not overlap that one assumes a significant difference existing between the scores.[8]

In interpreting difference scores, one could make two types of errors: (1) Interpret an observed difference as a true one when in fact it was due to random error; or (2) interpret an observed difference as due to chance when in fact a true difference exists. (In statistical terminology these are referred to as Type I and Type II errors, respectively.)

The first type of error may be considered as one of overinterpretation; the second type, as underinterpretation (Feldt, 1967). If one follows the commonly suggested procedure of interpreting the scores as not different if the $X \pm 1S_e$ bands of the two scores overlap, then the chance of the first type of error is quite small (around .16 if the S_e of the two tests are equal). This type of interpretative guideline, if followed, increases the chances of making the second type of error. Publishers and educators evidently feel that the first type of error is more costly, and so risks of making it should be minimized. (See Feldt, 1967, for a further discussion of this point.)

GAIN SCORES

A special type of difference score that has received considerable attention is a gain (or change) score. In education we often wish to know how much our students have learned (gained) from a particular instructional process. Many of the advocates of accountability and program evaluation are prone to use gain scores.

Statistically, one can estimate the reliability of a gain score by using Formula (5–12). In measuring gain, the r_{xx} would be the pretest, r_{yy} the posttest (which may be the same test or an equivalent form), and r_{xy} the correlation between the pretest and posttest. One particular problem with gain scores, however, is that r_{xy} is usually reasonably high, thus reducing the reliability of the gain scores. One could, of course, attempt to construct intentionally a posttest so that r_{xy} would be low and r_{diff} high, but then one is faced with the logical dilemma of whether the difference score is really a change on whatever characteristic was being measured on the pretest. For if

---

[8] Formulas for computing the standard error of difference scores can be found in any basic text on test theory or in the first edition of this text.

r_{xy} is low, maybe the pre- and posttests are not really measuring the same thing and therefore the difference is not a gain. Bereiter (1963) refers to this as the unreliability-invalidity dilemma. There are many other troublesome aspects of measuring gain. We refer you to Cronbach and Furby (1970), Cronbach, Gleser, Nanda, and Rajaratnam (1972), Harris (1963), Overall and Woodward (1975), and Stanley (1971) for more technical treatments of this topic.

The major points to be kept in mind are that (1) difference scores are less reliable than single scores; (2) gain scores are in general the least reliable of all difference scores; (3) although difference or gain scores may be too unreliable for use with individuals, they may be reliable enough for making decisions about groups (group means are always more reliable than individual scores because the random errors of the individual scores tend to cancel themselves out, thus making the mean reasonably accurate); and (4) anyone who intends to use difference (or gain) scores for important educational decisions would be well advised to study the references given in the preceding paragraph.

Reliability of Criterion-Referenced Tests

As we mentioned in Chapter 3, the purpose of a norm-referenced test is to discriminate among individuals or compare them to each other. The purpose of a criterion-referenced test is to compare each individual to some standard. In criterion-referenced interpretation of test scores we are not interested in student variability. In fact, if all students received a perfect score on a mastery test, we would be happy. Yet, since classical reliability depends upon the existence of differences among students' observed scores, the reliability of such a mastery test would be undefined.

Let us review the basic definitional formula (Formula 5–3) for reliability, but rewrite it slightly as follows:

$$r_{xx} = \frac{S_t{}^2}{S_x{}^2} = \frac{S_t{}^2}{S_t{}^2 + S_e{}^2}$$

If the variability in true scores is reduced, the ratio is reduced and classical reliability goes down. At the point where $S_t{}^2$ (true-score variance) is reduced to zero, reliability is zero except for the situation where $S_e{}^2$ (error-score variance) is also zero so that everyone receives the same observed score. Then the denominator would be zero, and the ratio would be undefined.

Thus, classical estimates of reliability are not completely appropriate for criterion-referenced measures, particularly for that subset of criterion-referenced measures that are called mastery tests. Yet the concept of a precise measure—one that has a small standard error of measurement—is still important. We do wish to measure with as much precision as possible, and we should have estimates to tell us what precision we have obtained.

Whereas in classical test theory we are interested in the precision of the score, in criterion-referenced interpretation we are sometimes interested in the precision of the score but at other times we are only interested in the precision of the decision. For example, in mastery testing our decision is to categorize individuals as masters or nonmasters. We are really more interested in the precision of the decision than in how precise a score is. Different mathematical formulations are needed to estimate the reliability of a decision than to estimate the reliability of a score.

More work still needs to be done in the conceptual and operational definitions of reliability where norm referencing is not used. For both criterion-referenced and gain-score measurements, where we may not be interested in maximizing the differences between individuals, classical reliability estimates yield values that present a very pessimistic picture of the precision of the measuring instrument; excessive emphasis should not be placed on them in judging the technical adequacy of such scores. Lord's (1957) conceptualization of the standard error of measurement is probably a more useful approach in judging the precision of a criterion-referenced test.[9]

Reliability and Test Use

A question often asked in measurement courses is: How reliable should a test be in order for it to be useful? This question cannot be answered in a simple manner. It depends upon the purposes for which the test is to be used. No major decision should be made on the basis of a single test. If the decisions the scores will help make are extremely important and/or irreversible, then the reliability of the measure is of more concern than if the decision is not quite so important and/or tentative and reversible. If a measure is to be used to help make decisions about individuals, then it should be more reliable than if it is to be used to make decisions about groups of people. Although there is no universal agreement, it is generally accepted that standardized tests used to assist in making decisions about *individuals* should have reliability coefficients of at least .85. (Classroom or teacher-constructed measurement devices may often have lower reliability than this. Thus, one should not be making important decisions based on only one test.) For *group decisions*, a reliability coefficient of about .65 may suffice. These are only guidelines. There are no absolutes; one should use the best test available. A

[9] Various formulas have been developed for estimating the reliability of criterion-referenced tests. Discussion of these is beyond the scope of this book. We refer interested readers to Hambleton and Novick (1973), Huynh (1976), Livingston (1972), Subkoviak (1976), and Swaminathan, Hambleton, and Algina (1974).

more relevant factor is the consideration of how good a decision can be made without the help of the test data. If there is very little other information on which to base a decision, and a decision must be made, it may be helpful to use a test with low reliability rather than none at all. (A test with low reliability may still have some *validity* and can therefore be useful.) On the other hand, if a good decision (or accurate prediction) can be made without any test data, it may not be worthwhile to give a test, even though it is reliable.

In standardized test selection a crucial matter for the reader of a test manual is to be able to understand the reliability information reported. This, of course, implies that reliability data must be reported in the test manual. A knowledge of the concept of reliability, different estimates of reliability, and effects upon these estimates should help lead to such an understanding.

The kinds of reliability data that one should expect to find in a test manual depend on the type of test and on how one expects to use it. For general aptitude tests the most imporant kind of reliability estimate would be a stability estimate. Because aptitude test results are used to help make long-range predictions, it is important to know how stable the aptitude results are. (If the test scores are not stable, they cannot predict themselves, much less a criterion.) For multiple aptitude tests it is also essential to have data on the reliabilities of the subtests and the difference scores. Equivalence and internal consistency estimates are also of value for interpreting any aptitude test, since one should have some information regarding the homogeneity of the content and the degree to which the scores are dependent upon particular questions.

For achievement tests, equivalence reliability estimates seem almost essential. One wants to infer from the responses to a specific set of items the degree to which a person has mastered the essential skills and/or knowledge in a much larger universe. In addition, it would be valuable to have some indication about the homogeneity of the content. Thus, internal consistency estimates should also be provided. As with multiple aptitude tests, achievement test batteries should provide data on subtest reliabilities and on the reliabilities of difference scores. Inasmuch as most achievement tests are intentionally designed to fit the curriculum, and students learn those materials in differing amounts and rates, one would not expect these scores to remain constant. Hence, long-range stability coefficients would be rather meaningless.

For noncognitive measures, the types of reliability information needed varies. For example, if one wishes to use an interest test to predict long-term job satisfaction, then one must assume that interests are stable, and information relevant to this assumption is needed. On the other hand, if one wishes to obtain a measure of a transient personality characteristic (such as temporary depression), high-stability coefficients would not be expected. Instead, one might look for internal consistency reliability.

In addition to indicating the type(s) of reliability estimates obtained, the manual must also provide other information. It is essential to know the characteristics of the sample on which the reliability estimates were computed.

One should know the sample size, its representativeness, and the mean and standard deviation of sample scores.

Standard errors of measurement (and how they were obtained) should be provided. Separate age and/or grade estimates should be reported. Even within an age or grade level, different S_e should be reported (for example, an aptitude or achievement test should report separate S_e for students performing at the high, middle, and low levels).

VALIDITY

The degree of validity is the single most important aspect of a test. Validity can be best defined as the degree to which a test is capable of achieving certain aims. When discussing validity it is useful to think of two general types of aims: (1) for making predictions about the individual tested, and (2) for describing or representing him. A test is used as a *predictor* when the focus is on some behavior we are interested in predicting. Predictive use is dependent upon criterion-related validity (see next subsection). A test describes or *represents* when the test items themselves are similar to the behaviors we wish to measure. Tests that represent can further be differentiated as *samples* or *signs*. The distinction is based on the degree to which one can *define* the behavorial domain being sampled. If the items are drawn from a clearly defined universe, we speak of this as a sample. If the universe is not clearly defined, we speak of the test as a sign. Samples *describe* the domain, signs help *explain* the domain. For tests to serve as samples we need high content validity, to serve as signs we need high construct validity (see next subsection).

Validity is sometimes defined as truthfulness: Does the test measure what it purports to measure? In order for a test to be valid, or truthful, it must first of all be reliable. If we cannot even get a bathroom scale to give us a consistent weight measure, we certainly cannot expect it to be accurate. Note, however, that a measure might be very consistent (reliable) but not accurate (valid). A scale may record weights as 2 pounds too heavy each time. In other words, reliability is a necessary but not sufficient condition for validity. (Neither validity nor reliability is an either/or dichotomy. There are degrees of each.)

Since a single test may be used for many different purposes, there is no single validity index for a test. A test that has some validity for one purpose may be invalid for another.

Kinds of Validity

While many different authors have used many different terms for validity (Ebel, 1972, p. 436), the latest *Standards for Educational and Psychological Tests and Manuals* (American Psychological Association, 1974) delimits only three kinds of validity:

1. Content validity
2. Criterion-related validity
3. Construct validity

We will discuss each of these plus a fourth kind of validity, face validity.

CONTENT VALIDITY

As mentioned earlier, one purpose of a test is to describe or represent a person. A test serves as a sample if the items are drawn from a clearly defined universe. Content validity is related to how adequately the content of, and responses to, the test samples the domain about which inferences are to be made. Lennon (1956, p. 294) defines validity as

> The extent too which a subject's responses to the items of a test may be considered to be a representative sample of his responses to a real or hypothetical universe of situations which together constitute the area of concern to the person interpreting the test.

Content validity is particularly important for achievement tests. Typically we wish to make an inference about a student's degree of attainment of the universe of situations and/or subject matter domain. The test behavior serves as a sample, and the important question is whether the test items do, in fact, constitute a representative sample of behavioral stimuli.

In judging content validity, one must first define the content domain and universe of situations. In doing so, one should consider both the subject matter and the type of behavior or task desired from the pupils. Notice in the definition by Lennon quoted above that content validity is ascribed to the subject's responses rather than to the test questions themselves. Both content and process are important. The test user makes inferences to a *behavioral* universe. (For simplicity in writing we will from now on call the universe to which we wish to infer the content domain. Remember, however, the inferences are to *behavior*.)

There has been some debate about how explicitly the content domain needs to be defined. Some of our discussion in Chapter 3 on norm- and criterion-referenced measurement was related to this debate. The section of Chapter 2 on the behavioral specificity of objectives is also related. It is probably desirable in most cases to have the domain defined as specifically as possible in terms of a complete, finite, set of behavioral objectives. This is easier for some subject matter areas than others. For example, elementary school mathematics may be more easily defined totally than British literature. The more thoroughly defined the domain, the closer we come to being able to build a domain-referenced test (see Chapter 3). But for many subject matters we cannot define the total domain with complete specificity. This, of course, means we would not have perfect content validity, but it does not necessarily mean that the content validity is inadequate. A reasonable expectation is that the test constructor specify with considerable detail the subject matter topics and pupil behaviors the test is designed to sample. We will talk more in Chapter 7 about test blueprints or tables of specifications for achievement tests. These are two-way grids designed to aid in constructing tests so that all appropriate topics and behaviors will be sampled in the proper proportions. If these grids are both carefully constructed and carefully followed in building the test, this will do much to ensure adequate content validity.

There is no commonly used numerical expression for content validity. It is typically determined by a thorough inspection of the items. Each item is judged on whether or not it represents the specified domain. Although a detailed, systematic, critical inspection of the test items is probably the single best way to determine content validity, it does have some drawbacks. It is subjective and does not yield any quantitative expression. Two individuals— whether or not they have the same understanding of the content domain— may well make different judgments about the match of the items to the domain. Of course, inter-judge agreements of ratings could be calculated (see Tinsley & Weiss, 1975).

The task of subjectively judging content validity is made easier if the author of the test defines the universe and the sampling process. Displaying the table of specifications and the number of items from each category would greatly facilitate this judgment. In addition, the procedures followed in setting up the table of specifications as well as the methods used for classifying the items should be described. These procedures might include using curriculum specialists as expert judges and reviewing current texts, curricular guides, and the like.

In addition to expert judgment, there are other procedures for judging content validity. One method, similar to one discussed previously under reliability, indicates the close relationship between one type of reliability and content validity. Recall that in reliability we wished to know how confidently we could generalize from the particular score obtained to the score we might have received under different conditions. Likewise, in content validity we are interested in how adequately we can infer from a particular score to a larger domain. In either case we wish to *generalize*. Thus, building two tests over the same content, giving both to the same set of pupils, and correlating the results tells us something about both equivalent form reliability and content validity. In fact, Ebel (1975b) has suggested that instead of content validity we might better use terms such as "content reliability" or "job sample reliability."

As Brown (1976) points out, in one sense content validity is a general property of a test. If a test *author* defines the content domain and writes items to represent the domain, he succeeds to some degree in attaining his goal. From the point of view of a test *user*, however, content validity is situation-specific. Does the test measure the behaviors considered important? It should be emphasized that an achievement test may have high content validity for one user and have low content validity for another.

For example, not all teachers (even those teaching the same course titles in the same grade) are necessarily teaching the same domain of subject matter. For that reason they should construct their own evaluation instruments to ensure that their tests have adequate content validity for their particular courses. Obviously, they should help in the selection of standardized achievement tests because they are best able to judge the content validity in relation to the subject matter they are teaching.

CRITERION-RELATED VALIDITY

Criterion-related validity pertains to the empirical technique of studying the relationship between the test scores and some independent external measures (criteria). Some writers make a distinction between two kinds of criterion-related validity: concurrent validity and predictive validity. The only procedural distinction between these pertains to the time period when the criterion data are gathered. When they are collected at approximately the same time as the test data, we speak of concurrent validity. When they are gathered at a later date, we have a measure of predictive validity.

A second distinction is a logical rather than a procedural one, and is based not on time but on the purpose of testing. In predictive validity we are actually concerned with the usefulness of the test score in *predicting* some future performance. In concurrent validity we are asking whether the test score can be *substituted* for some less efficient way of gathering criterion data. Thus, whether criterion-related validity should be expressed as concurrent or predictive, depends on whether we are primarily interested in *prediction* or in assessment of current status.

Although concurrent and predictive validity differ in the time period when the criterion data are gathered, they are both concerned with prediction in a *generalizability* sense of the term. In criterion-related validity as in content validity and reliability we wish to determine how well we can *generalize* from one score to another. In reliability we were asking how confidently we could generalize to another measure of the same characteristic. In content validity we wished to generalize from a sample to a total domain. In criterion-related validity we are asking how confidently we can generalize (or predict) to how well a person will do on a *different task*. For example, a college admissions test may include verbal analogy items. Admission officers are not directly interested in how well a student can perform on these items, but rather they wish to measure this characteristic because it predicts a relevant criterion: college success.

The distinction between a test as *representing* versus *predicting* is not completely clear. The same test could be used for both purposes. A test sampling the mathematics concepts taught in grade 7 could be used as a description of level of achievement in seventh-grade mathematics; it could also be used to predict success in eighth-grade mathematics.

MEASURING THE CRITERION   In studying criterion-related validity, one must look closely at both the conceptual and operational (measurement) aspects of the criterion. For example, suppose we wish to determine the degree to which scores on a certain aptitude test predict "success in school." Success in school is, then, the criterion. How do we measure success in school? Traditionally, educators have used grade-point average (GPA) as the operational definition of school success, but most realize that this is not a completely adequate definition. Other criterion measures, such as graduation versus withdrawal, are possible. Similar situations exist if we are trying to predict success on a job. In this case, supervisor ratings are often used as a criterion measure, but they also have many inadequacies. If a test score did not correlate well with the ratings, one would not know for sure whether the test did not predict on-the-job success or whether the supervisor could not rate it accurately, or both.

One of the hardest tasks in a study of criterion-related validity is to obtain adequate criterion data. Gathering such data is often a more troublesome measurement problem than constructing the test or predictive instrument. *Criterion measures, like all other measures, must have certain characteristics if they are to be considered adequate.* (See Brown, 1976, pp. 101–102.) First of all they should be *relevant*. That is, the criterion measure should actually reflect the important aspects of the conceptual criterion. There is no point in obtaining a criterion measure that really does not reflect the criterion. The degree of relevance of the criterion measure is a value judgment, and not everyone will agree on any specific case. Some educators, for instance, argue that success in college should mean the amount of knowledge possessed after four years in college and that grades are a good (or at least the best available) measure of such knowledge. Others believe that amount of knowledge is a good definition of success, but feel that the grading system employed does not allow one to infer amount of knowledge from GPA. Still others may feel that success in college means marrying well, making good contacts, or something else. To these people, grades would be an irrelevant criterion measure.

A second desired characteristic of a criterion is that it be *reliable*. Just as test reliability affects the degree of correlation between it and the criterion, so does the reliability of the criterion affect the correlation. A general theoretical relationship is that the maximum relationship one can obtain between two variables is equal to the square root of the product of their respective reliabilities. Or

$$r_{xy} \leq \sqrt{(r_{xx})(r_{yy})}$$

where r_{xy} = correlation between predictor (x) and criterion (y)
r_{xx} = reliability of the test
r_{yy} = reliability of the criterion

Thus, the reliability of the criterion affects criterion-related validity every bit as much as the reliability of the predictor.

A third characteristic of the criterion measure is that it be free from bias or contamination (Brogden & Taylor, 1950). Criterion contamination occurs when the criterion score is influenced by the knowledge of the predictor score. Suppose that in September a ninth-grade math teacher gives and scores a test designed to predict success of his pupils in ninth-grade math. If his knowledge of these predictor scores consciously or unconsciously affects the grades (criterion scores) he assigns at the end of the year, then we have criterion contamination. The best way to avoid this problem is to make sure the rater supplying the criterion scores has no knowledge of the predictor values.

CONSTRUCT VALIDITY

Construct validity is the degree to which the test scores can be accounted for by certain explanatory constructs in a psychological theory. If an instrument has construct validity, people's scores will vary as the theory underlying the construct would predict. A simplified example may help.

If one is interested in studying a construct like creativity, it must be because he hypothesizes that people who are creative will *perform* differently from those who are not creative. It is possible to build a theory (or theories) specifying how creative people (people who possess the construct creativity) behave differently from others. Once this is done, creative people can be identified by observing the behavior of individuals and classifying them according to the theory. (They could be rated rather than classified.)

Now, suppose one wished to build a paper-and-pencil test to *measure* creativity. Once built, the creativity test would be considered to have construct validity to the degree that the test scores are related to the judgments made from observing behavior identified by the psychological theory as creative. If the anticipated relationships are not found, then the construct validity of the test is not supported.

A lack of a relationship could occur for several reasons. For example, the test may really not measure the construct of creativity, or the psychological theory specifying how creative people behave may be faulty. Theoretical psychologists are probably more apt to believe that the test rather than the theory is faulty. Even though this is the more probable reason, it is suggested that psychologists should be a little more willing to reexamine their theories if empirical evidence does not support them.

Construct validity is an important concept for those educators and psychologists who are doing theoretical research on various constructs. Individuals with such interests surely need to delve further into the topic than we have in these few paragraphs. We suggest Anastasi (1976), Brown (1976), or Cronbach and Meehl (1955) as good references for further study.

FACE VALIDITY

Occasionally content and construct validity are confused with face validity. The latter is not really validity at all in the technical sense of the word. Face validity is simply whether the test looks valid "on the face of it." That is, would untrained people who look at or take the test be apt to think the test is measuring what its author claims? Face validity often is a desirable feature of a test in the sense that it is useful from a public relations standpoint. If a test appears irrelevant, examinees may not take the test seriously, or potential users may not consider the results useful. (Occasionally, in assessment in the affective domain, one wishes to conceal the purpose of assessment in order to diminish faking. In these cases, reduced face validity leads to increased criterion-related or construct validity.)

Methods of Expressing Validity

As mentioned before, there is no common numerical expression for content validity. The methods to be discussed below are used in expressing both criterion-related and construct validities. However, it should be kept in mind that one must obtain many indices before feeling justified in suggesting that any degree of construct validity has been demonstrated.

CORRELATION COEFFICIENTS AND RELATED EXPRESSIONS

The Pearson product moment correlation coefficient (r) is probably the most common procedure used in reporting validity. A fairly standard notation is to use the symbol r_{xy} for correlations representing validity coefficients. (Recall that r_{xx} is used for reliability.) The x subscript stands for the test score (predictor); the y subscript for the criterion measure. For example, a correlation coefficient of .60 ($r_{xy} = .60$) between Scholastic Aptitude Test scores (X) obtained in eleventh grade and college freshman GPAs (Y) may be reported. This correlation would indicate a substantial relationship for this type of prediction and therefore we could say that the Scholastic Aptitude Test has considerable predictive validity with regard to college freshmen grades.

The relationship between the test and the criterion is often expressed using algebraic modifications of the correlation coefficient. One such expression is $(r_{xy})^2$, that is, the squared correlation between the test and the criterion. A squared correlation is called a *coefficient of determination*. An often-heard expression is that $(r_{xy})^2$ indicates the proportion of criterion variance accounted for by the test. Thus, in the example above, where $r_{xy} = .60$, $(r_{xy})^2 = .36$, this would mean that 36 percent of the variation in college freshman GPA can be accounted for (predicted) from knowledge of the aptitude test scores.

Another statistic often reported is the *standard error of estimate* $(S_{y.x})$. The symbol is read "the standard deviation of y for a given value of x." It can be computed by

$$S_{y.x} = S_y \sqrt{1 - (r_{xy})^2} \tag{5-13}$$

where S_y = criterion standard deviation. The value $S_{y.x}$ can be used to set confidence limits about an estimated criterion score, just as the standard error of measurement (S_e) is used in setting confidence limits about a true score.[10] The equation (commonly called a regression equation) used to estimate the criterion score (Y) is

$$\hat{Y} = r_{xy} \left(\frac{S_y}{S_x} \right) (X - \bar{X}) + \bar{Y} \tag{5-14}$$

Of course, in order to use this equation (or compute any correlational data), one must have data for a single group of people on both the X and Y variables. If we have such data why would we be interested in predicting Y from X? Why not just look at the Y score to see what it is? The answer is that we build the equation from one group's scores to use in predicting Y scores for other similar groups. The group we use for test validation purposes should not be the same as the group for which we use the test in decision making. For example, suppose we wish to validate a Scholastic Aptitude Test (X) for the purpose of predicting college success (Y) (operationally defined as a college GPA). We would gather data on the Scholastic Aptitude Test for high school (say grade 12) students. We would follow these people through college and determine their college GPA. We would then have the X and Y data. We would use this information for assistance in predicting col-

---

[10] Some people prefer to use a statistic called the *coefficient of alienation*,

$$\frac{S_{y.x}}{S_y} = \sqrt{1 - (r_{xy})^2}$$

which is not influenced by the unit of measurement. This coefficient of alienation gives a ratio of the size of the error of estimate relative to the size of the error one would get if the validity of the test were zero or if one had to predict a person's Y score from no knowledge of his X score.

lege GPA for *future* groups of high school students. If we gathered Scholastic Aptitude Test data in 1976, college GPA data in 1980 (or more likely, GPA data in 1978 at the end of the sophomore year), then we could use these data to predict college GPAs for the 1981 high school graduating class.

Suppose we wish to predict Melinda's college GPA from knowledge of her score on a Scholastic Aptitude Test. Assume her aptitude test score (X) is 52, $\bar{X} = 50$, $r_{xy} = .60$, $S_y = 0.8$, $S_x = 10$, and $\bar{Y} = 2.4$. Melinda's predicted GPA score would be

$$\hat{Y} = .60 \left(\frac{.8}{10} \right)(52 - 50) + 2.4 = 2.496 \cong 2.5$$

It would be desirable to know how much confidence can be placed in this predicted GPA. Since the standard deviation of the GPA distribution (S_y) is .8, by using Formula (5–13) we see that $S_{y.x} = .8\sqrt{1 - (.60)^2} = .64$. Recall that $S_{y.x}$ is the estimated standard deviation of the Y (criterion) scores for all people with a given X score. In this case, we are saying that the Y-score distribution for all people with an X score of 52 will have a mean of 2.5 ($\hat{Y} = 2.5$) and a standard deviation of .64 ($S_{y.x} = .64$). By assuming that this distribution of Y scores is normal, we say that about 68 percent of the people with an X score of 52 will obtain a GPA (Y score) of 2.5 ± .64. Ninety-five percent of them will obtain a GPA between 2.5 ± 2 (.64). In setting confidence limits on Melinda's GPA, we can say that the chances are about 68 in 100 (odds of about 2 to 1) that Melinda's actual GPA will be between 2.5 ± .64. We can be about 95 percent confident (odds of 20 to 1) that her actual GPA will be between 2.5 ± 2 (.64). Theoretically, we assume that $S_{y.x}$ will be the same for every value of X (this is called the assumption of homoscedasticity), so we would use the same value of $S_{y.x}$ found in the example above (.64) in setting confidence bands about any predicted Y score. The 68 percent confidence band is always the predicted Y [$\hat{Y}$] ± $1S_{y.x}$; the 95 percent confidence band is always $\hat{Y}$ ± $2S_{y.x}$; and the 99 percent confidence band is $\hat{Y}$ ± $2.58S_{y.x}$.

We know that criterion-related validity depends upon the reliability of the test and criterion scores. We also know that in many instances the reliabilities of the test and criterion scores are low. In an attempt to compensate for these low reliabilities, test publishers occasionally employ a statistical manipulation called the *correction for attenuation*. This correction tells us what the relationship would be had there been perfectly reliable measures. However, it is certainly subject to misinterpretation. Naïve users may easily be led by these corrections into believing that a test is a better predictor than is warranted. In general, we are opposed to such statistical manipulations being reported in a test manual. If they are reported, however, the uncorrected validity coefficient must also be reported, and the manual should caution the user with regard to the interpretation of the statistic.

Several other points should be made before leaving this section on expressing validity using correlational procedures. Recall two points made in Chapter 4: correlation does not signify cause and effect, and the Pearson product moment correlation coefficient is a measure of linear relationship. If we believe the relationship between X and Y is not linear, we should use some other correlation coefficient.

Finally, this section and the example in it were written as if one were predicting a person's Y score (and therefore making a decision about that person) on the basis of a single piece of data (X score). That should seldom, if ever, occur. We used the single-X example because it is easier to conceptualize. Typically, a test user would want to make decisions based on a variety of predictor data. Equations similar to (5–14) exist to assist us in such predictions. They are called multiple regression equations, indicating the use of more than one X score per person. For example, we might wish to predict college grades from both knowledge of high school rank (HSR) and a Scholastic Aptitude Test. Both of these variables would then be used as data in the equation. If we thought that other variables would assist in the prediction, we would use them also. Perhaps data on a scale measuring academic motivation would increase our ability to predict. Perhaps data on race or sex would assist. Any (or all) of this additional data could be used in an equation predicting college success. (Sometimes if variables such as race or sex are used they are termed moderator variables.)

EXPECTANCY TABLES

Ordinarily students and teachers find expectancy tables easier than correlation coefficients to understand and interpret. A hypothetical expectancy table is given in Table 5–3. Column 1 gives the Scholastic Aptitude Test score in percentile rank form. The numbers in columns 2, 3, and 4 of the table represent the percent of people within each of the five categories of the test who achieved college freshman GPAs of D or higher, C or higher, and B or higher, respectively. Although such a table is usually understood by high school students, two limitations (or possible misinterpretations) should be noted. First, the column giving the size of the group is important. From column 5 we can see that the percentages for the last row were based on only ten people. Percentages based on such a small numbr of people are subject to extreme fluctuation. Second, the table should not be interpreted as if a person in the bottom fifth (0–19) on the Scholastic Aptitude Test has no chance of receiving a GPA of C or greater, or that a person in the middle fifth (40–59) has no chance of receiving a GPA of B. The table shows only that of the group sampled, no students fell in these cells of the table. Using a different sample, we would expect to find slight deviations in our predictions.

Counselors would be well advised to build expectancy tables such as

TABLE 5-3   Sample Expectancy Table[a]

(1) PERCENTILE RANK ON THE SCHOLASTIC APTITUDE TEST (NATIONAL NORMS)	CHANCES IN 100 OF A FRESHMAN OBTAINING AN AVERAGE GRADE OF			
	(2) D, or higher	(3) C, or higher	(4) B, or higher	(5) Size of Group (n)
80–99	99	81	32	100
60–79	95	52	12	100
40–59	80	15	—	60
20–39	50	—	—	30
0–19	30	—	—	10

[a] Expectancy table for first-year GPA, based on Scholastic Aptitude Test scores of freshmen entering Central College in the fall of 1976.

Table 5–3 for their own school system.[11] The tables can be very useful in helping students make decisions about college attendance. However, one must remember that just as there can be errors in prediction with regression equations, so there can be with expectancy tables. Like correlation data, expectancy tables do not prove cause and effect and can be built using more than one predictor variable.

DISCRIMINANT STATISTICS

Other methods of expressing validity employ various statistics describing the degree of difference between groups (t tests, F tests, the discriminant function, and the percent of overlap are examples of this type of statistic). To learn to compute these statistical values requires more statistics than are presented in this text. However, the test user need only understand that these procedures allow for a numerical expression of the degree to which various groups perform differently on the test. If we wish to use a test to differentiate (classify) people with various psychiatric disorders (as in the Minnesota Multiphasic Personality Inventory) or to differentiate between various occupational interest groups (as in the Strong Campbell Interest Inventory), it is important to know how successful the test is in that endeavor.

The percent of overlap is one of the more common methods used by test publishers to express the difference between groups. If two groups have a 30

[11] See the Psychological Corporation's Test Service Bulletins 38 and 56 for information on how to construct expectancy tables.

percent overlap on a test, 30 percent of the total number of people in the two groups have scores higher than the lowest score in the better group and lower than the highest score in the poorer group. Assume in Figure 5–1 that there are 50 people in Group A and 50 people in Group B. Of these 100 people, 30 (30 percent) have scores in the lined area, so there is a 30 percent overlap.

Another way of expressing overlap is to determine the percent in the lower-scoring group who exceed the mean of the upper-scoring group. This is illustrated in the solid portion of Figure 5–1. As can be seen, one obtains a much smaller percent of overlap when it is defined in that fashion. When reading studies that report an overlap statistic, one has to note carefully which definition the author is using.

Factors Affecting Validity

Many factors can affect any of the validity measures—validity coefficients, expectancy tables, and those measures reporting group differences—previously discussed. Of course, a main factor affecting validity measures is the actual relationship between the two variables we are measuring. If height is actually unrelated to intelligence, then the *measures* of height and intelligence should be unrelated. However, it is possible for two variables to *actually* be highly related but our *measures* of them in a particular *sample* of people indicate the contrary. This could occur for several reasons. For example, there may be an actual relationship between knowledge of eighth-grade mathematics and success in ninth-grade algebra. Yet a *test* of eighth-grade mathematics may not correlate with ninth-grade success. This might be because the test is too hard or too easy, it might be because the students did not try while taking the test, and/or the test may simply be a poor test of knowledge of eighth-grade mathematics. These same things could all be true of the criterion measure also.

As already stated, the reliabilities of both test (predictor) and criterion measures are important. The less reliably we can measure either the test or the criterion, the lower the validity coefficient. Recall that $r_{xy} \leq \sqrt{r_{xx}\, r_{yy}}$.

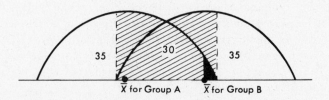

35   30   35

X̄ for Group A   X̄ for Group B

FIGURE 5–1   Diagram showing percent overlap between groups using two different definitions.

Since often r_{yy} is fairly low, r_{xy} must be fairly low. Another factor is the heterogeneity of the group(s) with respect to both test data and criterion measures. As with reliability coefficients, other things being equal, the more heterogeneous the group the higher the validity coefficient. Thus, it may not be reasonable, for example, to expect the Miller Analogies Test and grades in a doctoral program to be highly related, since the doctoral candidates are fairly homogeneous with respect to both variables. A low correlation due to homogeneity is especially likely to occur when the group on which the correlation has been obtained has already been screened (selected) on the basis of the test (or some other measure that correlates with the test score). For example, if all those who took an algebra aptitude test took algebra regardless of their test score, we would anticipate obtaining a higher correlation between test score and grade than if only those who scored in the upper half of the test could take algebra. For group-difference statistics such as percent overlap, significant differences are more likely to be found if each group is homogeneous but different from the other group(s).

The problem of *interpreting* validity coefficients on groups already screened or selected is particularly troublesome. Ideally, in investigating the validity of an instrument for predicting job performance or educational success, one should use scores from an *unselected* group of applicants. For example, one should study the relationship between the scores on a scholastic aptitude test of all applicants to college and their later success in college. But many colleges will not allow all applicants to be admitted. (Probably no employer would hire all applicants unless there were a real shortage.) Thus, the validity study must be conducted with a more homogeneous group than the group of future applicants on which we will be making decisions.

A paradox exists with respect to validity. In evaluating a test to see whether it will assist us in decision making, we want the test to have high validity coefficients on *unselected* groups. However, if we then *use* the test data to help make wise selection decisions, the validity coefficient among the selected individuals may be quite small.

If we originally evaluate the usefulness of a test using a *selected* group, or if for legal or other reasons (see the section on fairness of tests to minorities in Chapter 19) we are forced after the fact (i.e., after we have used it for selection purposes) to prove the test is valid, the good *use* of a test decreases the validity coefficient. That is, if we accurately select *out* those individuals who would not succeed and select *in* only those individuals who will succeed, we are successfully decreasing the validity coefficient among the selected *in* group. As Fricke (1975) points out, good personnel practices will produce low correlation coefficients among the selected individuals. Unfortunately many users of tests do not understand this and at times incorrectly assume that low correlations among selected individuals indicate that the test was invalid for making the original selection decisions.

In addition to the decreased correlation due to the restriction of range that occurs following selection, the shape or form of the relationship between the predictor and criterion variables also plays an important role. The scattergrams in Figure 5–2 illustrate these points. Let X be the predictor and Y the criterion. Assume that the horizontal line a represents the minimum criterion score necessary to consider an individual successful. Let the vertical line b represent the predictor score necessary to be selected. The elongation and general slope of the oval shapes indicate the degree of relationship between X and Y. If the pattern of scores is quite elongated (very little scatter around a line) and sloping, the correlation is high. If there is considerable scatter, the relationship is low. If the slope is zero, there is no relationship. In Figure 5–2(a) and (b) the overall correlation between X and Y is quite high (although for Figure 5–2(b) we would not use the Pearson product moment correlation coefficient). After restricting the range through selection we have a much lower degree of relationship in Figure 5–2(a), but it is still positive. There is essentially no relationship between X and Y in Figure 5–2(b) after selection (for scores to the right of line b). This would be the case in situations where one needed a certain amount of characteristic X in order to be successful in endeavor Y, but "more of X" wouldn't help one be more successful in Y. This might be true, for example, if X were a measure of reading comprehension and Y a job requiring that one can read well enough to comprehend instruction manuals but in which further skills in reading are irrelevant. One could *validly* use the reading test to select out those who could

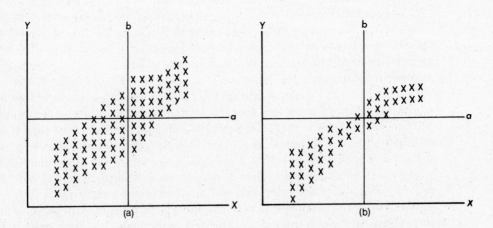

FIGURE 5–2   (a) Scattergram showing a high degree of relationship between X and Y for total range of X scores and a smaller degree of relationship for scores to the right of line b. (b) Scattergram showing a high degree of relationship for the total range of X scores and zero relationship for scores to the right of line b.

not read at a high enough level to perform their tasks. But, after one *wisely* used the test for that purpose there would be no correlation between X and Y for those accepted applicants.

Thus, one can see that just as the size of the reliability coefficient can be affected by so many variables, so too can the validity measures. To interpret validity data correctly, it is necessary to be aware of these various factors.

Let us take one more example to illustrate these interpretation problems. Suppose one finds a correlation of 0.20 between college GPA and some measure of success as a teacher. (In this example GPA is the predictor variable X and success as a teacher is the criterion variable Y.) How should one interpret this fairly low correlation? Individuals not aware of the factors discussed in this subsection might assume that the data indicate that knowledge of subject matter is irrelevant to teaching success. This, of course, is a possibility, but there are many other possible (and more likely) reasons for the low correlation. Perhaps grades do not actually measure knowledge of subject matter. Perhaps our measure of teaching success does not actually measure what we really mean when we think of a successful teacher. Perhaps neither our measure of X or Y is reliable. Perhaps our sample is too restricted in range on either the X or Y variable. Or perhaps a relationship exists such as that depicted in Figure 5–2(b) and we have only graduated (or hired) teachers to the right of line *b*. (Once teachers know enough mathematics they can teach it, but to know a lot more advanced mathematics is irrelevant for teaching success.)

Before one could reasonably infer which of all these "perhaps" statements is most likely, he would need information on the grading practices of the college, the reliability of the GPAs, the reliability and at least the *content* validity of the measure of teaching success, and the variability of the sample studied on each measure. To really know *empirically* the degree to which knowledge of subject matter influenced teaching success, one would have to be willing to let people teach with all degrees of knowledge from none on up. Rather than do that many of us probably would rather assume that one can *logically* infer knowledge of subject matter is related to teaching success and that the low correlation cited above is due to one or more of the many factors discussed.

Validity and Decision Making

Let us assume that a test manual reports a correlation coefficient of .50 between scores obtained on a mathematical aptitude test administered in the eighth grade and scores in a ninth-grade algebra course. Will this information have any effect on the kind(s) of educational decisions made? What if the school's policy is to have all students take ninth-grade algebra in heterogeneous classes? In this case the benefits derived from the test score information could be used only for instructional purposes. If the school's policy is to have all students take ninth-grade algebra and if students are also grouped homogeneously, then the test score information can be used for both instructional and administrative purposes. If the school's policy is to permit students to select either ninth-grade algebra or general math, then the test score information could be used for instructional, administrative, and counseling purposes. For any of these decisions—instructional, guidance, or administrative—the important question is whether or not better decisions could be made by using test score results in addition to other data already available (for example, teacher recommendations and previous school grades). This is an empirical question, one we would not necessarily expect the ordinary classroom teacher or counselor to answer. However, all educators should be cognizant of the factors that are likely to make test score information useful and efficient.

1. *Availability of other data. Tests should be used only if better decisions can be made with than without the data.* This increase in decision making is often referred to as incremental validity (Sechrest, 1963). How much better the decisions would be using the test data than if they were based on chance alone is not the relevant consideration (see Cronbach & Gleser, 1965). One never, or almost never, is forced to make an educational decision on the basis of no information. If fairly valid decisions can be made without test data, then the probability that the test data will improve the accuracy of the decision decreases. If the probability of making a correct decision without the test data is very low, then it may well be beneficial to give the test, even though it has only a modest correlation with the criterion.

2. *Cost of testing and faulty decisions.* Decisions are subject to two kinds of errors: (1) false rejections, that is, predicting failure when success would have occurred; and (2) false acceptances, that is, predicting success when failure is the result.[12] The value of a test is dependent upon the difference between the cost of testing (including such factors as the cost of purchasing the test, student and examiner time, and scoring) and the savings in the cost of errors. In the "algebra" example, a student could take algebra and fail or not take algebra even though he could have passed it. To decide whether the test information is worth gathering is dependent upon the cost of these errors and whether the reduction in these costs is greater than the cost of gathering the data. The concepts of available data, incremental validity, and cost effectiveness often lead to *sequential* testing and decision making. In the "algebra" example, one may well be willing to use already available data such as previous grades to make decisions for a fair number of individuals. (For example, in a particular school one may decide that *all*

---

[12] Some authors use the terms false positives and false negatives for these two errors. The terms used here seem less confusing.

students with less than a B average in seventh- and eighth-grade math should *not* take algebra. There may be another set of students for whom the school personnel are willing to recommend ninth-grade algebra without the knowledge obtained from a mathematical aptitude test.) Only those students for whom a decision could not be made would take the aptitude test. In general, in sequential testing and decision making one uses already available data first, gathers relevant data that are fairly moderate in cost for more decisions, and uses expensive data-gathering techniques to make decisions about only a few individuals. Figure 5–3 illustrates a basic sequential decision-making strategy.

Once data are gathered, the decision regarding where to set the cutoff score is dependent upon the relative cost of the two errors. If a false rejection is expensive as compared to a false acceptance, then the cutoff score should be lower (that is, the selection ratio should be higher) than if the reverse is true. Suppose, for example, we have the relationship between Y (success in college defined as a GPA equal to or greater than 2.0) and X (some numerical value derived from a combination of variables such as test score information or past grades) represented by the scattergram shown in Figure 5–4(a). Here each tally above the horizontal line (defining success in college) and to the left of $X = 4$ (the minimum admission score) would represent a false rejection. Every score below the horizontal line and to the right of the X cutoff score would be a false acceptance. The other tallies would represent correct decisions.

If the decision maker equated the costs (utility values) of the two kinds of errors, then the proper approach would be to minimize the total errors and therefore to set the cutting score at 4, as is shown in Figure 5–4(a). This would give six false rejections and five false acceptances (or 11 total errors). If, however, it was decided that false rejections are three times as costly as false acceptances (in terms of loss to society or whatever), then the proper

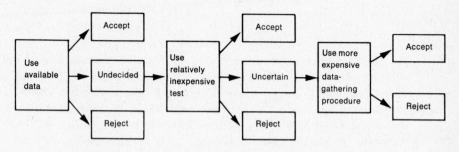

FIGURE 5–3   A basic sequential decision-making strategy.

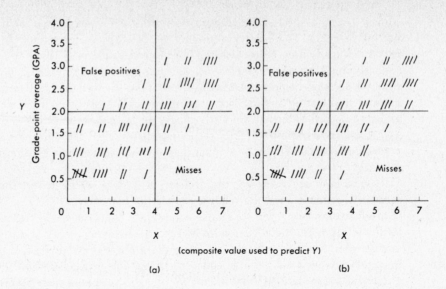

FIGURE 5–4   Scattergrams depicting (for the same data) false rejections and false acceptances for cutting scores of 4 and 3, respectively, when a GPA of 2.0 is required for success.

cutoff score should be changed. If the cutoff score were kept at 4, one would have

6 false rejections at a cost of 3 units each = 18 cost units
5 false acceptances at a cost of 1 unit each = 5 cost units
                                               23 cost units

A cutoff score of 3, as in Figure 5–4(b), would produce 15 total errors but only 21 cost units, as follows:

 3 false rejections at a cost of 3 units each = 9 cost units
12 false acceptances at a cost of 1 unit each = 12 cost units
                                                21 cost units

This simple example illustrates again that test information does not make decisions but is used (often in conjunction with other information) to help us set probability values. There are many decision strategies other than the simple one illustrated here that one might adopt. In some cases, for example, one might decide that false rejections are not costing anything and one simply wants to obtain the highest possible ratio of successes to failures *among those selected*. Or, more likely (especially in industry), one may want to maximize some *mean level of output*. Thus one would *not* simply count a success as a success but weight the *degrees* of success differentially (likewise for failures). In the latter case, one would decide whether the cost of testing was worthwhile by comparing the mean utility value for all those hired using the test to help make decisions versus the mean utility value of those one would hire without the test data. If this *difference* is greater than the cost of the test, then it is cost effective to give the test. The general point to keep in mind is that once we have set some utility values on the various outcomes of the alternatives, we can combine probabilities and utilities to arrive at better decisions. Of course, we need to keep in mind that although from a theoretical measurement point of view we ideally obtain data such as the data presented in Figure 5–4, we often do not in practice. Colleges typically simply do not admit, and industries do not hire, people below the cutting score. Thus, we do not know what the data to the left of the cutting-score line are really like. It is possible to mathematically make estimates of these data, but these estimates are not too satisfactory.

3. *Selection ratio.* In the example dealing with ninth-grade algebra, it was pointed out that if all students were required to take ninth-grade algebra, the test data would be of no value for selection purposes. If conditions are such that almost everyone is to be selected, then the data will not be so valuable in selection decisions as in cases where the selection ratio is lower.

4. *Success ratio.* Another factor affecting whether test data are likely to improve decision making is the success ratio (the proportion of people selected who succeed). The success ratio depends in part upon the selection ratio. Other things being equal, the smaller the selection ratio, the larger the success ratio. The success ratio, however, is also highly dependent upon base rates (Meehl & Rosen, 1955). *Base rates* refers to the proportion of people in the general population who fall in a certain category. If 99 percent of the general ninth-grade population can succeed in ninth-grade algebra, one can predict success with 99 percent accuracy simply by predicting success for everyone. It would take a very valid test to enable one to predict more accurately than that. If only 1 percent can succeed, an analogous situation exists. Base rates in clinical psychology are often so high or low (for example, the proportion of people who commit suicide) that tests cannot improve prediction. In educational decisions the base rates are often somewhat closer to 50 percent, the value that best enables a test score to improve the predictive accuracy.

Validity and Test Use

Just as people want to know how reliable a test should be, they also want to know how valid a test should be. The same answer must be given: it depends upon the purposes for which the test is to be used. Naturally, one should select the best test possible. Suppose, however, that no test is very valid for our purposes. Does that mean we should not test? To decide, we must answer the incremental validity question raised in the preceding section:

How much better decision can we make by using the test information in addition to all other information than we could make just from the other data alone? Once that question is answered, we must inquire whether this increase in accuracy of prediction is sufficiently greater to justify the use of the test. Theoretically, this could be answered by cost analysis procedures if we could specify the cost of faulty decisions. It should be stressed here that, in education, a test is seldom used to assist in just a single decision. As Cronbach (1971b, p. 496) stated: ". . . in educational testing the information is usually placed in the student's file and used for many later decisions: admission, choice of major, selection of courses, career planning, etc. A test with multiple uses can repay a cost that would be unreasonable if a test were to be used once and forgotten."

Validity is a matter of degree, and a test has many validities, each dependent upon the specific purposes for which one uses the test. Eventually the validity of any test is dependent upon how it is used in the local situation; therefore educators and personnel directors should, where feasible, conduct their own validity studies.

Publishers of standardized tests also have a responsibility to conduct and report research on the validity of a test. Just as for reliability, the kinds and extent of validity data that one should expect to find in a test manual depend upon the type of test and the use(s) the publishers advocate for it. As discussed previously, content validity of achievement tests is by far the most important type of validity. Aptitude, interest, and personality measures probably, depending upon their use, should have evidence of criterion-related validity. If one wishes to use test data as evidence to support or refute a psychological theory, then construct validity is necessary.

In addition to reporting the type(s) of validity evidence, the manual must also provide other relevant information. The characteristics of the group(s) from which the evidence was obtained must be reported in detail. Tables of specifications and their rationale should be given in support of content validity claims; standard errors of estimates should be reported for validity coefficients; and a large number of studies should be reported if one wishes to make a claim for construct validity.

Three points should be reemphasized when thinking about validity and test use. First, it is extremely unlikely that any test will ever have perfect validity for any decision. Some errors are almost bound to occur. Our goal is to minimize errors in decision making, but one should *not* conclude that a test is invalid because it is possible to point to incorrect decisions made with the use of test data (for example, "I scored 88 on an intelligence test and a counselor told me I couldn't succeed in college but I now have a Ph.D.; therefore all intelligence tests are invalid."). The crucial question in validity is *not* whether errors will be made in individual cases—the answer will invariably be yes. The crucial question is whether fewer errors will be made by using a test in addition to other data than would be made using just the other data.

Second, although the examples used here have tended to be for selection decisions, remember that many decisions are for placement or classification rather than selection. It is necessary for all these kinds of decisions to have some data supporting the criterion-related validity of a test. But at times the discriminant statistics data are more relevant than correlational data.

Finally, when we gather information that will be useful in decision making we are, in one sense of the word, using the data to make predictions. We predict what will happen if we decide on various alternative strategies. But, as Ebel (1975b, p. 2) points out, we are really more interested in *using* the data than making the predictions per se.

"There is an enormous difference between an army general's use of information about the strengths and movements of enemy forces in order to defeat the enemy and his possible, but most improbable, use of the same information to predict which army was likely to be victorious."

Likewise, in education we would be well advised to concentrate on how to upset negative predictions. We typically use the predictive information not primarily for the purpose of making a passive prediction but rather to direct action toward desirable outcomes. This goes along with what we said earlier about the difference in predictive validity prior to using the test and the predictive validity after one *used* the test data for wise decision making. We should be striving to use adaptive strategies that will result in upsetting negative predictions that would have resulted under traditional treatments. But to do this we need to have the test data in order to identify which students need special attention. If we can use the data to make decisions that result in positive outcomes for individuals for whom we *originally* predicted negative outcomes, we should feel gratified. But we should not conclude from this that the test either was not valid or did not serve a useful function. The test did just what it was designed to do—identify individuals who needed special attention.

Validity of Criterion-Referenced Tests

The issue of the validity, like the reliability, of criterion-referenced tests has not yet been adequately dealt with by psychometricians. Since criterion-referenced tests are used primarily in the area of achievement testing, the major concern is the content validity of the test. In this respect criterion-referenced tests should always match or excel norm-referenced tests. Why? Because the *universe of behaviors or achievement is usually more narrowly defined in criterion-referenced tests, and the rules for sampling from this universe (item-generating rules) are often more precisely defined.* (These concepts will be discussed in more detail in Chapter 7.) The content validity of criterion-related tests thus constructed is almost assured. As Osburn noted, "what the test is measuring is operationally defined by the universe of content as embodied in the item generating rules" (Osburn, 1968, p. 101). Such a test would have what Mosier (1947) termed *validity by definition* or what Ebel (1961) referred to as *meaningfulness*.

However, if results of criterion-referenced tests are to be used in instructional decision making, some empirical (criterion-related) validity evidence ought to be provided.[13] We practically always wish to "generalize beyond the universe of content defined by the item generating rules" (Jackson, 1970, p. 13). For example, if one is using the results of a mastery test to decide whether to allow a student to proceed with the next unit of study, some evidence ought to be provided to show that people just below the cutoff score do not do so well in the subsequent material as do people above the cutoff score.

If one uses correlational approaches to establish the criterion-related (predictive or concurrent) validity of criterion-referenced tests, the potentially small variability of criterion-referenced test scores (discussed earlier) will attenuate the validity coefficient just as it would the reliability coefficient. For this reason the discriminant statistic approaches mentioned earlier are likely to be more useful. (See Hambleton and Novick (1973), C. W. Harris et al. (1974), Millman (1974), and Swaminathan et al. (1975), for more complete discussions of the validity of criterion-referenced tests.)

SUMMARY

The principal ideas, conclusions, and implications presented in this chapter are summarized in the following statements:

1. Reliability is the degree of consistency between two measures of the same thing.
2. Some examples of sources of inconsistency, or error variance, are trait instability, sampling error, administrator error, scoring error, and errors within the person.
3. The standard error of measurement (S_e) is the estimated standard deviation of a person's observed scores about his true score. Traditionally, when we know a person's observed score we can place a confidence band of $\pm 1S_e$ about this score and say that we are about 68 percent confident that his true score would be in that range.
4. One can estimate a person's true score from knowledge of his observed score, the group mean, and the reliability of the measuring instrument for that group. The predicted true score is always closer to the mean than the observed score. In other words, we predict a regression toward the mean.

---

[13] The terms *criterion-referenced testing* and *criterion-related validity* can be confused. *Criterion* has a different meaning in each term. For the former it refers to some measure of proficiency on the test itself. In the latter case it refers to a different characteristic, which is estimated from the test score.

5. There are many estimates of reliability. Those discussed in this chapter are categorized as measures of (a) stability, (b) equivalence, (c) stability and equivalence, or (d) internal consistency.

6. Measures of stability are obtained by administering a test to a group of individuals, readministering the same test to the same individuals at a later date, and correlating the two sets of scores. Any change in score from one time to another is treated as error.

7. Measures of equivalence are obtained by giving two forms of the test to the same group of individuals on the same day and correlating these results.

8. Measures of equivalence and stability combine the previous two procedures.

9. All measures of internal consistency require only one administration of the test.

10. Scorer reliability may be estimated by having a sample of papers scored independently by two different scorers and by correlating the results.

11. The different methods of estimating reliability consider different sources of error. Which should be used depends upon how one wishes to use the results of the test.

12. In general, longer tests are more reliable.

13. Internal consistency estimates should not be used for speeded tests.

14. Reliability will be higher when a test is given to a heterogeneous group.

15. Difference scores are less reliable than single scores. A gain score, a special type of difference score, is particularly unreliable.

16. Traditional estimates of reliability depend upon true-score variance. For criterion-referenced measures, where we are less interested in true-score variability than we are in norm-referenced measures, the traditional estimates of reliability are not completely appropriate.

17. Reliability is a necessary but not sufficient condition for validity.

18. Validity can be defined as the degree to which a test is capable of achieving certain aims. Since a single test may have many different purposes, there is no single validity index for a test.

19. Educators typically categorize validity into three kinds: content, criterion-related, and construct validity.

20. Content validity is related to how adequately the content of the test samples the domain about which inferences are to be made.

21. Criterion-related validity pertains to the technique of studying the relationship between the test scores and independent external criterion measures.

22. In order to study criterion-related validity, it is important to have a good measure of the criterion. This measure should be relevant, reliable, and free from bias.

23. Construct validity is the degree to which the test scores can be accounted for by certain explanatory constructs.
24. Various methods of expressing validity include the correlation coefficient, the coefficient of determination, the standard error of estimate, the coefficient of alienation, expectancy tables, and various discriminant statistics.
25. Various factors affect validity, such as the reliabilities of the predictor and criterion measures, the group heterogeneity, and the shape of the relationship.
26. Various factors affect whether a test is valid enough to be useful in decision making, such as the (1) availability of other data (2) cost of testing and faulty decisions, (3) selection ratio, and (4) success ratio.
27. The content validity of criterion-referenced tests should match or excel that of norm-referenced tests.
28. The correlational approaches to determining validity are not appropriate for criterion-referenced tests to the extent that the variability of the score distribution is constricted. Therefore, discriminant statistic approaches are more likely to be useful.

CHAPTER SIX
Norms, Scores, and Profiles

In Chapter 4 we discussed some basic descriptive statistics, including measures of central tendency, variability, and relationship. Measures of relative position are discussed in this chapter.

We often wish to. compare a person's performance to the performance of others. Using well-defined norm groups and converting the original obtained scores to derived scores helps in this comparison. If we wish to portray two or more scores for the same person (or groups of people), we do so by means of a profile. Norm groups, types of scores, and profiles are discussed in this chapter. After studying this chapter, the student should be able to—

1. Know the basic definitions of the terms presented.

2. Appreciate the value of a norm group as an aid in interpreting test scores.

3. Evaluate the adequacy of a set of norms in terms of recency and representativeness.

4. Judge what would constitute a

relevant norm group for a specified purpose of testing.

5. Recognize when one should use different norm groups.
6. Judge the adequacy of the norms description in a test manual.
7. Distinguish between norms and standards.
8. Interpret various types of derived scores.
9. Recognize the limitations of grade equivalents.
10. Interpret various profiles.

NORMS

The terms *norm, norm group,* and *norms* are often used in educational measurement. *Norm* is sometimes used as a synonym for average, and is the mean (or median) score for some specified group of people. This specified group of people is called the *norm group* or reference group. There may be more than one such specified norm group for any test. A table showing the performance of the norm group(s) is called a *norms table,* a set of *norms,* or (more commonly) *norms.* Norms tables typically show the relationship or correspondence between *raw scores* (the number correct on the test) and some type of *derived scores.* (See Table 6–1 as an example of the types of norms tables found in manuals.) Before discussing several types of derived scores, let us first consider the need for norms, how to obtain an appropriate norms group, some various types of norm groups, what test manuals should report about norms, and how to use norms.

The Need for Norms

We discussed briefly the differences between norm and criterion-referenced measurement in Chapter 3. Criterion-referenced measures have a place in specific types of instructional training programs, but, in general, normative referencing is of more value. There are very few educational situations in which criterion referencing *alone* is sufficient. Even in the situation where the test itself is composed of all behaviors to which we wish to infer, we usually desire normative data.

Suppose we have a 100-item test composed of all possible permutations of multiplying two one-digit numbers. If Johnny took this test and got 75 answers correct, we could clearly make a criterion-referenced statement: Johnny knows 75 percent of the material. But to know how others performed on the test would certainly help us to interpret his score. If others of his age and education can typically receive 100 percent, and have been able to do so for two years, his score would take on quite a different meaning than if he is the only one in his age group who can score higher than 50 percent on the test.

Norms, then, are important in that they tell us how others have performed on the test. We have no clear idea of the meaning of a person's score in and of itself. It must be compared with other scores.

FALL GRADE 11	BOYS (N = 5350 +)			RAW SCORES						
Percentile	Verbal Reasoning	Numerical Ability	VR + NA	Abstract Reasoning	Clerical S and A*	Mechanical Reasoning	Space Relations	Spelling	Language Usage	Percentile
99	49-50	39-40	87-90	48-50	70-100	66-70	57-80	98-100	55-60	99
97	48	38	84-86	47	64-69	65	54-56	96-97	52-54	97
95	46-47	37	81-83	46	59-63	63-64	51-53	93-95	49-51	95
90	44-45	35-36	77-80	45	56-58	61-62	48-50	90-92	46-48	90
85	42-43	33-34	74-76	43-44	54-55	59-60	46-47	87-89	43-45	85
80	40-41	32	70-73	42	52-53	58	44-45	84-86	41-42	80
75	38-39	30-31	67-69	41	50-51	57	42-43	81-83	39-40	75
70	36-37	29	64-66	40	49	56	39-41	78-80	37-38	70
65	34-35	27-28	60-63	39	48	54-55	37-38	75-77	35-36	65
60	32-33	25-26	57-59	38	47	53	35-36	73-74	33-34	60
55	30-31	24	54-56	37	45-46	51-52	33-34	70-72	32	55
50	27-29	22-23	50-53	36	44	50	31-32	67-69	30-31	50
45	25-26	21	47-49	35	42-43	49	28-30	64-66	29	45
40	23-24	19-20	43-46	33-34	41	47-48	26-27	61-63	27-28	40
35	21-22	17-18	39-42	32	40	45-46	24-25	58-60	25-26	35
30	18-20	15-16	35-38	30-31	39	44	22-23	55-57	23-24	30
25	16-17	14	32-34	28-29	37-38	41-43	20-21	52-54	21-22	25
20	14-15	12-13	28-31	24-27	35-36	38-40	18-19	49-51	19-20	20
15	12-13	10-11	24-27	19-23	33-34	35-37	17	46-48	17-18	15
10	9-11	9	20-23	14-18	30-32	31-34	15-16	42-45	14-16	10
5	7-8	7-8	17-19	11-13	24-29	27-30	12-14	37-41	12-13	5
3	6	6	14-16	8-10	15-23	24-26	11	32-36	10-11	3
1	0-5	0-5	0-13	0-7	0-14	0-23	0-10	0-31	0-9	1
Mean	28.2	22.9	51.1	33.9	44.3	49.2	32.3	67.7	31.0	Mean
SD	12.5	9.8	20.9	10.8	11.3	10.9	13.1	17.7	11.6	SD

* Clerical Speed and Accuracy.

SOURCE: Reproduced by permission. All rights reserved. Copyright 1947, 1952 © 1959, 1963, 1966, 1968, 1973 by The Psychological Corporation, New York, N.Y.

An Appropriate Norm Group

A norm group, to be appropriate, must be *recent, representative,* and *relevant.*

RECENCY

Such rapid changes are taking place in education that test norms can quickly become outdated. This is particularly true in the area of achievement tests. If we do a better job of instructing, or change our curricular emphasis, how ninth-grade students achieve in a social studies test three years from now might be quite different from the achievement of present ninth-graders. Of course, as the content of a curriculum changes, not only the norms but the test itself becomes outdated. This is usually obvious to a test user who is competent in his subject matter.

A less likely detected obsolescence of norms occurs when the content of the test is still relevant but the characteristics of the reference group have changed. This may be true, for example, in a college that changes from a restricted to an open admissions policy. A prospective freshman may have quite a low test score in comparison with that of freshmen admitted under a restrictive policy and be quite high relative to that of freshmen admitted under on open policy. Many other less obvious changes in society could also make an older reference group no longer appropriate.

One caution we will mention here is that one cannot always judge the recency of the norms group on a published test by looking at the copyright date of the test manual. Any change in the test manual allows the publisher to revise the copyright date of the manual and thus it is not an indication of the recency of the norms.

REPRESENTATIVENESS

There are two sources of error in any normative statement about a person's score (Angoff, 1971, p. 548). One, the error of measurement, was discussed in Chapter 5. It is due to the imprecision or unreliability of the test or testing process. The second, the sampling error, is due to the inadequacies of the sample. A *population* refers to a specified *group* of individuals (for example, all fifth-graders in the United States). A *sample* is a smaller number of people selected from the population and actually tested. We will consider in the next section the relevance of the population sampled. In this section we are concerned with the adequacy of the sample.

One consideration of importance in sampling is the size of the sample. Any sample should be large enough to provide stable values. By "stable" we mean that if another sample had been drawn in a similar fashion, we would obtain similar results. Most of the more popular published tests have samples of adequate size.[1]

Another important factor is the kind of sampling. A large sample alone is not sufficient. If a sample is biased, making it larger does not solve the problem. The sampling procedure must be correct. Space does not permit us to delve into sampling techniques extensively. In general, however, stratified random sampling is the best procedure where the stratification is done on all relevant independent variables. The relevant independent variables would vary from one kind of test to another, but examples might be such things as age, sex, socioeconomic status, race, size of community, and geographic location of the subject. Perhaps the most troublesome problem in sampling is that one is dependent upon the cooperation of the sample chosen. If cooperation is poor, so that the proportion of the original sample for which one obtains scores is too low, then the obtained scores may be from a biased sample. Fortunately, most schools cooperate with agencies desirous of building a norm group. Unfortunately, the agencies do not always tell us what proportion of the originally chosen sample did cooperate and how they differed from the noncooperators.

A sampling procedure too frequently employed is to sample by convenience rather than by a particular technical sampling procedure. For example, schools in which one has professional contacts or those that have previously cooperated are often chosen because they are convenient. Such a chosen sample *may* not be biased, particularly if one appropriately weights the data in such a sample. Nevertheless, the likelihood that such a sampling procedure will produce biased results is great enough that we should be leery of norms built in such a fashion.

RELEVANCE

The relevance of the norm group is dependent upon the degree to which the population sampled is comparable to the group with which users of the test wish to compare their students. If, for example, we wish to compare a student's ability with that of students who intend to go to college, then the norm group should be a sample of students who wish to go to college and not a sample from a general population. Since a test may be used for several different purposes, it is usually necessary to have more than one norm group. Some of the more common types of norms will now be discussed briefly.

---

[1] The stability of the sample is not dependent only on the number of students. It is also dependent upon clustering procedures. Thus, for example, the number of *schools* sampled, as well as the number of *students*, is relevant to the stability estimates. More technical details with regard to sampling can be found in Angoff (1971).

Types of Norms

NATIONAL NORMS

The type of norms most commonly reported by test publishers and used by educators are *national norms*. These norms are almost always reported separately by the different age or educational levels for which the test is constructed. Occasionally they are reported separately by sex. National norms can be used with all types of tests but are probably most useful for general scholastic aptitude and achievement tests. They assist in keeping one from forming too parochial a view. Suppose Johnny attends a school district where the students all come from professional homes. The school, Johnny's parents, and Johnny himself may get quite an unrealistic picture of him if he were to be compared only to others in that district. He may be in the bottom fourth of that district but in the top 10 percent nationally.

Most major test publishers who report national norms have employed reasonably satisfactory sampling procedures. Nevertheless, there is still the obvious limitation of school cooperation, some tendency to choose samples of convenience, and the always present sampling error. Thus "national norms" are not completely comparable to each other, and it is not really possible to compare a pupil's scores on two different tests unless the data were *gathered on the same sample*. Many testing companies do use the same sample for norming both an aptitude and achievement battery, thus allowing intertest comparisons. (There have been attempts to equate the scores on various tests normed on different samples. One of the most thorough of these was the Anchor Test Study (Jaeger, 1973) which provided comparable national norms for seven widely used reading achievement tests. There have been scholarly debates about the adequacy of such equated norms. Technical problems abound in such endeavors. At any rate, as soon as one of the seven tests was revised, the norms became obsolete.)

One other point should be mentioned. National norms for educational tests are most often gathered in school settings. Since 100 percent of the population is not in school, we do not have a truly national sample. The higher the grade level, the lower the proportion of children that are in school, and the more biased the sample. This is not really a handicap in making educational decisions, but it is a point we need to remember if we wish to interpret the data as literally representative of the nation.[2]

Thus, as useful as national norms may be, they certainly do have some limitations. The most serious one is that often they simply do not provide

---

[2] Related to this point, we must remember in any international comparisons of achievement that the samples are drawn from schools, and the United States has a greater proportion of youth attending school than do other countries. In such studies, we are often comparing the top 75–85 percent of our youth to the top 20–30 percent of the youth in some other country.

the comparison data or permit us to make the interpretation we need. If a student planned to take automobile mechanics at Dunwoody Technical Institute, we would be much better able to counsel him if we could know how his aptitude in auto mechanics compared with students presently in Dunwoody.

SPECIAL GROUP NORMS

For many decision-making purposes, highly specific norms are the most desirable. Norms such as "first-year education students at state colleges," "high school juniors," or "students who have taken two years of French" may be the comparison we are most interested in. We are apt to want such special norm groups for specific aptitude tests such as Mechanical, Clerical, and Musical, and for specific subject-matter tests such as first-year Spanish, Music Appreciation, and Chemistry. Such special norm groups are also useful for tests designed for the physically or mentally handicapped. Intelligence tests designed for the blind or deaf obviously need to have special group norms.

One test frequently used by educators involves a special type of norm group that needs some explaining. The College Board Scholastic Aptitude Test (SAT) uses what is called a "fixed reference" group. This fixed reference group comprises the approximately 11,000 people who took the test in 1941. A common set of items (an anchor test) used in a previous test is included in each new SAT test. Then, through a series of equating procedures, the new form can be equated back to the 1941 test.[3] By using this fixed reference group, changes in the candidate population over time can be detected. There is, of course, a danger in misinterpreting the scores. A person who scores 500 on the SAT is scoring at the mean. But it is a very special mean, one calibrated to be equal to that of the 11,000 students who took the test in 1941.

LOCAL NORMS

Publishers do not always provide the special group norms one is most interested in, and sometimes test users have to provide their own special group norms. These are typically referred to as "local" norms.

By using local norms, one can make the across-test comparison mentioned earlier in this chapter. If one wishes to make some interschool comparisons, or intercity comparisons, local norms are better. Not that one could not make such comparisons using national norms, but the users may find it more difficult to make the comparison with the data in that form. If test scor-

---

[3] The various techniques of equating and calibrating test scores will not be dealt with in this book. The interested reader is referred to Angoff (1971).

ing is done by machine—whether by a test company or locally—local norms can be constructed easily. In general, it is worth the slight extra charge to have these local norms prepared. This facilitates test score interpretation to the teacher, the parent, the student, and the community.

SCHOOL MEAN NORMS

If one is interested in comparing the mean performance of a classroom (or total school district) to other schools, he must use school or total district mean norms. It is *not* appropriate to compute a mean for a school district and interpret it by using the norm tables based on individual pupil performance. The variability of school means is far less than the variability of individual scores, and the individual norm tables would therefore give an underestimate of relative school performance for above-average schools and an overestimate of relative school performance for below-average schools. Many test publishers provide school mean norms for those people who wish to make such comparisons. If not provided, such comparisons cannot be made (of course, the local district can compute the school means for those schools in that district and build local school mean norms for those specific schools).

What Test Manuals Should Report

The user of test information must be very cautious in his interpretation of the norms provided by the test publisher. Questions like the following must be considered: How representative are the norms? What were the characteristics of the standardization and norming sample? How old are the norms? Are the norms useful for the kinds of comparisons to be made? These questions must be satisfactorily answered before one can correctly and meaningfully use the norm data, but test manuals at times do not seem to provide the data necessary to answer them. If not available in a manual, it is possible that the information may be found in a technical supplement. At any rate, one should not accept the norms on faith.

A manual may state that it has a "national" sample without providing the data necessary for the user to judge for himself the adequacy of the sample (norms). The norm group must necessarily consist of those who are willing to be tested, and the test manual should state the refusal rate. The user must then decide how this will affect his interpretations. Many older tests were often normed so that the norm data really represented, say, only the Midwest, or only the East Coast, or only the Far West. Generally, the newer tests, particularly those published by the larger reputable companies, have adequate norm data. Highly sophisticated sampling procedures have been worked out so that a representative sample can be obtained if the publishers are willing to go to the effort to achieve such an end.

Using Norms

Normative data aid greatly in the interpretation of test scores, but there are also dangers of misinterpretation or misuse of norms. It would be a misuse, for example, to interpret national norms as special group norms, or vice versa. Perhaps the greatest mistake is to interpret norms as standards: *Norms are not standards.* Norm information tells us how people actually perform, *not how they should perform.* Comparing a person's score with a norm group does not automatically tell us whether that person's score was above or below the level at which it *should* be. It tells us only how he performed in comparison to others. A description in relative terms is not an evaluation.

One of the most ridiculous but frustrating criticisms of the schools is the complaint that there are so many students "below norms"! For example, half the sixth-graders read "below grade level"! Terrible? Of course not. If "norm" is used as a synonym for "average," half the students *must* be below the norm. There is no way the schools can do such a good job that less than half the people will be below average.

Also, when evaluating output—such as scores on an achievement test—one must consider input. Input includes such things as previous instruction on the variable being measured, as well as family, community, and school characteristics. We will talk more about the relationship between input and output in the section on accountability in Chapter 18. But output should always be interpreted in relation to input. As we mentioned in Chapter 1, we would evaluate two fifth-graders' scores quite differently if the year before one scored at the third-grade level and the other at the fourth-grade, fifth-month level.

One final point: The output on standardized achievement tests should be interpreted in view of the local curricular and instructional objectives. If the local objectives differ from the ones followed by the test maker, then the national norms will not be so appropriate or informative as they might be if the local and national test objectives were highly similar. More will be said about this in Chapter 15, "Standardized Achievement Tests."

TYPES OF SCORES[4]

To know a person's observed score (raw score) on a measuring instrument gives us some information about his performance. As already stated in Chapter 4, to know how that person's score compares with the mean score of an identifiable group norm (group) is of more value. If one has an indication of the variability of the distribution of scores in the norm group as well, much more information is obtained. If a person's raw score is changed into a score

[4] A book by Lyman (1971) treats test scores in more detail than we do and would be an excellent supplementary source.

that *by itself* gives normative or relative information, we can present the information more efficiently since the mean and standard deviation need not also be reported. Such expressions as *kinds of scales, kinds of norms, types of scores,* and *derived scores* all refer to those various transformations of raw scores into scores that have normative or relative meanings.

Derived scores are useful, then, in comparing a person's score to those of others, that is, in making interindividual comparisons. A second use is in making intraindividual (with-individual) comparisons. It is not possible for example, to compare directly the test score, GPA, and IQ measures as the values are currently listed for individual 1 in Table 4–1. It is first necessary to transform all data into comparable units. (Of course, comparability of the norm groups is also necessary.)

Let us illustrate with the following example the importance of derived scores in interpreting data. Assume Irwin, an eleventh-grade boy, has received the following *raw scores* on the Differential Aptitude Tests (DAT).

	Verbal Reasoning	Numerical Ability	Abstract Reasoning	Clerical S & A
Raw Score	32	29	32	42

	Mechanical Reasoning	Space Relations	Language Usage—I: Spelling	Language Usage—II: Grammar
Raw Score	42	36	64	30

These data, in and of themselves, tell us nothing about how Irwin compares to others of his age, since we have no idea how other children score. But do they even tell us anything about whether Irwin is better in one subtest area than another? No, since we do not know the total number of questions on each subtest, nor whether some subtests have easier questions than the others. Some type of derived score is necessary for both inter- and intra-individual interpretation.

Another use of derived scores is to assist in a meaningful combination of data. At times one wants to combine various pieces of information to make a single decision about an individual. An example would be to combine results of term papers, quizzes, and examinations to arrive at a final grade. The question is: How does one weight the various pieces of data? By converting all scores to derived scores, a weighting scheme can be carried out.

The types of derived scores that teachers are most likely to use themselves and/or find used in reporting standardized test results are percentiles, linear z and T scores, normalized z and T scores, stanines, grade equivalents, and deviation IQ scores. These will be explained, and advantages and disadvantages will be discussed.[5]

[5] The literature on transformed scores is not consistent with regard to terminology. In general, normalized z scores are not used as such but are only found as an intermediate step to normalized T's. Some refer to a normalized T score with just the symbol T and use Z to refer to what we have called a "linear" T.

Percentiles and Percentile Ranks

A *percentile* is defined as a point on the distribution below which a certain percent of the scores fall. A *percentile rank* gives a person's relative position or the percent of students' scores falling below his obtained score.[6] To illustrate the computation of percentiles, consider the data in Table 4–2. There are 50 scores. If one wanted to compute the 80th percentile (P_{80}), he would want to find a point below which 40 (80 percent of 50) of the scores lie and above which 10 of the scores lie. We see that 40 scores lie below 77.5 (the upper theoretical limit of 77) and 10 scores lie above 79.5 (the lower theoretical limit of 80). P_{80} falls somewhere in the range of 77.5 to 79.5. Convention suggests that we designate P_{80} as falling halfway between these two points, so $P_{80} = 78.5$. As one more example, let us compute the 50th percentile (P_{50}). We wish to find the point below which and above which 25 (50 percent of 50) scores lie. We note that both the 25th and 26th scores are 55. Thus, $P_{50} = 55$. (Note that this value is the same as the median found in Chapter 4, which it should be.)

Percentiles have the advantage of being easy to compute and fairly easy to interpret. (Occasionally, people will confuse percentiles with percentage correct, but the distinction can be easily explained to most people.) In explaining a national norm percentile rank to a child, one would say, for example, "Your percentile rank of 85 means that you obtained a score higher than 85 out of every 100 students in a representative sample of eighth-graders in the nation."

As with other derived scores, both intra- and interindividual comparisons can be made from percentiles. For example, looking at a percentile norm table (see Table 6–1) for the DAT values given earlier for Irwin, we find the following percentiles:[7]

	Verbal Reasoning	Numerical Ability	Abstract Reasoning	Clerical S & A
Raw Score	32	29	32	42
Percentile	60	70	35	45

	Mechanical Reasoning	Space Relations	Language Usage—I: Spelling	Language Usage—II: Grammar
Raw Score	42	36	64	30
Percentile	25	60	45	50

We can now see how Irwin's scores in each subtest compare with those of other eleventh-grade boys (interindividual comparison) as well as see how

---

[6] Statisticians differ somewhat in the precise definitions of these terms, but these differences are minor and need not concern us. Some use the terms *percentile* and *percentile rank* interchangeably.

[7] Some would call these "percentile ranks." The DAT manual refers to them as "percentiles."

his scores in the different subtests compare with each other (intraindividual comparison). As can be seen, the order of Irwin's raw scores was meaningless information.

Percentiles have a disadvantage in that the size of the percentile units is not constant in terms of raw-score units.[8] For example, if the distribution is normal, the raw-score differences between the 90th and 99th percentiles is much greater than the raw-score difference between the 50th and 59th percentiles (see Figure 6–1). Thus, a percentile difference does not really represent the same amount of raw-score difference in the middle of the distribution as it does at the extremes. Any interpretation of percentiles must take this fact into account. We can be more confident that differences in percentiles represent true differences at the extremes than at the middle of a normal distribution. A type of derived score that does not have this limitation is the linear *standard score*.

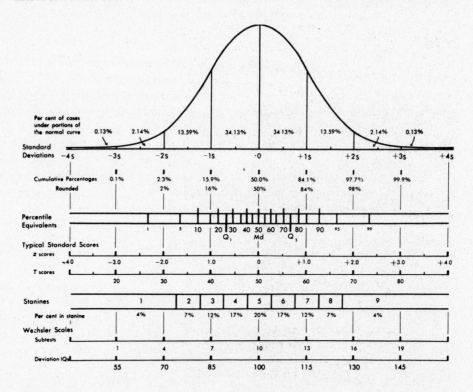

FIGURE 6–1   Chart showing the normal curve and its relationship to various derived scores. (Reproduced and adapted by permission. All rights reserved. Copyright 1947, 1952, © 1959, 1963, 1966, 1968 by The Psychological Corporation, New York, N.Y.)

[8] Except in the unusual case where the raw-score distribution is rectangular.

Linear z and T Scores

Linear scores are transformed scores for which the resulting set of values has a distribution shape identical to the original raw-score distribution. In other words, if the original raw scores are plotted on one axis and the transformed scores on another, a straight line will connect the plotted points. The linear z score is the basic standard score. The formula for a z score is

$$z = \frac{\text{raw score} - \text{mean}}{\text{standard deviation}} = \frac{X - \bar{X}}{S_x} \tag{6-1}$$

As can be seen from the formula, a person whose raw score was equal to the mean would have a z score of zero. If a person has a raw score that is one standard deviation above the mean, his z score would be $+1.0$. Thus, z scores are standard scores with a mean of zero and a standard deviation of 1.

Linear T scores are derived scores with a mean of 50 (the T score if $z = 0$) and a standard deviation of 10. The formula for a T score is

$$T = 10z + 50 = 10\left(\frac{X - \bar{X}}{S_x}\right) + 50 \tag{6-2}$$

There is no theoretical advantage for the T score over the z score, or vice versa. One is simply a linear transformation of the other. Practitioners often prefer T scores because then negative numbers and decimals can generally be avoided.

Table 6–2 shows the computation of the linear z and T scores for individual 1 in Table 4–1. (The means and standard deviations are provided. Computation of all these values has not been demonstrated thus far in the text. As practice, you may want to verify these values.)

When scores are *normally* distributed there is a precise mathematical relationship between z and T scores and other derived scores. Recall that in a normal distribution, approximately 68 percent of the scores fall between $\pm 1 S_x$, 95 percent between $\pm 2 S_x$, and 99.7 percent between $\pm 3 S_x$. Since a z score has a standard deviation of 1, approximately 68 percent of the z scores will be between ± 1, 95 percent between ± 2, and 99.7 percent between ± 3 in a normal distribution. As Figure 6–1 illustrates, when a person scores one standard deviation above the mean, he has a z score of 1 ($T = 60$), and is at about the 84th percentile.

Most norm groups for standardized tests are quite large, and the distribution of their scores often approaches normality. Thus, linear z and T scores for most standardized tests can be interpreted as if they relate to percentiles, as shown in Figure 6–1. Classrooms of 50 pupils, however, *do not* typically present normal distributions, and the relationship depicted in Figure 6–1 would not be accurate.

TABLE 6–2   Computation of Linear z and T Scores for Individual 1 in Table 4–1

	RAW SCORE	MEAN	STANDARD DEVIATION	z	T
Test Score	83.0	56.96	21.4	1.2	62
GPA	3.6	2.80	.4	2.0	70
IQ	120.0	109.96	7.0	1.4	64

$$\text{Test Score:} \quad z = \frac{83 - 56.96}{21.4} = \frac{26.04}{21.4} = 1.2$$

$$\text{Test Score:} \quad T = 10(1.2) + 50 = 12 + 50 = 62$$

$$\text{GPA:} \quad z = \frac{3.6 - 2.8}{.4} = \frac{.8}{.4} = 2$$

$$\text{GPA:} \quad T = 10(2) + 50 = 20 + 50 = 70$$

$$\text{IQ:} \quad z = \frac{120 - 109.96}{7.0} = \frac{10.04}{7.0} = 1.4$$

$$\text{IQ:} \quad T = 10(1.4) + 50 = 14 + 50 = 64$$

Normalized z and T Scores

When raw scores are *normalized*, the shape of the distribution of the transformed (normalized) scores is normal, regardless of the shape of the original distribution.[9] Test publishers often provide normalized scores, and the wise test user should be able to discern the difference between these and linear-transformed scores. If normalized z and T values are given, then the relationship between these values and percentiles as shown in Figure 6–1 is accurate, regardless of the shape of the raw-score distribution. Thus, knowing that a person had a normalized z of 1, we would know that he was at about the 84th percentile. This interpretation could not be made with a linear z of 1 unless the original raw-score distribution was normal. (It should be emphasized that the relationships shown in Figure 6–1 hold for a normal distribution of raw scores, not for all raw-score distributions.)

Stanines

Stanines are derived scores with a mean of 5 and a standard deviation of 2. Only the integers 1 to 9 occur. In a normal distribution, stanines are related to other scores as shown in Figure 6–1. As can be seen, the percentages

[9] It is not an objective of ours that readers of this text be able to normalize raw scores. However, for those of you who wish to do so, proceed as follows: Rank the raw scores, convert them to percentiles (percentile ranks), and look up the corresponding z score in a conversion table (found in almost any basic statistics or test theory text). One converts a normalized z to a normalized T by using Equation (6-2) in this chapter.

of scores at each stanine is 4, 7, 12, 17, 20, 17, 12, 7, and 4, respectively. Whether or not the original distribution is normal, stanine scores are typically assigned so that the resultant stanine distribution is the 4, 7, 12, 17, 20 . . . 4. Thus, a plot (histogram) of the stanines would approach a normal distribution and we can think of stanines as normalized scores.

There is no particular advantage of stanines over other types of derived scores. They do represent the finest discrimination that can be made on one column of an IBM card. The major reason we present them is that they are frequently used in reporting the results on standardized tests, and a competent teacher should be able to interpret such scores.

Grade Equivalents

Grade equivalents can be best explained by an example. If a student obtains a score on a test that is equal to the median score for all the beginning sixth-graders (September testing) in the norm group, then that student is given a grade equivalent of 6.0. If a student obtains a score equal to the median score of all beginning fifth-graders, then he is given a grade equivalent of 5.0. If a student should score between these two points, linear interpolation would be used to determine his grade equivalent. Because most school years are ten months, successive months are expressed as decimals. Thus, 5.1 would refer to the average performance of fifth-graders in October, 5.2 in November, and so on to 5.9 in June.

Grade equivalents suffer from at least four major limitations. One of these limitations is the problem of extrapolation. When a test author standardizes his test, he normally does not use students of all grade levels in his normative sample. Suppose a particular test is designed to be used in grades 4, 5, and 6. Ordinarily the norming would be done on only these three grades.[10] Now, if the median sixth-grader receives a grade equivalent of 6.0, then half the sixth-graders must have a grade equivalent higher than this. How much higher, 7.0, 7.8, 9.0, 12.0? We do not know. Since the test was not given to students beyond the sixth grade, there is no way to know how well they would have done. However, we can estimate—and that is just what is done. A curve can be constructed to show the relationship between raw scores and grade equivalents, as in Figure 6–2. The actual data (that is, the median raw scores for each grade) are available only for grades 4, 5, and 6. However, the curve can be extrapolated so that one can guess at what the median raw scores would be for other grade levels. The extrapolation procedure is based on the assumption that there would be no points of inflection (that is, no change in the direction) in the curve if real data were available. This is a very unrealistic assumption.

[10] Some publishers would norm on a wider range—perhaps grades 3 through 8. The problem of extrapolation would still exist, but to a lesser degree.

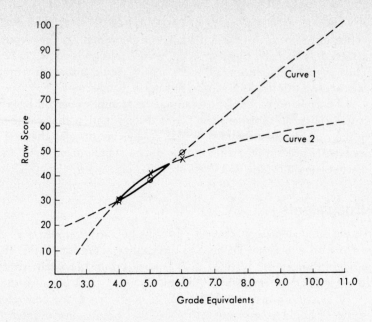

FIGURE 6–2   Curves for determining grade equivalents from raw scores. ○ = population median raw scores for grades 4–6; X = sample raw scores for grades 4–6.

Another problem in extrapolation relates to sampling error. Look at the two curves in Figure 6–2. Let us assume that curve 1 is accurate for grades 4 through 6. That is, given the whole population of students in these grades, the median raw scores would fall as indicated by the circles on curve 1. However, due to sampling error (that is, not having a group with the same median as the population) within grades 5 and 6, we may obtain the medians shown by the X's on curve 2. The differences between the medians of the two curves are well within the range of sampling error we might expect. Now when these two curves are extrapolated, we get completely different estimated grade equivalents. For example, a raw score of 60 is given a grade equivalent of 7.0, using curve 1 (the one we assumed accurate), whereas it would get a grade equivalent of about 10.3 if curve 2 were used. Thus small sampling errors can make extrapolated grade equivalents very misleading.

A second limitation of grade equivalents is that they give us little information concerning the percentile standing of a person within his class. A fifth-grade student may, for example, because of the differences in the grade equivalent distributions for various subject matter, have a grade equivalent of 6.2 in English and 5.8 in mathematics and yet have a higher fifth-grade percentile rank in mathematics.

The third limitation of grade equivalents is that (contrary to what the numbers indicate) a fourth-grader with a grade equivalent of 7.0 does *not* necessarily know the same amount *or* the same kinds of things as a ninth-grader with a grade equivalent of 7.0. For example, a bright fourth-grader who can do very well on an arithmetic test involving speed and accuracy may perform as well as the average seventh-grader. A weak ninth-grader may be poor in speed and accuracy and perform at the seventh-grade level on a test demanding those skills. Yet those two respective students, receiving equal scores on an arithmetic test, do not know the same things about mathematics in a more general sense.

A fourth limitation of grade equivalents is that they are a type of norm-referenced measure particularly prone to misinterpretation by the critics of education. As we have mentioned before, norms are not standards, and even the irrational critics of education do not suggest that everyone *should be* above the 50th percentile. Yet we continually have people talking as if all sixth-graders should be reading at or above the sixth-grade equivalent!

Grade equivalents remain popular in spite of their serious inadequacies. Teachers are under the impression that such scores are easily and correctly understood by both children and parents. This is unfortunate. It is probably not too dogmatic to suggest that grade equivalents, although useful if used in conjunction with other kinds of scores such as percentiles, should never be used alone.

Deviation IQs

The intelligence quotient (IQ) is one of the most misunderstood concepts in measurement. Much of this confusion exists because of a lack of understanding of intelligence tests. (In Unit IV we will consider what an aptitude or intelligence test supposedly measures, and how the scores can be interpreted usefully.) Part of the confusion, however, exists because people do not understand the type of score typically used to report the results of intelligence tests, that is, the IQ. Originally, the IQ was actually a quotient (a ratio). It was found by dividing a person's mental age by his chronological age and then multiplying by 100 ($IQ = MA/CA \times 100$). The problem was in determining a person's mental age. This was accomplished differently on various tests, but essentially the process was similar to obtaining grade equivalents. Thus, if a student obtained a raw score equal to the median raw score of all 9-year-olds, he would be given a mental age of 9 years.

The ratio IQ had many inadequacies. One weakness was that the standard deviations of the IQs were not constant for different ages so that an IQ score of, say, 112 would be equal to a different percentile at one age than another. A second problem was that opinions varied about what the maximum value of the denominator should be. When does a person stop growing intellectually—at 12 years, 16 years, 18 years? Because of these various inadequacies of the ratio IQ, most test constructors now report *deviation* IQs. Deviation

IQs are computed separately for each age group within the norm sample. These are not literal intelligence quotients. They are transformations much like the z or T values (usually normalized) discussed earlier. Typically, these deviation IQs have a mean of 100 and a standard deviation of 15 or 16, although some tests have standard deviations as low as 12; others, as high as 20. The fact that standard deviations vary from test to test is just one of the reasons that we cannot compare two individuals' IQ scores unless they have taken the same test. A score of 128 on a test with a mean of 100 and a standard deviation of 12 has a higher z score than a score of 130 on a test with a mean of 100 and a standard deviation of 16.[11]

Expectancy Scores

In Chapter 1 we discussed the difference between measurement and evaluation. A test score represents measurement. When one makes an interpretation or judgment about the score, that is evaluation. One could, and often should, make different evaluations of the same test score made by different students. To interpret a test score, one should have information about other relevant variables. For an achievement test one such relevant variability is scholastic aptitude. Many test publishers norm their scholastic aptitude and achievement tests on the same sample. They can then provide a derived set of scores that indicate the *expected* score on an achievement test based on a scholastic aptitude score. (For some publishers the expectancy score is based on other variables as well, such as race and sex. The mathematical/technical techniques of the equating also differ across publishers. We shall not discuss these differences here.)

These expectancy scores help answer the question of whether a child's achievement is as high as could be reasonably expected. Discrepancy scores may be provided showing the difference between an individual's actual achievement and expected achievement.

Such discrepancy scores can be useful in dealing with an individual child. Such scores for groups of children can help in making curricular or instructional decisions about a class, building, or school district. However, such scores do need to be interpreted with caution. In the first place, there is considerable debate about whether aptitude tests are really much different from achievement tests. (We discuss this further in Chapters 14 and 15.) They most assuredly are *not* pure measures of *innate* ability. They are, in part, measures of developed ability, and some of the same environmental factors that influence the scores on achievement tests also influence scores on aptitude tests. Thus we should *not* form *fatalistic* expectations and conclude that children

---

[11] There are other types of scores, such as age equivalents and modal age norms. Such scores, when used, are usually described in sufficient detail in the test manuals. Since they are used so seldom, we do not discuss them in this text.

with low scholastic aptitude scores are innately stupid and therefore give up trying to teach them. (Actually, expectancy scores may keep us from doing this, for many students indeed *do* achieve higher scores than expected, thus showing it is possible.) Nevertheless, since schools do *not* have control over many of the factors that affect both scholastic aptitude and achievement scores, educators should not unduly chastise themselves for low achievement test scores if the expectancy scores are low, nor should they feel particularly virtuous about high achievement scores if the expectancy scores are high. The discrepancy between expected achievement and actual achievement is a better measure of school impact (or lack of impact) than achievement data alone.

A second caution regarding discrepancy scores is that, since achievement scores and expectancy scores are highly correlated, the difference scores are extremely unreliable. This is particularly important to remember when interpreting an individual pupil's discrepancy score. The difference has to be quite large before we interpret it as being due to more than chance variation.

PROFILES

When we wish to portray two or more scores for the same person (or groups of people), we do so by means of a *profile*. Of course any such comparison is meaningless unless the raw scores have all been converted to the same type of derived score based on the same norm group. When a test is composed of several subtests(like multifactor aptitude tests, achievement batteries, or many personality and interest inventories), then these subtests will have been normed on the same sample and meaningful profiles can be constructed. Some test companies norm different tests on the same sample, and derived scores from these tests could also be meaningfully compared.

In addition to a common norm group and type of derived score, some index of error should be portrayed on the profile (Brown, 1976, p. 199). This has been done in different ways (and sometimes not done at all), as we shall see in the examples to follow.

Profile sheets should also contain complete information about the test, such as the title, form, and level; the name of the person tested; the date of the test; and the raw scores from which the scaled scores were derived.

Figure 6–3 shows a profile on the Differential Aptitude Test (DAT). The scale used is a percentile scale, but it is plotted on a *normal percentile chart*. These are profiles for which the scores reported are in percentiles, but the dimensions are such that equal linear distances on this chart represent equal differences between scores. The distances between the percentiles correspond to those portrayed in Figure 6–1. The significance of differences is discussed in the text accompanying the profile in Figure 6–3. This discussion is for the student and is in nontechnical language, but it is related

PROFILING YOUR DAT SCORES

The numbers that tell how you did on each test are in the row marked "Percentile." Your percentile tells where you rank on a test in comparison with boys or girls in your grade in numerous schools across the country. If your percentile is 50, you are just in the middle—that is, one-half of the students in the national group did better than you and one-half did less well.

If your percentile on one test is 80, you are at the top of 80 percent of the group—only 20 percent made higher scores than yours. If you scored in the 25th percentile, this means about 75 percent of the group did better than you on the test. These percentiles indicate your relative standing among students of your sex and grade. They do NOT tell you how many questions (or what percent of them) you answered correctly.

Using the information printed in the "Percentile" row, you can now draw your aptitude profile on the chart provided. There are nine columns to be marked; in each of these make a *heavy short line* across the column at the level corresponding to your percentile on that test. (In some cases, the line you draw will coincide with a dotted or solid line already printed on the chart.) Then blacken each column for a distance of one-half inch above and one-half inch below the short line you have drawn, so that you end up with a solid black bar in each column. (For extremely high or low percentiles, you will not be able to blacken one-half inch in both directions without running off the chart.)

HOW BIG A DIFFERENCE IS IMPORTANT?

Since tests cannot be perfectly accurate, you should not overestimate the importance of small differences between two percentiles in comparing your aptitudes. The bars on your profile help by indicating the more important differences.

Look at the bars for any *two* tests and notice whether or not the ends of the bars overlap. If they do not, chances are that you really are better in the kind of ability represented by the bar that is *higher* on the profile chart. If the bars overlap, but not by more than half their length, consider whether other things you know about yourself agree with this indication; the difference may or may not be important. If they overlap by more than half their length, the difference may be disregarded; so small a difference is probably not meaningful. This method of looking at the overlap of bars works for any two abilities you want to compare, whether they are listed next to each other or several columns apart on the chart.

FIGURE 6–3   Individual report form for the Differential Aptitude Test. (Reproduced by permission. All rights reserved. Copyright © 1972, 1973 by The Psychological Corporation, New York, New York.)

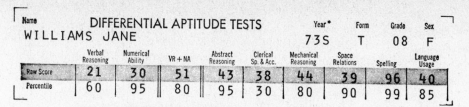

	Verbal Reasoning	Numerical Ability	VR + NA	Abstract Reasoning	Clerical Sp. & Acc.	Mechanical Reasoning	Space Relations	Spelling	Language Usage
Name: WILLIAMS JANE — Year*: 73S — Form: T — Grade: 08 — Sex: F									
Raw Score	21	30	51	43	38	44	39	96	40
Percentile	60	95	80	95	30	80	90	99	85

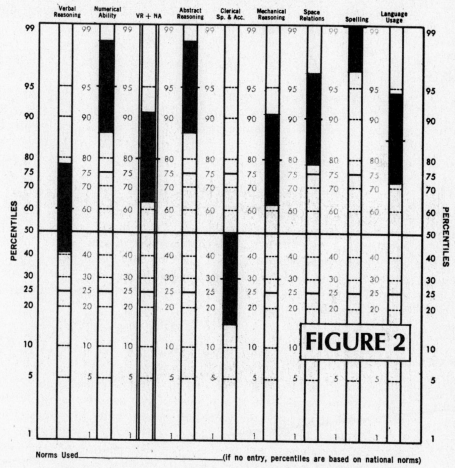

Norms Used_____(if no entry, percentiles are based on national norms)

*F — first (fall) semester testing and percentiles; S — second (spring) semester testing and percentiles.

FIGURE 6–3   (Continued)

to the discussion of the reliability and standard error of difference scores discussed in Chapter 5.

Figure 6–4 shows a profile for the Iowa Test of Basic Skills (ITBS). (The ITBS is discussed in Chapter 15.) This profile permits the charting of growth on the ITBS for an individual across seven different administrations of the test. The scaled scores are really grade equivalents, so a value of 65, for example, means the fifth month of the sixth grade—usually expressed as 6.5. Although this type of profile has the obvious advantage of showing growth, it also has some disadvantages:

1. The scaled scores are spaced close together so that the profile is flattened in appearance.
2. Grade equivalents are used; while useful for considering growth across time within a subtest, they can be misleading if one wishes to compare a student's subtest scores at one point in time. (See our discussion of grade equivalents.)
3. No provision has been made on the profile for displaying error of measurement.
4. There is no place to record the raw scores.

Increasingly, publishers of standardized tests will provide computer printed narrative test result reports to accompany the derived scores and profiles. For example, publishers of the Iowa Test of Basic Skills have prepared such reports for pupils, parents, and teachers (Mathews, 1973). Such reports offer information in a form easily understood by pupils and parents and are a useful supplement.

Profile Analysis

In addition to using profiles for making intraindividual comparisons, one might wish to compare the total profiles of two or more persons or to compare a single individual's profile against various criterion groups. The topic of such profile analyses is beyond the scope of this book. In general, multiple regression procedures could be used to weight and combine the separate scores so that a best prediction could be made of a single criterion. This approach is simply a mathematical extension of the regression procedure discussed in Chapter 5. Discriminant analysis procedures and similarity scores could be used if one wished to determine in which criterion group the individual's profile best fits. Interested readers should consult such references as Cooley (1971), Prediger (1971), and Rulon, Tiedeman, Tatsuako, and Langmuir (1967). Discriminant analysis procedures are most likely to be used with interest and personality inventories and are especially helpful in the counseling uses of test data.

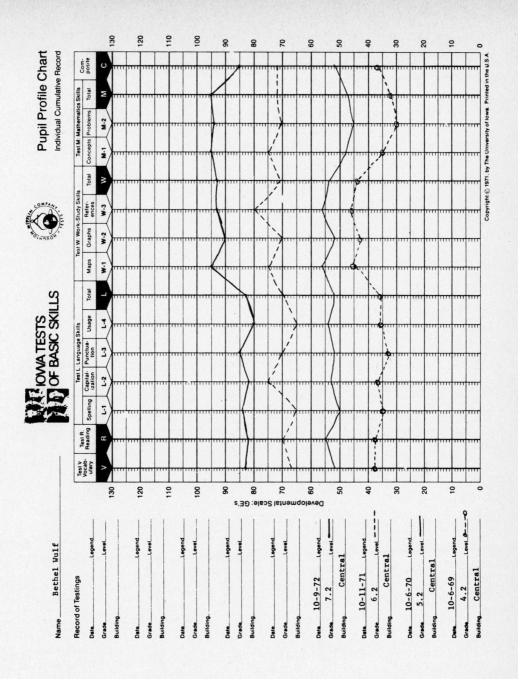

FIGURE 6–4   Pupil profile chart for the Iowa Test of Basic Skills. (Reproduced by permission of Houghton Mifflin Company.)

SUMMARY

The following statements summarize the major points of this chapter.

1. Normative data are an important aid in interpreting scores.
2. Norms should be recent.
3. Norms should be sampled from a larger population in such a manner that the sample is representative.
4. The population sampled should be relevant.
5. The type of norm most commonly used by test publishers is the national norm.
6. Special group norms or local norms are often more meaningful than national norms.
7. School mean norms must be used if one is interested in comparing a school district's performance to other school districts.
8. Norms are not standards.
9. A percentile rank for a person indicates the percent of students' scores falling below his obtained score.
10. Percentiles are easy to interpret, but have the disadvantage of unequal units.
11. Linear z and T scores are derived scores with means of 0 and 50 respectively.
12. Stanines are derived scores with a mean of 5 and a standard deviation of 2.
13. When scores are normally distributed percentiles, z, T, and stanine scores have the relationship depicted in Figure 6–1.
14. Grade equivalents have several major limitations. The technical limitations are due to extrapolation and lack of any information regarding the shape or variance of the grade-equivalent distribution. Practically, one is likely to *mis*interpret grade equivalents as indicating the actual grade level at which a person is performing and/or as standards of performance.
15. Deviation IQs are standard scores with means of 100 and, depending on the test, with standard deviations usually (but not always) of 15.
16. Profiles are useful aids in interpretation when we have several scores for the same individual.
17. In order to use profiles, scores must all be converted to the same type of derived score and be based on the same norm group. In addition, some index of error should be portrayed on the profile.

TEACHER-MADE
EVALUATION TOOLS

UNIT 3

CHAPTER SEVEN

Classroom Testing: The Planning Stage

© 1968 United Feature Syndicate, Inc.

Teacher-made tests are frequently the major basis for evaluating students' progress in school. One would have great difficulty in conceptualizing an educational system where the child is not exposed to teacher-made tests. Although the specific purposes of the tests and the intended use of the results may vary from one school to another or from one teacher to another, it is essential that we recognize the value that test results can play in the life of the student, parent, teacher, counselor, and other educators.

Classroom evaluation instruments are not restricted to the conventional pencil-and-paper achievement tests. Some of the more important instructional objectives cannot be evaluated by a pencil-and-paper test. Rather, we must use rating scales, check lists, and other observational techniques. The discussion in this chapter is concerned with teacher-constructed evaluation procedures in general, but primarily it focuses on teacher-constructed achievement tests, as do Chapters 8 through 11. Other teacher-made evaluation instruments will be considered in more detail in Chapter 12.

After studying this chapter the student should be able to—

1. Discuss the advantages of teacher-made tests over commercially published tests.
2. Understand the major problems associated with teacher-made tests.
3. Classify teacher-made achievement tests according to item format, nature of stimulus, and purpose.
4. Explain how purposes, content, method, timing, test length, item difficulty, and test blueprints relate to the planning of an evaluation procedure.
5. Construct a test blueprint.
6. Understand the importance of, and be able to construct, an item that matches an instructional objective.
7. Understand the differences between essay and objective tests.
8. Understand the factors to be considered in selecting a particular item format.
9. Evaluate the strengths and weaknesses of the essay and objective item.
10. Understand the factors to be considered when deciding upon the test's length.
11. Define and discuss item difficulty.
12. Follow the guidelines offered for preparing test items.
13. Discuss the six characteristics (abilities) a person needs to write good test items.
14. Specify the sources of ideas upon which to base test items.
15. List the criteria to be met when selecting ideas for test items.

WHY TEACHER-MADE TESTS?

Teachers have an obligation to provide their students with the best instruction possible. This implies that they must have some procedures whereby they can reliably and validly evaluate how effectively their students have been taught. The classroom achievement test is one such tool. At this point, you might ask, "If there are commercially available achievement tests, why is it so important that the classroom teacher know how to construct his own tests? Why doesn't he use the commercial tests?"

Schwartz and Tiedeman (1957, p. 110) stated that teacher-made tests are valuable because they—

1. Assess the extent and degree of student progress with reference to specific classroom activities.
2. Motivate students.
3. Permit the teacher to ascertain individual pupil strengths and weaknesses while the pupil is studying a particular subject-matter area.
4. Provide information for reporting purposes.
5. Provide immediate feedback for the teacher, who can then decide whether a particular unit or concept needs reteaching and/or whether individual pupils are in need of remedial instruction.
6. Provide for continuous evaluation.

Commercially prepared achievement tests could be used to obtain some of the information needed by the teacher, and they could be used to motivate students. But, even in those schools that use commercial tests, it is unusual for such tests to be administered more than once a year. In addition to providing more frequent evaluations, teacher-made tests are better in the sense that they are more relevant to a teacher's particular objectives and pupils. Who knows better than the classroom teacher the content covered in the course? Who knows better than the classroom teacher the needs, backgrounds, strengths, and weaknesses of his pupils? The classroom teacher, of course, is in the best position to provide answers to questions such as "Does Ilene know how to add a single column of numbers well enough to proceed to the next instructional unit?" or "What relative emphasis has been placed on the Civil War in contrast to the Declaration of Independence?" Not only is the classroom teacher able to "tailor" the test to fit his particular objectives, but he can also make it "fit" the class and, if he wishes, "fit" the individual pupils. Commercially prepared tests, because they are prepared for use in many different school system with many different curricular and instructional emphases, are unable to do these things as well as the teacher-made test.

Also, the content of commercially prepared tests tends to lag, by a few years at least, recent curricular developments. Teacher-made tests are more likely to reflect *today's* curriculum. This is especially true in subject-matter areas such as science and social studies, which change rather rapidly in contrast to, say, composition or literature.

Classroom test results may also be used by the teacher to help him develop more efficient teaching strategies. For example, Miss Atom may feel that her pupils must understand valence before they can be introduced to balancing chemical equations. Or, Mr. Divider may feel that his students must know the concepts of subtraction and multiplication before they can be introduced to long division. These teachers could develop their own tests, administer them to their students as pretests, and then proceed on the basis of the test results to (1) reteach some of the information they falsely assumed the students already knew, (2) omit some of the material planned to be taught because the students already knew it, and (3) provide some of the students with remedial instruction while giving other students some enriching experiences. The teachers could have obtained this information with a commercial test, only *if* that test reflected their particular objectives. Many times, such tests do not.

There are many instances when a teacher wants to sample thoroughly in a particular area. That is, he is interested in obtaining as much information as possible from a test in a specific content area such as refraction, reflection, absorption, magnetism, or valence. Normally, the commercial test will sample a variety of skills and knowledge rather than focus on any single aspect of the course content. Hence, the teacher who wants to sample thoroughly in a particular area can do this best by preparing his own test. Even if a teacher can find a commercial test that sampled a particular concept(s) to his liking, what would he do with the remainder of the test? It would be rather uneconomical to buy the total test for such a limited purpose. Yet the limited purpose is important and it should be evaluated. It is best evaluated by a well-constructed teacher-made test.

Classroom tests, because they can be tailored to fit a teacher's particular instructional objectives, are essential if we wish to provide for optimal learning on the part of the pupil and optimal teaching on the part of the teacher. Without classroom tests, those objectives that are unique to a particular school or teacher might never be evaluated.[1]

To this point we have attempted to explain why teacher-made tests are still necessary, even though there are good commercially prepared achievement tests available. However, in recent years there has been an attempt to build up item banks that can be used by the classroom teacher to prepare his test. Does this imply that teacher-made tests will be gradually discarded? We think not. At present these item banks—such as the Instructional Objectives Exchange (IOX) at UCLA (Popham, 1970b), Project COMBAT (Walter, 1970), the project for Comprehensive Achievement Monitoring (Gorth, 1969; Gorth, Grayson, Popejoy, & Stroud, 1969)—are not geared to provide the kind of service that would be required if large numbers of teachers were

[1] Our emphasis on the desirability and importance of the classroom teacher's being able to construct his own personal, unique, and relevant tests should *not* be construed as a deemphasis or an implied lack of value of commercial tests. On the contrary! Both serve a common function: The assessment of a pupil's skills and knowledge. But because they differ in scope, content, and use, we should capitalize on how they complement each other rather than argue that one is better than the other.

to avail themselves of the service. More important, however, is that such agencies would *not* encourage dispensing with teacher-made tests. They would provide only the raw materials, *not* the finished test. Teachers would still have to know how to build,[2] plan, score, and analyze the test. There is still a preponderance of schools having local, unique objectives that would not be measured by materials contained in these item banks, and teachers would have to write some items.

Another reason we feel that teacher-made tests will always have a place in the classroom is that agencies such as IOX will have only a limited number of items per objective. Teachers will *not* be able to make generalizations about their pupils' knowledge, skills, abilities, and performance from such a limited sampling of the subject matter. Item banks will, in the future, be of value to the classroom teacher. We do not think, however, that they will replace the need for the teacher's having knowledge of the processes involved in building a good achievement test.

DEFICIENCIES IN TEACHER-MADE TESTS

Students sometimes complain that they are fed up with tests that are ambiguous, unclear, and irrelevant. Comments of students such as "this was an exercise in futility," "I didn't know what the teacher was looking for," and "I studied the major details of the course but was only examined on trivia and footnotes" are not uncommon. Nor are they necessarily unjustified (see Planisek and Planisek, 1972). By and large, teacher-made achievement tests are quite poor. Let us briefly look at some of the major deficiencies commonly associated with teacher-made achievement tests. The deficiencies discussed below can be minimized by careful planning, by meticulous editing and review, and by following some simple rules of test-item construction.

1. *Ambiguous questions.* When a statement or word can be interpreted in two or more ways, we have ambiguity. In the essay test, words such as "discuss," and "explain" may be ambiguous in that different pupils interpret these words differently. Or in a true-false test the item[3] "The North American Indians were a backward people" might be true or false, depending upon the student's referent. In comparison to the Aztecs, the statement might be true. But if one were comparing the North American Indians with some aborigine tribe in New Zealand, the statement might be false. Students should not be required to guess at an answer because the question is ambiguous. The question should be worded in such a way that it is interpreted in the

---

[2] The teacher would still have to prepare a table of specifications so that he could "order" the appropriate test items.

[3] Item and question are used interchangeably. Item format refers to the type of item, such as true-false or multiple-choice.

same way by all students. Differential performance should be the result of differences in knowledge of the subject matter, *not* because of differences in interpretation of the item. Editing and some independent review of the test items by another teacher should help minimize ambiguity.

2. *Excessive wording.* Too often teachers think that the more wording there is in a question, the clearer it will be to the student. This is not always so. In fact, the more precise and clear-cut the wording, the greater the probability that the student will not be confused. The following item illustrates "window dressing." In its original form, we have extensive superfluous information in both the stem and responses, that contributes nothing to the clarity of the item. The "better" example asks for the same information in a more lucid fashion.

Poor: Miss Adder has taught seventh-grade algebra for 15 years. For some time she has been concerned about the fact that her brighter students had more difficulty than her average pupils in comprehending arithmetic concepts. She decided to do a study of the relationship between scholastic aptitude and academic achievement in algebra. She took her pupils' scholastic aptitude scores and, after computing a Pearson product moment correlation, found that $r = 0.00$. She therefore concluded that—
  A. The higher a person's scholastic aptitude score, the more likely he would be to receive low grades in algebra.
  B. The higher a person's scholastic aptitude score, the more likely he would be to receive high grades in algebra.
  C. The scholastic aptitude score will, in general, be of no help in predicting grades in algebra, since the correlation is not statistically significant.
  D. The scholastic aptitude score has no construct validity.
  E. The scholastic aptitude score is not reliable.

Better: The correlation between scholastic aptitude scores and grades in seventh-grade algebra is 0.00. How can this "fact" be interpreted?
  A. The scholastic aptitude test is not reliable.
  B. The scholastic aptitude test has no construct validity.
  C. The scholastic aptitude test will not be of any help in predicting grades in seventh-grade algebra.
  D. The higher a person's scholastic aptitude score, the more likely will he be to receive high algebra grades.
  E. The scholastic aptitude test will not be of any help in predicting GPA in the seventh grade.

3. *Lack of appropriate emphasis.* More often than not, teacher-made tests do not cover the objectives stressed and taught by the teacher, and do not reflect proportionally the teacher's judgment as to the importance of those objectives. Generally, teacher-made achievement tests are heavily loaded with items that call forth only the student's ability to recall specific facts and

information, such as "In what year was the Magna Carta signed? (1215)." "Quote the first five lines of any soliloquy studied this year." We do not negate the value of knowing certain specific facts and details such as the multiplication tables. We feel that knowledge of such information should be tested. But this is markedly different from having the student quote the first five lines from "To be or not to be. . . ." Why are so few of the test items constructed by classroom teachers devoted to measuring the higher mental processes such as understanding and application? Primarily because it is so much easier to prepare items that measure factual recall than it is to write test items that measure application, comprehension, synthesis, and evaluation.

4. *Use of inappropriate item formats.* Some teachers use different item formats (such as true-false, matching, or essays) solely because they feel that change or diversity is desirable. This feeling for the need of diversity should *not* govern the type of item to be used. There are, as will be discussed in later chapters, advantages and limitations associated with each type of item format. Teachers should be selective and choose the format that is most effective for measuring a particular objective.

CLASSIFICATION OF TEACHER-MADE TESTS

There are a variety of ways in which teacher-made tests (or for that matter commercially published tests) can be classified. One type of classification is based upon the type of item format used—*essay* versus *objective*. Another classification is based upon the type of stimulus material used to present the problems to the student—*verbal* and *nonverbal*. Still other classifications may be based upon the purposes of the test and the use of test results—*criterion referenced* versus *norm referenced*; *achievement* versus *performance*; and *formative* versus *summative* evaluation. We will now consider the various classification schemes in greater detail.

It should be recognized at the outset that the classification schemes to be discussed are not mutually exclusive. For example, a test may be of the essay type, but the student may be required to react to a picture or music that he hears, and the results may be designed to assist the teacher in correctly placing him at an appropriate step in the learning (instructional) sequence.

Classification by Item Format

There are several ways in which items have been classified by format— supply and selection type; free answer and structured answer; essay and objective. (See Ebel, 1972; Gronlund, 1976; Lien, 1971; Thorndike & Hagen, 1977.) We will classify item types into two major categories—*essay* and *objective*—and place the short-answer form under objective rather than essay. The short-answer form is really a compromise between the essay and other types of objective items. Short-answer items, as do essay items, require recall

(supply) rather than recognition (selection) skills, but they permit less freedom of response than do essay questions. Also, short-answer items can be
scored more objectively than essay questions.[4]

It is not possible to classify tests solely on the basis of whether or not
subjectivity is involved. Subjectivity is involved when *any* test is constructed
—deciding upon the purpose(s) of the test, deciding upon the kinds of questions to ask, deciding upon the difficulty level of the test, deciding upon
whether or not a correction formula should be used—and hence one *cannot*
say that an objective test does not involve some degree of subjectivity on the
part of the test maker. Also, even though some educators argue that essay
tests are more susceptible to subjectivity in scoring than are objective tests,
some techniques that can be used to make essay scoring more objective[5] will
be given in Chapter 8. At any rate, the two major types of teacher-made
achievement tests—objective and essay[6]—do differ quite markedly in the
degree to which they are amenable to objective scoring. It is primarily for this
reason that we favor the classification of teacher-made achievement tests
shown below:

A. Essay type
    1.   Short-answer or restricted response (about one-half of an 8½ ×
        11-inch page)
    2.   Discussion or extended response (about 2 to 3 pages)
    3.   Oral
B. Objective type
    1.   Short-answer
        a. Single word, symbol, formula
        b. Multiple words or phrase
    2.   True-false (right-wrong, yes-no)
    3.   Multiple-choice
    4.   Matching

Classification by Stimulus Material

We generally think of tests in terms of a series of verbal problems that
require some sort of verbal response. There are many instances, however,
where the stimulus material used to present the problem to the student need
not be verbal. In a humanities or art course, the stimulus materials can be
pictorial. In a music course, the stimulus material could be a recording of an

[4] Objectivity of scoring refers to the extent to which the personal judgment of the
scorer affects the score credited to a particular response.

[5] We agree that the reader or scorer reliability is somewhat lower in essay-type tests,
precautions notwithstanding.

[6] The oral examination, which is less popular today, could be classified as being of the
essay type.

instrument or symphony. In a woodworking course, the stimulus material might be the tools. Nevertheless, the student is still being tested to see what abilities, skills, and knowledge he possesses. Although nonverbal stimulus-material items are infrequently used in the classroom, this does not mean that they are not a good medium to use.

Classification by Purpose:
Criterion- versus Norm-Referenced Interpretation

As discussed in Chapter 3, the test score in a criterion-referenced interpretation is used to describe the status of the individual. Does Ilene know how to add a single column of figures? Does Allan know how to balance an equation? A norm-referenced interpretation of the test score permits the teacher to make meaningful comparisons among students in terms of their achievement. Hence, if the teacher wants to compare Ilene's performance in arithmetic to that of her peers, he would use norm-referenced interpretation.

Classification by Purpose:
Achievement versus Performance

The educational process is *not* restricted to achievement in such areas as reading, science, social studies, or mathematics. There are many instances where teachers are just as, if not more, concerned with what the pupil can *do*. For example, an art teacher might be as interested in seeing how well his students can draw or paint as he is in whether they know the distinction between form and symmetry. An instrumental music teacher no doubt would be as concerned with measuring his pupils' ability to play a musical instrument as he is in learning whether they know the difference between a treble and bass clef. And a woodworking teacher might be more concerned with ascertaining whether his students can operate a lathe than he is in knowing whether they know the parts of a lathe. Education is concerned with both what we know in an academic sense and how well we are able to apply our knowledge. For this reason, teachers could use achievement tests, performance tests, or a combination of the two, depending upon the subject matter. In Chapters 8 through 10 we will concern ourselves with teacher-made achievement tests. In Chapter 12 we will discuss performance tests.

Classification by Purpose:
Formative versus Summative Evaluation

Again, the item format used and the types of items written generally do not differ for tests used for formative and summative evaluation. What differ are the table of specifications and the frequency of testing. Since formative evaluation is designed to provide the teacher with continuous and immediate feedback so that he can govern his instructional strategy, teachers will test more frequently. With respect to the table of specifications, as in the case with criterion-referenced and diagnostic tests, there will be a very thorough sampling of a limited content area, whereas in summative evaluation there will be a more restricted sampling across a larger content area.

PLANNING THE TEACHER-MADE TEST

Good tests do not just happen. They require adequate and extensive planning so that the goals of instruction (objectives), the teaching strategy to be employed, the textual material, and the evaluative procedure are all related in some meaningful fashion. Most teachers recognize the importance of having some systematic procedure for ascertaining the extent to which their instructional objectives have been realized by their pupils. And yet, one of the major errors committed by teachers when preparing their classroom tests is *inadequate* planning. Too often, teachers feel that they can begin giving some thought to the preparation of their tests about one or two weeks before the test is to be administered. More often than not, they leave it until the last possible moment and rush like mad to prepare something. This is indeed unfortunate, for the test produced may contain items that are poorly conceived, poorly worded, ambiguous, and grammatically incorrect. The test may contain items that are either not scorable or have more than one correct answer. The test may be either too easy or too difficult. The test may be measuring trivial details rather than the more important pervasive outcomes of learning. Writing items that are valid, reliable, and objectively scorable requires time, energy, and adequate planning. Professional item writers are seldom able to write more than ten good items per day. It would therefore seem unrealistic to expect the ordinary classroom teacher to be able to prepare a 50-item test if he begins thinking about his test only a few days before it is scheduled. The solution to the problem lies in adequate planning and in spreading out the item-writing phase over a long period of time.

Ideally, every test should be reviewed critically by other teachers, to minimize the deficiencies noted earlier. Possibly the only way that the teacher can have confidence in his test is to have it prepared in sufficient time to permit a critical, independent review. And this requires that the classroom teacher adequately plan his test and write his test items in advance.

All the deficiencies discussed earlier are related in one way or another to inadequate planning. This is not to imply that careful planning will *ipso facto* remove these deficiencies; rather, without adequate and careful planning, one can be fairly certain that his test will not be very good.

Before the classroom teacher (or for that matter, the professional item writer) sits down to write his test items, he must ask himself a series of questions. The questions may be considered somewhat analogous to those on a check list used by commercial airline pilots, who would never attempt to take off before completing their check list. The two most general questions the classroom teacher must consider are: (1) What do I want to do? and (2) What is the best way in which I can accomplish my goal? Table 7–1 sets forth the kinds of questions that should be asked by the classroom teacher in the test-planning stage. In subsequent sections of this chapter we will consider the first seven questions contained in the check list. In the succeeding chapters we will concentrate on answers to the remaining questions—the techniques of writing essay and objective test items, assembling, reproducing, administering, scoring, and analyzing the test.

Purpose of the Test

You will recall that in Chapter 1 we discussed the many ways in which evaluation can aid both the pupil and the teacher. To be helpful, classroom tests must be related to the teacher's instructional objectives, which in turn must be related to the teacher's instructional procedures, and eventually to the use of the test results. But what are the purposes of the test? Why is the test being administered? To what use will the test results be put by the pupil, teacher, counselor, administrator, and parents?

**TABLE 7–1   Check List for the Planning Stage
in Preparing Classroom Tests**

---

1. What is the purpose of the test? Why am I giving it?
2. What skills, knowledge, attitudes, etc., do I want to measure?
3. Have I clearly defined my instructional objectives in terms of student behavior?
4. Have I prepared a table of specifications?
5. Do the test items match the objectives?
6. What kind of test (item format) do I want to use? Why?
7. How long should the test be?
8. How difficult should the test be?
9. What should be the discrimination level of my test items?
10. How will I arrange the various item formats?
11. How will I arrange the items within each item format?
12. What do I need to do to prepare students for taking the test?
13. How are the pupils to record their answers to objective items? On separate answer sheets? On the test booklet?
14. How is the objective portion to be scored? Hand or machine?
15. How is the essay portion to be graded? Global or analytical?
16. For objective items, should guessing instructions be given? Should a correction for guessing be applied?
17. How are the test scores to be tabulated?
18. How are scores (grades, or level of competency) to be assigned?
19. How are the test results to be reported?

Classroom achievement tests serve a variety of purposes, such as (1) judging the pupils' mastery of certain essential skills and knowledge, (2) measuring growth over time, (3) ranking pupils in terms of their achievement of particular instructional objectives, (4) diagnosing pupil difficulties, (5) evaluating the teacher's instructional method, (6) ascertaining the effectiveness of the curriculum, (7) encouraging good study habits such as frequent reviews,[7] and (8) motivating students. These purposes are not mutually exclusive. A single test can and should be used to serve as many purposes as possible. For example, a classroom achievement test in fifth-grade arithmetic can be used to diagnose student strength and weaknesses, to rank pupils, and to evaluate a particular instructional strategy. This, however, should *not* be construed as de-emphasizing the need for every classroom teacher to specify in advance the purposes to which his test results will be put. The classroom teacher should not hope that because a test can serve many masters, it will automatically serve his intended purposes. The teacher must plan for this in advance. For example, if the teacher wishes to use his test to ascertain whether each of his pupils has mastered certain essential knowedges and skills, the psychometric properties of the items will differ from those of items used when he is interested in ranking his students on those same objectives. For the former, the teacher would be more interested in having items that most students can answer correctly (that is, easy items) and he would want his test to have a rather narrow or restricted sampling of content. For the latter, the teacher would want the majority of items to be of average difficulty and to have a test that samples a wider range of subject-matter content.

A test can serve many purposes, but it cannot do so with equal effectiveness. It is essential that the teacher know the major use of the test results. Otherwise, we fear that he will not be able to prepare a test that will be most useful to him or his pupils.

What Is to Be Tested

The second major question that the classroom teacher, now turned test constructor, must ask himself is *what* is it that I wish to measure? Regardless of whether the teacher is preparing an achievement test, a rating scale or check list, or developing an observational schedule, he must know *what* he wants to measure. On the surface, this may appear to be a ridiculous question. Surely, you would say, the teacher knows what is to be tested. But does he *really* know what he wants to test? He may say that he is interested in testing for knowledge, skills, and attitudes, and you might surmise that he knows what he wants to measure. But what knowledge does he wish to measure?

[7] Gallagher and Gay (1976) reported that on a "surprise" final examination, students given frequent, short-answer quizzes during the course retained significantly more than students in two other experimental situations.

What skills is he interested in measuring? What attitudes does he wish to measure? Should the teacher test for factual knowledge or should he test the extent to which his students are able to *apply* their factual knowledge? The answer to this depends upon the teacher's instructional objectives and what has been stressed in class. If the teacher emphasized the recall of names, places, and dates, he should test for this. On the other hand, if in twelfth-grade chemistry he has stressed the interpretation of data, then his test, in order to be a valid measure of his teaching, should emphasize the measurement of this higher mental process. In this stage of thinking about the test, the teacher must consider the relationships among his objectives, teaching, and testing. The following check list should assist the test constructor:

1. Specify the course or unit content.
2. List the major course or unit objectives.
3. Define each objective in terms of student behavior.
4. Discard unrealistic objectives.
5. Prepare a table of specifications.
6. Decide upon the type of item format to be used.[8]
7. Prepare test items that match the instructional objectives.

Then, in order to further relate testing to teaching, the teacher should—

8. Evaluate the degree to which the objectives have been learned by the pupils.
9. Revise the objectives and/or teaching method and/or test on the basis of the test results.

Specifying the Course Content

Another important step for the teacher in the planning stage is to specify or outline the content of the course, since the content is the vehicle used to achieve the expected outcomes of instruction. Table 7–2 presents in general terms the outline for a college freshman course in Natural Science.

Specifying the Major Course Objectives

Undoubtedly, the most difficult step in the test-planning stage is the specification of objectives. Yet this is essential, for without objectives the teacher is at a loss to know what is to be measured. It is vital that the teacher, indi-

[8] We recognize that only the first five points are directly related to the *what* is to be tested. Since the "what" determines the "how," and since testing should be related to teaching, we have chosen to include the additional points at this time. We confine our discussion in this major section to only the first five points. We will consider the sixth and seventh points briefly in a later section of this chapter, and again in Chapters 8, 9, and 10.

TABLE 7-2   Course Content in Natural Science

MAJOR TOPICS
  I.   Methods of science; hypotheses concerning the origin of the solar system
  II.   Minerals and rocks
  III. Changes in land features
  IV.   Interpretation of land features
  V.   The plants of the earth
  VI.   Animal classifications
  VII. Populations and mechanics of evolution
  VIII. Variation and selection
  IX.   Facts of evolution and the theory that explains them
  X.   Evolution, genetics, and the races of man

Source: Courtesy of Dr. Clarence Nelson, Michigan State University.

vidually but preferably in consultation with other teachers (using a variety of sources such as those discussed in Chapter 2), specify in advance the *major* course objectives (goals or outcomes) for his pupils. Then the teacher can develop appropriate measurement tools to learn the extent to which his pupils have achieved his objectives. For example, one of the objectives in seventh-grade science might be "to understand the operating principles of a four-cycle internal combustion engine." The teacher who accepts this objective must not only teach this material but must also test his pupils for their *understanding* of the principles involved in the operation of the four-cycle engine. It would be inappropriate to test the students on their ability to label the operating parts *unless* this knowledge was also an instructional objective. We realize that it may be difficult to delineate all major course objectives. We also are aware that circumstances beyond the teacher's control might result in some of his instructional objectives not being taught. However, *those objectives for which learning experiences are provided, must be subjected to some form of testing and evaluation.*

Defining Behavioral Objectives

One of the major deficiencies in teacher-made tests results from inadequate attention being paid to the expression of instructional objectives in terms of student behavior. Too often, objectives are expressed as vague generalities, such as effective citizenship, critical thinking ability, or writing ability. It may be adequate for the ninth-grade social studies teacher to state one of his instructional objectives as "to develop effective citizenship." This objective, however, is too vague for the test constructor. The objective must be made more specific and must be expressed in behavioral terms. What is meant by "effective citizenship"? Does it mean that the student is honest and moral? If so, what is honesty and morality?

Vague, general goals often do not offer adequate direction to the teacher. As Chapter 2 pointed out, objectives should provide direction to the teacher so that he can prepare and organize appropriate learning experiences for his pupils. A good rule of thumb in writing objectives is to ask yourself, "Can my students do these things?" For example, can they—

1. Change Fahrenheit temperatures to Celsius?
2. Spell these words?
3. Explain how an internal combustion engine works?
4. Label the chambers of the human heart?
5. Divide with carrying?
6. Describe the three major branches of the federal government, and explain their duties and powers?
7. Quote the Declaration of Independence from memory?
8. Read a wet-bulb thermometer?
9. Give the past perfect tense of specified verbs?

It matters little whether goal 8 involves a skill, goal 7 concerns memory, or goal 3 measures understanding. What does matter is that each of these goals is very precise, observable, and measurable. Each of these very fine or specific subdivisions of some larger whole pertains to some aspect of human behavior. With goals phrased or expressed in this manner, the teacher knows *both* what to teach and what he is to test for.

Discarding Unrealistic Objectives

There are many desirable characteristics we may wish to develop in students, but we cannot always do so because attainment of such traits may be either unrealistic or impossible. As discussed in Chapter 2, the needs and capabilities of the learner must be considered when specifying relevant goals. A desirable goal for schoolchildren is for them to work independently. This would be more realistic and attainable for a third-grader than for a kindergarten child. By the same token it would be realistic for a fourth-grader to write cursively, but it would be both an unrealistic and generally unattainable skill for a nursery-school child. It is one thing to establish a list of goals and objectives. It is still another thing to adopt only those that are within the grasp and need of the pupil.

To help in developing a test that has adequate content validity, the teacher should develop some scheme whereby instructional objectives are related to course content and eventually to the kinds of test questions he proposes to use for measuring the degree of student mastery of these objectives. Such a scheme is referred to as a table of specifications.[9]

Table of Specifications

One of the major complaints made by students with regard to teacher-made tests is that they are often invalid. Students may not use the technical term "validity," but their comments—"we were tested on minute, mundane facts," "the material we were tested on wasn't covered in class nor is it in the text or assigned readings," and "we spent one-half of the course discussing the concepts of validity and reliability and yet only 5 percent of the test was devoted to these concepts"—all point out that the test lacked content validity. We recognize that there may be some instances where students are only displaying a "sour grapes" attitude and complain for the sake of complaining. But we know from looking at a plethora of teacher-made achievement tests that there is some justification for the complaints made. Although a table of specifications is no guarantee that the errors will be corrected, such a blueprint may help improve the content validity of teacher-made tests.

Did you ever see an engineer build a structure without using a blueprint? Did you ever see a plumber or electrician work in a new home without referring to some type of blueprint? Did you ever see a tailor make a suit without a pattern? We haven't. But we have seen some tests constructed by teachers and college professors who did not use some type of plan or guide or blueprint, and their tests reflected it.

The purpose of the table of specifications is to define as clearly as possible the scope and emphasis of the test and to relate the objectives to the content. For example, how does one proceed to construct a test on American history or literature or mathematics? The area to be tested must first be delimited further. The test must be balanced and should reflect the objectives of instruction. In other words, the test must be a valid measure of the pupil's knowledge, skills, and other attributes that the teacher sought specifically to teach. By ensuring that the test adequately covers the content and is directly related to the objectives, the teacher has satisfied the most important criterion of the test—content validity.

Who Should Prepare Specifications?

Some teachers argue strongly against involving students in the development of the table of specifications. These teachers contend that if students play a role in the decision-making process, education will be eventually run by the students rather than for them. We see nothing wrong in involving stu-

[9] The table of specifications is sometimes called the test blueprint, test grid, or content validity chart.

dents in the development of the table of specifications. In fact, where feasible, we encourage such student involvement, if for no other reason than to have students feel that they have played some role in planning the course. Our attitudes toward student participation should *not* be interpreted as condoning students' complete control. Nor should our remarks be regarded as an abrogation of the teacher's major and final responsibility. The *teacher* is the decision maker—not the students. Student input should be considered by the teacher in making his decisions and should be utilized only in an *advisory* capacity.

When to Prepare Specifications

Should the table of specifications be prepared just before the test is constructed or should it be prepared before the course has been taught? Ideally, and to be of most benefit, the table of specifications should be prepared *before* beginning instruction. It would be nice if it were considered part and parcel of the course preparation. Why? Because these "specs" may help the teacher be a more effective teacher. These specs should assist the teacher in organizing his teaching material, his outside readings, his laboratory experiences (if necessary)—all the resources he plans on using in teaching the course. In this way, the specs can help provide for optimal learning on the part of the pupils and optimal teaching efficiency on the part of the instructor. Hence, if the specs are to assist and be of value to the classroom teacher, they should be prepared *before* the instructional phase is begun. In a way, then, the specs serve as a monitoring agent and can help keep the teacher from straying off his instructional track.

Preparing the Table of Specifications

Once the course content and instructional objectives have been specified, the teacher is ready to integrate them in some meaningful fashion so that the test, when completed, will be a valid measure of the student's knowledge. Table 7–3 is an extension of the one-way grid of the course content in Natural Science (Table 7–2) and incorporates the course objectives. This extension is a two-way grid that simultaneously relates the course content to the behavioral objectives as defined by Bloom (1956).

One could, of course, delineate the course content into finer subdivisions. Whether this needs to be done depends upon the nature of the content and the manner in which the course content has been outlined and taught by the teacher. A good rule of thumb to follow in determining how detailed the content area should be is to *have a sufficient number of subdivisions to ensure adequate and detailed coverage.* The more detailed the blueprint, the easier it is to get ideas for test items.

You will notice in Table 7–3 that there are numbers in certain cells and blanks in other cells. If you were to total the last column or bottom row,

TABLE 7–3   Two-Way Table of Specifications for a Final Examination in Natural Science

| | OBJECTIVES[a] | | | | |
COURSE CONTENT	Knowl-edge	Compre-hension (Transla-tion, Interpre-tation, Extrapo-lation)	Applica-tion	Analysis	Total
1. Methods of science; hypotheses concerning the origin of the solar system	5	2		3	10
2. Minerals and rocks	5	5			10
3. Changes in land features	4	4	2		10
4. Interpretation of land features	2	2	6		10
5. Animal classifications	2	4	4		10
6. Plants of the earth	4	4	2		10
7. Populations and the mechanisms of evolution	3	3		4	10
8. Variation and selection		1	5	4	10
9. Facts of evolution and the theory that explains them		2	2	6	10
10. Evolution, genetics, and the races of man		3	4	3	10
Total	25	30	25	20	100

[a] Objectives are based on Bloom's taxonomy.
SOURCE: C. H. Nelson, 1958. *Let's Build Quality into Our Science Tests*. Washington, D.C.: National Science Teachers Association.

you would get 100. Now, what do all these numbers mean? The number 100 in the bottom right-hand cell (corner) is the total percentage (it can be, however, related to the number of items on the test) or numerical value or worth of the test. The numbers at the bottom of each column indicate the percentage of the test devoted to a particular objective. Hence in this hypothetical test 25 percent of the test items measured knowledge, 30 percent of the items measured comprehension, and so forth. The numbers in the last column signify the percentage of items that were allocated to each content area. In this case it was decided that each content area would be weighted equally, and hence 10 percent of the items were written for each content area. The boldface number 5 tells you that 5 percent of the total test was devoted to the measurement of "knowledge" in methods of science. At this point you might ask: "Who determines the weights?"—that is, who determines the proportion of items that are designed for each content area and for each objective?

Determination of Weights

You will recall that one of the major advantages of the teacher-made versus commercially published test is that the teacher-made test can be tailor-made to fit the teacher's unique and/or particular objectives. In this way, Mr. Molecule, who wishes to stress the gas laws in eleventh-grade physics, can do so while Mr. Element, who wishes to stress heat and mechanics, is also at liberty to do so. Each teacher can prepare a test that is valid for his students. Because the classroom teacher—more so than any other person—knows the relative emphasis placed upon the various instructional objectives, it naturally follows that he should have the major responsibility in assigning the various weights to the cells in Table 7–3. There is no hard-and-fast rule that can be prescribed for the teacher to use in determining the weights to be assigned to the various cells in the table of specifications. Experience is his best resource. All that we can say is that the weights assigned should reflect the relative emphasis used by the teacher when he taught the course.

As an example we give a very simplified illustration of how a classroom teacher can initially determine the weights to be assigned to a particular cell in the table of specifications. Assume that Mr. Atom will spend five class periods on a unit in hydrogen and he wants to prepare a test on this unit. Mr. Atom plans to spend one period (20 percent of the time) discussing the physical properties of hydrogen; one and one-half periods (30 percent) on the chemical properties of hydrogen; one-half period (10 percent) on the preparation of hydrogen; and two periods (40 percent) discussing the uses of hydrogen. These values are represented as the row totals in Table 7–4. In teaching this unit, Mr. Atom will be concerned with three behavioral changes: the ability to recall information; the ability to understand basic concepts and principles; and the ability to apply information, concepts, and principles in new situations. The relative emphasis placed on each of these behavioral (instructional) objectives will be 40, 30, and 30 percent, respectively. These values are represented as the column totals. Mr. Atom must now assign values to each of the 12 cells. This could be done by multiplying the row totals by the column totals. For example, the cell involving recall of information in physical properties would have a weight of $.20 \times 40 = 8\%$; the cell incorporating application and uses would have a weight of $.40 \times 30 = 12\%$. This procedure is repeated for each cell and is illustrated in Table 7–4. Mr. Atom now has a blueprint *both* to guide him in teaching this unit and in constructing a test on this unit.

TABLE 7–4   Table of Specifications for a Chemistry Unit on Hydrogen

| | INSTRUCTIONAL (BEHAVIORAL) OBJECTIVE | | | |
CONTENT, PERCENT	Recall of Information	Understanding Concepts	Application in New Situations	Total, Percent
Physical properties	8	6	6	20
Chemical properties	12	9	9	30
Preparation	4	3	3	10
Uses	16	12	12	40
Total	40	30	30	100

There arises now the question of how firm the assignment of weights in each cell should be. We take the position that the initial weights in each cell should be considered as tentative. It is only after the course has been taught that the weights can be considered as definite. And, because conditions may vary from one class to another, the final weights may be somewhat different for different classes taught by the same teacher. This, however, does not mean that the teacher should depart from his original "specs" because he finds it difficult to write items designed to measure the higher mental processes. As Tinkelman (1971, p. 56) wrote: "If a test blueprint rests upon a sound judgmental basis, the test constructor has the professional obligation to obtain items of satisfactory quality and in sufficient numbers to satisfy blueprint specifications."

Without a well-thought-out and prepared table of specifications, there is a great possibility that the test, when finally constructed, will lack content validity. If you look at the typical teacher-made final examination constructed by, say, a social studies teacher, you would see that many items test for the recall of names, places, and dates. Does this mean that the social studies teacher is not concerned with developing critical thinking? Does this in fact imply that the teacher stressed *only* the knowledge of isolated facts and skills? Not necessarily! The apparent undue emphasis on recall of factual material or computational skills that occurs in so many teacher-made tests probably occurs because of the difficulty of writing test items that measure the higher mental processes of comprehension, application, analysis, and interpretation.

Tables of Specifications for Criterion-Referenced Tests

As we mentioned in Chapter 3, the major difference between criterion- and norm-referenced tests is whether we interpret a person's score by comparing it with a specified behavioral criterion of proficiency (90 percent of the items answered correctly) or by comparing it with the scores of other people (Allan did better than Jack). However, *both* norm- and criterion-referenced test scores are related to *content*; therefore, in building an achievement test whose scores will be norm-referenced, we must be as concerned with content validity as when building a test whose scores will be criterion-referenced. In both cases, there is a domain of relevant tasks or behaviors from which we wish to sample. In both cases, we should use a table of specifications to ensure that our sample of test items is representative of the domain of behaviors. The major difference is that for the specific types of instructional decisions where one usually finds criterion referencing to be of more value, the content domain is quite narrow or limited in focus. For those educational decisions where one is likely to find a normative interpretation of the score most useful, the domain of tasks is usually more broad. Thus, when building a test whose scores will be interpreted by comparison with some specified criterion, we may well have only one cell in the table of specifications. The domain is so narrow that it need not be subdivided. For example, we might build a criterion-referenced test on the task of adding two single-digit whole numbers. A table of specifications for such a test would not need to be subdivided. If a test had a broader focus—that is, was designed to measure addition of whole numbers, fractions, and decimals—then one would build a table of specifications so that each subtype of addition problem was represented. This would be true whether one wished to interpret the scores in an absolute or relative fashion.

In summary, the use of a test blueprint or table of specifications will help ensure that (1) only those objectives actually involved in the instructional process will be assessed, (2) each objective will receive a proportional emphasis on the test in relation to the emphasis placed on that objective by the teacher, and (3) no important objective or content area will be inadvertently omitted. Much time and effort are (or can be) expended in preparing a table of specifications. In the long run, however, it will be time and effort well spent, as it can aid immensely in the preparation of test items, in the production of a valid and well-balanced test, in the clarification of objectives to both teacher and students, and in assisting the teacher to select the most appropriate teaching strategy. Better classroom tests would be built if more careful attention were paid to the precise statements of test specifications (Ebel & Damrin, 1960, p. 1508).

Distributing the Table of Specifications

Naturally, the table of specifications should be used by the teacher. But it *should also be given to the students* (especially those in the upper elementary grades and above) during the first week of school and should be discussed thoroughly with them.[10] This can help minimize, if not eliminate, future misconceptions, misunderstandings, and problems.

Too frequently, teachers prepare or outline their course of instruction and fail to distribute it to the students. Why? Are they ashamed of it? If they are, it cannot be very good and should be revised immediately. If it *is* good, is the student entitled to know his teacher's objectives? Definitely yes! Is it not conceivable that a prior knowledge of the table of specifications might result in the student's placing less emphasis in those areas that would contribute little to his total score, thereby concentrating on the more important objectives of instruction? Yes, he might! Is this bad? Not necessarily so. If it will help motivate the student to concentrate on the major course objectives, isn't this good? We think so.

Using the Table of Specifications

We have already discussed how the table of specifications can assist the teacher vis-à-vis his instructional strategy and in preparing valid evaluation instruments. Especially since the "age of accountability" there has been some concern voiced by educators that teachers will be prone to "teach for the test." It could therefore be interpreted that teachers who prepare and follow a table of specifications may be prone to follow this practice. As we said in Chapter 2, if the teacher has an appropriate set of instructional objectives, he should teach his pupils to realize these objectives. It is not wrong to "teach for the test" in this sense. In fact, we would be most pleased if teachers would take the time to develop appropriate instructional objectives, teach them, and then test to see the extent to which they were realized by their pupils. This is markedly different from teaching the test items per se.

Relating the Test Items to the Instructional Objectives

Obtaining a "match" between a test's items and the test's instructional objectives is *not* a guaranteed outcome of a test blueprint or table of specifications. The test blueprint only indicates the number or proportion of test items to be allocated to each of the instructional objectives specified. For example, on a unit test in, say, the characteristics of a test, the teacher may decide that 10 percent of the test will consist of items dealing with psychometrics. But we are still lacking needed information for preparing a valid test. The table of specifications will tell us that 10 percent of the test items will deal with psychometric characteristics of a test, but it does *not* tell us what psychometric properties will be dealt with. What specific learning outcomes do we

[10] This would also allow the students to voice opinions concerning course content and the relative emphasis. If changes are made as a result of this interaction, the pupils should be given a revised set of "specs."

wish to measure—validity, or reliability, or objectivity? All of these pertain to a test's psychometric properties. And if we are dealing with the concept of validity, what aspects are we concerned with measuring? Do we wish to see whether the pupils can define validity? Whether they can name the different types of validity? If so, the test item should be of the *supply* rather than the *select* type; that is, the student provides the answer (as in a short-answer or completion item or the essay) in contrast to choosing from an answer provided (as in the matching, true-false, or multiple-choice item). On the other hand, if we are interested in measuring the student's ability to *compute* a correlation coefficient (which is the manner in which criterion-related validity is expressed), our test item should be such that we ask the student to *compute* a correlation coefficient rather than have him provide a verbal description of how one computes a coefficient of correlation and not have him select the correct formula for computing a correlation coefficient from a list of formulas. Following are some examples of learning outcomes expressed in terms of specific behavioral objectives, with accompanying test items designed to measure the learning outcome. (A note of caution is appropriate here. Although the examples to follow are basically knowledge-type items, this does *not* mean that "matching" cannot nor should not concern itself with the higher mental order processes.) Some of the examples illustrate "matches," whereas others do not. See whether you are able to correctly identify those that do and do not match.

Example 1

Learning outcome (L.O.): The student will be able to define (in one or two sentences) technical terms used in a tests and measurements course, such as validity, reliability, objectivity, CRT, and NRT.

Test item (T.I.): In one or two sentences, define the following the terms:

1. CRT
2. Validity
3. Objectivity
4. NRT
5. Reliability

Do we have a "match" between the learning outcome and test item?

Example 2

L.O.: The student will be able to list four types of reliability.

T.I.: Which of the following are types of reliability?

1. Stability
2. Concurrent
3. Internal consistency
4. Equivalence
5. Content

Do we have a "match"?

Example 3

L.O.: The student can perform mouth-to-mouth resuscitation on a drowning victim.
T.I.: Describe the correct procedure for administering mouth-to-mouth resuscitation on a drowning victim.
Do we have a match?

Example 4

L.O.: The student will be able to perform a tracheotomy using proper instruments and techniques.
T.I.: Select, from the following list, those instruments used to perform a tracheotomy.
Do we have a "match" between the learning outcome and test item?

Of the four examples given, only the *first* example displays a "match" between the learning outcome (L.O.) and the test item (T.I.). The second is not an example of a "match" because the L.O. specified that the student would be able to list or name the four types of reliability, whereas the T.I. asked that the student be able to *recognize* different types of reliability. The T.I. calls for *selection*, whereas the L.O. calls for listing. In the third example there is no match because describing something is *not* valid evidence that the person can *do* something. In the fourth example we have the situation where there is no congruence between what the L.O. specifies and what the T.I. requires the student to do. The L.O. did *not* ask the student to demonstrate his ability to select the instruments used in a tracheotomy. Although, on the surface, one might say that those examples illustrating the lack of a "match" between the test item and learning outcome illustrate minor, insignificant, semantic differences between the L.O. and the T.I; however, even the smallest difference is unacceptable if one wishes to be a "stickler" and say that to have a valid measure of a L.O., there must be a perfect match. And we are insistent that, wherever possible, each and every test item be related to, or "match," each and every instructional or learning outcome.

Note that we said, wherever *possible* there must be a "match." Where would we be willing to deviate? Example 3 is an example of a situation where one could *not* match the L.O. to the T.I. How can one demonstrate whether he is able to correctly apply mouth-to-mouth resuscitation on a drowning victim unless he happens to come upon a drowning victim. It is readily evident that you can't go out and drown someone. At the same time, you should not ask the student being tested to describe either orally or in writing what he would do and how he would do it. What then can you do if you are teaching a course in lifesaving or first aid and this is an important learning outcome? In such instances, you could have a simulated situation and use a mannikin or even another live human and ascertain whether the student can demonstrate his knowledge. In any event, where it is impossible to obtain a "match" because of situations beyond the examiner's control, it is important that the student perform the main intent despite the artificiality of the situation.

The major step, then, in preparing relevant test items is to *carefully analyze the behavior called for in the learning outcome.* Is the learning outcome to have the student demonstrate his knowledge of, or ability to *name, identify, compute*? Is it to reflect knowledge at the lower mental process level (recall or recognition or application) or at the higher level of mental process such as synthesis or evaluation? In the examples given above, the learning outcomes were very specific. One can, if he wishes, have a general learning outcome—one that is *not* specifically related to course content. An example of a content-free learning outcome would be as follows:

> The student will be able to identify (recognize) the function of a given tool.

Then an example of a valid or relevant content-free test item would be as follows:

> What is the function of _____?

The virtue of having content-free learning outcomes is that they can serve as models upon which content-specific learning outcomes can be written. In other words, they are a frame or shell which is then built upon. A major limitation of the content-free learning outcome is that it may result in the item writer losing sight of the fact that before a test item can be written, the learning outcome(s) must be made very specific; otherwise the item may not "match" the instructional objective.[11]

Selecting the Appropriate Item Format

Now that the teacher has decided on the purpose of the test and *what* he is interested in measuring—both in terms of the objectives and content— he must decide on the best *way* of measuring his instructional objectives. (This, of course, does not preclude "mixing" different, but *appropriate*, item types on a test.) We are still not dealing with the actual writing of test items. Rather, we are concerned at this time only with the different types of essay and objective test items. We are still in the planning or "get ready" stage.

As will be evident in our discussions of the various item formats, some are less appropriate than others for measuring certain objectives. For example, if the objective to be measured is stated as "the student will be able to organize his ideas and write them in a logical and coherent fashion," it would be inappropriate to have him select his answer from a series of possible answers. And, if the objective is to obtain evidence of the pupil's factual recall of

---

[11] Even though our consideration of this important topic was brief, this is not to be construed that it is not too important. Rather, it is essential. For those interested in a more detailed consideration of matching items with objectives, we refer you to Mager (1968).

names, places, dates, and events, it would not be efficient to use a lengthy essay question. Although there are instances where the instructional objective can be measured by different item formats, the teacher should select the least complicated one.

The discussion of the advantages and limitations of the various item formats as well as the actual preparation of essay and objective test items will be found in Chapters 8 through 10. Inasmuch as it is important for the classroom teacher to give some thought to whether he should use an essay or objective test, before he actually sits down to write test items (that is, he must engage in some sort of item format planning), we will at this time discuss the major differences between the essay and objective test. In addition, we will discuss some of the more general factors the classroom teacher should consider when deciding upon the type of test to use.

Differences between the Essay and Objective Test

Ebel (1972, pp. 123–138) noted the following differences between the two major types of teacher-made tests—essay and objective.[12]

1. Essay tests require an individual to organize and express his answer in his own words. In the essay or "free response" item, the student is not restricted to a list of responses from which he is to select his answer. Objective tests, on the other hand, require that the individual either supply a brief answer (one or two words) or choose the correct answer from among several alternatives. Many people seem to think that admitting this difference implies the superiority of essay exams, but this is not necessarily so. As Ebel pointed out:

> . . . producing an answer is not necessarily a more complex or difficult task, or one more indicative of achievement, than choosing the best of the available alternatives. . . . if the populace had a clear choice between a man good at making statements but weak on decisions, another weak on making statements but good at making decisions, is there any doubt which they should choose? (Ebel, 1972, p. 125–126)

Nevertheless, we do occasionally wish to measure ability to organize and to write cogently, and essay tests are superior for that purpose.

2. An essay test consists of fewer questions but ones that call for more lengthy answers. An objective test would have more questions but ones taking less time to answer. Adequacy of sampling, efficiency, and reliability are therefore likely to be superior in objective tests.

3. Different skills and processes are involved in taking the tests. In the

[12] For a more elaborate treatment of these differences and similarities see Ebel (1972, pp. 124–144).

essay test, the student spends most of his time thinking and writing. In the objective test (especially the multiple-choice) most of the student's time is spent on reading and thinking.

4. The quality of the essay test is dependent largely upon the skill of the reader (the person grading the answer); that of an objective test, upon the skill of the test constructor.

5. Essay tests are relatively easier to prepare but more difficult to grade accurately (reliably). It undoubtedly takes less time to prepare a 2-hour essay examination than it takes to prepare a 2-hour objective examination. In fact, some teachers believe (and govern themselves accordingly) that essay questions may be prepared while the teacher is on his way to school and may be then written on the blackboard. Although this is possible, it does not lead to the preparation of good essay questions.

6. Essay tests afford both the student and grader the opportunity to be individualistic. Objective tests afford this freedom of expression (item writing) only to the test-maker.

7. On objective tests the examinees' tasks and the scorers' criteria tend to be more explicit.[13]

8. Objective tests are more susceptible to guessing; essay tests are susceptible to bluffing. The seriousness of both problems, however, has been grossly overestimated. Blind guessing seldom occurs on objective tests, and when it does, it is not likely to result in a large change in a student's position with respect to the norm group. Bluffing is relatively easy to detect *if* the reader has some skills in reading essay exams and knows what answers he is looking for.

9. The score distribution in the essay test may vary from one reader (scorer) to another; on the objective test, the distribution is determined almost completely by the test.

Two popular misconceptions not supported by empirical evidence are that (1) essay tests assess certain skills such as analysis and critical thinking better than objective tests, and (2) essay tests contribute to better pupil study and work habits.

Misconceptions of the validity of different types of item formats have resulted in much debate about the relative merits of one type of examination over another. Rather than argue whether essay tests are better than objective tests, or vice versa, we should understand the strengths and weaknesses associated with each type (essay and objective) and capitalize on their strengths. Tyler expresses our feelings aptly:

There is indeed, no need for recognizing any general conflict between these

---

[13] Although the task for the examinee and the criteria for grading can be made more explicit in essay tests, they seldom are.

two types, the objective and essay test. No good purpose can possibly be served by arguing their general advantages and disadvantages, while much harm can thereby be done by appealing to established prejudices. The intelligent point of view is that which recognizes that whatever advantages either type may have are *specific* advantages in *specific* situations; that while certain purposes may be served by one type, other purposes are best served by the other; and, above all, that the adequacy of either type in any specific situation is much more dependent upon the ingenuity and intelligence with which the test is *used* than by *inherent* characteristics or limitation of the type employed. (Tyler, 1933, p. 519)

Factors to Consider When Selecting an Item Format

If a classroom teacher were to ask us, "If it were the teacher's prerogative to use an essay or objective test, or, if an objective test, the supply (completion, short-answer) or select-type (true-false, matching, multiple-choice), which item format would you recommend?" we would say, "It depends upon many things."

Although we are unable to provide you with a definite set of rules, we are able to give you some suggestions for your consideration and deliberation. You, the test user, must make the final decision as to the item format(s) you will use. Your decision of the type of item format to be used should be governed by such factors as (1) the purpose of the test, (2) the time available to prepare and score the test, (3) the number of pupils to be tested, (4) the physical facilities available for reproducing the test, and (5) your skill in writing the different types of items.

1. *Purpose of the test.* The most important factor to be considered is what you want the test to measure. To measure written self-expression, you would use the essay; for spoken self-expression, the oral. If you wish to measure the extent of the pupil's factual knowledge, his understanding of principles, or his ability to interpret, we would prefer the objective test because it is more economical and tends to possess higher score reliability and content validity. If your purpose is to use the test results to make binding decisions for grading purposes or admission to college or for classification or selection, we recommend the objective test because of greater sampling of content and more objective scoring. If you want to see whether the pupils can produce rather than recognize the correct answer, you would use the completion or short-answer *supply* type rather than the matching, or true-false, or multiple-choice *recall* type objective test.

2. *Time.* It will take less time to prepare five extended-response essay questions for a 2-hour grade 12 history test than it would to prepare 75 multiple-choice items for that same test. However, the time saved in preparing the essay test will be used up in reading and grading the responses. When *all*

factors are considered, it takes approximately the same amount of time to prepare and score an essay test (or to prepare and hear the responses in an oral test) for a class of 30 students as it does to test the students with an objective test. The time element, then, becomes of concern in relation to *when* the teacher has the time. If he is rushed before the test is to be administered, but will have sufficient time after it has been given, he might choose to use an essay examination. But, if he must process the results within two or three days, and he has no additional readers, he should use the objective test, *provided* he has sufficient time to write good objective items.

3. *Numbers tested.* If there are only a few pupils to be tested and if the test is not to be reused, then the essay or oral test is practical. However, if a large number of pupils are to be tested and/or if the test is to be reused at a later time with another group, we recommend the objective test—it's much harder to remember 75 objective items than it is to remember 5 or 6 essay topics.

4. *Physical facilities.* If stenographic and reproduction facilities are limited, the teacher is forced to use either the essay test, with the questions written on the board, or the oral test; or he can use the true-false or short-answer item by reading the questions aloud. However, multiple-choice items must (because of their complexity and/or amount of material to be remembered) be mimeographed or reproduced mechanically. We believe that all tests should be mechanically reproduced if possible.

5. *Age of pupils.* Unfortunately, there are still some teachers who believe that a good test is characterized by many different item formats. They no doubt feel that this introduces an element of novelty or that a change of pace will result in keeping the pupils' motivation high. This *may* be true for older pupils, but is definitely *not* so for younger pupils. In fact, we believe that changing item formats with accompanying changes in directions to be followed will, for younger children especially, result in confusion in adapting to new instructions, and whatever novelty might be introduced will be at the expense of valid and reliable test results.

6. *Teacher's skill.* Teachers will be prone initially to frustration and disappointment when writing test items, possibly more so with one item format than another. But, as will be seen in later sections, some item formats are easier to write than others, and teachers do a better job with one type than another. In fact, Ebel (1975a) found that teachers are able to write more discriminating multiple-choice than true-false items.

Because of the differences in teachers' skills in writing different types of items, we urge you to try your hand at writing all item formats. Item writing is a skill that can be improved with practice.

Every item format has its advantages and limitations (see Table 7–5). To be able to take advantage of an item type while at the same time minimizing its deficiencies should be every item writer's prayer. However, it requires

TABLE 7–5   Evaluation of Various Item Types

FACTOR	ESSAY OR ORAL	SHORT-ANSWER	TRUE-FALSE, MATCHING, MULTIPLE-CHOICE
Measures pupil's ability to select, organize, and synthesize his ideas and express himself coherently.	+ +	+	−
Discourages bluffing.	− −	−	+ +
Potential diagnostic value.	− −	−	+ +
Answer cannot be deduced by process of elimination.	+ +	+ +	−
Can be rapidly scored.	− −	+	+ +
Can be scored by machine or untrained person.	− −	−	+ +
Scoring is reliable.	− −	−	+ +
Independent of verbal articulation (fluency).	− −	+	+ +
Provides for good item pool.	− −	+	+ +
Takes relatively little time to prepare.	+	+	−
Measures higher mental processes.	+ +	−	+ +
Provides for broad content sampling.	− −	+	+ +
Measures application in novel situations.	+ +	+	+ +
Provides for adequate sampling of objectives.	− −	+	+ +
Measures originality.	+ +	+	− −

SOURCE: Adapted with permission from R. L. Thorndike and E. Hagen, *Measurement and Evaluation in Psychology and Education* (3d ed.). New York: Wiley, 1969, p. 71. By permission of John Wiley & Sons, Inc.

more than prayer and hope to write good items. It requires careful construction but, even more important, it also requires careful planning.

The various item formats are compared in Table 7–5. The (+) indicates a slight advantage; the (+ +) a marked advantage; the (− −) a marked disadvantage; and the (−) a slight disadvantage of that item type for that factor.

Some Additional Details

Once we have decided upon the purpose of the test and have at least tentatively decided upon the item format(s) to be used, we still must answer five questions before we are able to sit down and begin writing test items. They are: (1) How long should the test be? (2) How difficult should the test be? (3) When and how often should tests be given? (4) Should every pupil answer every item? (5) Should the nature of the stimulus (the item) be pictorial or verbal?

Test Length

There is no ready-made formula that can be used to determine the minimum number of items that should be used for the test to be valid. Although the teacher's intent is to allow each student sufficient time to demonstrate his knowledge of the subject, there must be, for practical reasons, a time limit imposed on all classroom tests. If not, there will be some students who would spend the whole day on a 2-hour examination while others will finish within 45 minutes, the average student being able to complete the test in the allotted time. The length of the test will vary according to its purpose, the kinds of items used, the reliability desired, and the age and ability of the pupils tested.

1. *Purpose.* If the test is only for a unit of work rather than for the total term's or year's work, it will require fewer items. Why? Because the unit test will be concerned with fewer content areas and objectives, and hence fewer items will be needed to achieve adequate content sampling. For diagnostic (rather than prognostic) purposes, there will generally be a need for more items, inasmuch as the teacher is concerned with a more thorough and intensive coverage in a diagnostic test than he would be in a survey achievement test. The length of a test will also be dictated by whether the test is to be used for frequent formative evaluation, which is a necessary condition for individually prescribed instruction (IPI), or for summative evaluation. In IPI, there is constant testing. However, there are techniques where the precision of a criterion-referenced test can be increased using a minimum number of items (Novick, 1973; Novick & Lewis, 1973).[14]

2. *Kinds of items used.* The essay question will require more time than the objective item. Short-answer items will require more time than true-false items. True-false items will require less time than multiple-choice items (Frisbie, 1971). Some general guidelines that we can offer about test length in relation to the kind of item format used are as follows:

A. For the four- or five-response multiple-choice item used in the higher elementary and senior-high grades, the majority of students should be able to respond to the item in about 75 seconds. Hence, if the testing period is 50 minutes, the teacher can plan on using 35-five-response multiple-choice items. Although only about 44 minutes are used for actual testing, the remaining time is needed to distribute and collect the test, give directions, and clarify any questions that the students might have. Naturally, the complexity of the subject matter and objectives being measured, the fineness of the discrimination needed, and the number of alternatives will affect the time needed for the pupil to respond to the item (Frisbie, 1971).

---

[14]For a discussion on the test length and setting of passing scores for criterion-referenced tests, see Millman (1972, 1973).

B. For a short-essay response (about a half-page), most students can answer about six questions in a 1-hour testing period.[15]

C. For the longer essay (2 to 3 pages), most junior- and senior-high pupils can answer about three questions in 1 hour. For students in the fourth or fifth grade, one might only be able to ask two "long" essay questions in a 1-hour testing period.[16]

D. For the short-answer, matching, or true-false item, a rough guideline is that it will take the pupil about 50 seconds to respond to each item. Therefore, in a 1-hour testing period, the teacher can reasonably expect to give a 60-item test.

E. For every pair of four-response multiple-choice questions answered, the student is able to answer three true-false items (Frisbie, 1971).

With the exception of the 3:2 ratio for multiple-choice to true-false items, all other limits are not supported by empirical research but are based upon the authors' personal experience and conversations with teachers. We strongly recommend that the teacher consider these times as suggestive only, and early in the term he should administer a test to his pupils, record the actual time required for the majority of his pupils to complete the test, and govern himself accordingly for future tests with these pupils. Remember—you do not want to hurry the student, but you must impose some arbitrary time limits.

3. *Reliability desired.* Recall from Chapter 5 that (other things being equal) the longer the test, the more reliable it tends to be, since random errors cancel each other out. The degree of reliability desired will influence test length.

4. *Pupil's age.* By and large, young children tend to read, write, and maybe even think slower than older children. Also, young children tend to become restless and tire more readily than older children. Hence, tests for primary-grade pupils cannot be as long as tests for junior- and senior-high pupils.

5. *Ability level of pupils.* Just as young children need more time to respond to a test item than do older children, slow-learning children also require more time than average or gifted children. The teacher must know his pupils and be governed not only by the type of item format used, but also by the students' characteristics insofar as the length of the test is concerned.

It should be readily evident now why we initially stated that there is no formula the classroom teacher can use to determine the length of his test. We

---

[15] These estimates, of course, would vary according to the nature of the questions and the content area.

[16] If the teacher feels that he must use a longer essay test and if the ability and/or age level of his pupils dictate a shorter testing time, he should divide the test and administer it on successive days.

have offered some suggestions regarding the time needed by pupils to read and respond to different item formats. But these are *suggestions* only and must be interpreted in the light of a variety of factors and conditions. Gauging the amount of time needed to complete a test is something that develops with experience. Much depends on the nature of the content and the skill of the teacher in writing clear, concise, unambiguous items. Each teacher must, through experience, determine time limits that are practical for his students and his test. When in doubt, be overgenerous in setting time limits.

Item Difficulty[17]

The classroom teacher can make his test very easy, very difficult, or in between. There are some teachers who feel that they can purchase the respect of their students by giving them easy tests. They are wrong! There are some other teachers who feel that the more difficult the test, the better; that a difficult test will separate the sheep from the goats; that a difficult test will command respect from pupils and parents. They are also wrong. About the only positive thing that we know about difficult tests is that they tend to make pupils study harder (Marso, 1969; Sax & Reade, 1964). The concept of difficulty or the decision of how difficult the test should be depends upon a variety of factors: notably (1) the purpose of the test, (2) the ability level of the students, and (3) the age or grade level of the students. (These are the same factors that must be considered in planning the number of items as well as the item format to be used.) Disregarding these factors for a moment, we do not think that it is bad to give a very easy test occasionally if for no other reason than to instill some feelings of confidence and self-respect in the slow-learning student. On the other hand, we recommend the use of an occasional hard test to challenge the brighter students and/or show them that they are not so bright as they think they are. There is a time and a place for the more difficult test—it is especially valuable for the good students so that they will be prepared for such exams as the College Boards (and will not become paranoiac when they do not do as well on them as they did on teacher-made tests). But be careful not to make the difficult test so excessively difficult that you really frighten the students.

What we are attempting to say is that there must be a good reason for giving either a very easy or a very difficult test. We abhor the custom of giving hard tests solely for the sake of difficulty itself. We concur with Hedges (1966) who said, "what such teachers are really saying is that they either refuse or are unable to give tests appropriate for their students at a particular stage of their development."

The concept of difficulty has more meaning for the objective type of test

[17] Item difficulty is expressed in terms of the number of examinees who answer an item correctly. This will be discussed more fully in Chapter 11.

than it does for the essay or oral examination. In the former, the answer is either right or wrong; in the latter, there can be varying degrees of correctness. Item difficulty is also of more concern when we want the test to discriminate among pupils in terms of their achievement than if the test is designed to be used as a *diagnostic* or *mastery* test. In a diagnostic arithmetic test given in an average class, we might reasonably expect the majority of pupils to do well and have only a few relatively low scores (an "easy" test). In a diagnostic test we are *not* interested in comparing the relative standing of Ilene and Lori; rather, we want to know the strengths and weaknesses of *both* girls so that we can recommend appropriate remedial instruction if and when it is warranted. In a mastery test we would also expect the test to be relatively easy because, presumably, the teacher taught in such a way that certain minimal essentials (skills and/or knowledge) were learned or mastered by all or a great majority of his pupils. If the test is being used as a pretest (that is, given to the students before a particular unit or concept is introduced) to help develop effective teaching materials and/or strategies, we would expect most students to do poorly because they have not as yet been *taught* the material. Hence, for *mastery, diagnostic,* and most *pretests,* we are less concerned with difficulty because it is *not* our intent to differentiate or spread out people according to their achievement level.

Regardless of what the pupils' scores are, we get the information we want —the pupils' strengths and weaknesses; the extent of their prior knowledge; and an indication of the extent to which they have mastered certain basic fundamentals. Generally, we would not be very concerned with the difficulty level of items in any test other than one designed to measure relative achievement. But, there are many instances where our intent is to discriminate among pupils. For selection and classification purposes, we ordinarily want a test that produces a spread of scores.

To obtain information that will enable the teacher to differentiate (discriminate)[18] among his pupils in terms of their relative achievement, the teacher should prepare questions that, if no guessing occurs, about one-half the pupils would be expected to answer correctly and about one-half would be expected to answer incorrectly (the test is then said to be of average difficulty).

We believe that even a test used for discrimination purposes should consist of a few very easy and a few very difficult items. If this policy were adopted, the poorer students could be motivated to continue, especially if the easy items were at the beginning of the test, while the brighter students could be challenged. *But, by far, the majority of the items should be of average difficulty.*

[18] The extent to which we know how well the students are being differentiated by the items is referred to as *item discrimination.* Item discrimination will be discussed in greater detail in Chapter 11.

In summary, how difficult a test should be depends to a large extent upon its purpose (that is, how the test results will be used). If the test results are to be used to describe the status of the individual pupils (criterion-referenced), the concept of item difficulty has little meaning. However, if the test results are to be used to differentiate among pupils in terms of their achievement, the concept of test and item difficulty has meaning. This is still another reason that teachers must know what use will be made of the test results.

When to Test

Teachers often ask, "When should I test my students? Should I test every week? After the unit has been completed? Once or twice a semester?" Some teachers prefer to test on small segments of the course at frequent intervals. Other teachers prefer testing less frequently and on larger units of the course. The majority of teachers usually govern themselves by the marking and reporting schedules of their school. As of now, there is no evidence to show that a test based on a small segment of the course is better than a test that samples a larger unit of the work. We prefer frequent testing because it can provide a more reliable basis for evaluation, in addition to keeping both teachers and students better informed of student (and teacher) progress. However, we realize that too-frequent testing might impinge upon instructional time.

Once again, the uses of the test results will determine the frequency of testing. In most objectives-based instructional programs where formative evaluation procedures are appropriate, pupils are (or should be) given short, criterion-referenced tests frequently to apprise the teacher of the pupils' performance and identify those in need of additional or remedial instruction.

If pretests, posttests, and delayed posttests are being used to feed continuous information to the teacher to guide him in his instructional program, then frequent testing will be needed. If teachers use the results of tests to determine whether the student has mastered the material and is ready to proceed to the next unit of instruction, then frequent testing may be needed, depending upon the number of steps involved in the program.

The nature of the pupils may also affect the frequency of testing. Teachers dealing with the slow learner, the child in need of remedial instruction, and the very bright child may test at frequent intervals. Our opinion is that the teacher should determine the frequency of testing, for he is in the best position to make this decision. In general, we recommnd that tests be administered at least twice a semester and, where feasible, as often as possible since more frequent evaluation is superior to less frequent evaluation (Gallagher & Gay, 1976; Gaynor & Millham, 1976; Martin & Srikameswaran, 1974). We disagree with those critics of testing who contend that testing time detracts from teaching time. This may be so if poor tests are used or if the teacher does not use the results of the tests to obtain information on the pupils' strengths and weaknesses. But if valid tests are used and if teachers take the time to analyze the nature of both the correct and incorrect responses, test results can be an effective and valuable source of information for both teachers and learners.

Should Every Pupil Answer Every Item?

Conventional testing practices require that every pupil attempt (or be administered) every test item. Considering the heterogeneity in ability and aptitude among the pupils in the typical classroom, such a procedure is highly inefficient. And if the tests are administered to obtain group rather than individual results or for group rather than individual decision making, such a procedure is also inefficient. Valid and reliable group information can be obtained using a matrix sampling approach where no one pupil receives all the test items.

But what about the instance where the teacher wants to have information on the individual pupils in his class to govern his instructional strategy? Does he have to administer every item to every pupil? No! He can employ *tailored testing*, which is really building or administering a test that is fitted to the individual pupil.

Nature of the Stimulus: Verbal or Pictorial?

The nature of the test-item stimulus is highly dependent upon the nature of the content being tested (for example, a performance test in woodworking lends itself better to use of nonverbal stimuli) and the age of the pupils tested (very young children cannot read). For young children we recommend using lots of pictures, a minimum of verbal material (unless one is measuring reading or reading readiness), and a simple vocabulary appropriate to the students' age and ability, lest the test become a reading or general aptitude test.

SOME GENERAL CONSIDERATIONS IN WRITING TEST ITEMS

Regardless of the item format used, there are two essential ingredients that every test item must possess—validity and reliability. Validity and reliability of the individual items as well as the test as a whole can be achieved only when (1) each test item is expressed in clear, unambiguous language; (2) the students are not given any clues to the correct answer; (3) the scoring is objective; and (4) a table of specifications has been prepared and followed.

The different item formats are susceptible to different types of errors. These specifics will be dealt with when we consider the preparation of the essay question and the different types of objective items in the chapters to follow. However, there are some general factors that should be considered by the item writer regardless of the item format. These will be discussed at this time. Some have already been mentioned, and some will be elaborated upon in Chapters 9 and 10, but we feel that they bear repetition because of their importance in writing good test items.[19]

Preparing the Test Item

1. *Carefully define your instructional objectives.* Without well-defined, specific, and clear instructional objectives, it will be very difficult to provide for optimal learning on the part of the student and optimal instruction on the part of the teacher. And since a teacher-made test—regardless of the item format—is prepared specifically to measure the extent to which the instructional objectives have been realized, one cannot begin the preparation of a valid test without carefully defined instructional objectives.

2. *Prepare a test blueprint, keep it before you, and continually refer to it as you write the test items.* You will recall that the test blueprint or table of specifications relates the course objectives to the subject-matter content. It tells you the kinds of information you want to obtain. The test item is an outgrowth of one or more cells of the table of specifications. Continually refer to your test blueprint to help ensure that you will have a test with adequate content validity. It is much easier to build content validity or adequate sampling into your test as you write the test item than it is to refer to your blueprint after writing the items and then finding that some cells have been overrepresented while others have been underrepresented in proportion to the emphasis placed during the instructional phase. Starting with the test blueprint should make your task easier in the long run.

Remember! Make sure that each and every test item is "matched" with the instructional objective(s) it has been designed to measure. The best test items may still result in your having an invalid test if the items do not reflect the instructional objectives.

3. *Formulate well-defined questions.* Some of the criticisms leveled against tests are the result of questions that are vague, ambiguous, and too global. Not only may such questions cause the student difficulty in that he is unsure of what the teacher is looking for, but they may also cause the teacher problems in reliably scoring the answer (especially the essay and short-answer).

4. *Avoid excessive verbiage.* Verbal overload must be controlled lest the test become one of reading ability or general intelligence. Teachers, in their attempt to clarify, too often confuse rather than elucidate by excessive wording. We agree with Bornstein and Chamberlin[20] (1970), who said "the langu-

---

[19] See Tinkelman (1975) for examples of good and bad test items.

[20] Although the research and subsequent recommendations were based on multiple-choice items, it is applicable to any item format and therefore is considered here rather than under the writing of multiple-choice items in Chapter 10.

age used on multiple-choice achievement test items should be no more complex than is necessary to test the examinees' knowledge of the subject matter."

5. *The test item should be based on information that the examinee should know (or be able to deduce from the context) without having to consult a reference source.* We all know that even the best test contains only a sample of the possible questions that can be asked. And we are all aware that no one student can commit *all* the course content to memory. We should therefore *not* expect the student to have an encyclopedic mind. The course objectives upon which the test is based should *not* test minutiae unless those minute details are vital to meeting the course objectives. For example, in a course in pharmacology we should not expect students to memorize the dosages or limits of normal values or toxicity of every drug that is on the market. There are, of course, certain drugs that are frequently used or dispensed and we might expect the student to know the characteristics of them. We should only test on information that is within the daily working knowledge of the examinee. Naturally, if certain formulae, for example, are needed to solve a problem, and a course objective was *not* to commit formulae to memory, they should be provided to the examinee. The crux of this issue, of course, is getting agreement as to what the basic minimal skills are.

6. *Use the most appropriate stimulus.* Although the actual test item may be verbal, if the test item is based upon some external stimulus, the stimulus need not be verbal. There are many instances in achievement testing where equipment configurations can only be presented pictorially or where the material in, say, economics might be clearer if presented in graphic or tabular form rather than by means of a verbal description. When this is the case, the nature of the stimulus is nonverbal. But the test constructor must think about the most effective method of presenting the stimuli *before* the item is written. Otherwise, the test results may be unreliable and invalid. A question you might pose at this time would be whether there is any difference between illustrated and verbal items insofar as pupil achievement is concerned. Yes, there is. Schwartz (1955) compared illustrated items with written items and found, as might be expected, that illustrations were better in the lower grades than in the upper grades. Washington and Godfrey (1974) used a sample of airmen and reported that (a) with respect to difficulty and discrimination, illustrated items generally resulted in better performance than when matched written items were used, and (b) the best type of illustrated item was the *table* or material that can be expressed in numerical form. Accordingly, we recommend that at least for the lower elementary grades and for some specialized technical content areas, serious consideration be given to using an illustrated stimulus, a minimum of verbal material (unless one is measuring reading or reading readiness), and a vocabulary that is appropriate to the students' age and ability, lest the test become a general aptitude or reading test.

7. *Try to avoid race and sex bias.* Many persons, both within and outside the education profession, have criticized tests (the attacks have been

directed primarily at standardized tests) claiming that they exhibit a race and sex bias. Although we will discuss this issue more thoroughly in Chapters 14, 15, and 19 when we consider standardized tests and inventories, we believe that teachers should be aware of, and concerned with, these issues so that they will strive to develop tests that are as free as possible from race and sex bias.

It goes without saying that we are in favor of taking all possible precautions in using words or vocabulary that are free from racial or sexual biasing or stereotyping. Teachers must correctly select words that are not differentially understood by different ethnic groups or by males and females. For example, if all the story problems on a teacher-made mathematics test involved males engaged in athletic events or females engaged in homemaking activities, this would be an example of sex stereotyping. If one used the vocabulary of the black inner-city youth and if these words were not understood by other students unfamiliar with this vocabulary, this would be an example of inappropriate vocabulary *unless* one was specifically testing for the pupils' knowledge of these words.This last point needs to be emphasized! If vocabulary knowledge or understanding of a concept is the learning objective being tested and it is seen that one ethnic or racial or sex group does better on the test because they really know more or understand better, we would *not* call the test biased. But, if one group did better on a test because of the language used, the test may be biased. Actually, if a teacher follows the guidelines offered in this chapter for writing test items, there should be little bias of the latter type in his/her tests.

Finally, we should stress that the furor over race and sex bias in achievement tests has been raised without the protagonists presenting any good (valid) empirical evidence to demonstrate the detrimental effects on the examinee's performance. As will be seen in later chapters, there are factors such as the examinee's personality, the difficulty and discrimination of the test items, and the ambiguity of wording that affect an individual's test performance.

8. *Write each test item on a separate card.* Often when writing test items, teachers write one item after another on a sheet of paper. We encourage you to write each test item on a separate card. Why? This will permit you to record any item analysis data (this will be discussed in Chapter 11) directly with the item, and will be the beginning of a test file that can be used to yield items for future tests.

To assist in checking the test items against the test blueprint so as to obtain content validity, we suggest that the item be keyed to the objective and content area measured, the key being placed in either the upper right- or left-hand corner. Finally, with each item on a separate card, it is easy to sort the cards so that all item formats are together.

9. *Prepare a scoring key or guide, preferably as the item is being written.* By preparing your scoring key in advance, it may be possible to see that some of the items are ambiguous and should be revised.

10. *Prepare more items than you will actually need.* Every teacher should prepare extra test items to replace those discarded in the review process. For an essay test, we suggest that you prepare about a 25 percent overage of items. For an objective test, we suggest about 25 percent extra items be written for each cell in the test blueprint. For example, assume in Table 7–3 that we had a 100-item objective test. If 5 percent of the test is devoted to knowledge of methods of science, you should prepare six items. We are quite certain that some of your original items will have to be replaced. But even if you are fortunate and have to replace only two or three objective items, the remainder can be used as the base for a later test.

11. *Write the test item as soon as possible after the material has been taught.* The best time to write an item dealing with a particular behavioral objective (outcome) is immediately after covering the material in class. It is at this time that the item appears in its complete context and the relationship of the item to a particular objective is most clear. Even if the teacher only sketches out two or three items when the material is presented in class, over a period of time he will have a sizable pool of tentative items that can be refined later and incorporated into his test. By writing the items over a long period, the teacher avoids some of the problems discussed earlier. Good item writing takes time, and for the ordinary classroom teacher, time is at a premium. If, however, items are written on a frequent basis (preferably daily) the last-minute rush can be overcome in part.

12. *Prepare the items well in advance to permit reviews and editing.* Very seldom is an item writer, be he a classroom teacher or a professional, fortunate enough to prepare a test item that does not require at least some slight revision or modification. Ideally, the review phase and subsequent editing should occur some days after the item has been written. This will allow the item writer to look at his items with a fresh perspective so that, hopefully, he will be able to see some errors that he may have originally missed when he read the item just after writing it. One of the major faults of poor items is that they often do not communicate effectively the item writer's intent. The item writer knows implicitly what he is trying to measure—the pupil must be told explicitly. By having the editing phase occur a few days after the items have been written, the initial implicit clarity may be found to be cloudy. The best approach, of course, would be to have a fellow teacher (one who teaches the same subject matter) review the test items and directions.

13. *Avoid specific determiners.* Don't give the test-wise student any undue advantage over the naïve but equally knowledgeable student. Don't give test-wise students clues to the correct answer, such as a pattern or position effect in multiple-choice tests, or in true-false items using certain words such as "never" or "always."

14. *Be careful when rewording a faulty item.* The item writer must be very careful in reworking an item that has been found to be faulty lest he alter the particular objective the item was originally written to measure. Subtle

changes in the behavior measured are likely to occur when we rewrite some of the distracters in the multiple-choice item (Gronlund, 1971) and when we change a completion item to a multiple-choice item, or vice versa (Knapp, 1968).

What Does It Take to Be a Good Item Writer?

The process of writing good test items is not simple—it requires time and effort. It also requires certain skills and proficiencies on the part of the item writer, some of which can be improved by formal course work; others require considerable practice. Rules, suggestions, guidelines, and textbooks may be useful, but they are *not* the panacea for writing valid test items. Just as a surgery course in third-year medical school does not prepare the student to be a certified surgeon, no single course in tests and measurements will produce an innovative item writer. There is no doubt, however, that all these aids will be of some assistance, *provided* the item writer is willing to devote the necessary time and energy to the preparation of test items. In the long run, practice of the rules of item writing will help achieve perfection.

To be a good item writer, one should be proficient in six areas.

1. *Know the subject matter thoroughly.* The greater the item writer's knowledge of the subject matter, the greater the likelihood that he will know and understand *both* facts and principles as well as some of the popular misconceptions. This latter point is of considerable importance when writing the selection type of item in general, and the multiple-choice item in particular (because the item writer must supply plausible although incorrect answers).

2. *Know and understand the pupils being tested.* The kinds of pupils the teacher deals with will determine in part the kind of item format, vocabulary level, and level of difficulty of the teacher-made test. For example, primary school teachers seldom use multiple-choice items because young children are better able to respond to the short-answer type. The vocabulary level used for a class of gifted children may be very different from that used with a class of educable but mentally retarded children. The classroom teacher who knows and understands his pupils will generally establish more realistic objectives and develop a more valid evaluation device than will the teacher who fails to consider the characteristics of his students.

3. *Be skilled in verbal expression.* Some of the major problems or deficiencies of teacher-made achievement tests are related to problems of communication—ambiguous wording, poor choice of words, and awkward sentence structure. The item writer must be scrupulously careful at expressing himself verbally. It is essential that the item writer clearly convey to the examinee the intent of the question. In an oral examination, the pupil may have the opportunity to ask for and receive clarification of the question. In the traditional classroom pencil-and-paper test, this is not possible. We agree with

Ebel (1951, p. 187) that "it is probably true that no sentences are read with more critical attention to meanings, expressed and implied, than those which constitute test items."

4. *Be thoroughly familiar with various item formats.* The item writer must be aware that there is more to item writing than knowing that the major types of tests are either the essay or objective type. He must be knowledgeable of the various item formats—their strengths and weaknesses, the errors commonly made in writing this or that type of item—and the guidelines that can assist him in preparing better test items.

5. *Be persevering.* Writing good test items, regardless of their format, is both an art and a skill that generally improves with practice. Nevertheless, there are very few, if any, professional item writers who are so gifted, able, and blessed to write an item that requires absolutely no editing or rewriting. Depending upon the skill of the item writer, the number of items that need rewording or will be rejected will vary. The important thing is that classroom teachers who are trained as teachers rather than item writers should be persevering and not give up hope, even though the task seems overbearing.

6. *Be creative.* The abundance of sterile, pedantic items normally found on teacher-made achievement tests results from the reticence of teachers to be creative. Tests need not be somber and imposing. Teachers can be novel! Occasionally, in the item stem or descriptive material (or pictorial) upon which some items are based, there can be some humor injected. For example, in an arithmetic test, why not in a verbal problem for addition say "Mr. Adder" instead of Mr. Jones? At the same time that we urge you to be creative, we must caution you not to become too creative, since your enthusiasm might lead to the preparation of items that no longer test for, or are related to, the instructional objective for which they have been written. Also, be careful in your attempt to become creative that you do not become overly verbose.

Ideas for the Test Items

It would indeed be fortunate if the classroom teacher could consult his favorite genie to give him ideas for his test items. Before one is able to prepare a test item, he must have ideas. While the test blueprint specifies the content areas to be covered and the relative emphasis to be placed on each area and instructional objective, it does *not* directly give the item writer ideas that he can develop into test items. These the item writer must supply on his own. Where, then, does the classroom teacher get ideas? Primarily from the textbook or syllabus, other tests, journal articles, and questions raised by his pupils in class. It is not too difficult to develop ideas for measuring factual recall of information. It becomes progressively more difficult as one climbs the hierarchy in the taxonomy (Bloom, 1956) and as one tries to invent appropriate novel situations. The final selection of ideas to be developed into test items is dependent upon (1) the purpose of the test, (2) the test blueprint, (3) the importance of specific material covered in class, and (4) the items' ability to discriminate between those students who do and do not know the material. Each of these factors must be considered.

Constructing Criterion-Referenced Tests

The procedures (and principles to be followed) for writing criterion-referenced test items do *not* differ appreciably from those to be considered when writing norm-referenced test items. *Both* criterion- and norm-referenced tests should be developed with a table of specifications; *both* should be concerned with validity and reliability (although the procedures used to compute reliability may differ, and the type of validity deemed important may also differ); and *both* should be used to help make decisions about the individual, differing only in the context within which these decisions are made.

Two general approaches have been used frequently for the construction of criterion-referenced tests: (1) the empirical approach and (2) the universe-defined approach.[21] In the empirical approach, items are selected on the basis of their ability to differentiate between pupils who have been taught the material and those who have not been taught the material (this will be discussed in greater detail in Chapter 11). Examples of the "universe-defined" approach are Ebel's (1962) content standard method, Bormuth's (1970) linguistic transformation method, and Osburn's (1968) and Hiveley, Patterson, and Page's (1968) item-form methods. The goal of all these methods is to define the universe of all possible items in a given domain so that one may be able to generalize from an individual's test score on a representative sample of items to a statement about his proficiency level in the total domain. Bormuth (1970) suggested developing a set of rules that operationally define the transformation of instructional materials into items to eliminate item-writer bias. Many criticisms have been raised about the utility of this model (Cronbach, 1970b; Diederich, 1970; Mehrens, 1970). Osburn (1968) and Hiveley et al. (1968) described versions of an "item-form" procedure for the construction of universe-defined tests. Osburn's (1968) method emphasized the generation of a population of items that directly mirror the logical structure of the subject-matter content in some domain rather than the learning outcomes of the sort usually embodied in instructional objectives. This therefore necessitates that the instructional objectives be of a global nature. Hiveley et al. (1968) also used the item-form approach, but their model differs from Osburn's in that instructional objectives are directly transformed into item forms without going through the subject-matter structure. Thus, for each skill, a series of domains is specified, and within each domain are listed the skills to be tested. For each skill, an item form consisting of a "general form"

[21] See Jackson (1970) and Millman (1973) for a review of literature on constructing criterion-referenced tests.

and a series of "generation rules" is developed. Unfortunately, there are few domains other than mathematics where it would be possible to specify item-generation rules of the type he proposed. It would appear that a combination of the Osburn-Hiveley models would be best. If so, the test constructor will have his domain (collection of item forms) from which test items can be selected and the teacher will have his domain that clearly specifies what is to be taught. However, much work remains to be done.

SUMMARY

The principal ideas, conclusions, and recommendations presented in this chapter are summarized in the following statements:

1. Teacher-made test results are often the major basis for evaluating student progress.
2. All teachers have an obligation to assess the validity and reliability of their instructional procedures. The teacher-made test is one procedure for accomplishing this.
3. Although paper-and-pencil tests are the most frequently used formal evaluation procedure, some important instructional objectives can be evaluated only by observational techniques.
4. Classroom tests, despite some of their limitations, will never be replaced because they (a) tend to be more relevant, (b) can be tailored to fit a teacher's particular instructional objectives, and (c) can be adapted better to fit the needs and abilities of the students than can commercially published tests.
5. A major deficiency of teacher-made tests is that they suffer from inadequate planning.
6. Teacher-made tests may be classified on the basis of item format, nature of stimulus material, and purpose.
7. Classroom tests may be classified as either essay or objective. Objective tests may be classified as supply or select type.
8. The test-planning stage must consider two general questions: (a) What is the purpose of the test? (b) What is the best means whereby the purpose can be achieved?
9. In developing a specific measuring instrument, the first task is to review the instructional objectives. Following this, the objectives are expressed in terms of student behavior. Then a table of specifications or test blueprint should be constructed.
10. The table of specifications ideally should be prepared by the pupils and teachers. It should relate the content to the instructional objectives.
11. There should be a match between every item and every instructional objective.
12. The essay test is especially appropriate for measuring the pupil's ability

to synthesize his ideas and express them logically and coherently in written form. Its major limitations are that it has limited content sampling and low scorer reliability.

13. The objective test permits the teacher to obtain a broader sampling of content in a given time, has higher scorer reliability, and is less susceptible to bluffing than is the essay test.

14. Both the objective and essay test have important roles to play in evaluating pupil achievement.

15. In the planning stage, before a test item is written, a variety of factors —such as the test's purpose, type of item format, length, difficulty, and nature of the stimulus material—must be considered.

16. The determination of appropriate item difficulty depends upon the purpose of the test. In general, achievement tests should be of average difficulty. A test that is either too difficult or too easy provides the teacher with little meaningful information.

17. The two major considerations that item writers must consider relate to (a) clarity of communication from the item writer to the examinee, and (b) writing the item so that the answer is not given away.

18. Skilled item writers know their subject matter thoroughly, understand their pupils, are skilled in verbal expression, and are familiar with the various item formats.

19. Criterion-referenced item writers employ procedures and principles essentially similar to those used by norm-referenced item writers.

20. The two most commonly used approaches for constructing criterion-referenced tests are the empirical approach and the universe-defined approach. In the former, items are selected on the basis of their ability to discriminate between pupils who have been taught the material and those who have not. In the latter, items are generated on the basis of item-generation rules.

CHAPTER EIGHT

The Essay Test: Preparing the Questions and Grading the Responses

© 1970 United Feature Syndicate, Inc.

The "get-ready" or planning stage discussed in Chapter 7 is vital if one wants to develop a valid test of pupil achievement. It is in this planning stage that the purposes of the test are set forth, the table of specifications—which relates the course content to the instructional objectives—is prepared, thought is given to the kind of item format to be used, and decisions are made about the length and difficulty of the test. The next step is to write test items. We must now translate our behavioral objectives into test questions that will elicit the types of behavior we are interested in measuring. One type of test item is the essay question.

The distinctive features of the essay question are: (1) the examinee is permitted freedom of response, and (2) the answers vary in degree of quality or correctness (Stalnaker, 1951).

Since there are demonstrable advantages as well as limitations associated with essay examinations, and since for many teachers the essay examination is the one used most frequently (whether appropriately or inappropriately), it seems advisable to try to develop procedures that will maximize the advantages and at the same time minimize the limitations of essay examinations. In this chapter we consider (1) the two major types of essay questions, (2) the various mental processes that can be elicited with essay questions, (3) the advantages and limitations of the essay question, (4) the reasons that essay tests are still so popular with teachers despite the many criticisms leveled at them, and (5) some suggestions on how to prepare and grade the essay question.

After studying this chapter the student should be able to—

1. Understand the differences between the restricted and extended-response essay questions.

2. List the two most serious limitations of essay questions and discuss methods of combating these limitations.

3. Discuss the reasons that essay tests are so popular, pointing out which reasons are supported by empirical research and which are mainly hearsay.

4. Follow the guidelines offered when constructing essay questions.

5. Differentiate between global and analytical scoring.

6. Follow the guidelines offered when grading essay questions.

7. Discuss the similarities between the essay and oral question.

8. Appreciate the value of, and need for, the essay question in classroom tests.

9. Do a better job in constructing and grading the essay question.

CLASSIFICATION OF THE ESSAY QUESTION

Essay questions are subdivided into two major types—*extended* and *restricted* response—depending on the amount of latitude or freedom given the student to organize his ideas and write his answer. Children of average ability (in grades 3–6) wrote better compositions in the structured mode, whereas children of higher ability did better in the unstructured mode (Servey, 1966).

Extended Response

In the *extended*-response type of essay question virtually no bounds are placed on the student as to the point(s) he will discuss and the type of organization he will use. An example of an extended-response essay question would be:

Describe what you think should be included in a school testing program. Illustrate with specific types of tests, giving reasons for your test selection. Your essay should be about 300 to 400 words in length (2 to 3 pages).

In answering this question, the pupil may select those aspects of the school testing program that he *thinks* are most important, pertinent, and relevant to his argument; and he may organize the material in whichever way he wishes. In short, the extended-response type of essay question permits the student to demonstrate his ability to (1) call upon factual knowledge, (2) evaluate his factual knowledge, (3) organize his ideas, and (4) present his ideas in a logical, coherent fashion. It is at the levels of synthesis and evaluation of writing skills (style, quality) that the extended-response essay question makes the greatest contribution.

Restricted Response

In the *restricted*-response essay question, the student is more limited in the form and scope of his answer because he is told specifically the context that his answer is to take. An example of the *restricted*-response essay question is:

Pavlov found that sometimes dogs he had conditioned to salivate when a bell rang failed to do so. How do you account for this? Your answer should be about one-half page in length.

This question is more restrictive than the example given for the extended-response essay in that the student need only address himself to one specific area rather than discuss a variety of alternatives.

By aiming the student at the desired response we minimize somewhat the problems of reliable scoring (which will be considered in detail in a later section), and we may possibly make scoring easier. But by restricting the student's response we give up one of the major advantages of the essay question—a measure of the student's ability to synthesize his ideas and express them in a logical, coherent fashion. Because of this, the restricted-response type of essay is of greatest value for measuring learning outcomes at the comprehension, application, and analysis levels, and its use is best reserved for these purposes.

Examples of Different Types of Essay Questions

One can make a further or more elaborate classification of essay questions on the basis of the types of mental activities required of the pupil. Weidemann (1933, p. 82) classified the essay examination into 11 major categories. Arranged from the simple to higher mental processes, these categories are as follows: (1) *what, who, when, which,* and *where;* (2) *list;* (3) *outline;* (4) *describe;* (5) *contrast;* (6) *compare;* (7) *explain;* (8) *discuss;* (9) *develop;* (10) *summarize;* and (11) *evaluate.* Monroe and Carter (1923) used 20 categories. We prefer their scheme because the question itself describes specifically the nature of information to be recalled by the student in answering the question.

It will be readily evident when you read the examples given below that some of the classifications are related more to the *restricted* response; others, to the *extended* response. However, it is very difficult to classify each of Monroe and Carter's 20 categories as either restricted or extended, since the nature of the question posed will, in many instances, determine whether it calls for a restricted or an extended response. What is more important, however, are some examples of kinds of questions that can be posed.

1. Comparison of two things:
   Compare norm- and criterion-referenced measurement.
2. Decision (for or against):
   Should the death penalty be abolished? Defend your answer.
3. Causes or effects:
   Why did fascism develop in Italy and Germany but not in the United States or England?
4. Explanation of the use or exact meaning of some phrase or statements in a passage:
   In Arms and the Man *Bluntschli says, "Nicola is the ablest man I've ever met in Bulgaria." Explain the meaning of the word "ablest."*
5. Analysis:
   Does the Gulf of Tonkin resolution suffice as an explanation of U.S. involvement in Indochina? Support your answer with reasons.
6. Statement of relationships:
   Why does validity imply reliability but not the converse?
7. Discussion:
   Discuss Canadian Confederation under the following headings:
   a. The important reasons for a union
   b. The Confederation Conference
   c. The reasons for a choice of a federal union
   d. The important terms of the B.N.A. Act
   e. The division of powers between the Dominion and Provincial governments
8. Reorganization of facts:
   Trace the development of the industrial (in contrast to the laboratory) preparation of nitric acid.

9. Formulation of new question (problems and questions raised):

   Assuming that (1) the East and West will continue in their arms buildup, (2) more of the smaller nations will develop nuclear arms, and (3) minor skirmishes will be on the increase, what are some of the problems that man will have to face in the next decade? Discuss at least three such problems.

10. Criticism (as to the adequacy, correctness, or relevancy of a printed statement):

    Criticize or defend the statement: "The central conflict in Barometer Rising *is between Geoffrey Wain and Neil Macrae."*

ADVANTAGES AND LIMITATIONS OF THE ESSAY TEST

Over the past 50 years there have been many claims and counterclaims made regarding the superiority of the essay test over the objective test. As will be seen in a later section, many of these claims and counterclaims are not substantiated by research.

Advantages of the Essay

The advantages of the essay examination most frequently cited are that (1) it is relatively easier to prepare an essay test than to prepare a multiple-choice test; (2) it is the only means that we have to assess an examinee's ability to compose an answer and present it in effective prose (Ebel & Damrin, 1960); (3) it tests the pupil's ability to *supply* rather than select the correct answer; and (4) it helps induce a "good" effect on student learning.

Limitations of the Essay

The two most serious limitations of essay tests are (1) their poor (limited) content sampling, especially in the extended-response type of essay; and (2) their low reader reliability. Regardless of the thoroughness with which an essay test is constructed, you cannot sample the course content so well with six lengthy essay questions as you could with 90 multiple-choice questions. Not surprisingly, some students do better on some questions while others do better on others (Godshalk, Swineford, & Coffman, 1966; Gosling, 1966; Young, 1962). Thus a student's raw score (and relative score) will depend to some extent on the particular questions asked. The more questions, the less likely a student's score will suffer because of inadequate sampling of content and the greater the likelihood that the test will be reliable. Therefore, essay tests that contain several questions requiring short answers are preferable to a test that asks only one question requiring a lengthy answer.

The second major problem, that of reader reliability, can be minimized by careful construction of the questions and by setting up specified scoring procedures. To give you some idea as to the magnitude of the problem of reader reliability, let us relate the study of Falls (1928), which, though a study of reader reliability of an actual essay, gave results highly similar to results of essay tests. In 1928, Falls had 100 English teachers grade copies of an essay written by a high school senior. The teachers were required to assign both a numerical grade to the essay as well as to indicate what grade level they thought the writer was in. The grades varied from 60 to 98 percent and the grade level varied from fifth grade to a junior in college! With this type of variation across readers, it is no wonder that measurement specialists are concerned about the adequacy of essays (or essay tests) as evaluation procedures. If a score is so dependent upon who reads the paper rather than on the quality of the written exposition, it is probably not a very accurate reflection of the student's achievement.[1]

A third problem or limitation of essay test questions is that the student does not always understand the questions and therefore is not sure how to respond. (This problem also occurs in objective items but to a much lesser degree.)

A fourth limitation of the essay examination relates to the amount of time needed to read and grade the essay. Even if one were able to ensure that reliable scoring could be obtained, reading essays is very time consuming and laborious. Unlike objective items, essays can be read only by the teacher and/or competent professionals and not by clerks or teachers' aides. This is still the case, even though there has been research conducted to study the feasibility of grading essays by computer (Page, 1967; Whalen, 1971).

WHY ARE ESSAY TESTS STILL POPULAR?

As Coffman (1971) pointed out, "Essay examinations are still widely used in spite of more than a half century of criticism by specialists in educational measurement." The fact that an essay question has been reintroduced into the 1977 College Board English Composition Test, after a six-year lapse, and in the new ETS Basic Skills Assessment Program, suggests that despite some serious limitations, an expanded use of essay questions is underway.

Given the potential disadvantages of essay tests—poor predictive validity, limited content sampling, scorer unreliability, and scoring costs—why are they still in use? Why are essay tests so popular? Many reasons have been advanced for their popularity and importance in classroom testing. Perhaps one reason is that teachers are unaware of their limitations. However, there are other reasons—some with which we agree and others with which we

---

[1] See also Eells (1930), who showed that teachers scoring the same set of papers on a several-month interval between readings did *not* agree with their original judgments of the papers' quality. See also Coffman and Kurfman (1968), Marshall (1967), and Starch and Elliott (1912).

disagree. For some, we have evidence to support our claims. For others, we have no such evidence.

Acceptable Claims—Supporting Evidence

1. *Essay tests can indirectly measure attitudes, values, and opinions.* In the extended-response essay, the student is allowed latitude to select whatever ideas he wishes and to expound on his ideas in whatever manner he chooses. For example, to the question, "What does ecology mean to me?" the student will undoubtedly reveal certain attitudes and values in his response. He is more likely to reveal his true feelings in his essay response than if he were asked his attitudes about ecology on an attitude scale because, in the latter, he might be conscious of providing a socially acceptable answer. There is some evidence that the extended-response essay serves as a projective technique (Sims, 1931).

2. *Good essay tests are more easily prepared than are good objective tests.* We are *not* saying that good essay questions are easy to prepare. They aren't (even though some teachers feel that they are and give little attention to their preparation). However, in contrast to writing good objective items designed to measure the higher mental processes, it is easier, per unit of testing time, to prepare a good essay examination. For example, in a 2-hour testing period, a high school teacher can give six extended-response essay questions or he can give a 90-question, five-response, multiple-choice test. Now it may only require 1 or 2 hours to write a good essay question for a total of 6 to 12 hours preparation time. However, it takes an average of 1 hour to write a good five-response multiple-choice test item that measures more than factual recall. It takes time to generate plausible (even though incorrect) alternative answers in the multiple-choice item. At least 90 hours would be spent preparing a good 90-item multiple-choice test that measures the higher mental processes. Actually, about the same amount of time is needed to write a good essay question as to write a good multiple-choice item. But, since only a few essay questions are needed for a test, in comparison to the number of objective items, *essay tests* are easier to prepare than objective tests.

No doubt the factors of cost, time, and difficulty in writing multiple-choice test items to measure the higher mental processes make and keep the essay test popular.

3. *Essay tests provide good learning experiences.* Developing one's ability to select ideas, organize them, synthesize them, and express them in written form is an important educational objective. By writing essays, students are given practice in organizing their ideas, expressing their thoughts, and thinking through solutions to problems. Essay tests are a good learning experience for students (Vallance, 1947), especially when teachers take time to write comments on the papers.

Acceptable Claims—No Supporting Evidence

1. *If achievement is measured only by the selection type of objective test, there may be deleterious effects insofar as teaching methods are concerned.* Recognizing the problems involved in reliably grading essays, teachers might make no effort to teach for anything other than the students' ability to *select* the correct answer. If this were the case, an important educational objective would be ignored.

2. *Essay tests require the student to express himself logically, coherently, and in good English.*[2] The essay question, especially the extended-response essay, is the only medium to assess self-expression ability.

Rejected Claims—Justifying Evidence

1. *The essay test and only the essay test can be used to measure the higher mental processes of organization, analysis, and evaluation.* A common *misconception* prevails among many teachers that the essay and *only* the essay can be used to measure the higher mental processes. As of now, however, we can cite no evidence to substantiate the claim of proponents that the essay test is superior to the objective test for measuring learning outcomes involving the higher mental processes.

This does not mean that essay tests are useless and should be abolished from our classroom testing programs. The essay test is appropriate for measuring such objectives as attitudes, opinions, self-expression skills, and understanding. Essay tests are probably the best procedure for measuring some characteristics, such as writing ability, and the ability to create, synthesize, and evaluate ideas. But some objectives such as analysis and comprehension can perhaps be better (more objectively) measured by using the objective type of item. As an example, we use two questions cast in different formats but measuring the same skills with each item format.

The Setting or Background Information

A little mining town in Pennsylvania gets all of its water from a clear mountain stream. In a cabin on the bank of the stream above the town one of two campers was sick with typhoid fever during the winter. His waste materials were thrown on the snow. In the spring the melting snow and other water ran into the stream. In several days after the snow melted, typhoid fever and death struck the town. Many of the people became sick and 144 people died.[3]

---

[2] For an excellent review of the literature on the judging of writing ability by essay tests, see McColly (1970).

[3] Louis M. Heil et al., "The Measurement of Understanding in Science," in *The Measurement of Understanding,* Forty-fifth Yearbook of the National Society for the Study of Education, Part I, ed. Nelson B. Henry (Chicago: University of Chicago Press), pp. 129–130.

Essay Question

Does the incident described above show how the illness of one person caused the illness and death of many people? Support your answer using scientific facts or principles. [Your answer should be about 300 to 400 words in length (2 to 3 pages).]

Objective Question[4]

Part A. Directions: Below is a list of statements about the story. If you were to say that the man's sickness caused the sickness and death in the town, you may believe some or all of the statements. If a statement says something that an intelligent person should believe, then mark it as true.

Part B. Directions: If you were to decide that the man's sickness caused the sickness and death in the town, you would want to be sure about several things before you made that decision. Read the statements below again and check ($\sqrt{}$) the three which you believe are the most important to be sure about before you should decide that the man's sickness caused the sickness and death in the town. Do not check more than three.

Part A I believe the statement is true		Statements	Part B
YES	NO		
————	————	A. Water in mountain streams usually becomes pure as it runs over rocks.	————— a
————	————	B. Typhoid fever germs in drinking water may cause typhoid fever.	————— b
————	————	C. All of the drinking water of a small town like this one came from the mountain stream.	————— c
————	————	D. In a small town like this one there would not be nearly so many people sick at the same time with typhoid as the story tells.	————— d
————	————	E. Typhoid germs were the only kind of germs in the water.	————— e
————	————	F. There was no other possible way of getting typhoid—such as an impure milk supply in the town.	————— f
————	————	G. Typhoid fever germs did not get into the stream from some source other than the sick man.	————— g
————	————	H. A person by himself, like the camper, can get typhoid.	————— h

2. *Essay tests promote more effective study habits than do objective tests.* As of now, there is no proof that essay tests are superior to objective tests insofar as motivation and study habits are concerned. Different skills are

[4] Heil et al. (1946), p. 130.

involved when the student *supplies* rather than *selects* the answer. Study habits for the student studying for an essay test could conceivably be different if he were studying for an objective test (Alker ,Carlson, & Hermann, 1967; Biggs, 1971; Millman, Bishop, & Ebel, 1965; Stalnaker, 1951; Terry, 1933). Although Meyer (1935) found that students studied differently for essay than for objective tests, Douglass and Tallmadge (1934), French (1965), Terry (1933), and Vallance (1947) questioned the superiority of essay questions as catalysts or stimulators of effective work and study habits. No doubt some of the discrepancy between the findings of Meyer and French may be attributed in part at least to the improvement in the writing of the objective type of items. More recent research (Hakstian, 1971) demonstrated that, regardless of the item format (essay versus objective), students did *not* prepare differently in terms of time spent studying, organization of materials, and techniques employed.

RESTRICT THE USE OF ESSAY TESTS TO APPROPRIATE SITUATIONS

There are many instances where an essay test is used to measure factual recall or simple understanding of a concept or principle. No doubt you are all familiar, from your experience in taking essay tests, with items such as "Define valence," "Define kinetic energy," "What are mutations?" "What is a pronoun?" and so forth. This is a *poor* use of the essay examination. The major advantage of the essay examination is that it gives the student the opportunity to decide for himself *what* he wants to say (select ideas that he feels are most relevant to his discourse), *how* he wants to say it (organization of ideas), and then present his thoughts in his own words. If one of our instructional objectives is "the student will be able to select, integrate, and write effectively," the only way that we are able to measure the student's achievement is to have him write on a number of different topics and then grade his performance. For this objective, the essay is the most appropriate and valid medium. It is *not* appropriate to use the essay examination for the "what, who, where, when" situation (the objective test is vastly superior from the standpoint of adequate content sampling and reliable scoring). It boils down to this: If you want to see how well a student is able to express himself (be it on a writing sample in English composition or a discourse on the inevitability of the Civil War), by all means use the essay test. If you are more concerned with one's thoughts or feelings about an issue and how he defends them rather than in a correct or incorrect answer (although you could, if you wished, be interested in the latter in some instances), by all means use the essay. If you are interested in measuring the student's ability to criticize, to state cause-and-effect relationships, and to apply principles in a novel situation, you could use either the essay or objective test. *But do not use the essay test to measure rote memory of facts or definitions.*

WRITING GOOD ESSAY QUESTIONS AND PREPARING GOOD ESSAY TESTS: SOME GENERAL CONSIDERATIONS

You will recall that the essay test places a premium on the student's ability to produce, integrate, and express his ideas, and allows the student to be original and creative. These are the major distinguishing factors between the essay and objective item insofar as the purposes served by the test are concerned. A well-prepared essay question should give the student the opportunity to reveal those skills and abilities that you are interested in measuring. Just writing a question in the essay format does *not* guarantee that these skills will be tapped. For example, to measure understanding of "response set," the question "compare the halo, leniency, and severity effects" will require very little on the examinee's part other than the regurgitation of factual material.

Although we cannot give any "pat" answers to the question, "In a given amount of testing time, how can the essay test yield the most valid and reliable sample of the examinee's achievement?" we can offer some suggestions that, if followed, may help make this goal attainable.

1. *Give adequate time and thought to the preparation of essay questions.* In the essay test, fewer questions can be asked in a given testing time than if one were to use objective items. Hence, "goofs" made in preparing essay questions loom greater than those committed in an objective test. (One or two ambiguous questions in a 100-item objective test will have significantly less effect than would one poor essay question worth 20 points.) And yet, we have seen teachers walk into the classroom and with little or no advance preparation write a single test item on the blackboard, such as "Discuss the Monroe Doctrine." Faults, such as failure to delimit the problem, ambiguity of wording, and the global nature of the question, are all directly related to inadequate thought being given to the preparation of essay questions. Although the idea for an essay question and the preliminary wording may come more quickly than for a true-false or multiple-choice item, the teacher should allow himself sufficient time to edit each question so that he is satisfied that (1) it is measuring the intended objective, (2) the wording is simple and clear to the students, and (3) it is reasonable and can be answered by the students. Unless, however, adequate time has elapsed from the preliminary planning to the final writing of the essay question, it is very doubtful that the teacher can prepare a valid essay examination.

2. *The question should be written so that it will elicit the type of behavior you want to measure.* On the surface, this statement appears to be both obvious and easy to do. It is not. If a teacher is interested in learning the extent to which his history class students understand the difference between the League of Nations and the United Nations, he should not frame a question such as "What do you think of the U.N. in comparison to the League of Nations?" Framed this way, by and large, he will elicit the

students' *opinions* of, rather than their understanding of, the two organizations. (This does not mean that essay questions should not be used to measure opinions and beliefs. But it does mean that if one is interested in measuring understanding, he should not ask a question that will elicit an opinion.)

3. *A well-constructed essay question should establish a framework within which the student operates.* We recognize that there must be a "trade-off" of some sort in making the essay questions sufficiently specific and detailed to remove any possible sources of ambiguity[5] and yet give the student sufficient latitude to demonstrate his abilities. Latitude of response should not be interpreted as complete freedom of response. The teacher preparing essay tests must carefully tread the path between highly specific essay questions and too-general questions that confuse the student and for which no answer can be adequately given in the allotted time. We recognize that in our attempts to "aim" the student, we might remove one of the virtues of the essay examination—to measure the student's ability to select, integrate, and express his ideas. We take the position that we would rather remove some of the uniqueness of the essay test if by doing so we would be able to prepare essay questions that tell the student precisely what is wanted and what direction his answer should take.

Quite often, it is this lack of a framework that gives rise to the difficulty encountered by the student in knowing exactly what it is the teacher expects him to do. And, absence of a framework makes it more difficult for the teacher to grade the response reliably, since he may get a variety of answers to the same question, depending upon how the student interpreted it. This lack of a framework is primarily responsible for the common belief that you can bluff your way through an essay exam. As Perry (1963) wrote:

> "But sir, I don't think I really deserve it, it was mostly bull, really." This disclaimer from a student whose examination we have awarded a straight "A" is wondrously depressing. Alfred North Whitehead invented its only possible rejoinder: "Yes sir, what you wrote is nonsense, utter nonsense. But ah! Sir! It's the right kind of nonsense!"

Among the many ways in which a framework to guide the student may be established are (a) delimiting the area covered by the question, (b) using words that themselves give directions, (c) giving specific directions, or "aiming" the student to the desired response, and (d) indicating clearly the value of the question and the time suggested for answering it.

a. *Delimit the area covered by the question.* A high school chemistry teacher could ask an essay item such as "Describe the operation of a fire extinguisher." If he did, he might receive answers describing the operation

---

[5] To measure attitudes and values, we might want some ambiguity, but *not* to measure achievement.

of a soda-acid extinguisher or a foam type of extinguisher. The answers might be based on the chemical changes that take place, on the physical manipulations involved, or a combination of these and other factors. Some students might illustrate their answer with chemical equations, some might prepare a labeled diagram of the fire extinguisher, some might do both, and some students might do neither. Regardless of the manner or nature of the response, the student should know exactly what he is to do. This lack of specificity often gives rise to problems of validity. If, for example, the chemistry teacher is interested in learning the extent to which his pupils understand and can explain the operation of the soda-action type of fire extinguisher, he should rephrase his question:

With the aid of a diagram, explain the operation of the soda-acid type of fire extinguisher. Label the diagram. Write the equation(s) showing the reaction that takes place when the extinguisher is put into operation.

b. *Use descriptive words.* Words such as "define, outline, select, illustrate, classify, and summarize" are reasonably clear in their meaning. On the other hand, "discuss" can be ambiguous. Hence, if the word "discuss" is used, there should be specific instructions as to what points should be discussed.

It is also advisable for teachers to define the meaning of words such as "explain," "compare," and "contrast." Otherwise, differences in response to an essay question may reflect differences in semantic interpretation rather than differences in knowledge of the material among the pupils tested.

The vocabulary used should be as clear and as simple as possible so that the task required of the examinee will be as clear as possible. Although some students may not know the answer, *all* students taking the test should have a clear idea of what it is they are being asked to do.

c. *"Aim" the student to the desired response.* The purpose of any test is to assess the student's knowledge. In the essay test, we have an opportunity to see how well the students are able to organize their knowledge and express themselves logically and coherently. We are *not* measuring general intelligence. For the restricted-response essay, the examiner should write the question so that the student's task is defined as completely and specifically as possible. That is, the student is "aimed" at the response. He knows the specific factors the examiner wishes him to consider and discuss in his answer. Some might interpret this as being contradictory to "the essay question gives the student freedom of response" (see page 204). We do not think so. The student must still select, integrate, and express his ideas, even though his range may be more restricted. All we are really doing when we aim the student to the desired response is say, in effect, "we would like you to do your thinking and organization along these lines." We feel that the student is still permitted latitude even though he has been "aimed." An example of a question that does *not* "aim" the student is discussed in an interesting fashion by Calandra (1964).[6] We quote in part:

Some time ago, I received a call from a colleague who asked if I would be the referee on the grading of an examination question.

It seemed that he was about to give a student a zero for his answer to a physics question, while the student claimed he should receive a perfect score and would do so if the system were not set up against the student. The instructor and the student agreed to submit this to an impartial arbiter, and I was selected.

I went to my colleague's office and read the examination question which was, "Show how it is possible to determine the height of a tall building with the aid of a barometer."

The student's answer was, "Take the barometer to the top of the building, attach a long rope to it, lower the barometer to the street, and then bring it up, measuring the length of the rope. The length of the rope is the height of the building."

Now, this is a very interesting answer, but should the student get credit for it?

[6] Special permission granted by *Current Science*, published by Xerox Education Publications, © 1964, Xerox Corp.

I pointed out that the student really had a strong case for full credit, since he had answered the question completely and correctly.

On the other hand, if full credit were given, it could well contribute to a high grade for the student in his physics course. A high grade is supposed to certify that the student knows some physics, but the answer to the question did not confirm this.

With this in mind, I suggested that the student have another try at answering the question. . . .

Acting in terms of the agreement, I gave the student six minutes to answer the question, with the warning that the answer should show some knowledge of physics. At the end of five minutes, he had not written anything.

I asked if he wished to give up, since I had another class to take care of, but he said no, he was not giving up. He had many answers to this problem; he was just thinking of the best one. I excused myself for interrupting him, and asked him to please go on.

In the next minute, he dashed off his answer which was:

"Take the barometer to the top of the building and lean over the edge of the roof. Drop the barometer, timing its fall with a stopwatch. Then using the formula, $S = \frac{1}{2} AT$ squared, calculate the height of the building."

At this point, I asked my colleague if he would give up. He conceded.

In leaving my colleague's office, I recalled that the student had said he had other answers to the problem, so I asked him what they were.

"Oh, yes," said the student. "There are many ways of getting the height of a tall building with the aid of a barometer. For example, you could take the barometer out on a sunny day and measure the height of the barometer, the length of its shadow, and the length of the shadow of the building, and by the use of simple proportion, determine the height of the building."

"Fine," I said. "And the others?"

"Yes," said the student. "There is a very basic measurement method that you will like. In this method, you take the barometer and begin to walk up the stairs. As you climb the stairs, you mark off the length of the barometer along the wall. You then count the number of marks, and this will give you the height of the building in barometer units. A very direct method.

"Of course, if you want a more sophisticated method, you can tie the barometer to the end of a string, swing it as a pendulum, and determine the value of g at the street level and at the top of the building.

"From the difference between the two values of g the height of the building can, in principle, be calculated."

Finally he concluded, "If you don't limit me to physics solutions to this problem, there are many other answers, such as taking the barometer to the basement and knocking on the superintendent's door. When the superintendent answers, you speak to him as follows: 'Dear Mr. Superintendent, here I have a very fine barometer. If you will tell me the height of this building, I will give you this barometer.' "

The intent of this humorous but yet so realistic parable was to convey the message, "Ask a stupid question (that is, one so ambiguous and non-directive that nearly any type of answer would be acceptable) and you get a stupid answer."

Let us assume that a twelfth-grade teacher of Canadian history was interested in measuring the extent to which his pupils know and understand the terms of the Quebec Act, how it was received by various groups, and the permanent effect of the Act. We seriously doubt that he would elicit this response were he to frame the question as, "Discuss the Quebec Act of 1774," even though most of his students might know the answer. The question as written is so ambiguous that almost any answer could be given, including "it was one of the most important Acts in Canadian history." On the other hand, one student might concentrate on the terms of the Act; another might discuss the reactions of the clergy or habitants to the Act; another might discuss the political factors leading up to the Act; and still another might discuss the permanent effects of the Act. Each treatment might be well done and appropriate, but how are the answers to be scored?

The "better" example given below illustrates how this same essay question could be written so that it aims the student and still permits him some freedom of response and an opportunity to evaluate his ideas.

Better: Discuss the statement "The Quebec Act of 1774 has been described as one of the most important measures in Canadian history." In your answer, refer to (1) the terms of the Act; (2) how the Act was received by (a) the French clergy, (b) the seignors, (c) the habitants, (d) the Thirteen Colonies, and (e) the British; and (3) the permanent effects of the Act. Your answer should be about 300–400 words in length (2–3 pages).

Note: Don't be afraid to use long instructions or even give hints if this might help "aim" the student to the desired response. For the extended-response essay, the amount of structuring will vary from item to item, depending upon the objective being measured. The student should be given as much latitude as possible to demonstrate his synthesis and evaluative skills, *but the item should give enough direction* so that it is evident to the student that the question elicits these skills.

d. *Indicate the value of the question and the time to be spent in answering it.* In addition to making explicitly clear to the student what is expected of him, it is desirable that each question should indicate the approximate length of time the student is to spend answering it, as well as the value of the question in relation to the total test score. The student can then govern himself accordingly in deciding where he should place his emphasis in responding to the various essay questions.

4. *Decide in advance what factors will be considered in evaluating an essay response.* At this time we are not concerned with the substantive material desired in an essay response. This will be discussed in the section Grading Essays. What we are concerned with here is whether or not spelling, punctuation, composition, grammar, quality of handwriting, and clarity of

expression are to be considered in evaluating a pupil's response and hence in the score assigned to that response. If they are, this should be made very clear to the students *before* they begin their examination. An example of such directions is as follows:

> These questions are a test of your judgment, knowledge, and ability to present such knowledge in an appropriate matter. Cite specific facts to substantiate your generalizations. Be as specific as possible in illustrating your answers. Do not neglect to give dates where they are necessary for a fuller understanding of your response. Clearness of organization as well as the quality of your English will be factors considered in scoring your answers. (Solomon, 1965, p. 149.)

Our contention is that the "ground rules" of the test, especially the weighting of the questions and the subparts of the question(s), as well as information on the general criteria to be used in grading the test response, should be made known to the student *beforehand* with sufficient time so that he can organize and plan his study habits more effectively.

We feel strongly that, with the exception of an English or composition test, a student should *not* be marked down for misspelled words, faulty grammar, and poor handwriting. Similarly, he should *not* be rewarded (given extra marks) for displaying proficiency in these factors. This does not mean that the teacher should not note and (if he has the time) correct these errors. He should! Nor does this imply that teachers of other subjects (other than literature, English, or composition) should not correct spelling, grammar, and punctuation errors and comment on the quality of handwriting. They should! What it does mean is that unless this is an explicit course objective, it should not be considered in grading the pupil's answer.

5. *Do not provide optional questions on an essay test.* Three major reasons can be given why optional questions should not be given on an essay test: (a) It is difficult to construct questions of equal difficulty; (b) students do *not* have the ability to select those questions upon which they will be able to do best; and (c) the good student may be penalized because he is challenged by the more difficult and complex questions.

Unless all pupils are asked "to run the same race" by answering the same questions, it will not be possible to make valid comparisons of achievement among them (DuCette & Wolk, 1972; Futcher, 1973; Stalnaker, 1936; Swineford, 1956; Vernon & Millican, 1954).

Should the teacher be more lenient in grading those students who have selected the more difficult questions? Should he rate more severely the students who have answered the easy questions? It is not possible to compare students who, in essence, have taken different tests. Another reason against permitting a choice of questions is that if the students know this, they will be less motivated to study *all* the material, reasoning (whether correctly or incorrectly depends upon what they studied and the questions asked) that if they have a choice of questions, they should be able to find *some* questions that they will be able to answer moderately well.

With some possible exceptions (discussed in the next paragraph), we find no compelling reasons or arguments to support the claim that permitting students a choice of questions will be fairer because it will permit each student equal opportunity to do well. All factors considered, it is *not* beneficial to the student to give him options. Remember—the purpose of a test is not to show how well a student can do if allowed to select his own questions; rather, it is to ascertain his proficiency when responding to a representative set of questions.

There are, of course, extenuating circumstances where a partial choice of questions is justified. There may be some classes where the students are not presented with or taught common materials. For example, a high school chemistry class where the method of instruction was independent study might contain some students who spent the whole year working on the gas laws, some who worked on organic derivatives, and some who studied the toxological effects of DDT. In this same class, some students might have used a common text, others library references, and still others no text. In such a situation, having a common examination would be grossly unfair, and no doubt would be an invalid assessment of the pupils' competency. Or, there may be five chemistry classes taught by team-teaching wherein there are deviations from the common syllabus. Depending upon the nature of the course content, there may be a set of common questions for all students to answer, but there may also be a choice of questions to accommodate inter- and intraclass variations.

We are aware that a limitation of the essay exam is its limited sampling of content. We also recognize that having optional questions will help the "lucky" student who fortuitously only studied 20 minutes but was examined on what he studied. Then what solution is there? You are damned if you give optional questions and you are damned if you don't! Little can be done about the lucky student, but there is something that can and should be done about the limited sampling of content. The best solution to this problem is not to change the "ground rules"; rather, it is to obtain as many different samples of achievement as possible on as many different occasions as possible—that is, more frequent testing where *all* students answer the *same* questions. This is especially pertinent for those teachers who rely primarily upon essay examinations to assign final course grades.

6. *Use a relatively large number of questions requiring short answers (about one-half page) rather than just a few questions involving long answers (2–3 pages).* We prefer having many short, restricted-response essay questions, for a variety of reasons: (a) They will provide for a broader sampling of content, thereby reducing the error associated with limited sampling (reread "Reliability" in Chapter 5 if you don't know why). (b) They tend to discourage bias on the part of the teacher who grades for quantity rather than

quality. (c) The teacher will be able to read the answers more rapidly and more reliably because he has a mental set of what he should be looking for. (d) It is easier to "aim" the student to the desired response.

7. *Don't start essay questions with such words as "list," "who," "what," "whether."* These words tend to elicit and (rightly so) responses that require only a regurgitation of factual information. If this is the only way that you can begin the question, it is likely a short-answer (one or two lines) recall question and *not* an essay question as we have defined it.

8. *Adapt the length of the response and the complexity of the question and answer to the maturity level of the student.* A common fault of teachers using essay questions is that they expect too much from their students. The depth and breadth of discussion anticipated for sixth- and tenth-graders should be markedly different for the two groups, since sixth-graders are unable to conceptualize, organize, and express their thoughts as effectively as tenth-graders should be able to do. We might give a doctoral candidate a 6-hour examination on only one item, such as "Discuss the Civil War." But you would surely agree that this topic is too complex even for an undergraduate history major.

9. *Use the novel type of question wherever feasible.* To answer a question discussed in the textbook or in class requires little more than a good memory. But, to apply that same principle or thought process to a *new* situation requires a higher level of learning. Too many teachers think that they are measuring understanding and application when, in reality, they are only measuring factual recall.

An ingenious teacher can make any achievement test interesting to the examinee by casting the items in novel situations. For example, to measure the students' understanding of the halo effect, the teacher could write the following question:

The data presented in the table below [Table 8–1] are scores (the maximum value for each question is 10 points) on a unit test given by Mr. History to four students

TABLE 8–1   Grades Assigned by Mr. History

| Pupil | MARKS ASSIGNED TO QUESTION | | | | | |
	1	2	3	4	5	Total
Bill	8	9	9	8	8	42
Ruth	7	7	7	10	7	38
Irv	4	4	5	4	4	21
Beth	3	3	4	3	2	15

in his independent study course. Bill and Ruth are just average in ability as measured by conventional intelligence and achievement tests, but are well-behaved students and *never* challenge Mr. History Irv and Beth have excellent records as students and have each won a Merit Scholarship for next year, but they constantly challenge Mr. History on his interpretation and overgeneralization of facts. On the basis of the information presented, would you say that Mr. History exemplifies the "halo," "severity," or "leniency" syndrome? Support your answer. Your answer should be about 200 words in length (1½ pages).

To answer this question correctly, the student must (a) call forth his knowledge of the terms *halo, severity,* and *leniency,* (b) be able to interpret the data presented in the table, (c) integrate his information with the factual material, and (d) express his answer effectively in writing.

10. *Prepare a scoring key.* What is a good response to an essay question? What is an excellent response to an essay question? What points should the student discuss in his answer? Are there some points that are more important than others? As has already been mentioned, one of the more serious problems of the essay test is the subjectivity of scoring and consequent unreliability of scoring. Scoring can be made more reliable and more objective if the classroom teacher writes out in advance what he considers an "acceptable" or "model" answer. Or, if he wishes, he may read a sample of papers to determine various standards of quality. What is important, however, is that the "model" answer must be available *before* the set of papers is graded. Actually, we prefer that the teacher write out the "ideal" answer as the item is being written because it may bring to light ambiguity, unrealistic expectations, or other deficiencies.

Summary

We have suggested that it is essential to control all elements in the structure of the essay test that have no relevance to the pupil's performance if we hope to obtain a valid measure of his competence. To accomplish this, we should restrict the completely free response and "aim" the student in the direction that we wish him to take in answering the question. Three major factors should be considered in constructing essay tests: (1) the wording of the questions, (2) the use of many relatively short questions, and (3) requiring all students to answer the same questions.

We will now attempt to synthesize the previous discussion by listing the major factors to be considered when writing essay questions. We will then trace through, step by step, the development of a "good" essay question.

Table 8–2 should be used both as a preliminary and final check list rather than as a compilation of *the* rules to be followed in writing good essay questions.

TABLE 8–2   Check List for Writing Essay Questions

	YES
1. Is the question restricted to measuring objectives that would not be assessed more efficiently by other item formats?	✗
2. Does each question relate to some instructional objective?	✗
3. Does the question establish a framework to guide the student to the expected answer?	
a. Is the problem delimited?	✗
b. Are descriptive words such as "compare," "contrast," and "define" used rather than words such as "discuss" or "explain"?	✗
c. For the restricted-response essay in particular, is the student "aimed" to the answer by appropriate subdivisions of the main question?	✗
4. Are the questions novel? Do they challenge the student? Do they require the student to demonstrate originality of thought and expression?[a]	✗
5. Are the questions realistic in terms of—	
a. difficulty?	✗
b. time allowed the student to respond?	
c. complexity of the task?	✗
6. Are all students expected to answer the *same* questions?	✗
7. Is there a preponderance of short-answer (restricted-response) questions?	✗
8. Has a model answer been prepared for each question?	✗

[a] Originality need not be an objective for every essay question.

A Final Comment

It is imperative that teachers *teach their students how to take essay tests.* Other than a brief discussion in Chapter 11 on preparing the testing conditions and preparing the students emotionally, we have emphasized the construction of good classroom achievement tests and have paid relatively little attention to the preparation of students on how to take examinations. Although adequate preparation should be undertaken, regardless of the type of item format, it is of paramount importance insofar as the essay test is concerned. The student *may* have the knowledge and skills, but he must be *taught* how to organize and present his ideas most effectively. And in the essay test the pupil must understand the meaning of words (which, hopefully, are directive) such as *compare* (should the answer contain *both* similarities and differences or only similarities?), *contrast* (means only differences), and *list* (means only a listing without any attempt to organize). Student practice in writing essays, although not specifically related to the improvement of the essay test, per se, should result in the teacher's getting a more valid estimate of the student's competency.

AN EXAMPLE OF THE STEPS INVOLVED
IN WRITING A GOOD ESSAY QUESTION

Now that we have offered some suggestions for constructing an essay question, we will illustrate the steps one goes through in developing a good essay question. Remember our earlier comment that test construction is not an exact science and that writing good examination questions requires some ingenuity on the teacher's part.

Miss Social Studies, *before* teaching the unit on the Civil War to her twelfth-grade American history class, began to give some thought to the kinds of essay questions that she would use on her unit test the following week. After looking through the textbook and her teaching notes and materials, she prepared the following question:

List the events immediately preceding Lincoln's call to arms on April 12, 1861.[7]

When she first looked at this question it appeared acceptable. But when she went back to her table of specifications, she saw that she wanted to prepare an essay question that involved more than factual recall. She wanted a question that involved the higher mental processes of synthesis and evaluation. (Parenthetically, had she referred to her test blueprint before writing the item, she could have saved herself some time. But, better late than never.)

Miss Social Studies went back to her desk and prepared the following question as a replacement for the first one written:

What were the main issues that caused Americans to be divided and which eventually led to the Civil War?

On further reflection, Miss Social Studies saw in the revised item an undue emphasis upon the recall of factual material ("what"), and she decided that such an item would be better measured by a series of multiple-choice items. Miss Social Studies was not dismayed, but was beginning to get a clearer perspective of what she really expected from her students, so she went back to her desk and formulated this question:

There has been much debate and controversy among historians as to whether or not the Civil War was unavoidable. Some historians go so far as to say that it was a stupid war. Do you agree that the Civil War was *inevitable*? Why? Why not? Support your reasons with facts.

[7] Adapted with permission of Frank F. Gorow (1966).

Miss Social Studies rejected her latest question because she felt that it didn't "tap" the students' analytical skills. With this in mind, Miss Social Studies reworked the question as follows:

Although historians have argued about the inevitability of the Civil War, let us assume that there *never* was a Civil War in the United States. How do you think this would have affected the development of the United States subsequent to 1865? In your answer consider the slavery issue, the development of the West after 1865, economic factors, and our relations with European nations after 1865.

Miss Social Studies now had reached the point where she had a "good" essay item. The item was specific, related to the course objective, and was sufficiently delimited to give some direction to the student in preparing his response. But Miss Social Studies could make the item even more interesting to the students by setting the question in a novel situation and by involving the student. And she did do all these things when she reworked the question to read:

It is the morning of April 14, 1861. President Lincoln has called his cabinet into an emergency session to discuss the recent events. YOU have been invited to the cabinet meeting. As the meeting progresses, telegrams begin arriving, telling of the defeat of the northern troops by the experienced southern troops. Each cabinet member is asked his opinion on what to do. President Lincoln listens to all his cabinet and then turns and faces you. He asks YOU two questions: (1) What, if any, are the alternatives to war? and (2) What might happen if we don't go to war?

Your response should consider the development of the West after 1865, the social and economic factors, and U.S. relationships with European nations.[8]

Miss Social Studies is now finally happy and she has every right to be pleased with her question because it satisfies the major criteria of a "good" essay question. Before she is able to "put the question to bed," she still has to indicate the suggested time to be spent answering the question, indicate the value of the question, and inform the students whether or not spelling, punctuation, grammar, and handwriting will be considered in grading the answer.

[8] It should be recognized that this is only an example of the steps that the teacher goes through to prepare a valid essay question. As written, the question is very complex and would take a great deal of time to answer. In fact, we seriously doubt whether more than two or three such questions can be asked in a 2-hour testing period. We also recognize that by attempting to cast the item in a novel situation, we may be accused of excessive window dressing. There is no doubt that the same abilities could have been tapped by asking just two questions and giving the directions the student is to take. Our intent here is only to provide an illustration. However, we would not discourage having one such "window-dressed" question occasionally.

GRADING ESSAYS

In the essay test (in contrast to the objective test), the measurement of a student's ability does *not* end with his answer, but depends to a large extent upon the person who reads his answer and assigns a grade to that answer, as well as upon the grading method used.

After the teacher is satisfied that his questions (1) reflect his course objectives and (2) are carefully and accurately prepared, his next task is to make certain that he (or whoever might read the responses) exercises as much objectivity as possible in grading the responses. The effectiveness of an essay examination depends to a large degree on how well it is graded. An ill-conceived, poorly prepared essay test cannot be salvaged by even the most refined, valid, and reliable grading standards, *but* the most careful planning and construction can be ruined by improper grading procedures and standards. We cannot overemphasize the importance of reliably grading essay tests.[9] Unreliable grading has been one of the major and most valid criticisms leveled against their use.

In grading essay responses, one must (1) use appropriate methods to minimize biases,[10] (2) pay attention only to the significant and relevant aspects of the answer, (3) be careful not to let personal idiosyncracies affect grading, and (4) apply uniform standards to all the papers. Undoubtedly, the uniformity of grading standards (hence the reliability of the scores) is probably the most crucial aspect of essay grading. For without uniformity there is no valid way of comparing students. Moreover, without uniformity one cannot be certain that he has a valid measure of the student's achievement. Two commonly used methods have been developed for grading essay examinations—the *analytical* method and the *global* method. Which one should be used will depend to a large extent on the use and/or purpose of the test, the time and facilities available for reading the papers, and whether the essay is of the restricted- or extended-response type.

Analytical and Global Methods of Grading Essays

In the analytical method the ideal answer to a question is specified in advance.[11] In the global method the ideal answer may be specified in advance,

[9] See Van Der Kamp and Mellenbergh (1976) for a somewhat technical discussion of how to obtain reliable teacher ratings; Phillips (1976) for reliably grading free-response answers in career and occupational development; Mullis (1976) for scoring writing tasks; and Martin (1976) for scoring free-response mathematics items.

[10] Huck and Bounds (1972) reported a significant interaction between the graders' handwriting neatness and the neatness of the essay answer they were grading. To minimize this, they recommend analytical scoring (this is discussed in the next section).

[11] Although the model answer can be prepared just before the papers are graded, we strongly recommend (for reasons noted earlier) that it be prepared when the question is written. We would be remiss if we did not point out that, as of now, there is no empirical evidence to show that preparing the "ideal" answer results in higher reliability, although it helps make the scoring criteria explicit. Many factors other than the use of an "ideal" answer influence the grades assigned by the reader to an essay response.

although it need not be. Other than that, there is no similarity between the two procedures.

Analytical Method

In the *analytical* method (sometimes called the "point-score" method), the ideal or model answer is broken down into specific points. The student's score is based upon the number of points contained in his answer. In addition, component parts such as "effectiveness of expression," "logical organization," and "support of statements" are specified and assigned points of values. In a sense, then, we end up with a check list than can be used quite objectively. (For those interested in a scoring guide and check list for an essay question on the Civil War, a good example and prototype can be found in the 1964 College Entrance Examination Board Advanced Placement Examination in American History.)

If there are different points, should the teacher assign numerical values to each point and, if so, should there be different values for the different points? For example, to a question on the Civil War, should a student who mentions "growth of railroads and desire for federal subsidies" receive two points and the student who mentions "the Spanish American War" receive one point? We recommend that the teacher not be concerned with the weighting of the various points within the essay question inasmuch as research has shown it to be of negligible value (Stalnaker, 1938). This does *not* mean that essay questions per se should all be assigned the same point values in the test. Factors to be considered in assigning point values to the respective essay questions include (1) the time needed to respond, (2) the complexity of the question, and (3) the emphasis placed on that content area in the instructional phase.

As the teacher (reader) reads the responses to a particular question, he gives points for those component parts contained in the answer. For many years the analytical method was considered by measurement experts to be more reliable than global scoring because it was believed that the key provided a better basis for maintaining standards (uniformity) from reader to reader and from paper to paper. However, Gosling's (1966) studies did not show consistent results.

Ideally, the analytical method prevents or minimizes the influence of extraneous material, be it right or wrong. In actual practice, however, controlling for human variability is difficult to achieve, even though a detailed scoring guide is employed, because of the fallibility of the human reader. The major advantages of the analytical method of grading are as follows: (1) It can yield very reliable scores when used by a conscientious reader. (2) The very process of preparing the detailed answer may frequently bring to the teacher's attention such errors as faulty wording, extreme difficulty and/or complexity of the question, and unrealistic time limits. Hence, if the model answer had been prepared before the test was administered, the question could have been reworded or the time extended. (3) The fine subdivision of the model answer can make it easier to discuss the grade given to the student. One of the problems with essay examinations is that if a subjective impression is used to assign a grade, it is difficult to communicate and even justify at times. But the teacher could point out which pertinent facts were omitted from the pupil's answer. Thus the pupil could see that the teacher was fair in his grading—and this is worth something today! Two major limitations of analytical scoring are: (1) It is very laborious and time consuming; (2) in attempting to identify the elements, undue attention may be given to superficial aspects of the answer (Diederich, 1967, pp. 582–583).

Although the analytical method may be used for both extended- and restricted-response types, it is recommended primarily for the latter inasmuch as responses will tend to be very specific and not too lengthy. It is also more reliable for the latter for the same reasons.

Global Scoring

In *global* scoring (sometimes referred to as the *holistic* or *rating* method), the ideal answer is *not* subdivided into specific points and component parts; it simply serves as a standard. Papers that are less than ideal and vary across the quality continuum should be selected as other standards or anchor points. The rater is then instructed to read the response rapidly, form a general impression, and, using some standard, assign a rating to the response. The crux of this method is to select papers to serve as anchor points that vary in quality, and to train readers to go rapidly through a response and give some general or global impression of the quality of the response.

ESTABLISHING STANDARDS OR ANCHOR POINTS   Regardless of the scale values employed (that is, one could grade a response as "good," "average," and "poor," or one could make finer or less fine discriminations), the procedure employed to establish the scale values is the same. The teacher could prepare a variety of answers corresponding to the various scale points, or he could select papers from those already written and let the actual responses establish the various anchor points. (See National Assessment of Educational Progress, 1970b.)

READING THE RESPONSES   Depending upon the degree of discrimination required, papers may be read on a 2-point "acceptable-unacceptable" scale or on a 5-point "superior-inferior" scale. Four or five rating categories are probably sufficient for most purposes, although Coffman's (1971) review of research performed at ETS suggested that *with trained readers* as many as 15 categories can be used without slowing up the reading rate or decreasing reliability.

Although the training period should make readers consistent in applying the prescribed standards, it is suggested that occasional checks be made. Let us assume that one wishes to employ a 5-point scale such as

1. Superior quality
2. Above-average quality
3. Average quality
4. Below-average quality
5. Inferior quality

On a rapid reading of the response, the reader would assign it to one of five piles, depending upon the quality of the answer in relation to the different samples.[12] For example, a student whose paper was judged to be "average" would be placed in pile 3. It would then be a simple clerical task to assign score values to the papers in the various piles.

With global reading, each set of responses should be read and classified at least twice—preferably by a different reader the second time, who would assign an independent rating. This is not an undue hardship nor is it overly time consuming, since global rating is considerably faster than analytical rating once the standards have been established.

The global approach is very effective when large numbers of essays are to be read. It can be used by the classroom teacher who has as few as 30 papers to read. However, it might be more difficult to select papers for anchor points when only a limited number of papers are available to begin with (this would be especially true if the class were quite homogeneous). We suggest that when only a few papers are to be read, the teacher make a preliminary reading and assign each paper (actually each question being read) to one of the piles. Then, each question should be reread one or two times, and those found to have been misclassified should be reclassified.

Some Suggestions for Grading Essay Tests

After taking the steps previously discussed for the preparation of good essay questions, the guidelines offered below should help increase the reliability of the grading.

1. *Check your scoring key against actual responses.* If a teacher prepares a model answer when the essay question is prepared, it is conceivable that he may be overly optimistic with regard to the clarity of the question

---

[12] In the ETS and NAEP procedures, an actual numerical value is assigned to the paper rather than placing it in a pile and then assigning a value. This is done to permit an independent second reading. In a variation of the global method described by Sims (1931), the papers are first assigned to one of five piles, ranging from very superior to very inferior, and then the papers in each pile are reread and necessary shifts are made.

and/or the nature of the responses to be elicited by the question. Before actually beginning the grading process, it is suggested that a few papers be selected at random, to ascertain the appropriateness of the scoring guide. If it is seen that most students are giving responses different from those established *a priori*, this may be due to the students' misinterpretation of the intent of the question. For example, if the question was intended to measure "interpretation," but the responses indicate that the answers are at a lower level of understanding, the scoring criteria can be revised. *Once the grading has begun, the standards should not be changed, nor should they vary from paper to paper or reader to reader.*

2. *Be consistent in your grading.* It is one thing to say that all questions should be graded uniformly and another thing to actually achieve uniformity. Graders are human and therefore fallible. They may be influenced by the first few papers they read and thereby grade either too leniently or too harshly, depending upon their initial mind set. For this reason, once the scoring criteria have been checked out against actual responses and once the grading has begun, teachers should occasionally refer to the first few papers graded to satisfy themselves that the standards are being applied consistently. Otherwise, the grade a student receives is dependent on the chance appearance of his paper in the order in which the papers are read.

3. *Randomly shuffle the papers before grading them.* It is generally assumed that a student's essay grade will be influenced by the position of his paper, especially if the preceding responses (answers) were either very good or very poor (Follman, Lowe, & Miller, 1971; Hales & Tokar, 1975; Ross & Stanley, 1954). For example, an essay answer that is worth, say, a B might receive only a C if many of the previous papers were very good and received B's. On the other hand, this same answer could receive an A if many of the preceding papers were of only average quality. Hales and Tokar (1975) showed this was so and recommended shuffling the papers randomly prior to grading to try to minimize the effects of the preceding grades.

4. *Grade only one question at a time for all papers.* To reduce the "halo" effect (the quality of the response to one question influencing the reader's evaluation of the quality of the response to the next question), we strongly recommend that teachers grade one question at a time rather than one paper (containing several responses) at a time. In addition to minimizing the halo effect, such a procedure will make it possible for the reader to become thoroughly familiar with just one set of scoring criteria, concentrate completely on them, and not be distracted by moving from one question to another.

5. *Grade the responses anonymously.* In every classroom there are teacher's "pets" or the teacher may have a higher opinion of some students' abilities. Regardless of the reason, it is only natural that the teacher might favor the response of one student over that of another even though the answers are of equal quality. We recognize that this is a natural tendency,

but a student's grade should *not* be influenced by his teacher's bias. In the selection type of objective test, we are protected from our biases because the answer is either right or wrong. This is not so in essay tests, even though a scoring guide is employed. Therefore, to protect the student from reader bias, we advise that the teacher not know whose paper is being graded.

Another reason for preserving anonymity (even though it is unrelated to the reliability of grading essays) is that it can promote and/or maintain a healthy classroom atmosphere. There are, no doubt, some students who feel that they are subjected to prejudice of one form or another, and these students would argue that the grades they receive are a reflection of their teacher's biases toward them. But, if the papers were graded anonymously, not only would this protect the teacher, but it would also indicate to the students that their teacher is treating them fairly.

Anonymity can be obtained in a variety of ways. One way would be to have the student write his name on an envelope attached to the answer booklet and have only the clerical staff record the grades on the student's record sheet. Another way would be to have the student write his name on the back page of the test booklet rather than on the front page. We assume, of course, that if this procedure is adopted, the teacher will not look at the name before he grades the paper. Still another way would be to have students select a card with a number on it, write their name on the card and only their number on the paper. The teacher would then match the numbers and names when he records the grades. We recognize, of course, that even though the teacher might take pains to have the students' responses remain anonymous when he grades the papers, it may be that he will recognize a student's handwriting. In such cases, we can only hope that the teacher will be completely objective in his grading.

6. *The mechanics of expression should be judged separately from what the student writes.* For those teachers who feel that the mechanics of expression are very important and should be reflected in the grade given the answer, we strongly suggest that they assign a proportion of the question's value to such factors as legibility, spelling, punctuation, and grammar. The proportion assigned to these factors should be spelled out in the grading criteria and the students should be so informed. It the teacher wishes, he may assign separate subscores to each factor. In any event, the teacher must be careful not to let such factors influence his evaluation of the answer's subject-matter content.

For those teachers who contend that they are not influenced by how a person writes, but only by what he writes, we can only say be careful! It has been shown that when teachers are told to *disregard* spelling, punctuation, and grammatical errors, they still assign lower grades to papers containing such errors (Scannell & Marshall, 1966).

7. *Try to score all responses to a particular question without interruption.* One source of unreliability is that the scorer may vary markedly from one

day to the next and even from morning to afternoon of the same day. We would be very unfair to our students if we allowed a personal argument with one's spouse, a migraine headache, or an upset stomach to influence the grade we give a student for his answer. Our scoring is valid only to the degree that it is based upon the quality of the subject's answer and *not* on the reader's disposition at a particular moment.

Although we recommend that all responses to a particular question be read at the same time, we do *not* suggest that there should be no short breaks during the reading period. There must be some short diversionary periods so that the reader will not become fatigued and grouchy. What we are suggesting is that, in order to keep the standards clearly in mind, the set of papers should be graded without excessive interruption and delay. If a lengthy break is taken, the reader should reread some of the first few papers to refamiliarize himself with his scoring standards so that he will not change them in midstream. This is especially important in global reading.

8. *If possible, have two independent readings of the test and use the average as the final score.* A double reading by two independent readers will make the scores more reliable (Swineford, 1956). If independent readings are done, the scores should not be recorded on the test booklet, but should be written on a separate sheet. Seeing the scores from the first reading could markedly influence the scores on the second reading, and thus defeat the aim of maintaining independent scoring.

When it is not possible to have two different teachers grade the essay responses, but it is possible to have the same teacher grade the papers twice, this should be done with an interval of several days elapsing between the two readings so that the teacher, in essence, begins his second reading with new perspective. Once again, the scores should not be recorded on the test booklet for the reasons mentioned earlier.

We recognize that it is difficult for the ordinary classroom teacher to find the time to do one reading of a set of essay papers, so where will he find the time to read the papers twice? Also, we realize that it is difficult to get two independent readers to grade the essay responses. This does not preclude us from recommending it when it is feasible. We strongly recommend that two independent ratings by competent readers be obtained when the results of the examination are to be used to make important decisions such as the awarding of a scholarship or admittance to graduate school.

9. *Provide comments and correct errors.* You will recall that some of the purposes of testing are to provide the student with information regarding his progress, to motivate him, and to teach him even though it may be in an indirect fashion. Although it is time consuming to write comments and correct errors, it should and must be done if we are to help the student become a better student. Also, the teacher may become a more effective teacher if he makes a tally of the kinds of errors committed and then attempts to analyze the reasons for these errors. Isn't it possible that the students did

not do well because they were not taught well? However, unless the teacher has made some sort of tally of the types of errors made by his students, it will be very difficult to analyze the errors and initiate remedial measures should they be called for.

Another value of providing comments and noting errors is that this approach will make it much easier for the teacher to explain his method of assigning a particular grade to a particular paper. There are some instances when the student does not understand why he received the grade he obtained. But, with a detailed scoring guide as well as with appropriate comments, it should be much easier for the teacher and student to communicate.

Regardless of the type of test used, a test that is used *only* to assign grades is of little value for developing an effective teaching-learning situation. The test per se will be of little help to either the teacher or the student. That is why we feel strongly that the teacher should make comments, correct errors, and analyze the errors made.

10. *Set realistic standards.* Unfortunately, some teachers use tests as a punitive device rather than as an instructional and evaluation tool. Such teachers contend that unless one makes a test exceedingly difficult, the pupils will not work hard.[13] On the other hand, there are some teachers who will bend over backwards to make the test as easy as possible, feeling that in this way they will be able to purchase the students' respect and affection. Being overly lenient, in our opinion, is just as bad as being a "hard-nose." We have little to say on the matter other than both types of teachers may, in the long run, do more damage than good and that such teachers hold a very distorted view of the evaluation process. A teacher whose grades are significantly higher or lower than those of his colleagues teaching the same subject matter to the same kinds of students should reflect for a moment to see whether or not he is at fault. And if he is, he should correct the problem. The only bit of practical advice that we can offer at this time to avoid being caught in the "generosity/hard-nose trap" is that essay readers should use *all* the scale points when they grade the pupils' responses. Although this may not completely prevent the problem, it should help reduce it.

In summary, the evidence on grading essay tests or questions suggests that, with special precautions, the papers can be scored reliably, but most of the time these precautions are either not known to the teacher or they are ignored, with the end result that reader reliability is low. If a teacher uses essay questions as an evaluation tool, we believe that he has the professional

---

[13] We are not against establishing standards if they are realistic. Pupils will not rebel against realistic expectations even though they may not always achieve them. In setting forth in the scoring guide the minimal acceptable standards for a particular grade, we urge teachers to consider their students' age and ability levels, and the nature of the examination questions. Avoid being a "hard-nose" solely for the sake of letting the students know who is the boss.

obligation to spend the necessary time to grade the answers as reliably as humanly possible.

We do not deny that some valid criticisms can be leveled at essay tests. True, the questions may be ambiguous, the students may be able to bluff their way through an essay test, the grading may be dependent as much on the idiosyncracies of the reader as on the quality of the response. This does *not* mean that the essay test question should be removed from either teacher-made or commercially published tests. The fault lies in the construction and scoring of the essay examination and is not inherent in the essay item per se. It would indeed be unfortunate if essay questions were abolished from achievement tests, because they perform an important function in measuring one of our more important educational objectives—the ability to select and synthesize ideas and express oneself in writing.

French stated the point well when he said:

> So, if we psychometricians can encourage testing and further clarification of those aspects of writing that objective tests cannot measure, encourage the use of readers who favor grading the particular qualities that are desirable to grade, and see to it that the students are aware of what they are being graded on, we can enlighten rather than merely disparage the polemic art of essay testing. (French, 1965, p. 596.)

THE ORAL QUESTION

The oral approach, rather than the oral exam, is frequently used by the classroom teacher. Every day, pupils are asked questions by their teachers. Although the results of these questions may not be (although they may be and sometimes are) used by the teacher to help assign a final course grade, both teachers and pupils can, if they wish, profitably use the results obtained to improve the teaching-learning situation. Oral questioning provides immediate feedback to both pupil and teacher.

The oral question is a variation of the essay question. Although not so popular in American schools as in foreign schools, and although more frequently used in final examinations of graduate students or in the senior comprehensives of college students than as a measurement device for schoolchildren, it deserves brief mention because of its utility in the classroom, especially in the primary grades.

Both oral and essay examinations have certain limitations and advantages that they share in common.

Limitations in common
1. Both provide for a very limited sampling of content.
2. Both have low rater reliability.
Advantages in common
1. Both permit the examiner to determine how well the pupil can syn-

thesize and organize his ideas and express himself (be it in written or spoken form).

2. Both are not so dependent as the multiple-choice form on the ability of the pupil to *recognize* the correct answer; rather, both require that the pupil know and be able to *supply* the correct answer.

3. Both permit free response by the pupil.

Oral tests, in addition, may result in pupil trauma and embarrassment, which does not help instill or maintain motivation. Moreover, they are very costly and time consuming (only one student can be tested at a time); may not be equally fair to all pupils; often encourage lack of planning; and do not permit or provide for any record of the examinee's response to be used for future action by the teacher and pupil *unless* the examination process is recorded. Even so, listening to a "playback" can be time consuming. Finally, the oral examination may be advantageous to the highly articulate students. Such students may know very little but can express their limited knowledge so eloquently that, although they do not correctly answer the question, they make a good impression and are often given a grade higher than warranted.

The major advantage of the oral test is that it permits detailed probing by the examiner and hence may be very useful in the diagnostic sense. In fact, a very qualified examiner can actually elicit responses that may be indicative of a student's thinking process. Oral exams are also useful in the sense that the pupil can ask for clarification. As noted earlier, one of the major disadvantages with the essay and objective types of questions is that they are very susceptible to ambiguity in wording. In the oral examination, ambiguity also may be present, but the pupil can ask to have the question rephrased. Many times, incorrect responses are given *not* because of the pupil's lack of knowledge but because of ambiguous wording or misinterpretation of what was asked for. The oral approach, as mentioned earlier, may be traumatic for the pupil. However, it may also be very settling and reassuring, depending upon the examiner. Examinations are (or should be) intended to reveal as much as possible about the pupil's understanding of the subject matter. If for some reason a pupil becomes very nervous or "uptight," he shouldn't be penalized. Unfortunately, the examiner is unable to calm a student in a written examination, but an alert oral examiner often can do this by either rephrasing the question or by reassuring the nervous pupil. Oral examinations are also valuable for testing physically handicapped students who are unable to take written tests or in those situations where the objective is to see how the pupil will conduct himself before a group of people (for example, a course in public speaking).

SUMMARY

The principal ideas, suggestions, and recommendations made in this chapter are summarized in the following statements:

1. The essay is the only test procedure that the teacher can use if he wants to see whether his students can express themselves effectively in written form.

2. The two major types of essay questions are the extended- and restricted-response types.

3. A variety of different mental processes and skills can be measured by the essay.

4. Many of the "claimed" advantages of the essay over the objective test are not substantiated by research. The major advantages are that (a) they permit the teacher to assess the extent to which the student is able to compose an answer and present it in effective prose, (b) they are easier to prepare, and (c) they make teachers emphasize certain pupil skills.

5. The two most serious limitations of essay questions are their poor content sampling and their low reader reliability.

6. Adequate planning and conscientious scoring minimize the faults of essay tests.

7. Essay tests should be restricted to measuring the higher mental processes. They should *not* be used to measure factual recall.

8. A well-constructed essay question should provide a framework to guide the student in preparing his answer. The problem should be delimited, worded so that the student knows exactly what is expected of him, and realistic with respect to the complexity of the question and the time allowed the student to answer it.

9. All students should be required to answer the same questions.

10. Content sampling may be improved by having many relatively short essay questions.

11. Avoid starting essay questions with "who," "when," "where," and "what."

12. Adapt the complexity of the question and the length of response to the maturity level of the students.

13. Use a novel type of situation wherever possible.

14. The two most commonly used methods to grade essays are the *analytical* and the *global* approaches.

15. Both global and analytical methods require the preparation of a model answer. Preferably, this should be done early, to check on the realism of time allotted, the complexity of the question, and the clarity of wording.

16. The analytical method is recommended for the classroom teacher when only a few papers are to be graded.

17. The global method is recommended when large numbers of papers have to be graded.

18. If possible, try to have two independent ratings for each question.

19. Grade essays without knowing the identity of the student.

20. Grade one question at a time. This will tend to reduce the "halo" effect.

21. If more than one factor is being judged, such as legibility of handwrit-

ing, spelling, and knowledge of the subject matter, these other factors should be judged independently from *what* the student wrote.

22. Try to score all the responses to a single question without interruption.

23. The teacher should make comments and correct errors in order that the test may be used as a learning device.

24. Teachers should avoid the penalty and generosity errors. That is, they should not be overly strict or overly lenient in their grading standards.

25. The oral question is a variation of the essay. It is well suited for testing students who are unable to write because of physical handicaps.

26. There is a place in our schools for essay tests that are carefully constructed and reliably graded. Rather than argue whether essay tests are superior to objective tests, we should focus our attention on how *both* can be used most effectively.

CHAPTER NINE

Writing the Objective Test Item: Short-Answer, Matching, and True-False

The planning stage discussed in Chapter 7—defining instructional objectives carefully in behavioral terms, preparing and using a test blueprint, formulating well-defined problems or questions, preparing a scoring key in advance, and having the items reviewed independently—provided us with some guidelines to follow in our attempt to obtain a valid measure of pupil achievement. In Chapter 8 we discussed the essay as a testing medium. We are now at the stage where we consider the various types of objective formats that can be used. As will be evident after studying this chapter and Chapter 10, there are advantages and limitations associated with each item format.

Because clarity of wording is so vital in writing good test items, we will elaborate further on our previous discussion. In addition, we will discuss in this chapter some of the factors to be considered when writing the objective-type item, regardless of format. We will then present some guidelines to follow when preparing the short-answer, matching, and true-false item. In Chapter 10, we will discuss the preparation of the multiple-choice item.

After studying this chapter, you should be able to—

1. Understand the steps to be considered when writing the objective-type item.
2. Understand why clarity of expression is so important in test items.
3. Recognize how irrelevant clues to the correct answer can easily creep into objective items.
4. Define and discuss the following objective-type formats: short-answer, matching, and true-false.
5. Differentiate between the various types of short-answer items.
6. Apply the guidelines offered for constructing short-answer items.
7. Apply the guidelines offered for constructing the matching exercise.
8. Apply the guidelines offered for constructing true-false items.
9. Write better short-answer, matching, and true-false items.

OBJECTIVE-TYPE TESTS

The objective-type item was no doubt developed to overcome the criticisms leveled against the essay question—poor content sampling, unreliable scoring, time-consuming to grade, and encouragement of bluffing—discussed in Chapter 8. All objective-item formats may be subdivided into two classes: *supply* type (short-answer) and *select* type (true-false, matching, and multiple-choice). The *supply* and *select* types of objective-item formats are sometimes called *recall* and *recognition*, respectively. All are objectively scored, once an answer key has been constructed.

One of the virtues of the objective item is that it is an economical way of obtaining information from a pupil because, in general, it takes less time to answer than an essay question. Because of the lessened amount of time needed for pupils to respond to objective items, many questions can be asked in a prescribed examination period and more adequate content sampling can be obtained, resulting in higher reliability and better content validity. In addition, objective items can be scored more easily and more accurately. Finally, objective items *may* create an incentive for pupils to build up a broad base of knowledge, skills, and abilities.

Some very vocal critics of the objective-type item contend that the objective type test does not measure the higher mental processes, but rather encourages rote memory, encourages guessing, and neglects the measurement of writing ability. Objective items often are used to measure rote recall of facts, dates, names, and places. But, as will be evident after you have studied this and the next chapter, objective items can be written so that they measure the higher mental processes of understanding, application, analysis, and interpretation.

SOME GENERAL CONSIDERATIONS IN WRITING OBJECTIVE ITEMS

We have already discussed in Chapter 7 those qualities needed to be a good item writer: (1) a thorough understanding of the subject matter, (2) a thorough understanding of the pupils to be tested, (3) skill in verbal expression, (4) familiarity with the different item formats, (5) perseverance, and (6) creativity. But even if teachers possess these traits, they must be cognizant of some of the pitfalls involved in writing objective items. (In Chapter 7 we also discussed some general guidelines for writing good test items.) Teacher-made achievement tests are generally deficient in several ways. The most common fault is related to *ineffective communication.* We will now offer some general guidelines for writing objective items. These will then be followed by guidelines for a particular item format.

1. *Test for important facts and knowledge.* Some teacher-made objective tests consist of items testing for material contained in a footnote or asking questions on other trivia. It is no wonder, then, that pupils taking such tests memorize details and specific facts rather than concentrate on developing an understanding of the material.

We recognize that the knowledge of many specific facts is both important and necessary—such as knowing the alphabet, addition facts, the multiplication table, and the like. But how important is it for students to know the name of the ship that Columbus was on when he discovered America, or the date (and/or time) when Edison invented the light bulb? Teachers who teach and test for the ability to recall or supply trivial details are practicing pedagogically unsound methods.

2. *Tailor the questions to fit the examinees' age and ability levels as well as the purpose of the test.* The vocabulary used should be commensurate with the age and ability of the examinees. Teachers working with slow learners should use more simple vocabulary than those working with average or bright children. Similarly, the type of objective item format to be used (as well as the manner in which answers are to be recorded) is, in part, dependent upon the age and ability level of the pupils. For example, the slow learner might not be able to comprehend the tasks involved in a matching exercise, but would have less difficulty with the short-answer format. Primary school children might be able to handle items that involve simple matching, but would have difficulty with the multiple-choice format. Elementary school children might be better able to handle "knowledge of facts," and "simple applications and understanding" than interpretation of a complex reading

passage. We do *not* mean to imply that achievement tests for younger children should test only for the factual recall of knowledge. They should not! All we are saying is that the abilities taught and tested should be realistic for the pupils.

In a criterion-referenced test, the intent is to *describe* the individual in terms of his competencies or abilities. In a norm-referenced test, the purpose is to *compare* the pupil with other pupils. Depending upon the purpose of the test, the difficulty level and discrimination power of the items may differ. For example, an achievement test used to rank pupils should be neither too easy nor too difficult if it is to retain its power to discriminate validly among pupils in terms of their achievement. But in a mastery test given *after* instruction (posttest), we might expect the majority (if not all) of the pupils to be able to answer the items correctly. By the same token, the mastery test given *before* instruction (pretest) may prove to be more difficult and discriminating than when it is used as a posttest.

The beauty of the teacher-made test in contrast to the commercially prepared achievement test is that the teacher-made test can be designed specifically to *fit* the needs of the pupils and the teacher's instructional objectives. For this reason, it is important that the teacher have a thorough understanding of his pupils and tailor the test questions to the intended audience and purpose appropriately.

3. *Write the items as clearly as possible.* Lack of clarity may arise from a variety of sources, such as the inappropriate choice of words used, the awkward arrangement of words, and excessive verbiage. What is clear to the item writer is often vague and ambiguous to the examinee reading the question. A good rule of thumb to follow is to ask yourself: "Does the question as written ensure that the examinee will understand the task he is to perform?"

Poor: Columbus discovered America in _____.

As written, the question is ambiguous because the examinee does not know whether the teacher wants to know the year, the date, or the name of the ship. If interested in seeing whether the pupils know the year in which Columbus discovered America, the question should be rewritten as follows:

Better: In what year did Columbus discover America? (1492)

Ambiguity can often occur when qualitative rather than quantitative language is used. Words such as "hot," "few," "many," and "low" can mean different things to different people. Wherever possible, we advocate the use of quantitative language.

Poor: <u>T</u> F   The correlation between scholastic aptitude test scores obtained by high school seniors and their later college grades is high.

Better: <u>T</u> F   The correlation between scholastic aptitude test scores obtained by high school seniors and their later college grades is about .50.

The "poor" example is ambiguous, depending upon how the examinee interprets "high." Although a correlation of .50 may be high for Bill, it may not be high for Irv, or vice versa, and they would respond accordingly.

Clarity can also be improved by using good grammar and sentence structure. Selecting words that have a precise, exact meaning will help achieve clarity by removing ambiguity. However, in their attempt to achieve clarity, teachers too often resort to using sentences that contain many qualifying statements, qualifiers, parenthetical statements, repetition of words, and the like. Sentence structure, like test directions, should be clear and simple. Long sentences should be broken up into smaller sentences. Vocabulary should be as simple as possible. If qualifiers are needed, they should appear immediately *after* the word or statement they are to qualify. Again, what may be implicit to the examiner *must* be made explicit to the examinee. The following example—written by a twelfth-grade civics teacher to ascertain whether his students know that, in the United States, all cases of impeachment are tried by the Senate—is poor because it is ambiguous. If the students had studied various governments, they would not know to which country the question applied. Also, because of its ambiguity, there would be more than one correct answer. In rewording such an item, the teacher must be careful not to introduce qualifiers that will make the sentence awkward.

Poor: Impeachment cases are tried by the _____.
Better: According to the U.S. Constitution, all cases of impeachment are tried by the (<u>Senate</u>).

or

According to the U.S. Constitution, all cases of impeachment are tried by the
<u>A</u>. Senate.
B. Supreme Court.
C. Judicial Committee.
D. House of Representatives.

If the purpose of a test item is to measure understanding of a principle rather than computational skill, use simple numbers and have the answer come out as a whole number. A fifth-grade teacher who wants to learn whether his students understand the meaning of "discount" could either have his students supply or select the definition, or he could present them with a verbal problem. In any event, his test item should be presented clearly and concisely.

Poor: Mr. Jones is entitled to a 14½ percent discount at the ABD department store. One day, Mr. and Mrs. Jones decide that, because of Mr. Jones' recent raise, they are able to afford a new table for their family room. The old table is now 15 years old and is decrepit. They decide, after visiting other stores and comparing prices, to buy one at the ABD store. The table they purchase is priced at $105.49. How much does Mr. Jones pay for the table? ($90.19)

This item is full of window dressing that bears no relationship to the problem and involves computations that are not simple whole numbers. It is better rewritten as:

Better: Mr. Jones was given a 15 percent discount on a table that is priced at $80.00. How much did Mr. Jones pay for the table? ($68.00)

Clarity often can be better achieved by using a few well-chosen words than by writing excessively, as illustrated in the "poor" example above. The intent of the test item is (or should be) to measure the instructional objectives, be they knowledge of facts, comprehension, understanding, or other mental processes—*not* reading ability, verbal fluency, or general intelligence. Another golden rule in item writing is to *come to the point as quickly, clearly, and simply as possible.*

4. *Avoid lifting statements verbatim from the text.* Lifting statements verbatim from the text and omitting one or two words to make a short-answer item, or inserting a negative to get a true-false item that is false is poor testing. Statements lifted out of context may lose most of their intended meaning and may result in ambiguous items. This is especially so for true-false items. Also, such an item-writing procedure might result in poor study habits on the part of the pupils. The use of textbook language in a test encourages the pupils to memorize rather than to understand the subject matter.

Poor:
T F   Content validity is related to how adequately the content of the test samples the domain of subject matter about which inferences are to be made.
Better: An arithmetic test that relates the course content and instructional objectives to a test blueprint is said to have what type of validity?
    A. Content
    B. Construct
    C. Predictive
    D. Concurrent

5. *Avoid using interrelated items.* Some tests consist of a series of items in which the correct answer to one is necessary for the pupil to get the correct answer to another item. Teachers should avoid writing items that have this type of dependency. An example of interdependent items follows.

X	Y
8	7
6	9
11	11
13	13
12	10

Questions 1 to 6 are based on the data presented above.

1. $\bar{X} = (\underline{10})$.
2. $S_x = (\underline{2.61})$.

.

.

.

6. If $r_{xx} = .75$, what is the value of the standard error of measurement of X?
    ($\underline{1.31}$)

Interdependent items are grossly unfair, since they may penalize the student who knows how to compute the correct answer to one question but gets an incorrect answer because of an incorrect answer to another question. Let us assume that Allan knows that the formula for the standard error of measurement is $S_x \sqrt{1 - r_{xx}}$. However, if Allan computed the value of S_x incorrectly in item 2, he would obtain the wrong answer to item 6, even though he had the necessary knowledge and skills. If the teacher wants to learn whether his students know how to compute S_e, he should give them hypothetical values to substitute into the formula. Or if the teacher's intent is to see whether the students know the formula for the standard error of measurement, he can test this without reference to the answer of a preceding item.

We are not advocating the removal of computational problems from teacher-made tests. On the contrary, in science and mathematics courses it is important that the student be able to engage in the arithmetic processes needed to compute a value in the gas laws, to be able to balance equations, and to solve quadratic equations. Nor are we advocating that teachers should not ask a series of questions on a set of common materials. It is more economical when a series of items can be asked on a common set of materials. What we are saying is that a pupil should get only *one* item wrong and not two or more because of an error in his arithmetic on a previous item. The use of interrelated or interdependent items should be avoided.

6. *There should be only one correct (or best) answer.* Having more than one correct answer encourages students to quibble, argue, and challenge the "correctness" of their wrong answers. We are *not* opposed to students questioning the appropriateness of the answer keyed as correct. In fact, we encourage it. Done in a constructive and positive fashion, it can be a meaningful learning experience for both pupil and teacher. However, teachers who frequently change their answers contribute little to establishing and maintaining harmonious classroom relationships. And, if many "double-keyed" (two answers are correct) items are deleted, it may affect the test's validity.

Somewhat related to this point is the case where there is some disagreement among experts in the field as to *the* correct answer. For example, some cardiologists may believe that cholesterol is a major cause of heart attacks but other cardiologists may disagree. Generally, we prefer that teachers not write items where there is no single correct or best answer. However, when different opinions are held, the item should cite the authority(ies) holding a particular view.

Poor:	T F	A major cause of heart attacks is cholesterol.
Better:	T <u>F</u>	According to White, a major cause of heart attacks is cholesterol.

7. *Avoid negative questions whenever possible.* Indiscriminate use of the negative should be avoided. Since the pupil has to change his normal thought processes, he may overlook the negative aspect and answer the item incorrectly even though he knows the correct answer. Also, it takes the examinee longer to answer a negative item than a comparable one stated positively, and more errors are introduced (Wason, 1961; Zern, 1967). Whenever a pupil overlooks the negative because of carelessness, the validity and reliability of the test are lowered. If negative questions are to be used, the negative should be made explicit (by underlining or using all capital letters) so that the examinee does not overlook the negative statement. Double negatives confuse the student and contribute nothing to valid evaluation. In fact, we can think of no instance where the double-negative item should be used. It is not inconceivable that a double negative may be used in a cautious statement, but it should never be used as a test item. We recommend that, whenever possible, originally written negative statements be expressed positively.

Poor:	T <u>F</u>	A United States congressman is not elected for a 2-year term.
Better:	<u>T</u> F	A United States congressman is elected for a 2-year term.
		or
	T <u>F</u>	A United States congressman is elected for a 6-year term.

For the multiple-choice item, avoid using such words as "not," "never," and "least." If such words must be used, attention should be drawn to them.

Poor stem: It would never be inappropriate to use essay questions for measuring. . . .

Better: It would be appropriate to use essay questions for all of following except
- A. skill in organizing material.
- <u>B.</u> knowledge of facts and principles.
- C. understanding of factual material.
- D. skill in providing unique solutions to problems.

Best: It would be appropriate to use essay tests—
     A.   to measure knowledge of facts and principles.
     B.   to measure skill in organizing material.
     C.   to encourage good study habits.
     D.   if grading time is at a premium.

8. *Do not give the answer away.* A pupil should get the correct answer to a test question only because he has learned the material. Unfortunately, there are many instances where test-wise (but not necessarily knowledgeable) students obtain the correct answer because of some irrelevant clue(s). Some of the more common types of irrelevant clues are (a) having information in the stem of one item provide the answer to another item; (b) lack of parallelism between stem and responses in the multiple-choice item; (c) the length of the correct response (in multiple-choice items); (d) the position and pattern of the correct answer; (e) grammatical clues such as an "a" or "an" preceding a blank in the short answer or at the end of the stem in the multiple-choice; (f) using textbook language verbatim; and (g) using technical jargon. Look at the following examples of two items from the *same* test.

Item 8.   The "halo" effect is most pronounced in essay examinations. The *best* way to minimize its effects is to
     A.   provide optional questions.
     B.   "aim" the student to the desired response.
     C.   read all the responses for one question before reading the other questions.
     D.   permit students to write their essay tests at home where they will be more at ease.
Item 37.   The "halo" effect is more operative in
     A.   essay tests.
     B.   true-false tests.
     C.   matching tests.
     D.   short-answer tests.
     E.   multiple-choice tests.

The student could obtain the correct answer to item 37 because the answer is in the stem of item 8.

Poor: Among the causes of the League of Nations' becoming ineffective were—
     A.   the Western-bloc nations distrusted the Eastern nations.
     B.   the Eastern-bloc nations distrusted the Western nations.
     C.   the European nations opposed the appeasement tactics of England.
     D.   differing views on punishing belligerent nations and protecting internal rights.

To answer this item correctly, the student need only look for a response (answer) that contains two or more reasons, since the stem calls for a plural ("were") response. To prevent such a clue, all responses should contain two or more reasons, or the stem should be reworded as "The League of Nations became ineffective because. . . ."

Teachers writing multiple-choice items may resort to placing qualifiers in the correct answer so that it is completely and unequivocally correct (or best). But, they fail to provide these qualifiers in the incorrect responses and this often provides a clue to the test-wise student. When it is not possible to prepare a multiple-choice item with all the possible answers of approximately equal length, write the responses so that in some instances the longest answer is the correct one, and vice versa. Then, length will no longer be a clue to the correct answer.

A test assembled in haste may give irrelevant clues if a particular pattern to the position of the correct answer is established (Jones & Kaufman, 1975). For example, the items, when assembled, may contain the correct answer at either the beginning or end; the correct answer may follow a pattern in true-false tests such as T,F,T,F, . . . T,F; or, in multiple-choice tests, it may be A,D,C,B, A,D,C,B. Random assignment of the correct response as well as having approximately an equal number of true-false statements or having approximately an equal number of correct answers for each response position (A,B,C,D,E) in the multiple-choice item will minimize pattern clues.

9. *Get an independent review of your test items.* Many of the flaws found in teacher-made tests can be spotted by having an independent review made of the items. Preferably, this review should be made by a teacher who teaches the same subject matter. Such a review will permit the item writer to obtain another opinion about the difficulty of the items, the adequacy of content sampling, the plausibility of the distracters (in a multiple-choice item), the adequacy of the scoring key, and the technical quality of the items. Of course, unless the test has been planned and the items written well in advance of the time the test is scheduled, such a review is not possible.

The following item attempts to present most of the major flaws found in teacher-made objective items.

Poor: Test standardization is the process whereby a common set of administrative and scoring directions are established. It is usually the major distinguishing factor between the teacher-made and commercially published test. Many steps are involved in test standardization. Some of these steps are rigorously adhered to while others are not. Of the following steps in test standardization, the one usually neglected is
   A.   finding the mean of the group.
   B.   not trying out each item in a pretest.
   <u>C.</u>   not furnishing adequate validity information.
   D.   not furnishing adequate reliability information.
   E.   to report the standard deviation of the standardization sample.

The item contains double negatives, has excessive verbiage, is grammatically incorrect, and has two possible correct answers. Choice A begins with a participle (finding), choice E begins with an infinitive (to report) and choices B, C, and D begin with a negative. The negatives here might also be a source of confusion, since the examinee is clued to look for something that is neglected (in itself a negative).

Better:　Some steps in test standardization follow. The step *most often neglected* is
A. finding the group mean.
B. trying out each item in a pretest.
C. furnishing adequate validity information.
D. reporting the standard deviation of the standardization sample.

A Check List for Writing Objective Test Items

Have you ever kicked the tires on your automobile? Do you normally have your car checked over before embarking on a trip? When offered a new type of cheese, have you ever nibbled at a small piece to see if you like it before taking a larger portion? Certainly you have done something analogous to one or more of these. Why? As a precaution! Just as no commercial pilot would ever think of taking off from a runway before he has completed a detailed check list pertaining to his plane, so should no teacher administer a test before he has thoroughly checked out the items he has written.

Table 9–1 is a summary of the points discussed above. It presents a list of the more important factors to be considered when writing objective test items, regardless of their format. If any of your objective items "fail" this check list, you should go back to the actual textual discussion.

WRITING SHORT-ANSWER ITEMS

The short-answer item is classified as a supply-type objective item. It is easily recognized by the presence of a blank(s) in which the student writes his answer to the question. The three common varieties of the short-answer form are (1) the *question* variety, in which the item is presented as a direct question; (2) the *completion* variety, in which an incomplete statement is used; and (3) the *association* variety. Examples of each variety follow.

1. *Question variety:*
   In what city was the first experimental psychology laboratory located? (Leipzig)
2. *Completion variety:*
   The first experimental psychology laboratory was located in the city of (Leipzig)
3. *Association variety:*
   After each city, write in the name of the state in which the city is located.
   Detroit (Michigan)
   Chicago (Illinois)
   Boston (Massachusetts)

TABLE 9–1   Check List for Writing Objective Test Items

FACTOR	YES
1. Are the instructional objectives clearly defined?	×
2. Did you prepare a test blueprint? Did you follow it?	×
3. Did you formulate well-defined, clear test items?	×
4. Did you employ "correct" English in writing the items?	×
5. Did you specifically state all necessary qualifications?	×
6. Did you avoid giving clues to the correct answer? For example, grammatical clues, length of correct response clues?	×
7. Did you test for the important ideas rather than the trivial?	×
8. Did you adapt the test's difficulty to your students?	×
9. Did you avoid using textbook jargon?	×
10. Did you cast the items in positive form?	×
11. If negative items were used, did you draw the students' attention to them?	×
12. Did you prepare a scoring key? Does each and every item have a single correct answer?	×
13. Did you review your items? Yourself? Another teacher?	×

In each form the pupil answers with a word, phrase, mathematical symbol, chemical formula, or other required entry. This type of item is somewhat of a compromise between an essay item and the other types of objective items. Sloppy phrasing and/or an imprecise scoring key could result in questions that cannot be scored with complete objectivity. For example, suppose a teacher writes the following item:

Poor: The capital of Canada is (<u>Ottawa</u>).

One correct answer is "in Ontario." Another correct answer is "where the Prime Minister lives." If the key specifically states that Ottawa is the only correct answer, then the scoring would be objective, but the determination of the key would be very subjective indeed. Would "Ottawa" be counted correct? We do not wish to belabor the point of this lack of objectivity. Proper wording can alleviate most problems of this type.

Better: The name of the capital city of Canada is (<u>Ottawa</u>).

Another aspect of short-answer items which makes them somewhat of a cross between the essay and other objective items is that, like essay items, they require recall rather than recognition. While recalling a correct answer and recognizing a correct answer are indeed two different behaviors, studies have indicated that correlations between scores on two tests differing in recall versus recognition forms are quite high. (See Cook, 1955.)

Advantages and Limitations of the Short-Answer Item

Short-answer items are particularly useful in mathematics and the sciences, where a computational answer is required or where a formula or equation is to be written, such as:

Write the formula for sulfuric acid. $\underline{H_2SO_4}$
Solve: $x + 2 = 4$. $x = \underline{2}$.

Short-answer items are also useful in spelling and foreign language evaluations, where specific bits of information are usually tested. There are, of course, instances in science and mathematics when understanding, application, and problem-solving skills can be measured with a short-answer item, as illustrated below:

A soldering iron takes 1.1 amperes when used on a 110-volt circuit. Its resistance is (100) ohms.
The sum of twice a number and 5 is 39. What is the number? (17)

To solve the first problem, the student would have to know the formula $I = E/R$. He would then have to substitute into the formula the values given and solve for R. This would require that he be able to divide and multiply with decimals. To solve the second problem, the student would first have to introduce an unknown to stand for the number he is looking for. He would then have to translate the verbal problem into an equation such that $2X + 5 = 39$. Then he would solve for X.

To test for the knowledge of definitions and technical terms, use the short-answer item. Generally, when we are interested in testing for the student's knowledge of definitions or technical terms, we feel more confident that we are getting a valid reading when the student *supplies* rather than selects the answer.

Still another advantage of the short-answer or constructed response test over the multiple-choice test, is that, for first graders at least, individually administered constructed-response tests predicted end-of-year performance, as well as a group-administered 4-foil, multiple-choice test. And despite the fact that the constructed-response tests may be more time consuming and difficult, it was preferred by teachers who said that they (1) were easier to administer, (2) eliminated copying, (3) motivated the pupils who felt that they were receiving individual attention, and (4) provided more diagnostic information (Niedermeyer & Sullivan, 1972).

Some of the disadvantages associated with the short-answer item are as follows:

1. They are limited to questions that can be answered by a word, phrase, symbol, or number. There are very few instances when an abstraction, generalization, or interpretation can be adequately presented by the examinee in one or two words. This, no doubt, accounts for the fact that the preponderance of short-answer items measure little more than factual recall.

2. It is almost impossible to write good short-answer items that require the student to exhibit synthesis and interpretation so that one and only one answer will be correct.

3. Because short-answer items are best for measuring highly specific facts (dates, names, places, vocabulary), excessive use may encourage rote memory and poor study habits.

4. Scoring can be quite tedious and somewhat subjective. The scoring may not be quick, easy, routine, and accurate because of the variety of acceptable answers. Also, because of the multiplicity of plausible answers, clerks cannot be used as scorers. Frequently, the scorer must decide whether a given answer is right, wrong, or partially right. This can lead to bias in scoring, and hence it lowers test validity. Test reliability may also be affected.

Suggestions for Writing Short-Answer Items

1. *For computational problems, the teacher should specify the degree of precision and the units of expression expected in the answer.*

Poor: The value of π is (3.1?   3.14?   3.142?).
Better: The value of π (to 6 decimals) is (3.141593).

In science and mathematics it may be just as important for the student to know and use the correct unit of expression as the procedure involved in arriving at the answer. If units of expression are important, the teacher must make it clear in the instructions to the student that the correct unit of expression is to be used. Otherwise, the student could just give the numerical answer.

Following is a set of directions that specifies the manner in which answers are to be expressed:

Directions: This science test consists of 60 questions, some of which require computations to be made. For those questions involving computations, you *must* (1) carry out your answer to two decimals, and (2) express the answer in proper units such as pounds, grams, or volts.

2. *Omit important words only.* A short-answer exercise involves more than just having one or more blanks in a sentence. The words that are to be omitted when writing the exercise must be important or key words. The student should be asked to supply an important fact. If verbs, pronouns, or

adverbs are omitted, a variety of plausible answers will be received, but the item may no longer possess content validity. Look at the following example.

Poor: Columbus (discovered) America in 1492.

As the question was originally written, answers such as "left," "sailed to," "discovered," "came to" would all have to be considered correct.

3. *Avoid excessive blanks in a single item.* We reiterate that what is explicit to the tester must also be made explicit to the examinee. Item writers are prone to forget that although they may have the intent of the item in mind when they write it, excessive omission of key words may result in the item's losing its specific meaning. Omitting too many key words may turn an achievement test into an intelligence test or a guessing game. Overmutiliation can only result in the item's being ambiguous and confusing. An item writer may have the tangent-ratio concept in his mind when he prepares the following item: *The ratio of the   to the   is called the   . But how is the examinee to know this? Might he not answer "opposite side," "hypotenuse," and "sine" for the three respective blanks? If the teacher wishes to learn whether his students know the formula for the tangent, he should ask this or he should rewrite the item as:

The tangent is the ratio of the (adjacent side) to the (opposite side).

4. *Have the blanks occur near the end of the sentence.* When the blank is at the beginning or middle of the sentence, the essential point of the question may be overlooked or forgotten by the time the student reads the item. This is especially true when dealing with complex material and/or testing young children who have a limited attention and retention span.

Poor: The _____ is authorized by the U.S. Constitution to try all cases of impeachment.
Better: The U.S. Constitution states that all cases of impeachment will be tried by the (Senate).

The essential point of the question—who is responsible for trying impeachment cases—should come as close to the beginning of the item as possible so that students can focus their attention on the problem and not have to reread the material to see what they are being asked to do.

5. *Generally speaking, it is advantageous to use the direct question rather than the incomplete statement.* The direct question is preferred because (a) it may be easier to phrase the question so that it is less ambiguous and does not provide irrelevant clues, and (b) it is more natural to pupils who are used to answering the teacher's questions in class rather than answering the teacher's incomplete statement. When the item writer uses the direct-

question approach, he will tend to write the item more clearly because he has to clarify in his own mind exactly what it is he intends to measure.

6. *To test for the knowledge of definitions and/or the comprehension of technical terms, use a direct question in which the term is given and a definition is asked for.* Quite often when writing the definition, the item writer will provide the student with a clue to the correct answer.

Poor: What is the statistical term that describes the consistency with which all the items in a test are measuring the same thing? (coefficient of internal consistency)

Better: What is internal consistency reliability? _____

The latter is to be preferred because the word "consistency" in the poor example may provide the student with a clue to the correct answer.

7. *Don't skimp on the answer space provided.* If the student is asked to fill in a blank or to give a short answer to a question, the teacher should provide sufficient space for the pupil to record his answer. But be careful— an irrelevant clue to the correct answer might be given by the length of the blank provided. To minimize this, we suggest that all blanks be of uniform length, regardless of the length of the answer. And, to make scoring easier, we suggest that for those tests that require only a single word, number, formula, or symbol, *all* blanks be in a single column, either at the right- or left-hand side of the page. Where the item may have more than one blank to be filled in, such as "The tangent is the ratio of the_____(1)_____to the_____(2)_____," the blanks can be numbered and the pupil instructed to write his answer in the corresponding numbered blank at the side of the page. (We will discuss test layout in greater detail in Chapter 11.)

8. *Avoid giving irrelevant clues.*

A Check List for Writing Short-Answer Items

The material previously discussed is summarized in Table 9–2. We strongly urge you to refer to it (and the discussion) when writing short-answer items.

WRITING THE MATCHING EXERCISE

In the traditional format, the matching exercise consists of two columns—one column consists of the questions or problems to be answered (premises); the other column contains the answers (responses). The examinee is presented with the two lists and is required to make some sort of association between each premise and each response. He pairs the corresponding elements and records his answers.

Directions: In the blank to the left of each situation described in column A, write the letter of the type of reliability coefficient (column B) that is most appropriate. You may use a letter in column B once, more than once, or not at all.

Column A

(G) 1. Scores on the Stanford-Binet are correlated with scores on the WISC.

(D) 2. The method most often used to estimate the reliability of teacher-made tests.

(C) 3. Generally provides the lowest reliability estimate.

(D) 4. Results most affected by speeded tests.

(A) 5. A scholastic aptitude test is administered to high school freshmen and again to the the same students as seniors.

Column B

A. Stability
B. Equivalence
C. Stability and equivalence
D. Split-half
E. K-R 20
F. K-R 21
G. None of the above

There are many modifications of the matching exercise that can be used.[1] For example, the student may be given a map on which certain locations are assigned letters or numbers. These letters or numbers are then to be matched

[1] Gerberich (1956) lists 38 versions of the matching exercise.

TABLE 9–2   Check List for Writing Short-Answer (Supply-Type) Items

FACTOR	YES
1. Can each item be answered in a word, a phrase, with a symbol, formula, or short sentence?	X
2. Do the items avoid the use of verbatim textbook language?	X
3. Is each item specific, clear, and unambiguous?	X
4. Are any irrelevant clues avoided? Grammatical? Length of blank? Other?	X
5. Do computational problems indicate the degree of precision required? Whether or not the unit of measurement is to be included in the answer?	X
6. Do the blanks occur near the end of the sentence?	X
7. Have only key words been omitted?	X
8. Was excessive mutilation kept to a minimum?	X
9. Have direct questions been used where feasible?	X
10. Are the items technically correct?	X
11. Is there one correct or agreed-upon correct answer?	X
12. Has a scoring key been prepared?	X
13. Has the test been reviewed independently?	X
14. Is this format most efficient for testing the instructional objectives?	X

with the names of cities, lakes, rivers, continents, or other entities. Or the student may be given a diagram of a piece of electrical equipment such as a voltmeter with the various parts assigned numbers. His task would then be to match the name of the part with the number on the diagram.

A variation of the traditional or simple matching exercise is the classification variety.[2] Here, a classification scheme (parts of speech, types of rocks) is presented and the examinee classifies each statement according to the scheme. This variation is well suited to topics dealing with criticism, explanation, and understanding. Following is an example of a classification exercise.

Directions: Items 1–7 each contain a complete sentence. Determine whether the sentence is simple, compound, complex, or compound-complex. Using the key below, write the letter of the type of sentence it is in the blank to the left of the sentence.

Key: A. Simple sentence
B. Compound sentence
C. Complex sentence
D. Compound-complex sentence

(C) 1. The teacher said that his answer was correct.
(A) 2. They made him chairman.
(D) 3. After I had gathered the information, I turned it over to him and he started the report.

.
.
.

(B) 7. I warned her, but she was persistent.

Advantages and Limitations of the Matching Exercise

The matching exercise is well suited to those situations where one is interested in testing the knowledge of terms, definitions, dates, events, and other matters involving simple relationships. It is well suited to the "who," "what," "when," "where," types of learning. Dates may be matched with events, authors with book titles, and tools with their uses. In many learning situations, we try to stress the association between various ideas; for example, Columbus discovered America in 1492; Fleming discovered penicillin; Bell invented the telephone. Here, the matching exercise, when properly constructed, is a very valuable measurement tool.

Some of the major advantages of matching exercises are as follows:

1. Because they require relatively little reading time, many questions can be asked in a limited amount of testing time. This then affords the opportunity to have a larger sampling of content and, other things being equal, a resultant reliability that is higher than if fewer questions were asked.

[2] It is sometimes classified as a key type of multiple-choice exercise.

2. Like true-false or multiple-choice items, matching exercises are amenable to machine scoring. Even if they are hand-scored, they can be scored more easily than say the essay or short-answer and can be scored by clerks, paraprofessionals, and even the students, since there should be just one correct answer.

The two major deficiencies associated with simple matching exercises are as follows:

1. If sufficient care is not taken in their preparation, the matching lists may encourage serial memorization rather than association.
2. It is sometimes difficult to get clusters of questions that are sufficiently alike that a common set of responses can be used.

As in all achievement tests, clarity of the items is to be *maximized*; irrelevant clues and confusion should be minimized. Some of the more common faults of teacher-made matching exercises are (1) the directions are vague, (2) the sets to be matched are excessively long, (3) the list of responses lacks homogeneity, (4) the material is set up so that it is not simple for the student to respond, and (5) the premises are vaguely stated. Following are some suggestions to guide the item writer in his efforts to write a valid matching exercise.

Suggestions for Constructing the Matching Exercise

1. *If at all possible, have the response list consist of short phrases, single words, or numbers.* Putting the lengthier questions in the premise column at the left-hand side of the page will make for easier reading by the pupil, who normally reads from left to right. He would read the lengthier problem first and then just scan the short responses to find the correct answers.

2. *Each matching exercise should consist of homogeneous items.* A single matching exercise, to be most valid, should consist of items that deal with only a single concept, classification, or area. For example, in a single matching exercise do not include items that involve book authors, titles, inventors, and inventions. *Have separate homogeneous lists.* When the lists are lacking in homogeneity, we are likely to measure verbal association, which can be readily answered by students who have only a superficial knowledge of the subject matter.

Obtaining homogeneity in the lists may be easier to say than to accomplish. In fact, violation of this prescription is one of the more frequent ones committed by those using the matching exercise. Why? Because what may appear to be homogeneous for fifth-graders may be very heterogeneous for tenth-graders. Look at the following matching exercise. Is there a lack of homogeneity in the lists?

		Column A	Column B
(C)	1.	Discovered penicillin	A. Armstrong
(B)	2.	Discovered America	B. Columbus
(A)	3.	First astronaut to walk on the moon	C. Fleming
(J)	4.	Invented the cotton gin	D. Glenn
(F)	5.	First explorer to sail around the Cape of Good Hope	E. Jefferson
(D)	6.	First U.S. astronaut to orbit the earth	F. Magellan
			G. Newton
			H. Salk
			I. Washington
			J. Whitney

You will notice that our list of responses in column B consists of explorers, inventors, and scientists, with two astronauts thrown in (they might be termed "explorers"). To a group of elementary (especially primary grade) pupils, the lists might appear to be very homogeneous, but to a group of older children, the lists would be very heterogeneous. Hence, if this matching exercise were to be used in the higher grades, there should be four matching exercises written: one for the questions on explorers, a second for the questions on inventors, a third for the items on scientists, and a fourth for the items on astronauts. The finer the discrimination to be made, the more difficult it is to prepare sufficiently long homogeneous response lists. Following is a matching exercise based on *only* the concept of validity.

		Statement	Type of Validity
(A)	1.	To construct a spelling test, a teacher uses the words commonly misspelled in his students' themes.	A. Content validity
(B)	2.	A teacher wonders whether the spelling of dictated words is the same as spelling the same words when writing a theme.	B. Construct validity C. Criterion-related validity
(C)	3.	A test manual reports a correlation of 0.76 between the IQ and that obtained from the Stanford-Binet.	D. None of the above
(C)	4.	Production records are compared to supervisors' ratings.	
(A)	5.	A table of specifications is constructed.	

3. *Keep each list relatively short.* The item writer must achieve a happy balance between having the lists too long or too short. Long lists require that the student spend too much time reading and looking for the answer. Excessively long lists also lend themselves to concentration or emphasis on one or two objectives, which can adversely affect the validity of the test. The number of premises and responses in each list for a single matching exercise should ordinarily range from 5 to 12, the optimum size being 5 to 8 items per matching exercise (Shannon, 1975). An exercise that consists of 20 premises

and 20 responses requires the student to make 400 different comparisons—a rather lengthy and tedious task. And the economy to be achieved by using a matching exercise is no longer realized.

Short lists are also preferred because lists that are long make it more difficult to maintain the homogeneity of the material. Finally, short lists are to be preferred because, in an excessively long list, the pupil may inadvertently miss the correct answer, thereby reducing the validity of the test.

4. *Avoid having an equal number of premises and responses.* If the student is required only to make a one-to-one match, it is conceivable that for an eight-item exercise, the student who knows seven of the eight answers can get the eighth answer correct solely on the basis of elimination. A good rule of thumb to follow is to have two or three more responses than premises.

Somewhat related to this point is the practice of writing matching exercises in which the student can use any one response once, more than once, or not at all. We encourage this to help minimize guessing.

5. *Arrange the answers in some systematic fashion.* For the convenience of the student, words should be listed in alphabetical order; dates and numbers, in either ascending or descending order. The simpler we can make the task for the examinee, the more effective the item is likely to be.

Directions:		Under column A are listed famous wars and battles. Under column B are listed dates of these wars or battles. Place the letter of the appropriate date in the blank to the left of the battle or war.		

		Column A	Column B	
(A)	1.	Battle of Hastings	A.	1066
(F)	2.	Crimean War	B.	1759
(B)	3.	Plains of Abraham	C.	1777
(C)	4.	Saratoga Campaign	D.	1812
(E)	5.	Waterloo	E.	1815
			F.	1861
			G.	1904
			H.	1914

6. *Avoid giving extraneous irrelevant clues.*

7. *Explain clearly the basis on which the match is to be made.* Although it would appear self-evident that the student matches something with something, *how* he is to match is not always clear. For example, if a list of authors and a list of book titles are presented to the examinee, is he to match title with author, or vice versa? If a list of inventors and a list of inventions is given, is the student to match invention with inventor or inventor with invention? Although it does not make any difference *how* the match is accomplished when a single statement in one list is matched with a single answer in the other list (the one-to-one match), confusion can result when any single response may be used once, more than once, or not at all. It is there-

fore essential that the student be given *explicit* instructions so that he will know what he is to do and how he is to do it.

Here is a set of directions that convey the essence of the examinee's task:

Directions: In the blank to the left of each author in column A, write the letter of the book title in column B that he wrote. You may use a letter in column B once, more than once, or not at all. The first item is answered as an example.

	Column A		Column B
(A) X.	Arthur Hailey	A.	*Wheels*
(D) 1.	Eric Segal	B.	*Main Street*
(E) 2.	Irving Wallace	C.	*Winds of War*
(H) 3.	Joseph Wambaugh	D.	*Love Story*
(C) 4.	Herman Wouk	E.	*Seven Minutes*
(F) 5.	Leon Uris	F.	*QB VII*
		G.	*The Winding Staircase*
		H.	*The New Centurions*

Ordinarily, a separate set of instructions will be needed for each matching exercise, to ensure that the student understands exactly what he is to do.[3]

8. *Maintain grammatical consistency.* Use all proper names or all common nouns; all singulars or all plurals; all men or all women. Do not have the name of one woman among ten men and ask for the name of the actress who won the Academy Award in 1963. Mixing the lists may provide an irrelevant clue.

9. *Every response in one column should be a plausible answer to every premise in the other column.*

A Check List for Writing the Matching Exercise

Table 9–3 presents the check list to be used when preparing the matching exercise. In addition, the suggestions previously given for writing the objective item should be considered.

WRITING TRUE-FALSE ITEMS

The true-false (or it may be referred to as the alternate-response) item is essentially a two-response multiple-choice item in which only one of the propositions (answers) is presented and the student judges the truth or falsity of the statement. Some of the more common variations of the true-false item are (1) yes-no, (2) right-wrong, (3) cluster variety, and (4) correction variety. The right-wrong and yes-no varieties (the yes-no format

---

[3] Because of space limitations, we do not always have a separate set of directions for the various examples discussed in this chapter.

© 1968 United Features Syndicate, Inc.

© 1968 United Features Syndicate, Inc.

TABLE 9–3   Check List for Writing Matching Exercises

FACTOR	YES
1. Have you given the student clear, explicit instructions?	✕
2. Are the response and premise lists both homogeneous?	✕
3. Is one list shorter than the other?	✕
4. Are both lists between 5 and 12 entries?	✕
5. Are the premises longer and more complex? The responses simple and short?	✕
6. Did you arrange the responses in some systematic order?	✕
7. Do both lists of a matching exercise appear on the same page?	✕
8. Are your lists relatively free of clues?	✕
9. Did you have your materials reviewed independently?	✕

is often used to measure attitudes, values, beliefs, and interests) are essentially similar to the traditional true-false format except that the nature of indicating the answer is different. The right-wrong or yes-no varieties are more useful for testing young children, who are better able to comprehend the concept of right-wrong than true-false. Following are some illustrations of the true-false item and the cluster and correction variations.

TRUE-FALSE VARIETY   The student is presented with a declarative statement that is true or false.

T F   The mean would be greater than the median in a distribution of the income taxes paid by Americans in 1972.

CLUSTER VARIETY   In the cluster variety, there is one incomplete stem (statement) with several suggested answers. Each of the suggested answers is to be judged as true or false. The cluster variety permits the item writer to ask many questions, using a single stem and thereby conserving on space and reading time. Sometimes the cluster of statements will refer to a drawing, graph, or photograph.

The arithmetic mean is
T F   (a) a measure of central tendency.
T F   (b) less affected by extreme scores than is the median.
T F   (c) used to express the correlation between two variables.

CORRECTION VARIETY   In the correction variety, the subject is required to make every false statement true by crossing out the incorrect portion (it may be a word or phrase) and replacing it with the correct word or phrase. We recommend that the portion of the statement to be judged true or false be underlined. Otherwise, there may be instances when the student will judge the accuracy of the statement in a different light and will make a correction that was not an instructional goal for the teacher. For example, assume that Miss Adder wanted to see whether her students knew that the square root of 64 is 8. If she prepared her item as

T F   The square root of 64 is 9.

one student might cross out the "64" and substitute "81"; another might cross out the "9" and substitute "8." Since Miss Adder's intent was to measure knowledge of the square root of 64, she should rewrite her item as

T F   The square root of 64 is 9.

Then the student knows that he is to determine whether or not "9" is the square root of 64.

Another variation of the correction variety is frequently used in the language arts. Here a single sentence is presented and broken up into segments. For each of the designated segments, the student must determine whether it is right or wrong. He then can be asked to correct the error(s). Like the simple correction type, this variation is economical from the standpoint of space needed and time required to read and respond on the part of the pupil. However, it is quite difficult to write sentences that contain errors but which still seem sensible before they have been corrected.

(A)	(B)	(C)	(D)	A	B	C	D
Doesn't/	them children know/	it ain't right/	to steal?				
Don't	those	isn't					

In the preceding example, sections A, B, and C are incorrect. The subject indicates this by blackening in the spaces A, B, and C. (Of course there could be a true-false under each of A, B, C, D, but this method consumes more space.) As noted earlier, the pupil could also be instructed to correct the incorrect parts of speech.

True-false items, while very popular in the early days of testing, have lost much of their popularity. They are seldom used in standardized tests, and most authors of measurement texts speak disparagingly of them. For example, Ahmann and Glock (1971, p. 94) stated that "the advantages accrued by using true-false test items are outweighed by the limitations also present." Stanley (1964, p. 216) suggested that one should "restrict the use . . . to situations in which other test forms are inapplicable." Wesman (1971, p. 94) concurred with Stanley and said: "On balance, unless there are compelling reasons to do otherwise, the test constructor would do well to favor other forms of items." Ebel (1965b, 1972), one of the few who favor the true-false item, suggested that many of the weaknesses of this item format (ambiguity, measures triviality) are *not* inherent in the form of the item; rather, the weaknesses are due to *misuse* and lack of skill on the part of the item writer. Ebel (1970, p. 288) presents a cogent argument and concludes that there is "no necessary reason why true-false items should be more trivial, irrelevant, or badly written than other forms of test items." Furthermore, he contends that if true-false items do about the same job, and discriminate about as well in tests of equal length (in minutes), why should they not be used?

Ebel makes the following observation in defense of using true-false tests:

> Acquisition in command of knowledge is . . . the central purpose of education. All knowledge is knowledge of propositions. . . . The essential purpose of logical reasoning is to test the truth or falsity of deductive propositions. Propositions are expressed in sentences. These sentences may be true or false. This is the stuff of which human knowledge (and true-false tests) are made. (Ebel, 1965b, p. 125.)

He disagrees with the recommendation that classroom teachers should give preference to writing multiple-choice over true-false items (Ebel, 1975a).

Versatility of the True-False Item

Many of the so-called faults of true-false items—such as "they only measure trivia," "they are most susceptible to guessing," "they encourage students to memorize rather than understand," and "they do not measure the higher mental processes"—are more the fault of the item *writer* than the item format per se (Ebel, 1975). True-false items need not encourage and reward verbal *memory*. They *can* be written so that they measure comprehension, understanding, application, deduction, and problem solving (Jenkins & Deno, 1971). And true-false tests can be, and are, highly reliable (Ebel, 1970; Frisbie, 1974). But special talents are needed to write valid true-false items (Storey, 1966; Wesman, 1971). Following are some examples to illustrate the versatility of the true-false item.

TESTING FOR FACTUAL KNOWLEDGE

T F   The variance equals the average squared deviation score.

To answer this item correctly, the student need only recall the definition of variance. He does not have to know how to compute the variance, nor does he have to understand the concept of variance to answer the item correctly.

TESTING FOR COMPREHENSION OR UNDERSTANDING[4]

T F   Kinetic energy is found in a wound spring.

Here, the student would have to know more than the textbook definition of kinetic energy. He would have to *understand* what kinetic energy is and relate the concept of kinetic energy to the type of energy found in a wound spring.

TESTING FOR APPLICATION

T F   Test XYZ has a reliability of .84 and a standard deviation of 10. Its standard error of measurement is 4.

TESTING FOR DEDUCTIVE SKILL

T F   If the ceiling height of an organ chamber is 20 feet, one can install an organ with a 30-foot stop.

Here the student must know something about the physics of sound and the relationship between pitch and open-ended pipes; that is, that an open pipe will produce twice the pitch of a closed pipe.

TESTING FOR PROBLEM-SOLVING ABILITY

T F   Given the general gas law, where $PV/T = k$, where $k = 2$, $P = 5$, and $T = 50°C$, then $V = 20$.

There are some who think that since a critical element in the solution to this type of problem is *knowledge* (T is absolute temperature) rather than problem-solving ability per se, it should not be classified as problem solving. We must emphasize that as one goes beyond the "knowledge of facts" in Bloom's *Taxonomy* (1956), and approaches problem solving and analytical skills, it is necessary for the student to have some basic knowledge.

Advantages and Limitations of True-False Items

The major advantages of true-false items are that they—

1. Are good for young children and/or pupils who are poor readers.

---

[4] Our examples of items to measure understanding, application, deduction, and problem solving would be little more than factual recall of information *if* the student had studied these same or comparable items in class or in the textbook.

2. Can cover a larger amount of subject matter in a given testing period than can any other objective item; that is, more questions can be asked. A student can answer three T–F items for every two multiple-choice items (Frisbie, 1971; Oosterhoff & Glassnapp, 1974). But the time ratio depends upon the content as well as the difficulty/comprehension factor of the item. Measuring factual information will generally show less time-to-respond variability than measuring comprehension (Frisbie, 1971). We must also be aware that the "trade-off" value of obtaining broader content sampling with true-false items may result in more measurement error and hence lower test reliability.

3. Generally provide high reliability per unit of testing time.[5]

4. Can be scored quickly, reliably, and objectively by clerks.

5. Are particularly suitable for testing beliefs in popular misconceptions and superstitions.

6. Are adaptable to most content areas.

7. May provide a salvage pool for those multiple-choice items that should be discarded because only two of the responses provided are selected by the majority of students. The true-false item needs only one good response to a stem.

8. Can, if carefully constructed, measure the higher mental processes of understanding, application, and interpretation.

The major disadvantages of the true-false item are that—

1. Pupils' scores on short true-false tests may be unduly influenced by good or poor luck in guessing.

2. True-false items are more susceptible to ambiguity and misinterpretation than any other selection-type objective item, thereby resulting in low reliability. In fact, on an item-per-item basis, true-false tests tend to have the lowest reliability.

3. They lend themselves most easily to cheating. If a student knows that he is to take a T–F test, it doesn't require much effort to work out a system in which one of the better students signals a T versus F answer.

4. They tend to be less discriminating, item for item, than multiple-choice tests.

5. When the correction-for-guessing formula is used, multiple-choice items are easier than true-false items (Oosterhoff & Glassnapp, 1974).

6. They are susceptible to an acquiescence response set; that is, subjects tend to develop a pattern of responding (true) in a somewhat automatic form without really giving thought to the item.

[5] This should be interpreted very carefully. It does *not* mean that T-F tests have the highest reliability. Oosterhoff and Glassnapp (1974) said that one needs 2½ to 4½ times as many T-F as multiple-choice items to get equivalent reliability. However, *more* T-F than multiple-choice items can be asked and answered per unit of testing time.

7. There are many instances when statements are *not* unequivocally true or false; rather, there are degrees of correctness. For example, the boiling point of water depends upon the pressure. The statement "water boils at 212°F" would be true only at sea level. Many true-false items require qualifiers, which in themselves may provide an irrelevant clue. Because of the phenomenon of degree of correctness, good true-false items are difficult to write.

8. Specific determiners (a type of irrelevant clue) are more prevalent in true-false items than in any other objective-item format. Specific determiners generally appear because the item writer wishes to have a completely true or false statement.

In conclusion: When very young children and/or persons with limited vocabulary and reading speed are to be tested; if one desires broad content sampling in a relatively short testing time; if one wants a test that can be scored accurately, quickly, and objectively by clerks, the true-false item is recommended. Although writing true-false items to measure the higher mental processes can be both difficult and time consuming, it is less difficult to write a good true-false item than to write a good four-response multiple-choice item.

Suggestions for Writing True-False Items

1. *Use simple, clear language.* Ambiguous statements resulting from loose or faulty wording are a frequent cause of faulty true-false items.

T   F   All men are created equal.

On the surface, a teacher writing an item on the Declaration of Independence might think that this is an unambiguous item. As stated in the Declaration of Independence, the item is true. But a student could interpret the item in terms of mental ability, pain threshold, physical strength, or other characteristics and mark the item false. If the teacher wants to know whether his pupils understand "equality" as stated in the Declaration of Independence, he should write the item as follows:

<u>T</u>   F   The Declaration of Independence states that all men are created equal.

Ambiguity is often present when an item deals with qualitative terms such as "more," "few," "heavier," "lighter," and the like. Since these words are somewhat vague, indefinite, and imprecise, they may be interpreted differently by different people. It is suggested that, wherever possible, *quantitative* rather than qualitative terminology be employed.

Poor: <u>T</u>   F   Humphrey received a large number of votes in the 1968 presidential election.

How much is "large?" Is it 30 or 40 or 46 percent? A student could answer a test item incorrectly because of his interpretation of the qualitative terms used.

Better: T̲   F   Humphrey received more than 40 percent of the votes in the 1968 presidential election.

2. *True-false items must be based on statements that are clearly true or clearly false.* It is not uncommon to find T-F items consisting of two statements, part of which is correct, the other part wrong. Consider the following example:

<table>
<tr><td></td><td>(1)</td><td>(2)</td></tr>
</table>

Poor: / Whales are mammals, / and / with the exception of humans, they are the most intelligent mammals/.

Statement (1) is correct; but statement (2) is false.

Better: Whales are the most intelligent mammals.

When a true-false item does not satisfy the condition of being completely true or clearly false, we inject an element of ambiguity or trickiness into the item. Whenever the knowledgeable student is confused by the wording and answers incorrectly because he reads too deeply into the question and recognizes that there are possible exceptions, we have a faulty item. Trying to doctor up a true-false item that is not unequivocally true or false by inserting a series of qualifiers or exceptions will likely result in a more confusing item.

We recognize that there are some statements, especially generalizations, which need not be wholly true or false. When this is the case, we recommend a variation of the true-false item—true, false, sometimes—be used. For example, we would want to have stability in an aptitude test. But in a personality test we might not want to have stability. Therefore, to write an item regarding the stability of test scores, we recommend the following item format.

T   F   S̲   Stability of test scores is essential for a test to be valid.

There are some instances where the correct answer depends upon a particular frame of reference. For example, borderline intelligence may have an IQ range on one test that differs from the designation of borderline intelligence on another IQ test. When this is the case, the student must be given the frame of reference used.

Poor: T   F   The limits of borderline intelligence are 70–79 IQ.
Better: T̲   F   On the WAIS (Wechsler Adult Intelligence Scale), the limits of borderline intelligence are 70–79 IQ.

3. *Avoid trick questions.* One of the easiest and surest ways of disenchanting and "souring" students toward tests and teachers is to have a test full of trick questions, such as

T <u>F</u>   O. Henry was William Sidney Porter.

The "trick" here is that Porter's middle name is spelled Sydney.

T <u>F</u>   The Magna Carta was signed in 1215 BC.

The "trick" here is that the Magna Carta was signed in 1215 AD.

T <u>F</u>   The Battle of Armageddon was a famous battle.

The "trick" here is that Armageddon has not yet been fought. According to the Revelation of Saint John the Divine in the New Testament, it *will* be a great battle between the powers of good and evil.

We must remember that students are under pressure when they take tests. They tend to read very rapidly and pay little attention to "tricky" wording. More important, one of our objectives in giving tests is to see what the student has learned; *not* whether he can be tricked. In addition to jeopardizing the affective relations between student and teacher, "trick" questions affect the test's validity.

4. *When the true-false item is used to test for cause-and-effect relationships, we strongly recommend that the first proposition in the statement always be true, with the subordinate clause* (reason or explanation) *being written as either false or true.* The student could be told that the first part of the statement is true and that he is only to judge the truth of falsity of the subordinate clause.

T <u>F</u>   Marble rarely, if ever, contains fossils *because*
                         (true)
              it is a metamorphosed igneous rock.
                  (true or false)

5. *Word the item so that superficial knowledge suggests a wrong answer.* This does not mean that the wording should be ambiguous or overly complex. Rather, it means that the wording should be such that the student who has only superficial knowledge may answer incorrectly.

6. *Make the wrong answer consistent with a popular misconception that is totally irrelevant to the item.*

7. *Avoid specific determiners.* We have previously stated that irrelevant clues must be avoided. However, because specific determiners tend to be more prevalent in the true-false item than in other objective-item formats, we feel it bears some additional discussion. Achievement tests should not be

measures of test-wiseness. In the true-false test, the teacher, in his attempt to write an item that is clearly true, may use such qualifiers as "usually," "some," "generally," "should," "sometimes," and "may" to make the statement true. On the other hand, the teacher who wishes to ensure falsity in an item may use qualifiers such as "always," "never," "none," and "all." Pupils learn very quickly that the odds are in their favor to mark test items as true or false, depending upon the qualifiers used. In the long run, they will be right more times than they are wrong. If the true-false item cannot be rewritten to avoid the use of specific determiners, we recommend that a different item format be used.

8. *Avoid lifting statements verbatim from the text.* All textual material should be rephrased or put in a new context to discourage rote memory.

9. *Avoid making true statements consistently longer than false statements.* Teachers, in their attempt to ensure absolute truth in a statement will employ qualifying statements that make the item longer. Pupils readily learn to recognize this irrelevant clue. To minimize this effect, the item writer should vary the length of both true and false statements.

10. *For the correction type of true-false item, underline the word(s) to be corrected.*

11. *Have approximately an equal number of true and false statements.* Some students have a tendency (response set) to mark items that they are unsure of as "true," while other students mark the items "false." By having approximately an equal number of true and false statements in the test, we limit the influence of response set on the validity of the test score. But having exactly the *same* number of true-false statements could be a clue to the testwise student. Ebel (1965) and Frisbie (1974) suggested having more false than true statements since there is evidence that false statements tend to be more discriminating. Also, students who don't know the answer have a propensity to answer false (Frisbie, 1974).

Somewhat related to both this point as well as an earlier one regarding the wording of the item are the findings that the difficulty of a true-false item can be affected by the phraseology employed, that is, a true-affirmative statement (three is an odd number), a false-affirmative (six is an odd number), a true negative (six is not an odd number), and a false-negative (three is not an even number). Peterson and Peterson (1976) reported that true-affirmatives are easier than false-affirmatives and that false-negatives are easier to verify than true-negatives. They question the suggestion made that true-false tests should have more false items and recommend using negative phrasing be it a true-negative or a false-negative wording that is employed.

A Check List for Writing True-False Items

Table 9–4 presents a check list for preparing true-false items. We urge you to review the material previously discussed for writing the objective type items.

TABLE 9–4   **Check List for Writing True-False Items**

FACTOR	YES
1. Is each item expressed in clear, simple language?	×
2. Did you avoid lifting statements verbatim from the text?	×
3. Have negative statements been avoided where possible?	×
4. Have specific determiners such as "all," "may," "sometimes," been avoided?	×
5. Have double-barreled items (part true, part false) been avoided?	×
6. Have trick questions been removed?	×
7. In the correction type true-false, is the word(s) to be corrected clearly indicated?	×
8. Is each item clearly true or false?	×
9. Are there approximately the same number of true and false items?	×
10. Have the items been edited?	×
11. Have the items been independently reviewed?	×

SUMMARY

The principal ideas, conclusions, and recommendations presented in this chapter are summarized in the following statements:

1. Objective test items must be written as simply and clearly as possible so that all examinees will be able to make the same interpretation of the items intent.

2. Test items should be tailored to fit the age and ability level of the examinees.

3. Textbook language, technical jargon, and excessively difficult vocabulary should be avoided wherever possible. Otherwise, we have a test of verbal fluency or general intelligence.

4. Irrelevant clues should be avoided. The test-wise student should not have any undue advantage over the comparably knowledgeable but non-test-wise student.

5. There should be only one correct or best answer. We prefer the correct answer variety inasmuch as it is difficult to obtain agreement, even among experts, on what is the "best" answer.

6. Test items should be reviewed, preferably by a fellow teacher.

7. Important ideas rather than trivial details should be stressed. Otherwise, we encourage rote memory.

8. The short-answer item is well suited to those objectives and content areas where the answer can be provided by a word(s), symbol, number, or formula.

9. For short-answer items (a) omit only key words, (b) avoid over-mutilated sentences, (c) use the direct question format where feasible,

(d) avoid giving irrelevant clues, and (e) for numerical problems, tell the student the degree of precision desired and indicate whether the unit of expression is expected in his answer.

10. For matching exercises (a) keep the lists relatively short (5 to 12 entries in each list), (b) keep each list homogeneous, (c) arrange each list in some systematic fashion (for example, order by length of response, or in ascending or descending order for dates and numbers), (d) have both lists appear on the same page, and (e) have one list shorter than the other.

11. For true-false items (a) avoid double-barreled items (part true, part false), (b) avoid negative questions where possible, (c) avoid double negatives, (d) have an approximately equal number of true and false statements to counteract the effects of the examinee's response set, and (e) restrict their use to items for which the answer is clearly true or false.

CHAPTER TEN

Writing the Objective Test Item: Multiple-Choice and Context-Dependent

Multiple-choice items are the most popular and versatile of the selection-type objective item. They are widely adaptable to different content areas and objectives and can be used to measure rote memory as well as complex skills. (See Mosier, Myers, & Price, 1945.) No doubt, such adaptability and versatility is responsible for these items being the stock in trade of many commercially prepared achievement and aptitude tests.

The measurement of the higher mental processes can be attained objectively. Our discussion in Chapter 9 and some of our discussion in this chapter concern the use of single, independent test items to measure complex achievement. There are, however, some cases in which items based upon an external source (such as a graph, diagram, table, chart, or verbal passage) are more suitable for measuring complex achievement. Items based on such external sources are called *context-dependent* and are considered in this chapter.

After studying this chapter, the student should be able to—

1. Define and discuss the multiple-choice format and some of its more frequently used variations.
2. Understand why the multiple-choice format is so popular.
3. Discuss the advantages and limitations of the multiple-choice format.
4. Understand and apply the guidelines offered when writing the multiple-choice item.
5. Define and discuss the following context-dependent item formats: pictorial, interlinear, and interpretive exercises.
6. Understand and apply the guidelines offered when writing items based upon pictorial materials.
7. List the two most serious limitations of the interpretive exercise as a measure of complex learning.
8. Understand and apply the guidelines offered for writing the interpretive exercises.
9. Write better multiple-choice items.

THE MULTIPLE-CHOICE ITEM

The multiple-choice item consists of two parts: (1) the *stem*, which contains the problem; and (2) a list of suggested answers (responses or options). The incorrect responses are often called *foils* or *distracters*; the correct response, the *key*. The stem may be stated as a direct question or an incomplete statement. From the list of responses provided, the student selects the one that is correct (or best).[1]

[1] A possible variation is to have multiple-choice questions that allow the examinee to choose as many options as are correct. This variation is the same as the true-false cluster variety discussed on page 262. It is generally *not* preferred because it may lead to scoring problems.

Distracters is sometimes spelled with an o: *distractors*. We prefer the first spelling, which is usual in measurement texts.

Some items can be written more clearly in one format than in the other. The direct question format has several advantages: (1) it forces the item writer to state the problem clearly in the stem; (2) it reduces the possibility of giving the examinee grammatical clues; and (3) it may be more easily handled by the younger and less able students because less demand is placed on good reading skills. One disadvantage of the direct question form is that it may require lengthier responses.

There appears to be some disagreement regarding the relative superiority of the question variety over the incomplete statement variety. Whereas Dunn and Goldstein (1959) reported no advantage, Board and Whitney (1972) found that items of the incomplete statement format were more difficult and lowered the test's reliability. Regardless of the empirical research, one thing is clear. If the incomplete statement form is used, the stem must be clear and meaningful in and of itself and not lead into a series of unrelated true-false statements.

Variations of the Multiple-Choice Format

The four most frequently used variations of the multiple-choice item are (1) *one correct answer*, (2) *best answer*, (3) *analogy type*, and (4) *reverse type*.[2]

One Correct Answer

This is the simplest type of multiple-choice item. The student is required to select the *one* correct answer listed among several plausible, but incorrect, options.

Directions: Each of the questions or incomplete statements below is followed by several answers. From these, you are to choose the *one* answer that answers the question or completes the statement correctly. Place the letter of your answer (A,B,C,D,E) in the blank at the left of the item.[3]

---

[2] Some other variations of the multiple-choice item are the *association, substitution, incomplete-alternatives, combined response,* and *multiple-response* varieties. Excellent descriptions and illustrations of these variations can be found in Thorndike (1971c) and Gerberich (1956).

What might more properly be referred to as a *procedure,* rather than a format, per se, is the answer-until-correct variety. Although this procedure may result in higher test reliability (Gilman & Ferry, 1972; Hanna, 1975), it consumes more time per item and may lower the test's validity (Hanna, 1975). Because of the paucity of research, we do not recommend the A-U-C procedure at this time.

[3] If answer sheets are used, the student would be directed to blacken in the corresponding space on the answer sheet. The example would then illustrate how this is done.

<u>(C)</u>   If 36 percent of a test's variance is error, what is the test's reliability co-efficient?

     A. 0.36
     B. 0.40
     C. 0.64
     D. 0.80

Best Answer

The preceding item has *one* and *only* one correct answer. There can be no argument that there are two correct answers, with one being "more correct" than the other. But look at the following item:

> A test manual reports a Kuder-Richardson reliability of .95 for 25,000 children. We can conclude that the scores on this test are
> A. highly valid.
> B. highly reliable.
> C. suitable for use in guidance.
> <u>D.</u> highly internally consistent.

Although both B and D are correct, D is the *best* answer.

There are times where it is more difficult, if not impossible, to express one unequivocal right answer within the limits of the multiple-choice format. For example, "the major purpose of the United Nations," does not lend itself to the single-correct-answer format. And yet, there still may be one answer that is "best." When this is the case, the best-answer variation is useful. The directions are similar to those of the single correct answer *except* that the student is told to select the *best* answer.

Analogy Type

The analogy type of multiple-choice item is more frequently found on commercially prepared aptitude and achievement tests than on teacher-made tests. There is no reason, however, why it cannot be used for teacher-made tests. When used occasionally, it introduces novelty.

In this format, the student is required to deduce the relationship that exists between the first two parts of the item and then apply it to the third and fourth parts. Normally, the third part is given and the missing fourth part is selected from the list of options on the basis of the relationship existing between the first two parts.

Irregular curvature of the lens: astigmatism: deficiency in thyroid secretion:
    A. cretinism
    B. hybridism

C. hydrocephaly
D. mongolism

Reverse Multiple-Choice Type

This format is the opposite of the single correct answer in that all but *one* of the answers are correct. It is sometimes called the negative variety of multiple-choice item. As will be discussed in a later section (pp. 281–282), one of the most difficult tasks in writing multiple-choice items is to provide wrong answers (distracters) that are plausible and homogeneous. In some cases it is easier to construct three or four options that are true about a given fact than it is to prepare an adequate number of plausible distracters. When this is the case, the reverse multiple-choice format may be used. However, we do not recommend its use unless absolutely necessary. And, if this format is used, the students' attention should be drawn to the fact that they are to select the incorrect answer.

ADVANTAGES AND LIMITATIONS OF MULTIPLE-CHOICE ITEMS

There are several major advantages of multiple-choice items:

1. Possibly the most outstanding advantage is their versatility. Multiple-choice questions can measure factual recall, but can also measure the student's ability to reason, to exercise judgment, and to express himself correctly and effectively.

2. They can be scored quickly and accurately by machines, clerks, teacher aides, and even students themselves.

3. They are relatively efficient. True-false and matching items are slightly more efficient (in terms of the number of questions that can be asked in a prescribed time and the space needed to present the questions), whereas the essay question is far less efficient.

4. The degree of difficulty of the test can be controlled by changing the degree of homogeneity of the responses. If, for example, one is giving a test to discriminate among pupils in terms of their achievement, then he should use items that are neither too difficult nor too easy. Knapp (1968) conducted a study that compared three versions of multiple-choice items and found that the choice of responses often drastically affected the item difficulty.

5. Compared to true-false items, multiple-choice questions have a relatively small susceptibility to score variations due to guessing.[4]

---

[4] The probability of guessing a correct answer depends upon the number of options. For a three-option item, the chances are 1 in 3; for a five-option item, the chances of guessing the correct answer are 1 in 5.

6. They can provide the teacher with valuable diagnostic information, especially if all the responses are plausible and vary only in their degree of correctness.

7. They usually provide greater test reliability per item than do true-false items.

8. Multiple-choice items are easier to respond to and are better liked by students than true-false items. Students feel they are less ambiguous than true-false items.

9. Of all the selection-type objective items, the multiple-choice item is most free from response sets (the tendency for an individual to give a different answer when the *same* content is presented in a different form). For a fuller discussion of response set, see Cronbach (1950).

In spite of their popularity, multiple-choice items are not without their critics (see Hoffmann, 1962). These critics are not opposed to multiple-choice exercises alone. They object to all objective-type items, suggesting that such formats almost invariably lead to the asking of trivial, ambiguous questions that may well handicap the really able students. Two important facts, however, detract from the critics' credibility: (1) the critics supply no empirical evidence supporting their contentions; and (2) they offer no alternative methods of assessment and appear unaware of the serious limitations of essay testing. We agree, however, that there are deficiencies or limitations associated with multiple-choice items. Some of the more serious limitations of the four- or five-option multiple-choice items are as follows:

1. They are very difficult to construct. Teachers cannot always think of plausible sounding distracters (incorrect alternatives), and if only one good distracter is listed, they wind up with a multiple-choice item with as large a guessing factor as for a true-false item.

2. There is a tendency for teachers to write multiple-choice items demanding only factual recall. This tendency is probably less for multiple-choice items than for other objective-type items, but it still persists.

3. Of all the selection-type objective items, the multiple-choice item requires the most time for the student to respond, especially when very fine discriminations have to be made.

4. Research has shown that test-wise students perform better on multiple-choice items than do non-test-wise students, and that multiple-choice tests favor the high-risk–taking student (Rowley, 1974). Also, students who are skillful in recognizing ambiguity do better than students who do not (Alker, Carlson, & Hermann, 1967).

5. Some professional educators have voiced their concern about the validity of multiple-choice tests. Barzun (1947), Getzels (1960), and Hoffmann (1962) contend that the multiple-choice item punishes the more able student and rewards the less able student. One of the reasons given by these critics

for the multiple-choice item discriminating against the more able student is that ambiguity is found in multiple-choice items. We contend that an item is ambiguous because of the item writer and *not* because of the item format per se.

SOME SUGGESTIONS FOR WRITING MULTIPLE-CHOICE ITEMS

Although any test item is good or bad depending upon the clarity of expression, the multiple-choice item must have, in addition to a stem that is clear and free from ambiguity, a correct answer and a set of plausible responses (distracters). The value of a multiple-choice item depends to a large degree on the skill with which the various distracters are written. It will be readily evident when reading these guidelines that a common theme pervades the writing of all test items, regardless of the format used. Two basic questions that an item writer must continually ask himself are: (1) did I communicate well? and (2) did I provide any clues to the correct answer? Because it is so important that the item writer communicate effectively and not give the answer away, we will repeat some of the suggestions discussed in the previous chapters. (See Board and Whitney, 1972, for a discussion of the effects of item-writing flaws on a test's difficulty, reliability, and validity.)

1. *The essence of the problem should be in the stem.* The stem should contain the central problem so that the student will have some idea as to what is expected of him and some tentative answer in mind before he begins to read the options. There are some exceptions, such as in a literature test; here, if the objective is to ascertain the pupil's understanding of the main theme in a story or poem, the stem may be short and the options long. An easy way to ascertain whether or not the stem is meaningful in and of itself is to cover up the responses and just read the stem. If the stem is well written, it could easily become a short-answer item by drawing a line after the last word. If it would not be a good short-answer item, something is wrong with the stem.

Poor stems: Consumer cooperatives
                Work
                Reliability

The stem must consist of a statement that contains a verb. The "poor" stems illustrated above do not convey the intent of the question to the student.

Better stem: Which of the following best describes what happens when work is done?

2. *Avoid repetition of words in the options.* The stem should be written

so that key words are incorporated in the stem and will not have to be repeated in each option. This will save reading time on the part of the student as well as help focus the student's attention on the problem. It will also conserve space.

Poor: Test reliability
        A. may be improved by increasing the length of the test.
        B. may be improved by including a larger number of items with high difficulty indices.
        C. may be improved by shortening the test.
        D. may be improved by changing the test to one of absolute standards of performance.

Better: The reliability of a test may be improved by
        A. increasing the length of the test.
        B. decreasing the length of the test.
        C. changing the test to one of absolute standards of achievement.
        D. including a larger proportion of items with high difficulty indices.

3. *Avoid superfluous wording.* As mentioned earlier, many teachers feel that elaborate explanations make the item clearer when, in reality, they may cause it to be more difficult because of possible ambiguity. The stem should be concise, clear, and free of "window dressing." Although the research on violation of this guide is inconclusive vis-à-vis the item's validity, reliability, difficulty, and discriminaton power (Board & Whitney, 1972; Dudycha & Carpenter, 1973; Schmeiser & Whitney, 1975), we still favor avoiding verbal overload if for no other reason than that it demands extra reading time on the examinee's part and thereby reduces the number of items that can be asked in a given testing time.

4. *When the incomplete statement format is used, the options should come at the end of the statement.* All test items should present the problem to the student as *early* and clearly as possible. The following two items measure the student's knowledge of the concept of reliability coefficients.

Poor: The coefficient of (1) stability, (2) equivalence, (3) stability and equivalence, (4) internal consistency is used to study the homogeneity of test items.

Better: A statistic used to study the homogeneity of test items is called the coefficient of
        A. stability.
        B. equivalence.
        C. internal consistency.
        D. stability and equivalence.

In the "poor" example, the student's continuity of reading is impaired, and this may result in confusion. In the "better" example, the essence of the problem is presented early and clearly. Also the examinee need not engage in extensive rereading of the item to see what it is he is expected to do.

5. *Arrange the alternatives as simply as possible.* Although the responses could be placed after the stem in run-on fashion, it is preferable to list them in some order *below* the stem (alphabetical if a single word, in ascending or descending order if numerals or dates, or by length of response). This makes it easier for the examinee to read the material. Also, in the incomplete statement format, where each response completes the sentence, listed alternatives are easier to consider separately than if placed in paragraph fashion, as in the preceding "poor" example.

6. *Avoid highly technical distracters.* Occasionally, teachers will attempt to make a test item more difficult by using either unfamiliar or difficult vocabulary. They may do this either in the stem or in the distracters. This, of course, should be avoided. As we have said throughout Chapters 8 and 9, the difficulty of an item should be related to the content and instructional objectives, *not* to the vocabulary used.

7. *All responses should be plausible and homogeneous.* One of the advantages of the multiple-choice over the true-false item is that the examinee is required to select the correct or best answer from among the many answers provided, thereby reducing the probability of guessing the correct answer. The student should be forced to read and consider all options. No distracter should be automatically eliminated by the student because it is irrelevant or a stupid answer. Every distracter should be grammatically consistent with the stem so that no clues are given to the correct answer.

Poor: Which of the following men invented the telephone?
  A. Bell
  B. Salk
  C. Morse
  D. Pasteur
  E. Marconi

This question is concerned with an inventor in the field of communications. Therefore, for the distracters to be plausible, all should deal with inventors in the field of communications who lived at about the same time. It is true that all five persons listed in the example discovered something, but their discoveries differ markedly. Only Bell, Marconi, and Morse were inventors in the field of communications. Salk is in virology and Pasteur was a bacteriologist. Only Bell, Morse, and Pasteur lived at about the same time. The distracters offered the student here are definitely not plausible, nor do they offer a realistic challenge to the students' knowledge.

Better·   Which of the following men invented the telephone?
     A. Bell
     B. Morse
     C. Edison
     D. Marconi

We have emphasized that all distracters should be plausible and appealing to the student. Unless each distracter attracts some pupils who have certain misconceptions, the test is not functioning effectively. But how does the item writer get such distracters? This is, without a doubt, one of the most difficult aspects of preparing good multiple-choice items. Teachers, in their attempts to write plausible distracters, could (1) guess at the plausibility of the distracters on the basis of their experience and knowledge of how pupils behave, (2) administer a completion test and use the most frequently occurring errors as plausible distracters, or (3) administer a completion-type test and select as distracters those errors that best discriminate among the high- and low-scoring students. It makes little difference which of these approaches one uses to obtain plausible distracters, inasmuch as there is no significant effect on the test's validity (Frisbie, 1971; Owens, Hanna, & Coppedge, 1970). We have found it useful to use the completion type of format, because a large number of incorrect yet plausible responses are obtained. When a teacher is trying to conjure up typical errors in, say, mathematics—be they computational or because of misunderstanding—what is a better source than actual errors most often made by the students? We cannot think of a better pool of errors that represents *genuine* misunderstanding and/or confusion among pupils.

8. *Avoid making the correct answer longer than the incorrect one.* Jones and Kaufman (1975) found that a "guessing" response set resulted from a *position* and *length* response set, the frequency of "guessing" varying according to the number of items answered correctly by the student as well as the frequency of the position and length of the distracters. Board and Whitney (1972) reported that this item-writing flaw benefited the poor student more than the good student and reduced the test's validity and internal consistency. We recognize that *occasionally*, because of the need for qualifying words, the correct answer often is longer than the incorrect distracters (Chase, 1964). If this is the case, lengthen the distracters with qualifiers so that they will also look more plausible. Since students tend to select the response that is more elaborate and detailed, the item writer should avoid having the correct answer the longest one in every instance.

9. *Avoid giving irrelevant clues to the correct answer.* We have already discussed the situation in which the length of the response can be a clue to the correct answer. Other clues may be of a grammatical nature, such as the use of an "a" or "an" at the end of the statement; asking for the name of a male, but having all but one of the distracters with female names; using a singular or plural subject and/or verb in the stem, with just one or two

singular or plural options. At times, a key word in the stem repeated in the correct option will provide a clue. Any clues that assist the examinee in making the correct association on some basis other than knowledge are to be avoided. Following is just one example of an unintentional clue provided the student. Can you find the clue?

Which of the following diseases is caused by a virus?
  A. Gallstones
  B. Scarlet fever
  C. Typhus fever
  D. Typhoid fever
  E. Viral pneumonia

The clue is "virus" in the stem and "viral" in response E. The item is also defective in that gallstones is not a disease.

The item writer should also be on his guard to make sure that there are no overlapping items such that the information presented in one item may provide a valuable clue for answering another item.

Still another clue is provided when the correct answer assumes some definite pattern or position. Some teachers like to place the correct answer in the first or second position, while others prefer the third or fourth position. All positions should be used with approximately equal frequency and be randomly assigned throughout the test lest students become "test-wise." Again, we must admit that there are no definitive research findings related to having a random distribution of correct responses. Some researchers have shown that a "pattern effect" does not alter the item's difficulty (Hopkins & Hopkins, 1964; Marcus, 1963; Wilbur, 1966), while others have shown that a guessing response-set might be induced (Jones & Kaufman, 1975), thereby affecting the item's psychometric properties.

10. *Consider providing an "I don't know" option.* Strong arguments can be advanced against the use of this option—low ability students tend to avoid it, the average or higher ability students use it more frequently than lower ability children (Finley & Berdie, 1970). That is, the higher ability students, who are willing to admit their lack of knowledge and not guess at an answer, are being penalized. Also, use of this option may be a reflection of the pupils' personality (Sherman, 1976). Why, then, even consider this option?

If the test results are to be used in a judgmental or summative evaluation sense, this option will probably be ineffective. However, if the test results are to be used in a formative evaluation sense to assist in instructional guidance of the pupil, and the test score is not going to affect a student's grade, then it is to the pupil's advantage to be honest and mark "I don't know" rather than to guess at the answer. To guess correctly could result in a student's being placed in an instructional sequence at too high a level. For tests used, then, for instructional guidance as opposed to final evaluation, including an

"I don't know" option may be beneficial to both pupils and teachers. Of course, pupils have to be taught that it is to their advantage to use this option rather than guess blindly at an answer.

Are we contradicting ourselves here, since in Chapter 11 we encouraged students to attempt all the items? Really not. We still claim that if an "I don't know" option is *not* provided, it is to the students benefit to guess at answers he is unsure of. However, if such an option *is* provided and the test results are used for formative evaluation, it would be to the student's benefit to use it.

11. *There should be only one correct or best answer to every item.* This requirement, like many others, is obvious, but it is frequently ignored or disregarded by many teachers who prepare their own classroom achievement tests. We have seen, and occasionally we ourselves have even prepared, test items where "experts" would fail to agree on the single correct answer. In fact, even though there were innumerable review sessions held with the exercises of the National Assessment of Educational Progress project (Finley & Berdie, 1970), there were still one or two items that were found to be unscorable because either the answer provided was not clearly correct and/or there were two correct answers. Quite often, the disagreement about a correct or best answer occurs because of ambiguity in the stem, which results in different pupils making different interpretations of the intent or meaning of the question. For example, look at the following item.

Choose the man who doesn't belong in the group.
 A. Bell
 B. Salk
 C. Sabin
 D. Pasteur

The pupil who is thinking about virologists would select item A because Bell was not a virologist. Another pupil could reason that the item calls for the identification of scientists, and hence he would also select A, but for a different reason. Still another pupil could select B if his classification scheme was United States citizens. How could the teacher score the different responses?

We prefer writing the multiple-choice item—any test item, in fact—so that there is one and only one correct response rather than a "best" answer. In those cases—such as controversial issues—where the "best" answer is to be selected, this should be made clear to the students in the test directions as well as in the item itself.

12. *Avoid using "all of the above" as an option.* This option is seldom justified as a viable option on the typical multiple-choice test, since items using this option were found to be easiest especially when this alternative was keyed as the correct response (Mueller, 1975). If a student is able to recognize that just one answer is incorrect, he can automatically disregard this option. And, if on the typical four-option multiple-choice item the student is able to

recognize that at least two of the responses are correct, he can automatically select this option and get credit for having complete information, even though this may not be the case. Despite the contradictory evidence regarding the effect of option combinations (A and B; B and C) on the item's difficulty and discrimination power (Boynton, 1950; Hughes & Trimble, 1965; Mueller, 1975; Wesman & Bennett, 1946; Williamson & Hopkins, 1967), we recommend the "combination" option over the "all of the above" option. Following is an example of an item that makes the student consider various combinations and which serves somewhat the same function as one with an "all of the above" option.

Mr. Adder wants a 50-item test to measure mathematical reasoning. He is unable to write more than 40 items that measure mathematical reasoning, so he adds 10 items that measure computational skill. By adding these 10 items, Mr. Adder
  A. decreases validity.
  B. increases validity.
  C. increases reliability.
  D. increases validity and increases reliability.
  E. decreases validity and increases reliability.

13. *Use the "none of the above" option sparingly.* Some teachers use this option to "cure" multiple-choice item susceptibility to guessing and/or emphasis on measuring recall. Using this option will *not* remove the guessing factor. Rather, it can only lower its effect. For example, if a multiple-choice test consists of 100 items of a four-option format, and if each option occurs with equal frequency, the student has a 1 in 4 chance of guessing the correct answer. If "none of the above" is included, the student has a 1 in 5 chance of guessing the correct answer. But the process of obtaining the correct answer may still involve recognition rather than recall. For example, the pupil could look at each of the options and, if he didn't "recognize" the correct answer, he could select the "none of these" option as the correct answer. This option helps the teacher who wants to reduce the effects of guessing but does not change the item's emphasis on recognition.

   This does not mean that the "none of these" option is useless. In some areas, such as spelling or punctuation or arithmetic, where there is an absolute standard of correctness, the "none of these" option could be used either as a useful distracter or the correct answer. We can only say that this option should be used very infrequently and, when it is used, it should be the correct answer some of the time. For the "none of the above" option to be most useful, pupils must be convinced that it is a viable response. We suggest that it be used early in the test as a correct answer for some of the easier items. Then the student will see that he *cannot* automatically ignore it as a plausible correct answer. If it is *never* the correct answer, the test-wise student is given an irrelevant clue. Also, its use should be limited to those items where there is a single correct answer rather than a "best" answer. For example, what do we do with the pupil who selects E as the answer to the question

What is the value of π?
A. 0
B. 1
C. 2.17
D. 3.14
E. None of the above

Is the student right or wrong? It depends. As written, the student could argue that the "keyed" answer of 3.14 is not the absolute value of π. If "none of the above" were not an option in this question, there could be no argument about the best answer.

The research evidence on the "all or none of the above" options is inconclusive. When all three types of complex alternatives were used (all of the above, none of the above, or a combination of two foils such as A and B or A and C), it was found that they were more effective as distracters than were substantive alternatives. Also, the highest response rate was obtained when a combination of complex distracters was used. In addition, items containing this complex alternative tended to be the most difficult (Mueller, 1975). Does this then suggest that we are in favor of using complex alternatives? Not necessarily! We feel that they may have a place as foils in multiple-choice tests but we should heed Mueller's cautions and caveats, to wit, (1) "the disproportionate use of complex alternatives as correct answers may have seriously affected the item difficulty and discrimination," and (2) because the combination complex alternative contained several discrete kinds of alternatives, "it is impossible to determine from this study the differential effectiveness of the various kinds of combination complex alternatives" (Mueller, 1975, p. 141).

14. *Use three to five options.* A question frequently asked by teachers is: "How many distracters should be written for a multiple-choice item?" There is no magic number and it depends upon whom you ask. There are some (Costin, 1970; Grier, 1975; Tversky, 1964) who say that a three-option test is just as reliable and discriminating as a four-option test; that it requires less time to construct because it's easier to come up with two plausible distracters than with three or four; that it requires less reading time on the examinee's part, thereby permitting more questions to be asked per unit of testing time and thus permitting greater content sampling to be achieved. However, a basic assumption underlying the use of the three-item option is that maximum reliability can be achieved *only* if the number of test items is increased. On the other hand, some researchers (Ramos & Stern, 1973) as well as many authors of measurement and evaluation texts (Ahmann & Glock, 1971; Hedges, 1964; Micheels & Karnes, 1950; Thorndike & Hagen, 1977; Torger-

son & Adams, 1954) recommend using four or five options. Who is right? Actually, everybody! Theoretically, the larger the number of plausible distracters, the greater the reliability of the test item. But we must be practical, too! The number of distracters to be used should be governed by such factors as (a) the age of the children tested and (b) the nature of the material being tested.

a. *Age of children.* The multiple-choice item places somewhat of a premium on the examinee's powers of retention and reading comprehension. Not only must the examinee be able to read the stem and options, but he must also remember the central problem so that he will not need to reread the stem with each option. Therefore, younger children should be given multiple-choice items with fewer options than older children because the comprehension span of the younger children is more limited. There is no set formula that one can employ to determine the number of options to use. We can only suggest on the basis of our experience working with younger children that second-graders appear able to handle two- or three-choice items without too much trouble; third- and fourth-graders should be able to handle the three- or four-choice item; students in the middle school (sixth grade) and above should have little difficulty handling the four- or five-choice item.

b. *Nature of the material.* There are some subjects such as spelling or mechanical arts for which two or three distracters may be the maximum that can be written and still be plausible. Why, then, waste your time trying to conjure up distracters that are not plausible, that just take more space and reading time? You shouldn't! Two plausible distracters are to be preferred over four or five implausible ones. If no pupil chooses some of the distracters, they contribute nothing to the test and only take up valuable time that could be better used by including more items.

There is no empirical evidence to suggest that every item in a multiple-choice test should contain the same number of options. A decade ago, when test-scoring machines were less flexible and when the correction for guessing was very popular, it was necessary to have similar multiple-choice item formats. But, today, it is no longer necessary because scoring machines and computers can be programmed to handle a variety of item formats (as well as variations within a format), whether or not the correction for guessing is used. As stated earlier, the effectiveness of the distracters is more important than their number. In fact, it has been shown that when the number is reduced, there is little effect upon test reliability (Williams & Ebel, 1957). Teachers would be better off thinking up fewer good distracters than many poor ones. This would not only make the test more valid, but the time that would be spent trying to dream up additional distracters would also be put to productive use in writing more and better items.

15. *Avoid overlapping options.* Sometimes the teacher, in his haste to prepare distracters, may heed the caution to make them plausible but may commit the error of the overlapping options (if one option is correct, another

option also has to be correct, since one may incorporate the other). The following example is really a two-option rather than a four-option item.

The average weight of the adult United States female is
  A. less than 104 pounds.
  B. less than 110 pounds.
  C. more than 117 pounds.
  D. more than 120 pounds.

The choices are really between B and C. If A is correct, then B must also be correct. And, similarly, if D is correct, then C must be correct also. To prevent such overlapping in options, the item should be rewritten as:

The average weight of the adult United States female is
  A. less than 104 pounds.
  B. more than 119 pounds.
  C. between 110 and 116 pounds.
  D. between 117 and 119 pounds.
  E. between 104 and 109 pounds.

16. *To measure the higher mental processes, cast the item in a novel situation.* Many teachers do not realize that if they have used a particular example in class to illustrate understanding or interpretation, they *cannot* use this same item on a test to measure the mental process taught in class. If they do, they are only measuring recall. For example, if a teacher has taught his students that area equals length times width, and he wishes to test them to see whether they *understand* and can *apply* this principle, he should use a question (assuming it or another comparable question was not discussed in class or in the textbook) such as the following one:

Assume a quart of paint will cover 50 square feet. How many quarts of paint will you need to paint the walls of a room that is 10 feet × 10 feet × 10 feet?
  A. $\frac{4}{5}$
  B. 2
  C. 8
  D. 20
  E. 80

17. *Use the multiple-choice item where most appropriate.* Although the multiple-choice item has many valuable features, there are some subjects for which it is less suitable than other item formats. For computational problems in mathematics and science, we recommend the short-answer format. Where fact and/or opinion are to be measured, the true-false item should be used. When it is difficult to write plausible distracters, but there are many homogeneous items, the matching exercise is superior. The multiple-choice format

has wide applicability, but it is not always the best choice. We reiterate one of the basic tenets of test construction—*use the item format that measures the objective most directly and efficiently.*

A Check List for Writing Multiple-Choice Items

Table 10–1 presents the essential elements to be considered in writing multiple-choice items. Of course, the general considerations for writing any test item, discussed on pages 195–199, should be referred to.

In summary, then, even though the research dealing with the effect of poor item-writing practices on item difficulty and discrimination and the test's validity and reliability is inconclusive and sometimes contradictory (Board & Whitney, 1972; Dunn & Goldstein, 1959), we still recommend that teachers be cognizant of the various types of errors as well as some techniques whereby such errors can be minimized or prevented. Why, if there is no demonstrable deleterious effect? Because we feel that poor item-writing practices serve to

TABLE 10–1 Check List for Writing Multiple-Choice Items	
FACTOR	YES
1. Has the item been clearly presented? Is the main problem in the stem? Has excess verbiage been eliminated?	×
2. Has the item been cast so that there is no repetition of key words or phrases for each option?	×
3. Do the options come at the end of the stem?	×
4. Have the responses been arranged in some systematic fashion, such as alphabetical or length of response?	×
5. Are all distracters plausible? Are the number of distracters related to the examinees' age level? To the subject matter? To the time available for testing?	×
6. Have all irrelevant clues been avoided (grammatical, rote verbal association, length of correct answer, etc.)?	×
7. Are the correct answers randomly assigned throughout the test with approximately equal frequency?	×
8. Has an "I don't know" option been considered?	×
9. Is there only one correct (or best) answer?	×
10. Has "all the above" been avoided?	×
11. Has the "none of these" option been used sparingly? Only when appropriate?	×
12. Have overlapping options been avoided?	×
13. Have negative statements been avoided? If used, has the negative been underlined or written in capital letters?	×
14. Have the items been reviewed independently? By you?	×

obscure (or attenuate) differences between good and poor students chiefly by making the latter look more like the former than their performance (scores) on "error-free" tests would suggest. We are also of the opinion that even though there may not be a statistically significant effect on the psychometric properties of a test or a test item, we should not feed our critics with ammunition (sloppy test construction) to support their contention that tests and testing are invalid and therefore should be herewith and forthwith removed from the classroom. Finally, although some item-writing errors may not have an effect upon pupil performance or the psychometric properties of a test or test item, some do. And if teachers become sloppy in some areas, it won't take too much to have them become sloppy or unconcerned in those areas that are even more important.

WRITING CONTEXT-DEPENDENT ITEMS

Up to this point, our discussion of the various item formats dealt primarily with independent units; that is, the essence of the problem was presented in the stem. In addition, the stimulus mode previously illustrated has been the conventional verbal approach. Occasionally, however, the essential elements of the problem need not be verbal for a pencil-and-paper test. Many different kinds of stimuli—pictures, graphs, tables, diagrams, film strips, tape recordings, and the like—can be used, even though the examinee's response mode is in marking an answer on a piece of paper. Items that are based upon an external source—be it pictorial or verbal—are called *context-dependent*. A teacher interested in learning whether his pupils can read and interpret a graph or table, interpret a poem or short story, identify a painting, recognize a musical composition, read the dials on a piece of electrical equipment, and the like would provide this material to the student. The student would then use it as his frame of reference to answer items based on this external material. In the next section, we will discuss the *pictorial form* (the medium used to present the problem) and two types of context-dependent items—the *interlinear* exercise and the *interpretive* exercise—which can be, but need not be, based upon pictorial materials. Objective test items can be based upon pictorial materials, verbal materials, or a combination of the two.

Objective Test Items Based upon Pictorial Materials

The *pictorial form*[5] is very useful for younger children and those with reading difficulties. Kindergarten children can be shown different-colored pictures and asked to identify various colors. First-graders can be shown a picture having various lengths of string and asked to select the longest (or shortest or in-

[5] The pictorial form is a medium used to present the material to the examinee. It is *not* an item format. Different item formats may be used wtih pictorial materials.

between length) string. For measuring a young child's ability to count, to measure, and to discriminate, pictorial material is an excellent medium. To measure some of the more complex skills such as reading a graph, using an income tax table, and using an index, pictorial materials are ideally suited.

In some instances the item writer would have to include a great deal of information in the stem or introductory material to remove possible ambiguity. In some cases, a picture would have been worth many hundreds of words and the problem would have been much clearer to the examinee had a pictorial medium been employed to present the problem. Is it not easier to classify rocks from pictures of rock samples than it is to classify them on the basis of verbal descriptions of their properties? Would it not be easier for the examinee to classify a tissue sample in pathology with a slide or picture of that tissue specimen than it would be if a verbal description were used?

In addition, pictorial materials lend a degree of realism to the test situation and introduce an element of novelty and interest. These, however, should *not* be the underlying reasons for using such materials. Pictorial materials, or for that matter any medium, should be used only when they are the most appropriate and effective method of presenting the problem. Pictorial materials do not always improve the test item. If a verbal presentation suffices, it should be used rather than a pictorial medium, and vice versa. Item writers should also be on their guard *not* to make the pictorial material overly complicated and/or ambiguous. In fact, if needed, the pictorial material should be clarified verbally.

Test constructors using pictures must be careful that they use materials that are common to the experiential background of the children being tested. We are well aware of the fact that children differing in their background also differ in their familiarity with certain objects. And just as in writing verbal tests we must be careful lest we test for reading ability, in using pictorial tests we should *not* test for unfamiliarity of the stimulus being used.

If pictorial materials are so good, why are they seldom used in teacher-made tests? Primarily because (1) *good* relevant pictorial materials are hard to find; and (2) pictorial materials often have to be adapted slightly, but most teachers are not artistically inclined.

Following are some examples of test items based upon pictorial materials. In some instances, they call only for simple knowledge; in others, higher reasoning processes are involved.

True-False Test Items

The following items are designed for first-grade children who have just completed a unit on telling time.

Directions: In the picture below, there are four clocks. I am going to tell you some things about these clocks. If they are right, draw a line through the letter Y. If they are wrong, draw a line through the letter N.

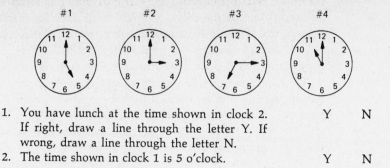

| #1 | #2 | #3 | #4 |

1. You have lunch at the time shown in clock 2.   Y   N
   If right, draw a line through the letter Y. If
   wrong, draw a line through the letter N.
2. The time shown in clock 1 is 5 o'clock.   Y   N

Short-Answer Test Items

Based upon the pictures of the clocks, the following short-answer questions could be written for a group of second- or third-graders.

1. What time is it on clock 2? (<u>3 o'clock</u>)
2. What clock shows the time that is closest to 12 o'clock? (<u>4</u>)

Multiple-Choice Items

Assume that an eighth-grade science teacher is interested in learning the extent to which his students understand the concept of kinetic energy. He could present them with a series of verbal descriptions and ask them to select the correct answer; he could have them write a short essay describing kinetic energy; or he could present the material in pictorial form as illustrated below.

(<u>A</u>)   Which of the following has the greatest kinetic energy?
(<u>B</u>)   Which of the following *could* have the greatest kinetic energy?
(<u>D</u>)   Which of the following would *never* exhibit kinetic energy?

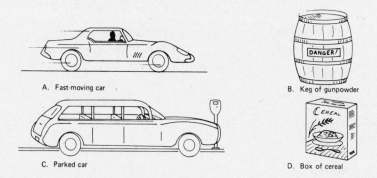

A. Fast-moving car   B. Keg of gunpowder

C. Parked car   D. Box of cereal

Items 34 through 36 have reference to the *letters* locating certain places on the accompanying map.

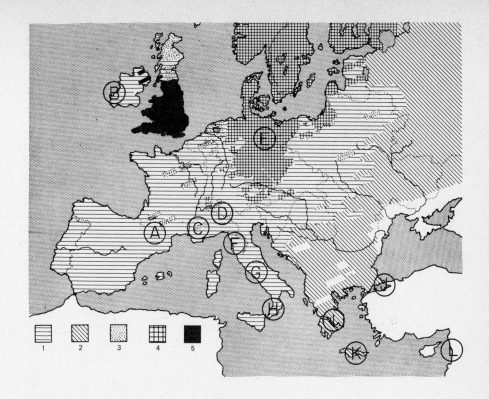

34. Where did Luther post his "Ninety-five Theses"?
    1. A   2. B   3. C   4. D   5. E
35. During the "Babylonian Captivity" one of the claimants to the papacy resided at which of the following designated places?
    1. A   2. B   3. C   4. D   5. E

The Interlinear Exercise

The *interlinear* exercise is analogous to the correction true-false item discussed on page 262. It is somewhat of a cross between the essay question (the student is given some latitude of free expression in that he decides what is to be corrected and how it is to be corrected) and the objective item (the answer can be objectively scored). It is a semiobjective test of writing ability developed to overcome the unreliability of scoring the essay test. In the interlinear exercise, the student is given a piece of prose that may contain spelling, grammatical, and punctuation errors. He must read the material, recognize the errors, and then correct the errors so that the material will be a better piece of prose. An example of an interlinear exercise with the changes made by the student is presented below.

Billy ain't a good boy. When he has went to the store, he don't look out for cars.
    isn't   goes   doesn't

One of these days, him going to get hurt bad. He not only ignores his parents, but
he is   *badly*

he also laughs at him.
them

In scoring this exercise, only those elements (errors) introduced in the material by the item writer are considered. Other revisions or editing are disregarded. Although we have an element of objective scoring, there is still some subjectivity, since we are still dealing with free-response materials. However, if a detailed scoring key is provided and followed, scorer reliability can be quite high.

The Interpretive Exercise

The *interpretive* exercise consists of either an introductory statement, pictorial material, or a combination of the two, followed by a series of questions that measure in part the student's ability to *interpret* the material. All test items are based on a set of materials that is identical for all pupils.

In the past, the interpretive exercise was seldom used by the classroom teacher. It was used most frequently in commercially published reading comprehension and ability tests. No doubt one of the reasons that it was seldom used in teacher-made tests was that it is rather difficult and time consuming to prepare. However, such exercises are finding their way into teacher-made tests in greater numbers because of their many distinct advantages over the traditional items (Ebel, 1951; Wesman, 1971). The reasons for their growing popularity are:

1. The structuring of the problem assists both examiner and examinee. Both approach the problem with the *same* frame of reference.
2. They lend themselves to the measurement of understanding, interpretation, and evaluation.
3. Complex material can be measured with a series of different items based upon a single introductory passage, graph, chart, or diagram.
4. They minimize the influence of irrelevant factual material.
5. They lend themselves to a variety of item formats and modes of presentation.

At the same time it should be mentioned that such exercises are not free of problems and/or deficiencies. If they are based on a paragraph, they make a heavy demand on reading skill, and therefore they are not too suitable for very young children and for those students who have reading problems. They are very difficult to prepare, especially those dealing with complex topics. Because of the time needed to administer them, one is restricted somewhat in the number of items that can be asked in a given time, and hence the reliability of the test per unit of time is reduced. For that reason alone, the interpretive exercise should not be used to measure factual knowledge. In view of the amount of time needed by the teacher to prepare the introductory material upon which the items are based, as well as the additional time needed by the students to read and comprehend the introductory material, we suggest that (from an economic standpoint) more than one item should be written for each set of introductory materials.

In comparison to the essay question, the interpretive exercise has two limitations as a measure of complex learning (Gronlund, 1976). First, the results indicate to the teacher only that the student is or is not able to function at higher levels—*not* whether the pupil has the ability to integrate these skills in a different situation. Second, the interpretive exercise indicates only whether the pupil can *recognize* the answer—*not* whether he can supply evidence to demonstrate his problem-solving skills and his organizational ability. "To measure the ability to *define* problems, to *formulate* hypotheses, to *organize* data, and to draw conclusions, supply procedures such as the essay test must be used" (Gronlund, 1976, p. 225).

Following is an example of an interpretive exercise based on a map that measures the students' ability to read and interpret the map. The actual item and ensuing discussion is taken from the pamphlet *Multiple-Choice Questions: A Close Look* (1963).[6] Although the items are written in the multiple-choice format, the item writer is free to use whichever format he wishes.

In the following questions you are asked to make inferences from the data which are given you on the map of the imaginary country, Serendip. *The answers in most instances must be probabilities rather than certainties.* The relative size of towns and cities is not shown. To assist you in the location of the places mentioned in the questions, the map is divided into squares lettered vertically from A to E and numbered horizontally from 1 to 5.

[6] From *Multiple-Choice Questions: A Close Look.* Copyright © 1963 by Educational Testing Service. All rights reserved. Reproduced by permission.

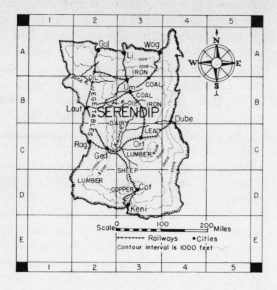

(B)   Which of the following cities would be the best location for a steel mill?
    (A) Li   (3A)
    (B) Um   (3B)
    (C) Cot   (3D)
    (D) Dube   (4B)

A map of an imaginary country, such as that shown above, offers numerous possibilities for questions which measure important understandings. One could ask several questions requiring an understanding of the symbols used on the map. To determine student comprehension of the meaning of contour lines, for example, one might ask which railroad has the steepest grades to climb. Similar questions can be developed which require knowledge of the factors influencing population distribution, economic activities and so on.

The question reproduced beneath the map requires knowledge of the natural resources used in producing steel and an awareness of the importance of transportation facilities in bringing these resources together. It was part of a general achievement test given to high school seniors.

The student who knows that iron is the basic raw material of steel and that coal commonly provides the necessary source of heat would proceed to locate deposits of these resources in relation to the cities listed in the question. He would be able to eliminate Cot immediately, since there is no iron or coal in its vicinity, although Cot might be an attractive choice to students who mistakenly think that copper is a basic ingredient of steel. Both Li and Dube are located reasonably near supplies of iron, and therefore might be attractive choices. Um, however, is the more clearly "correct" response, because not only are deposits of iron and coal nearby, but they are more readily transportable by direct railroad routes.

Suggestions for Writing Interpretive Exercises

In order to have a valid and reliable interpretive exercise, the item writer, of course, must follow the basic tenets of good test construction, such as clearly communicating to the student the intent of the question and making certain that no irrelevant clues are provided the student. However, two additional tasks are required: (1) the selection and/or preparation of the introductory material, and (2) writing test items that are *dependent* upon the introductory material and call upon the higher mental processes to answer the questions. The suggestions that follow are restricted to the interpretive exercise. Depending upon the item format used, the material previously discussed is also pertinent, but it will not be repeated here.

1. *Carefully select the material to be interpreted so that the interpretations to be made will be significant and representative of course content and objectives.* This stage is analogous to selecting the topics for which independent items will be written. For the interpretive exercise, the introductory material (be it verbal or pictorial) *is the topic.* There are a variety of excellent sources for introductory verbal materials, such as digests, summaries, and abstracts of articles. Although these sources may not be completely appropriate as they stand (one will seldom find introductory material that is completely relevant to the instructional goals without at least some minor revision), they do provide good raw material for the item writer to use in developing materials that will be most appropriate and meaningful. If the material selected is adapted, it must be within the experiential background of the pupils, it must be within their reading ability, it must be brief and yet say something, and it must measure specifically what it is the teacher wants the student to interpret. In many instances the preparation of the introductory material and the writing of the test items go hand in hand.

The teacher must *think ahead* before he prepares the test items. He must decide in advance whether he wants to place some, much, or no emphasis on the student's prior knowledge. This is very important inasmuch as the item writer, depending upon the decisions made, can prepare the introductory material accordingly. Although the major emphasis in the interpretive exercise is on the material to be interpreted, we must recognize that it is the item writer and *not* the items that govern what is and what is not to be included in the introductory material. In other words, the item writer must have the purpose of the test clearly in mind before he prepares the introductory material.

The following steps for the preparation of the introductory material should be of assistance.

a. Look through materials that contain a reading passage, to see whether they might be appropriate for having interpretive exercises prepared on them.

b. Make certain that the material used is completely *new* to all students.

Otherwise, you are measuring prior knowledge and/or mental ability.

c. Write some items based upon the selected material.

d. See whether there are some instructional objectives that you would like to measure but are unable to do so because the material does not lend itself to such items. Rewrite the material so that you can develop certain kinds of items. In the rewrite stage, remove any irrelevant material that is not related to the items written and can be removed without destroying the continuity of the passage.

e. Ask yourself whether you could prepare some additional good items by further rewriting of the passage.

f. Revise the passage until you are satisfied that it is brief but still clear, that it has continuity, that it is interesting, that it is appropriate to the reading level of the pupils, that the pupils have been exposed to the tasks called for by the items, and that you have been able to get full mileage from the selection. You may be very surprised to find that the final selection bears little resemblance to the original passage.

The teacher must try to achieve a happy balance between having the introductory material too easy and too difficult. If the introductory material is too easy, the items that are prepared may require nothing more than reading skill. On the other hand, if the introductory material is too complex, it may well be that the test is a measure of general intelligence and/or verbal comprehension unrelated to the instructional objectives. This balance is not easy to achieve and requires considerable skill and practice. What is important, however, is that the teacher consider the age and ability level of his students, the course content, and the instructional objectives to be measured.

Just as one might say that the essence of the multiple-choice exercise lies in the quality of its distracters and that the essential ingredient of the essay lies in the specificity of the framework established by the item writer, one can say that the essence of the interpretive exercise lies in the adequacy of the introductory material (be it prose or pictorial) presented to all examinees. It is therefore vital that the material be selected and/or prepared very carefully. The item writer has *control* of what he wishes to present and how much information he wishes to give the student. Hence he is able to measure the degree of proficiency possessed by the examinee.

2. *Keep the introductory material brief.* Other things being equal, for younger children and for children who have difficulty in reading we prefer the interpretive exercise based on pictorial materials. For children in the higher grades, one could use either written material or pictorial material, or a combination of the two. Although reading ability is required in any test except the oral examination, the teacher must be very careful that he does not make the interpretive exercise primarily a test of reading ability or general intelligence. Although brevity is desirable, if the introductory material is verbal it must contain all information needed to measure the pupils' interpretive skills.

3. *Be novel and creative in preparing introductory materials.* In the interpretive exercise, creativity and/or novelty are very important. But teachers must be careful that they do not become too creative or too novel. They must reach a happy compromise of instilling something new and different but not introducing too much novelty so that they fail to measure instructional objectives that are relevant.

4. *Base the items on the introductory material.*[7] This does *not* mean that the teacher construct items that are answered *directly* in the introductory material. Such items measure only reading ability and/or memory (Garren, 1976; Pyrczak, 1974, 1976; Tuinman, 1974). At the same time, he should not write items that are irrelevant to the introductory material. Such items may be a measure of general intelligence. The items prepared should be such that they are based upon the introductory material. It does not matter whether the pupil must call forth basic knowledge not purposely presented in the material, as long as the interpretive skill measured has some foundation in the introductory material.

5. *Write true-false or multiple-choice items to measure interpretive skills.* Once again we say that the short-answer item is *not* designed to measure complex achievement efficiently. Although the essay item could be used, it also would be inefficient. Of the selection-type objective item, the true-false or multiple-choice format could be used. In general, we prefer the multiple-choice format because of its greater versatility (Furst, 1958; Jenkins & Deno, 1971; R. E. Smith, 1968, 1970; Wesman, 1971). However, there are times when the true-false item is preferred because of its simplicity.

6. *Regardless of the item format used, the guidelines previously discussed should be followed.* Even though the essence of the problem is contained in the introductory material rather than in the item stem, the item writer must still be cognizant of the importance of clarity and the effect of irrelevant clues. The use of verbal or pictorial introductory materials, no matter how good, is no substitute for well-constructed test items.

7. *If pictorial materials are used, they should be relevant and of high quality.* Any diagrams, charts, graphs, maps, and the like should be well drawn, clear, and easily recognized (read) by the examinee. Sloppy materials may confuse the student, thereby affecting test validity.

8. *If the interpretive exercise uses key-type items, make certain that the categories are homogeneous and mutually exclusive.* The key-type item is a cross between multiple-choice and matching items. It is similar to the matching exercise in that it uses a common set of responses to classify each of the

---

[7] Pyrczak (1974, 1976) and Tuinman (1974), among others, showed that supposedly context-dependent reading tests were in fact not so, because specific clues were present that enabled the examinee to answer the item correctly *without* reading the associated material upon which the item was supposedly based. Pyrczak and Tuinman have developed formulas for determining the degree to which test items based upon a particular reading passage are, in fact, *dependent* on that passage.

statements or items. Because the student makes some sort of classification of the statement, it is vital that the key contain distinctly separate categories so that there is no possibility of having two correct answers because one category overlaps another category. The following example[8] illustrates the use of mutually exclusive and homogeneous categories.

Items 12–16 are based upon the following preliminary information and experiment.

Preliminary information: In the presence of gaseous oxygen Solution X is purple. When gaseous oxygen is absent, Solution X is a colorless liquid. Yeast is a plant.

Experiment: Five drops of Solution X were placed in each of four (4) small tubes. A brass screw was dropped into each tube to serve as a platform. Four pieces of filter paper were rolled; one was dipped into glucose solution; one was dipped into a yeast suspension; one was dipped into a yeast suspension to which glucose had been added; one was dipped into water. Each of the pieces of rolled filter paper was placed into one of the tubes. A cork was then inserted into each tube. The tubes were placed in a drawer and were left there for an hour. At the end of the hour the tubes were examined. The color of Solution X at the end of the hour is recorded in the table below for each tube.

Tube	Filter paper dipped into:	Color of Solution X
1	Glucose solution	Purple
2	Yeast suspension	Pale purple
3	Yeast suspension + glucose	Colorless
4	Water	Purple

For items 12–16 select your response from the list below, numbered 1 through 8.
1. Statement of an observational fact.
2. An experimental assumption, that is, something which must be assumed about the experiment or experimental materials, in order to interpret the experiment.
3. An immediate conclusion.
4. A conclusion, interpretation, or generalization that can be formulated on the basis of the data.
5. A statement that can be contradicted on the basis of the data.
6. A prediction, deduction, or an expectation.
7. A statement which is probably false, but which cannot be contradicted on the basis of these data.
8. The statement may be true, but the truth of the statement cannot be established on the basis of these data.

12. Carbon dioxide is produced by yeast.
    A. 1   B. 2   C. 4   D. 7   E. 8
13. The amount of oxygen utilized by yeast per unit time is related to the available food supply.

[8] We are grateful to Dr. Clarence Nelson, Office of Evaluation Services, Michigan State University, for permitting us to use this example from his test file.

A. 1   B. 2   <u>C</u>. 4   D. 7   E. 8

14. If the gases in Tube 3 were collected and run through a phenol red solution, the phenol red would change from red to orange or yellow.

    A. 2   B. 3   C. 4   <u>D</u>. 6   E. 7

15. At the end of the experiment the liquid in the bottom of Tube 3 was colorless.

    <u>A</u>. 1   B. 2   C. 3   D. 5   E. None of these

16. Gaseous oxygen is the only substance which affects the color of Solution X.

    A. 1   <u>B</u>. 2   C. 3   D. 5   E. 7

9. *Get the most mileage out of the interpretive exercise.* It would be ridiculous to spend countless hours looking for and preparing the introductory material and then ask just one question on the material. And it would be ludicrous from the examinee's point of view to read the introductory material and then be asked only one question. Such a procedure would be a very inefficient use of testing time, both for the examiner and the examinee. It would be analogous to delivering a 1-pound package with a semitrailer truck. We cannot provide a formula that relates the number of items to the length of the introductory material. All we can say is that the teacher should ask several significant questions for each interpretive exercise. Of course, content validity should not be sacrificed by asking too many questions. Other things being equal, we favor short introductory materials with a relatively large number of test items based on the material. This will provide for more adequate content sampling in a limited amount of testing time, recognizing that the interpretive exercise requires more time than the conventional objective item. Be careful though! Do not overload the test with interpretive exercises. Writing of a large number of interpretive exercises can severely upset the balance of the test and result in a test that lacks content validity.

SUMMARY

The principal ideas, conclusions, and recommendations presented in this chapter are summarized in the following statements:

1. Multiple-choice items are the most popular and flexible of the objective-type *selection* item.
2. The criticism that the multiple-choice test rewards the poorer student and penalizes the more able student is not supported by empirical evidence.
3. Ambiguity in multiple-choice items can be avoided by carefully preparing the test item.
4. Four commonly used variations of the multiple-choice format are the one correct answer, the best answer, the analogy type, and the reverse type.

5. Of all the selection-type objective items, the multiple-choice item requires the most time for the student to respond.

6. The multiple-choice item is the least efficient objective item for measuring factual recall. The multiple-choice item is ideally suited for measuring the higher mental processes.

7. Two of the major deficiencies in teacher-made multiple-choice items are ambiguity and imprecise (or superfluous) wording.

8. Multiple-choice questions can be presented as either direct questions or as incomplete statements. Regardless of the form used, the options should come below the stem.

9. The options should be arranged as simply as possible. If numbers, they should be in ascending or descending order; if single words, alphabetically; if phrases, in order of length.

10. Highly technical distracters, negative statements, and textbook jargon should be avoided.

11. All responses should be plausible and homogeneous. One way to increase the difficulty of the test is to increase the homogeneity of the distracters.

12. Avoid giving the student clues to the correct answer. Some of the usual clues to the correct answer are (a) making the correct answer longer than the incorrect ones, (b) having overlapping items, and (c) giving grammatical clues.

13. There should be only one correct or best answer for every item.

14. Avoid "all of the above" as an option.

15. Use "none of the above" sparingly. To avoid irrelevant clues, this option should be the correct answer only some of the time. We suggest that this option be used only with the correct answer variety of multiple-choice question.

16. In general, we recommend that four or five options be used. The distracters must all be plausible. In addition, the age of the pupils tested, the nature of the material, and the time available for testing will influence the number of distracters.

17. Independent review of the items will generally improve their quality.

18. Items that depend upon information presented in pictorial material or in a reading passage are called *context-dependent* items. Interlinear and interpretive exercises are examples of context-dependent items.

19. Pictorial materials are very well suited to younger children and those with reading difficulties.

20. If pictorial materials are used, they should be familiar to children coming from different backgrounds.

21. Pictorial materials are often the only testing medium possible for measuring certain skills, such as ability to read a chart, table, or graph.

22. If pictorial materials are used, they should be of high quality and related to the content and objectives being measured.

23. The true-false and multiple-choice formats are best suited for interpretive exercises.
24. A major problem with the interpretive exercise is the selection and subsequent revision of the introductory material upon which the items are based.
25. The introductory material for the interpretive exercise should be brief, yet meaningful.
26. The number of items to be written for a particular interpretive exercise will depend to some extent on the length of the introductory material. It would be foolish to have a one-page article and then ask just one or two questions on it. Get the most mileage out of the material, but *not* at the expense of content validity.

CHAPTER ELEVEN

Assembling, Reproducing, Administering, Scoring and Analyzing Classroom Achievement Tests

In Chapter 7 we discussed the "get-ready" or planning stage in preparing classroom tests. In Chapters 8 through 10 we discussed the preparation of essay and objective-type items. We are now at the "get-set" and "go" stages where we begin assembling our ingredients (test items) into the final product (the test). All the planning and preparation for the test that has taken place will be in vain if we "goof" in these next stages. The care, time, and effort expended in this mixing or blending stage will be positively related to the goodness of the final product. Extreme care must be exercised in planning the test—delineating the course objectives and expressing them in terms of pupil behavior, preparing the table of specifications or test blueprint—and writing the test items if a teacher is desirous of obtaining valid measurement of his pupils' achievement. However, there are other aspects that must be considered in teacher-made tests besides those mentioned under planning and the techniques of item writing.

In the "get-ready" and "go" stages of teacher-made achievement tests, the teacher must consider such questions as

1. How should the various item formats be organized in the test?
2. How should the various items within a particular format be organized?
3. How should the test be reproduced?
4. Should pupils be encouraged to answer all test items, even those they are unsure of?
5. What kinds of directions should the student be given?
6. Should the students record their answers directly in the test booklet or should a separate answer sheet be used for objective-type tests?
7. Should a correction-for-guessing formula be used in objective tests?

In addition, the teacher must also pay some attention to the analysis of the test items and to the interpretation of the test results. Unless the teacher is certain that his test is valid and reliable, it would indeed be ludicrous to use the test results to make decisions—be they group or individual, instructional, administrative, or counseling.

This chapter is devoted to a consideration of the major questions posed above. After studying this chapter, the student should be able to—

1. Appreciate the importance of paying careful attention to the assembly, reproduction, administration, and scoring aspects of classroom tests.
2. Differentiate between scoring and grading.
3. Follow the guidelines offered when assembling the various item formats into a test.
4. Appreciate the importance of having clear, concise directions for the student.
5. Follow the guidelines offered when writing test directions.
6. Appreciate the importance of encouraging all students to attempt all test items even though they may be unsure of the correctness of some of their answers.
7. Recognize the major limitations of the correction-for-guessing formula.
8. Understand the various approaches to, and opinions about, trying to control for guessing.
9. Apply the correction-for-guessing formula.
10. Follow the guidelines offered when laying out and reproducing the test.
11. Recognize the importance of physical and psychological conditions in test taking.

12. Understand why cheating must be discouraged, and know how to minimize it.

13. Understand the importance of teaching all students how to take tests; that is, make them all test-wise.

14. List the four major points to consider in scoring the test.

15. Understand the instructional and learning value of feedback.

16. Understand the importance of analyzing a test.

17. Understand the difference between item difficulty and item discrimination.

18. Compute and evaluate a difficulty index.

19. Compute and evaluate a discrimination index.

20. Understand the relationship between difficulty and discrimination.

21. Understand the major uses of item analysis data.

22. Recognize the limitations of item analysis data.

23. Be acquainted with the opinions about, and methods of, computing item analysis data for criterion-referenced tests.

GETTING THE TEST READY

Objective tests, especially multiple-choice tests and some variants of the true-false item, *cannot* be administered orally. Neither can the items be written on the blackboard a few minutes before the examination is scheduled to begin. The test must be reproduced. The reproduction process used—be it hectograph (such as ditto), mimeograph, or some offset process—is not important. The material need only be legible. What is important, however, is to have similar item formats grouped together; to have clear and concise directions; and to decide upon the manner in which the pupils are to record their answers. The test-taking conditions should be such that every pupil is given maximum opportunity to perform at his highest level. The steps to be discussed below may appear obvious. However, you would be surprised at the large number of errors teachers make, errors that do not enhance their opportunity to obtain valid and reliable measurement of the pupils' achievement.

Arranging the Test Items

One can digress from a recipe for making a cake and still end up with a cake. But what kind of cake will it be? Will it be moist and tasteful, or will it be a tasteless blob? It is hard to tell positively, but we would be willing to bet that, in the long run, the cook will not be too pleased with his or her efforts. By the same token, various test items can be thrown together to make a test. But how valid and reliable will the results be? Again, we cannot say positively, but it is likely that validity and reliability will be seriously impaired.

Throughout our discussion on the writing of the various item formats, we have emphasized and reemphasized that the task given the student must be as clear as humanly possible. One way to achieve this is to group all items of the same format together rather than to intersperse them throughout the test. Such a grouping is advantageous for a variety of reasons: (1) Younger children may not realize that the first set of directions is applicable to all items of a particular format and may become confused; (2) it makes it easier for the examinee to maintain a particular mental set instead of having to change from one to another; and (3) it makes it easier for the teacher to score the test, especially if hand scoring is done.

We also recommend that the various item formats be presented in such a way that the complexity of mental activity required by the student will progress from the very simple to the very complex. For example, simple recall as measured by the completion type of item should precede the interpretive exercise or the unrestricted essay. Gronlund (1971, p. 238) suggested the following scheme:

1. True-false or alternative-response items
2. Matching items
3. Short-answer items
4. Multiple-choice items
5. Interpretive exercises
6. Essay questions

Within each item format, the exercises should, wherever feasible, be grouped so that those that deal with the same instructional objective (such as "knowledge of terms," "application of principles," and "synthesis") are grouped together. Such a grouping can help the teacher ascertain which learning activities appear to be most readily understood by his pupils, those that are least understood, and those that are in between. There is no empirical evidence to suggest that grouping items of similar content will lead to more valid and reliable measurement (Marso, 1970) or that it will help ensure positive pupil motivation.

A suggestion given by nearly all authors of measurement texts is that within each item format the items be grouped so that they begin with the very easy and progress in difficulty. But does the arrangement of items in order of difficulty from easy to hard affect the examinees' anxiety and/or test performance? There are some (Sax & Cromack, 1966; Towne & Merrill, 1975), who, like Cronbach (1970a), believe that a "sequence effect" (the proportion of students who answer an item correctly may be influenced by the difficulty of the preceding item) is present and that an examinee's motivational level may be altered by the "discouragement resulting from failure on a particular item." As of now, however, the empirical evidence is inconclusive (Hambleton & Traub, 1974; Klosner & Gelman, 1973; Marso, 1970;

Olson & Barickowski, 1974; Sirotnik & Wellington, 1974). Nevertheless, we recommend, as do others (Sax & Cromack, 1966; Towle & Merrill, 1975) that for lengthy tests and/or timed tests, items should progress from the easy to the difficult if for no other reason than to instill confidence in the examinee, at least at the beginning. Most students approach a test with anxiety and apprehension. We can imagine nothing more traumatic or frustrating for a student than to sit down to a test for which he has diligently prepared himself and find that he is *not* able to answer the first five questions. If the test were to begin with two or three easy items that almost everyone could answer correctly, even the less able students might be encouraged to do their best on the remaining items.

The test items should be so arranged that they are easily read by the examinees. This means that the reproduction should be legible and that the items will not be crowded together.

If diagrams or drawings are used, they should be placed *above* the stem. If placed below the stem, there will be a break in the examinee's reading continuity between the stem and the options. As we recommended before, if the illustrative material is considered to be part of the problem, the problem should be placed early in the stem.

Finally, one point previously discussed bears repetition: Arrange the items in such a way that the correct answers follow a random pattern.

In summary, then, the organization of the various test items in the final test should—

1. Have separate sections for each item format.

2. Be arranged so that these sections progress from the easy (true-false) to the difficult (interpretive exercise and essay).

3. Group the items within each section so that the very easy ones are at the beginning, and the items progress in difficulty.

4. Space the items so that they are not crowded and can be easily read.

5. Keep all stems and options together on the same page; if possible, diagrams and questions should be kept together.

6. If a diagram is used for a multiple-choice exercise, have the diagram come *above* the stem.

7. Avoid a definite response pattern to the correct answer.

Writing Test Directions

You might have a car that is well tuned and aligned, and has good tires and a good battery, but it will be of little use to you in reaching your destination if you do not know in what direction to drive. An analogous situation may, and frequently does, occur when a teacher takes the time to prepare good test items, develops a scoring key, organizes the items into a test so that some of the technical faults mentioned earlier are minimized, but fails to consider the preparation of simple, clear directions. Occasionally the test instructions given students are vague and/or incomplete with regard to (1) the manner in which the pupil is to respond, (2) the time to be allotted to the various sections, (3) the value of the item, and (4) whether or not the pupil should guess at any answers he may be unsure of (Furst, 1958; Gronlund, 1976; Travers, 1955). The directions provided should be clear and concise and should tell the student *what* he is to do, *how* he is to do it, and *where* he is to record his answers. Except for young children, the written test directions should be so explicit that the student can begin the test without any additional oral instructions. If this criterion is not met, the directions are not sufficiently clear and should be revised.

1. *Each item format should have a specific set of directions.* In addition to a general set of instructions, there must be a specific set of instructions that are applicable to a particular item format. For computational problems the student should be told the degree of precision required; whether or not he is to express his answer in the proper units (such as volts, ohms, square feet), whether or not he should show his work and, if so, where he should show it. For responses that require a short answer (one or two sentences), the pupil should be informed whether or not his anwers are to be in complete sentences and whether spelling, grammar, and legibility of handwriting will be considered in grading the answer.

2. *For objective tests at the elementary level, give the student examples and/or practice exercises so that he will see exactly what and how he is to perform his task.* Although we contend that students be given practice taking tests, we do *not* mean to imply that coaching or specific instructions be given inasmuch as this can well produce invalid scores (Evans & Pike, 1973).

3. *Students should be told how the test will be scored.* Not only should students be given clear, concise directions on how to take the test, they should also be given clear, concise information on how the test will be scored. They should be told, for example, if on an essay examination in social studies, whether such factors as spelling, punctuation, and grammar, will be considered, and if so, what proportion of the question's value will be assigned to these factors. Or, on an arithmetic test, they should be told whether they will receive part scores for showing a correct procedure even though they may have obtained an incorrect answer. When pupils know the "ground rules" they can operate accordingly. For example, they can be more careful in their computations, or, if a guessing factor is being applied they may have more "omits" (Traub and Hambleton, 1974, found that the way a test is scored had a significant effect on the number of items omitted).

4. *Above the second grade, all directions should be written out.* For some groups, especially younger children, slow learners, or pupils with reading problems, the directions may be read aloud in *addition* to being printed and available to each examinee.

Although we could give the specific directions to be employed with the various item formats, we have chosen to give a set of directions (see Table 11–1) for just one type of examination—a final examination consisting of four-option multiple-choice items—where the responses are to be recorded on a separate answer sheet and no guessing correction will be made. Different formats and methods of recording the answers would entail slight modifications of these instructions.

The directions given in Table 11–1 could be used for senior high school students. The wording, of course, would have to be modified for younger children. As we said earlier, the directions could be read to the students, but they should be available to the student for reference when needed.

TABLE 11–1   General Directions for a Multiple-Choice Test

General Directions: DO NOT open your test booklet until you have read, understood, and carried out the directions below. SINCE YOUR ANSWER SHEET WILL BE SCORED BY MACHINE, IT IS ABSOLUTELY NECESSARY THAT YOU MARK YOUR ANSWER CORRECTLY TO AVOID ERRORS IN THE GRADE YOU RECEIVE.

Specific Directions: This final course examination consists of 75 multiple-choice items, each worth one point. You will have 2 hours to complete the test. Read each question carefully and decide which of the alternatives (answers) given best completes the statement or answers the question.

1. On your answer sheet,[a] *print* in the appropriate spaces your name, the name of the examination, and the date.

2. Be extremely careful to mark your answer to each item in the appropriate space on the answer sheet by darkening the letter corresponding to the answer you select.

3. Do any necessary figuring or scribbling on the blank paper furnished. Do NOT mark any answers in the test booklet. Answers are to be marked on the answer sheet only.

4. *Keep the marked part of your answer sheet covered at all times.*

5. Mark only *one* response per item. If you mark more than one answer per item, if you make stray dots on the answer sheet, or if you fail to erase completely an answer you wish changed, *your response to that item will not be counted.*

6. Note that the items have only FOUR responses. Be careful not to use the fifth-response position on your answer sheet.

7. Your score on this examination will be the number of answers you have marked correctly. Try to answer every item, but do not spend too much time on any one item.

8. Are there any questions about what you are to do and how you are to do it? You may now begin. Good luck!

THIS EXAMINATION CONSISTS OF 75 ITEMS ON 8 PAGES.
BE SURE YOU DO NOT OVERLOOK ANY ITEMS.

---

[a] If separate answer sheets are not used, the directions given in this table would have to be altered accordingly.

Instructions for Guessing

Guessing is recognized as a major and persistent source of error in cognitive tests of achievement and aptitude (faking rather than guessing has been a problem in affective tests and will be discussed in Chapter 16), and a variety of procedures have been devised—applying a correction formula, giving explicit instructions, employing confidence weighting scoring schemes—to combat this problem (see Bauer, 1973; Wood, 1976).

Some teachers feel that students should *not* answer any item they are unsure of, and they advocate the use of a correction formula to discourage students from guessing blindly. Other teachers feel just as strongly on the opposite side of the continuum. Who is right?

We contend that, on the basis of the research evidence available, *students should be instructed to answer every item and that no correction for guessing should be applied.*[1] Our position is based upon the following arguments:

1. If students are instructed to answer only those items that they are certain of, we can expect to find students differing in their interpretation of "certainty," and hence the instructions will be interpreted differently.

2. Some students, because of their personalities, are prone to guess regardless of the penalties imposed and the instructions given them not to guess (Bauer, 1971; Hritz, Drugo, & Jacobs, 1970; Kogan & Wallach, 1967; Slakter, 1968a,b; Slakter, Koehler, Hampton, & Grennell, 1971; Swineford & Miller, 1953; Waters, 1967). By instructing the student to omit all items he is uncertain of, we are penalizing the timid, insecure student and rewarding the "gambler," who will get a score higher than he deserves because he had the response-set to guess (see Cronbach, 1950) and was able to get some correct answers by chance.

In our opinion, having instructions not to guess and/or applying a correction formula will not equalize test-taking conditions among the examinees because differences in test scores among students may be due to personality differences (Sheriffs & Boomers, 1954; Jacobs, 1971) in their propensity to guess as well as differences in their achievement (Ebel, 1968). Neither instructions nor penalties will remedy this.

3. The correction formula (this will be discussed under "Recording and Scoring the Answers") is based upon a rather tenuous assumption, namely, that the student who does not know the correct answer will guess *blindly* among the options provided and will therefore select the correct answer a given number of times on the basis of chance alone. That this assumption is very tenuous and possibly invalid has been shown by Cureton (1966a),

---

[1] Crocker and Benson (1976) found that correction-for-guessing was *not* appropriate for criterion-referenced tests in general, and mastery tests in particular. In fact, Jacobs (1975) felt that students taking CRTs be advised to adopt different test-taking strategies than when taking NRTs.

Little (1962), and Shimuzu (1965). If students are motivated to do their best, if the items are of appropriate difficulty, if the students are given sufficient time to answer all items, and if the items have plausible and attractive distracters, we feel that very little blind guessing will occur. We feel that instructing students to omit those items they are not completely certain of, and then applying a correction formula, implies that students should be discouraged from making intelligent guesses. But isn't much of life based upon making educated guesses? Don't the meteorologist, the internist, and the automobile mechanic often make educated guesses? How often do people have full, absolute information upon which to base a decision? "In everyday life, persons are continually guessing on the basis of partial knowledge, but they hope to guess right a fair share of the time" (Traxler, 1951, p. 329).

The correction formula does *not* handle those students who guessed the correct answer on the basis of partial information or those students who guessed the wrong answer because of misinformation and/or the plausibility of the distracters (Abu-Sayf, 1975). When pupils get the correct answer by eliminating some implausible distracters and guessing from the remaining ones, the formula *undercorrects* for guessing. When pupils get the wrong answer because of *misinformation*, the formula *overcorrects* for guessing (Nunnally, 1967). Slakter (1968a) reported that the nonguesser is penalized by the application of the standard correction-for-guessing formula. In any event, the formula does not always do what it is intended to do—make valid corrections for wild guessing.

4. A "guessing" response set is *not* static (Jones & Kaufman, 1975) but varies according to (1) the extent of occurrence of specific determiners, (2) the number of items the examinee answers correctly, and (3) the *type* of determiners—for example, position versus length (the former is much stronger in inducing a guessing response set).

5. There is lack of agreement among psychometricians about the value of the correction formula insofar as validity and reliability are concerned. (See Diamond and Evans (1973) for a 40-year review of the research on formula scoring; see also Holmes, Michael, & Michael, 1974; Reilly, 1975.)

6. Confidence weighting has been proposed as a method for minimizing guessing. In confidence weighting, the examinee not only selects what he believes is the correct answer, but he also indicates the degree of confidence he has in the answer selected. Then, on the basis of the examinee's answer selection and expression of confidence, appropriate weights are applied. This approach, however, is not too appealing because scoring tends to become complex. But even if computer facilities are available (which in many schools they may not be), confidence weighting does *not* improve predictive validity (Bernhardson, 1967; Hopkins, Hakstian, & Hopkins, 1973).[2]

[2] Miles (1973) reports that signal detection theory *may* provide a useful and viable approach. More research, however, is needed.

So then, what is the status or opinion regarding the use of correction formulas or confidence weighting schemes? It would appear that it depends upon whom you ask, when you asked them, the *type* of validity or reliability you were referring to, and so forth. As mentioned earlier, and we hope that we have supported our position, we do not favor applying a correction formula.

If all pupils have sufficient time to, and in fact do, answer all items, the correlation between the corrected and uncorrected scores is perfect. Although the magnitude of the scores will change, there will be no change in the students' relative ranking (Tinkelman, 1971). Furthermore, every student should be encouraged to answer every item even though he may guess blindly at some of the answers. This may not be pedagogically sound and acceptable, but we feel that such instructions will help equalize the test-taking behavior for all students and will not give any preferential advantage to the blind guesser.

Regardless of one's position on the guessing issue, one thing is of paramount importance: *When interpreting a test score, the teacher must be cognizant that the obtained score is dependent, in part at least, upon the guessing instructions given the pupils.* For example, a score obtained on a test where students were told that they should not guess and/or a correction formula will be applied, penalizes students who have a tendency to gamble and take risks. Also, since a test score is in part a reflection of the individuals' need for social approval, their motivation, and their anxiety, these factors must be considered in interpreting their test score since their propensity to guess is affected or influenced by their personality.

Should Students Change Their Answers on Objective Tests?

Although this point is not directly related to the written instructions the teacher prepares for his classroom test, this question is frequently asked by pupils before, during, or after the test. We feel that it deserves some mention, albeit briefly.

A myth that has persisted for some time is that students taking an objective test should not change their answers when they review the test before handing it in, the reason being that the first answer is usually the correct answer. Empirical evidence does *not* substantiate this myth. In fact, most studies have shown that, by and large, students profit from changing an answer (Foote & Belinsky, 1972; Jacobs, 1972b; Lynch & Smith, 1972, 1975; McMorris & Gregory, 1976; Mueller & Schwedel, 1975; Mueller & Wasser, 1977; Pascale, 1974; Reiling & Taylor, 1972; Smith & Moore, 1976).

No one really knows why students may or may not change answers. Whether it is due to their personality (McMorris & Gregory, 1976) or to their obtaining more insight or some other factor(s) on rereading the item is not clear (Jarrett, 1948). What is clear, however, is that we strongly urge teachers to de-emphasize the conventional caution that "the first answer is invariably the best answer." Do we then advocate that students be instructed and encouraged to change their answers on a test? Not necessarily! What we do advocate, and what appears to be clear, is that pupils should be encouraged to review the test and their answers, that they should carefully reread each question, and if on further consideration they obtain a better understanding of the item and/or are able to recall additional information the second time through, or feel that they answered incorrectly the first time, then by all means they should change their original answer. A change based on such factors will tend to *raise* rather than lower the pupil's score.

REPRODUCING THE TEST

It is important that enough copies of the test be prepared so that each student can have his own. Careful attention to the reproduction phase will not only make it easier for the examinee, but may also make scoring much easier, especially when objective items are used. To assist both examinee and examiner, we suggest the following practices (recognizing that some points have been previously discussed):

1. Space the items so that they are not crowded. In multiple-choice items, reading the stem becomes very difficult when items are tightly crammed together with options. For multiple-choice tests, the options should be placed in a vertical column *below* the test item rather than in paragraph fashion.

2. For the alternate-response test, have a column of T's and F's at either the right- or left-hand side of the items so that the student need only circle, underline, or cross out the correct response. This is better than having the student write T or F. When writing rapidly, examinees, especially young children, often make the letters T and F look alike. As mentioned earlier, for very young children we recommend the use of "yes-no" rather than true-false.

3. For matching exercises, have the two lists on the *same* page.

4. For the multiple-choice item that uses a *key* list, try to keep all items using a particular key on the same page. If this is not possible, the key should be repeated on the new page.

5. For the interpretive exercise, the introductory material—be it a graph, chart, diagram, or piece of prose—and the items based on it should be on the same page. If the material used is too long, facing pages should be used.

6. All items should be numbered consecutively. For the matching and multiple-choice item, the material in the list to be matched and/or the options to be used should be *lettered*.

7. For the short-answer items (1 to 2 words), the blank should be numbered and the responses recorded in blanks (vertically arranged and numbered

to correspond to the number of the blank) on one side of the answer sheet used. For example:

1. The Spearman-Brown formula is used   1. (split-halves)
   for the (1) reliability.

It is essential, of course, that adequate space be provided the student to write his answer. Young children especially vary in the size of their handwriting, so it is difficult to accurately say that 1, or 1½, or 2 inches of space should be provided.

8. If the responses are recorded directly on the test booklet, it will make scoring easier if all responses to objective items are recorded on one side of the page, regardless of the item format used.

9. If work space is needed to solve numerical problems, provide this space on the *answer* sheet or test booklet rather than having examinees use scratch paper. Majors and Michael (1975) found that seventh-graders did better when they did their computations in the test booklet's work space than when scratch paper was used. There are too many opportunities for making recording-type errors when an answer from one place must be transferred to another place.

10. All illustrative material used should be clear, legible, and accurate.

11. When feasible, and especially if large numbers of copies are needed, use a mimeograph or offset method of reproduction rather than a hectograph process, which becomes illegible after many copies have been prepared.

12. Proof the test carefully *before* it is reproduced. If possible, try to have the test reviewed independently, preferably by a teacher who teaches the same subject. If errors are found after the test has been reproduced, they should be called to the students' attention *before* the actual test is begun.

ADMINISTERING THE TEST

The physical conditions should be as comfortable as possible and the examinees should be as relaxed as possible even though the evidence is inconclusive regarding the effects of physical conditions on test performance (see Anastasi, 1976; Boggs & Simon, 1968; Holen & Newhouse, 1976; Ingle & DeAmico, 1969; Mowsesian & Heyer, 1973; Shapiro, 1975; Thorndike & Hagen, 1977; Trentham, 1975).

Even though reliability formulas are typically not used to estimate the error variance due to different physical conditions, this does not imply that the errors are nonexistent, nor does it detract from the fact that we are obligated to provide students with optimal testing conditions (Donlon, 1975). If we know that conditions are not what we would like them to be, the interpretation of the pupils' scores must be made accordingly. This is especially true for very young children whose test performance can be adversely affected by the test conditions present (Trentham, 1975).

Psychological Aspects

Individuals usually perform better at any endeavor, including test taking, if they approach the experience with a positive attitude. Yet teachers frequently fail to establish a positive mental attitude in the pupils tested. No human being can do his best when he is tense and nervous, and tests do induce tenseness, more so in some pupils than others. At present, the research on the general mental attitude and motivation of individuals and the correlation of these traits with test performance is inconclusive. We do know, however, that test anxiety affects optimum performance (Osterhouse, 1975; Sarason, Hill, & Zimbardo, 1964; Weiner & Kukla, 1970; Weiner & Potepan, 1970). It is the task of the teacher to prepare the student emotionally for the test. Students should be motivated to do their best (Yamamoto & Dizney, 1965). They should be convinced in their own minds that, in the long run, the test results will be of value to them—that the test results will help identify their strengths and weaknesses. Pupils should believe that test results are designed to *improve* their knowledge and skills, and that tests are *not* punitive measures contrived by the establishment or a grouchy teacher. Teachers, of course, must be careful that in their attempts to motivate the students they do not end up making the students more anxious. We feel that if students are made aware of the benefits they will derive from accurate test results, this should do much toward setting the proper emotional climate.

Students may easily develop negative attitudes toward tests when their teachers "spring" tests on them. Ideally, the schedule of tests to be administered during the year, semester, or quarter should be announced to the students as early as possible.

Let's face it! To many students, tests are a traumatic experience. To some students, they are the "club" the teacher uses to keep them in line. Too often, confidence in teachers is dissipated and even ruined because of the kinds of tests they give, and because of the reasons why tests are used. There is no need for this kind of student reaction. But it can be remedied only if teachers work earnestly to reassure students and convince them that test results are as useful to them as to the teacher.

Before the test begins (actually throughout the year), the teacher should reassure his students, put them at ease, and answer any questions they may have. Once the test has begun, however, the teacher must make certain that all distractions are kept to a minimum.

Some Additional Considerations

When administering the test, the teacher should make sure that the students understand the directions and that answer sheets, if they are being used with the younger pupils, are being used correctly. In addition, the teacher should keep the students informed of the time remaining (for example, writing the time left on the blackboard at, say, 15-minute intervals). Careful proctoring should take place so that cheating is eliminated, discouraged, and/or detected. We have seen many teachers in public schools as well as in college who define proctoring as "being present in the room." They are physically present, but spend their time reading a novel, writing a letter, completing a report, or grading papers.

To minimize cheating, a variety of procedures could be used—using alternate seats, having equivalent forms, scrambling the items—but these are not practical for the ordinary classroom test, nor do they necessarily result in a decrease in cheating (Houston, 1976). In fact, scrambling the items *may* produce a test with different properties from that of the original test. The single, *most* effective method to minimize cheating is by careful proctoring. Considering the prevalence of cheating on exams, it is obvious that many teachers do not take their proctoring responsibilities seriously enough. Students should be made to realize that cheating is dishonest and, if detected, will result in their failing the course. But the best way to detect cheating is to observe students during the examination—*not* by being preoccupied at one's desk.

Some educators have suggested the honor system as a deterrent to cheating. Prior to the scandal at the Air Force Academy in Colorado in 1965, the military academies were used as examples of how effective this method can be. However, as most educators now realize, the honor system really does not work very well.

DeCecco (1968, p. 640) pointed out: "Failure to prevent cheating may have serious deleterious effects on student achievement: (1) When cheating occurs with impunity, honest achievement goes unrecognized or punished and reduces student motivation to achieve; (2) there is no way to assess validly or reliably what the student has and has not learned; and (3) ingenuity in devising ways to cheat becomes more important than attainment of the instructional objectives."

Test-wiseness is a recognized source of variance on educational tests which reduces the test's validity. (For a review of the literature on test-wiseness, see Nilsson and Wedman (1974).) Ebel (1965b, p. 206) stated that "more error in measurement is likely to originate from students who have too little, rather than too much, skill in taking tests." If Ebel is correct, and we believe he is, then teachers must either construct "test-wise–free" tests by having clear instructions and a minimum of clues, or identify those students who are low in test-wiseness and instruct them in the principles of being test-wise or how to take tests (Crehan, et al., 1974; Diamond, Ayrer & Green, 1977; Slakter, et al., 1970) so that all pupils are working under similar conditions. Slakter et al. (1970) reported that students could be taught test-wiseness by means of a programmed approach. Gaines and Jongsma (1974), Jongsma and Warshaver (1975), and Woodley (1975) showed that test-wiseness rules and strategies can be taught and may be better than practice in specific item types, a strategy offered by Callenbach (1973) who reported a significant improvement in the reading scores of second-graders given instruction and practice in test-taking skills. It is clear that test-wiseness can be taught (the methods may differ) to children as young as 4 or 5 years old (Oakland & Weilert, 1971). At present, for college students at least, there are many books available for preparing them to take tests (Manuel, 1956; Juola, 1968). More important than having books or programmed materials, however, is our belief that test-wiseness skills should be an integral part of the instructional phase.

RECORDING AND SCORING THE ANSWERS

In Chapter 8 we discussed the scoring of the essay test in a fairly detailed fashion. Our ensuing discussion will therefore be restricted to the recording and scoring of answers to objective-type tests.

Is it better for the pupil to record his answers directly on the test paper or should he use a separate answer sheet?[3] Which method is easier for the teacher to score accurately and reliably? It depends upon the item format used, the age and ability level of the pupils, and the nature of the content. Generally speaking, separate answer sheets will provide more accurate and reliable scores, especially if they are machine-scored, although as mentionad earlier, for tests involving numerical answers being computed it might be better to have pupils record their answers directly in the test booklet rather than use a separate answer sheet.

There are essentially three types of scoring processes: (1) hand scoring, either in the booklets themselves or on separate answer sheets; (2) machine scoring; and (3) self-scoring answer sheets. This means therefore that there are also three methods by which the pupil can record his answers. The manner in which the answers are to be recorded, and hence scored, will be governed (in part at least) by the availability of special scoring equipment, the speed with which test results are needed, and the monetary resources available to have the answer sheets scored by an independent scoring service.

Hand Scoring

For the completion-type item, the teacher may prepare a scoring key by writing out the answers on a test paper or he may make a separate strip key that corresponds to the column of blanks provided the student. With either of these methods, the teacher can place the scoring key next to the pupils' responses and score the papers rather quickly.

Pupils, of course, may use a separate answer sheet, which is hand-scored. A punched key, which is nothing more than the regular answer sheet with

---

[3] For a discussion on the effect of type of answer sheet used on test performance, see Hayward (1967).

the correct responses punched out, can be placed over the pupils' answer sheet and the teacher or pupil can count the number of blackened spaces to determine the number of items answered correctly. The teacher must check to see that no paper contains more than one mark per item.

The carbon booklet is another technique that may be used to record and score responses. The pupil records his answer on the top sheet, and these marks are transferred directly to a scoring sheet below. Should the student wish to alter a response, he completely fills in the square of the original answer. After the test has been completed, the teacher need only separate the two answer sheets and count the number of responses in the squares to ascertain the number of items answered correctly.

An adaptation of the carbon booklet is the silver-overlay answer sheet. Here, the correct answers are previously placed in the appropriate squares, and the total answer sheet is covered by a silver overlay that conceals the correct answers. The student erases the square he feels corresponds to the correct answers. This procedure has not found its way into commercially published tests as yet but it is used quite effectively in classroom testing because it provides immediate feedback. Research has also shown that such a self-scoring procedure results in a higher split-half reliability than the conventional right-wrong method (Gilman & Ferry, 1972).

The pinprick method is similar to both the carbon booklet and the silver overlay techniques. Instead of checking the answer by placing an "X" in the appropriate square or by erasing the appropriate square, the subject sticks a pin in the square (or circle) near the answer he thinks is correct. Squares (or circles) corresponding to the correct answer are printed on the back page so that when the booklet is torn open the number of pinholes falling within the designated squares indicates the subject's score.

Machine Scoring

The simplest way to score select-type objective-test items is to have the student record his answers on a separate answer sheet and then have the answer sheet machine-scored.[4] Although separate answer sheets make scoring easier and generally more reliable, they are *not* recommended for the young and slow-learning children because of the inconclusive evidence regarding their use with young children (Beck, 1974; Cashen & Ramseyer, 1969; Clark, 1968; Gaffney & Maguire, 1971; McKee, 1967; Moore, 1960; Muller, Calhoun & Orling, 1972; Ramseyer & Cashen, 1971). When a separate answer sheet is used, the pupil must remember the question that he is answering (especially if he skips one), the answer selected, and then transfer this accurately to the answer sheet. Such a task may be too demanding for very young children (kindergarten and first-graders definitely). If separate answer sheets are used, stu-

[4] For a thorough discussion on scoring answer sheets by computer, see Baker (1971a).

dents have to be taught how to use an answer sheet, should be given practice with it, and should be given examples on the test. It would be helpful for the teacher to also give examples on the use of the answer sheet before the test begins, using the blackboard. Then, any questions or problems that exist can be dealt with before the test begins.

When feasible, we recommend the use of a separate machine-scorable answer sheet for efficiency and accuracy.[5] For example, with the IBM 1230 scoring machine, approximately 900 answer sheets can be scored in 1 hour. With the Digitek optical scanning equipment about 1200 papers can be scored every hour. A disadvantage of machine scoring is that, unless directions are given explicitly and followed by the student, scoring errors will occur. The errors can be minimized by a preliminary screening; however, the time required for correcting sloppy and/or smudgy papers may prove to be costly. This need for remarking or correcting can be almost entirely eliminated by careful administrative directions prior to taking the test.

Although schools with either small testing programs or with a small enrollment would not be in a position to justify the expenditure of funds to purchase or lease elaborate, sophisticated test-scoring equipment, simpler versions are available to them. In the past few years, small, relatively inexpensive scoring machines have appeared, with prices varying from about $1000 to about $3000. Information on these machines can be obtained by writing directly to the manufacturers.

For volume users, commercial firms will provide test-scoring services for a very nominal charge. It is also possible to have the papers scored by some state universities or large school districts for a small charge. Those persons considering the processing of separate answer sheets by machine should compare the costs and services offered so that they will be able to process their answer sheets most economically. (Some agencies will, in addition to scoring the answer sheets, provide printouts of the pupils' raw and standard scores, percentiles, and test score distributions, print out the mean, median, and test reliability, and provide item analysis data.)

Some General Considerations for Scoring Objective-Type Tests

Regardless of whether the pupil records his answer directly in the test booklet or on a separate answer sheet, whether the responses are scored by hand or machine, there are still certain precautions that the teacher can take to ensure that his scoring key is properly prepared. Some of the points have been discussed earlier but deserve repetition here because, if adopted, they may avoid needless quibbling between teacher and student.

[5] For an interesting discussion on the legal, ethical, and psychometric factors involved in using separate answer sheets, see Stake, Womer, and Hills (1966).

1. The scoring key should be prepared and checked well in advance. One way to check on the correctness of the scoring key is to have another teacher either check your key or prepare his own and compare the two keys. Another way to check on the adequacy of the scoring key, especially for completion items, is to select the papers of a few of the more able students and compare their responses with the key. This "dry run" may indicate some discrepancies in the scoring keys that are the result of ambiguity in the item and/or an answer that is correct but was not anticipated. Naturally, any time a correct but unanticipated answer is received, the key should be corrected accordingly.

2. If factors other than the correctness of the answer (such as spelling, grammar, or legibility of handwriting) are to be considered, they should be given a separate score.

3. Generally speaking, each item should have equal weight.[6] Although empirically weighting each option might result in a better test (psycho-metrically speaking), this will be the case *only* if no items are omitted or the "omits" are appropriately weighted (Raffeld, 1975). Needless problems will be avoided if each objective-test item is assigned the *same* point value. Trying to justify that one item is worth two points, another one point, and still another one-half point is very difficult. With differential weighting employed, the teacher is really saying that knowledge of one concept is more important than knowledge of another concept. If the teacher believes that this is so, he should sample more heavily in these areas rather than use differential weights.

4. Whether students should receive credit for partial knowledge is another perplexing problem that, though not restricted to only objective-type tests in general or multiple-choice tests in particular, deserves some consideration. Without a doubt this question has received considerable attention in the past but particularly within the past decade. Once again we have those who argue strongly on the side of credit for only a correct answer and those who argue just as vehemently that if on a computational problem the student demonstrates knowledge of the process and concepts but makes a simple arithmetic error, the student should be given at least partial credit. And what about the student who, when a confidence scoring model is used, selects the correct answer but is not too confident in his choice. Should he receive partial credit? If a confidence weighting system is used, such a student will receive partial credit. We believe that for some tests (e.g., essay, problem-solving) students should receive partial credit for partial knowledge. For objective tests, however, such a complicated scoring formula is not warranted.

[6] For a comprehensive survey of the research on weighting, see Stanley and Wang (1970). See also Echternacht (1976), Hakstian and Kansup (1975), Kansup and Hakstian (1975), Patnaik and Traub (1973), and Raffeld 1975).

Correction for Guessing[7]

Although the correction for guessing is still popular with commercially prepared achievement tests, its popularity is on the decline insofar as teacher-made tests are concerned. We have already stated that we do *not* favor the application of a correction formula. Pupils don't like it, many teachers are hard-pressed to defend it, and research findings question its value (Rowley & Traub, 1977). In fact, Lord (1964) contends that formula scoring should be restricted to (used in) (1) very difficult tests, (2) those cases where examinees have differential guessing rates, and (3) multiple-choice tests having fewer than five options. However, if a teacher does not agree with us, and has informed his students that they will be penalized for guessing, he must apply a correction formula. The standard correction-for-guessing formula is

$$\text{Score} = R - \frac{W}{n-1}$$

where R = number right
W = number wrong
n = number of options

In a true-false test where $n=2$, the formula becomes $S = R - W$. In a three-choice multiple-choice test, the formula becomes $S = R - (W/2)$.

Some research (Ebel, 1965a; Hambleton et al., 1970; Hanna, 1975; Hopkins et al., 1973; Koehler, 1974) has demonstrated that with more complex scoring procedures (for example, confidence scoring, empirical weighting, probabilistic scoring, and the like), it might be possible to reduce blind guessing. But even with these more sophisticated techniques, we must still recognize that whether or not a student obtains a higher and/or more valid score depends to a great extent on his personality and response set (Hansen, 1971; Jacobs, 1971). Even if this were not so, we feel that with the extra time needed for the pupil to respond to the item, the gain in reliability (Ahlgren, 1969; Pugh & Brunza, 1975) would not be commensurate with the time and effort expended (Koehler, 1971). Yes, counteracting the effects of guessing on selection-type objective tests is a persistent problem for which no satisfactory solution has as yet been devised, although Traub and Hambleton's (1972) research on reward for "omits" shows promise and is better than imposing a guessing penalty (Waters & Waters, 1971). But we agree with Thorndike (1971c, p. 61), who said ". . . the happiest solution to the guessing problem lies not in correcting for guessing but in preventing it."

[7] For a thorough review, see Diamond and Evans (1973).

TESTING THE TEST: ITEM ANALYSIS

Would you like to buy some product that had not undergone any type of quality control check? It depends, of course, upon the product, its cost, and other factors. You might say that quality control would be more important for an electrical device, which could cause death from electrocution, than for a bottle of glue. Would you not agree that decisions made on the basis of test results—selection, classification, admission, and grading—are important enough that some type of quality control check should be made on the tests teachers use? Definitely yes!

If teacher-made achievement test results are to be used for decision-making purposes, it is important that the tests give information as accurate as possible. If they do not provide accurate data, teachers should want to know this so that they could (1) place less emphasis on the data in decision making and (2) improve their measuring instruments for use in future evaluations and decision making. More often than not, teachers prepare, administer, and score a test, return the test papers to their students, possibly discuss the test, and then either file or discard the test. Ebel (1965b, p. 15) suggests that one of the common mistakes of teachers is that they do not check on the effectiveness of their tests. This is probably because (1) teachers do not always understand the importance of accurate evaluation; (2) teachers are not aware of the methods of analyzing tests; or (3) teachers feel that test analysis is too time consuming. We certainly hope that by now you realize that important decisions are often based on classroom achievement tests and that accuracy is therefore important.

Evaluate with Respect to Measurement Criteria

There are certain criteria (reliability, validity, objectivity, difficulty, and discrimination) that evaluation instruments should possess. Teachers do not have the time to check all aspects of these characteristics for all evaluative instruments, but many of them can be checked for most instruments without consuming a great deal of teacher time. For example, reliability can and should be checked for major evaluative instruments, such as the end-of-semester exams. The scorer reliability of essay exams can be checked by correlating the values given by two or more readers. The difficulty and discrimination indices of the test items used should be checked every time a test is administered.

For achievement tests, the validity of most concern to educators is content validity. As was mentioned under the section on planning (see pages 174–179), a blueprint should be constructed for every test so that the test content will be appropriate to the course objectives. As we will see in Chapter 12, teacher-constructed instruments such as rating scales, sociograms, or observational techniques are in a sense checked for content validity when the teacher rethinks whether the characteristics rated or the behavior observed are really relevant to his educational objectives and decision making. Other teachers and students, and at times even parents, can be valuable resource people in examining the validity of any measuring instrument.

Objectivity and efficiency can be easily examined on any instrument. Discrimination and item difficulty, a related variable, can be checked by a procedure known as item analysis. While something analogous to item analysis can be performed on any instrument, it is most useful for objective tests. We will limit our discussion of item analysis to objective tests using multiple-choice items. Many of the principles discussed are applicable to true-false and matching items.

Item Analysis

Item analysis is the process of examining the students' responses to each test item to judge the quality of the item. Specifically, what one looks for is the difficulty and discriminating ability of the item as well as the effectiveness of each alternative.[8]

When an item writer prepares test items, he must make some judgments regarding the difficulty level, discrimination power, and content validity of his items. Normally, the item writer makes some "gut level" decisions (he may incorporate the views of others) about content relevance, but difficulty and discrimination indices require some quantitative evidence. Some of the evidence obtained in the National Assessment of Educational Progress vividly demonstrated that there were many instances where professional item writers misjudged the difficulty of their test items (Finley & Berdie, 1970). If this can happen with professionals, we can expect that classroom teachers, for a variety of reasons, will make invalid estimates of the psychometric properties of their test items (Ryan, 1968). That is why we recommend that some quantitative evidence to support the difficulty and discrimination indices of test items be obtained. Such estimates can be obtained from item analysis.

Still another value accrues from performing an item analysis. Many teachers fail to reuse test items. Often those teachers who do reuse test items use both the better and poorer items. It is indeed unfortunate when a teacher fails to reuse his better test items (or reuses poor items) on subsequent tests. The time, effort, and energy expended in the planning and writing of test items is wasted if the good items are discarded. Even if the better items— those that possess content validity and which discriminate between high and low achievers—were only filed, they could at some future date be reused. It is ridiculous for teachers to have to write new items every time they prepare a test. Over time, they should have built up a test file of the better items to

---

[8] Hoffman (1975) introduced a new item-analysis index, e, the index of efficiency, which is the ratio of observed discrimination to maximum discrimination.

be reused. However, in order to build this test file, it is necessary to know how the item behaves.

You will recall from our previous discussion of item difficulty that for a norm-referenced test to provide valid and useful information, it should be neither too easy nor too difficult, and that each item should discriminate validity among the high- and low-achieving students. The procedure used to judge the quality of an item is called *item analysis*.

There are a variety of different item-analysis procedures (see, for example: Cureton, 1966; Davis, 1964; Engelhart, 1965; Henrysson, 1971, Oosterhoff, 1976b. See also Baker (1977) for a discussion, albeit technical, on advances in item analysis).[9] In general, the simpler procedures as described in an Educational Testing Service bulletin (1960) are as effective as the more statistically complicated ones for purposes of analyzing classroom tests (Henrysson, 1971, p. 145).

In conducting an item analysis of a classroom test, one should follow the steps listed below. (See Educational Testing Service, 1960.)

1. Arrange the test papers from the highest score to the lowest score.

2. From the ordered set of papers, make two groups: Put those with the highest scores in one group and those with the lowest scores in the other group. There are some statistical reasons (Kelley, 1939) why one should place the best 27 percent of the papers in one group and the poorest 27 percent in the other group. But, for classroom tests, it really is not too important what percentage is used (D'Agostino & Cureton, 1975). If the class is small (say 40 or fewer students), there would be too few papers in the top and bottom 27 percent to obtain very reliable item-analysis indices. In the typical type of classroom situation it is quite appropriate to simply divide the total group into the top and bottom halves.

3. For each item, count the number of students in each group who choose each alternative (in the completion or true-false item, it would be the number who answered the item correctly).

4. Record the count as follows for each item (assume a total of 40 papers, 20 in each group, for this example, in which the asterisk indicates the correct answer).

| | ALTERNATIVES | | | | | |
	A	B	C*	D	E	Omits
Upper group	0	0	20	0	0	0
Lower group	4	2	8	3	3	0

[9] Those persons interested in computer-generated item-analysis procedures should consult Schittjer and Cartledge (1976).

5. For each item, compute the percentage of students who get the item correct. This is called the *item difficulty index* (p)[10], which can range from .00 to 1.00. The formula for item difficulty is:

$$\text{Difficulty} = \frac{R}{T} \times 100$$

where R = number of pupils who answered item correctly
T = total number of pupils tested

In the example in step 4, $R = 28$ (this is the total number of students who answered C, the correct answer), and $T = 40$ (the number of students tested). Applying the formula,

$$\text{Difficulty} = \frac{28}{40} \times 100 = 70\%$$

There are some who like to express difficulty and discrimination as decimals rather than percentages. In this case, one would only compute R/T.

If one did not divide the total group into two halves but put the top 27 percent in the upper and the bottom 27 percent in the lower group, one could obtain an estimate of item difficulty by dividing the number of persons in the two groups who answered the item correctly by the total number of people in those two groups. (Be careful! *Not* the total number of students tested!)

6. Compute the *item discrimination index* for each item by subtracting the number of students in the lower group who answered the item correctly from the number in the upper group who got the item right, and dividing by the number of students in either group (for example, half the total number of students when we divide the group into upper and lower halves). In our example,

$$\text{Discrimination} = \frac{R_U - R_L}{(1/2)T} = \frac{20 - 8}{20} = .60$$

This value is usually expressed as a decimal and can range from -1.00 to $+1.00$. If it has a positive value, the item has positive discrimination. This means that a larger proportion of the more knowledgeable students than poor students (as determined by the total test score) got the item right. If the

---

[10] Difficulty can be expressed as either *average test difficulty* or *item difficulty*. Average test difficulty is defined as the ratio between the average score and the total test score. For example, if on a test where the maximum score was 100, the average score was 70, we would say that the average test difficulty is 70/100 = .70. If all pupils who took the test received a perfect score, the average test difficulty would be 100/100 = 1.00; if no pupil answered any item correctly, the average test difficulty is 0/100 = .00.

value is zero, the item has zero discrimination. This can occur (1) because the item is too easy or too hard (if everybody got the item right or everybody missed the item, there would be zero discrimination) or (2) because it is ambiguous. If more poorer than better students get the item right, one would obtain a negative discrimination. With a small number of students, this could be a chance result, but it may indicate that the item is ambiguous or miskeyed. In general, the higher the discrimination index, the better, recognizing that there are situations where low discrimination is to be expected. For classroom tests, where one divides the class into upper and lower halves as we have done, one would hope that most of the items would have discrimination indices above .20. (If one uses the upper and lower 27 percent, one should expect higher values, since there is more difference between the groups.)

7. Look at how the distracters (incorrect options or alternatives) worked by using the same process specified above. For the distracters, we hope to get *negative* values. That is, more poor students than good students should choose incorrect answers.

Quite often, a visual inspection is all that is needed to evaluate the effectiveness of the distracters. Look at the following example, which is taken from an actual test and measurement examination.

TOPIC	OBJECTIVE
Table of Specifications	Understanding

12. In planning a test, the table of content and process objectives is *least* useful in
   A. relating content to behavioral objectives.
   B. deciding whether to use essay or objective items.
   C. judging relative emphases to be given to different objectives.
   D. judging relative emphases to be given to different content areas.
   E. gearing the test to the instruction it follows.

ITEM 12		TEST 3200[a]			NOV 1970		
	A	B*	C	D	E	OMIT	
U	0	83	0	0	17	0	DIFF 24
L	42	50	8	0	0	0	DISC 33

[a] Numbers below are *percentages*.

It is readily evident in the example (even if the discrimination index were not provided) that the item discriminates in a positive direction. Alternatives A and C are effective in the sense that they attracted more students from the lower group than from the upper group. But alternative D is a poor distracter because it attracted no one and therefore is useless. This visual inspection suggests that alternative D be replaced or revised. Alternative E is also poor because it attracted a higher proportion of the better than poorer students. The item writer must ask himself, "Why were the brighter students attracted to E?" Was it because of ambiguity? Was it because there were two equally correct answers? Was it because of carelessness on the part of the examinees? It would appear that the better students misread the question that asked for the *least* useful aspect of the table of specifications. Without a doubt, "E" is a very useful aspect of the table of specifications.

A reasonable hypothesis is that E was selected in greater proportion by the better students because of poor reading rather than a weakness in the item or distracter. Given the small number of students who took the test, the item could be used again before making any changes in either the stem or E.

In the item analysis below, where the asterisk indicates the correct answer, the item is discriminating in a *negative* direction.

| | Alternatives | | | | | |
	A	B	C	D	E*	Omits
Upper 20 students	0	1	7	2	4	6
Lower 20 students	0	1	5	3	6	5
Total	0	2	12	5	10	11

What is the "ideal" discrimination index? Generally, for a norm-referenced test, the higher the discrimination index, the better. *What is the "ideal" difficulty index?* Teachers would like their classroom achievement tests to have appropriate difficulty because test difficulty is related to *discrimination power*. If an item is so easy that everyone answers it correctly, or so hard that no one can answer it correctly, it cannot discriminate at all and adds nothing to test reliability or validity. So, then, what is the "ideal" index of difficulty that the teacher should strive to obtain? The designation of the "ideal" difficulty level is dependent upon many factors, the most important ones being the purpose of the test and the type of objective items used.

If the purpose of the test is to see the extent to which fourth-grade students have *mastered* the multiplication table, the teacher (after completing this unit) might expect all his test items to have a difficulty value approaching 1.00. That is, he would expect most, if not all, of his students to answer each item correctly. But, if the purpose of the test was to achieve maximum discrimination among his pupils in terms of a final examination on the year's work, he would not expect his students to obtain perfect or near-perfect scores. Rather, he would want a spread of scores and would want items

---

[11] If chance didn't operate, such as in completion items, we would expect an examinee of average ability to answer about one-half the items correctly.

having a medium level of difficulty,[11] the range of difficulty being rather restricted (Cronbach & Warrington, 1952).[12]

In the long run, what is more important than the level of difficulty is to have a test that possesses adequate content validity. In addition, we want a test in which, for each item, a larger proportion of the better able than less able students can answer the item correctly.

Although a general rule of thumb is to prepare a test for which the mean is halfway between a chance and perfect score, Lord (1952) showed that for tests where guessing can occur, more reliable results can be obtained if the test as a whole is just a bit easier. This reduces the effect of chance guessing and increases test reliability. Lord gave the following guide for preparing tests with different item formats:

Item Format	Ideal Average Difficulty for a Maximally Discriminating Test
Completion and short-answer	50
Five-response multiple-choice	70
Four-response multiple choice	74
Three-response multiple-choice	77
True-false (two-response multiple-choice)	85

You should remember that the chart values are "ideal" values if the purpose is to get a test that is *maximally* differentiating among pupils.

A word of caution—or how not to make a test more difficult. For motivational purposes, we should have both some very easy and *some very difficult items.* But, if one is preparing a test to select one scholarship winner to Michigan State University, he might want to have a test that is quite difficult. However, in attempting to write more difficult items, we must be very careful not to resort to (1) ambiguity of wording, (2) emphasis on trivial details such as "What did Columbus eat for breakfast on the day he sighted America?," and (3) outright trickery. Emphasis on the trivial aspects of the course content will invariably lead students to memorize details at the expense of the more important learning outcomes, such as comprehension or analysis. Therefore, by emphasizing the trivial, we are not only contributing to undesirable learning outcomes, but we are also lowering the test's content validity—*unless* the one and only course objective was to teach rather insignificant details.

Other things being equal, the more positive and usually more profitable approach to use to increase test difficulty is to have more items calling for the application of the higher mental processes, such as application of principles, understanding of concepts, analysis, synthesis, and the like (Smith, 1970).

[12] For a more intensive treatment of the effect of population homogeneity and item heterogeneity on item difficulty, see Cronbach and Warrington (1952), Lord (1952), and Tinkelman (1971).

Using Item-Analysis Results

Item analysis data have several values: (1) They help one judge the worth or quality of a test; (2) they can be of aid in subsequent test revisions; (3) they can be used to build a test file for future tests; (4) they lead to increased skill in test construction; (5) they provide diagnostic value and help in planning future learning activities; (6) they provide a basis for discussing test results; and (7) they can be a learning experience for students, if students assist in, or are told the results of, item analysis.

Although item difficulty, item discrimination, and the response frequency of the distracters are useful in judging the adequacy of the test already given, they are probably more useful in helping revise the test (or the items) for future occasions. Very poor items should be discarded or, better yet, rewritten. Lange, Lehmann, and Mehrens (1967) showed that items can be improved, without too much effort, through using item analysis data. Revising these poor items is probably more economical than simply discarding them and attempting to write new ones. (We realize, of course, that some items are so poor that it would be better to prepare new ones than to try and patch them up.) By keeping a record of item-analysis data (one of the reasons we suggested that each item be written on a separate card), one can refer to it on subsequent revisions and determine the effectiveness of the changes. This continual revising and rechecking process leads to increased skill in test construction in that a teacher gradually learns what methods of wording and what type of distracters will work best. It is important to recognize that *careful inspection of the item itself is needed before making any changes.*

Another use of item analysis data relates to its impact on instructional procedures. If students all do poorly on some items, it may be due to poor teaching of that content. By carefully looking at the content of the hard items, a teacher can identify those areas in which students are not learning, so that in future classes he can do a more effective job by emphasizing the relevant material. Also, wrong answers *do* give valuable information not provided by just looking at correct answers (Powell & Isbister, 1974).

Providing Feedback to Students

It always has been, still is, and hopefully will continue to be, our firm conviction that not only should test papers be returned to students, but that every teacher should incorporate the discussion of the individual test items as part of their instructional strategy. We feel that it is essential for teachers to discuss the test for a variety of reasons, some of which are (1) to correct errors on the part of the student, some of these errors being the result of poor study habits or sloppy test-taking skills, (2) to motivate pupils to do better on subsequent tests, (3) to demonstrate to pupils those instructional objectives that are being stressed and tested so that they can organize their study habits accordingly, and (4) to permit students to discuss why a particular answer is keyed as the correct answer, that is, to clear up possible misconceptions and misunderstandings they may have. We recognize that providing feedback may destroy the security of items for future use. But, balancing test security against the potential value of feedback, we favor feedback.

The important thing is that feedback is extremely useful in the teaching-learning process. Although it might be considered by both teachers and pupils as time consuming and detracting from the time available for learning new material, we are firmly convinced that it is more important to learn the material covered well before moving on to new areas. As of now, there appears to be some disagreement as to the time when this feedback should be given (Anderson, Kulhary, & Andre, 1971; Jacobs & Kulkarni, 1966; Kowalski, Ranthawan, & Hunt, 1974). Some feel that it is more effective if done as soon as possible after the test has been given so as to correct errors immediately, before they have a chance to solidify in the pupils' minds. Others say that feedback can be delayed for up to one week without serious dilatory effects. Still others feel that delayed feedback is best and that it enhances retention (Kippel, 1975; Sassenrath, 1975; Sturgis, 1973; Surber & Anderson, 1975). The evidence bearing on the question of feedback time is inconclusive. What is conclusive, however, is the research that demonstrates that pupils given feedback, regardless of the delay, perform significantly better on similar-type items at a later date (Wexley & Thornton, 1972).

Feedback will be dealt with more fully in Chapter 17, where we will discuss reporting to parents, pupils, and teachers.

Interpreting Item-Analysis Data

Item-analysis data should be interpreted with caution (Cronbach, 1970; Furst, 1958; Gronlund, 1976; Helmstadter, 1974). Discriminating power is not analogous to item validity; the discrimination index is not always related to the quality of the item; and item-analysis data are very tentative.

1. *Item-analysis data are not analogous to item validity.* In order to judge accurately the validity of a test, one should use some external criterion. You will recall from our discussion of the item analysis procedure that no external criterion was used. The total test score was used to select the better and poorer groups. In other words, a form of circular reasoning was employed. In reality, we used an *internal* criterion. Therefore, it would appear that we were studying the internal consistency of the items rather than their validity.

2. *The discrimination index is not always a measure of item quality.* Generally speaking, the index of discrimination tells us about the quality of an item. In general, a discrimination index of .40 is regarded as satisfactory. However, one should not automatically conclude that because an item has a low discrimination index it is a poor item and should be discarded. Items with low or negative discriminating indices should be identified for

more careful examination. Those with low, but positive, discrimination indices should be kept (especially for *mastery* tests). As long as an item discriminates in a positive fashion, it is making some contribution to valid measurement of the students' competencies. And as long as we need some easy items to instill proper motivation in the examinees, such items are valuable. There are a variety of reasons that an item may have low discriminating power: (a) The more difficult or easy the item, the lower its discriminating power—but we often need such items to have adequate and representative sampling of the course content and objectives; (b) the nature (or purpose) of the item in relation to the total test will influence the magnitude of its discriminating power. Remember that we are dealing with the total test score as our internal criterion. Hence, if on an eleventh-grade physics test Mr. Magnet wants to measure various objectives and different content areas such as heat, light, magnetism, and electricity, he would need a variety of different items. If only 5 percent of his course deals with "the ability to apply principles" and this is spread over the various content areas, these "application" items might have low discriminating power because the major portion of the test may be measuring, say, "knowledge and understanding." Removing these low discriminating items could seriously impair test validity. As long as Mr. Magnet teaches for "application," he is obliged to test for application. In this case, since the typical classroom test measures a variety of instructional objectives, we might expect to find that "low positive indices of discrimination are the rule rather than the exception" (Gronlund, 1976, p. 270).

3. *Item-analysis data are tentative.* Some teachers assume that difficulty and discrimination indices are fixed. This is *not* true. Item-analysis data are influenced by the nature of the group being tested, the number of pupils tested, the instructional procedures employed by the teacher, and chance errors. Our judgment of the quality of an item should be predicated more by the fact of whether or not it measures an important instructional objective rather than by the magnitude of its difficulty and discrimination indices. As long as the item discriminates positively, is clear and unambiguous, and is free from technical defects, it should be retained at least for possible future use. Naturally, if a better item is developed, the newer one should be used.

4. *Avoid selecting test items purely on the basis of their statistical properties.* One of the better ways to select test items is to choose those that have appropriate difficulty and discriminating power for the intended purpose of the test. This does *not* mean that statistical analysis should be the overriding factor, especially in teacher-made achievement tests in the elementary grades where the item statistics are computed on only about 30 pupils, and hence may not be too reliable. Another reason for not selecting test items solely on the basis of their statistical properties, even if a sufficiently large sample was used, is that item difficulty can be affected by guessing, the location of the correct answer among the alternatives, and the serial location of

the item in the test (Huck & Bowers, 1972). Still another reason for being cautious is that in some cases the statistical selection of test items results in a test that is unrepresentative and biased. Cox (1964) conducted a study to learn what, if anything, would occur if a test were composed of items selected *purely* on their statistical properties. The major implication of this study is that if only item-analysis data are used to select the "better" test items for future use, the new test may be biased in that it may not evaluate the instructional objectives in the same proportion as would the original item pool; that is, the content validity is actually lowered. Cox recommended that the most discriminating items *within* each taxonomical category be selected, rather than select the most discriminating items from the entire pool of items where the taxonomical structure is ignored. This, then, means that in the planning stage the teacher would specify the number of items measuring each instructional objective and then write items for the total item pool accordingly. Then, within each category, a specified number of items would be selected for inclusion in the final form of the test. Unless this were done, the teacher would never be certain that his final form of the test would validly measure the instructional objectives specified in the test blueprint in the planning stage. Finally, as Whitely and Dawis demonstrated (1976, p. 336), ". . . test difficulty may depend on the tendency of items to interact in context as well as on their individual difficulties."

In our opinion, item-analysis data provide a valuable service in selecting good test items. But, they should be used as a "flag" to identify items that may require more careful examination. We must temper our predilection to select only items bearing certain statistical properties. We do not deny the value of item analysis, but statistical efficiency is *not* the *sine qua non*. We agree with Neill and Jackson (1976) who said that even after an item analysis is completed, items must still be carefully reviewed to ensure adequate content sampling, readability, conciseness, and lack of ambiguity. A good rule of thumb is to use rational procedures as a basis for initial selection of test items and then use statistical techniques to check on your judgment.

Item Analysis for Criterion-Referenced Tests

In criterion-referenced tests, especially mastery tests, the concept of difficulty and discrimination is antithetical to the philosophy underlying the mastery concept—that all or nearly all students should pass the item. And, if in criterion-referenced tests this is the case, should we be concerned with an item analysis procedure in order to identify the nondiscriminating items when ideally there should be none? A more important question, however, is whether we should be concerned with identifying those items that may be in need of revision.

There are those who contend that the conventional item analysis procedure for NRTs is inappropriate for CRTs because in CRTs there is no variability, and these techniques depend upon variability. And there are some who say that conventional procedures can be used because pre- and posttest scores can be used to obtain reliability. And, there are some, like Harris and Stewart (1971, p. 3) who contend that "item difficulty techniques cannot be properly used in constructing tests to assess skill in mastery when the population of performance (content) is specifically defined." Cox and Vargas (1966) used upper and lower 27 percent groups for pretest and posttest items and concluded that selection based on the difference in percentages passing the item on the pre- and posttest yielded good items. Brennan and Stolurow (1971) presented a variety of decision rules that can be applied to either pretest data only, posttest data only, or pre- and posttest data for the purpose of suggesting to the evaluator that either the test item or the instructional method, or both, are in need of further study or possible revision. Their procedure thus assists the teacher in making decisions about *both* his test items and his teaching method. We feel that more research is needed before any conclusive answer can be obtained with regard to the usefulness of conventional item analysis procedures for criterion-referenced tests. It may well be that conventional item analysis is appropriate but that we will have to interpret the data in a slightly different manner. Popham and Husek (1969) advocated that for criterion-referenced tests less attention be paid to discrimination and difficulty.

Even if we dispense with the traditional item analysis for CRTs, we must still be concerned with ascertaining whether the items in a CRT behave similarly, inasmuch as they are supposed to measure a well-defined domain. How, then, does one go about selecting appropriate items for a CRT? Popham (1972) proposed using an index of homogeneity based upon a chi-square technique, but this requires the administration of a pre- and posttest, a procedure that is neither economically efficient nor possible in many cases. Pettie and Oosterhoff (1976) proposed an adaptation of Popham's method to compute item difficulty that did not require an index of variability and only required a single test administration. Further research is needed, however, before the validity of this procedure can be established.

We believe that, regardless of whether a test is criterion- or norm-referenced, we should *not* discard an item that does not discriminate "if it reflects an important attribute of the criterion" (Popham & Husek, 1969, p. 6). Popham and Husek stated that with either a criterion- or norm-referenced test, a negative discriminating item should be looked at carefully. In criterion-referenced tests as well as in norm-referenced tests, a negative discriminator may be due to a faulty item, ineffective instruction, or inefficient learning on the part of the pupil.

SUMMARY

The principal ideas, conclusions, and recommendations presented in this chapter are summarized in the following statements:

1. All tests items should be prepared early enough to have a thorough critical review and editing, preferably by another teacher.
2. Test items should be grouped according to item format, and ordered according to difficulty within each format.
3. All test directions must be simple, clear, and concise. If diagrams or illustrative material are used, they should be of good quality and be accurate.
4. Students should be told how the test will be scored.
5. Test directions should be written out. They may also be given orally, but they should be available for student reference when needed.
6. Every student should have his own copy of the test.
7. Any questions that students have should be clarified before the test begins.
8. Teachers should proctor the test diligently and conscientiously. Otherwise, cheating may occur and the results will be invalid.
9. Pupils should be taught how to take tests.
10. Students should be encouraged to answer every test item. The correction-for-guessing formula should *not* be used for classroom achievement tests.
11. Pupils should be encouraged to review the test and change answers.
12. Responses may be made either directly on the test or on a separate answer sheet. Separate answer sheets should not be used for children below grade 3 unless special instructions and practice have been given. Answers to numerical problems should be recorded directly in the test booklet.
13. Teachers should attempt to provide optimal physical conditions. Also, they should consider the pupils' psychological reactions to test taking.
14. Each item should be given *equal* weight. Differential weighing should be avoided. (Essay tests, however, are a different matter.)
15. For some tests and for some purposes, students should receive partial credit for partial information.
16. Test results should be discussed with the class as a whole and/or with individual pupils.
17. Pupils should be motivated to do their best on tests.
18. Teachers should use basic item-analysis procedures to check the quality of their tests. The results of item analysis should be interpreted with caution.
19. Some measurement people feel that conventional item-analysis procedures are not applicable to criterion-referenced tests. More research is needed in this area.

CHAPTER TWELVE
Other Teacher-Made Evaluation Procedures

The primary way that teachers obtain data concerning their pupils' achievements and attainments is by their daily contacts with students. Teacher observations of daily behavior and the tests they give constitute the major impact upon teacher evaluations of student achievement. In fact, recent research has shown that observing overt classroom behavior (at least for second-graders) is not only useful in predicting school progress at the end of the school year but also leads to a better understanding of the child's progress (McKinney, Mason, Peterson, & Clifford, 1975). In Chapters 8 through 11 we considered just one procedure for evaluating student behavior—teacher-made cognitive tests. However, there are certain elements of practical work that cannot be tested by the conventional paper-and-pencil test but can only be measured with observational tools and techniques. In addition, education is, or at least *should* be, concerned with more than cognitive objectives or work samples of products. Our future society depends as much on the affective behavior of its citizenry as it does on its intellectual prowess. We, as educators, must therefore recognize that pencil-and-paper achievement tests are only one of the methods of evaluation available to teachers. Tests must be supplemented with other procedures if we are desirous of measuring or describing the multi-facets of human behavior. Tests periodically measure certain outcomes of instruction (primarily those in the cognitive domain) under contrived conditions. But as Stake and Denny (1969, p. 380) said, "needed but not available are reliable classroom observation techniques and instruments . . . the affective component of instruction is almost neglected in the current instructional-assessment schedules." These noncognitive instructional objectives should be measured continuously in more natural settings. (One could argue that the normal classrooms, and even the playground, are not completely natural and realistic settings, although they are much less restricted than test-taking conditions.) Direct observation of performance is the appropriate technique in a variety of learning situations from kindergarten to college, where the instructional objective is "to do. . . ."

This chapter covers methods of evaluation other than testing. Many of these methods depend upon the observation of pupils and their behavior. In general, the methods to be discussed here are less adaptable than achievement tests to the criteria of measurement procedures discussed in previous chapters. However, as observation becomes more systematized and less like everyday perception, such evaluation can become quite accurate. The topics to be discussed in this chapter are (1) evaluating procedures and products, (2) measurement and evaluation in the affective domain, (3) observational tools and techniques, (4) advantages of observation, (5) participation charts, (6) check lists, (7) rating scales, (8) anecdotal records, (9) evaluating personal-social adjustment by sociometric methods, and (10) attitude scales. These topics are related both to methods of observing and methods of recording behavior. Because in many of the procedures the student does not record any response and/or is unaware that data are being collected, and even when the student does record a response, there is no "right" or "wrong" answer, these procedures are sometimes referred to as *nontest* procedures (Payne, 1968, p. 30).

After studying this chapter, the student should be able to—

1. Discuss the two major problems in evaluating products and processes.
2. Recognize the difference between procedures and products.
3. Appreciate the importance of educators being knowledgeable about affective behavior.
4. Recognize that many of the arguments advanced by educators for minimizing the importance of, and need for, affective measurement are not valid.
5. Understand the problems associated with affective measurement and

why affective scales lack psychometric elegance in comparison to cognitive measures.

6. Understand the advantages and major limitations of observations.

7. Follow the suggestions offered for improving observations.

8. Differentiate between an observational tool and an observational technique.

9. List, define, and discuss the uses of six nontesting methods of evaluation: participation charts, check lists, rating scales, anecdotal records, sociometric methods, and attitude scales.

10. Develop and use effectively participation charts and check lists.

11. Discuss the four major types of rating scales.

12. List the major sources of error in rating scales and understand their effects.

13. Follow the suggestions offered for improving rating scales.

14. Follow the suggestions for improving raters.

15. Follow the suggestions for improving ratings.

16. Understand the advantages and limitations of anecdotal records.

17. Follow points offered for effectively constructing and using anecdotal records.

18. Understand the myriad of issues related to, and the need for resolving, the storage of anecdotal record data controversy.

19. Discuss the different sociometric devices used to evaluate personal-social adjustment.

20. Use sociometric data.

21. List six limitations of sociometric data.

22. Follow the guidelines provided and be able to construct a good attitude scale.

23. Know the three major approaches for constructing attitude scalese.

EVALUATING PROCEDURES AND PRODUCTS

The primary function of education is to effect some change on the part of the learner. This change may be in the cognitive, affective, or psychomotor domain. In this unit, we focus our attention on the measurement of behavioral changes in the cognitive domain—knowledge of facts, understanding, application, and the higher mental processes of synthesis and evaluation—with teacher-made achievement tests. There are, however, many times when we want to evaluate not only what a person knows but what a person can do. We are interested in performance because, so often, what a person knows is *not* a good predictor of what a person can do. And measuring what a person can do requires both an instrument (performance test) and a procedure.

Performance tests are techniques that try to establish what a person can do as distinct from what he knows. Work samples and skills samples are major procedures, but we may also be interested in those tasks involved in generating (making or producing or creating) the product so that we will be able to diagnose weaknesses in either the instructional system, the learning process, or both.

Procedure refers to the steps followed in doing some task. In typing, procedure refers to one's posture, finger placement on the keys, looking at the material to be typed rather than at the keyboard, strike, and so forth. The *product* refers to the end result. In typing, the product would be the typed letter. In language arts, it could be the theme written, the speech delivered, or the poem read aloud to the class. In many instances, it is very difficult to separate the procedure from the product. For example, in basketball, is dribbling a procedure or a product? Is singing a procedure (process) or a product?

The pupils' ability to *do* or *make* something is an important instructional objective, especially in such courses as home economics, industrial arts, the physical and biological sciences, and public speaking. The student in chemistry and physics should be able to work with laboratory equipment just as the student in woodworking must work with a hammer and saw. The student taking a laboratory course in the biological sciences should be facile in operating a microscope, just as he should be able to list the steps to be followed in preparing a tissue specimen. Products and processes are not relegated solely to the nonacademic areas, although they are generally of more concern to technical and vocational teachers. Yet most of our commercially prepared achievement tests and usually the majority of teacher-made achievement tests pay little attention to products and processes. Why? Primarily for two reasons: (1) Measuring pupil performance tends to be more subjective than measuring pupil achievement; and (2) because of the complexity of measuring one's performance, such tests tend to be more difficult to administer, score, and interpret (Ahmann & Glock, 1971, p. 212). This, however, should not deter us from measuring performance and product, since they are important instructional objectives. As you read this chapter, it will be evident that there have been successful attempts to develop valid and reliable instruments to measure noncognitive skills.

Although procedures and products are interrelated (a particular procedure must be followed to bake a cake, weld a bead, antique a piece of furniture), they are generally separate entities that can be observed, measured, and evaluated independently. As Gronlund (1976, p. 439) pointed out: "In some areas . . . it might be more desirable to rate *procedures* during the early phases of learning, and *products* later, after the basic skills have been mastered."

The importance of process evaluation can be illustrated by using typing as an example. A student who has "played around" on the typewriter prior to his first formal typing course may, by the end of the second study week, outperform all his peers in terms of a product—typing faster and more accurately. However, he may be using such an inefficient process (for example, hunt and peck) that his chances of any further product improvement are severely limited. Similar examples exist in most subject matters. Music, art, home economics, physical education, shop, and science all require correct processes in order for the products to achieve real excellence.

Process evaluation is also very important in the affective domain. Observation of a student while he is performing a particular task can provide useful information concerning his attitudes about the task. Observational techniques are particularly valuable in assessing processes.

All evaluation—be it of knowledge, procedures, or products, or formative versus summative—requires that some criterion of correctness be established a priori by the evaluator. For procedural evaluation, we are generally concerned with both efficiency and accuracy. For example, to ascertain whether his students are able to operate a microscope, the teacher would first have to delineate the steps involved and then observe each and every student to see how well these steps were followed. For accuracy, he might use as a criterion the precision with which the slide is focused. There are some skills, however (because of their complexity), that preclude the establishment of a set of rigid procedural steps that must be followed in a prescribed order. In such instances, the teacher must establish his own criteria and then subjectively compare the pupil's performance against them. This, in a sense, is what a music, book, or drama critic does when he writes his review.

The evaluation of both products and processes can be either subjective or objective, or a combination of the two. It depends upon what is being evaluated. For example, in art, the teacher is exercising a certain degree of subjectivity when he says that the shading is too weak. On the other hand, the art teacher is being objective when he says that the lines are crooked. Whenever a product or process can be broken down into separate, specific categories, it generally lends itself to more objective measurement. This is so because a global interpretation of the value or goodness of a product may vary from time to time, depending upon the mood of the evaluator.

Problems in Evaluating Procedures and Products

The two major problems encountered in evaluating procedures and products are reliability and validity.[1] In order to have valid measurement, the teacher must know specifically what qualities of the product or process are to be evaluated. Teachers are too often prone to rate a speech, debate, the singing of a song, or some product on just general impressions. In other words, it is an evaluation predicated upon *affect*, or feeling. Such visceral or "gut level" decisions are *not* appropriate when valid and reliable measurement is desired. Why? The teacher's feelings toward a student at a particular moment in time may markedly influence his evaluation of the procedure or product. If he

---

[1] Crocker (1974), among others, feels that for observational rating scales, more attention should be paid to *construct* validity.

likes the student, he may be overly generous; if he does not like the student, he may be overly severe in his rating. This not only affects the quality of measurement, but also has a marked influence on the student's motivation to learn. The best way to overcome this is to make a listing of all *significant* qualities of the product before evaluating the product or process, and then to follow this listing religiously.[2]

In any free-response exercise—art, music, writing—the essential ingredient needed to obtain valid measurement is to develop a thorough scoring system and to use it with well-trained scorers. Knight (no date) said, "given conceptually simple scoring dimensions defined with a minimum of esoteric language, it appears feasible to have persons without specific training in art to make relatively complex judgments about art works."

How Does One Evaluate Procedures and Products?[3]

To evaluate a procedure or product, we must first *observe* the procedure employed or the product made by the student. Then, on the basis of some scale, we ascertain the degree to which the steps followed or the product made are acceptable. The scales one can use are check lists, rating scales, and ranking methods. However, to have valid procedure and product evaluation, we must first have valid and reliable observation.

After specifying the evaluative criteria to be used (the teacher must be satisfied that the criteria are related to the instructional objectives), the teacher must decide upon the weight to be assigned to each criterion. The weight assigned to each step or characteristic should reflect the instructional emphasis placed on each criterion. For example, the presentation of any report generally involves three major factors: (1) content, (2) organization, and (3) presentation. Each of these can be further subdivided into smaller units. For example, presentation can be subdivided into five units:

1. Stereotyped diction
2. Clear, concise diction
3. Diction at the appropriate level
4. Too soft-spoken
5. Emphasis on significant points

The teacher may think that content is the most important part and assign one-half of the total score to that feature. He may think that organization and presentation are equally important and assign one-fourth of the grade to each

---

[2] This is analagous to the test blueprint stage in cognitive tests.

[3] A good annotated bibliography on performance testing is *Annotated Bibliography on Applied Performance Testing* published by the Center for the Advancement of Performance Testing.

of these. Each component and each subcomponent are then assigned some numerical value that has been predetermined by the teacher. For excellent illustrations of weighted objectives and scales for specific subjects, see Henry (1946).

Evaluating a process or product can range from the very subjective to the highly objective. Wherever possible, the objective (and preferably quantitative) approach should be used. There are times, when on the surface at least, it appears that subjective ratings are the only ones possible to make, but steps can sometimes be taken to increase their objectivity. These steps will be discussed in a later section.

MEASUREMENT AND EVALUATION IN THE AFFECTIVE DOMAIN

Traditionally, public education has been primarily concerned with cognitive learning. And evaluation of our schools and educational products has generally used as the major criterion the degree of success that students had in learning the cognitive skills and content taught. In fact, most accountability programs—be they at the local, state, or national level—use some type of achievement test(s) as their major evaluative instrument. There are, however, other skills and behaviors—affective and psychomotor—that should be of concern to every classroom teacher, administrator, school board member, parent, pupil, and to any others associated with education.

We feel that *both* parents and educators should be as concerned with affective behavior—with (1) developing a future society with healthy personalities, (2) preparing students so that they will be able to participate effectively in our society vis-à-vis their roles as citizens, and (3) producing a citizenry that is happy and satisfied in its vocational and avocational pursuits—as they are with teaching students to read, write, and compute.

We feel that since the affective disposition of the student has direct relevance to his ability to learn, his interest in learning, and his attitudes toward the value of an education, educators in general, and classroom teachers in particular, should know something about affective measurement, especially attitudes. Quite often, learning difficulties are related to a student's attitudes. How often you have heard:

> Johnny is a bright enough boy but he just isn't interested in school.
> I wonder what's wrong with Ruth? She is above average in ability, and though she performs poorly in science and mathematics, she does very well in French.
> Allan is very interested in science but despises literature.

Often students have learning difficulties in, say, spelling or reading or mathematics because they *think* or *feel* that they can't learn the material.

Is it not conceivable that, if teachers had a better understanding of a student's affective behavior (as well as a good understanding of the student's cognitive and psychomotor behavior), some learning difficulties could be alleviated or at least ameliorated by correcting the student's inferiority complex?

If affective development is so important to the individual's growth, development, and behavior as an effective adult, and if one's attitudes and values play such an important role in a person's cognitive development, why the reluctance on the part of teachers to develop, administer, and use affective measures in their classrooms?

The Dearth of Affective Measurement

Despite increased attention to the teaching of, concern about, and measurement of affective behavior within the past decade, interest in some of the affective components of pupil behavior such as attitudes, values, and beliefs, is still relatively weak in contrast to cognitive behavior. Why? There are many reasons, both teacher-related and technical, that have inhibited appropriate emphasis on affective measurement, thereby resulting in the affective domain assuming a secondary, if not subservient, role in U.S. education. Some of these reasons are as follows:

1. The lack of a systematic approach to measuring affect. There are many locally constructed attitude scales that unfortunately do not have a sound theoretical rationale. Until this problem is remedied, attitude measurement will be suspect with respect to its validity.

2. Some teachers do not want to become involved in teaching (and hence measuring) affective outcomes, contending that they should be taught in the home or church, *not* in school. These teachers feel that only cognitive or psychomotor skills should be taught in the school. No doubt, teachers adopting this stance are worried about getting involved in controversial issues, especially in this age of "invasion of privacy" and individual rights. But we feel that this reasoning is a "cop-out." We feel that schools *must* involve themselves in the affective domain. We do not live in a "value-free" society.

3. Lack of time is the lament of many teachers who say that they are sufficiently harassed now just teaching the cognitive skills. They feel that if they were to devote any time to the affective objectives, it would decrease the amount of time needed to teach cognitive skills and knowledge.

4. Lack of faith in the validity and reliability of affective measures. Many teachers claim that (a) affective behavior *cannot* be measured by pencil-and-paper tests, and (b) affective scales are highly susceptible to faking and response sets. Research, however, has shown that affective behavior can be measured with pencil-and-paper tests, albeit with lesser validity and reliability than for cognitive tests. Also, because a person can fake does *not*

imply that he *will* fake. Finally, there are techniques that can be used to help control for response sets and styles. (These will be discussed in greater detail in Chapter 16.)

5. Lack of awareness of the relationship between affective traits and learning.

6. Lack of knowledge about affective measurement.

7. Lack of knowledge about how to effectively utilize affective information of pupils in planning the teacher's instructional strategy.

8. The shift of emphasis in recent years to behavioral objectives has contributed, in part at least, to even more emphasis being placed on cognitive objectives which are easier to delineate, observe, and measure than are traits such as tolerance, empathy, honesty, and so forth.

9. Artificiality of the situation is another problem inherent in affective measurement. Many persons believe that the information provided by conventional self-report or observational techniques regarding an individual's affective behavior is invalid. They feel that because of the artificiality of the situation, any similarity between what a person says he would do in a real situation and what he actually does in that situation is purely coincidental. We agree that considerable reliance must be placed on *inference.* The degree of our trust depends to a large extent on the individual's answering the questions truthfully, which in turn depends upon the type of information requested. The more personal, confidential, and potentially threatening the questions asked, the greater the likelihood of invalid responses. But if proper rapport is established between teachers and students, if pupils are shown how the information will be used to provide for maximal learning, and if pupils are assured of the confidentiality of their responses, we feel that fairly reliable information can be obtained. Also, we believe that since most of the affective variables within the classroom tend to be general, rather than private, and tend to be nonthreatening, they should lend themselves to somewhat valid assessment.

10. Stability of affective outcomes—or one should say the questionability of the stability of affective behavior—is used as a reason by some educators to de-emphasize the importance of affective measurement in the classroom. Some teachers say that although attitudes tend to be quite stable in adults, they are very unstable in children. Generally speaking, this may be the case. If so, this supports our belief that attitudes are amenable to change and therefore should be of concern to classroom teachers.

11. There is disagreement regarding whether verbally expressed opinions can be regarded as valid indicators of "real" attitudes. In part, this problem concerns the relationship between verbal and nonverbal overt behavior. In other words, does an individual suit his actions to his words or to the items found on the attitude scale? Discrepancies between verbally expressed attitudes and overt behavior have been well documented in the literature. It has also been shown that even observations of overt behavior may not neces-

sarily provide an accurate index of a person's attitudes. For example, an individual may profess strong religious beliefs and attend church regularly. Does this mean that the person is really religious? Not necessarily! He may be attending church regularly as a means of gaining social acceptance.

12. There is also some disagreement concerning the relationship between one's "public" and "private" attitudes. Is the attitude toward, say, abortion that a person may express in conversation with a very close friend the same as that expressed in conversation with a person(s) of just recent acquaintance? Is the attitude expressed to a person(s) whose position or feelings you know the same as those expressed to one whose feelings you don't know or whose feelings are different from yours?

We concur that some of these reasons for the dearth of measurement in the affective domain are valid. As yet there is no unifying theory and no systematic approach to measuring affect. Yes, teachers are busy teaching cognitive objectives. Yes, affective measurement is more difficult to engage in, is less valid and reliable, and is more controversial than the measurement of cognitive skills and knowledge (Fishbein, 1967; Summers, 1970). But we feel that despite the validity of some of the reasons given above by educators to support their belief for de-emphasizing the affective domain, this is not prima facie evidence for neglecting this area in our classrooms.

One has to know something in order to be successful at something. But how often have we seen very knowledgeable individuals who are unsuccessful, or misguided, or confused and frustrated? And what about the approximately 65 to 75 percent of the variance in GPA that is *not* accounted for by either achievement or aptitude tests? Are these not sufficient reasons for educators, parents, and pupils to be concerned with affective behavior? We believe they are!

OBSERVATIONAL TOOLS AND TECHNIQUES

Systematically observing students in natural or simulated (the former is preferable) settings is a very useful technique for gathering data about students' performance and about their affective behavior. This procedure is being used more frequently today despite the methodological problems— sampling behaviors to be observed, defining the domain of behaviors to be studied, selecting and training observers, validity and reliability of observational measures—associated with observational tools and techniques. For example, what pupils should be studied? All the pupils? Those that are continually causing problems? When should pupils be observed? Who should do or make the observations? What inferences can one draw from a limited sample of behavior? These are just some of the problems that must be faced by the user of the observational method.

In those situations in education where no tangible product is produced, such as participating in class discussion, but where an important instructional objective needs to be evaluated, teachers must depend on their observation of the pupils' behavior and then make valid inferences as to whether the goal or instructional objective was achieved. Because the evaluation of a pupil's performance—be it playing a piano sonata or delivering a speech—may, depending upon the nature of the task, involve a great deal of subjectivity and immediate judgment of its worth (the pupil can't replay the sonata the *same* way), obtaining valid and reliable evaluation is extremely difficult. There are so many instances where these types of judgments must be made and where formal pencil-and-paper testing procedures are not appropriate that it behooves us to consider the use of observational tools and techniques and to look at some ways in making them as valid and reliable as humanly possible, recognizing that we will not achieve the same degree of success as we would in measuring cognitive skills.[4]

Classroom teachers continually observe their students. And much valuable data can be gathered by observing students' behavior. The observations, however, are typically informal and unsystematic, carried on without benefit of specific planned procedures.[5] Since so much of what teachers "know" about and do for children is based on their observations, it is important that these observations be as accurate and reliable as possible.[6] Scientists are rigorously trained in observation. They are taught the value to be derived from accurate observations and are willing to have their observations (actually findings) checked by other scientists. Teachers should be taught to appreciate the value of systematic observations and should receive training similar to that given scientists (Noll & Scannell, 1972).

The terms *observation tools* and *techniques* are not synonymous, although they are used interchangeably by many persons. An observation technique generally implies the use of a particular observational tool such as a check list, rating scale, participation chart, or anecdotal record. However, the process of observing and recording an individual's behavior is what is meant by the term observational technique. The observational technique has certain limitations associated with it. Because it requires the observation of some form of behavior, it may be subject to the idiosyncracies of the observer. The observer should be completely objective and come as close as possible to being a mechanical recording device—recording the actual behavior (for example,

---

[4] See Herbert and Attridge (1975) for an excellent review and synthesis of the literature. They identified 33 criteria that observational systems should satisfy.

[5] It should be noted that there are numerous classroom observation schedules available for research. (See Borich and Malitz, 1975, for their discussion of the validity of these measures.) Brophy, Coulter, Crawford, Evertson, and King (1975) feel that classroom observation scales are a convenient and reliable way to obtain descriptive measures of classroom processes.

[6] See McGaw, Wardrup, and Bunda (1972) and Medley and Mitzel (1963), for discussions on sources of error in observations.

Johnny laughed when Billy told a joke) without attempting to synthesize or interpret the behavior.

Advantages of Observations

There are several advantages of observational data:

1. Frequent observation of a student's work (and work habits) can provide a continuous check on his progress. The teacher can detect errors or problems as they arise and take corrective action quickly.
2. Observational techniques are not so time consuming or threatening for the pupil as are achievement tests.
3. Observational data provide teachers with valuable supplemental information, much of which could not be obtained in any other way.

Some Suggestions to Help Make Valid Observations

In spite of the difficulties in obtaining accurate and significant data from observations, teachers continually do observe and make decisions based on these observations. Therefore, it is essential that the observations made (which involve *both* the tools and the techniques) satisfy the same criteria expected of a written, cognitive test, or for that matter, any good measuring device—validity, reliability, objectivity, and practicality of construction, administration, and scoring. Specifying what behavior(s) to observe and determining a time schedule for such observation will improve the data considerably. Also, training the observer with the necessary skills needed to make systematic and objective observations cannot be overemphasized. To help make observations more valid, we offer the following suggestions:[7]

1. *Plan in advance what is to be observed and prepare an observational list, guide, or form to make the observations objective and systematic.* The observer must know what he is looking for *before* he goes into the classroom or library, or onto the playground.

One of the major difficulties in observations is to determine or specify a meaningful and productive set of behaviors to be observed. This determination, like deciding what content to put in an achievement test, must be dependent upon the objectives one wishes to evaluate and the decisions one hopes the data will help determine. However, it is often somewhat more difficult to specify what observed behaviors are relevant than it is to specify what questions should be asked on a test or what characteristics should be judged on a rating scale.

[7] Some of these are also suggestions for constructing cognitive tests. Although discussed earlier, we believe they bear repetition.

What we observe and the significance of the observed behavior are two different aspects. For the former, we must delineate our course objectives and ask ourselves two basic questions: (1) What is the purpose of the observation? (2) What traits should be observed? It is true that the latter aspect—what the behavior signifies—is important and is related to what we observe. This may be easy enough to determine in a psychomotor skill area (the significance of a person watching the typewriter keys or looking at the basketball while dribbling is obvious enough), but the significance of isolated bits of behavior in the affective domain is more difficult to determine. One way to avoid this is not to specify in advance what categories of behavior to observe. This, however, takes us back to an unsystematic procedure and could lead to a teacher saying something like: "The students were using class time for independent study, so there was no behavior for me to observe!" Of course, the students were behaving. It is just that the teacher had no idea what to look for. Behaviors that could be observed (but which weren't) would be such things as chewing nails, looking out the window, talking out of place, doodling, and pushing a fellow student.

Even though observational tools are not tests in the conventional sense, they are still used to attain the same overall objectives—(1) to tell us whether people differ, (2) to permit us to make valid predictions about future behavior, (3) to provide the user with information that will permit him to undertake appropriate action to correct or modify undesirable behavior—and therefore it is essential that we know in advance *what* will be observed and *why* we are observing this or that behavior.

2. *The teacher should concentrate on only one or two behaviors.* With a class of 30 students it is impossible to observe all the different kinds of behavior occurring at a given time. More reliable data will be forthcoming if the teacher observes or concentrates on just one or two behaviors at a time. For example, in a football game the teacher may limit his observations to just perseverance and sportsmanship, although he may also be interested in co-operation and aggressiveness. He cannot concentrate on all four traits at any one time. For those who contend that he may miss something significant by concentrating on only one or two behavioral incidents, we maintain that if a behavior pattern is typical, it will recur. If it does not, we can assume that it is insignificant. Naturally the teacher should be on the alert for unanticipated incidents that may be important in obtaining a better understanding of the pupil. Generally, however, we favor the concentration on just one or two aspects at a time.

3. *Use clear, unambiguous terminology.* Unless the terminology used is clearly defined and accompanied by a description of the type of behavior attendant to, or associated with, that behavior, reliable observations will be difficult to obtain.

4. *Each item should be mutually exclusive.* When this criterion is not

met, the observer will encounter difficulty in classifying and/or appropriately coding the observation made.

5. *The observer must be cognizant of sampling errors.* If we observe Ruth at 9:20 A.M., we cannot necessarily infer from her behavior at that time how she would behave at other times. To minimize errors that may occur due to sampling, a technique called *time sampling* is often employed. In time sampling, a teacher develops either systematically or randomly a schedule for observations to ensure that each pupil is observed at many different times during a day, week, or semester. Thus, Ruth's observation schedule may call for an observation at 9:15–9:20 A.M. on Monday; 10:20–10:25 A.M. on Tuesday; 2:30–2:35 P.M. on Wednesday, and so forth. Allan's observational schedule would be on a different but comparable schedule.

We recommend that there be frequent, short observations distributed over a period of several weeks and at different times of the day. This should provide for a more representative sample of the pupil's behavior.

6. *Coordinate the observations with your teaching.* Systematic observation requires that observation and teaching be coordinated. When the teacher is planning his instructional strategy, he should also plan his observations so that the two will be related. Otherwise there is great danger that invalid observations will result.

7. *Extensive observations should be selective.* We recommend that extensive observations be confined to only those few selected students (the slow learner, the hyperactive child, the autistic child, the "loner") who are in need of special help.

8. *Record and summarize the observation immediately after it has occurred.* This is more difficult than it appears to be. Pupils, especially the younger ones, may become disturbed when their teacher makes notes. More important, however, is that when pupils know they are being observed, their resultant behavior *may* be atypical.[8]

9. *Make no interpretations concerning the behavior until later on.* Too often, trying to interpret a pupil's behavior when a particular behavior is observed will interfere with the objectivity of gathering the observational data.

10. *Have categories and coding schemes that are simple to use, that call for behaviors easily observed, and that deal with behaviors that can be conveniently recorded.* When an observer must infer a particular behavior from a series of different (and sometimes unrelated) behaviors, we run the risk of invalid inferences being drawn. We are well aware of the fact that any observation requires the observer to make some type of judgment. What we imply by this caution is that the degree of observer inference be reduced as

[8] If the observer is unobtrusive and avoids giving the pupils the feeling that judgments are being made, the observer's presence will have little effect on the validity of the pupil's behavior observed. (See Heyns & Lippitt, 1954, p. 399; Kerlinger, 1967, p. 506.)

much as possible during the actual observational period. Inferences, in an ideal setting, should occur only *after* the data have been gathered and coded.

TYPES OF OBSERVATIONAL TOOLS

Participation Charts

An important instructional and educational objective is to have students voluntarily participate in activities—be it a debate, a group report, work on a social committee, or in athletics. Yet this important objective is seldom evaluated in some systematic and rigorous fashion even though it occurs daily in our classrooms. How well does Lori participate in a group discussion? Does Shelly tend to participate more in larger groups than in smaller groups? Does Ilene tend to engage in athletic activities more than in social activities? Is Allan a leader or a follower? Is Bill independent in his thoughts and convictions or does he tend to go along with the group's feelings? By means of a participation chart, the teacher can plot a pupil's growth throughout the year and then make some evaluative judgment about the pupil's behavior.

It should be noted that the participation chart per se does *not* indicate *why* some pupils do and do not participate in group activities, and/or *why* they participate in one type of activity but not in another. Nor will the data collected by means of a participation chart help explain why some pupils use this medium to gain attention from their peers. Nevertheless, because group participation is needed to participate effectively in our society (the conforming nonconformists notwithstanding), teachers should be concerned with its measurement. If it is found that some students are isolates or "loners," it may be possible for the teacher to help the student. Figure 12–1 is an example of a participation chart that measures pupil involvement in discussion. The example contains a tally of the participation by four students in a group discussion. In the course of the discussion, the teacher would check

---

Objective: Discussion of the importance of the U.N.

Extent of contribution	Group Members			
	CHARIS	LEROY	DAVE	JEANETTE
Significant*	/ /	/	/ / /	/ / /
Secondary	/ / /	/ /	/	/
Doubtful				/
Irrelevant	/	/ /	/	

* Significant: introduces new ideas in the discussion
  Secondary: introduces important but minor idea
  Doubtful: insufficient evidence to evaluate contribution—need more information
  Irrelevant: introduces irrelevant ideas and contribution detracts from discussion

---

FIGURE 12-1   Measuring participation in a small group.

off each point (statement) made by each pupil. In Figure 12–1 the tally indicates that Charis dominated the discussion in that she raised or introduced six points. Of these six points, the teacher judged that two made a significant contribution to the discussion, three made a secondary contribution, and one point was irrelevant. Each of the other three members of the group introduced five points to the discussion. But note that of LeRoy's five points, two were irrelevant.

Whether or not the behavior of any of the students in this particular group is good, bad, or indifferent should not be the issue. What is important is that if the teacher is interested in observing the behavior of students in a small discussion group, he must use some type of participation chart to give him the desired information. And, as we noted earlier, he should use a time-sampling plan to gather this information. It would also be advantageous to use an event (topic or issue discussed) sampling to obtain a fuller picture of the individual's behavior.

It will be readily evident that the teacher engaged in evaluating pupil participation will be occupied in his task. This leads us to making the following recommendations for teachers using participation charts:

1. Try to rate participation in *small* group settings rather than in large class discussions. It is just too difficult to concentrate when there are many pupils involved.

2. The teacher should only observe and not partake in the discussion. Noting and recording the behavior of the participants is a full-time task. By entering into the discussion, the teacher may overlook something significant.

3. The behavior noted should be recorded immediately after it has happened. Delaying notation until the end of the discussion lends itself to bias and selective perception on the part of the observer.

Check Lists

A check list consists of a listing of steps, activities, or behaviors that the observer records when the incident occurs. It is similar in appearance and use of rating scales (rating scales will be discussed in greater detail in the next section) and is classified by some as a type of rating scale (Guilford, 1954). It should be emphasized that a check list enables the observer to note only whether or not a trait or characteristic is present. It does not permit the observer to rate the quality of, degree to which, or frequency of occurrence of a particular behavior. When such information is desired, the check list is definitely *inappropriate*.

Check lists are adaptable to most subject-matter areas. They are useful in evaluating those learning activities that involve a product, process, and some aspects of personal-social adjustment. They are most useful, however, for evaluating those processes that can be subdivided into a series of clear, distinct, separate actions, such as welding a bead, making a mortise joint, or operating a microscope.

The values to be derived from check lists (actually, from any observational tool) depend upon the skill and care with which the check list is constructed. When properly prepared, check lists (1) force the observer to direct his attention to clearly specified traits or characteristics, (2) allow interindividual comparisons to be made on a common set of traits or characteristics, and (3) provide a simple method to record observations.

An example of a check list for constructing a test is as follows:

_____ 1. Specifies the behavioral objectives to be measured
_____ 2. Prepares the test blueprint
_____ 3. Determines the item format to be used
_____ 4. Decides upon the length of the test
_____ 5. Decides upon the difficulty of items
_____ 6. Writes the test items
_____ 7. Edits the items
_____ 8. Has the items independently reviewed
_____ 9. Prepares a scoring key

If one of the course assignments was to have students demonstrate their competency in preparing a test, the instructor could use this check list to note whether or not his students followed a prescribed procedure. In those instances where a sequential order is necessary to certify competence, the teacher can easily record the order in which each of the steps was made.

An example of a check list to measure personal and social adjustment is presented in Figure 12–2.

The check list illustrated in Figure 12–3 is a good example of a performance check list.

Pupil _____   School and Grade _____
Setting _____   Date _____
                              Observer _____

Directions: Listed below are a series of characteristics related to "concern for
        others." For the pupil listed above, check those characteristics that are
        applicable.

_____ Sensitive to the needs and problems of others
_____ Prefers to play with younger children
_____ Respects the views and opinions of his peers
_____ Helps other students when they have problems
_____ Respects the property of other children
_____ Willingly accepts suggestions
_____ Works cooperatively with other children
_____ Is a "loner"
_____ Resents criticism

FIGURE 12-2   A check list recording concern for others.

STUDENT'S ACTIONS	Sequence of Actions	STUDENT'S ACTIONS (Continued)	Sequence of Actions
a. Takes slide	1	ah. Turns up fine adjustment screw a great distance	
b. Wipes slide with lens paper	2	ai. Turns fine adjustment screw a few turns	
c. Wipes slide with cloth		aj. Removes slide from stage	16
d. Wipes slide with finger		ak. Wipes objective with lens paper	
e. Moves bottle of culture along the table		al. Wipes objective with cloth	
f. Places drop or two of culture on slide	3	am. Wipes objective with finger	17
g. Adds more culture		an. Wipes eyepiece with lens paper	
h. Adds few drops of water		ao. Wipes eyepiece with cloth	
i. Hunts for cover glasses	4	ap. Wipes eyepiece with finger	18
j. Wipes cover glass with lens paper	5	aq. Makes another mount	
k. Wipes cover glass with cloth		ar. Takes another microscope	
l. Wipes cover with finger		as. Finds object	
m. Adjusts cover with finger		at. Pauses for an interval	
n. Wipes off surplus fluid		au. Asks, "What do you want me to do?"	
o. Places slide on stage	6	av. Asks whether to use high power	
p. Looks thru eyepiece with right eye		aw. Says, "I'm satisfied"	
q. Looks thru eyepice with left eye	7	ax. Says that the mount is all right for his eye	
r. Turns to objective of lowest power	9	ay. Says he cannot do it	19,24
s. Turns to low-power objective	21	az. Told to start a new mount	
t. Turns to high-power objective		aaa. Directed to find object under low power	20
u. Holds one eye closed	8	aab. Directed to find object under high power	
v. Looks for light			
w. Adjusts concave mirror			
x. Adjusts plane mirror		**NOTICEABLE CHARACTERISTICS OF STUDENT'S BEHAVIOR**	
y. Adjusts diaphragm		a. Awkward in movements	
z. Does not touch diaphragm	10	b. Obviously dexterous in movements	
aa. With eye at eyepiece turns down coarse adjustment	11	c. Slow and deliberate	✓
ab. Breaks cover glass	12	d. Very rapid	
ac. Breaks slide		e. Fingers tremble	
ad. With eye away from eyepiece turns down coarse adjustment		f. Obviously perturbed	
ae. Turns up coarse adjustment a great distance	13,22	g. Obviously angry	
af. With eye at eyepiece turns down fine adjustment a great distance	14,23	h. Does not take work seriously	
ag. With eye away from eyepiece turns down fine adjustment a great distance	15	i. Unable to work without specific directions	✓
		j. Obviously satisfied with his unsuccessful efforts	✓

SKILLS IN WHICH STUDENT NEEDS FURTHER TRAINING	Sequence of Actions	CHARACTERIZATION OF THE STUDENT'S MOUNT	Sequence of Actions
		a. Poor light	✓
a. In cleaning objective	✓	b. Poor focus	
b. In cleaning eyepiece	✓	c. Excellent mount	
c. In focusing low power	✓	d. Good mount	
d. In focusing high power	✓	e. Fair mount	
e. In adjusting mirror	✓	f. Poor mount	
f. In using diaphragm	✓	g. Very poor mount	
g. In keeping both eyes open	✓	h. Nothing in view but a thread in his eyepiece	
h. In protecting slide and objective from breaking by careless focusing	✓	i. Something on objective	
		j. Smeared lens	✓
		k. Unable to find object	✓

FIGURE 12–3 Check list for evaluating skill in the use of the microscope. (From Ralph W. Tyler, "A Test of Skill in Using a Microscope," *Educational Research Bulletin*, 9:493–496. Bureau of Educational Research and Service, Ohio State University. Used by permission.)

The student's goal is to find a specimen present in a culture. The teacher's goal is to see whether the student is able to operate a microscope so that the specimen is located. The student is provided with all the necessary materials and the teacher observes his actions, numbering them in the order of their occurrence. In addition, you will note that there are sections devoted to (1) areas that require further training, (2) the student's behavior, and (3) the mount.

Some Suggestions to Consider when Using Check Lists

1. Use check lists only when you are interested in ascertaining whether a particular trait or characteristic is present or absent.
2. Clearly specify the traits to be observed.
3. Observe only one child at a time and confine your observations to the points specified on the check list.
4. Have a separate check list for each child. If you desire to obtain an overall impression of the class, the individual observations can be recorded on a master check list.
5. The teacher must be trained how to observe, what to observe, and how to record the observed behavior. The directions given the observer must be very specific and clear. Raters should be told to omit recording those behaviors for which they have insufficient information to make a valid judgment.

Rating Scales

Rating scales resemble check lists but are used when finer discriminations are needed. Instead of just indicating the presence or absence of a trait, a rating scale enables the user to indicate the status or quality of what is being rated. Rating scales provide systematic procedures for obtaining, recording, and reporting the observer's judgments. Rating scales may be filled out while the observation is being made, immediately after the observations are made, or (as often is the case) when teachers fill out forms for students. In the latter case the scales are filled out long after the observation and are really based on remembered or perceived behavior.

Uses of Rating Scales

As with other methods of evaluation, rating scales should be constructed (or selected) so that they measure specified outcomes or goals of education deemed to be significant or important to the teacher. Since rating scales, like the other observational methods discussed in this chapter, tend to be less reliable, valid, and efficient than tests, they should not be used to evaluate outcomes that can be more easily and validly assessed through other procedures.

Rating scales are most helpful in evaluating procedures, products, and personal-social development (see Gronlund, 1976, pp. 439–442). Such procedures as those necessary in typing, working with laboratory equipment, shopwork, or athletic skills cannot be easily measured via pencil-and-paper tests. Many instructional objectives involve the completion of a product, which in itself should be evaluated. In home economics, it may be making a dress. In music, it may be playing an instrument. In English it may be writing a theme or giving a speech.

Probably the most common use of rating scales in education is in the evaluation of personal-social adjustment. It is not uncommon for teachers to rate their students periodically on various characteristics such as punctuality, enthusiasm, cheerfulness, cooperativeness, consideration for others, and the like. One of the problems of such evaluations is that, though supposedly based on observations, the observations have been spread over a long period of time. Such ratings are often broad impressions of perceived behavior rather than of actual behavior. That is, they are likely to reflect the teacher's biases concerning the student rather than the student's actual behavior. The suggestions previously offered about effective use of check lists and cautions to be applied are appropriate here also.

At the college level, particularly within the past decade, there has been increased use of rating scales for evaluating teacher effectiveness and course content. As might be expected, college faculties have tended to denigrate the value of these data, especially the use of tacher rating scales, claiming that the scales are invalid and unreliable.[9] Unfortunately for the skeptics, there is a tremendous body of literature that shows student rating scales to be very reliable (Barsell & Magoon, 1972), and that generally, teaching does improve from students' ratings of their teachers' classroom behavior (Trent & Cohen, 1973).

Types of Rating Scales

Although there are a variety of rating scales (see Guilford, 1954, pp. 263–301), we will consider the following: *numerical, graphic, comparative* (sometimes referred to as product scales), and *paired comparisons. Ranking* procedures are also often considered as a type of rating scale and will be considered in this section. The major practical advantage of rating scales over other observational techniques such as anecdotal records is that rating scales take little time for the teacher to complete and can therefore be used with a large number of students. In addition, they tend to be very adaptable and flexible.

[9] For an excellent review of this controversial issue, see Doyle (1975). See also Aleamoni (1974); Greenwood, Bridges, Ware, & McLean (1974); Lehmann (1974); Menges (1973); Sockloff & Papacostas (1975); Warrington (1973).

NUMERICAL RATING SCALES   This is one of the simplest types of rating scales. The rater simply marks a number that indicates the degree to which a characteristic (or trait) is present. The trait is presented as a statement and values from 1 to 5 (the range is arbitrary, but we strongly recommend that it be a maximum of 10, since finer discriminations are too difficult to make) are assigned to each trait being rated. Typically, a common key is used throughout, the key providing a verbal description. For example, a key might be as follows:

5 = outstanding
4 = above average
3 = average
2 = below average
1 = unsatisfactory

A numerical rating scale might be as follows:

Activity: Participation in School Activities
1. How active is the student in class projects?
   1   2   3   4   5
2. How well does the student relate to his peers?
   1   2   3   4   5
3. To what extent does the student participate in discussions?
   1   2   3   4   5

GRAPHIC RATING SCALE   The graphic rating scale is similar to the numerical rating scale in that the rater is required to assign some value to a specific trait. This time, however, instead of using predetermined scale values, the ratings are made in graphic form (a position *anywhere* along a continuum is checked). The rater is no longer restricted to any particular point, but can record anywhere between points. An example of a graphic rating scale is presented in Figure 12–4.

One advantage of the graphic rating scale is that if a number of traits are rated on the same page with a common set of categories, a behavioral *profile* can be constructed. Graphic rating shares the disadvantages associated with numerical rating. For classroom use, neither of the two scales has any particular advantages over the other, although the numerical scale may be somewhat easier to construct. The important point for either is that the numbers or periodic points on the lines must be described sufficiently so that every rater has the same understanding of their meaning.

In the two types of rating scales discussed above, the rater considers only one trait at a time and checks a response he believes to be *most* descriptive of the ratee's trait, either by arriving at some numerical score or by indicating the degree or quality of the trait along a continuum. Any of three other

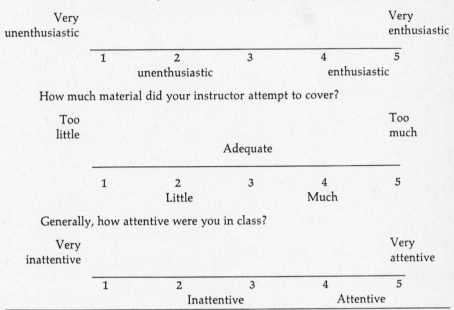

Directions: Following is a list of characteristics that are descriptive of your instructor. Please rate your instructor for each characteristic listed below along the continuum from 1–5. You are encouraged to use points between the scale values. Mark an "X" at the appropriate place along the continuum.

How enthusiastic was your instructor in presenting the course material?

| Very unenthusiastic | | | | Very enthusiastic |

| 1 | 2 | 3 | 4 | 5 |
| | unenthusiastic | | enthusiastic | |

How much material did your instructor attempt to cover?

| Too little | | Adequate | | Too much |

| 1 | 2 | 3 | 4 | 5 |
| | Little | | Much | |

Generally, how attentive were you in class?

| Very inattentive | | | | Very attentive |

| 1 | 2 | 3 | 4 | 5 |
| | Inattentive | | Attentive | |

FIGURE 12-4   Example of a graphic rating scale to rate instructors.

formats also can be used: (1) a comparative scale, (2) ranking procedure, (3) paired-comparison scales.

COMPARATIVE RATING SCALE   This type of scale provides the rater with several standard samples of different degrees of quality with which to compare the sample being rated. The scale is used chiefly for products and is often called a *product scale.* An example of such a scale is presented in Figure 12–5. The rater's task is to compare the pupil's product (in this case, handwriting) to a carefully selected series of samples of the product. The pupil's product is then assigned the scale value of the sample product it most closely resembles. (As you will recognize, this procedure is similar to the global procedure in scoring essays.)

There are very few commercially published product scales such as the one illustrated in Figure 12–5. This means, therefore, that in the majority of instances the teacher will have to prepare his own product scale. The pro-

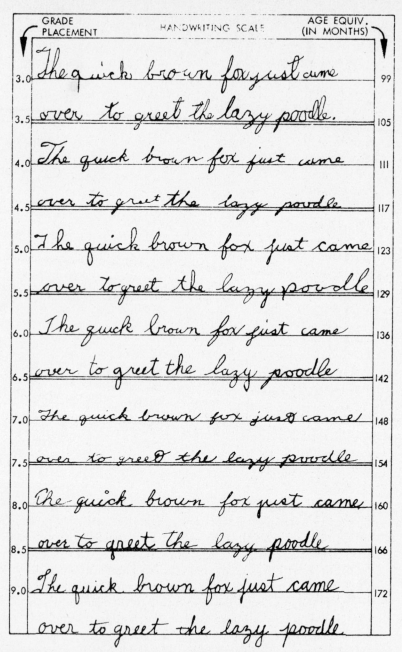

Figure 12–5 Handwriting scale used in the California Achievement Tests. (Copyright © 1957 by McGraw-Hill, Inc. Used by permission of the publisher, CTB/McGraw-Hill, Del Monte Research Park, Monterey, CA 93940.)

cedure discussed in selecting samples for scoring essays by the global method (see pages 229–230) is appropriate for developing such scales.

RANKING   A scale is sometimes used in lieu of the typical rating techniques. In this procedure the rater, rather than assigning a numerical value to each student with regard to the characteristic, ranks a given set of individuals from high to low on the characteristic being rated. A useful procedure to help ensure that pupils are validly ranked is to rank from both extremes toward the middle. Here, the subjects ranked first and last are identified; then the student ranked second best and the one second from the bottom, and so forth. Although this simplifies the task for the teacher, the ranking method becomes very cumbersome when large numbers of students and/or characteristics are to be ranked. Also, the serial position of the trait(s), the characteristic(s), or behavior(s) to be ranked (that is, where it appears on the scale) affects the ranking such that those traits appearing early tend to be ranked higher.

We recommend that the number of traits to be ranked be limited to a maximum of seven. Also, the number of persons to be ranked should be limited. Trying to rank too many traits and/or persons will make the task so cumbersome that the validity and reliability of the measure will be affected (Wagner & Hoover, 1974).

Without a doubt, there can be a marked difference between the rating and ranking methods. The difference in results can be shown by the following example. Suppose two different fourth-grade teachers were to judge their students on their "ability to get along with others." If a rating procedure were used, one set of students might come out with much higher ratings due to a generosity characteristic of one teacher. If each teacher were forced to rank his students from high to low, this generosity effect (or conversely, a severity effect) could be avoided. However, another source of error becomes possible. The student ranked fifth in one class may actually be superior with respect to the characteristic to the person ranked fifth in the other class because the two classes differ. In addition to this problem, ranking is very hard to do (students at the extremes cause no problem; students near the middle are very hard to rank because they are so very similar), and teachers resent having to make such discriminations. Also, if teachers perceive all their students as very superior (or inferior), they would like to have the opportunity to say so rather than rank them. In general, rating scales are preferred to ranking for evaluating social-personal adjustment and development, and when dealing with large numbers of students. Rankings, when used, are probably most appropriate for evaluating student products. We prefer, however, classifying the product as superior, average, and inferior, rather than using the ranking method.

PAIRED COMPARISONS   Another technique somewhat like the ranking method is the *paired-comparison* method, which (although more precise) is more time consuming. In this method each student is paired with every other student and the rater indicates which of the two students is superior on the trait being rated. The rater then has only to make a tally of the number of times each pupil is rated superior, to make his ranking. This procedure tends to produce more reliable results and should be used whenever high reliability is of concern.

Sources of Error in Rating Scales

There are several common sources of error in rating scales. Errors may be due to the scale itself (ambiguity), the personality of the rater, the nature of the traits being rated, and the opportunity afforded the rater for adequate observation. By "ambiguity" we refer to wording and meaning of the traits being measured—such that the rater may be uncertain as to what it is he is really being asked to rate. Two teachers rating students on "aggressiveness" may be making ratings on quite different characteristics. To one teacher, "aggressiveness" may be a positive trait, suggesting that the student is appropriately self-assertive. To the other teacher, aggressiveness may connote hostility. This suggests that such terms as "honesty," "effective citizenship," and "personality" must be clarified for the rater. Unless all pupils are being rated on the *same* attributes, the ratings will be invalid and unreliable.

Ambiguity of the frame of reference is another problem of rating scales. When criteria such as "superior," "good," "inferior" are used, what do these words really mean? What is "good?" Is doing the 100-yard dash in 20 seconds "good?" It depends. For a 60-year-old man it is good. For a 70-year-old cripple, it is outstanding. For a 16-year-old boy it may be poor. Quality must be interpreted in terms of the nature of the trait being rated and the age and ability of the ratee.

As mentioned earlier, the problem of ambiguity may be reduced quite extensively by breaking up the behavior to be measured into a series of specific, observable, and measurable traits, by describing fully what the trait represents; and by giving examples of the different kinds of behavior associated with differing levels of the trait.

In addition to the sources of error associated with the rating scale, there are also sources of error associated with the raters. Some of these are the *halo effect, severity effect, central tendency error,* and *logical error.* If a student were to ask us "what are the characteristics of an ideal rater?" we would respond that he must be competent, objective, and well trained in the use of the scale. Personal bias must be controlled if we wish to obtain reliable ratings.

The *halo effect* occurs when the rater's general impressions of a person influence how he rates him on individual characteristics. If we like a person and think that she is good-looking and studious, we are apt to rank her high on other traits that may be quite unrelated to good looks and studiousness. Or if we have a generally unfavorable attitude toward a person, we are apt to rank him (note the gender change) *low* on all traits. In one study where college students rated well-known personalities, it was found that about 20 percent of the variance was due to the halo effect (Blumberg, DeSoto, & Kuethe, 1966). In another study it was found that the degree of composite halo exhibited by teachers when rating pupils was affected by the race and sex of *both rater and ratee* (Jaeger & Freijo, 1975). One way to minimize the halo effect is to reverse the "high and low" or "desirable and undesirable" positions on the continuum. This, however, may confuse the naïve rater (Guilford, 1954).

Raters who favor the high end of the continuum (the desirable end) are committing the *generosity* error. Less frequent in occurrence, but a response set with some people, is the tendency to favor the low end of the continuum—that is, to be overly harsh. This is called the *severity error*. Still another type of response set is the person who avoids using the extremes and favors the middle positions—that is, he rates everybody about "average." This is called the *central tendency error*.

The leniency, severity, and central tendency errors all arise because raters do not use uniform standards. Three raters may know a set of students equally well and indeed perceive them about the same. Yet on a five-point scale, one rater may give the students a mean rating of 4.3; another rater, a mean of 1.7; and the third, a mean of 3.0. The first rater is likely too lenient and the second too severe. The third may be about right. However, if the third rater gives practically all 3s, only a few 2s and 4s, and no 1s and 5s, he is probably committing the error of central tendency. That is, he is not differentiating among the students as much as he should.

A fourth type of rater error, which is not related to response set, is called *logical error*. *Logical* error is closely related to the halo effect, but is *not* due to personal bias. Rather, it occurs when two traits such as intelligence and socioeconomic status or achievement and aptitude are closely related, and the rater is influenced in the rating of one by the presence (or absence) of the other. When a rater bases his ratings for an individual on a general relationship he *thinks* or *knows* exists, in the population, he has committed a logical error (Gronlund, 1976, p. 443).

There are still two other factors that can affect the validity of a rating: (1) the rater's attitude, and (2) the rater's opportunity for adequately observing the person (and traits) being rated.

ATTITUDE OF RATERS   Accurate observation is a very time-consuming chore, especially if large numbers of students are to be involved. Unless teachers truly believe that there is some value to be derived from ratings, they may consider them only as another administrative chore and not do a conscientious job.

Possibly more serious than any of the errors previously discussed are the errors a rater makes because he does not know well enough the person he is rating. In the elementary grades the teacher gets to know his students fairly well, even if his knowledge is confined to the classroom setting. In junior and senior high school the teachers see their students less frequently. As would be expected, teachers are more familiar with those students who are at the extremes (very gregarious, very withdrawn, very uncooperative). However, they may be asked to rate a student who is not at the extremes and/or one they do not know too well. The authors of this book, professors at a large university, often have had requests from prospective employers (and employees) to fill out rating sheets for students they hardly know. The only reasonable thing to do is to refuse to rate the person on those characteristics about which you have little or no knowledge.

Ways to Improve Data from Rating Scales[10]

Although data from rating scales are often not too reliable, random error can be reduced by improving the rating scale, improving the raters, or improving the rating method. The following suggestions should be helpful.

IMPROVING THE RATING SCALE

1. Identify the domain of particular behaviors (traits)—be it a psychomotor skill, or some performance task—that you wish to rate.[11] Make sure they are educationally significant. Also make sure that they occur in the school setting so that the teacher can observe them.

2. Clearly define the traits to be rated and the scale points to be used. Many of the problems and errors associated with rating scales are due to undefined trait characteristics and poorly designated scale points. One way of avoiding some of these problems is to avoid the use of labels and technical jargon such as "hostility," "reticence," and "aggressiveness." A simple rule of thumb is break down the trait into several smaller components, each of which is quite limited and specific. For example, personality can be broken down into emotional adjustment, social adjustment, wholesomeness, and similar attributes. Social adjustment can then be subdivided into many specific components, such as "playing with other children," "sharing with other

---

[10] See Van Der Kamp and Mellenbergh (1976) for a somewhat theoretical discussion on how to obtain reliable teacher ratings.

[11] Some traits are more amenable to reliable rating than others. In general, when traits can be expressed as simple, unitary aspects of behavior and can be operationally defined, they will be amenable to reliable rating. The more complex the behavior, the more difficult it is to obtain high inter-rater reliability (Horrocks & Schoonover, 1968, pp. 447–448).

children," "respecting other children's property," and "working cooperatively with other children." Ratings can then be made on each of the specific components, but it may be necessary to break the subcomponents into still finer divisions. For example, "works with children" could be further delineated as "helps others," "accepts suggestions," "provides ideas," and "accepts majority rule." The more specific the behavior to be rated, and the more descriptive the response options (points along the scale or continuum), the greater the likelihood that raters will be on the same "wavelengths" and will exercise uniformity. Also, they will have a clearer idea as to what observations are to be made and considered in their rating.

3. Sample carefully from the domain of traits to permit generalizability.

4. Avoid technical jargon. If slang will help convey the intent, by all means use it.

5. Express the traits to be rated as questions rather than as declarative statements.

6. For the graphic and descriptive graphic rating scales, the continuous line should follow immediately after the question (trait to be rated) or be placed below the question.

7. Determine how discriminating you want the ratings and divide the continuum accordingly. We recommend that the continuum be subdivided into three- to seven-point intervals, although some people feel that as many as nine can be used effectively (Guilford, 1954). Further subdivisions will make for such fine discriminations that the rater will not be able to rate the trait validly.

IMPROVING THE RATER

1. Conduct a thorough training session. In the training session, point out the value of accurate and honest ratings. Point out the kinds of errors commonly committed by raters and how they might be avoided, or at least minimized. Discussing such things as "halo effects" can reduce their effects. Have some "dry runs" to give the raters practice.

2. Motivate the raters to do as accurate a job as possible.

3. Select persons who can provide objective, unbiased ratings. Avoid persons who are either overly critical or solicitous. Avoid people who have an "axe to grind." Select persons who are aware of children's developmental patterns.

IMPROVING THE RATING

The validity of obtained ratings will be improved if care is taken in the construction of the scale and the selection and training of the raters. In addition, there are several factors that can help improve the validity of the rating, but which are not necessarily related to improvement of the scale of raters per se.

1. Encourage raters not to rate those traits or persons for which they have insufficient knowledge to make a valid rating. Two ways in which this can be done are (1) to provide an "insufficient information" point on the scale (this will then suggest to the rater that he need not rate every trait); and (2) to require the rater to provide evidence for his ratings, especially those at the extremes.

2. Combine (or average) judges' ratings.[12] In general, the larger the number of independent ratings and raters, the higher the reliability. Why? Because individual errors and biases should cancel out each other. Also, multiple observations should provide for a more representative sample of the ratees' behavior. This is especially true in junior and senior high school, where an individual teacher has only limited contact with his students.

3. Rate only one trait or characteristic at a time. For example, if a rating scale consists of 15 traits, and 30 pupils are to be rated, all 30 pupils should be rated on trait 1 before proceeding to trait 2. This will permit the rater to give his undivided attention to the trait and should provide for more reliable measurement.

4. The numerical rating scale should be used to rate only those characteristics that can be categorized into a small number of subdivisions and where there is good agreement among raters on what kind of behavior is represented by "outstanding" or "average," or other descriptions assigned to the numbers on the scale. More often than not, there is considerable variation in the interpretation of scale values, and hence the scale is often less valid than anticipated.

5. To reduce the influence of the halo effect and response set, vary the directionality of the scale. That is, for some ratings, have the first position indicate a desirable trait, the last an undesirable trait, and vice versa.

6. Avoid making the extremes so atypical of behavior that few raters will use these points.

7. Make the meaning of the intermediate levels closer to the neutral or average level rather than the extreme points (descriptions). This may induce raters to use the total continuum rather than just the middle position.

8. Control the effect of extraneous variables. Be on guard to confine the rating to, and only to, the attributes being measured. Do *not* be influenced by a pretty binder or a professional typing job when rating an essay or term paper. "Don't judge a book by its cover" is very apropos, since too often we are unduly influenced by extraneous factors, the result being invalid data.

Anecdotal Records

Anecdotal records are records of specific incidents of student behavior. Over a period of time, anecdotal records can provide the teacher with a

---

[12] See Werts, Joreskog, and Linn (1976) for a description of a model to analyze rating data on multiple dimensions by multiple raters.

longitudinal picture of the changes that have taken place in a particular pupil.

While normally restricted to the area of social adjustment, anecdotal records may be used in many other contexts. For example, Johnny, who has appeared to be uninterested in arithmetic, might come to school one day and tell the class a new way of working with multiplication facts. Or Mary, who has been most uncoordinated in her physical education class, may one day ask her teacher if she could be permitted to demonstrate an intricate tumbling act (and, incidentally, perform it perfectly). Or Allen, who has been most careless in the science lab, may suddenly become careful for a few days and then reverts to his former behavioral traits. All these examples illustrate that anecdotal records should possess certain characteristics:

1. They should contain a factual description of *what* happened, *when* it happened, and under *what circumstances* the behavior occurred.
2. The interpretation and recommended action should be noted separately from the description.
3. Each anecdotal record should contain a record of a *single* incident.
4. The incident recorded should be one that is considered to be *significant* to the pupil's growth and development.

By and large, anecdotal records are typically less formal and systematic than the data obtained through other observational techniques. Time sampling is not employed. Rather, incidents are noted as they occur. For this reason the data from anecdotal records are ordinarily not so reliable as those obtained from other observational tools.

Advantages of Anecdotal Records

The major advantage of the anecdotal record is that, if properly used, it can provide a factual record of an observation of a single, significant incident in the pupil's behavior that may be of assistance to the teacher in developing a better understanding of the growth and development of that pupil. Other advantages of anecdotal records are that they—

1. Record critical incidents of spontaneous behavior (in a *natural* setting), many of which do not lend themselves to systematic measurement.
2. Provide the teacher with objective descriptions rather than make him rely on vague generalizations.
3. Direct the teacher's attention to a single pupil.
4. Provide for a cumulative record of growth and development, if collected over time.
5. Can be used by the counselor as a source of information upon which to base his discussions with the pupil.

6. Can be used as a supplement to quantitative data obtained from other tests so that the teacher will better understand the behavior of his pupils.

7. Provide for a more thorough description of the pupil's behavior than will check lists, rating scales, or sociograms because they contain the setting in which the behavior was observed. Many teachers consider these more complete descriptions of behavior better suited to understanding and guiding pupils than the other observational tools available.

Limitations of Anecdotal Records

We have already mentioned that one of the more serious limitations of anecdotal records is that they tend to be less reliable than other observational techniques because they typically tend to be less formal and systematic and ordinarily do not employ time sampling. Some other limitations of anecdotal records follow.

1. They are time consuming to write.

2. If collected over a period of time for many students, they can create a storage problem.

3. It is difficult for the observer to maintain objectivity when he records the incident observed. Observers are human and are prone to include interpretive words or phrases in their descriptions. This can be minimized by thoroughly training teachers in the manner of recording and reporting incidents.

4. Too often the incident is described without including the situation in which the behavior was observed. When incidents are read out of context, they may lose their meaning. Look at the following anecdotal records[13] to see how an incident described out of context can be subject to misinterpretation:

Incident without setting: While Frank was reading his lines, George continuously made faces at the other cast members, whispered loudly to students offstage, and created such a disturbance that Frank was forced to stop reading.

Although this anecdotal record is objective and factual, and describes just a single incident, it is open to misinterpretation. On the surface, after reading this description, the reader would no doubt picture George as a nuisance, an attention-getter, a potential troublemaker. Why? Because there is no setting that gives the reader any option but drawing this conclusion.

Setting: George and Frank are bitter rivals in all school activities. Both are very good students. Today tryouts were being held after school for the junior class play. George

[13] The two anecdotal records are from Schwartz and Tiedeman (1957, pp. 199, 202).

and Frank were both on stage prepared to read their lines for the lead part in the play, a part both boys wanted very much. I told them I would select the lead on the basis of their reading of the lines.

Would you still interpret the incident as evidence that George is a nuisance or troublemaker? Or would you interpret the incident as one that might be expected in the light of the competition between the two boys and the eventual reward? We venture to say that you would interpret George's behavior differently after reading the additional information.

    5. Teachers tend to use anecdotal records as a method of recording only undesirable incidents. They neglect the positive incidents.

    6. Anecdotes present only a verbal description of the incident. They *do not reveal causes.*

Using Anecdotal Records Effectively: Suggestions for Preparation

The major problem in using anecdotal records is to be *selective* in deciding what incident, action, or event should be recorded and which ones should or could be ignored. We offer the following suggestions:

    1. The teacher should restrict his observations to those behaviors that cannot be evaluated by other means. Anecdotal records should not be used to record information about the student's knowledge of subject matter, for which pencil-and-paper achievement tests are more reliable and efficient. By the same token, the anecdotal record should not be used for product or process evaluation, since rating scales and check lists are more appropriate. Anecdotal records should be restricted to those situations from which we wish to obtain data on how the pupil behaves in a natural situation.

    2. Records should be complete. There are several different styles of anecdotal records. All, however, contain the following parts: (a) identifying information—pupil's name, grade, school, and class; (b) date of the observation; (c) the setting; (d) the incident; and (e) the signature of the observer. Some contain a section for the interpretation and recommendation for action, while others restrict themselves only to the factual data.

    3. Anecdotal records should be kept by all teachers and not be restricted to only the child's homeroom teacher. Behavior occurs in the classroom, in the playground, in the library, in the halls and restrooms, in the music room, on the bus, and other locations. Therefore, all teachers should write anecdotal records. It should not matter where the behavior occurred or who witnessed it. What is important is that the incident be recorded. The validity of the anecdotal record will be enhanced with a variety of common information gathered from different sources. The homeroom teacher should welcome rather than resent anecdotes submitted by other staff members. In fact, the school principal should elicit the cooperation of his staff in providing other

teachers with this information. This is especially important in the junior- and senior-high grades, where the student is in his homeroom only for a short amount of time during the school day. Here, the homeroom teacher is heavily dependent on outside sources.

4. The behavioral incident or action should be recorded as soon as possible after it has happened. Some teachers feel that if they jot down some brief notes, they can complete the anecdotal record at some later time. It should be remembered that any lapse of time places heavy reliance on the teacher's memory, which may become blurred if too much time elapses.

8. Anecdotal records could be compiled on slips of paper, cards, or any material readily handy. We recommend that some standard form be used for filing. Also, we recommend *against* using slips of paper, since they can be easily lost or misplaced. A large sheet of paper is preferred because it permits the teacher to write his interpretation on the same sheet as the description of the setting and incident.

9. Anecdotes should have interpretive value. A jumbled collection of anecdotes is of little value. They must be collated, summarized, and interpreted. If, for example, Ilene has only one record of aggressiveness, this is inconsequential. On the other hand, if Ilene has been observed to display aggressive behavior on 9/6, 9/14, 10/12, 10/13, and 11/21, in a variety of different settings, this behavioral pattern does become significant.

10. Anecdotal records must be available to specified school personnel. We have already indicated that we feel strongly that the anecdotal record should be shared with other teachers and especially with the school counselor if there is one. Also, this material should be incorporated in the student's folder with other information gathered by means of tests. We also believe that a general summary should be shared with the parents, and with the pupil if he is old enough to understand it. Other than for school personnel, parents, and the students, the anecdotal record should be considered as confidential information.

11. Anecdotal records as an educational resource should be emphasized The success of any measurement program depends upon the attitudes and cooperation of the teachers involved. Because anecdotal records depend so heavily on the willingness of teachers to do a good job, it is essential that teachers develop an appreciation for the value of anecdotal records in helping them obtain a better understanding of their pupils. (Indirectly, this should result in the development of better-adjusted students.)

12. Anecdotal records should not be confined to recording negative behavior patterns. In fact, the anecdotal record should record significant behaviors regardless of their direction. Only in this way can the teacher obtain a valid composite picture of the student.

13. As in writing good test items, the teacher should have practice and training in making observations and writing anecdotal records.

Storing Anecdotal Records

Although the storage of information will be discussed more fully in Chapter 19, we would like to refer to it briefly at this time inasmuch as it bears on the collection and storage of anecdotal records.

It would appear to us, at least, that we are dealing with a variety of questions: (1) What information should be kept in, or recorded in, the anecdotal record? (2) How long should information about a student be kept? (3) Where should the anecdotal records be stored? (4) Who should have access to the information? Let us consider each of these questions briefly.

We contend that information is, or should be, gathered for the purpose of making decisions that will be of benefit to the pupil. As for the kinds of information to be gathered and kept, we believe that only those data that have a *direct* bearing and relevance to the students' growth and development be kept. We see no use for, or need for information concerning the number of times Clarence picked his nose, *unless* picking one's nose has some predictive validity in the educational domain.

How long one should or can keep this information is analogous to asking "How hot is hot?" Who can say how long information on, say, a rebellious, hostile third-grader should be kept? We would surmise that it should be retained until this behavior problem no longer manifests itself. But how long is that? We are cognizant of the fact that records cannot be kept *ad infinitum.* Therefore, we believe that, if possible, records should be stored at least while the student is enrolled in a particular school.

Where the information should be stored is simply answered. All data pertaining to a student's behavior should be kept under lock and key.

To us, at least, the issue is much broader than it appears. It really has to do with the professional competence and integrity of educators. If we are to provide for maximal student learning, then we must use all available resources to achieve that end. And this could, and often does, require the collection and storage of different kinds of data.

EVALUATING PERSONAL-SOCIAL ADJUSTMENTS BY SOCIOMETRIC METHODS

A variety of instruments and approaches are available for evaluating personal-social adjustment. Some of these include teacher observations and the use of check lists, rating scales, and anecdotal records previously discussed. Others involve peer ratings, self-report, sociometric techniques, and projective tests. Some of the tools required can be developed and used by the ordinary classroom teacher without additional training. Others, such as projective tests, should be administered and interpreted only by skilled clinicians. Because of the limited training of teachers in clinical procedures, we will focus our attention on various teacher-made sociometric techniques such as peer appraisal, nominating procedures, and social distance scales. In Chapter 16 we will consider other aspects of personal-social development, such as interests and personality.

Sociometry is concerned with how an individual is seen and accepted by his peers. Sociometric techniques have been, and are constantly being, used by students. When they choose up sides for a game of baseball or a spelling bee, they are using sociometry. When they elect class officers, select the yearbook editor, the high school beauty queen, and the ugliest senior, they are employing sociometry.

The sociometric approach to studying personal-social adjustment is quite economical in time and money. The essential ingredient is to devise a series of questions that will elicit a student's *true* feelings about other members in his class. Following are some suggestions to help you prepare the questions.

1. Write questions in clear, unambiguous language adapted to the age level of the student. Avoid technical jargon.

2. Write questions that will elicit *true* feelings about a student's peers. Some examples of "good" questions are: "Whom would you like to sit next to in class?" "Who is your best friend?" "Whom would you like to have work with you on the social committee?"

3. Decide in advance what use will be made of the results, as this will determine the kinds of questions to be asked. For example, if a teacher wants to know what would be the most harmonious group to work on a social committee, he would not ask the question, "Whom would you like to sit next to in class?"

Peer Appraisal Methods

A teacher's observation of pupil behavior is of limited value. He observes the pupil in a special setting where the student may well be behaving somewhat differently than he would in other situations. For example, Jim may be very cooperative in the formal classroom setting but very independent on the playing field. Also, the teacher is necessarily observing from a certain frame of reference. Peer appraisal can be a very good supplement in the evaluation program. In evaluating such characteristics as popularity, leadership ability, power, and concern for others, fellow students are often better judges than teachers.

Peer appraisal could be obtained by using any of the rating scale methods previously discussed. If each student filled out a rating form for every other student, considerable data would be available. However, in obtaining peer appraisal, it is usually desirable to simplify the task, since students are doing the actual work. (If one is dealing with younger students, it is absolutely necessary to make the task as simple as possible.) Students are untrained and generally unmotivated raters. To expect a student to fill out 30 different rating sheets without becoming quite careless or bored is asking a lot! Typically, then, the task is simplified to a *guess who* or *nominating* technique.

Whenever peer ratings are desired, two major principles must be adhered to: (1) The traits to be rated should be within the student's experiential background. Asking "Who is the most popular student?" is markedly different from asking "Who will be the most successful student?" The language used should also be simple. (2) Complete anonymity and confidentiality must be maintained so that students who receive "poor" ratings will be protected from further embarrassment and possible harassment, as well as to ensure that we will obtain true responses from the students.[14]

"Guess Who" Technique

In the "guess who" technique, each pupil is given a list of descriptions and asked to name the pupil(s) who best fits each description. The descriptions used are dependent upon the traits one wishes to measure. If one wishes to assess cheerfulness, the description might be as follows:

> This person is always happy.

If one wishes to assess leadership qualities, a possible description would be

> This person is an effective leader.

In the "guess who" technique, one simply tallies the number of times each person was named for each description. When the tally is completed, the teacher can readily see which pupils are mentioned most frequently, seldom, or not at all for each characteristic. Data regarding who named whom are also available but are seldom used in the "guess who" technique.

Nominating Technique

The nominating technique is very similar to the "guess who" method except that the questions are slightly different. Instead of choosing a name to fit a description, the student is asked to nominate the person(s) with whom he would like to work, sit by, study, or play.[15] Again, what one wants to measure determines what kinds of questions are asked. We could, for example, measure perceived competence, power, or social acceptance. Occasionally, students are asked to nominate whom they would *least* like to sit by, play with, and so on. This is generally not recommended; it could hurt group morale. The nominating technique provides data relevant to the existing

[14] In addition, a sociometric test should be administered as informally as possible.
[15] Children in the elementary grades might be limited to two or three choices; those in the upper grades, to four or five.

social relationships in the class. With this technique we are interested in *who made* the nomination as well as *whom was nominated*. Reciprocal relationships are looked for.

Suppose we have asked fourth-graders to list their first and second choices of fellow students with whom they would most like to play. The results can be tabulated in a matrix like the hypothetical one shown in Figure 12–6. (We have assumed a small class for convenience of illustration.) The pupils' names are listed both on the side and on the top. The names along the side represent the person *doing* the nominating. The two people chosen are indicated by placing a "1" under the name of the first choice and a "2" under the name of the second choice. The totals along the bottom of Figure 12–6 indicate the

Chooser / Chosen →	Allan	Bill	Beth	Diana	Fred	Irv	Jake	Ilene	Lori	Machell	Ruth	Susan
Allan		2				1						
Bill			(1)			(2)						
Beth		(1)							2			
Diana	1									2		
Fred											2	1
Irv		(2)									(1)	
Jake	2										1	
Ilene									(2)		(1)	
Lori								(2)		(1)		
Machell			1						(2)			
Ruth						(1)		(2)				
Susan								(2)		(1)		
1st choice	1	1	2	0	0	2	0	0	1	2	3	0
2d choice	1	2	0	0	0	1	0	3	2	1	1	1
Total	2	3	2	0	0	3	0	3	3	3	4	1
Mutual choices	0	2	1	0	0	2	0	2	2	2	1	0

Date: April 17, 1972.

FIGURE 12–6 Matrix showing students' choices of play companions.

number of times each person was nominated. Mutual choices are circled, ignoring the distinction between first and second choices. Notice that mutual choices are always an equal number of cells from the main diagonal (the straight line running from upper left to lower right, which divides the figure).

Although the choices could be weighted so that the first choice will count more than the second choice, we prefer to use a simple count rather than a weighting procedure for a variety of reasons: (1) Different weighting systems have shown that no one scheme is superior to another (Gronlund, 1959); (2) it is difficult to ascertain whether there was much difference between the first and second choice or that they were about equal and could have been decided by a flip of a coin; and (3) it is difficult to ascertain the strength of preference among different students.

The number of choices that an individual pupil receives on a sociometric question is used as an indication of his social acceptance by his peers. From the data presented in Figure 12–6, we can identify the students who are most popular (referred to as *stars*); those who receive no choices (called *isolates*); and those who receive only a single choice (called *neglectees*). Ruth is a *star*. She received the most nominations. (Three of the four were first choices.) Bill, Irv, Ilene, Lori, and Machell all received three nominations—one more than the average. Susan is a *neglectee*, since she received only one nomination. Diana, Fred, and Jake are *isolates*, receiving no nominations. Notice that of the 24 nominations made, there were 12 mutual choices. There were eight opposite-sex choices (this is normal for fourth-graders). By using similar matrices for other nominations, such as choices for seating, working, or playing companions, the teacher can obtain some valuable insights into the group relationships present in his class.

The Sociogram

The sociogram dates back to the work of Moreno (1934). It is really just a graphic picture of the data matrix presented in Figure 12–6. The general procedure is to place the "star"(s) at the center, the "isolates" on the periphery, and the other students between the center and periphery in relation to the strength of their choice. Drawing a sociogram can be quite complex.[16]

Using Sociometric Data

As we stressed before, one gathers evaluative data to aid in decision making. Obtaining sociometric data is no exception. Although the reasons behind the nominations are unknown, teachers can use the results for organizing classroom groups and to improve the social climate in the classroom. The

---

[16] For a thorough discussion on the construction, interpretation, and uses of the sociogram, see Jennings (1948) and Gronlund (1959).

results can also be used to improve the social structure of the group by breaking up cliques and/or helping the isolates become more acceptable to their peers. Further study may be needed to determine *why* some students are isolates. Often, teachers can assist isolates into becoming integrated into the group by providing them with more opportunity for social contact with the group and thus improving their social skills. Although sociometric techniques differ from the other observational techniques discussed earlier (in sociometric tests, the data are gathered about individuals from their peers rather than from teachers or observers), all provide data necessary to obtain a better understanding of pupil behavior.

To be most effective, decisions based on sociometric data should be implemented as soon as possible. For example, if the teacher wants to establish a social committee to work on a Halloween party, he should, after asking for the information, (1) form the groups as quickly as possible, and (2) form groups reflecting the students' choices. Unless individual preferences are honored, students will quickly lose interest and subsequent data may be invalid. Of course, there are some instances where individual preferences cannot be honored, such as occurs when one pupil is chosen first by every other pupil.

Some other ways in which sociometric data can be used by teachers and researchers are as follows:

1. To study the effects of certain experiences on group structure
2. To study the relationship between group structure (acceptance) and such factors as sex, religion, color, and age
3. To study the stability (or lack of it) of group structure

Limitations of Sociometric Data

Several points need to be considered when interpreting sociometric data.

1. The data are only as valid as the rapport that exists between the student and teacher and the student's willingness to be honest.

2. The data only reveal relationships. They do *not* establish causal relationships. In fact, more often than not, sociometric data raise more questions than they give answers to. Why did no one choose Diana as a playmate? Is she too aggressive and domineering? What can I, as a teacher, do for Diana so that she will be accepted by the other students? How can I break up a clique?

3. The group relationships depicted are dependent upon the kinds of questions asked. For example, Bill may wish to play with some peers but work on a class project with other peers.

4. The relationships are not necessarily stable, especially in younger children. They may, and often do, vary during the school year. (Maybe Jake

has just moved into the school. In another three months he could be a *star*.) In fact, the picture obtained from sociometric data tends to be specific to a given day, and the choices made may be to a specific activity. This is important to remember, since social situations change rapidly. We therefore suggest that sociometric data be collected at frequent intervals and that the matrix be labeled as to the date collected and the activity sampled.

5. It should not be assumed that the "star(s)" is the most well-adjusted pupil. It indicates only that he or she is acceptable to the majority of his or her peers.

6. Sociometric data should be interpreted in the light of what we know about child development. For example, we would expect boy-girl choices in the primary grades, but not in the intermediate grades. Isolates and cliques should be interpreted with reference to such things as their cultural, social, racial, and religious backgrounds.

MEASURING ATTITUDES

Although affective measurement encompasses the totality of the individual's personality, of which attitudes are just a segment, we will focus our attention on the measurement of attitudes since many aspects of personality assessment are beyond the scope of the classroom teacher.

Attitudes are learned. Because they are learned, they can be changed if deemed necessary. However, before one can alter, modify, or reinforce something, he must know the status of that "something." Despite the methodological problems associated with attitude measurement, teachers should know something about attitudes and how they can be measured. The remainder of this chapter will consider (1) the definition of attitudes, (2) the general characteristics of attitude scales, and (3) the different methods of measuring and constructing attitude scales that are within the scope of the classroom teacher and can be used by the teacher to develop a better understanding of his pupils.

What an Attitude Is

Attitudes are predispositions to respond overtly to social objects. This statement is alluded to, in part at least, by the numerous definitions posited by psychologists. There are, however, two schools of thought concerning the structure of attitudes: *unidimensional* and *component*. Proponents of the unidimensional approach subscribe to the following definition of an attitude: "an enduring system of positive or negative evalutions, emotional feelings, and pro or con tendencies with respect to a social object." (Krech, 1962, p. 177.) A slight modification is made by Campbell (1950), who defines an attitude as "a syndrome of response consistency with regard to social objects." Both definitions, however, and both schools of thought deal with feelings—

likes or dislikes, affinities for or aversions to something. The second position, which is held by *component* theorists, contends that attitudes are more than (or should be concerned with more than) one dimension. Component theorists believe that we must consider the various components associated with an attitude. A comprehensive definition of the component theorist is provided by Zimbardo and Ebbesen (1970, p. 7), who define the affective, cognitive, and behavioral components of an attitude as follows:

> The affective component consists of a person's evaluation of, liking of, or emotional response to some object or person. The cognitive component has been conceptualized as a person's beliefs about, or factual knowledge of, the object or person. The behavioral component involves the person's overt behavior directed toward the object or person.

Attitudes, per se, are *not* directly observable but are inferred from a person's overt behavior, both verbal and nonverbal. You cannot see prejudice but you can observe the behavior of one who is prejudiced. Thus, on the basis of observations of a person's consistent behavior pattern to a stimulus, we would conclude that he displays this or that attitude (Shaw, 1973).

General Characteristics of Attitudes

Relevant to, and to be considered in, attitude measurement are certain traits or characteristics. These characteristics are as follows:[17]

1. Attitudes are evaluative and can be represented on some continuum of "favorableness."
2. Attitudes have a specific social referent, which may be either a concrete or an abstract object.
3. Attitudes vary in intensity (strength of feeling) and direction. Two persons may have the same attitude toward abortion, but they may differ in how strongly they feel about the issue. Or they may be at completely opposite ends of the "favorableness" continuum but with the *same* degree of intensity. (For example, on the abortion issue, Allan may strongly agree while Ilene may strongly disagree. Both Allan and Ilene feel strongly about their position, but they are diametrically opposed.)
4. Attitudes vary in affective saliency; that is, there are some attitudes (such as to abortion) that are accompanied by or connected with a person's emotions.
5. Attitudes represent varying degrees of embeddedness or interrelatedness to other attitudes. As would be expected, attitudes related to similar objects such as integration and equality of education are more likely to be

[17] See Shaw and Wright (1967) for a fuller treatment of the characteristics of attitudes.

interconnected than attitudes toward dissimilar objects such as capital punishment and women's liberation.

6. Attitudes are relatively stable, especially in adults. This does not mean that they cannot be changed or modified. Rather, it is more difficult to change the attitudes of an adult than of an adolescent or young child. The fact that attitudes are relatively stable supports the belief of many social psychologists that attitude scales can provide reliable measures, albeit possibly less so than for tests of cognitive skills or knowledge.

Although we must develop techniques to express these traits in numerical terms, the only ones that have received any attention are those of magnitude, intensity, and direction. Much work still remains to be done, and as Scott (1968, p. 208) has said, with reference to these characteristics, ". . . most of them have not been operationalized satisfactorily, let alone scaled."

In summary, we still have a long way to go to make attitude measurement as respectable, as valid, as reliable, and as objective as cognitive assessment. But we should do the best job possible with the techniques at our disposal.

Constructing Attitude Scales

We must be concerned with the validity and reliability of any psychometric scale, test, or inventory. Possibly of more relevance, however, in attitude measurement is the need for making certain that the method of measurement does *not* affect the trait(s) being measured.

The two major approaches to, or methods of, measuring attitudes are by *observation* of subjects in a normal (or simulated situation) and by *self-report* inventories and scales. Self-report techniques are most often used to measure attitudes even though users are cognizant of the fact that these techniques are susceptible to faking. In contrast to observations, self-report approaches tend to be more valid and reliable. We will now consider some general guidelines to be held in mind when constructing attitude scales as well as the different types of attitudes scales that we feel are within the knowledge and skill domain of classroom teachers, recognizing that in most instances all but the simplest scales should be left to professionals.

General Guidelines for Constructing Attitudes Scales

Any test, scale, or inventory—be it cognitive, affective, psychomotor, or performance—is no better than the items used. Previously we provided suggestions for writing cognitive-type items. Some of these principles or suggestions also pertain to the writing of attitude scale items, such as clarity of wording. Some of the suggestions provided below pertain to any type of attitude scale, whether Thurstone or Likert, whereas others are more relevant to a particular type of scale.

1. Use statements that refer to the *present* rather than the past. You are generally more interested in attitudes toward an issue that is presently popular than one that is just of historical value.

2. Write direct statements in clear, simple language. Use simple rather than complex sentences.

3. Avoid factual statements or those that may be interpreted as factual.

4. Avoid using "universal" words such as "always, never, all, none."

5. Restrict the use of words such as "only, just, merely," as much as possible.

6. Make each statement brief, preferably less than 20 words.

7. Avoid statements that are ambiguous and may be interpreted in a variety of ways.

8. Each statement should be unidimensional, that is, should be related to only a single concept. Avoid double-barreled statements; for example, "I don't like to go to parties because I'm nervous in crowds." If the subject responds in an affirmative manner (or it could be in a negative way), you don't know whether (1) he dislikes parties, (2) he is nervous, or (3) both apply.

9. Avoid statements that are likely to receive universal endorsement or rejection. Select statements that cover the total continuum of favorableness. Remember! You are trying to differentiate among people's attitudes. Try to write items that you would guess one-half of the people would agree and one-half would disagree with the statement. Hence, the item, "I like to associate with nice people" wouldn't be a good attitude item, whereas "Sometimes I don't like to associate with nice people" would be.

10. Try to have an equal number of positively and negatively worded items. This will help minimize the occurrence of a response or acquiescence set.

11. Randomly allocate the statements to the attitude scale, making certain that you do not have more than four or five positive or negative items in sequence.

12. Don't restrict yourself to a three-point continuum, but don't exceed seven points.

13. Don't restrict yourself to an "agree-disagree" continuum. The trait being measured, such as the value of a particular course, may better lend itself to a "valuable-valueless" continuum. Feelings of favorableness, interest, and value are appropriate bipolar continua.

14. Write more statements than will actually be needed.

15. Do everything to ensure the individual's privacy. Otherwise the validity of the response obtained is questionable.

Types of Self-Report Attitude Scales

Attitude scales, like interest and personality tests (these will be discussed in Chapter 16) are classified in terms of their method of *construction*. There are three major procedures or techniques for constructing attitude scales: *sum-*

mated rating scales, such as the Minnesota Scale for the Survey of Public Opinion (Likert type); *equal-appearing interval scales*, such as the Thurstone and Remmers scales (Thurstone type); and *cumulative scales* (Guttman type). In addition, the Semantic Differential Technique,[18] though not a type of scale construction, per se, is a technique used to measure attitudes.

In the Likert, Thurstone, and Guttman methods, statements are written and assembled into a scale and the subject responds (either positively or negatively) to each statement. On the basis of the subject's responses, an *inference* is made about the respondent's attitude towards some object(s). In the Semantic Differential, the subject rates a particular attitude object(s) on a series of bipolar semantic scales such as good-bad, sweet-sour, strong-weak. Each of these approaches to constructing attitude scales is different. Each has its advantages and limitations. As Zimbardo and Ebbesen (1970, p. 123) said, each of the techniques makes different assumptions about the kind of test items used and the information provided, even though there are some assumptions that are basic and common regardless of the method used. For example, each method assumes that subjective attitudes can be measured quantitatively, thereby permitting a numerical representation (score) of a person's attitude. Each method assumes that a particular test item has the *same* meaning for all respondents, and therefore a given score to a particular item will connote the same attitude. "Such assumptions may not always be justified but as yet, no measurement technique has been developed which does include them." Since the Guttman method is too complex and beyond the scope of this book, we will consider only the Thurstone, Likert, and Semantic Differential.

The Thurstone Method of Attitude Scale Construction

A large number of statements expressing various degrees of positive, neutral, and negative feelings toward some institution (the U.N., the U.S. Senate, school, labor unions) or group (blacks, Jews, Puerto Ricans) are written. (For a good source of items ask people to write (give) their opinion about the object for which an attitude scale is being developed.) For example, to develop an attitude scale towards mathematics, many items such as the following are written:

> Mathematics is boring
> Mathematics is interesting
> Studying mathematics is a waste of time

Then, a group of knowledgeable judges (the larger the number in the group, the better) are asked to sort *each* statement into one of an "11-pile" con-

---

[18] See Maguire (1973) for a comprehensive discussion of the Semantic Differential as a technique for constructing attitude scales.

tinuum (ranging from extremely favorable to neutral to extremely unfavorable). The *statements* in each pile are ranked, *not* the personal opinion or judgments of the judges. For example, let us assume that we are interested in constructing an attitude scale toward labor unions. One of the items written was "Labor unions have benefited the working man." Although a judge may despise labor unions and what they stand for, he is to assign this statement in terms of whether it is a favorable, neutral, or unfavorable statement about labor unions and then decide, if the statement is not neutral, how positive or negative the statement is *disregarding his personal feelings*. This procedure is then repeated with all the statements pertaining to labor unions, each judge making an independent assignment. This sorting procedure is what is referred to as the method of *equal-appearing intervals*. Although there may be some variation in the ranking of each of the statements, only those statements that demonstrate high interjudge agreement are retained. The median value and interquartile range $(Q = Q_3 - Q_1$, which is used as a measure of interjudge variability) are computed, and all items for which there is marked disagreement are rejected (marked disagreement suggests that the item is ambiguous). The remaining items must then have values that are evenly distributed over the range of scale values, should have relatively small Q values, must be relevant to the trait being measured, and must be internally consistent. These items (it is suggested there be about 20 items on the scale) are then arranged in random order. The subject then checks those statements with which he agrees. His score is an average of the scale values of the statements checked.

Some words of caution are appropriate at this time. (1) We assume that each statement is independent of, and unrelated to, any other statement in the scale. (2) Research has vividly demonstrated that scale values are affected significantly by the judges' attitudes. (Hovland & Sherif, 1952; Thurstone & Chave, 1929.)[19]

The Thurstone method of attitude scale construction produces scales that tend to demonstrate adequate reliability (.75 or better). One of the disadvantages is the complex method of finally arriving at or preparing a scale of 20 to 25 items. The scales are easy to administer and score and are adaptable to a variety of institutions or groups, once a basic prototype has been established. This variation is often referred to as the Remmers' scales.

Remmers' method is a Thurstone-type scale. To avoid the inordinate amount of time needed to build a separate scale for every attitude object, Remmers devised a series of master scales. With these master scales, the same statements can be used for similar objects. For example, in our illustration of writing items to measure attitude toward mathematics,

1.   Is boring

[19] As Hovland and Sherif (1952) demonstrated, this is especially true when judges with extreme views are used.

2. Is interesting
3. Is a waste of time

the teacher could use such statements to measure attitudes toward school or any school subject.

The major difference between the master and specific scales is that the former tend to be more general and rather than having the statements listed randomly, they are presented in order of decreasing favorableness.

The Likert Method of Attitude Scale Construction

The Likert method appears to be the most popular. Likert scales are easier to construct and score than either the Thurstone- or Remmers-type scales. Other advantages of the Likert scale are that it (1) produces more homogeneous scales, (2) yields essentially the same results as the more laborious Thurstone-type scales, (3) allows the subject to indicate the degree or intensity of his feelings, and (4) permits greater variance.

The major distinction between the Thurstone and Likert methods of attitude scale construction pertains to the use of judges. The Thurstone method involves judges, but the Likert method does not require judges to sort the statements. Both are concerned with *unidimensionality*, that is, making sure that all the items measure the *same* thing. In the Likert method the researcher or test constructor collects or writes a large number of statements (varying in degree of positive and negative feelings) about an object, class of persons, or institution. The preliminary scale should *not* have many neutral items, nor should it have many items at either end of the continuum. The preliminary scale is then given to a large number of subjects who respond to each item by means of a five-point[20] scale ranging from "strongly agree" to "neutral" to "strongly disagree." The items are then each weighted from 1 to 5 and a total score obtained. Correlations are then computed between each item and the total score. Only those items that demonstrate a high correlation with the total score are retained. This method of selecting the final items to be used in our scale attempts to produce a scale that is internally consistent. The Likert method helps assure unidimensionality and often yields reliabilities that are higher than those obtained using an equal-appearing interval scale.

Osgood's Semantic Differential

As mentioned earlier, the Semantic Differential is not a method of attitude scale construction, per se. Rather, it is a *way* of measuring attitudes. Whereas

[20] The number of categories is variable. Masters (1974) found that when opinions are widely divided on an issue, increasing the number of categories had little effect on internal consistency. However, when opinion is not widely divided, a small number of categories can result in low reliability.

the Thurstone and Likert scales require the subject to indicate his degree of agreement or favorableness or liking to a set of items reflecting a particular attitude, the semantic differential asks subjects to *rate* a particular object along some type of bipolar semantic scale (sweet-sour). Osgood's research identified three general factors of meaning measured by the semantic differential: an *evaluative* factor, a *potency* factor, and an *activity* factor. In the evaluative factor, which is not only the *strongest* factor identified, but the one recommended for studying affect, there are 28 bipolar adjectives (scales) having high factor loadings. (Osgood, Suci, & Tannenbaum, 1957.) The 28 adjective pairs on the evaluative factor are:

Good–Bad	Beautiful–Ugly
Sweet–Sour	Clean–Dirty
High–Low	Calm–Agitated
Tasty–Distasteful	Valuable–Worthless
Kind–Cruel	Pleasant–Unpleasant
Bitter–Sweet	Happy–Sad
Empty–Full	Ferocious–Peaceful
Sacred–Profane	Relaxed–Tense
Brave–Cowardly	Rich–Poor
Clear–Hazy	Nice–Awful
Bright–Dark	Fragrant–Foul
Honest–Dishonest	Rough–Smooth
Fresh–Stale	Fair–Unfair
Pungent–Bland	Healthy–Sick

One can use *all* or just a subset of the 28 scales (the user must consider the age of the respondents and choose only words whose meanings are known to them). Each attitude object is responded to along a seven-point continuum. To get the most reliable attitude score, the sum or average of the ratings is computed (Shaw & Wright, 1967).

An example of a semantic differential to, say, abortion would be as follows:

ABORTION

Good____:____:____:____:____:____:____:Bad
Kind____:____:____:____:____:____:____:Cruel
Brave____:____:____:____:____:____:____:Cowardly

The subject then checks the blank on the continuum that most closely corresponds to his feeling about the stimulus word. Any number of stimulus concepts—concrete or abstract; referring to groups, people, or institutions—might be used.

In developing a semantic differential, one should proceed as follows:

1. Identify the concept(s) to be rated. Although the number and type will vary according to the *purpose*, the concepts should be related to each other.

2. Choose appropriate bipolar scales. We are interested in the subjects' *connotative* rather than their descriptive meaning.

3. Design a response sheet so that the concept being rated appears at the top (preferably in CAPS) with the scales listed below.

(a) Have only 1 concept/page.

(b) Reverse the "favorableness" of the scales so that some are in a positive direction, some in a negative direction.

(c) Although the scale points can vary from 3 to 9, Osgood found that a seven-point scale was most effective. For young children, however, a five-point scale may be best.

4. Consider the respondents' age in determining the number of concepts to be rated at a single sitting, the number of scales to be used, and the type of scales used. The younger the group, the fewer the number of concepts and scales one would use.

5. Assign a numerical value to each scale point. Then, depending upon the point checked, a total score can be obtained for each concept being rated. For example, on a seven-point five-scale differential, for a single concept the score for any individual can range from 7 to 35.

In summary, we have considered the need for and importance of educators being knowledgeable in attitude measurement. We have also discussed the various approaches to constructing attitude scales and have provided some suggestions or guidelines for developing statements for attitude scales. The approaches considered in this chapter are well within the capabilities of the classroom teacher and require no formal course work, although one might wish to refer to other textbooks on measuring attitudes such as Bills (1975), Edwards (1970), Shaw and Wright (1967), and Zimbardo and Ebbesen (1970).

SUMMARY

The principal ideas, conclusions, and recommendations presented in this chapter are summarized in the following statements:

1. Tests should not be the only means of measurement. They need to be supplemented by other procedures such as rating scales, anecdotal records, and sociometric methods. In fact, some data *cannot* be gathered by conventional paper-and-pencil tests.
2. Classroom teachers need to know about their pupils' affective behavior in general, and attitudes in particular, so that they will have a better understanding of their pupils.
3. Affective measurement is sorely lacking in our schools despite the fact that there has been some interest evidenced in the past few years.

4. A variety of teacher-related and technical factors have inhibited appropriate emphasis on affective measurement.

5. Observational techniques are particularly useful in evaluating performance skills and products and some aspects of personal-social adjustment.

6. All observational techniques are limited because (1) the observer may be biased; (2) the scale used might be poorly constructed; (3) they are time consuming; and (4) the subjects might behave in an abnormal fashion if they know they are being observed.

7. A check list is a type of rating scale that is useful in rating those behaviors where the only information desired is the presence or absence of a particular characteristic.

8. Rating scales are most helpful in evaluating procedures and products.

9. Rating methods provide a systematic method for recording the observer's judgments.

10. Rating scales can be classified into numerical, graphic, comparative, and paired-comparisons rating scales.

11. Ranking methods are a form of rating scale and are well suited to evaluating products.

12. There are several sources of error in rating scales. Some of the most common are errors due to ambiguity, halo effect, leniency or severity effects, errors of central tendency, and logical error.

13. Control of rating scale errors is a major consideration in constructing and using these scales. Errors can be minimized by (1) selecting only educationally significant characteristics, (2) limiting ratings to observable behavior, (3) clearly defining the characteristics and scale points, (4) limiting the number of scale points, (5) encouraging raters to omit the rating of those characteristics for which they have insufficient information, (6) thoroughly training raters in how to observe, and (7) pooling, wherever possible, the ratings from several raters.

14. The least structured of our observational techniques is the anecdotal record. Anecdotal records are recorded incidents of specific student behavior. Good records describe events rather than evaluate them.

15. Anecdotal records provide for a description of behavior in a natural setting.

16. Limitations of anecdotal records are that (1) they are time consuming to write; (2) data should be gathered continuously, to be most valuable; (3) they may not present a representative sampling of the pupil's behavior; and (4) it is sometimes difficult to prepare objective descriptions of the behaviors thought to be important and those that are irrelevant to the student's growth.

17. Anecdotal records can be improved when (1) the behavioral aspects to be observed are determined in advance, (2) the setting in which the observation was noted is fully described, (3) the record is made as soon as possible after the observation, (4) each anecdote is restricted to a single,

educationally relevant incident, (5) both positive and negative aspects of a student's behavior are noted, (6) the anecdote reports rather than interprets (interpretation should be done separately), (7) a variety of incidents occuring under different conditions are collected before making an inference, and (8) observers are trained on *what* and *how* to observe.

18. Peer appraisal can be a very good supplement in an evaluation program. In evaluating such characteristics as popularity, sportsmanship, leadership ability, and concern for others, fellow students are often better judges than teachers.

19. Peer appraisal methods include the "guess who" technique, the nominating technique, the sociogram, and social distance scales.

20. The "guess who" technique requires pupils to name those classmates who best fit each of a series of descriptive behaviors. The number of nominations received by each pupil on each characteristic indicates his popularity or reputation with his peers.

21. The nominating technique is very similar to the "guess who" except that the questions asked are slightly different. Also, nominees and nominator are identified and therefore it is possible to see reciprocal relations. The data can be expressed in tabular form or pictorially (sociogram). The number of choices a pupil receives is an indicant of his social acceptance.

22. Sociometric tests are most helpful in obtaining a better understanding of personal-social adjustment.

23. Sociometric data can be used to arrange (or rearrange) groups, to improve the pupils' personal-social adjustment, and to evaluate the effect of various experiences on pupils' social relations.

24. When sociometric techniques are used, it is important that the pupil understand what he is to do and know that anonymity will be preserved.

25. Sociometric data are *specific* rather than general. They apply to the kinds of questions asked and the number of choices made. Sociometric choices for young children tend to be less stable than for older children.

26. Sociometric data do not provide for causal explanations.

27. Social distance scales indicate the "degree" of acceptance.

28. Attitudes are a predisposition to respond overtly to social objects in terms of some favorableness or liking continuum.

29. The two major approaches to studying or measuring attitudes are by observation and self-report.

30. The three self-report approaches used to construct attitude scales are the Thurstone, Likert, and Guttman methods. The Semantic Differential is a way of measuring attitudes. The simplest, both in terms of construction and scoring, is the Likert method.

STANDARDIZED EVALUATION PROCEDURES

UNIT 4

CHAPTER   THIRTEEN
Introduction to Standardized Tests

In this unit we are going to discuss various types of standardized tests and their uses and misuses. Test publishing is a large enterprise in our society and, in general, educators feel that standardized tests serve as useful aids in educational decision making.

In this introductory chapter to the unit we present a definition and classification of standardized tests, outline their potential functions, and discuss factors to consider and sources of information relevant to test selection. After completing this chapter, the student should be able to—

1. Define standardized tests.
2. Classify standardized tests.
3. Comprehend the functions of standardized tests.
4. Understand what factors need to be considered in selecting tests.
5. Use some basic information sources when selecting standardized tests.

DEFINITION AND CLASSIFICATION OF STANDARDIZED TESTS

In order to facilitate understanding of standardized tests in education, it would probably be wise to discuss what *standardized tests* are. As defined in Chapter 1, they are *commercially prepared* by measurement experts. They provide methods for obtaining samples of behavior under *uniform procedures*. By a "uniform procedure" we mean that the same *fixed set of questions* is *administered* with the *same set of directions* and timing constraints and that the *scoring* procedure is carefully delineated and uniform. Scoring is usually objective, although a standardized achievement test may include an essay question, and certain unstructured personality inventories are scored in a fashion that is not completely objective. Usually a standardized test has been administered to a norm group (or groups) so that a person's performance can be interpreted in a norm-referenced fashion. However, there are some inventories, such as the Mooney Problem Check List, that do not have norms but are ordinarily considered as standardized. And some of the diagnostic achievement tests and "criterion-referenced" achievement tests do not have norms. Some writers seem to think of criterion-referenced tests as not being standardized. But if commercially prepared and if administered and scored under uniform conditions, they fit the definition given above, and we will consider them in this text.

The term standardized does *not* connote that the test necessarily measures what should be taught or at what level students should be achieving. However, with the current popularity of criterion-referenced tests, commercial publishers are marketing some achievement tests that perhaps do connote at least minimal standards.

There are many ways in which standardized tests can be classified. For example, they can be classified according to administrative procedures, such as individual versus group administration, or as oral instructions versus written instructions. However, the most popular broad classification is according to *what* is measured. We will employ the following classification of tests:

1. Aptitude tests (general, multiple, and special)
2. Achievement tests (diagnostic, single subject matter, and survey batteries)
3. Interest, personality, and attitude inventories

Often the first two categories are considered to contain tests of maximum performance; the third, tests of typical performance. Some classify aptitude and achievement tests as cognitive measures, and interest, personality, and attitude inventories as noncognitive or affective measures. Because the noncognitive measures have no factually right or wrong answers, some people prefer to refer to them as inventories rather than tests. This change in terminology may lessen the anxiety of the test taker. Whether or not these measures are referred to as tests or inventories, they do fit the definition of standardized tests given earlier. The word "test" is used in this chapter to simplify the language. However, it should not be used in the *titles* of noncognitive measures.

FUNCTIONS OF STANDARDIZED TESTS IN SCHOOLS

The functions of standardized tests are many and varied; however, as stated in Chapter 1 regarding all measurement devices, one can in essence sum up their functions by saying they should help in decision making. But are there some specific functions for which standardized tests are best qualified? Yes, of course. Although different authors use different systems of classifying these functions, we will use the two-way classification as shown in Table 13–1. The functions, as listed in the table, will be explained in more detail within each of Chapters 14, 15, and 16 in this unit. Note that interest, personality, and attitude tests serve fewer instructional purposes, although these tests can be very useful in the guidance functions of the school.

For all the specific functions mentioned, it should be remembered that the *ultimate* purpose of a standardized test is to help in making decisions. Some examples of the kinds of decisions that might be made better by using standardized test results are as follows:

1. Do the pupils in Miss Perriwinkle's third grade need a different balance of curricular emphasis?
2. Is it advisable for Erskine to take a remedial reading course?
3. Should Billy take a college-preparatory program in high school?
4. Is the phonics method of teaching reading more effective than the sight method?

If knowledge of a test result does not enable one to make a better decision than the best decision that could be made without the use of the test, then the test serves no useful purpose and might just as well not be given. However, if one used and interpreted test information correctly, it would be impossible to make poorer decisions using the additional information.

SELECTING STANDARDIZED TESTS

Because a test, once selected by a school, is ordinarily used for many years, it certainly behooves the purchaser to delve into the problem of test selection to a considerable extent. Some of the many questions that always arise in public schools are, "What kind of information is needed?" "How should this information be obtained?," and if it is agreed that test information would be helpful, "Who should select the tests?" One way to stimulate test use is to

TABLE 13-1   Purposes of Standardized Tests[a,b]

PURPOSES	KINDS OF TESTS				
	Apti-tude	Achieve-ment	Inter-est	Person-ality	Atti-tude
Instructional					
Evaluation of learning outcomes	X	X	?	?	
Evaluation of teaching	X	X			
Evaluation of curriculum	X	X	?		?
Learning diagnosis	X	X			
Differential assignments within class	X	X	?	?	?
Grading	?	?			
Motivation		?			X
Guidance					
Occupational	X	X	X	X	X
Educational	X	X	?	?	X
Personal	?	?	X	X	X
Administrative					
Selection	X	X	?		
Classification	X	X	X		
Placement	X	X	?		
Public relations (information)	X	X	?		
Curriculum planning and evaluation	X	X			
Evaluating teachers	?	?		?	
Providing information for outside agencies	X	X			
Grading	?	?			
Research	X	X	X	X	X

[a] An X indicates that a test can and should be used for that purpose.

[b] A ? indicates that there is some debate concerning whether or not a test can serve that purpose.

have all on the professional staff who will ever use the test results help in the test-selection process. If teachers are expected to use test information, then they should assist in selecting the tests; if guidance personnel will be using test results, then they should be involved; and if the principals also plan to use the test results to help them in certain decisions, then they should assist in the test selection. Test selection should be a cooperative venture by all the professional staff who intend to use the test information.

Purposes of Testing

In attempts to decide which test(s) to select, the first task should be a detailed examination of the purposes for which the testing is to be done. If general uses of the test results are not known in advance, the best decision would be not to test. If one will only administer the tests, obtain the results, and file them away in a vault, it makes little difference which test is administered.

When specific uses are delineated, then test selection can occur in a more sensible and systematic fashion. Quite often one can easily decide what general kind of test is most desirable. Aptitude and achievement tests and interest, personality, and attitude inventories are not used for exactly the same specific purposes. Although Table 13–1, for example, shows that all kinds of tests may be used for occupational guidance, obviously not all serve the same *specific* purpose equally effectively. Many purposes could fall under the heading of occupational guidance, and adequate test selection demands specific preplanning. Knowing that a test is to be used for the purpose of comparing Johnny's interests to the interests of people in various professional occupations would make the selection much easier.

Even knowing precisely the purposes for which one is testing, though, does not necessarily make selection automatic. Suppose you are a seventh-grade mathematics teacher and you wish to measure the achievement of your students in mathematics so that you can evaluate (1) whether or not they have learned enough material to undertake the eighth-grade math curriculum and (2) whether you have been an effective teacher. Furthermore, suppose you wish to use a standardized test, in addition to your own classroom test, to help make the evaluations. How do you decide which of the many standardized seventh-grade mathematics tests to administer? To make this decision, you must be precise in considering your purposes. One difference in all the tests from which you might choose is that they do not all cover the same mathematics content. Some of the tests will cover "modern math"; others will cover the content taught in traditional courses. To make a decision among these tests, you have to decide what your specific objectives are and exactly what area of mathematics you wish to test. Although this is a problem of content validity and has been mentioned in Chapter 5, it is also a problem of determining just exactly *why* you wish to use the test. *It cannot be emphasized too strongly that the most important steps in test selection are to determine exactly why you are giving the test, what type of information you expect from it, and how you intend to use that information once you have it.*

Sources of Information

Once you have determined specifically what sort of information you want to obtain from a test, how can you find out what tests will give this information, and how should you choose between them? There are many sources of information that can assist in this decision. Some of these are Buros' *Mental Measurements Yearbooks* (1938, 1941, 1949, 1953, 1959, 1965, 1972) and his *Tests in Print* (1974), publishers' catalogs, specimen tests, professional journals, measurement texts, and bulletins published by testing corporations.

A good place to start is the *Seventh Mental Measurements Yearbook* (Buros, 1972). This latest edition lists most of the published standardized tests that were in print at the time the yearbook went to press.[1] Those tests not reviewed in earlier editions (and those previously reviewed that have been revised) are described and criticized by educational and psychological authorities. Each school district should own a copy of this book and use it extensively in the test selection process.

Tests in Print (1974) is a comprehensive test bibliography and index to the first seven books in the *Mental Measurements Yearbooks* series. For each test mentioned in *Tests in Print* the following information is included:

1. Test title
2. Appropriate grade levels
3. Publication date
4. Special short comments about the test
5. Number and type of scores provided
6. Authors
7. Publisher
8. Reference to test reviews in *Mental Measurements Yearbooks*

Test publishers' catalogs are a particularly good source for locating new and recently revised tests. These catalogs provide basic information about the purpose and content of the test, appropriate level, working time, cost, and scoring services available. An important piece of information that is not provided in all publishers' catalogs is the copyright date (or norm date).[2]

After locating some promising tests by searching the *Mental Measurements Yearbooks* and the publishers' catalogs, it is essential that the tests be examined before you make a final selection and order large quantities. Most publishers will send, for a very nominal price, specimen sets of tests. These sets usually include the test booklet, answer sheet, administrator's manual, and technical manual, as well as complete information on cost and scoring services. Careful study of the set is essential in determining whether or not that test will meet your specific purposes. For example, a seventh-grade modern math teacher may receive a brochure describing a modern math achievement test. From published reviews as well as from the descriptive literature provided, this test appears to be appropriate. But is it? Even though the professional reviewers laud the test from a technical standpoint and praise its

[1] *The Eighth Mental Measurements Yearbook* is scheduled to be published in 1978.
[2] Addresses of test publishers are listed in Appendix A.

modern content, it is still quite conceivable that this test may be inappropriate. This seventh-grade teacher may stress fundamental operations in set theory, but the test may only have two items devoted to testing this concept. The teacher may skim over binary operations, but over 25 percent of the test may be devoted to this. The teacher may stress commutative, associative, and distributive properties without resorting to technical jargon. The test, however, although measuring these same properties, may assume the pupils' understanding of this mathematical language. This disparity between what the test is designed to measure and what the teacher actually teaches will not be evident except by detailed examination of the test and the test manual.

In addition to the information that can be obtained from a specimen set, several publishers have regional representatives who will visit the school and answer any questions the testing committee may have about their tests. It would be wise to consider inviting such representatives to a testing committee meeting prior to making a final selection. These representatives typically are quite well qualified, often having an M.A. or a Ph.D. degree in the field of educational measurement.

Other sources of information are the test reviews found in the professional periodicals. Journals such as the *Journal of Educational Measurement*, the *Journal of Counseling Psychology*, and *Measurement and Evaluation in Guidance* typically carry reviews of some of the more recently published or revised tests. *Educational and Psychological Measurement* publishes a validity studies section twice a year. The bulk of the articles in this section are reports of studies using various standardized instruments for predictive purposes. Textbooks on measurement also typically include information on various tests.

It should be obvious by now that there is an abundance of sources of information about tests. These sources should be used to a considerable extent. It makes test selection both easier and better.

Characteristics of Tests and Manuals

Several characteristics of tests and test manuals need to be considered when selecting tests. Some of the data regarding these characteristics may be found in published reviews—such as in Buros' yearbooks; some may be found in publishers' catalogs; some must be obtained from the technical manuals; and, unfortunately, all relevant information is just not available for some tests. The American Psychological Association's *Standards for Educational and Psychological Tests and Manuals* (American Psychological Association, 1974), is a guide that recommends certain uniform standards for developers as well as standards for the *use* of tests.[3] These standards are intended to apply to

[3] Although published by APA, these standards are the collaborative effort of the American Psychological Association, the American Educational Research Association, and the National Council on Measurement in Education.

any systematic basis for making inferences about characteristics of people. The Standards make recommendations on six specific topics for developers and four for users.

Developers
    A.   Dissemination of information
    B.   Aids to interpretation
    C.   Directions for administration and scoring
    D.   Norms and scales
    E.   Validity
    F.   Reliability and measurement error

Users
    G.   Qualifications and concerns of users
    H.   Choice or development of test or method
    I.   Administration of scores
    J.   Interpretation of scores

The importance of the individual recommendations made in the standards is indicated by three levels: essential, very desirable, and desirable. We have discussed or will discuss many of the points made in the standards at different places in this text. Nevertheless, serious developers, selectors, and users of tests should review these standards with care. Most reputable publishers pay close attention to the standards in developing their tests and preparing their manuals. If the publishers have good data on the norms, reliability, validity, and other characteristics of their tests, they typically provide the information in the manual. If the manual does *not* have such information, it seems reasonable to infer that the test developer did not do an adequate job in investigating these important qualities of the test or that the data are such that the publisher prefers not to report them.

Cost

The cost of testing should be only an ancillary factor to be considered when deciding which test is to be employed. Other things being equal, of course, the teacher or counselor should select the test that will have the lowest per-pupil cost in terms of administration and scoring. However, the factor of cost should not be a primary factor in selecting test A over test B. Validity, reliability, norms, an adequate manual, and the like are all more important than cost. Just as in any purchase, one test at 10 cents may be a good buy, while another at 6 cents may be too expensive. We should consider what we are getting for our money rather than how much it will cost us to provide an adequate and meaningful testing program in our school.

Format

Just as we should not judge a book by its cover, we should not judge a test by its initial appearance. Nevertheless, other things being equal, we should select the test that is most attractive in appearance and that is printed in clear type of a size appropriate for the grade level. In addition, if pictures or illustrations are used in the test, they should be of high quality. Too often we find tests used at the preschool or primary level containing illustrations that are fuzzy, hazy, and ambiguous. When the quality of reproduction is such that pupils might answer incorrectly because of the illustrations used rather than because they do not know the correct answer, it is advisable to find a better test.

SUMMARY

The major points of this chapter are summarized in the following statements:

1. Standardized tests are commercially prepared instruments for which administrative and scoring procedures are carefully delineated by the authors. Typically norms are provided as interpretive aids.
2. Standardized tests are classified as follows: (a) aptitude tests, (b) achievement tests, and (c) interest, personality, and attitude inventories.
3. Standardized tests serve as aids in instructional, guidance, administrative, and research decisions.
4. Test selection should be a cooperative venture by all the professional staff who intend to use the information.
5. In test selection, the first step is to determine the purposes for which testing is to be done.
6. The *Mental Measurements Yearbooks, Tests in Print,* publishers' catalogs, specimen sets, professional periodicals, and measurement textbooks are all fruitful sources of information concerning tests.
7. In selecting and using tests, one should consider the following characteristics of tests and test manuals:
   a. Availability of information
   b. Ease of interpretation
   c. Administration and scoring
   d. Norms and scales
   e. Validity
   f. Reliability
   g. Qualifications of users
   h. Cost
   i. Format

CHAPTER FOURTEEN

Standardized Aptitude Measures

This chapter is divided into six major sections. An introductory section covers (1) definitions of intelligence, (2) the structure of intelligence, (3) the etiology of intelligence, (4) the stability of intelligence, (5) intelligence versus aptitude, (6) aptitude versus achievement tests, and (7) the classification of aptitude tests. The second section introduces the reader to some individually administered intelligence tests; the third section covers group tests of general aptitude; the fourth, multifactor aptitude tests; the fifth, special aptitude tests. The final section is devoted to discussing some of the uses of aptitude test results.

After studying this chapter, the student should be able to—

1. Know some of the basic definitions of intelligence.
2. Understand some of the theories of the structure of intelligence.
3. Understand that both genetics and environment affect aptitude test scores.

4. Interpret the data on the stability of intelligence.

5. Compare the terms intelligence, aptitude, and achievement.

6. Know some of the more popular individual intelligence tests and recognize their advantages and limitations.

7. Know some of the more popular group tests of intelligence.

8. Evaluate a general aptitude test.

9. Discuss the concept of culture-fair testing.

10. Understand the desired characteristics of a multiple aptitude test.

11. Know some of the more popular multiple aptitude tests.

12. Evaluate a multiple aptitude test.

13. Recognize the existence of special aptitude tests and the purposes they are designed to serve.

14. Recognize some instructional, guidance, and administrative uses of aptitude test results.

INTRODUCTION

That the school should assist each pupil "to achieve the maximum of which he is capable" is a motto often heard in educational circles. But behind that simplistic well-meaning phrase lurk perplexing problems. How do we know what a person's capabilities are? Can we define *capacity*? Can we measure capacity? Does a person have a general capacity to acquire knowledge, or are there many different capacities, each specific to a given type of knowledge? Is capacity constant over time? If not, what conditions affect capacity? These are all relevant questions. Unfortunately, psychologists do not agree on all the answers. Nevertheless, for the past 75 years psychologists have been using various labels such as *capacity*, *intelligence*, *potential*, *aptitude*, and *ability* to identify a construct that appears to be useful in helping to predict various kinds of behaviors. The tests that have been designed to measure this construct (or set of constructs) vary considerably because test authors may not define a construct the same way or indeed may be talking about different constructs.

Definitions of Intelligence

In discussing definitions of intelligence it is useful to consider the common-sense, psychological, and operational or measurement definitions of the term. Most of us use the term intelligence in everyday language. We think we can differentiate between highly intelligent individuals and those at the opposite extreme. We make these layman's differentiations on the basis of the individuals' behaviors. If a person can time after time select an effective course of action under difficult situations, we are apt to conclude that person is intelligent.

Definitions of *intelligence* by psychologists generally fall into one or more of three categories: the capacity to (1) think abstractly, (2) learn, or (3) integrate new experiences and adapt to new situations. Some of the older, more common definitions of *intelligence* consider it as an ability or capacity (Binet & Simon, 1916; Stoddard, 1943, Terman, 1916; and Wechsler, 1944). Some (e.g., the Stoddard and Wechsler definitions) go far beyond what *tests* of intelligence actually measure.

A more recent definition is given by Cleary, Humphreys, Kendrick, and Wesman (1975, p. 19). They define intelligence as . . .

> the entire repertoire of acquired skills, knowledge, learning sets, and generalization tendencies considered intellectual in nature that are available at any one period in time.

Under this definition intelligence is not a *capacity*, but rather a *behavioral trait* that is dependent upon past learning. Cleary et al. claim that an intelligence test contains items that sample such acquisitions and that the definition is not circular since "there is a consensus among psychologists as to which kinds of behaviors are labeled intellectual" (p. 19). Although there is room for some debate about that last point, most psychologists would probably concur. The reason for potential debate is that intelligence is an "open" concept. That is,

> ". . . the number of activities legitimately characterized as indicators has never been listed—would indeed hardly be capable of being listed." (Butcher, 1968, p. 27)

(Even if we could agree completely on a list of behaviors, we might well disagree on how these are structured. In the next subsection we will discuss various theories on the *structure* of intelligence.)

Other more recent definitions would, like Cleary's, tend to emphasize acquired behaviors rather than ability or capacity. This is good in that it helps us avoid a "reification" of the concept. Intelligence is not something people have, like brains and nervous systems. Rather it is a description of how people behave.

The *operational* definitions of intelligence are those tests that claim to measure the concept. Operationally, intelligence is what an intelligence test measures. Though often scoffed at by people who do not understand the concept of operational definitions, this statement is neither meaningless nor bad. If a test samples the acquired behaviors psychologists agree can be labeled intellectual, then the test would be considered a *good* operational definition of intelligence; if not, it would be considered a *poor* operational definition. Although the various intelligence tests differ somewhat from each other with respect to what behaviors they measure, the correlations among the scores from such tests are typically quite high.

Recall (from Chapter 5) that a test describes or represents when items are similar to the behaviors we wish to measure. These tests that represent are either *samples* or *signs*—the former if the items are drawn from a clearly defined universe, the latter if not. Since intelligence is an open concept and the universe of "intellectual behaviors" is not clearly or totally defined, intelligence tests are *signs*, not samples. For tests to serve as signs, we need high construct validity, and the data gathered in the process of construct validation help us to understand the concept. The reading of this chapter plus the validity information in the technical manual of any intelligence test you are using will aid in your understanding of what is being measured by that particular test and how that information is likely to be useful.

In order to understand more fully the uses and misuses of the various instruments typically identified as intelligence or aptitude tests, it is first necessary to study briefly the various theories of the structure and development of intelligence.

Theories of Intelligence Structure

The formal movement in testing intelligence began in the latter part of the nineteenth century. Sir Francis Galton, an English biologist, began to apply the principles of variation and selection set forth by his cousin Darwin in relation to the measurement of physical and mental traits and devised many instruments for this purpose. He believed that tests of sensory discrimination and reaction time were estimates of intellectual functioning, and his tests were largely of this type. James McKeen Cattell, an American psychologist, also theorized that differences in sensory keenness, reaction speed, and the like would reflect differences in intellectual functioning. Cattell (1890) first introduced the term *mental test* in 1890. His tests measured such things as muscular strength, speed of movement, sensitivity to pain, weight discrimination, and reaction time. One of the major reasons that Cattell preferred these measures to what might be termed higher mental functions was that he was convinced these characteristics could be measured with more precision.

Whereas other psychologists such as Jastrow (1901) followed the leads of Galton and Cattell in measuring similar functions, Binet and Henri (1896) began their research by measuring such characteristics as memory, attention, and comprehension. In other words, they measured complex functions rather than the unitary characteristics (such as reaction time) previously employed. Although their research involved many different kinds of tasks, they conceptualized intelligence as a very general trait, defining it as the ability to adjust effectively to one's environment. In 1905, Binet and Simon (1905) developed the first individual intelligence test (the Binet Scale), designed to be a global measure of intellectual level.

Although many other psychologists have also conceptualized intelligence as a general characteristic, several opposing theories have developed. The controversy of whether mental ability can meaningfully be measured via a single score still continues. A variety of positions have been taken in the past 60 years (see Humphreys, 1967; McNemar, 1964; Resnick, 1976).

Spearman (1927) developed a two-factor theory, suggesting that intelligence is composed of a general factor (g) and many specific factors (s_1, s_2, . . . s_n). Using factor analytic methods, Thurstone (1933) developed a theory of multiple factors (f_1, f_2, . . . f_n), which led to his test of Primary Mental Abilities. Vernon (1961) suggested a hierarchical structure of abilities, starting with a general factor that is divided into two major group factors: verbal-educational and kinesthetic-mechanical. These major group factors are a little less general than Spearman's g, but more general than Thurstone's group factors. Under each major group factor there are minor group factors; and under each of these are specific factors.

R. B. Cattell (1963, 1971) has proposed a theory that suggests that intelligence is composed of both a fluid component and a crystallized component. The fluid component is the more general, and a person with a large amount of fluid intelligence would do many different tasks well. It is conceptualized as abstract, essentially nonverbal, and relatively culture-free mental efficiency. Crystallized intelligence is more closely linked to the culture or environment and represents one's ability to achieve in more specific tasks related to the culture.

Guilford (1959, 1967, 1969), in a structure-of-intellect model, postulated many factors of intelligence. He categorized these factors under three broad dimensions according to (1) the process or operation performed, (2) the kind of product involved, and (3) the kind of material or content involved. He then subclassified under each of these dimensions five operations, six types of products, and four types of content. Looking at the three main headings as faces of a cube, he ended up with 120 ($4 \times 6 \times 5$) cells within the cube, each representing a different aspect of intelligence. (See Figure 14–1.) Thus a person could conceivably be capable of divergent thinking on symbolic content when the product is an implication and not be so capable when the product is a transformation. Guilford claimed to have demonstrated empirically that 82 of the 120 different structure-of-intellect factors exist (Guilford, 1967). He argued that each factor should be tested separately and that tests giving a single score are somewhat misleading.

Although Guilford's model has received considerable favorable attention, most psychologists consider it to be of more theoretical interest than practical value. Just because the model is *logical*, it does not follow that tests could be constructed to correspond to every cell of the cube. And even if such tests could be constructed, they would not necessarily be of any value. Vernon (1964) and Hunt (1961) are both very pessimistic about the predictive value of any such tests. Hunt states flatly (p. 301) that tests of these highly specific factors have no predictive value in any situation.

Piaget (see O'Bryan & MacArthur, 1969; Pinard & Sharp, 1972) believes

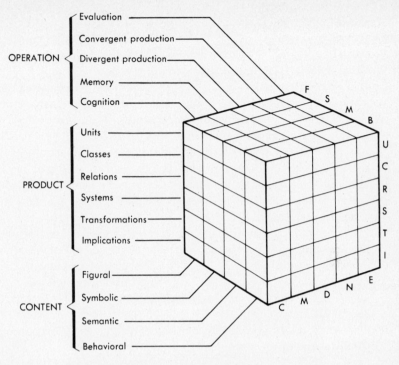

FIGURE 14-1 Guilford's "three faces of intellect." (Reproduced by permission of the author and McGraw-Hill Book Company from J. P. Guilford, *The Nature of Human Intelligence*. New York: McGraw-Hill Book Company, 1967.)

that a child's intelligence develops in sequential stages, each stage identifiable by ways of thinking. Piaget divides the evolution of thought into four major periods: sensorimotor (birth to age 1½ or 2 years), preoperational (from 1½ to 7), concrete operational (from 7 to 11 or 12), and formal operational (from 11 or 12 to 14 or 15).

Jensen (1968a, 1970a, 1973a) advocates a two-level theory of mental ability. Level I ability consists of rote learning and memory. It is the ability to register and retrieve information. It does *not* include any transformation, coding, or other mental manipulation between input and output. Level II *is* characterized by such mental manipulations, conceptualizations, reasoning, and problem solving. Level II is similar to the general factor (g) or Cattell's concept of fluid intelligence.

From the preceding discussion it should be readily evident that there are many different theories concerning the structure of intelligence.[1] Some

---

[1] We have curtailed this discussion drastically. Whole books have been written on the subject; many of the best known are cited in this text.

theorists believe that intelligence is a general attribute; others think that there are many different aspects to intelligence. However disconcerting it may be, one must accept the fact that psychologists cannot agree on the real nature of intelligence. While theoretical psychologists generally adopt the view that there are specific factors of intellect, most believe there is also a general factor. There are two primary reasons why many psychologists feel that the concept of general intelligence cannot be abandoned. First, whenever a whole battery of current cognitive tests is given to a sample of people, there results a set of positively correlated scores. This phenomenon of correlation among separate tasks is one of the most pervasive and stable findings of psychology and ". . . virtually forces attention to the questions of general intelligence." (Resnick, 1976, p. 7.) Second, a general factor of intelligence is the best predictor of future general academic performance. It is primarily for the latter reason that most practical psychologists are still very inclined to use tests of general intelligence.

The major point you should have gleamed from the above discussion is that psychologists are in considerable disagreement about the structure of intelligence (aptitude). As a result of this lack of agreement, there are a wide variety of tests that are often subsumed under the phrase *intelligence* tests (as we shall see later, *scholastic aptitude tests* is often a preferred term). They do not all measure exactly the same thing. A rather important implication is that when selecting and interpreting an intelligence test, one must be completely aware of the author's definition of intelligence.

Etiology of Intelligence: Heredity or Environment?

Because psychologists cannot agree on what intelligence is or how many intellectual factors there are, obviously they cannot agree on the etiology of intellectual differences. The score on any test of ability is a result of how well a person performs on that instrument at a particular time. An intelligence test measures acquired behavior. An acceptance of this statement does *not* rule out genetic influence. Being able to run the 100-yard dash in 9.2 seconds is also acquired behavior, but speed may in part be genetically based. Being able to throw a 16-pound shot put 50 feet is acquired behavior, but strength may in part be genetically based. Likewise, scoring well on an intelligence test is due to acquired behavior, but intelligence may in part be genetically based.

Ignoring for purposes of this discussion the possibility of chance errors, we must ask the questions: Why was that person able to perform as he did? Is the behavior on an aptitude test due to an individual's heredity or environment? Or does it really matter? For some purposes of testing, the preconditions affecting the test performance may not be relevant. If the purpose of a test is to use the results simply to predict some future behavior, then the question of the usefulness of the test is an empirical one. However, one seldom wants solely to predict. In fact, as stated before, educators are, or should be, in the business of attempting to upset negative or unfavorable predictions by changing the school environment. (This is not always easy, if at all possible.) If we are effectively to change our educational process as a result of the predictive evidence, then it may well be helpful to understand why a person performs as he does. For this reason, some understanding of the heredity-environment controversy is necessary.

A tremendous amount of research has been done in an attempt to resolve the heredity-environment controversy. Many of these studies compared correlations on intelligence test scores between identical or fraternal twins reared together or apart, and between other subjects hereditarily linked but in different environments. Erlenmeyer-Kimling and Jarvik (1963) reviewed 52 such studies, yielding over 30,000 correlational pairings. The average correlations of their studies are shown in Table 14–1.

Most, but not all, psychologists would interpret such data as being supportive of a strong genetic base for performance on intelligence tests. Without going into detail, it may be said that by far the most popular current opinion is that there is an interaction between heredity and environment. The original question, "Which one of these factors affects an intelligence test score?" was replaced by "Which one contributes the most?" This question, in turn, was replaced by "How do heredity and environment interact to affect test scores?" Psychologists do not as yet have the complete answer to this, and since the publication of a paper by Jensen (1968b), some have returned to the question of *how much*. Whether heredity contributes about 80 percent to the variance of scores on an intelligence test in the population and environment 20 percent, as some suggest, is hotly debated. (These estimates are called heritability ratios.) Schoenfeldt (1968) obtained estimates of heritability in his research as low as 0.26 and concluded that ". . . genetic components are not as large a proportion of the total variance as previously believed" (p. 17). The debates about heritability ratios arise in part because psychologists look at different

TABLE   14–1   Summary of Comparative Data on IQ Correlational Studies

CATEGORY	MEDIAN COEFFICIENT
Foster parent-child	.20
Parent-child	.50
Siblings reared together	.49
Fraternal twins	.53
Identical twins reared apart	.75
Identical twins reared together	.87

mathematical formulas in computing the ratios. We cannot delve into those problems in this text. We can briefly discuss some problems in interpreting these ratios. First, it must be emphasized that these are estimates of the proportion of total *variance* (see Chapter 4) of a trait (say, intelligence) that is attributable to heredity in a population of people. Such a ratio tells us nothing about what proportion of a *single* individual's intelligence is due to heredity, nor can that be determined. Jensen (1969a), for example, states this clearly, yet many of his readers misunderstand him and some (unfairly) take him to task for an incorrect position to which he does not subscribe. Since the heritability ratios apply to populations, they only apply to a particular population at a particular point in time. As social conditions vary, so should heritability estimates. For example, if all U.S. citizens lived in environments that were *equal* (not necessarily identical) with respect to their impact on intellectual development, then none of the variance in the intellectual differences could be due to environment; all would be due to genetic differences; and the heritability ratio would be 1.0. If our environments are becoming more equal, then the heritability ratio should be getting higher. Some environmentalists have trouble accepting this mathematical fact. They would like to have environments (with respect to impact on intellectual development) become more equal but hate to think of the proportion of variability as being increasingly genetic in origin.

Some individuals like to ignore the heritability estimates debate entirely. Since both genetics and environment contribute to our intelligence, and since they interact in this contribution, these individuals argue that it is pointless to talk about which factor contributes most. No one would suggest that the nervous system is immune from genetic influence. Likewise, no reputable writer would suggest that a person's environment does not at least partially influence his score on an intelligence test. Such things as severe malnutrition or extremely serious and prolonged intellectually deprived home environments, especially early in life, can inflict severe damage on intellectual growth.

One final point needs to be made. Many people seem to feel that it is better to accept the environmental side of the debate because it is more optimistic. If a person has a poor environment, we can change that and thereby increase his intelligence. If intelligence is genetically based, it is unchangeable. *Neither of the above statements is necessarily true.* Severe environmental deprivation can inflict permanent damage (see Ausubel, 1968, p. 246). And even if the damage were not necessarily permanent, it would not follow that we know enough about how to manipulate the environment to succeed in reversing the damage. Likewise, genetic does not mean unchangeable. A classic example is the low intelligence resulting from phenylketonuria (PKU), a gene-based disease. Special diets low in amino acid phenylalanine prevents the accumulation of toxic metabolic products in the brain, and intelligence can develop to a fairly normal level. Remember, high heritability of a trait should not be automatically equated with a low level of modifiability.

Social Class, Race, and Intelligence

In 1968 Jensen (1968b) published an article in the *American Educational Research Journal* entitled, "Social Class, Race, and Genetics: Implications for Education." In 1969 he published an invited paper in the *Harvard Educational Review* on the same general topic (Jensen, 1969a). These papers have caused more public controversy among educators and psychologists than any other two articles in recent history. The subsequent issue of the *Harvard Educational Review* carried rebuttals by other psychologists and a rejoinder by Jensen. The whole series of papers has been reprinted in paperback book form (*Harvard Educational Review*, 1969). Other recent references on this same topic are Block and Dworkin (1974a,b), Burt (1972), Cronin et al. (1975), Eysenck (1971), Gage (1972), Herrnstein (1971), Jensen (1970b, 1973a,b), Kamin (1974), and Shockley (1971, 1972). As Loehlin et. al. (1975, p. 3) point out, when questions on social class, race, and intelligence are examined in a society riddled with unresolved tensions in these areas, "it is not surprising that the result should be a massive polemic in which personal conviction and emotional commitment often have been more prominent than evidence or careful reasoning." It is difficult to discuss the controversy raised by the Jensen papers, especially in a brief space, without being misunderstood—and one certainly does not wish to be misunderstood on such an important and emotional issue. Yet, since the American public has been made aware of the debate through such popular periodicals as *Life, Newsweek, Saturday Review,* and *Time*, it seems that prospective teachers should have some awareness of the general argument and its importance. Jensen's original papers were scholarly reviews of the available evidence on causes of intellectual differences. He came to the conclusion that within the white race, the heritability index (i.e., the proportion of variance on intelligence test scores due to genetic reasons) is about .80. This conclusion parallels that of many other investigators, but of course is not accepted by all.

With regard to social class, most research shows a relationship between it and intelligence. Jensen suggested that "this relationship between SES [socioeconomic status] and IQ constitutes one of the most substantial and least disputed facts in psychology and education." He thinks it is likely that groups differing in SES would, on the average, differ in their genetic endowment of intelligence. Briefly, the rationale for this belief is as follows: If social mobility is in part a function of individual differences in ability, which in turn are in part genetically based, then status differences will tend to be associated with genetic differences. As Loehlin et al. (1975, p. 167) point out, this is not (contrary to what some people think) an assertion of hereditary castes as in an aristocracy. It is quite the opposite, since social mobility is the *key* to the genetic sorting-out process in each generation.

In general, the position on the relationship between SES and intelligence has not been attacked (Eckland, 1967; Gottesman, 1968; Herrnstein, 1973).

The more controversal part of Jensen's arguments is his position with respect to racial differences. Perhaps the clearest way to present his stance is to quote him directly.

> There is an increasing realization among students of the psychology of the disadvantaged that the discrepancies in their average performance cannot be completely or directly attributed to discrimination or inequalities in education. It seems not unreasonable, in view of the fact that intelligence variation has a large genetic component, to hypothesize that genetic factors may play a part in this picture. But such an hypothesis is anathema to many social scientists. The idea that the lower average intelligence and scholastic performance of Negroes could involve, not only environmental, but also genetic, factors has indeed been strongly denounced (e.g., Pettigrew, 1964). But it has been neither contradicted nor discredited by evidence.
>
> The fact that a reasonable hypothesis has not been rigorously proved does not mean that it should be summarily dismissed . . . the preponderance of the evidence is, in my opinion, less consistent with a strictly environmental hypothesis than with a genetic hypothesis, which, of course, *does not exclude the influence of environment or its interaction with genetic factors* [italics added]. (Jensen, 1969a, p. 82)

Some reactors agreed with Jensen, and some attacked his position with vigor. Many did not see how evidence on heritability could provide a basis for social or educational policy. Cronbach stated that Jensen ". . . does not see that, in writings for educators, it is pointless to stress heredity. The educator's job is to work on the environment; teaching him about heredity can do no more than warn him not to expect easy victories. Heritability of individual differences is not his concern" (Cronbach, 1969, p. 197).

Jensen countered this point as follows:

> I submit that the research on the inheritance of mental abilities *is* relevant to understanding educational problems and formulating educational policies. For one thing, it means that we take individual differences more seriously than regarding them as superficial, easily changed manifestations of environmental differences. (Jensen, 1969a, p. 239)

Anastasi (1973), who leans toward the environmental position, agrees with Jensen on the *importance* of the topic.

> It is only through a clear understanding of the operations of hereditary and environmental factors in behavior development that we can contribute toward effective decisions for the individual and for society. (p. 9)

As the controversy widened (Jensen has referenced 117 critiques and comments on his original article), Jensen (and others who supported his view) became the target of a variety of political and personal abuse (see Jensen

1973b). In the process of responding to his tormentors as well as the professional critiques, Jensen continued studying and writing. By 1973 he was willing to take a much firmer stand:

> In view of all the most relevant evidence which I have examined, the most tenable hypothesis, in my judgment, is that genetic, as well as environmental, differences are involved in the average disparity between American Negroes and whites in intelligence and educability, as here defined. All the major facts would seem to be comprehended quite well by the hypothesis that something between one-half and three-fourths of the average IQ difference between American Negroes and whites is attributable to genetic factors, and the remainder to environmental factors and their interaction with the genetic differences. (Jensen, 1973b, p. 358)

Clearly one does not need to accept Jensen's views. Indeed probably most psychologists do not. For those of you interested in exploring current opinions on this topic further we refer you to Loehlin et al. (1975). Several reviewers have considered it one of the most comprehensive and balanced reviews of the race and intelligence issue ever published. Their "final" conclusions are as follows:

1. Observed average differences in the scores of members of different U.S. racial-ethnic groups on intellectual-ability tests probably reflect in part inadequacies and biases in the tests themselves, in part differences in environmental conditions among the groups, and in part genetic differences among the groups. It should be emphasized that these three factors are not necessarily independent, and may interact.
2. A rather wide range of positions concerning the relative weight to be given these three factors can reasonably be taken on the basis of current evidence, and a sensible person's position might well differ for different abilities, for different groups, and for different tests.
3. Regardless of the position taken on the relative importance of these three factors, it seems clear that the differences among individuals *within* racial-ethnic (and socioeconomic) groups greatly exceed in magnitude the average differences between such groups. (Loehlin et al., 1975, p. 239)

They follow these conclusions by what they believe to be severe social and public policy implications. Two of these are as follows:

1. Given the large overlap in ability distributions, it would be both unjust and incorrect to label individual members of one group as inferior to members of another.
2. Although measured intelligence is an important variable, we must always remember that it is very far from being all-important in determining

what life will be like for most persons in the United States at the present time. It is easy to make too much of these differences—whatever their origin.

There is a great deal of *incontestable* evidence to demonstrate that there is a considerable overlap between groups. Jensen himself argues strongly that his paper is concerned only with group differences. Every psychologist knows that we *cannot* draw *any* definite conclusions about an individual's intelligence on the basis of his race or socioeconomic class. Unfortunately, some individuals, including teachers, do this, but hopefully readers of this book will not be among those. A wider discussion of how this problem affects testing and what steps have been taken to attempt to adjust for cultural differences is found in a later section (Culture-Fair Tests) and in Chapter 19.

Stability of Intelligence

Because intelligence is now generally considered to be influenced by both heredity and environment, it logically follows that as a person's environment changes, so might his intelligence—or so at least might his score on an intelligence test, which is an operational definition of intelligence.

The extent to which intelligence is a stable or variable construct is very important. If there were no stability to intelligence test scores, then the test would be a useless instrument. On the other hand, if intelligence test scores were completely stable, then we might adopt fatalistic attitudes concerning a student's educational prognosis.

Research findings[2] suggest that intelligence test scores are very unstable during the early years of a person's life. Bayley (1949), for example, found no relationship between intelligence measured at age 1 and age 17. Generally, preschool tests administered after the age of 2 years have moderate validity in predicting subsequent intelligence test performance, but infant tests have almost none (see, for example, McCall, Hogarty, & Hurlburt, 1972).

Certainly the tested intelligence of children under four years old is quite unstable.[3] It is hard to know whether this instability is primarily caused by imprecise measuring instruments, trait instability, or both. With increased age, the stability of intelligence test performance increases rapidly. Bayley (1949) found a correlation of .71 between mental age at age 4 and at age 17. "This justifies our taking preschool IQ's seriously" (Cronbach, 1970a, p. 231). In general, longitudinal studies have suggested that intelligence is a fairly stable characteristic after age 5. Bayley (1949) found the correlations between

[2] See for example Bloom (1964, pp. 52-94) and McCall, Appelbaum, and Hogarty, (1973) for excellent reviews of the longitudinal research.

[3] Data such as these have led one colleague to suggest that the best estimate we can obtain of a young child's intelligence is to take the average of his parents' intelligence. One would not have to lean heavily toward the hereditarian position to make this statement. Familial characteristics may be just as much due to environment as to heredity.

intelligence tests scores at ages 11 and 17 to be +.92.

Most of the research on the stability of intelligence has used individual intelligence tests. Longitudinal research using group verbal and nonverbal tests shows that (1) below age 10 stability in group test scores is less than for individual tests, (2) verbal group test scores are more stable than nonverbal scores, and (3) after grade 7 there is hardly any difference between the stability of individual and group verbal tests (Hopkins & Bracht, 1975).

In spite of the reasonably high stability coefficients for groups of children, individuals may show considerable growth or decline in intelligence test scores. Honzik, Macfarlane, and Allen (1948) reported that between ages 6 and 18, the scores of 59 percent of the children changed by 15 or more IQ points. Studies such as this should impress upon us the fact that, although scores on intelligence tests are reasonably stable and therefore useful as *guides* in both short- and long-term decision making, scores can and do fluctuate, and permanent decisions (or labeling) should not be done solely on the basis of intelligence test performance.

Several books (see, for example, Engelmann & Engelmann, 1968) and a few research studies (see Pines, 1969) have suggested that through proper intensive early stimulation, one can succeed in raising the intelligence of children. One study conducted by Hunt reported that having mothers of disadvantaged children watch the administration of intelligence tests and afterward coach their children on the test items resulted in an average gain of 30 IQ points! (Pines, 1969.) One must be very careful about drawing any conclusions from such data. It may be misleading to both theoreticians and practitioners. Biehler offered the following analogy to help clarify the point.

> Assume . . . that a particular child has extremely poor vision. If you helped this child memorize the materials used in testing his vision, would you be improving his sight? With training he could pass the test with a perfect score, but would he see any better? What might happen if on the basis of the test the child was placed in a situation in which he had to have perfect vision? Would he be able to perform satisfactorily? Or would it make more sense to get an *accurate* estimate of his sight and assist him to make the most of the actual vision he possessed? (Biehler, 1971, p. 447)

Ignoring the research where there is fairly direct teaching for the test, there is some evidence to suggest that a considerable change in environmental conditions is needed to affect a test score greatly after the first five formative years. This is one reason why there has been so much emphasis on programs like Project Head Start, "Sesame Street," or "Electric Company."

There has also been some controversy concerning the stability of adult intelligence. Wechsler (1955), testing a cross-sectional sample of adults, found that the verbal aspects of intelligence increase until age 30 and then begin gradually to diminish. However, his method of sampling was somewhat faulty because the educational levels of the various age groups were not comparable. The younger groups had a higher educational level than the older groups, and this could have accounted for the differences he found. Bayley (1955), using longitudinal evidence, concluded that there is continued intellectual growth until 50. A safe conclusion would be that general intellectual functioning does not automatically decrease with age. The environment of the adult may serve to increase or decrease his intellectual performance, but, barring health problems, the 50-year-old may well have as much intellectual ability as he had at age 25 (Jarvik, Eisdorfer, & Blum, 1973).

Intelligence versus Aptitude

We have not yet attempted to distinguish between the terms *intelligence* and *aptitude*. These two terms are used interchangeably by some; others suggest that subtle shades of meaning distinguish them. The distinctions have been made on two separate bases.

One distinction that has been made is whether the measure we obtain is considered a *general* measure. If so, the test frequently is called an intelligence test. If the test measures *multiple* or *specific* factors, then it is termed an aptitude test. Thus, we might conceptualize different measures of intelligence (aptitude) as lying on a continuum, with global measures falling at one end and specific measures at the other. At some point along the continuum we could arbitrarily change the label of the construct we are measuring, from intelligence to aptitude. Although this schema has been suggested by some, it certainly is not universally followed. It does present some difficulties because there are some tests, such as the Wechsler Adult Intelligence Test, that are considered measures of a general factor, yet report subscores.

Another distinction between the meaning of the two terms has a historical basis. During the time intelligence tests were first being developed, psychologists thought of intelligence as being an innate characteristic not subject to change. This assumption is invalid. However, the term *intelligence* unfortunately still carries to some the connotation of complete innateness. To avoid the implications of innateness, many test makers prefer to use the term *aptitude*. Because these aptitude tests are most useful in predicting future school success, some persons have suggested that the phrase *scholastic aptitude tests* is the most honest and descriptive. Other people prefer to refer to all such tests as measures of learning ability.

Authors do differ in their attempts to construct intelligence (aptitude) tests that are free from cultural and educational influences and which therefore supposedly measure innate ability more closely. Thus, some authors prefer the term *intelligence* to *aptitude*. However, these terms as used by authors certainly do not reflect the degree of success that test constructors have enjoyed in this endeavor. All test scores are influenced by both environmental and hereditary variables, regardless of whether the test is termed an intelligence or aptitude test.

In this book, both the terms *intelligence* and *aptitude* will be used. We will follow the general nomenclature used by the authors of the various tests. An author's use of a term does not necessarily reflect the position of the test on either the global-specific or innate-environmental continuum.

Aptitude versus Achievement Tests

Volumes have been written on the issue of the distinction between aptitude and achievement tests (see, for example, Green, 1974). To some psychologists the distinction seems clear enough; to others both types of tests seem to be measuring "achievement," and aptitude tests are only measuring one particular kind of achievement. There certainly is no hard-and-fast rule that allows us to distinguish an achievement test from an aptitude test by cursory examination of the test format. Further, both tests do measure behavior, and the behavior measured is, as discussed before, acquired rather than innate. However, aptitude and achievement tests do frequently differ along several dimensions. (1) General aptitude tests typically have broader coverage than achievement tests. (2) Achievement tests are more closely tied to particular school subjects. (3) Achievement tests typically measure recent learning, whereas aptitude tests sample older learning. (4) Studies generally show aptitude tests to have higher heritability indices than achievement tests. (5) The purpose of aptitude tests scores is to predict future performance, whereas the purpose of achievement tests is to measure the present level of knowledge or skills.

Although one is hard pressed to present definitions of achievement and aptitude that are acceptable to all people, the writers in general subscribe to the following definitions: *An achievement test is used to measure an individual's present level of knowledge or skills or performance; an aptitude test is used to predict how well an individual may learn.* However, it has often been said that the best way to predict future performance is to look at past performance. If this is true, and if aptitude tests are best able to predict future scholastic success, how do they differ from achievement tests? The common distinction that achievement tests measure what a pupil has learned (or past learning activities) and that aptitude tests measure ability to learn new tasks (or future performance) breaks down if past learning is the best predictor of future learning.

Thus, some people suggest that the difference is not in what the tests do but in the author's purpose and method of constructing the test. A certain achievement test may be a better predictor than a particular aptitude test for some specified purpose. If, however, the author originally constructed his test for the purpose of predicting future performance, then the test is called an aptitude test. If the purpose of the author is to measure recent learning, then the test is considered an achievement test, even though it may well be a very successful predictive instrument. This distinction also has some limitations because one would never administer a test solely to measure past learning. We always want to use tests to help us in making decisions. Decision making involves prediction. Thus, either explicitly or implicitly, achievement tests as well as aptitude tests are used to make predictions.

Aptitude and achievement tests are sometimes classified according to the degree to which the tasks within a test are dependent upon formal school learning. This distinction is a matter of degree. Some aptitude tests are more like achievement tests than others. As the test tasks become more and more dependent upon specific educational instruction, the test becomes more and more an achievement test. Thus, we have a continuation of the distinction between the terms *achievement* and *aptitude* on the innate-environmental continuum. Being more dependent on specific school instruction, achievement tests are more environmentally influenced than aptitude tests.

Cronbach (1970, pp. 281–283) suggested that aptitude tests can be arranged along a spectrum. Tests at one extreme are strictly measures of the outcomes of education—these resemble achievement tests in content and usefulness. Tests at the other extreme are those whose scores are fairly independent of specific instruction (intelligence tests). The so-called culture-free tests are examples of tests that are supposedly restricted to tasks where success is independent of differences in educational instruction. More will be said about these tests later. In general, the more content-oriented an aptitude test, the more useful it will be in predicting future school success in the *same content area*, but the less useful it will be in predicting general future learning.

In Chapter 6 we mentioned that publishers of some tests provide expectancy scores. These are derived scores that indicate the expected score on an achievement test based on a scholastic aptitude test score. Discrepancy scores are sometimes computed showing the difference between actual achievement and expected achievement. This may be useful for evaluation purposes. Publishers providing such scores should be using aptitude measures that are as independent of specific instruction as possible. Further, they need to explain carefully in their manuals the differences they perceive in the two constructs and the (typically low) reliability of the discrepancy scores.

In summary, several possible distinctions have been suggested between aptitude and achievement tests. If the author's purpose is to develop a predictive instrument, he will no doubt call it an aptitude test. If his purpose is to develop an instrument to measure past performance, he will call it an achievement test. For the latter goal the test items will be based on past school instruction; for the former goal that may or may not be the case. However, regardless of what an author calls his test, its uses may vary. Many achievement tests, like aptitude tests, are used to predict. This is ordinarily quite appropriate.

Classification of Aptitude Tests

There are a variety of ways in which aptitude tests can be classified. One type of classification is verbal versus performance (language versus nonlanguage)[4] tests. Although the terms *verbal* and *language* scales have similar connotations, performance and nonlanguage scales can be quite different. A performance scale usually requires the subject to manipulate objects to complete a specified task. (An example might be to fit together a puzzle.) Nonlanguage tests are those in which the subject is not required to use or understand the language. However, the subject need not be required to manipulate objects in a nonlanguage test. In spite of their differences, performance and nonlanguage scales are alike in that both are relatively independent of specific educational instruction. Test authors, however, do not always use these terms as appropriately as they should. In order to determine what a test demands, one should look at both the items themselves and the test manual, not only at the name of the tests or subtests.

For purposes of discussion, aptitude tests will be subdivided into four categories: (1) individually administered tests that give a general measure of intelligence[5] or (aptitude), (2) group-administered tests that give a general measure of aptitude, (3) tests that give measures of multiple aptitudes, and (4) tests that are measures of some specific kind of aptitude.

Often a person is looking for a single measure of ability that will enable him to make a general prediction about future vocational or educational success. Tests of general intelligence best suit this purpose. If one wants to make differential predictions, then a multiple aptitude test might be better. If one wants to predict success in a specific vocation or course, a specific aptitude test may be most appropriate. The next four sections will be devoted to a consideration of the four categories just mentioned.

INDIVIDUALLY ADMINISTERED TESTS OF GENERAL INTELLIGENCE

For the most part, educational institutions make use of group tests of intelligence. However, occasionally it is more appropriate to administer an individual test. All individual scales are valuable as clinical instruments. An examiner can observe the examinee's approach to problem solving, his reaction to stress, and his general test-taking behavior patterns, thereby having the opportunity to gain valuable information. Individual administration allows the

---

[4] Many consider *nonlanguage* to be a misnomer because mediation supposedly requires the covert use of verbal symbols. The use of nonverbal mediation, of course, is not what is meant by *nonlanguage tests*.

[5] The use of the term *intelligence* in no way implies that the authors of this book believe that intelligence test scores are solely measures of an innate characteristic. We know that is not true.

psychologist not only to observe more closely but also to control the behavior of the individual. This generally leads to more reliable measurement and a better understanding of the factors underlying the subject's behavior. Perhaps we should examine this statement more closely.

Control, as used here, has a positive connotation. One should control process variables such as the motivational level of the examinee. The outcome variables (responses) may also be controlled somewhat. However, this can be overdone. The amount of freedom a test administrator has in clarifying the questions so as to elicit the proper response is, appropriately, somewhat limited. When we suggest that individual administration leads to more reliable behavior, we are, of course, assuming that the test is correctly administered. Test scores could vary as a result of administrators' variability. However, administrators' reliability is high if they are correctly trained.

The most popular individual intelligence tests are the Stanford-Binet and the various Wechsler tests. These instruments, as well as examples of some infant and preschool scales and some performance scales, will be discussed in this section. However, because this book is designed to serve only as an introduction to standardized tests, these individual tests will not be covered in great detail.[6] Proper administration of individual tests requires considerable training. To be adequately trained, one needs a basic knowledge of psychology plus at least one course in individual testing with considerable practice under supervision.

Stanford-Binet

The present Stanford-Binet test is an outgrowth of the original Binet-Simon Scales. As previously mentioned, Binet was convinced that measures of simple sensory and motor processes were of little value as measures of intelligence. When Binet was charged with the task of identifying the mentally deficient children in the Paris schools, he collaborated with Simon to publish the 1905 Scale, which consisted of 30 tasks of higher mental processes arranged in order of difficulty. This scale was revised in 1908 and the tasks were grouped into age levels. For this reason, the Binet is referred to as an age scale. Thus, the score of a child could be expressed as a mental age. The test was again revised in 1911.

Although there were several American revisions of these scales, the one that gained the most popularity was the Stanford revision, published in 1916 (Terman, 1916). A second Stanford revision appeared in 1937, and a third revision in 1960 (Terman & Merrill, 1937, 1960). A new set of norms was published for the third edition in 1972. All three of the revisions followed essentially the same format. A series of tasks are designed at each of several age levels. For an average individual the administrator starts at a level just

[6] For fuller coverage of individual intelligence tests, see Anastasi (1976).

below the chronological age of the subject. He then works downward, if necessary, to lower age levels until the subject passes all the tasks within that age level. This is called the *basal* age. The examiner then proceeds upward from his original starting place to a level at which the subject misses all the tasks. This is called the *ceiling* age. An individual's total score (mental age) is computed by adding to the basal age appropriate weights for the items answered correctly up to the ceiling age.

The 1960 edition of the Stanford-Binet Form L-M (with its 1972 norms) is not really a revision but a combination of the best items of the two forms of the 1937 edition. It groups the tasks into age levels ranging from age 2 to superior adult. Between the ages of 2 and 5 the tasks are spaced at half-year intervals. From ages 5 to 14 the tasks are spaced at one-year intervals. There are four adult levels: one average adult and three superior adult.

Examples of tasks presented in the Stanford-Binet follow. Notice that emphasis is placed upon the knowledge of words and comprehension of written material throughout the test—especially at the higher age levels. The few instances of performance-type items are to be found at the lower age levels. In addition, scattered at the various age levels are tests designed to measure memory and ability to follow directions.

Year II

1. Three-hole form board: A 5-inch by 8-inch form board containing a cut-out square, circle, and triangle is shown to the child. The pieces are removed and the child is then asked to put them back.
2. Delayed response: Three small pasteboard boxes and a toy cat are used. While the child is watching, the cat is placed under the middle box. A screen is then placed in front of the boxes for about 10 seconds. After removal of the screen the child is asked to identify which box contains the cat. The procedure is repeated for each of the other two boxes.
3. Identifying parts of the body: The child is asked to identify various parts of the body on a large paper doll.
4. Block building: Using a set of 1 inch cubes, the examiner builds a four-block tower. He then asks the child to do the same.
5. Picture vocabulary: Eighteen cards with pictures of common objects are shown to the child. He is asked to name the objects.
6. Word combinations: The examiner is to note the child's spontaneous word combinations during the test. Two-word combinations such as *see man* are sufficient.

Year XIV

1. Vocabulary: This is the same as the vocabulary list for Year VIII. More correct definitions are required for passing at this level.
2. Induction: Six sheets of tissue paper are needed. The first one is folded once and cut on the fold, and the child is asked how many holes there will be when the paper is unfolded. This procedure is repeated for the next five

sheets, each being folded once more than the preceding one. On the sixth sheet, the child is asked to give the rule that tells how many holes there will be for the cut made on this sheet.

3. Reasoning: A reasoning problem (not mathematical) is presented on a card, which the examiner reads aloud while the child reads it to himself. A question is then asked to determine whether the child can reason through the problem.

4. Ingenuity I: Three "water jar problems" (where a child has two jars of different sizes and has to get an amount of water not equal to either size) are presented. The child is not allowed to use paper or pencil. Three minutes are allowed for each problem.

5. Orientation, Direction I: A child is given five sets of questions such as the following simplified hypothetical example: "You are facing north. If you turn left, what direction will you be facing?"

6. Reconciliation of opposites: The child is given five sets of paired words such as *big* and *small* or *fat* and *thin*. He is asked in each set to explain in what way the two words are alike.

Intelligence scores using the 1972 norms are computed as deviation IQ scores with a mean of 100 and a standard deviation of 16. In other words, they are derived scores (Dev IQ$=16z+100$). One can also obtain mental ages (MAs) for the Stanford-Binet. However, these are obtained using the same procedures as in the 1960 and 1937 editions. Thus, the traditional relationship between MA, CA, and IQ does not hold. For example, a child who, on his fifth birthday, achieves an MA of 5–0 would receive an IQ on the 1972 norms of 91. The rationale for *not* modifying the MAs with the 1972 norms was to maintain some continuity between the earlier and the present norms. However, this could cause some confusion among the users of the test.

By most technical standards, the Stanford-Binet is a soundly constructed instrument. Most of the reported reliability coefficients are over .90. They do, however, tend to be somewhat lower for the younger subjects. This test, like other intelligence tests, is most useful in predicting future scholastic success. The predictive and concurrent validity coefficients using such criteria as school grades and achievement test scores tend to fall between .40 and .75.

Perhaps the most limiting aspect of the test is that it is primarily a measure of verbal ability. The popularity of the test is indisputable. Thorndike (1975) reports that the test was administered to about 800,000 individuals a year from 1960 to 1972. The amount of research done on the Stanford-Binet can be attested to by the fact that Buros (1972, pp. 767–772) lists 986 references to professional journals and books regarding the test.

The Wechsler Scales

The major competitors of the Stanford-Binet are the Wechsler Scales. The first form of the Wechsler Scales, published in 1939, was known as the Wechsler-Bellevue Intelligence Scale. This scale was specifically designed as a measure of adult intelligence. The Wechsler Intelligence Scale for Children (WISC) was first published in 1949 and revised (WISC-R) in 1974. The original WISC was designed for ages 5 through 15, WISC-R spans the ages 6 to 16. In 1955 the Wechsler-Bellevue was revised and renamed the Wechsler Adult Intelligence Scale (WAIS). The Wechsler Preschool and Primary Scale of Intelligence (WPPSI) was published in 1967 and is designed for children of ages 4 to 6½.

WAIS

The WAIS (for ages 16 and over) is composed of eleven subtests grouped into two scales: verbal and performance. The six subtests comprising the verbal scale are as follows: information, comprehension, arithmetic, similarities, digit span, and vocabulary. The subtests of the performance scale are: digit symbol, picture completion, block design, picture arrangement, and object assembly.

An individual's score is based on the number of items answered correctly. For this reason, the WAIS is referred to as a *point scale*. (The items are not classified by age level, as in the Binet.) The raw scores for each subtest are transformed into standard scores with a mean of 10 and a standard deviation of 3. Thus, each subtest score is expressed in comparable units, permitting intra- and interindividual comparisons. Also, deviation IQ scores with means of 100 and standard deviations of 15 can be obtained for the verbal and performance scales as well as for the total. An interesting aspect of these deviation IQ scores is that they are obtained separately for different age groups. (This, of course, is always done for children's scales, but it is somewhat unique for adult scales.) The age 25 to 29 norm group performs better than any other group. Hence, adults in this age bracket must score higher (in raw score) on the test than those of any other age in order to receive the same deviation IQ. Computing IQs separately for different age groups was done intentionally so that, even if intelligence does decline with age, the average intelligence scores for each age group are equated. As mentioned earlier, however, it could well be that faulty sampling rather than a decline in intelligence with age was the cause of Wechsler's findings. Actually, the norm data of the WAIS has always been somewhat questionable. The norms are now somewhat out of date as well.

The WAIS is considered to give a very reliable measure of adult intelligence. The verbal and performance IQs have split-half reliabilities in excess of .93, and the total scale IQs have split-half reliability coefficients of .97 for the groups for which they were computed. The separate subtests, being quite short, have lower reliabilities. These range from about .60 to .96. Because the intent of Wechsler was to get a total or global measure of intelligence, he suggested that a profile interpretation of the scales for normal subjects would not be meaningful. There is some debate about the use of the subtest scores as clinical data.[7] Validity data are essentially lacking in the manual, although many studies support the usefulness of the test in predicting various criteria.

In general, the WAIS is considered to be a very good measure of adult intelligence, perhaps the best. It is, however, in need of revision. The item content as well as the normative information is somewhat outdated. A revision is currently in process. The revised WAIS should be published in 1979.

WISC-R

The WISC-R, which spans the ages 6 to 16, is a revision of the WISC, which was for ages 5 through 15. WISC-R follows the same format as the WAIS, giving subtest scores and verbal, performance, and total IQs. The subtests are the same as in the WAIS except that Digit Span is an alternate test (to be used if one of the other subtests is somehow spoiled during administration). Coding replaces a very similar Digit Symbol test and Mazes is added as an alternate in the Performance section. In administering the test, the verbal and performance subtests are alternated rather than administering all verbal subtests first.

The norms sample for the WISC-R was stratified on age, sex, race, geographic region, and occupation of head of household.

WPPSI

The WPPSI (for ages 4 to 6½) follows the same format as the WISC. There are 11 subtests, one of which is an alternate. Eight of these are downward extensions of WISC subtests. Sentences replace Digit Span in the Verbal section, and Animal House and Geometric Design replace Picture Arrangement and Object Assembly in the Performance section.

WPPSI has been standardized on a sample that includes 14 percent nonwhites. Its biggest faults are that (1) it is too difficult for the lowest performing 4-year-olds, and (2) the test is somewhat long for young children.

Comparison of the Stanford-Binet and Wechsler Scales

In terms of psychometric qualities such as validity and reliability, there is very little difference between the Binet and Wechsler scales. There are, however, some major differences between these tests. One of the major differences between the Stanford-Binet and the Wechsler is that the former is an age scale, whereas the latter is a point scale. Because the latest revision of the Stanford-Binet provides deviation IQs, there is some question of whether the work involved in building an age scale is really worthwhile. (See Stanley, 1960). An age scale is more extensive to norm. Most psychologists are in

---

[7] See Anastasi (1976) for a fuller discussion of the Wechsler as a clinical instrument.

agreement that point scales are preferable for adults. There is less agreement concerning which type of scale is preferable for children and young adolescents. However, many do prefer the age scale for children.

Another difference is in the norming procedure for adults. The Stanford-Binet was not designed to test adults. The standardization sample included only individuals through age 18. The WAIS was specifically designed to measure adult intelligence.

A third difference is that the Wechsler scales provide both verbal and performance IQs, whereas the Stanford-Binet provides only an overall IQ. Having separate verbal and performance tasks in the Wechsler tests makes it possible to obtain IQs for illiterates, individuals who have language difficulties, and individuals who come from impoverished environments (and therefore have a very limited verbal experiential background), by using the performance subtests. The Binet cannot be used for such individuals. In spite of these and other differences, however, the scores of the two tests correlate reasonably well. Studies show that the correlations between the various Wechsler scales and the Stanford-Binet are between .75 and .85.

Probably the most important points that educators should know about these two specific tests of intelligence are as follows:

1. They are highly reliable.
2. They are valid for predicting scholastic success.
3. The scores on the latest forms are derived scores with means of 100 and standard deviations of 16 and 15 for the Stanford-Binet and Wechsler scales, respectively.
4. One must be thoroughly trained to administer the tests and to interpret their results.

Individual Performance Scales

A test is called a *performance* test if the tasks require a manipulation of objects (for example, making geometrical configurations with blocks) rather than an oral or written response. This type of test is most helpful in assessing the level of intellectual functioning for people who have language disabilities. Those who speak only a foreign language, who are deaf or illiterate, or who have any type of speech or reading disability are unable to perform adequately on the instruments discussed in the preceding section. In some instances, then, performance scales must be used as replacements for other tests. It should be pointed out, however, that performance scales were originally conceived as supplements to rather than substitutes for the more verbally weighted tests. Some examples of performance scales are the Pintner-Patterson Scale, the Cornell-Coxe Scale, the Arthur Point Scale, the Cattell Infant Intelligence Scale, the Merrill-Palmer Scales (for preschoolers aged 2 and up), and the Leiter Adult Intelligence Scale. Although a variety of tasks can be, and are, used, some of the more commonly used subtests involve (1) manipulating small objects to form designs, (2) tracing and copying, (3) solving mazes or puzzles, (4) following simple directions, and (5) completing formboards.

Performance scales are most useful with young children and/or the mentally retarded because verbal tests are not very accurate for these groups. Although scales of this kind can be very helpful in assessing the level of intellectual functioning, they are not very predictive of immediate scholastic success, and they are seldom used in the schools.[8] If they are used, they should be given only by qualified personnel.

Infant and Preschool Mental Tests

As mentioned earlier, the measures of intelligence prior to age 5 do not correlate very well with the measures obtained at a later point in a person's life. This is not entirely due to imprecision of the measuring instruments. (Split-half and alternate form reliabilities of the tests used at early ages are reasonably high.) The low correlations between earlier and later testings of intelligence are also caused by the instability of the construct of intelligence from early childhood to adult and/or the nonidentity of the constructs being measured.[9] That is, the change in intelligence test scores may occur because the construct of intelligence is affected radically by environmental conditions; or the change may occur because the tasks on intelligence tests, being different at different age levels, actually measure different aspects of intelligence; or change may occur because of a combination of these and other factors that are continually interacting. Is, then, a change in score due to a qualitative or quantitative change in mental functioning? The question is a difficult one to answer, and the answer one gives depends in part upon which theory of the structure of intellect he accepts (see Stott & Ball, 1965).

Doing experimental research and armchair philosophizing on the reasons for the low correlations may be enjoyable and beneficial to the experimental and theoretical psychologists. Yet the practitioner has a legitimate point if he questions the value of early testing. Because early intelligence testing does not allow us to do an accurate job of predicting future development, the use must be justified on the basis of measuring present developmental status. That is, these tests are really similar to achievement tests, and their use must be justified, if possible, on that basis.

Because the nonspecialist will not be involved with infant testing, these kinds of tests will not be reviewed here. In terms of popularity, the Stanford-

---

[8] Performance tests measure abilities that are different from those measured by verbal tests such as the Stanford-Binet. Correlations between verbal and performance tests range from .50 to .80.

[9] Because the constructs measured at two different ages may, indeed, be different, many people would speak of the low correlation over time as a lack of validity rather than a lack of stability reliability.

Binet and WISC are two of the most popular tests for children under 6 (Stott & Ball, 1965). The WPPSI was not published at the time of the study referenced, but it has gained in popularity. The McCarthy Scales of Children's Abilities is appropriate for children from 2½ to 8½ years of age. Other tests used are the Columbia Mental Maturity Scale, the Bayley Scales of Infant Intelligence, the Goodenough-Harris Drawing Test, the Gesell Schedules, the Cattell Infant Intelligence Scale, the Ammons Picture-Vocabulary, the Peabody Picture Vocabulary Test, the Pictorial Test of Intelligence, and the Merrill-Palmer Scales.

A test based on the conservation aspect of Piaget's developmental theory of cognitive structure is the Concept Assessment Kit—Conservation. Most reviewers consider the kit useful for demonstrating Piaget's theory but not yet established enough to be considered more than an experimental test. (See Buros, 1972, pp. 810–813.) Students interested in more details on these preschool scales should check various editions of Buros.

Summary of Individual Tests

The field of individual intelligence testing is presently dominated by four tests: the Stanford-Binet, the WAIS, the WISC-R, and the WPPSI. These tests are technically sound and are useful both as predictors of future academic success and as clinical assessment devices. In comparing individual tests with the group tests to be discussed, we find that the major disadvantages are that individual tests are expensive to give and require a highly trained administrator. The major advantages are: (1) Individual tests are generally more reliable; (2) they are potentially more useful in clinical settings—a qualified administrator can learn more about a person from an individual test than a score indicates; (3) they can be used with individuals who may be unable for reasons of shyness, reticence, anxiety, or whatever to perform validly on a group test; and (4) although many individual tests are highly verbal in nature, they do require considerably less reading ability than most of the group tests to be discussed in the next section.

GROUP TESTS OF GENERAL INTELLIGENCE (Aptitude)

In educational institutions, group intelligence tests are used far more extensively than individually administered intelligence tests. They are much less expensive and generally give results comparable to those of the more time-consuming individual tests. Although in many schools the actual test administration may be performed by a counselor or someone else with special advanced training, most group tests are designed so that any teacher with a minimum of training (such as in-service training or a basic course in standardized testing) should be capable of the administrative task.

The first group intelligence test (the Army Alpha) was produced during

World War I when it became necessary to obtain a measure of general ability for one and a half million recruits very quickly. Because the Army Alpha required a reading level at about the sixth grade, and because many of the drafted men could not read at that level, the Army Beta was constructed. It was also a group test, but it required no reading on the part of the examinees. The directions could be given in pantomime if the subject could not understand spoken English.

The great demand for group tests can be attested to by the fact that within five years after the close of World War I, over 50 group tests of intelligence were in print. Although it is laudable that so many psychologists were willing to fill the need for group intelligence tests by providing their own, the hasty construction of some of these ill-conceived tests certainly did much in the long run to disenchant the public with psychological testing.

The distinction between verbal and nonverbal group tests that began with the Army Alpha and Beta has continued to this day. Many group tests, designed to give a measure of general intelligence, actually give scores on two subtests. These may be given such titles as verbal and nonverbal or language and performance scales. In considering the use of subscores, one must keep in mind the continuum from global to specific measures mentioned earlier. It is always hard to know just when to consider a test a measure of general intelligence and when to consider it a measure of multiple aptitudes. The classification is not solely dependent upon the number of subscores. (For example, the California Test of Mental Maturity has 12 subtests and 8 scores, and is classified in Buros as a general intelligence test. The Academic Promise Test has 7 subscores derived from only 4 subtests and is classified as a multi-aptitude battery.) The author's definition of intelligence and the method of constructing the test are primarily what determines the classification.

Most authors of tests that have two subscores such as verbal and nonverbal are really attempting to measure the same construct (general intelligence) with two separate procedures rather than attempting to obtain measures of two separate aspects of intelligence. Tests giving a whole series of subscores are typically attempting to measure different aspects of intelligence and are referred to as multifactor aptitude tests. These will be considered in the next section. We will discuss in this section the tests that are group administered and that are considered as measures of general intelligence even though they may report more than one score.

Besides differing on the general—specific and innate—environmental continua discussed previously, group tests are usually classified according to grade or age level. Some tests have different levels, each level being appropriate for certain grades. For school purposes there are advantages to using such tests. The same construct is being measured at all levels of the tests, and norm groups are chosen to be comparable from one level to another. This then permits one to compare measures obtained over a period of time.

It is impossible to review all appropriate group tests for each grade level. Because most group intelligence tests measure essentially similar skills (verbal and nonverbal), although they may employ a slightly different approach, we will discuss only briefly a few of the more commonly used tests. But first, one test, the Otis-Lennon Mental Ability Test, will be described in more detail so that the reader can ascertain some of the important considerations in selecting, administering, and interpreting a group intelligence test. Finally, there will be a short subsection on "culture-fair" tests. Prior to choosing any test for school use, it should be examined thoroughly.

Critical Evaluation of the Otis-Lennon Mental Ability Test

This thorough review should illustrate some of the important aspects to consider in test selection and use. The choice of the Otis-Lennon is not meant to imply that the authors of this book consider it the best test available. We have tried to point out previously in this book that a test must be evaluated in accordance with its intended use. No test is best for all possible uses. The Otis-Lennon is considered a technically well-constructed test, but so are many others. The Otis-Lennon has been chosen as a representative example of those well-constructed tests that cover a wide age range.

Grade Level and Content

The Otis-Lennon Mental Ability Test is designed for all grade levels from the last half of kindergarten through grade 12. There are six levels (with two parallel forms at each level) of the test, as follows:

LEVEL	APPROPRIATE GRADE RANGE
Primary I	Last half of kindergarten
Primary II	1.0–1.5
Elementary I	1.6–3.9
Elementary II	4.0–6.9
Intermediate	7.0–9.9
Advanced	10.0–12.9

The content of the Primary I and Primary II levels is identical. However, in the Primary I level, the pupil indicates his answer by circling an answer. In the Primary II level, the student shades in a small oval underneath his choice.

The Otis-Lennon was constructed ". . . to measure verbal, numerical, and abstract reasoning abilities. . . ." It is designed to be a predictor of scholastic success. The single score derived from the test can be thought of as an index of the verbal-educational component of Vernon's (1961) hierarchical structure-of-intellect model. There is no attempt to measure the second major group factor (kinesthetic-mechanical) of the model. The authors state that the test reflects ". . . a complex interaction of genetic and environmental factors. . . ."

Tables 14–2 and 14–3 show the breakdown of item types in the various

TABLE 14–2   Number and Percent of Items, Classified by Type, in Each Form of Otis-Lennon Primary I, Primary II, and Elementary I Levels

ITEM TYPE	PRIMARY I AND II LEVELS		ELEMENTARY I LEVEL	
	Number	Percent	Number	Percent
Pictorial/geometric classification	23	42	20	25
Pictorial/geometric analogies	0	0	20	25
Following directions	6	11	9	11
Quantitative reasoning	10	18	11	14
Picture vocabulary and general information	16	29	20	25
Total	55	100	80	100

Source: Taken from *Otis-Lennon Technical Handbook*, p. 10. (Reproduced by permission of Harcourt Brace Jovanovich, Inc., copyright 1969.)

levels of the Otis-Lennon. The items in the first three levels require no reading ability. Items similar to those found in the Primary I and II levels are shown in Figure 14–2. In each of the items in Part I or these two levels, the student is to mark the picture that is different. For the items in Part II, the student is to mark the picture according to the specific instructions read by the test administrator. Items similar to those in the higher levels are shown in Figure 14–3.

A reading-level analysis has been performed for the three higher levels. (This was not necessary for the three lower levels because they require no reading ability.) In general, the results suggest that the tests are not heavily dependent upon reading skill, although it is recommended that youngsters falling below a second-grade reading level should not take the Elementary II level (designed for grades 4 to 6.9).

Administration

DIRECTIONS   Each level of the Otis-Lennon has a manual for administration accompanying the test (the same manual is used for the last three levels). Separate specific directions are given, depending on whether the answers are to be marked in the test booklet (the only option at the Primary Levels) or on a separate answer card or sheet. All directions are clear and concise. For the first three levels the directions for each item are read orally by the examiner. No reading ability is required of the examinee. For the three highest levels, only the general directions are read. There is little doubt

TABLE 14–3 Number and Percent of Items, Classified by Type, in Each Form of Otis-Lennon Elementary II, Intermediate, and Advanced Levels

ITEM TYPE	ELEMENTARY II LEVEL		INTERMEDIATE LEVEL		ADVANCED LEVEL	
	Number	Percent	Number	Percent	Number	Percent
Verbal Comprehension	20	25	20	25	25	31
Synonym-definition	8		8		9	
Opposites	6		6		12	
Sentence completion	3		3		3	
Scrambled sentences	3		3		1	
Verbal Reasoning	32	40	32	40	25	31
Word-letter matrix	4		4		3	
Verbal analogies	15		15		13	
Verbal classification	4		4		0	
Inference	6		6		5	
Logical selection	3		3		4	
Figural Reasoning	15	19	15	19	15	19
Figure analogies	7		7		5	
Series completion	4		4		5	
Pattern matrix	4		4		5	
Quantitative Reasoning	13	16	13	16	15	19
Number series	7		7		7	
Arithmetic reasoning	6		6		8	
Total	80	100	80	100	80	100

SOURCE: Taken from *Otis-Lennon Technical Handbook*, p. 11. (Reproduced by permission of Harcourt Brace Jovanovich, Inc., copyright 1969.)

but that a typical teacher would be capable of administering the test correctly, provided the instructions are read carefully prior to the actual administration.

TIME LIMITS   For the Primary I and II levels, about 20 minutes actual testing time (30–35 minutes total testing time counting distributing materials and other preparation). For the Elementary I level, about 37 minutes testing time (55–60 minutes total). All three lowest levels are to be administered in two sittings—supposedly on the same day but not during the same half-day. (Of course, this is impossible for kindergarten students who attend only half-day sessions.)

Part I. Classification (The child must decide which picture does not belong with the others by abstracting the principle involved.)

(Pictorial)

(Geometric)

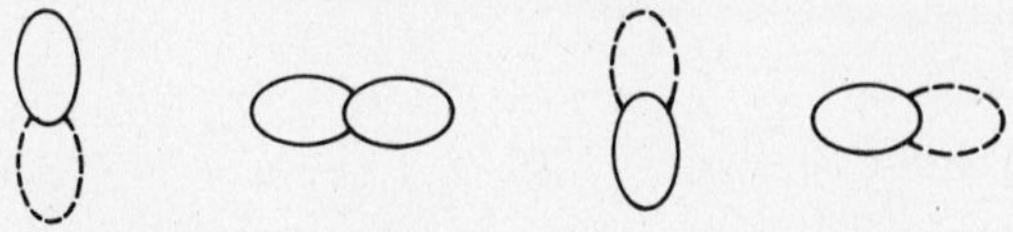

Part II. Verbal Conceptualization

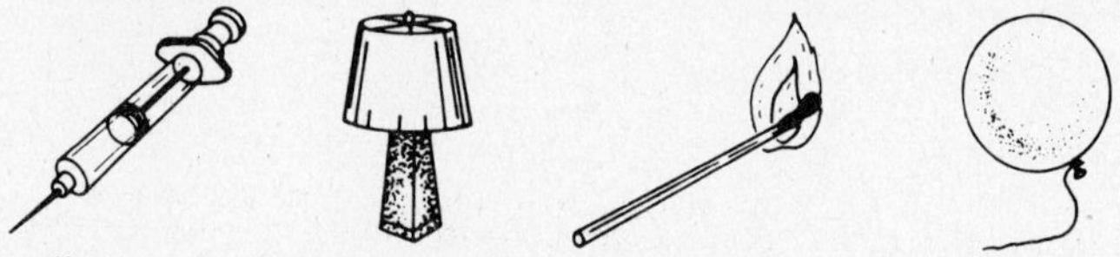

Direction to Pupils: Mark the picture that shows a *flame*.

Quantitative Reasoning

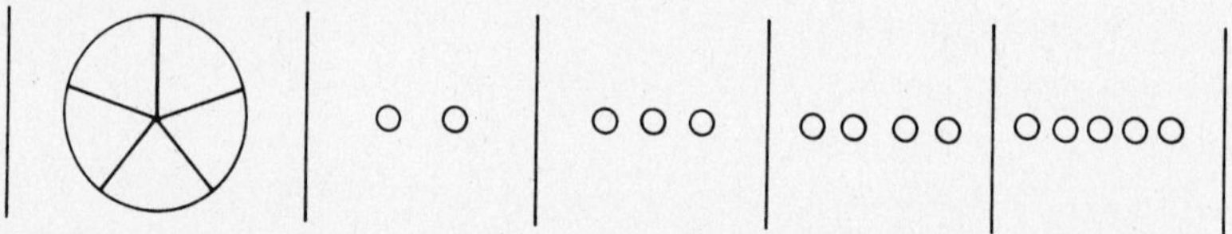

(Dictated orally) Look at the circle that has been cut into parts. Mark the picture that shows the same number of dots as there are parts in the circle.

General Information

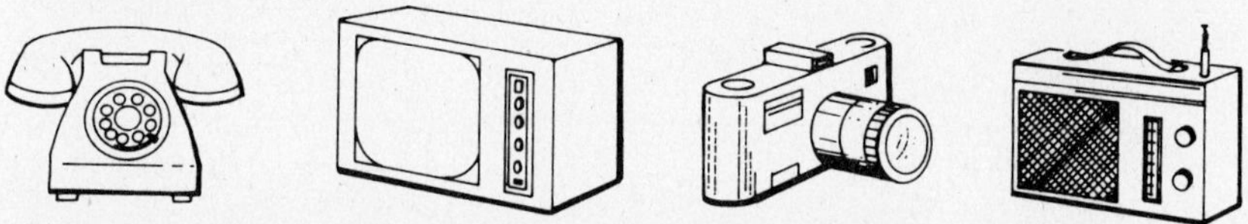

Direction to Pupils: Mark the picture of the thing we talk into.

Following Directions

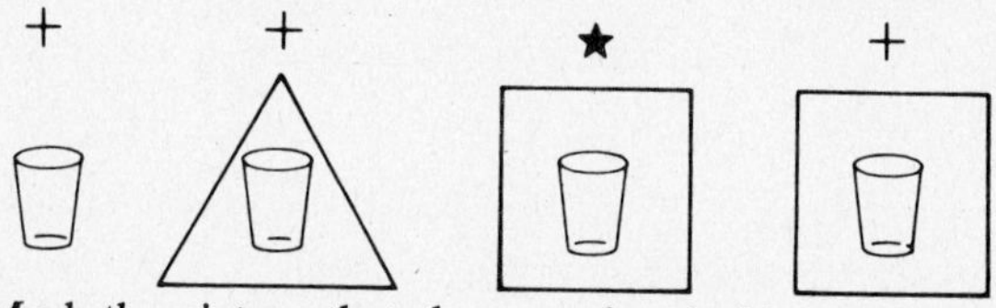

Direction to Pupils: Mark the picture that shows a glass inside a square with a cross on top.

FIGURE 14-2 Specimen items for Otis-Lennon Mental Ability Test, Primary I and II Levels. (Reproduced by permission of Harcourt Brace Jovanovich, Inc., copyright 1966, 1967.)

Verbal Reasoning   *Correct Response*

Which word below does *not* go with the others?

a—red b—green c—dark d—blue   (c)

Quantitative Reasoning

Which number is missing in this series?

1   2   ?   4   5   6   7

a—1 b—3 c—4 d—8   (b)

(Dictated orally) Look at the circle that has been cut into parts. Mark the picture that shows the same number of dots as there are parts in the circle.

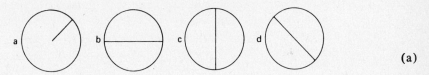

                 a   b   c   d   (d)

Figural Reasoning

Which picture does not belong with the others?

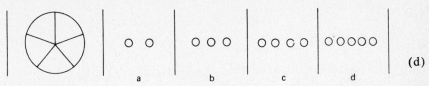

(a)

(b)

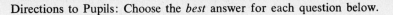

(a)

FIGURE 14–3   Specimen items for Otis-Lennon Mental Ability Test. (Reproduced by permission of Harcourt-Brace Jovanovich, Inc., copyright 1966, 1967.)

For the three highest levels, the testing time is 40 minutes (45–50 minutes total). The testing time appears to be ample. A special study showed that mean IQs were only about 1.8 points higher for students who took as long as they wished on the test. Correlations between timed and untimed administrations were above .98.

Scoring

The Primary I level must be hand-scored. The Primary II and Elementary I level booklets can be either hand-scored or machine-scored by the Measurement Research Center in Iowa City. The test booklets for the three highest levels must be hand-scored. The answer sheets may be scored by either hand or machine.

Types of Scores

The following derived scores can be obtained:

A. *By Age*

    1. Deviation IQs (normalized) with a mean of 100 and a standard deviation of 16. Provided for three-month intervals.
    2. Percentile ranks and stanines derived from the DIQ scores.
    3. Mental age equivalents (the median level performance of pupils of a given chronological age) provided for the three lowest levels. Appropriate interpretive cautions are mentioned in the administrator's manual.

B. *By Grade*

    1. Percentile ranks and stanines. Algebraically not empirically developed by interpolation for two different times of the school year. Available for testing one-half year above or below the grade range typical for a given level.

The meaning of the scores is quite well described in the administrator's manual. There is a section contrasting age and grade norms. All the scores mentioned above can be obtained through the basic HBJ scoring service. If requested, DIQs will be suppressed and will *not* appear on the HBJ report.

Norming

The standardization sample was selected to be representative of the entire United States educational system. The basic sampling unit was the school system. School systems were stratified on the basis of (1) enrollment; (2) type, that is, public, private, church related; (3) a socioeconomic index; and (4) geographic region. The final norms were based on roughly 200,000 pupils in 117 school systems from all 50 states. The weighted sample was very representative of the nation on the first three stratification variables. The North Atlantic region was somewhat underrepresented and the Southeast region somewhat overrepresented. A general conclusion is that the norming procedures compare favorably with other well-constructed aptitude tests.

Reliability

The reliability of the Otis-Lennon compares favorably with other well-constructed aptitude tests. The manual reports alternate-forms, split-half, Kuder-Richardson, and stability reliability estimates. Standard errors of measurement are computed from the alternate-forms reliability estimates. In addition, split-half reliabilities for school systems of varying size and socioeconomic level are reported.

Alternate-form reliabilities ranged from .81 to .94. (The .81 was for 5-year-olds.) Most of the estimates were above .90, the median being .92. The standard errors of measurement in DIQ points averaged about 6.0 for ages 5 to 9 and about 4.3 for ages 10 through 17. The median split-half reliability was .95 and the median K-R 20 was .94. Correlations between scores on the Otis-Lennon administered one year apart ranged from .80 to .94, the median being .87. Split-half reliabilities for special subsamples based on school system enrollment and socioeconomic level indicate little difference in reliability estimates for these different subgroups.

Validity

The technical manual devotes 16 pages (including 27 tables) to a discussion of the validity evidence on the Otis-Lennon. The discussion is organized under the categories of content, criterion-related, and construct validity. Under the section on content validity the authors state that the test measures facility in dealing with abstract concepts presented in verbal, figural, or symbolic form. From looking at the items and the breakdown of item types given in Tables 14–2 and 14–3, it appears that the tasks do represent what the authors claim they are measuring. Some might argue that this is really face validity rather than content validity. However, since they define aptitude as the ability to do these tasks, we feel that content validity is demonstrated.

Criterion-related validity evidence is based on studies showing the correlation of the Otis-Lennon with achievement tests and school grades. The bulk of the coefficients were in the .70s. Correlations with teacher grades fall within the .50 to .70 range in grades 1–8 and the .30 to .50 range at the high school level.

Construct validity evidence is based on studies showing the correlations between the Otis-Lennon and some readiness and many different aptitude tests. Most of these correlations are in the range of .70 to .90.

In summarizing the validity aspects of the Otis-Lennon, we feel it has as much evidence for its validity as most other group aptitude tests.

Format

The format of the tests is quite good. The test booklets for the first three levels are particularly pleasing. There could have been a bit more space between the questions in the three highest levels, but it is not so crowded as to confuse the students. The manuals (administrative and technical) are easy to follow and are written at such a level that teachers with a "one-course background" in tests and measurement should be able to understand them.

Interpretation and Use

In discussing uses of the Otis-Lennon, we will discuss only some of its more unique characteristics, not all the uses to which general aptitude tests can be put. They will be discussed in a later section.

First, we must commend the authors on the cautions they have mentioned in the manual. They stress again and again that the tests do *not* measure innate capacity and that test scores can and do change across time. They also clearly state that the assessment of mental ability rests upon the basic assumptions that all pupils have had equal opportunity to learn the types of things included in the test and are equally motivated while taking the test. They readily admit that these assumptions may not hold for youngsters who have experienced severe cultural deprivation. If the Otis-Lennon test is misused, it will hardly be the fault of the authors of the test manual.

A second aspect of the Otis-Lennon, related to interpretation and use, is that the various levels are equated via a scaled-score procedure so that students scoring almost at the top or bottom of a test can be administered the one at the next highest or lowest level.

Summary of the Otis-Lennon

This fairly thorough review of the Otis-Lennon was presented as an example of some of the aspects you should consider in choosing a group general aptitude test. The Otis-Lennon compares well with other tests of the same type.

Primary and Elementary Level (Grades K-8) Group Intelligence Tests

Although some individually administered tests attempt to measure the intelligence of very young children, group tests should ordinarily not be used for children under 5 (preschool children). Children of this age have difficulty following the detailed directions necessary for group-testing procedures and need individual supervision. For 5- and 6-year-olds, group testing is feasible, but it is necessary to keep the number within a group as small as possible. It is suggested that one not attempt to administer tests at the primary level to groups of more than 12 to 15 children.

Actually there is some difference of opinion on whether or not it is worthwhile to give intelligence tests to children in the very early grades. If only a few individuals are to be tested for specific reasons, individual intelligence tests are often used. As discussed earlier, the long-range reliability (stability) of these tests for young children leaves much to be desired. For this reason it is debatable just how useful the scores can be. Some persons, for example, argue that such measures can be helpful to the teachers in grouping their students. Others feel that any grouping should be very flexible and that scores on an intelligence test only serve the ill-advised purpose of making educators' decisions too rigid at this early school level. Decisions about grouping should be flexible. Using test information need not contradict this principle.

At any rate, there are several group tests that are appropriate for these early grade levels. These tests require little reading or writing on the part of the student. Responses are marked directly on the test booklets because it is difficult for young children to use separate answer sheets. Most of the items are of the type that require the student to mark the correct picture.

Tests at the elementary level (grades 4–8) give more stable results and are therefore more useful than primary level group tests. The tasks in these higher levels are generally more verbal in nature. All the tests mentioned below, except the Boehm, contain levels suitable for the elementary grades.

Examples of Primary and Elementary Level (K-8) Group Intelligence Tests[10]

ANALYSIS OF LEARNING POTENTIAL (ALP)   Harcourt Brace and Jovanovich, Inc., 1970. One form. Five levels: grades 1, 2–3, 4–6, 7–9, and 10–12. Two scores derived from the same total raw score: The Index of Learning Potential (ILP), which is expressed as percentile ranks and stanines based on age comparisons; and a General Composite Standard Score (GCSS), which is expressed as percentile ranks and stanines based on grade comparisons. For grades 4–12 a Reading Mathematics Composite Prognostic Differential score is available (this is a difference score between reading and mathematics).

Evidently conceptualized by the authors as something different from the traditional aptitude tests, the ALP is advertised as going "Beyond the IQ," "Not another mental ability test," and as "New wine in a new bottle." Re-

---

[10] Many of the tests described here also have appropriate levels through grade 12.

viewers are skeptical. It is considered to be a good test, but nothing so drastically new. Jensen (1972, p. 622) stated that ". . . the ALP measures nothing new. . . . It is old wine in a new bottle. But the old wine is excellent and the new bottle is indeed attractive." Cronbach (1972) and Jensen (1972) reviewed the ALP and found the title misleading and objectionable: It is not an "analysis" of anything, and is not a measure of learning potential (ability) as typically defined.

Boehm Test of Basic Concepts (BTBC)   The Psychological Corporation, 1969. Two forms. One level: K–2. Test composed of 50 items divided into two 25-item booklets. Testing time is from 30 to 40 minutes. The norms are the percent passing each item, by grade and socioeconomic level.

This test differs from the traditional group test of mental ability, although Buros (1972) classifies it as such. The publisher's catalog classifies it as a readiness test (Psychological Corporation, 1976). One could consider the test a cross between an aptitude test, a readiness test, a diagnostic test, and a criterion-referenced achievement test. This test is a picture test ". . . designed to appraise the young child's mastery of concepts that are commonly found in preschool and primary grade instructional materials and that are essential to understanding oral communications. . . . The BTBC is designed as both a diagnostic and a remedial or teaching instrument" (Psychological Corporation, 1976, p. 58). The fact that this test supposedly can serve as a useful guide in instruction of specific content makes it somewhat unique among the more traditional aptitude tests, which are not useful in *specific* instructional guidance. For thorough reviews of this test, we refer you to Buros (1972, pp. 625–629) and Dahl (1973).

The Henmon-Nelson Tests of Mental Ability   Houghton Mifflin Company, 1972 Revision. Primary Battery (Grades K–2) and Form 1 (Grades 3–12). The Primary Battery has three separate subtests: a Listening Test (general information), a Picture Vocabulary Test, and a Size and Number Test. Instructions and test questions are given orally, so reading skill does not influence test performance. There are three levels (3–6, 6–9, and 9–12) for Form 1. The overlap provides a choice when testing in grades 6 and 9. For both the Primary Battery and Form 1 the manuals provide DIQs for each age group; stanines and percentile ranks of DIQs; and stanines and percentile ranks of raw scores by grade.

High School, College, and Adult Level Group Tests

Many tests have levels appropriate for students from primary through grade 12. Some are designed for even higher levels. When choosing a test for a certain age level, one should be careful to assure that the ceiling on the test is adequate. If, for example, one were to administer a test to a group of above-average high school seniors, it would be best to use a test that is designed for college students as well as high school seniors so that the test has an adequate ceiling.

Two tests, not mentioned above, that are particularly useful in predicting college success at the undergraduates level are as follows (they are discussed further in Chapter 18):

Act Assessment Program   American College Testing Program. Revised annually. High school seniors and college freshmen. Four tests: English usage, mathematics usage, social studies reading, and natural science reading. Separate score for each test as well as a composite score. Scores reported in a variety of ways. Scored by publisher. Publisher provides extensive score reporting and research service for a fee.

College Entrance Examination Board Scholastic Aptitude Test (SAT)   Educational Testing Service. Revised continually. Candidates for college entrance. Scores are reported on verbal, mathematics, and English. In addition, separate scores on the reading comprehension and vocabulary sections of the verbal test are reported. Scores range from 200 to 800. Scored by publisher.

The two tests often used for predicting success in graduate school are the Graduate Record Examination Aptitude Test and the Miller Analogies Test. Because these are of little use to primary and secondary school personnel, they will not be discussed here.

Culture-Fair Tests of Intelligence

Intelligence tests have often been severely criticized for their "cultural biases." However, this term has been defined in so many ways one can never be completely sure what the criticism means. There are three common interpretations of cultural bias. To some individuals, a test is considered culturally biased if different subgroups obtain different mean scores on the test. To others, a test is culturally biased if it measures different constructs (or achievements) for different subcultures. Still others consider the issue of cultural bias in terms of differential prediction equations and/or different selection ratios or success ratios (see Chapter 5). (The whole Spring 1976 issue of the *Journal of Educational Measurement* focuses on the issue of bias in selection procedures.) The various technical definitions used by those whose focus is on prediction/selection issues are themselves contradictory. Many measurement experts prefer this third type of definition, since it focuses on the fair *use* of tests rather than on the tests themselves. (See Chapter 19 for more information on the fair use of tests.)

Of the first two interpretations, non–measurement specialists who are critics of testing are more apt to use the first type of definition (e.g., tests are unfair to blacks if the mean score for blacks is lower than the mean score for whites). Measurement specialists are more apt to prefer the second definition: A test is biased if it measures something different in different subcultures. Now a test biased in the second sense will probably (but not necessarily) be biased in the first sense. The logic is considerably less compelling in the opposite direction. To clarify these points, let us use two examples—one of physical measurement and one of psychological measurement.

If we wish to determine how fast individuals can run the 100–yard dash, we may measure this by timing people on this very task. Now, if blacks obtain a faster mean time than whites (or vice versa), the measure is biased under the first type of definition. However, if indeed the task is measuring the same thing for both races, it is not biased in the second sense.

If we wish to determine whether first-grade children know the rank order of a set of numerals, we might ask a question such as: Which of the following numbers represents the least amount: 13, 17, 19, 21? If a lower percent of Chicano students answer the question correctly than whites, the test is biased in the first sense. Is it biased in the second? It depends. If both the Chicano and the white students who miss the question do so because they do not know the concept of ranking numerals, then the question is *not* biased in the *second* sense. If, however, some of the Chicano students and none of the whites miss the question because they do not know the meaning of the word "least," then the question *is* biased in the sense that it is measuring knowledge of vocabulary for (some) Chicanos and knowledge of the rank order of the numerals for whites.

Clearly the second type of bias is bad. It leads to incorrect and harmful inferences to assume that a child (or a group) is inadequate in one area when in fact he has been measured (unknowingly) on something else. Test constructors try to avoid building tests that will have such biases. Research evidence (Jensen, 1976) would tend to indicate that publishers are generally quite successful in minimizing this type of bias, but they surely have not eliminated it (see Williams, 1974). (Publishers cannot build tests that are fair in the second sense for all possible uses/misuses. If one were to give an intelligence test in the English language to a child who spoke only Spanish, surely the test would be measuring something different from intelligence for that child! We can't blame publishers for such a ridiculous use or accuse them of building a culturally biased test.)

What about the unfairness of tests in the first sense—that is, of different means for different subcultures? We have already alluded to some difficulties with that definition, but it is nevertheless frequently used. Indeed, people have attempted to build tests that are "culturally fair" in that sense of the phrase. As already discussed, a person's environment (subculture) can affect his test score. People of different nations as well as people in different subcultures within the United States place different values upon verbal fluency, speed, and other aspects that influence the scores on intelligence tests. Suppose individuals in one subculture are less verbal than individuals in another subculture and that the test used requires verbal skills. Is the test fair to individuals of the first subculture?

Some people argue that intelligence testing is not fair to some groups. This argument is particularly set forth in the testing of the disadvantaged. Should typical intelligence tests be used with culturally disadvantaged? Or should we use tests that are culturally fair?

Psychologists have attempted in the past to develop tests that are free from cultural influences. Failing in this—for no test can be free from cultural influences—there has, more recently, been an attempt to develop tests that are equally fair to members of all cultures. Examples of tests of this type are the Culture-Fair Intelligence Test and the Davis-Eells Test of General Intelligence or Problem-Solving Ability. In attempting to achieve this cultural fairness, these tests have included tasks that involve nonsense material, or tasks that should be equally familiar or unfamiliar to all cultures. Figure 14–4

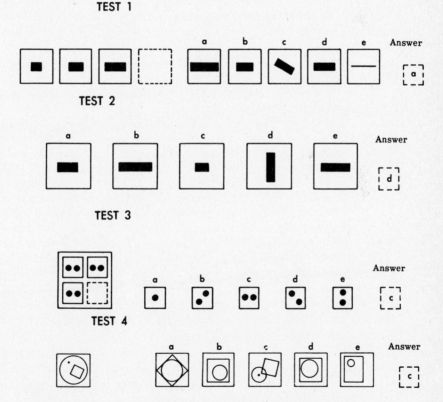

FIGURE 14–4   Sample items from Scale 2, Form A, of the Cattell Culture-Fair Intelligence Test. (Copyright © 1949, 1957, by the Institute for Personality and Ability Testing, 1602 Coronado Drive, Champaign, Illinois, U.S.A. All rights reserved. Reprinted with permission.)

presents examples of sample items taken from Scale 2 of the Cattell Culture-Fair Intelligence Test. Complete verbal directions are read to the subject so that he understands the task. These items do not appear to be unfair to any culture. However, the research evidence suggests that these tests are not culturally fair if, by this phrase, we mean groups from one culture score as well on the tests as groups from another culture.[11] It is very hard, if not impossible, to devise a test that will show no difference between such groups. (Contrary to what many critics believed, stress on verbal skills in our current tests is not the primary cause of group differences. Flaugher (1970) has cited a number of studies that show the greatest difference in the performances of blacks and whites is on nonverbal items.) Even if we could devise a completely culture-fair test, would it be a worthwhile attainment? Some argue yes. They say such a measure would be relatively independent of cultural influences and therefore as nearly correlated to innate ability as possible. Others argue that to mask existing group differences by eliminating all items measuring these differences is to delimit the usefulness of the test. Tannebaum, for example, in reviewing the Culture-Fair Intelligence Test, took the following position:

> In essence, then, it must be admitted that the long-pursued goal of demonstrating equality among national and international sub-populations on some measure of general ability has not been reached by this test. Is it, indeed, a goal worth pursuing? Even if it were possible to devise a test so antiseptic as to clean out inequality not only among sub-cultures but also among other groups showing differences in test intelligence, such as those classified by sex, age, education, geographic origin, body type, physical health, personality structure, and family unity—what kind of instrument would we then have? Since such a test must perforce be so thoroughly doctored as to omit tasks that reveal these group differences, or substitute others that show "no difference," what could it possibly measure? What could it predict? Covering up group differences in this way does not erase test bias. Rather, it delimits drastically the kinds of information one can gather about problem-solving strengths and weaknesses associated with groups as well as individuals. (Tannenbaum, 1965, pp. 722–723)

A somewhat different approach to developing a culturally fair instrument is a technique known as the *System of Multicultural Pluralistic Assessment (SOMPA)* developed by Mercer (1977). While the approach has much in common with some of the mathematical approaches to the fair use of tests, one can conceptualize the approach as a new measurement technique using a battery of instruments. The technique is used with children 5 to 11 years old and compares a child's score not only against a national norm group

---

[11] See the reviews in the *Fifth* and *Sixth Mental Measurements Yearbook* (Buros, 1959, 1965) of the two tests mentioned for substantiation of this sentence.

but also against the scores of children from a similar social and cultural background. Information for the assessment is gathered from two sources: a test session with the child and an interview with the child's principal caretaker, usually the mother. The test sessions with the child include administering the WICS-R, the Physical Dexterity Tasks, and the Bender-Gestalt test. Information obtained from the mother includes information on the "Sociocultural Modalities," which purportedly measure the distance between the culture of the home and the culture of the school, an Adaptive Behavior Inventory for Children, and a Health History Inventory. Using multiple regression equations based on the additional data, the WISC-R is "corrected." Mercer compares this correction to a golf handicap (Fiske, 1976). She feels that *uncorrected* scores should be used to determine immediate educational needs, whereas the *corrected* scores should be used to determine a child's "latent scholastic potential." Mercer wants to use the *corrected* scores to avoid labeling children as retarded and to use the *uncorrected* scores to make educational decisions. This may or may not work. Currently many states distribute special education funds on the basis of the number of children classified as retarded. Whether one can remove the label and keep the additional funding available for special educational needs is as yet undetermined.

The debate as to the usefulness of a culture-fair test or one mathematically "corrected" to equate for varying cultural backgrounds depends on how we wish to use the instrument. Some people wish to get a measure of innate ability (whatever that is) and argue as follows:

1. There are no genetic differences in intelligence among subcultures.[12]
2. Tests that are measures of innate ability will show no differences between subcultures.
3. Therefore, tests that show no differences between subcultures (or can be equated on the subculture) are tests that measure innate ability.

The logic breaks down in going from step 2 to 3. If A implies B, it does *not* follow that B implies A. We simply cannot (at the present time) obtain measures of innate ability.

Other people, who believe that we can never measure innate ability with a paper-pencil test, wish to use intelligence tests primarily as predictive instruments. If the environmental effects of one's culture are related to the criterion we are attempting to predict, then to eliminate these cultural differences would reduce substantially the validity of the test.

Paradoxically, there are a few psychologists and lay people who assert that tests are unfair to some subcultures and who also take the position that

---

[12] As mentioned earlier, this point has been debated by psychologists. However, there is certainly no compelling scientific reason to reject this assumption, and there are some good humanitarian reasons for accepting it.

all differences in intellectual functioning are due to environmental factors. Now, if there really were no genetic differences between people and if we used a measuring instrument that ruled out (or equated) environmental effects, then everyone would get exactly the same score on the test! Such a test would be completely useless. The question of whether we wish to build culture-fair tests is legitimately debatable, but only if we take the position that there are some nonenvironmental factors contributing to test performance.

Most measurement specialists take the position that if culture-fair tests could be developed, they would be in general less useful measures than the presently existing measures that are influenced by environmental factors. We will discuss further the testing of minority groups in Chapter 19.

MULTIFACTOR APTITUDE TESTS

As already mentioned, some psychologists contend that intellect is a general characteristic and that a single score can adequately represent the degree to which a person possesses intelligence. Others subscribe to a multifactor theory of intelligence, but argue that the measurement of these multifactors adds little, if any, to the predictive validity of single-factor tests. The advocates of multifactor testing generally support it on both theoretical and practical bases.

One of the early proponents of a multifactor theory of intelligence was Thurstone (1933). Using a statistical technique called multiple-factor analysis,[13] he found many different factors of ability and, in 1941, published the first multifactor test—the Chicago Tests of Primary Mental Abilities. (The name SRA Primary Mental Abilities has been given to later editions of this same test.) In the years since this early multifactor test was developed, the popularity of both a multifactor theory of intellect and the use of multifactor tests has grown. Many schools administer a multifactor aptitude test at some stage of a student's school career. What are the reasons for this popularity of multifactor tests? Is this popularity justified? What are the characteristics of these tests? What are their advantages and limitations?

The development of factor-analytic techniques was certainly the major technical development affecting the popularity of the multifactor theory. Rather than simply arguing whether intelligence is general, multifactor, or composed of many specific abilities, one can perform a factor analysis on many different kinds of ability tests. If only one factor is obtained, then we have some support for the theory of general intelligence. If many factors

[13] Factor analysis will not be covered in this book, other than noting that the intercorrelations between the tests determine the number of factors. If the tests are all highly correlated with each other, for example, then one would have only a single factor. If, at the other extreme, the tests do not correlate at all with each other, then we would have as many factors as tests. See, for example, H. Harmon (1960) for further discussion of this topic.

are obtained, this lends support to the multifactor theory. If one obtained as many factors as kinds of tests, this would support the specific aptitude theory.

Some of the multifactor tests have not actually been constructed through a factor-analytic procedure; rather, they have been constructed by choosing items that have high correlations with other items in the *same* subtest but low correlations with the items (and subtest scores) in the *other* subtests. This results in a set of subtests that are internally consistent but which have low intercorrelations with each other. This should be a major characteristic of any multifactor test. Of course, the use of test construction techniques to develop a multifactor test does not enable us to argue that obtaining a set of factors proves the actual existence of the factors within a person.

Another aspect that led to the increased popularity of multifactor aptitude tests was the vocational and educational counseling movement. The discovery of differential abilities within a person should certainly facilitate vocational and educational counseling. But does it? Some argue that identification of differential abilities will be helpful in counseling only to the extent that this knowledge allows us to differentially predict how well an individual will be able to perform in various educational curricula or vocational tasks. The degree to which multifactor tests enable us to differentially predict is an important aspect in determining their usefulness.

In general, the data indicate that multifactor aptitude tests are not very good for differential prediction.[14] This is not solely because of test inadequacies in subdividing intellect into its component subparts. The problem is that the criteria (for example, job success) are not solely dependent on specific aspects of intelligence. Thus, although we may be able to obtain measures of numerical ability and verbal ability that are distinct, there simply is not any criterion that differentially demands one aptitude and not the other. Therefore, there is little evidence of differential predictive validity.[15] Whether this makes the test no more useful than the less expensive and less time-consuming test of general intelligence depends on the degree to which one believes that a more precise description is useful in counseling, regardless of whether it increases predictability. As with any belief, there are differences of opinion on this. It is not a belief easily subjected to scientific verification.

Examples of Multifactor Aptitude Tests

Three of the most widely used multiple-aptitude batteries will be mentioned here. The Differential Aptitude Test, published by The Psychological Cor-

[14] See *The Use of Multifactor Tests in Guidance* (1957).

[15] Multifactor aptitude tests may increase in differential predictability as the more sophisticated analyses (such as multiple regression equations) are employed. However, to date, most of the validity evidence is reported using single correlations. Further discussion of this point is beyond the scope of this book.

poration, 1947–72, will be reviewed in some detail since it is used the most in the public schools.

Differential Aptitude Tests (DAT)

GRADE LEVEL AND CONTENT   The DAT has been designed for use in grades 8–12. There are two forms of the test (S and T), and each form has eight subtests: verbal reasoning (VR), numerical ability (NA), abstract reasoning (AR), clerical speed and accuracy (CSA), mechanical reasoning (MR), space relations (SR), spelling (Sp), and language usage (LU). The authors of the test also report a ninth score, VR + NA, which is interpreted as a measure of general scholastic aptitude. Examples of the practice items are shown in Figure 14–5. They are, of course, easier than the actual items in the subtests, but they are identical in form.

All the subtests are timed with limits as follows:

Standardized Aptitude Measures

Booklet I		Booklet II	
Verbal Reasoning	30 minutes	Mechanical Reasoning	30 minutes
Numerical Ability	30 minutes	Space Relations	25 minutes
Abstract Reasoning	25 minutes	Spelling	10 minutes
Clerical Speed and Accuracy		Language Usage	25 minutes
Part I	3 minutes		90 minutes
Part II	3 minutes		
	91 minutes		

Although all tests are timed, only the clerical speed and accuracy test is supposedly speeded. The manual suggests three alternative testing schedules (using two, four, or six sessions) so that the schools have some flexibility and can choose whichever schedule best fits their particular needs.

TYPES OF SCORES   Percentile ranks and stanines can be obtained for the eight subtests and for the combined raw scores on the verbal reasoning and numerical ability tests.

NORMING   The norm group includes more than 64,000 students from 76 school districts in 33 states and the District of Columbia. Separate sex and grade level (8–12) norms are provided. The testing of the normative sample was done in the fall. However, the authors also provide spring (second semester) norms for grades 8–11. These spring norms were obtained by interpolating between the fall norms of successive grades. The accuracy of these interpolated norms is debatable. It would be better to administer the test in the fall and to thus avoid having to use the spring norms. Special Catholic School Norms and Vocational School Norms are also available.

RELIABILITY   Split-half reliability coefficients computed separately for each sex and each grade are reported for both Forms S and T for all subtests except the clerical speed and accuracy subtest. Because this subtest is speeded (the others, remember, are timed but supposedly unspeeded), an alternate form reliability is reported. These reliability coefficients for the separate subtests range from .79 to .97 for boys and from .80 to .97 for girls. The mechanical reasoning subtest was the least reliable for girls, and the clerical speed and accuracy subtest was the least reliable for boys.

VALIDITY   The voluminous amount of validity data in the manual coupled with the authors' position concerning the importance of studies within each school system should serve as an impetus for such tasks as building local expectancy tables and prediction equations. However, in spite of such urgings, many educators unfortunately are apt to feel that with all that validity information there is no reason for them to conduct their own investigations.

The research on the prediction of course grades is summarized according to subject areas. English grades are best predicted by VR + NA and by the Language Usage and VR scores. Mathematics grades are best predicted by the VR + NA combination or by NA alone. Science grades can be best predicted by VR + NA, VR, NA, or Language Usage subtests. Social studies grades can be predicted about equally well, using VR + NA, VR, NA, or Language Usage subtests. The four major subject-matter areas can all be predicted with a fair amount of success. Median correlations (across all studies) between the best subscores on the DAT and the criterion course grades range from the upper .40s to the low .60s. However, all four major subject-matter areas can be predicted successfully using the same score: VR + NA. Thus, the *differential* validity of the DAT in predicting course grades is not very well substantiated.

The prediction of achievement test results follows essentially the same pattern as the prediction of course grades. Again, the subscores on the DAT are fairly good predictors, but they are not very adequate in differential predictions. The data showing the relationship between DAT scores and educational and occupational groups indicate the same thing.

The concurrent validity showing the correlation between the VR + NA score and tests of general intelligence reveal consistently high correlations. Their correlations, ranging mostly in the .70s and .80s, are as high as the correlations between most tests of general intelligence. Thus it certainly appears that the VR + NA score serves the same purpose as general intelligence test scores, and little would be gained by administering the DAT and a test of general intelligence in the same grade.

An interesting (and perhaps surprising to many) finding is the low correlations between the subscores on the DAT and the Kuder Preference Record scores. In general, interests and aptitudes are not highly correlated

VERBAL REASONING

For each sentence you are to choose from among five pairs of words to fill the blanks. The first word of the pair you choose goes in the blank space at the beginning of the sentence; the second word of the pair goes in the blank at the end of the sentence. When you have picked the pair to fill in the blanks, mark the letter of that pair on the Answer Sheet, after the number of the sentence you are working on. Here are some examples:

Example X.   ...... is to water as eat is to ......

A. continue —— drive
B. foot —— enemy
C. drink —— food
D. girl —— industry
E. drink —— enemy

Drink is to water as eat is to **food. Drink** is the first word of pair C and **food** is the second word of pair C, so the space under C has been filled in on line X of your Answer Sheet.

NUMERICAL ABILITY

This test consists of forty numerical problems. Next to each problem there are five answers. You are to pick out the correct answer and fill in the space under its letter on the Answer Sheet. If you do not find a correct answer among the first four choices, blacken the space under N as your answer. Choice N for every problem is **none of these**, which means that a correct answer is **not** among the first four choices. Only one answer should be marked for each problem. Do your figuring on the scratch paper you have been given, and reduce fractions to lowest terms. Here are some examples:

Example X.   Add

    13
    12

A   14
B   25
C   16
D   59
N   none of these

In Example X, **25** is the correct answer, so the space under the letter for **25**—B—has been filled in on line X of your Answer Sheet.

ABSTRACT REASONING

Each row consists of four figures called Problem Figures and five called Answer Figures. The four Problem Figures make a series. You are to find out which one of the Answer Figures would be the next (or the fifth one) in the series of Problem Figures. Here are two examples:

PROBLEM FIGURES   **ANSWER FIGURES**

Example X.

In Example X, note that the lines in the Problem Figures are falling down. In the first square the line stands straight up, and as you go from square to square the line falls more and more to the right. In the fifth square the line would be lying flat, so the correct answer—chosen from among the Answer Figures—is D. Therefore, the space under D has been filled in on line X of your Answer Sheet.

CLERICAL
SPEED AND ACCURACY

This is a test to see how quickly and accurately you can compare letter and number combinations. On the following pages are groups of these combinations; each test item contains five. These same combinations appear after the number for each test item on the Answer Sheet, but they are in a different order. You will notice that in each test item one of the five is **underlined.** You are to look at the **one** combination which is underlined, find the **same** one after that item number on the Answer Sheet, and fill in the space under it.

The following examples have been marked correctly on your Answer Sheet. Note that the combination marked on the Answer Sheet must be exactly the same as the one which is underlined in the test item.

Examples

V. <u>AB</u> AC AD AE AF

W. aA aB BA Ba <u>Bb</u>

X. A7 7A B7 <u>7B</u> AB

Y. Aa Ba <u>bA</u> BA bB

Z. 3A 3B <u>33</u> B3 BB

FIGURE 14–5   Examples of practice items from the subtests of the DAT. (Reproduced by permission. Copyright © 1972 by The Psychological Corporation, New York, N.Y. All rights reserved.)

MECHANICAL REASONING

Find the space for Mechanical Reasoning on the Answer Sheet.

This test consists of a number of pictures and questions about those pictures. Look at the two examples below, to see just what to do.

Example X

Which man has the heavier load?
(If equal, mark C.)

SPACE RELATIONS

This test consists of 60 patterns which can be folded into figures. To the right of each pattern there are four figures. You are to decide which **one** of these figures can be made from the pattern shown. The pattern always shows the **outside** of the figure. Here is an example:

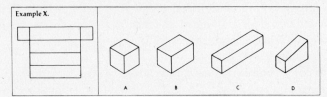

Example X.

In Example X, which one of the four figures—A, B, C, D—can be made from the pattern at the left? A and B certainly cannot be made; they are not the right shape. C is correct both in shape and size. You cannot make D from this pattern. Therefore, the space under C has been filled in on line X of your Answer Sheet.

SPELLING

This test is composed of a series of words. Some of them are correctly spelled; some are incorrectly spelled. You are to indicate whether each word is spelled right or wrong by blackening the proper space on the Answer Sheet. If the spelling of the word is **right,** fill in the space under R, for RIGHT. If it is spelled **wrong,** fill in the space under W, for WRONG. Here are some examples:

Examples

W. man   **Y.** catt

X. gurl   **Z.** dog

LANGUAGE USAGE

This test consists of a series of sentences, each divided into four parts lettered A, B, C, and D. You are to consider each sentence as an example of formal, written expression. In many of the sentences, one part has an error in punctuation, grammar, or capitalization. Decide which part, if any, is wrong. Then, on the Answer Sheet, fill in the space under the letter corresponding to the part of the sentence that contains an error. Be sure the item number on the Answer Sheet is the same as that of the sentence on which you are working.

Some sentences have **no** error in any part. If there is no error in a sentence, fill in the space under the letter N. Here are some examples of what you will find on the test:

Example X.   I just **/** left **/** my friends **/** house.
                    A   **B**   **C**   **D**

Figure 14–5   *(continued)*

and, as the DAT Manual points out, it is risky to base counseling on interest scores without having some information on a person's aptitude scores.

As mentioned in the introduction to this section on multifactor tests, one of the characteristics such tests should have if they are to be successful in differential prediction is low intercorrelations of the subtests. Although the average (across grades) intercorrelations for Form L of the DAT ar reasonably low, most users would probably wish lower intercorrelations.

To summarize the validity of the DAT is almost an impossible task. The authors are certainly to be commended for their complete and accurate presentation of validity data. The subscores of the DAT predict, quite well, a variety of secondary-school course grades and standardized achievement test results. They predict to a fair extent college course grades and job level within an occupational area. The evidence for differential validity is sketchy.

INTERPRETATION AND USE   The administration of the DAT in grade 8 or 9 can provide information that is relevant to the decisions a student must make concerning future educational plans. The general lack of differential predictive validity does not mean the test is useless. The subtests do predict a variety of criteria, and the descriptive value of the subtest scores is not to be underemphasized.

Many counselors are appreciative of the fact that students who would perform at a low level on a test of general intelligence may do well on some of the subtests of the DAT. Thus, the counselor can say something of a positive nature concerning the student's abilities, and the student leaves the counseling interview with a better self-concept than if one could only interpret the low score on a general intelligence test. The combined score (VR + NA) serves very well as a measure of general intelligence. A casebook prepared by The Psychological Corporation is of considerable value to counselors in interpreting the profile differences to students (Bennett, Seashore, & Wesman, 1951).

An optional service of potential value to counselors and students is the DAT/Career Planning Program. This program consists of a Career Planning Questionnaire and the DAT Career Planning Report in addition to the DAT itself. The Questionnaire collects data on student status, interest, and goals. A computer compares these with the results of the DAT and prints out an interpretive Report which may confirm the appropriateness of the student's occupational choices in terms of his abilities, interests, and plans; or which may suggest alternative occupational areas. It is suggested that the Report can be used by counselors in interviews with students and parents, and/or given to students for further discussion and study at home.

The DAT is certainly a well-constructed and well-researched instrument. However, as do other aptitude tests, it lacks the degree of differential predictive validity that multifactor aptitude tests ideally should have.

Academic Promise Test (APT)

Published by The Psychological Corporation (1961–1962), this test is designed for grades 6–9. There are seven scores: abstract reasoning, numerical, non-verbal total, language usage, verbal, verbal total, and total. Because three of the seven scores are totals, there are actually only four different areas tested. Three of the scores (abstract reasoning, numerical, and verbal) are downward extensions of their counterparts in the Different Aptitude Tests. Two forms are available. It is a well-constructed test with good validity and reliability. However, differential validity is not particularly high.

General Aptitude Test Battery (GATB)

This test, which is available from the United States Government Printing Office (1946–1970) is designed for grades 9–12 and adults. GATB has 12 tests and yields the following 9 scores: intelligence, verbal aptitude, numerical aptitude, spatial aptitude, form perception, clerical perception, motor coordination, finger dexterity, and manual dexterity. These aptitudes are not completely independent because some of the subtests are used in determining more than one aptitude score. A nonreading adaptation of the GATB, called the Non-reading Aptitude Test Battery, was published in 1969. It produces the same 9 scores from 14 tests.

The GATB has been widely used by the United States Employment Service (USES), and the tests are available to nonprofit institutions (such as public schools) for counseling purposes. Specific occupations have been grouped into job families, and multiple cutoff scores (a series of minimum scores) have been established for the three most relevant aptitudes for each family. These scores are used in predicting job success. The multiple cutoff approach has been criticized for its noncompensatory attributes and the fact that no relative probabilities of success are available to assist in guiding those individuals who exceed the cutoff scores in more than one job family.

The USES is continuing to do research on the GATB. It is considered by many to be a very well-constructed instrument. The total time required for testing is about 2½ hours.

SPECIAL APTITUDE TESTS

A special aptitude is usually defined as an individual's potential ability (or capacity to acquire proficiency) in a specified type of activity. Special aptitude tests were developed primarily for help in making vocational and educational selection decisions as well as for counseling. Compared to multifactor aptitude tests, they are probably more useful in selection (or placement) decisions by an institution, and generally less useful in personal counseling for individual decision making.

There are many kinds of special aptitude tests that could be discussed in this section. Most textbooks relegate to this section tests that really are not aptitude tests but that are ability tests, such as for hearing and visual acuity. We will follow this same practice. Thus this section will really contain a pot-pourri of special tests; the term *aptitude* will be used in a broad sense.

Because all readers will not be interested in the same areas, we will not spend a great deal of time on any particular test. The major purpose of this section will be to introduce the readers to the variety of special aptitude tests that exist. Those interested in a more thorough coverage of any test or area of testing should turn to the sources of information about tests discussed in Chapter 13.

Tests of Vision and Hearing

Although seeing and hearing abilities are not aptitudes per se, both sensory functions are important in various educational and occupational endeavors. The ability to see or hear can be predictive in the sense that an uncorrected deficiency will adversely affect performance on many kinds of tasks. It is now routine to screen all schoolchildren for visual or auditory deficiencies. We will not discuss tests in these areas because ordinarily the testing is not performed by classroom teachers. However, all school personnel should be alert to the detection of such deficiencies even though screening may have occurred. The screening is often not done as thoroughly as it might be, and students often are not aware of their own sensory limitations. Examples of vision and hearing instruments are the Eames Eye Test, the Snellen Chart, the Auditory Discrimination Test, and the Maico Audiometers.

Mechanical Aptitude Tests

Various mechanical aptitude tests measure many different traits, and even the same test sometimes will measure more than one function. Such traits as spatial ability, perceptual speed, manual dexterity, and mechanical reasoning are all, at times, classified under the general rubric of mechanical aptitude. For this reason, mechanical aptitude tests have low intercorrelations and cannot be used interchangeably. Most schools do not routinely give to all students any test of mechanical aptitude other than in those related aspects measured by the DAT (space relations and mechanical reasoning). It would be advisable, however, to use other tests in counseling with students who are interested in vocations requiring one or more of these various aptitudes. The ACER Mechanical Reasoning Test, the Revised Minnesota Paper Form Board Test, and the Bennett Hand Tool Dexterity Test are examples of other "mechanical aptitude" tests.

Clerical and Stenographic Aptitude Tests

Clerical aptitude, like mechanical aptitude, is not a unitary characteristic. There are many tasks that clerks must perform, and some of the more comprehensive clerical aptitude tests attempt to measure a variety of aptitudes. For example, aptitudes in verbal skills, alphabetical filing, grammar, and spelling are often considered important for success in clerical work. Again, as with mechanical aptitude, there are several subtests of the DAT related to clerical aptitude, and no other such tests are usually given to all the students in school. In the counseling of specific individuals, other clerical aptitude tests such as the Beginner's Clerical Test, the Minnesota Clerical Test, or the Short Tests of Clerical Ability may well prove useful.

Musical and Artistic Aptitude Tests

Several musical and artistic aptitude tests are available. These tests may be used by teachers in the specific areas or by counselors for certain individuals, but, in general, their use is not widespread. The Seashore Measures of Musical Talents (revised edition), the Wing Standardized Tests of Musical Intelligence, and the Musical Aptitude Profile are three of the most frequently used musical aptitude tests. The Meier Art Tests and the Graves Design Judgment Test are two frequently used art tests.

Aptitude Tests for Specific Courses and Professions

Aptitude tests developed for particular school subjects such as algebra and foreign languages have been used extensively in the past to help individual pupils with their curricular choice. However, in recent years this popular practice has diminished. Research has shown that such tests do not significantly increase the predictive validity over what can be obtained by a general mental ability test, the relevant subscores on multifactor aptitude tests, or achievement test batteries. Because these latter tests are usually given in the schools, it may well be a waste of time and money to administer special aptitude tests.

Many special aptitude tests, such as the Law School Admissions Test and the Medical College Admission Test, have also been developed in recent years for use in various graduate and professional schools. These tests are designed to be of appropriate difficulty (harder than general aptitude tests for adults) and emphasize the abilities of importance to the particular profession. While these tests are usually slightly better predictors than general aptitude tests, their major advantage lies in their security. Many general aptitude tests could be obtained in advance by an enterprising person desirous of obtaining a high score and thereby admission into a professional school. The security of the professional tests rules out this sort of enterprise as a factor in admission decisions.

Tests of Creativity

Some who subscribe to the general theory of intelligence suggest that creativity is an aspect of general intelligence and need not be measured separately. Others realize that, although tests of general ability are best able to predict future school success (that is, grades), it is likely that creativity is a distinct ability. Research seems to indicate that while one has to be reasonably intelligent to be creative, the converse does not hold. Butcher (1968) reports good correspondence between general aptitude and creativity test scores up to an IQ score of around 120, but above that there is little relationship between intelligence and creativity. In other words, a reasonably high level of intelligence appears to be a necessary but not sufficient condition for creativity. Although the majority of psychologists subscribe to the notion that creativity is something beyond (or different from) general intelligence, the problem is that it is hard to agree on constructual definitions of creativity, let alone operational definitions. Even if we could agree on an operational definition, it would be hard to indicate validity for the measure because of the lack of an adequate criterion measure. Does creativity imply a creative *process*, or a creative *product*? Or does the former lead to the latter? Is a creative person one who comes up with a variety of unique ideas, or is he one who has a variety of unique good ideas? That is, is there simply a quantity criterion or also a quality criterion for judging creativity? If one is asked, as in the Torrance Tests of Creative Thinking, to name as many uses of a cardboard box as one can think of, how should the results be scored? Torrance has created a scoring scheme, but it is doubtful if all would agree with it. As has been pointed out, the distinction between creative and asinine ideas is often hard to make. Most people feel that the production of a large number of unworkable ideas is of little use and to measure this type of creativity is a waste of time.

We feel that more research on attempts to measure creativity and to investigate its correlates is warranted. There is now available enough evidence to suggest that creativity is something unique and not necessarily correlated with ability to perform well in an academic setting. (However, it is a misconception that creative children do poorly in schoolwork. Research shows that, as a group, creative children do quite well in school.) There are many potential benefits available if one could effectively isolate and measure the construct of creativity. Creative people are important for an advancing society. If creativity can be further understood, if the identification of creative people becomes possible, and if creativity can be taught in the schools, our society is sure to benefit.

At the present time there are few creativity tests on the market. Those tests that do exist should be considered only as research instruments, and much more work is needed in the area before we can really feel comfortable with the results these tests give us. Fortunately, there is considerable investigation of this whole area, and it is possible that psychologists will soon have available more adequate tests. For further reading on this interesting topic, refer to Crockenberg (1972, pp. 27–46), Getzels and Jackson (1962), Guilford (1967), Hudson (1966), Torrance (1962, 1965), and Wallach and Kogan (1965).

Torrance Tests of Creative Thinking, Research Edition (TTCT)

This test, which is available from Personnel Press, Inc. (1966), consists of two forms, K through graduate school. There are two tests: a verbal test, called Thinking Creatively with Words; and a figural test, called Thinking Creatively with Pictures. Tasks involve such things as (1) asking all the questions one can think of about a picture, (2) suggesting changes in a toy that would make the toy more fun to play with, (3) listing as many uses as possible for a commonplace object, and (4) drawing a picture around a curved shape, and giving the picture a title.

There are four scores for each test: fluency, flexibility, originality, and elaboration. Fluency is the number of relevant responses given; flexibility is the number of different categories of response; originality is the sum of different credits, where some routine responses count zero, other less common responses count 1, and very uncommon responses count 2; and the elaboration score is based on the amount of detail used in the responses. The subscores are quite highly correlated, and it is doubtful whether considering the scores separately is more useful than simply considering two scores—verbal and pictorial.

The TTCT is definitely just a research instrument and the author makes this point in the manual. Unfortunately, the advertisements and the publisher's catalog do not make this clear.

USING APTITUDE TEST RESULTS

Considering all the types of aptitude tests discussed in this chapter (individual and group tests of general intelligence, multifactor aptitude tests, and special aptitude tests), one can confidently say that the average child will be given the opportunity to take (or be subjected to) at least three aptitude tests before graduating from high school. A collegebound student may easily take five or more. How are these tests being used? Are they helpful or harmful?

The public has been much concerned with the uses and possible misuses of aptitude tests. This final section, devoted to the uses of aptitude tests, will also contain warnings against potential misuses.

Table 13–1 lists some various purposes of standardized tests under four headings: instructional, guidance, administrative, and research. The use of aptitude tests under each of these categories will be discussed in more detail here.

Instructional Uses

The ability level of students in a particular class should enable a teacher to evaluate the appropriateness of his class materials. One should not teach the same kind of material in the same fashion to two classes, one in which the students have a mean IQ score of 85 and the other in which the students have a mean IQ score of 120. Neither should two students within the same class who differ considerably in ability have similar assignments. Thus, knowledge of general aptitude test scores enables a teacher to make better decisions about the kind of class material presented to each student.

As educators gain more knowledge in the area of aptitude-treatment interaction (see Cronbach & Snow, 1969), scores on aptitude tests should become even more helpful in designing instructional strategies. However, it is likely that if aptitude tests are to be maximally effective in such a task, they will need to be somewhat different from those currently most popular (Glaser, 1973). We should remember that current aptitude tests are much more useful for prognosis than for diagnosis.

An argument that has occasionally been voiced against the use of aptitude tests for instructional purposes is that teachers will use low aptitude scores as an excuse for not attempting to teach the students ("The students can't learn anyway" attitude). Unfortunately, it is probably true that some teachers do this. Aptitude test scores should be used in helping teachers form realistic expectations of students; they should not be used to help teachers develop fatalistic expectations.

However, in agreeing that this potential danger of testing exists, we do not think it should be overemphasized. The teachers in slum schools who do not try their hardest because of preconceived ideas that their students cannot learn have not obtained their ideas of student deficiency primarily from aptitude test scores. Such factors as the parents' educational level, socioeconomic status, race, and occupation all contribute to teachers' opinions concerning a child's aptitude. Goslin (1967), a noted sociologist, in a comprehensive survey of teachers' opinions about tests, found that less than one-fourth of the teachers felt that abilities measured by intelligence tests are more important than other qualities for predicting school success. He also found that teachers tend to view intelligence tests results as being more influenced by environmental factors than by innate capacities. Whether or not this is true, his findings would suggest that teachers are not likely to become fatalistic about a person's innate ability from intelligence-test score information. Goslin summarized the problems of teachers' opinions concerning the nature of intelligence as follows:

> Leaving for a moment the question of whether or not intelligence or aptitude tests actually measure innate capabilities to any substantial degree, we may conclude that there are likely to be certain advantages for the school

system and for pupils in it if teachers are unwilling to accept the presupposition that a pupil's score reflects his inherent (and therefore, presumably, unchangeable) abilities. How one reconciles this proposition with the facts in the situation, namely, that intelligence tests do measure innate abilities to some degree, however, is less clear. It is probably unrealistic to consider seriously attempting systematically to dupe teachers into thinking that tests do not measure innate abilities or that there are no such things as genetically influenced individual differences in capacity for learning. . . . In attempting to hide the fact that individual differences in learning capacity do exist, such a policy may result in teachers and others using less appropriate measures . . . to make inferences about the intellectual capacities of children. (Goslin, 1967, pp. 131–132)

Knowing that Denny has a measured IQ of 80, that his father is an unemployed alcoholic, and that his mother entertains men to pay for the groceries, the teacher may conclude (correctly or incorrectly) that Denny will have trouble learning in school. If the teacher accepts these factors in the spirit of a challenge and does his best—fine. If the teacher adopts a fatalistic attitude toward Denny—bad. However, there is no more compelling reason to blame the test for the improper attitude of the teacher than to blame his knowledge of all the other facts.

Let us make this point clear. *Aptitude tests can help teachers develop realistic expectations for their students*. While we, in no way, condone—in fact do condemn—teachers who develop fatalistic attitudes toward the learning abilities of their students, we do not think aptitude tests should be made the scapegoat. We admit this potential misuse of tests. There, however, is little evidence to suggest that teachers' attitudes toward the learning potential of their students are unduly influenced by test results. A 1973 Teachers Opinion Poll of NEA members shows, for example, that six teachers in ten thought that group IQ test scores predicted ability of physically handicapped pupils poorly or not at all. Three teachers in four thought the test predicted the ability of socially or culturally different pupils poorly or not at all. However, seven in ten thought the tests predicted the ability of pupils other than the handicapped very well or fairly well (Teachers Opinion Poll, 1974). Obviously, the teachers sampled in this poll are certainly not (as a group) overinfluenced by test results. Teachers are probably more apt to be unduly influenced by other factors with much less predictive validity. One must remember, however, that if we use any kind of data (including aptitude tests) to label children, we need to take care not to misuse the labels. *Labels must be treated as descriptions rather than as explanations*. Too often a label is treated as an explanation.

Improvement in aptitude test scores should not be used in evaluating learning outcomes or teaching because these scores should be relatively unaffected by formal school learning. However, knowing something about the ability level of the students in a class or school *can* help teachers determine whether the students are learning as much as is predicted from their ability level. While some people object to the term *underachiever* (for, really, it is just an overprediction), it is nonetheless helpful to know that a person is not performing as well as could be predicted on the basis of his ability scores. If a whole class or school is performing less well (say, for example, on a standardized achievement battery) than would be predicted from aptitude test scores, then this *may* be due to inadequate teaching. (See the section in Chapter 6 on Expectancy Scores.)

Guidance Uses

Aptitude tests can be useful in vocational, educational, and personal counseling. Once the training necessary for entrance into the occupation has been completed, it is generally true that tests of general intelligence are not very predictive of vocational success. However, these test scores are still useful in counseling because the educational requirements of some vocations do require considerable general ability. The correlations between general aptitude scores and success in training programs tend to run between .40 and .50 (Ghiselli, 1966). These correlations would be even higher if selections into the training programs were not based on the aptitude scores. (See Chapter 5.)

General aptitude tests often provide useful data for dealing with problem children. An overactive first-grader, if very bright, may be bored and needs to be challenged more. Or the child may be totally incapable of doing first-grade work and therefore causing trouble because of frustration. If the child is of average intelligence, perhaps emotional problems are the reason for the overactivity. An individually administered intelligence test can often provide the best data available for judging which of these competing hypotheses is most tenable.

Multifactor aptitude tests are often used in counseling to give students a better idea of their differential abilities. As discussed, the measurement of these differential abilities does not necessarily improve differential prediction, but it does lead to a fuller understanding of one's self.

For guidance, as for instructional purposes, there are some possible misuses of aptitude test scores. The problem of treating test scores as fatalistic predictors still exists. Counselors, teachers, and in fact all school personnel should remember that their job, in part, is to attempt to upset negative predictions.

A related problem to educators' becoming fatalistic is the development of a fatalistic attitude in children. A popular topic of conversation these days is the importance of developing a good self-concept in the students. There is no doubt that students should be self-accepting and feel that others accept them also. If a counselor interprets a low test score so that the student feels unworthy, then that is indeed unfortunate. One of the advantages of a multifactor aptitude test is that a student usually performs at an acceptable level on some of the subtests, and these scores can and should serve as morale builders for the students.

As with other possible misuses of test results, we feel this problem of low aptitude scores resulting in poor self-concepts can be overemphasized. Just as test scores are not the major factors in forming teachers' opinions about the learning abilities of children, so also low aptitude test scores are probably much less influential than other factors in contributing to an undesirable (inaccurately low) self-concept. Tests often seem to be blamed for educational problems that were not caused by the tests to begin with. To be sure, there is some relationship between what a person thinks he can achieve and what he will achieve. Nevertheless, it is a generally held position that counselors should help students obtain and accept an accurate self-concept, not an inaccurately high one. Proper interpretation of aptitude tests can be helpful in this endeavor.

Administrative Uses

There are many ways in which aptitude tests can be used by the administration. Some selection, classification, and placement decisions such as who should be admitted to kindergarten early, who should be placed in the enriched classes, who should be placed in the remedial classes, and who should be admitted to colleges are decisions that may be performed by counselors or school psychologists who rightly may not consider themselves as administrators. Nevertheless, these are administrative decisions.

As with almost any use of aptitude tests, there are accompanying potential misuses. Some persons charge that the major misuse of tests in administrative functions is that decisions made on the basis of test scores are often treated as if they were permanent, irreversible decisions. If a child is put into a remedial class in, say, grade 3, there is too often a tendency on the part of the administration, having made a decision once, to forget about it. The child then gets lock-stepped into a curriculum.

Now, although we do not support administrative inflexibility in the reconsideration of decisions, we should consider whether the use of test scores is really the causative factor of this inflexibility. We must admit that in some cases it is. Some people simply place far too much faith in test scores, and this results in too much faith in the correctness of decisions—so, they are made and then forgotten. However, not all, or not even most inflexibility can be charged to test-score misuse. Many of the decisions made would be incorrectly treated as permanent, even if there were no test score data on the students. It is worth noting that if a decision must be made, it should be based on as much evidence as possible. Not to use test information in making decisions because of possible misuse is cowardly, foolish, and even unprofessional.

There are also some who argue against the use of aptitude tests for various decisions because they do not think the decision has to, or should, be made at all. However, if a test is used to help implement a policy that is considered incorrect by some, there is no reason to blame the test. For example, a sizable group of educators is against ability grouping. If there is a policy, right or wrong, to group on the basis of ability, it is not incorrect to use an aptitude test to help decide who should be placed in what group. Some have argued that tests are unfair to different subgroups and therefore the test results should be ignored when doing ability grouping. However, although we do *not* advocate using *only* test data Findley (1974) reported that Carrager has shown that such a process would result in *less* separation of upper and lower SES students than if one uses other factors such as teacher grades, study habits, citizenship and industry, and social and emotional maturity in addition to test scores. As Findley explains ". . . stereotypes of upper and lower SES children held by school personnel result in further separation between groups than the tests alone would warrant" (1974, p. 25). We emphasize that this example is not meant to advocate ability grouping or making decisions using only test data. It does suggest that blaming *tests* for what one may consider harmful social separation is inappropriate. However, with respect to aptitude testing and grouping, we should make one important point. It is becoming increasingly clear that some educationally deprived children are being inappropriately labeled as retarded and placed in special classes. Any time one uses an aptitude test score, he must keep in mind the environmental conditions under which the child was reared. Whether or not special classes are desirable for mentally retarded children, it certainly is not desirable to *misplace* a child into such a special class.

Let us take another example. Some people are opposed to the use of scholastic aptitude tests in college selection decisions. It is sometimes unclear whether what they oppose is the notion of selecting college students on the basis of predicted success in college or whether they oppose the use of scholastic aptitude tests in assisting in that prediction. If the former, that is a philosophical point and should be argued separately from whether tests help in predicting success. If the latter, they should read the research literature. As Samuda states, "the evidence about college entrance tests as predictors is no longer a subject of legitimate dispute. The studies have been widespread, they number in the thousands, and the results are consistent. By and large, the higher the test scores, the more successful the students are in college" (Samuda, 1975, viii). In fact, there is also evidence that academic aptitude at time of college admission is significantly related to occupational level later in life (Lewis, 1975).

But don't aptitude tests serve to keep the lower SES students out of college? Were they not, in fact, designed to do that? The answer to both questions is *no*. With respect to the latter question, as Cronbach indicated in an excellent historical analysis, "Proponents of testing, from Thomas Jefferson onward, have wanted to open doors for the talented poor, in a system in which doors often are opened by parental wealth and status" (Cronbach,

1975, p. 1). With respect to the former, evidence suggests that the testing movement has accelerated the breakdown of classes by identifying able individuals from the lower strata who might otherwise have gone unnoticed (Tyler, L. E., 1976, p. 15). The reason some people may doubt this is that they read potentially misleading statements on this topic such as "Men with high test scores *tend to come from* economically and socially advantaged families" (Jenks, 1972, p. 221, italics added). What Jenks should have said is that people from upper SES groups *tend to score higher* than do children from lower SES groups. It has been estimated that of youths in the top quarter with respect to scores on intelligence tests 33 percent come from the working class, 42 percent come from the lower-middle, and 25 percent come from the upper and upper-middle classes combined (see Havighurst & Neugarten, 1975). Thus, lower SES students are not kept out of college because of their aptitude test scores. Fricke (1975, p. 110) demonstrated that if admission to the freshman class at the University of Michigan had been determined *entirely* by academic aptitude test scores of high school seniors, a *majority* of freshmen would have come from low SES backgrounds rather than the 10 or 15 percent that is typically the case. Using only the presumed "biased" test scores would not decrease but *increase* by a factor of four or five the number of low SES students. Again, we are not advocating using only test scores to make decisions. We are pointing out that it is not low test scores that are keeping low SES students (in general) out of college. At any rate, because of the proven validity of scholastic aptitude tests for predicting college success, if there is a policy, right or wrong, to limit college enrollment to those with some minimal level of scholastic aptitude, it is not incorrect to use aptitude test scores to *help* determine who should be admitted to college. Far too often the cry of test misuse is raised because the lamenter is against the policy that the correct use of test scores helps implement rather than because the test is not being correctly used under the existing policy.

The uses of aptitude test results for public relations and for providing information for outside agencies do have some very real potential pitfalls. Occasionally, press releases are made concerning how schools compare with each other in the average ability of their students. While this sort of public relations may momentarily "feather the cap" of some school official, the chances of the public understanding the release are dim indeed, and one is hard put to verbalize any real advantages of this sort of public release of information.

The issue of whether or not schools should provide an individual's aptitude test score to outside agencies is a cloudy one. The question is whether such information is to be treated as confidential. If so, then it should not be released without a student's permission. But does the consent have to be explicit, or can it be implied? For example, if a student applies for a job that requires security clearance, is the application to be interpreted as implied consent for the release of school records? This question cannot be discussed in great detail in this book. The safest procedure (both morally and legally), however, is not to release test information to any outside agency without the explicit consent of the student and/or his parents.

Another possible use of aptitude tests is for relevant supplementary information in curriculum planning and evaluation. An idea of the general ability level of the school should help educators decide, for example, how much relative emphasis to place on college preparatory curricula.

Finally, some administrators feel that aptitude tests can be useful in deciding which teachers to hire or promote. While there is obviously a relationship between aptitude test scores and the obtaining of a teacher's certificate, there is little known evidence suggesting a relationship between aptitude test scores and on-the-job performance for certified teachers. Thus, hiring or promoting on this basis has no merit.

Research Uses

Aptitude test scores can be used in many, many ways in research. Ordinarily the scores are used as independent variables in a research design. For example, in evaluating instructional procedures many researchers would want to use some aptitude measure as an independent variable. Some research—such as that investigating the environmental effects on intelligence—treats the scores as dependent variables. Because this book is not designed for the researcher, we will preclude further discussion of this topic.

SUMMARY

The major points of this chapter are summarized in the following statements:

1. The definitions, structure, etiology, and stability of intelligence are all unsettled issues in psychology.
2. Definitions of intelligence generally fall into one or more of three categories: the capacity to (a) think abstractly, (b) learn, or (c) integrate new experiences and adapt to new situations.
3. Theories regarding the structure of intelligence have ranged from the idea of a general factor of intelligence to the conceptualization of many specific factors. These various theories have resulted in many different kinds of tests, classified as tests of general intelligence, multifactor aptitude tests, and special aptitude tests.
4. Both heredity and environment affect intelligence-test scores.
5. In general, intelligence measures are not very stable in early childhood, but by the age of 5 or so they become quite stable.
6. The most popular individual intelligence tests are the Stanford-Binet and the Wechsler instruments. Specialized training is required to administer and interpret these tests correctly.

7. Individual tests can be better used with individuals who, for motivational or other reasons, do not perform accurately on group tests. Also, more clinical information can be obtained from individual tests.

8. Teachers are generally qualified to administer group tests of intelligence.

9. Various aspects to consider when choosing a test have been illustrated by the review of the Otis-Lennon.

10. Some attempts have been made in the past to build culture-fair intelligence tests. These results have largely failed if we define *culture fairness* as the equality of mean scores for various subcultures. Even if culture-fair tests could be devised, the usefulness of such measures is open to question.

11. Multifactor aptitude tests are used by the majority of school systems in either eighth or ninth grade. Although designed to be differentially predictive, they have not been very successful in that respect. Nevertheless, they have remained a popular tool of the counselors to assist students in understanding themselves better.

12. Aptitude test results can be used by teachers, counselors, and administrators. They can also be misused. Unfortunately, the negative attitude the public correctly displays toward test misuse has been overgeneralized and extended to the tests themselves.

CHAPTER FIFTEEN

Standardized Achievement Tests

What is an achievement test? How do standardized achievement tests differ from teacher-made achievement tests? Are there achievement tests for all subject matter areas? Will the Stanford Achievement Test be valid for my purpose? What use can be made of achievement test results? What are some of the factors that must be considered in the selection of a standardized achievement test? These are some of the questions that the classroom teacher, counselor, and school administrator can be expected to ask. This chapter presents information that will assist the test user to answer these and other questions.

In Unit III we discussed the teacher-made achievement test as one measurement tool available to the classroom teacher to aid him in making decisions about pupils. The material previously discussed—concepts of validity and reliability, scores, norms, planning the test, writing the test items, and analyzing the test—are equally pertinent to the preparation of a standardized achievement test. Hence, what you have already learned in previous chapters should provide a firm basis for understanding standardized achievement tests.

There are literally hundreds of standardized achievement tests available to the classroom teacher, counselor, school psychologist, and administrator. To try to cover a substantial portion of them here would be an exercise in futility. We have selected only a few of the more representative ones in order that we might comment upon their properties—properties that every user should examine when selecting a standardized test. The tests discussed here are generally of high quality. However, there are many other standardized achievement tests of equally high quality, and it should *not* be assumed that the tests discussed in this chapter are the best ones available. In the long run, the best test is the one that best measures the user's instructional objectives most validly, reliably, efficiently, and economically.

After studying this chapter, the student should be able to—

1. Understand the similarities and differences between standardized and teacher-made achievement tests.

2. Compare the three major types of standardized achievement tests— diagnostic, survey battery, and single subject matter—in terms of purposes, coverage, and construction.

3. Have a better conception of the newer type of standardized criterion-referenced tests and how they can be useful in the diagnosis of student learning problems as well as helpful in planning for optimal instruction.

4. Recognize that most standardized achievement tests are more similar than dissimilar.

5. Critically evaluate a standardized achievement test.

6. Understand the factors to be considered in selecting a standardized achievement test.

7. Understand and discuss the various instructional, guidance, and administrative uses of standardized achievement test data.

8. Recognize the supplemental value of standardized achievement test data to assist the teacher in his decision making.

HISTORICAL DEVELOPMENT OF ACHIEVEMENT TESTS[1]

The first objective educational or achievement test in the United States was developed by Rice in 1895. Rice's spelling test (consisting of 50 spelling words) was administered to over 16,000 pupils in grades 4 to 8. Because of the unexpectedly wide variation in results, Rice developed two more spelling tests so that he could be certain that the findings were the result of real differences in spelling ability rather than the result of the particular sample of words used. Although Rice is best known for his spelling test, he also devel-

[1] For a more complete discussion of the history of testing, see DuBois (1970).

oped tests in arithmetic and language. His major contribution to what is now called standardized achievement tests lay in his objective and scientific approach to the assessment of pupil knowledge. In 1908 Stone published his arithmetic reasoning test. In 1909 Thorndike published the Scale for Handwriting of Children. In addition to producing numerous scales and tests, Thorndike taught many students who were later to make their contribution to the field of measurement and achievement testing. Beginning in 1910 numerous studies indicated the unreliability of teachers' grading (Falls, 1928; Starch & Elliott, 1912, 1913a,b). These kinds of studies led to the search for, and development of, more objective procedures for testing and grading students.

Up to this time, with the exception of Fisher's Scale Book (Chadwick, 1864), all achievement tests were single-subject-matter tests. In the early 1920s and 1930s an important development was the publication of test batteries. In 1923 the first standardized survey battery, the Stanford Achievement Test, was published.[2] It was designed primarily for use at the elementary level. In 1925 the Iowa High School Content Examination, the first standardized survey battery for high school, was published. Since that time, hundreds of different standardized achievement tests (single-subject-matter tests, test batteries, diagnostic and prognostic tests) have been developed. Since the 1940s there has been a movement in test construction, from the specialized, single-subject-matter test to testing in broad content areas such as the humanities and natural sciences. In addition, more and more emphasis is now being placed upon the evaluation of pupil work-study skills, comprehension, and understanding rather than focusing on factual recall per se. In the 1970s emphasis is being placed on the development of standardized tests that are keyed to particular textbooks. This is becoming more and more common with reading textbook series, although a beginning has been made in the area of mathematics. The 1970s have also spawned an interest in the development of general criterion-referenced tests, diagnostic-prescriptive tests, and "tailored-to-user-specifications" tests. Also readily evident in the past decade is the variety of reporting formats used by test publishers. No longer do we just obtain raw and standard scores for individual pupils or the total class, but we can now get very detailed information about the responses of single pupils, of class groups, of school groups, and even of district groups.

DIFFERENCES BETWEEN STANDARDIZED AND TEACHER-MADE ACHIEVEMENT TESTS

Any test that has a representative sampling of the course content (that is, possesses content validity) and that is designed to measure the extent of

[2] A survey test measures general achievement in a given subject or area. A survey battery consists of a group of survey tests (different content areas) standardized on the same population.

present knowledge is an achievement test, regardless of whether this test was constructed by the classroom teacher or by professional test makers. The major (but not the only) distinction between the standardized achievement test and the teacher-made test is that in a standardized achievement test the systematic sampling of performance (that is, the pupil's score) has been obtained under prescribed directions of administration. They also differ markedly in terms of their sampling of content, construction, norms, and purpose and use. The comparisons between teacher-made and standardized achievement tests are summarized in Table 15–1.

TABLE 15–1 Comparisons between Standardized and Teacher-Made Achievement Tests

CHARACTERISTIC	TEACHER-MADE ACHIEVEMENT TESTS	STANDARDIZED ACHIEVEMENT TESTS
Directions for administration and scoring	Usually no uniform directions specified	Specific instructions standardize administration and scoring procedures
Sampling of content	Both content and sampling are determined by classroom teacher	Content determined by curriculum and subject-matter experts; involves extensive investigations of existing syllabi, textbooks, and programs (i.e., covers material covered in many, if not most, classrooms); sampling of content done systematically
Construction	May be hurried and haphazard; often no test blueprints, item tryouts, item analysis or revision; quality of test may be quite poor	Uses meticulous construction procedures that include constructing objectives and test blueprints, employing item tryouts, item analysis, and item revisions
Norms	Only local classroom norms are available	In addition to local norms, standardized tests typically make available national, school district, and school building norms
Purposes and use	Best suited for measuring particular objectives set by teacher and for intraclass comparisons	Best suited for measuring broader curriculum objectives and for interclass, school, and national comparisons

Sampling of Content

Standardized achievement tests normally cover much more material (that is, they have a wider range of coverage, although they need not have more items) than teacher-made tests because they are designed to assess either one year's learning or more than one year's learning. Teacher-made tests usually cover a single unit of work or that of a term. Standardized tests, in contrast to teacher-made tests, may not so readily reflect curricular changes, although test publishers attempt to "keep up with the times."[3]

The decision of whether to administer a commercially published standardized test or a teacher-made test is based to a large degree on the particular objectives to be measured. Norm-referenced standardized tests are constructed to measure generally accepted goals rather than specific or particular instructional objectives. Criterion-referenced standardized tests and teacher-made tests will usually measure more adequately the degree to which the objectives of a particular course for a particular teacher have been met. For example, let us assume that a teacher of eleventh-grade history feels that his pupils should have an awareness of social conditions prior to the French Revolution. If this area is atypical of the conventional curriculum in this course, it should be readily evident that the teacher-made test would be more valid than the best standardized test that did not concern itself with this objective. In other words, the test user must ask himself, "How valid is this test for my objectives?"

Construction

Another difference between standardized achievement tests and teacher-made achievement tests is in the relative amount of time, money, effort, and resources that are available to commercial test publishers. The following example of how a standardized achievement test is constructed by test publishers may indicate why the teacher-made test is seldom as well prepared as the standardized test.

First, the test publisher arranges a meeting of curriculum specialists and subject-matter specialists. After a thorough study and analysis of syllabi, textbooks, and programs throughout the country, a list of objectives is prepared—what information the student should have, what principles he should understand, and what skills he should possess. These decisions concerning objectives to be sampled by the test are then reduced to a test outline or table of specifications (based on the judgments of the various experts involved in the test planning) that guides the test maker in constructing the test. Then, with the assistance of classroom teachers and subject-matter experts, a pro-

---

[3] This is less of a problem with single-subject-matter tests than with survey batteries. It is easier (and often less expensive) to revise and renorm a single test than a survey battery.

fessional team of test writers prepares the items according to the specification outlined in the grid.[4] After careful review and editing, the tryout or experimental items are ready to be arranged in a test booklet. Then, the general instructions (and specific instructions, if there are subparts) to both administrators and pupils and the tryout tests are given to a sample of students for whom the test is designed. After the answer sheets have been scored, an item analysis is made to remove the poor items. In addition, comments from test administrators are noted insofar as they pertain to timing and clarity of instructions for both administrator and pupils. Then further editing is performed on the basis of the item analysis (or more items are written if too many need to be discarded and the content validity is rechecked) and the test is then ready to be standardized. After a representative sample of pupils has been selected, the refined test is administered and scored. Reliability and criterion-related validity evidence is obtained, and norms are prepared for the standardization sample.

This brief description should demonstrate how much time, effort, and expense go into the preparation of a standardized achievement test. Without minimizing the enthusiasm, interest, and dedication of the classroom teacher in constructing his own tests, we may say the teacher-made test seldom compares in technical aspects with a commercially made standardized test. The teacher alone constructs his test; the standardized test is constructed by test specialists in cooperation with experts in the subject matter area, curriculum specialists, and statisticians. The teacher has a limited amount of time that can be devoted to test construction; standardized test makers can spend as much as two or three years on the preparation of their test. The teacher has little, if any, opportunity to examine his items in terms of difficulty and discrimination; commercial test publishers have recourse to statistical tools in order to eliminate or to suggest ways to rewrite the poor items. The teacher, because he is unable to try out his test beforehand, does not have the opportunity to (1) clarify ambiguous directions and/or (2) alter the speededness of the test by either increasing or decreasing the number of items; the commercial test publisher tries out his items in experimental or preliminary editions and is able to ascertain how well the test and the items function. On the whole, then, it should be readily evident that commercial standardized achievement tests are superior in terms of technical features to teacher-made achievement tests. This does not imply that teacher-made achievement tests cannot be technically as sound as commercial tests. They can be, but because of the time, money, effort, and technical skill involved in preparing a good test, they normally are not.

The classroom teacher should not develop an inferiority complex because

---

[4] The publisher's inclusion of such a grid in the test manual would be very valuable to the user in ascertaining whether the test has content validity for him. Unfortunately, few publishers do so.

of the preceding remarks. He should recognize that he has been trained to be a teacher and not a test maker. Horst made the following comment regarding the teacher as a professional test maker:

> For some years considerable emphasis has been placed on the importance of teachers learning to develop objective measures of achievement based on subject matter. . . . The underpaid and overworked classroom teacher should not be expected to be a specialist in the development of measuring instruments. (Horst, 1966, p. 10)

Norms

Another feature distinguishing most standardized tests from teacher-made achievement tests is that standardized tests generally contain norms of one type or another: sex, rural-urban, grade, age, type of school (public, private, parochial). Their value is dependent upon the manner in which they have been constructed. With national norms, the classroom teacher, school psychologist, counselor, or others concerned with the pupil's education will be in a position to make numerous comparisons of the performance of individual pupils, classes, grades, schools, and school districts with the academic progress of pupils throughout the country. Naturally, the kinds of comparisons that can be made will depend upon the types of norms furnished by the test publisher. Although teacher-made tests may have norms, they usually do not.

Purposes and Use

Standardized achievement tests, especially survey batteries, by the nature of their construction have a broad sampling of content, and they may be too general in scope to meet the specific educational objectives of a particular school or teacher. Teacher-made achievement tests, on the other hand, will usually have narrow content sampling (although what is sampled may be covered thoroughly)—especially those tests prepared for just a single unit of material or for material covered in a single semester. This does not imply that the standardized achievement test is superior to the teacher-made achievement test. Because of the emphasis placed upon the various course objectives, the standardized achievement test may be superior to the teacher-made test in one instance and not in another. Both standardized and teacher-made achievement tests serve a common function: the assessment of the pupil's knowledge and skills at a particular time. However, because standardized and teacher-made achievement tests often differ in scope and content (as well as the normative data provided), they also differ in their uses. It is usually agreed that teacher-made achievement tests will assess specific objectives more satisfactorily than does the standardized achievement test. Teacher-made tests are generally better for making daily instructional decisions and for appraising student progress. Decisions related to placement, because they tend to consider a broad area; guidance and selection decisions, where normative comparisons are usually involved; and curricular and policy decisions, which invariably involve making comparisons, are usually best served by standardized tests. Diagnostic-type decisions that ultimately will involve some sort of remedial action can benefit from the information provided by *both* standardized and teacher-made tests. It should be noted, however, that all educational decisions—assignment of course grades, vocational and educational guidance, promotion, placement, teacher evaluation, instruction, and research, to mention just a few—should be based on as much empirical data as possible. Because the standardized and teacher-made achievement tests serve different purposes, school personnel should consider the supplemental value of standardized achievement test scores to teacher-made test scores and teacher observations and judgments, rather than argue that one measurement device is better than the other.

To compare the pupils in one school with those in another school, a standardized achievement test will be appropriate. To determine whether Johnny has learned his addition skills in Miss Jones' third grade may be better accomplished by using a teacher-made test. Thus the functions or uses of the two kinds of achievement tests vary. We will consider the uses of standardized achievement tests further in the concluding section of this chapter.

CLASSIFICATION OF STANDARDIZED ACHIEVEMENT TESTS

There are different kinds of standardized achievement tests: *diagnostic* tests, which are designed to isolate specific strengths and weaknesses of the individual in some particular field of knowledge; *single-subject-matter* achievement tests, which are concerned with measuring the pupil's educational accomplishments in a single content area; and *survey batteries*, which consist of a group of tests in different content areas standardized on the same population so that the results of the various components may be meaningfully compared.

These three types—diagnostic, single-subject-matter, and survey battery—of standardized achievement tests differ in their purposes, coverage, and construction. They differ primarily because they are designed to measure different aspects or segments of the pupil's knowledge.

Although we discuss criterion-referenced tests (CRTs) and it might therefore be construed that there are four types of standardized achievement tests, we have purposely avoided this classification scheme, since any of the three types could be either norm-referenced, criterion-referenced, or both.

Purposes and Use

All standardized achievement tests are designed to assess pupils' knowledge and skills at a particular point in time. This is true for diagnostic tests, single-subject-matter tests, or survey batteries, whether they be norm- or criterion-referenced. If we are interested in learning what Mary's specific strengths or weaknesses are, in, say, reading or spelling, we would use a diagnostic test.[5] If we are interested in making a somewhat thorough evaluation of Mary's achievement in spelling, we should use a standardized spelling test rather than the spelling subtest of a survey battery, because the survey battery subtest will ordinarily be shorter, thereby limiting its coverage. If we are interested in learning whether Mary is a better speller than she is a reader, we should use a standardized survey battery where the total test has been standardized on the same sample. If different subject-matter tests have norms based upon different samples, direct comparisons cannot be made because the samples might not be equivalent.

For guidance purposes, it may be advisable to use the results of both a survey battery (which will indicate the relative strengths and weaknesses in many different subject-matter fields) and a single-subject-matter test that gives more thorough information in a particular area. For example, pupils can initially be given a survey battery as a preliminary screening device. Then, certain pupils can be identified for more thorough investigation. These atypical pupils might then be given a single-subject-matter and/or diagnostic test in the area of suspected weaknesses. The use of such a sequential testing (that is, using the survey battery for an initial screening and a single survey test and/or a diagnostic test for only a few individuals) is an economical approach. Sequential testing is of great help to the classroom teacher or counselor in obtaining relevant data to assist school personnel in providing optimal learning conditions. In the end, everyone benefits—pupils, teachers, and counselors.

Coverage and Construction

Standardized achievement-test batteries attempt to measure pupils' knowledge in many diverse areas; single-subject-matter tests are restricted to only a single area of knowledge such as grade 11 physics or grade 4 spelling or grade 6 language arts. Both types of tests measure the important skills, knowledge, and course objectives. Normally, single-subject-matter tests are a little more thorough in terms of their coverage. For example, if a spelling test requires 1 hour and the spelling subtest of a battery requires 40 minutes, there is more opportunity for the single test to have more items and thereby to increase the content sampling.

Although the survey battery is more convenient to administer than an

---

[5] The teacher must interpret the results of a diagnostic test cautiously. The test does not provide an absolute and irrevocable explanation for the problem (deficiency or weakness) but only offers some suggestions. The psychometric quality of the data provided in these tests is typically inadequate.

equal number of single tests, and although for the most part it is fairly valid for the average classroom teacher, it does suffer from the possibility that some of the subtests may lack the degree of validity desired because the subtests contain a more limited sampling of tasks. The general consensus, however, is that, despite the more limited sampling of tasks, survey batteries are preferred over a combination of many single-subject-matter tests. This is so because the survey battery (1) gives a fairly reliable index of a pupil's relative strengths and weaknesses once it has been standardized on the same population, whereas this is seldom the case for single-subject-matter tests (even those prepared by the same publisher); (2) is more efficient timewise; and (3) is usually more economical.

Diagnostic tests may differ markedly from the survey battery or single-subject-matter test, depending upon the purposes they are to serve. If we recall that diagnostic tests are designed primarily to assist the teacher in locating or attempting to isolate the genesis of some deficiency, we would expect to find the diagnostic test to have a thorough coverage of a limited area. For example, both a standardized achievement test of arithmetic skills and/or the arithmetic subtest of a survey battery are concerned with measuring general goals and objectives of the arithmetic curriculum. Hence both types of arithmetic tests contain a variety of items on many different arithmetic topics. A diagnostic test, however, may be restrictive in the sense that it is concerned only with one or two aspects of arithmetic, such as addition and subtraction. In addition, the diagnostic test will be more concerned with measuring the components that are felt to be of importance in developing knowledge in a complex skill.

There is no appreciable difference among the various types of achievement tests in the technical and mechanical factors involved in their preparation. In many instances, it is not possible to identify the type of test from which an item comes on the basis of the item format. That is, a test item such as "What percent of 36 is 9?" could conceivably be found in a survey, a single-subject-matter, or a diagnostic test. About the only way in which one can attempt to distinguish among the various types of achievement tests is to make a study of the breadth or intensity of their coverage.

Summary

The major distinctions among the various types of standardized achievement tests are in their purpose and ultimate use (and for that reason, they differ slightly in the range of material covered). If an overall assessment in many different areas is desired and if comparisons are to be made for an individual's relative strengths and weaknesses in various subject-matter areas, a survey battery is desired. If only an assessment in a single area is desired, either a single-subject-matter test or a subtest of the battery will suffice. If the teacher is interested in obtaining a clearer picture of particular strengths and/or weaknesses, he should use a diagnostic test. If this is for individually prescribed instruction, one would use a CRT. If interindividual comparisons are to be made, one would use a norm-referenced test (NRT). It should be emphasized at this time that the final decision regarding the selection of one test over another should be made by the person(s) using the test. It is essential that the test be valid for the user's purposes—he is in the best position to know what use will be made of the test results.

EXAMPLES OF STANDARDIZED ACHIEVEMENT TESTS

In the preceding section we were concerned with comparing and contrasting the different kinds of standardized achievement tests. In this section we present some examples of diagnostic tests, criterion-referenced tests, single-subject-matter achievement tests, and standardized achievement-test survey batteries that are commonly used in the public schools. In addition, we also consider some of the factors that are relevant in determining the choice of one achievement test or battery over another.

Diagnostic Tests

Diagnostic tests are primarily concerned with the skills or abilities (for example, reading, arithmetic) that the subject-matter experts believe are essential in learning a particular subject. For example, an arithmetic diagnostic test will be concerned with factors that experts in teaching arithmetic think enter into the arithmetic process. Diagnostic achievement tests provide a variety of exercises and problems in a somewhat restricted range of instructional objectives, thereby giving the student considerable opportunity to commit errors that will be indicative of a potential deficiency. In other words, rather than asking one or two items on addition with carrying or counting off decimals in division, a variety of such problems are presented in a diagnostic test. Also, in addition to the greater number of items, diagnostic tests often have their items graded in difficulty.

Diagnostic tests have much in common with criterion-referenced tests because both attempt to obtain information about an individual's performance in highly specific skills and relate this information to instructional prescriptions.

The development of a good diagnostic test is predicated upon two major assumptions: (1) the ability to analyze skills or knowledge into component subskills, and (2) the ability to develop test items that will validly measure these subskills. In fact, a major weakness of diagnostic reading tests are the low reliabilities and high intercorrelations among the separate subtests. It goes without saying that the major problem in constructing a valid diagnostic test rests upon satisfying the assumptions noted above. The low reliability is particularly significant in some of the shorter diagnostic tests since these deficiencies reduce the test's diagnostic value.

Because reading is an integral component of the learning process, the majority of diagnostic tests are for reading. Diagnostic reading tests range from the conventional paper-and-pencil test, where the student reads a sentence and records the error in the sentence, to the oral procedure, where the examiner carefully notes, for example, mispronunciations, omissions, repetitions, substitutions, and reversals of letters. In the latter method—the "thinking aloud approach"—the examiner is in a better position to observe and record errors as they happen and thus to see whether there is any pattern to the errors. Not only understanding the kinds of errors made but also obtaining some insight into how the pupil responds and reacts can prove invaluable for future remedial work. For example, in the oral approach, the examiner may note that the pupil is nervous, wary, concerned, and so forth.

A diagnostic test not only will inform the teacher that a pupil is weak or deficient in reading or arithmetic, but it also will point out what areas are weak, such as word comprehension or addition with carrying. However, it will not establish causal relationships. In other words, the teacher might learn *what* the difficulty is but *not why* the problem is there. For example, let us say that Salvador is weak in algebra. This may be due to his intellectual ability, poor reading skills, psychomotor difficulties, poor study skills, emotional problems, inability to deal with polynomials, and so forth. The teacher must consider such factors to arrive at a reasonable solution to the problem. If not, he may only remedy the immediate algebra problem, but the etiological factors (having not been considered) may manifest themselves in other learning situations.[6]

The manuals of some achievement test batteries suggest that some of their subtests may be used for diagnostic purposes. We caution the user not to consider these subtests as diagnostic because, in many instances, the tests were not constructed to measure the components involved in a particular skill such as reading or arithmetic. Before a diagnostic test can be considered valid (1) the component skills subtests should emphasize only a single type of error (such as word reversal in a reading diagnostic test), and (2) the subtest difference scores should be reliable. This can be achieved only by having subtests that have high reliabilities in themselves and low intertest correlations. Achievement-test batteries or single-subject-matter tests seldom display these characteristics.

This does *not* mean that standardized achievement-test batteries cannot

---

[6] The diagnosis of learning problems requires trained specialists—school psychologists and often social workers, physicians, and psychiatrists. The remedial program to be initiated will require special-education teachers. Because of this, classroom teachers should leave this area to the specialists, especially for moderate or severe cases.

be used to diagnose group or class weaknesses. On the contrary! Curriculum evaluation would benefit greatly if achievement-test batteries were used for this purpose. Most achievement-test publishers provide various kinds of reporting services—item analysis data, grouping pupils of similar abilities, tailoring tests to textbooks, and so on—as well as prescriptive suggestions and materials for their tests. In the future we will witness greater use of computers for providing study assignments based on pupil test performance as well as suggestions to the teacher to improve his effectiveness and efficiency. Many of the states and local school districts undertaking assessment programs are using standardized achievement tests for curriculum evaluation.

Some of the more common questions asked about diagnostic tests by classroom teachers, counselors, and administrators are as follows:

Q. How does diagnostic testing differ from survey testing?

A. When one administers a standardized single-subject-matter test he is normally concerned only with the total score or possibly the subtest scores. Then appropriate decisions such as grouping or evaluation of the curriculum are made on the basis of the scores. In diagnostic testing, there is no single score. Rather, there is a detailed analysis (depending upon the test used) of the pupil's work habits. Then, instead of using the test results for, say, grouping, the teacher uses the analysis of test performance plus other information to outline a remedial teaching program.

Q. Are diagnostic tests standardized?

A. Diagnostic tests are standardized in the sense that the instruments are administered under uniform conditions and objectively scored. The fact that subjectivity enters into the interpretation or diagnosis does not detract from the diagnostic tests being considered standardized.

Q. Do diagnostic tests have norms?

A. Yes and no. Yes, in the sense that a distribution of scores may be presented to designate how students in general have performed. No, in the sense that we think of the norms being representative of a cross section of pupils throughout the country (national norms) who are in need of remedial instruction. The norms accompanying diagnostic tests are not necessarily based on the performance of only those students who are in need of remedial instruction. However, diagnostic test norms of a type may be provided by the test publisher. Such a norm(s) contains the classification of types of errors made. The important thing is that when norms accompany a diagnostic test, the sample on which the normative data are based must be clearly defined.

Q. What about diagnostic tests that have percentile or grade-equivalent scores?

A. Be wary of such scores.

Q. Should diagnostic tests be given to all students?

A. No! Only to those students who are having difficulty as evidenced from the teacher's observations and/or the results of a survey test. They are too time consuming to administer, score, and interpret.

Q. How difficult is it to administer a diagnostic test correctly?

A. Very difficult in comparison to other types of achievement tests. Not only must the examiner record the answer given (for young children) but also he must note the kind of error made (for example, leaving out a word when reading a sentence or reversing the letters in a word); he must record the student's thought processes if the student is asked to think aloud; he must note the attitude of the student throughout the test, to mention just a few. Considerable practice is necessary.

Q. Do diagnostic tests measure the major sources of pupil difficulty?

A. No! Even if it were possible (which we seriously doubt) to identify all the potential problem areas, time constraints would preclude a teacher from measuring all sources of difficulty. It should be remembered that any diagnostic test explores only *some* of the sources of difficulty in a particular area. And depending upon the test constructor's perspective, some skills deemed to be important to one author may not be considered as important to another author. For example, the authors of Level III of the Stanford Diagnostic Arithmetic test did not test the application of computational skills to verbally stated problems. If a teacher is interested in learning or probing specific deficiencies in analyzing problems, this test would not be appropriate.

It is not possible here to consider in very much detail the variety of diagnostic tests available to the classroom teacher. We have described some of the different methods used to construct diagnostic tests; we have attempted to caution the user to be wary in his interpretation of diagnostic test results (because they are not elegant psychometric instruments with high validity and complete normative data); and we have taken the view that the teacher must be certain every avenue has been explored in his attempt to remedy an evident defect. This section concludes with a very brief description of some of the more popular diagnostic tests available in the elementary grades. Possibly because of the technical difficulties involved, there is a paucity of valid diagnostic tests.

Reading Diagnostic Tests

Reading diagnostic tests generally measure such factors as reading rate, comprehension, vocabulary, visual and auditory discrimination, and motor skills. As will be evident when reading readiness tests are discussed, the skills measured by reading, reading readiness, and reading diagnostic tests are very similar, as we would expect. The major difference is in the range of material covered and the intensity of coverage.

Q. Do all reading diagnostic tests measure the same thing?

A. No! Although there are more similarities than differences among most standardized reading diagnostic tests, there are nevertheless some basic differences. For example, the Durrell Analysis of Reading Difficulty and the Gates-McKillop Reading Diagnostic Tests are both individually administered. Both measure various factors involved in the reading process, but do so in markedly different ways. In the Gates-McKillop, the subtests are analogous to power tests in that the exercises vary in their degree of difficulty. In the Durrell, this is not so. On the other hand, the Gates-McKillop has tests of the child's word-attack skills, but the Durrell does not.

The strength of the Durrell is in two sets of paragraphs; the Gates-McKillop has eight separate subtests.

Q. How valid are the interpretations that can be made with a reading diagnostic test?

A. This depends on the test—how the items were selected (or prepared), the test's psychometric qualities, and the adequacy of the norming group. For some tests like the Gates-McKillop, the training and experience of the examiner plays a vital role. The older Gates Reading Diagnostic Tests can be interpreted easily by classroom teachers. The types of interpretations that can be made are governed, to a large extent, by the range of material the test covers. The practical clinical value of the interpretation depends, to a large extent, on the check list of errors (and their validity) the publisher provides.

Stanford Diagnostic Reading Test (SDRT)   Harcourt Brace Jovanovich, Inc., 1976. Two forms. Four levels: Red Level (grades 1.6–3.5), Green Level (grades 2.6–5.5), Brown Level (grades 4.6–9.5), and Blue Level (grades 9–13, formerly Level III in the 1973 edition). Group administered. Six scores for Red Level, seven scores for Green and Brown Levels, and eight scores for Blue Level. Working time varies according to level but is approximately 2 hours for each level. There are timed and untimed tests in each level, the number of strictly timed tests increasing as one moves from the elementary grades to the high school and college level.

Factors measured in *all* four batteries are phonetic analysis, vocabulary, and reading comprehension, although different techniques are used to measure these factors depending upon the grade level. As might be expected, at only the upper grade levels are reading rate, scanning and skimming, and reading vocabulary measured. Some examples of the types of items used in the SDRT are presented in Figure 15-1.

Content and criterion-related (concurrent) validity were emphasized in the test's construction. K-R 20 reliability is reported using raw scores, and standard errors of measurement are reported for both raw and scaled scores. Although the manual reports only alternate-form reliabilities for selected subtests, it is indicated that this information will be available for all subtests in a series of special reports. Subtest intercorrelations are also presented for a single grade level within a grade-level range battery. On the whole, the revised SDRT displays adequate content and criterion-related validity and reliability.

Each of the subtest and total scores can be expressed and interpreted in terms of *both* a within-grade criterion-(content-) referenced mode (raw scores and Progress Indicators) or norm-referenced mode (percentile ranks, stanines, grade equivalents, and scaled scores). The stanine conversion is recommended and is used to prepare the pupil profile chart on the back page of the test booklet and on the *Individual Diagnostic Report*.

Progress Indicators, although not a test score per se, are cut-off scores that have been established for each SDRT Skill Domain and Item cluster to identify those pupils who have mastered or not mastered minimum competencies in those areas deemed to be vital in the reading process development sequence. The authors caution users *not* to consider the PI is an absolute standard but to interpret the score in terms of their instructional objectives.

A variety of reports—*Individual Diagnostic Report, Instructional Placement Report, Class Summary Report,* and *Item Analysis Report*—are available, and with the test manual provide helpful information to aid in both the interpretation of the pupils' or classes' performance as well as suggest appropriate instructional strategies. The manual is concisely written and is teacher oriented, although attention is also paid to how the test results can be used for making administrative decisions.

Users availing themselves of the publisher's scoring service are provided with an Instructional Placement Report that reports *level-based* rather than grade-based stanines. This type of reporting provides a profile analysis in terms of the pupil's basic instructional needs regardless of his grade placement. In addition, pupils are categorized or classified as members of a group —Remedial, Decoding, Vocabulary, Comprehension, Average, Superior— either as being in need of specific remedial instruction or as progressing satisfactorily. On each computer-generated IPR there are brief instructional strategies given.

The revised SDRT at each level reports or classifies the best items by objective and item cluster, provides the difficulty level for each item, and designates a Progress Indicator Cut-Off Score.

The revised SDRT is a well-constructed and standardized test. It is attractively packaged, has clear directions, provides a rationale underlying each of the subtests, and has an excellent manual to help the teacher. The type of instructional suggestions provided, as well as variety of strategies provided, do indeed make this a diagnostic-prescriptive test. Many of the deficiencies inherent in the previous edition such as reporting alternate-form reliabilities for each subtest have been corrected. Although users are cautioned about the kinds of interpretations that can be made with respect to difference scores, we would still like to see standard errors of measurement for difference scores reported. We would still like to see a measure of sight vocabulary and an Accuracy of Reading Score. However, despite these shortcomings, the thoroughness in which the test was constructed and standardized, the types of reporting services available, and the diagnostic-prescriptive orientation by far outweigh the deficiencies. Although the classroom teacher can administer, score, and interpret the test, we strongly recommend that, when feasible, an experienced reading specialist do the actual interpretation and, in conjunction with the classroom teacher, develop the appropriate corrective action.

Arithmetic Diagnostic Tests

With the exception of the teaching of reading, probably no subject has been more intensively studied than the teaching of arithmetic. Yet there have been

TEST 1: Auditory Vocabulary

Look at the first shaded box, box A, at the top of the page. (Demonstrate.) **Look at the pictures in the box. The pictures are of a rock, a dog, and a plant.** (Pause.) **Now I'm going to read a question to you about these pictures. Find the picture that answers the question. Ready? Here is the question: "Which one is an _animal_?" Which picture shows an _animal_?**

Pause. Encourage replies. Then say:

Yes, it is the second picture, the picture of the dog, because a dog is an animal. The answer space under the picture of the dog has been filled in to show that it is the right answer.

TEST 1: Auditory Vocabulary (continued)

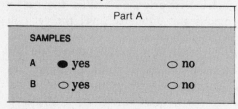

Look at the three words in line A, inside the shaded box. I am going to read a sentence to you. You are to choose one word from these three words that best completes the sentence. Here is the sentence: "To be glad is to be ... different ... happy ... silly." Which word best completes the sentence?

Pause for replies. Then say:

Yes, the best choice is "happy." That is why the space under "happy" has been filled in in your booklet.

TEST 2: Auditory Discrimination

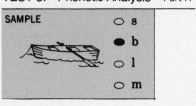

I am going to read two words to you. Listen to the words, and tell me if they begin with the same sound. The two words are: name ... night. Do "name" and "night" begin with the same sound?

Pause for replies. Then say:

Yes, they both begin with the same sound. That is why the space in front of "yes" has been filled in in your booklet.

TEST 3: Phonetic Analysis Part A

Look at the shaded box at the top of the page, where you see a picture of a boat. Think of the beginning sound of the word "boat" ... "boat." What is the first sound in "boat"?

Pause for replies.

Yes, it is /b/ ("buh"). "Boat" begins with the /b/ sound. Which letter in the shaded box stands for the /b/ sound?

Pause for replies.

Yes, it is "b" ("bee"); that is why the space next to the "b" has been filled in in your booklet. You will do the same with the other questions on this page. I will tell you what the picture is. Then you will fill in the answer space in front of the letter or group of letters that stands for the beginning sound or sounds of the word I say. Mark only one letter or group of letters for each picture. Does everyone understand what to do?

FIGURE 15–1   Sample items from the Stanford Diagnostic Reading Test. (Copyright © 1976 by Harcourt Brace Jovanovich, Inc. Reproduced by special permission of the publisher.)

TEST 3: Phonetic Analysis Part B

SAMPLE

- ○ p
- ○ d
- ○ h
- ● t

TEST 4: Word Reading

SAMPLES

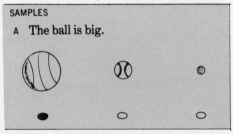

A   yes   cake   cow
     ○   ●   ○

B   dark   away   party
     ○   ○   ●

C   fun   hop   for
     ●   ○   ○

TEST 5: Reading Comprehension Part A

SAMPLES

A The ball is big.

●   ○   ○

TEST 5: Reading Comprehension Part B

SAMPLE

Pedro goes to the library to get

A   food   books   flowers.
     ○   ●   ○

FIGURE 15–1 *(continued)*

Look at the picture in the shaded box at the top of the page. (Demonstrate.) You see a picture of a cat. What letter tells the *ending* sound of the word "cat"?

Pause for replies. Then say:

Yes, "cat" ends with the /t/ sound of the letter "t." That is why the space next to the letter "t" has been filled in in your booklet. You'll do the same with the other questions on this page. I will tell you what each picture is. This time you will fill in the space next to the letter or group of letters that tells the *ending* sound or sounds of the word I say. You are to mark only one letter or group of letters for each picture. Does everyone understand what we're going to do?

We are going to look at some pictures and then find the words that tell about each picture. Look at the shaded box at the top of the page. (Demonstrate.) You see a picture of some children at a birthday party. (Pause.) Now look at the three lines of words below the picture. In each line, there is one word that goes with the picture. You are to pick out the word in each line that goes with the picture. Look at the first line. Read the words to yourself as I read them aloud: "yes ... cake ... cow." Which word goes with the picture?

Pause. Encourage replies.

Yes, the word "cake" goes with the picture. That's why the space under "cake" has been filled in in your booklet. (Pause.) Now look at line B. Read the three words to yourself. (Pause.) Which word goes with the picture?

Pause for replies.

Yes, the word "party" does. The three words are "dark," "away," and "party." The answer space under "party" has been filled in in your booklet. (Pause.) Now read the words in line C to yourself. (Pause.) Which word goes with the picture?

Pause for replies.

Yes, the right word is "fun." The children are having fun at the party. The space under "fun" has been filled in.

Look at the first shaded box at the top of the page. (Demonstrate.) Inside the box you see a sentence and three pictures. Read the sentence to yourself while I read it aloud: "The ball is big." One of the pictures goes with the sentence. Which picture is it?

Pause for replies.

Yes, the first picture is the one that goes with the sentence because the first ball is big. That's why the space under the first ball has been filled in in your booklet.

On this page, there are some stories for you to read. Look at the story in the shaded box. Read the first sentence to yourself as I read it aloud: "Pedro goes to the library to get ... food ... books ... flowers." Which word best completes the sentence?

Pause for replies. Then say:

Yes, "books" is the best answer. That is why the space under "books" has been filled in in your booklet.

very few new arithmetic tests in the past decade and even fewer new diagnostic tests. Certain fundamental skills in arithmetic are taught at the primary level, and regardless of the method of instruction employed, most diagnostic arithmetic tests employ similar kinds of items. Thus, only one such test will be reviewed.

Diagnostic Tests and Self-Helps in Arithmetic   California Test Bureau, 1955. Grades 3–12. One form. Untimed. Four screening tests and 23 diagnostic tests. No norms.

Each of the 23 diagnostic tests is accompanied by a self-help unit that is on the back of the diagnostic test. Six major areas are surveyed by the series: basic facts (five tests); fundamental operations with whole numbers (five tests); operations with percentages (one test); fundamental operations with decimal fractions (four tests); operations with measures (one test); and fundamental operations with common fractions (seven tests). The four screening tests are designed to measure pupil achievements in whole numbers, fractions, decimals, and general arithmetic skills and knowledge. On the basis of the pupil's performance on one (or more) of the first three screening tests, the appropriate diagnostic test(s) is administered. For example, if the pupil does poorly on Screening Test II, Screening Test in Fractions (the test author suggests that one or more errors is indicative of further testing), he would be given one or more of the Diagnostic Tests in Common Fractions. That is, if he had difficulty in the addition of like fractions, he would be given Test 12, Addition of Like Fractions. The screening test, because it contains only a few examples of the skills needed, would have to be supplemented by a separate test that contains many examples.

The diagnostic tests are essentially power tests that begin with very simple items and then progress in difficulty. Because there are many items dealing with the same concept or skill, the probability of committing an error is maximized, something that is desired in a diagnostic test. The separate diagnostic tests are cross-referenced to assist the teacher in locating the nature of the difficulty. For example, when a pupil multiples 640 by 23, he may arrive at an incorrect answer for a variety of reasons: (1) He may place the products incorrectly, (2) he may not add the columns correctly, or (3) he may not know how to add with carrying. Therefore, if his performance on the screening test suggested that the pupil had difficulty with multiplication, the teacher would have to see where this error was manifested. Because of the cross-referencing of the diagnostic tests, the pupil who multiplied 640 by 23 and arrived at an incorrect answer because he didn't add properly could be given Test 1, Addition Facts, and/or Test 6, Addition of Whole Numbers.

The diagnostic self-helps are keyed to the diagnostic test items. The self-helps are, in a sense, remedial exercises that have been worked out in detail. They indicate to the pupil the correct procedure to be used in answering that kind of item. For example, in Test 12, Addition of Like Fractions, the self-help exercises on the addition of fractions with no carrying would be as follows:

$\frac{1}{8}$
$\frac{1}{8}$
$\frac{2}{8} = \frac{1}{4}$ Add the numerators, 1 and 1
             Write the sum over a denominator 8

Then, $\dfrac{1+1}{8} = \dfrac{2}{8}$

Reduce $\frac{2}{8}$: $\dfrac{2 \div 2}{8 \div 2} = \dfrac{1}{4}$

After working through the self-help exercises, the pupil is encouraged to rework the items that he answered incorrectly.

No reliability and validity data are reported. The test author states that reliability was increased by having numerous items of the same kind. Content validity was stressed in constructing the test. The test author attempted to analyze the skills needed to perform a particular task. It would have been desirable to present more information about how these skills were analyzed, who did the analysis, and upon what basis the analysis was done. Do the self-help exercises contribute to learning? Do the diagnostic tests really assist the teacher in locating the nature of the pupils' difficulties or could essentially similar information be obtained from the arithmetic subtest of a standardized achievement test? Answers to these questions are absent from the manual.

The test manual contains numerous suggestions for the effective use of the test results. It also provides the user with a list of the more common errors in operations with whole numbers, common fractions, and decimals.

The Diagnostic Tests and Self-Helps in Arithmetic appears to do an adequate job in surveying specific weaknesses in fundamental arithmetic skills. The first four diagnostic tests contain 100 arithmetic operations involving digits 0 to 9. The basic facts, then, are covered thoroughly. However, there is inadequate provision for the measurement of arithmetic meaning or problem-solving ability. The value of these tests could possibly be increased by having some of the items responded to orally. In this way, the teacher, listening to the pupil "work the problem out loud," could obtain additional information regarding the pupil's work habits. Also, provision of a more complete error list could prove to be beneficial insofar as the teacher's instructional program is concerned.

Criterion-Referenced Standardized Achievement Tests

In recent years, accountability, performance contracting, formative evaluation, computer-assisted instruction, individually prescribed instruction, mastery learning, and the like, have spawned an interest in and need for new kinds of tests—criterion-referenced tests (CRTs), or, as some prefer to say, objectives-based tests.[7] Test publishers are now paying more attention to the development of CRTs since many educators believe that norm-referenced tests (because they are concerned with making *inter*-individual comparisons) are inadequate for individualized instruction decision-making purposes.

As mentioned earlier, the item-writing rules and principles are essentially the *same* for both CRT and NRT achievement tests. However, they do *differ* in purpose, use, and content sampling. In fact, traditional models for test construction and interpretation of NRTs appear to be less useful for CRTs (see Durnan & Scandura, 1973.)

As mentioned in Chapter 3, a multitude of definitions have been advanced for a criterion-referenced test. A common theme, however, is that the author of a C-R test must clearly specify a content domain and generate appropriate samples of test items from that domain.

As of now, the majority of criterion-referenced achievement tests are teacher-made. But in the past few years commercial test publishers have begun preparing such tests. Today commercially prepared standardized criterion-referenced achievement tests are generally in reading and arithmetic, although there are agencies available that will produce tailor-made criterion-referenced achievement tests in a variety of subject-matter fields at different grade levels (Westinghouse Learning Corporation, Instructional Objectives Exchange, Houghton Mifflin).

Criterion-referenced tests vary from the single test to a battery of "mini-tests" that are designed to measure the pupils' knowledge of the various instructional objectives in detail. Also, test and textbook publishers are beginning to prepare complete instructional systems using a survey test, a diagnostic test(s), and a set of prescriptions (suggested instructional activities). One of the most comprehensive instructional systems has been developed by Science Research Associates in Reading and Mathematics.

The SRA package or "lab" in reading[8] consists of 34 Probes or criterion-referenced diagnostic tests measuring instructional objectives normally covered in grades 1–4; six cassettes that make for self-administration of the Probes; a Survey Test that indicates the students' strengths and weaknesses and indicates what Probes, if any, should be taken; a Prescription Guide that keys the instructional objectives measured by a particular Probe (e.g., letter recognition, consonant blends, homographs) to major reading tests or supplementary activities; and a Class Progress Chart.

One commercial test publisher, Westinghouse Learning Corporation, currently has available an objectives-based testing program—School Curriculum Objective-Referenced Evaluation (SCORE)—where over 8000 in-

---

[7] One should *not* imply that norm-referenced achievement tests (NRTs) are not based on objectives. In order for an achievement test to be valid, be it a CRT or NRT, there must be instructional objectives on which the test items are based.

[8] The mathematics "lab" is similar in purpose and content.

structional objectives in reading, language arts, science, and social studies for grades K–8 have been cataloged and classified. To measure these objectives, over 20,000 test items are available.

SCORE differs from the conventional standardized test in that the program will tailor a test to the teacher's specifications. After a teacher selects his objectives, type of item format desired, item difficulty, and the like, Westinghouse Learning Corporation "creates" a test to measure the objectives identified with item characteristics meeting prescribed criteria. The items are then assembled and printed in a test booklet with accompanying directions. Or, if the teacher wishes, he can specify objectives that are unique to his course, and Westinghouse Learning Corporation will produce and print appropriate items. A variety of report forms—for example, class list, building summary, district summary, percentile distribution by building and district—are available.

California Test Bureau/McGraw-Hill exemplifies a newer approach in building criterion-referenced diagnostic tests in Reading and Mathematics (Prescriptive Reading Inventory [PRI] and Diagnostic Mathematics Inventory [DMI]).[9] The DMI and PRI are designed to identify pupils with difficulties in reading and/or mathematics. Then, after appropriate remedial instruction has taken place, the DMI or PRI is followed up with a criterion-referenced mastery test (Interim Evaluation Test) to ascertain the degree to which the pupil has mastered the minimal instructional objectives. Although untimed, each PRI test takes about 2¾ hours working time; the DMI for the lower grades (1.5–4.5) and upper grades (4.5–8.5) take about 2½ and 4 hours, respectively. In both the DMI and PRI, each test item is referenced to commonly used textbooks. In this way, the teacher is assisted in developing appropriate remedial instruction.

In both the DMI and PRI, objectives are arranged according to grade levels where they would normally be covered. Table 15–2 presents data describing the characteristics of the respective tests.

Content validity was stressed in the construction of the DMI, PRI, and the respective Interim Evaluation Tests. Extensive preliminary tryout data were gathered before the tests were published. Classroom teachers and curriculum specialists were used in the development of objectives and various criteria (see the Teacher's Guide for a full description of item development and selection) were employed to select the test items.

Both the DMI and PRI have a variety of reports available to pupils and teachers. The PRI has an Individual Diagnostic Map, an Individual Study Guide, a Program Reference Guide, a Class Grouping Report, and an Interpretive Handbook. The DMI has an Objectives Mastery Report, a Pre-Mastery

---

[9] We realize that the DMI and PRI, because they are diagnostic tests, could have been discussed earlier. However, since they are objectives-based in development and because of their relationship to the Interim Tests, we decided to cover the series together.

TABLE 15-2   Characteristics of Diagnostic Mathematics and Prescriptive Reading Inventories

	DMI	PRI
Grade Levels	Seven: Grades 1.5–2.5, 2.5–3.5, 3.5–4.5, 4.5–5.5, 5.5–6.5, 6.5–7.5, 7.5–8.5	Four: 1.5–2.5, 2.0–3.5, 3.0–4.5, 4.0–6.5
Number of objectives measured	325 in "new" and "old" mathematics programs (Because of overlap among the seven levels, a total of 714 objectives are tested)	90 (Because of overlap among levels, a total of 155 objectives are tested with the four levels)
Number of objectives per level	Varies from 37 to 138	Varies from 34 to 42
Number of items per level	Varies from 37 to 138	Varies from 123 to 162
Number of items per objective	1	Average of 3 or 4

Analysis, an Individual Diagnostic Report, a Group Diagnostic Report, a Mastery Reference Guide, a Guide to Ancillary Materials, and a Learning Activities Guide. The PRI's Interpretive Handbook and the DMI's Guides contain useful suggested activities and instructional strategies that teachers can use. All test questions are keyed to the appropriate objective being measured and most of the printouts reference the objective to a particular textbook page.

The Interim Evaluation Tests' (IET) objectives (and hence items) are organized as in the DMI or PRI. Each objective, be it in reading or mathematics, is measured with 4–6 items. Guidelines for determining whether the student has mastered the objective being tested, or needs to review an objective, are presented in the Examiner's Manual. This manual also suggests appropriate instruction activities that might be used to build mastery of the objective. A variety of output data are furnished. The test authors recommend that the IET (whether it be the total test, part of the test, or just a single objective section) "be administered not earlier than a full day and no later than a week" after appropriate remedial instruction has been given.

Use of the DMI or PRI and their respective Interim Tests permits a teacher to ascertain which students are in need of further instruction on a particular objective(s) and then to see whether, after remedial instruction, the student has mastered the objective(s). In a way, these tests can be considered as part of an individualized instruction program. The rationale underlying their development is that sound and extensive work was done to identify objectives and select items. The various reports issued to the teacher and the numerous suggested instructional aids offered are excellent.

However, we are very much concerned about the validity and reliability of a test that contains 1 to 4 items per objective. What can a teacher conclude if Irvin gets the right (or wrong) answer to "$2+2$"? Does this mean that Irvin would answer items of this type correctly? How far can we generalize? Has the total domain of this objective been delineated? Has there been sampling from this domain? We must caution the user of tests in general, and definitely diagnostic prescriptive tests in particular, to be very wary and to exercise extreme caution in his interpreting the test results. Implementing sometimes radical prescriptive surgery (remedial instruction) on the basis of limited data is precarious.

The Skills Monitoring Test from The Psychological Corporation is another example of a broad-range screening-test that covers a multitude of instructional objectives with as few as one item per objective. Then, on the basis of the student's performance, more intensive testing can be done with a series of tests covering a single objective. Presently, there is only an SMT for Reading which is designed for grades 3–5. Each grade level has a Skill Locator and from 40 to 60 one-page "Skill-Minis" containing 8–12 items on a single objective; a Teacher Handbook providing suggested activities; Class and Learner Skill Records, which permit progress monitoring; and a Grouping Guide, which assists the teacher in forming groups for appropriate instruction. A novel feature of the SMT pertains to the manner in which students respond. By means of chemically treated crayons and latent images, the student is able to obtain immediate feedback regarding the correctness of his answer. If the box he marks is the correct answer, the word "Yes" appears; otherwise he continues selecting responses until the correct answer is given.

Other standardized C-R tests commercially available are: Individual Pupil Monitoring System (IPMS) Mathematics and Reading and Customized Objective Monitoring Service—Reading and Mathematics (COMS) published by Houghton Mifflin, and the tests accompanying the Harper & Row Reading Series. The IPMS, like the SRA and CTB/McGraw-Hill tests discussed earlier, key their instructional objectives to commonly used textbooks. The COMS like SCORE "tailors" a test to the teachers' specifications using validated test items.

In summary, it is readily evident that test publishers have "jumped on the bandwagon" in the past few years to produce criterion-referenced standardized achievement tests. Presently these tests are primarily in reading and mathematics for the elementary grades, although we anticipate such tests in other content areas. And, in many instances, these tests are designed to provide diagnostic-prescriptive information (SRA, Psychological Corporation, and CTB tests), although SCORE and COMS typify the conventional purpose of achievement tests—be they criterion- or norm-referenced—to describe the knowledge and skills possessed by a pupil in some content area(s).

As discussed earlier, those responsible for constructing criterion-referenced tests still have to overcome many technical difficulties (although some success has been achieved) related to the validity and reliability of such tests, such as having enough items to measure an objective reliably and still keep the test length manageable. And in criterion-referenced tests we are faced with the problem of defining an acceptable level of performance as a criterion or standard of mastery. Doubtless a concerted effort will be made to remedy these difficulties because the increased concern for mastery learning, basic minimal competencies, and accountability will witness a larger number of standardized, commercially published criterion-referenced achievement tests.

Standardized Achievement Tests in Specific Subjects

Standardized achievement tests are available for nearly every subject (agriculture to zoology) and for every grade level (kindergarten to professional and graduate school). There are, for example, reading readiness tests; reading tests; arithmetic, spelling, and science tests; product scales; and vocational achievement tests. For the most part, reading and arithmetic tests (as well as readiness tests in these respective subjects) are restricted to the primary grades because (1) these skills are primarily developed there and the major emphasis in the first few years of formal schooling is on reading and arithmetic, and (2) the relatively uniform curriculum of the elementary school makes it possible for the survey battery adequately to cover the measurement of the important objectives of instruction. In the secondary grades, because of the nonuniform nature of the curriculum, specialized tests covering a particular course such as Latin, Greek, or psychology are the predominant type.

Reading Readiness Tests[10]

Usually the first type of standardized achievement test that a pupil receives is a reading readiness test. It is administered either at or near the end of the kindergarten year or very early in the first grade. This type of test is often considered one of the most important achievement tests that the child takes during his school years. It goes without saying that efficient and adequate reading skills play a vital role in subsequent learning. Hence anything that can be done (sectioning, placement, and remedial instruction) to provide optimal reading instruction should reap benefits insofar as future learning is concerned.

The major purposes of a reading readiness test are (1) to identify the

[10] Readiness, or prognostic, tests are sometimes considered aptitude tests because they are used to predict how well the individual will profit from instruction or training.

children who are not yet ready to begin reading,[11] and (2) to identify, for grouping purposes, the children who are at essentially the same level of readiness. This grouping will then assist the teacher in providing appropriate instruction. Reading readiness tests are not designed to predict reading achievement in, say, the sixth or seventh grade. They do provide valuable information insofar as reading ability in the first and second grades is concerned. In addition, reading readiness tests should not be confused with reading diagnostic tests. Although they may indicate weaknesses in certain general broad areas, such as word recognition or vocabulary, they are not designed to isolate specific reading defects.

There is a general consensus among reading specialists that a child's readiness to participate in reading and the extent to which he will learn how to read are dependent upon a variety of factors: (1) intellectual ability, (2) eye-hand coordination, (3) motivation to learn how to read, (4) perceptual and visual skills, and (5) knowledge of colors, names of common things, and concepts of time and space. Although there are variations among the many reading readiness tests commercially published, all have several of the following types of items:

1. *Motor skills.* The child is required to draw lines, complete a circle, underline words, go through a finger maze.

2. *Auditory discrimination.* The child is asked either to pronounce words after they have been read to him or to select which of several similar-sounding words identify a picture.

3. *Visual discrimination.* The child is required to choose similarities or differences in words, letters, numbers, or pictures.

4. *Vocabulary.* The child's knowledge of the meaning of words is assessed by asking him either to define the meaning of a word, name various objects of the same or different class, or to select the correct word to describe a picture.

5. *Memory.* The child may be asked to reproduce a geometrical figure to which he has been exposed for a certain length of time, he may be asked to repeat a story that has been read to him, or he may be required to carry out in sequence a series of instructions that have been presented to him.

The results from only a reading readiness test will not be sufficient to answer all questions about a child's readiness to learn to read, but they will provide valuable supplementary information to that gathered by observing the child. As we have constantly reiterated throughout this text, the results of any test are best considered as supplementary and complementary infor-

---

[11] Whether or not one is ready to begin reading depends upon a variety of factors such as aptitude, psychomotor skills, and mental attitude. For a discussion of these factors, see Gates (1947) and Harris (1961).

mation for decision making. Some questions that may be raised regarding reading readiness tests are as follows:

Q. If there is a high correlation between reading test scores and intelligence test scores, why administer a reading readiness test?

A. Yes, there is a high correlation between performance on a reading readiness test and an intelligence test. However, intelligence tests do not survey all the skills and traits the child must have in order to learn to read. Intelligence tests, by their very nature, are not designed to provide specific information on the child's ability to handle words, whether or not the child can use and manipulate words, whether or not the child has adequate muscular coordination. Reading readiness tests are specifically designed to assess those skills deemed important in the reading process. For this reason, it is recommended that a reading readiness test be administered to kindergarten children, and the intelligence test be postponed to the first or second grade.[12]

Q. Do all reading readiness tests measure the same thing?

A. No! Although many of them look as if they are doing so because they have vocabulary items, or paragraph reading, or reproduction of objects, there is usually something unique or different about each of the reading readiness tests available. For example, the Harrison-Stroud Reading Readiness Profiles has a test of auditory discrimination, but the American School Reading Readiness Test does not. The American School test authors felt that variations in performance could result from variations in administration and therefore deleted the measurement of this skill. This is true, but it is an insufficient reason for omitting such an important task. Steps could be taken to make the administration uniform, either by having explicit instructions or by having a recording of the instructions played to the pupils.

Q. How are items selected for reading readiness tests?

A. Once again, there are differences among the various tests. Some test authors, like Harrison and Stroud, attempted to make a task analysis. That is, they specified those skills felt to be important in the reading process and then prepared a test on the basis of this analysis. A somewhat different procedure was employed by the constructors of the Gates and American School tests. On the basis of previously used items and those suggested by experts in the field, they assembled a preliminary pool of items, administered the items, and then selected the items that were statistically sound. Both methods are valid, and no one can say that one is better than the other.

There is a growing trend for textbook publishers to develop tests for their reading series textbooks. In the past, the test materials have been presented in workbooks and were not readiness tests per se. Harper & Row, for example, has developed a series of readiness and achievement tests for one of their reading-text series—the 1966 Harper & Row Basic Reading Program. The child (in grades K–6) is first given a readiness test at the beginning of the

[12] Research has shown that reading readiness tests given in kindergarten predict reading achievement in grade 1 *better* than aptitude tests but that aptitude tests given in kindergarten predict reading achievement in grades 4 and 5 better than do reading readiness tests.

school year and, on the basis of his test score, is assigned to a particular reader. Then, after completing the reader, he is given an achievement test based upon the reader's content. Although these tests are not so elegantly standardized as other achievement tests, such tests do serve a valuable purpose.

Q. How do I know whether an existing test is valid for my purposes?

A. You don't until you study it carefully! You must study the test manual thoroughly and determine whether the test objectives are in agreement with your goals. All the test maker can do is indicate what he thinks is important. It is up to the user to judge not only whether he agrees with the test's purposes but also whether the manner in which the test was constructed was valid. For example, the authors of the American School Reading Readiness Test felt that auditory discrimination was not important. The Metropolitan Readiness Tests require the pupil to draw a man. The Harrison-Stroud and American School tests do not contain this type of item. If the user believes that auditory discrimination is important, he should consider a test other than the American. Similarly, if the user feels that the ability to draw a man is vital to the reading process, he would be advised to consider a test other than the Harrison-Stroud or the American. The user must also make a thorough analysis of the test items. He cannot judge the purpose of a subtest by merely looking at the items. As we mentioned earlier, both the Harrison-Stroud and the American School tests have items designed to measure the child's ability to follow directions. In the former, this type of item is found as a peripheral task, whereas in the latter there is a specific subtest designed to measure this skill. Once again, we reiterate—do not judge a test by the names of the subtests!

Q. When should a readiness test be administered?

A. School personnel often ask whether a reading readiness test (or any readiness test for that matter) can be administered prior to first-grade entrance and still have predictive validity. Rubin (1974) administered the Metropolitan Readiness Tests (MRT) to a group of pupils *prior* to kindergarten entrance and again prior to entering grade 1 and reported a one-year test-retest reliability of 0.65. She also found that the correlations between the Reading and Spelling scores on the Wide Range Achievement Test and Pre-Kindergarten MRT scores compared favorably with the correlations for the pre–first-grade and end-of-first-grade WRAT scores despite the 12-month interval between predictor and criterion measures.

The results strongly suggest that the MRT can be validly used in the first few months prior to kindergarten entrance to predict first-grade achievement in reading, spelling, and arithmetic (although not as well as for the latter two) instead of waiting to administer them at the end of kindergarten or early in the first grade as normally is the case. The implications of these findings, if they are substantiated by further research, are that: (1) pupils with school readiness deficiencies can be identified early, and consequently appropriate remedial instruction can be initiated prior to grade 1; and (2) pupils who are not ready for entering grade 1 can be identified.

Reading readiness tests employ a variety of procedures. All directions are given orally, although on one test, the Harrison-Stroud, one section is devoted to pupils doing the test independently. Numerous examples or practice exercises are provided so that the child will understand what he is to do and how he is to do it. All work is done in the test booklet. The examiner should constantly check the students to be sure that they understand the directions. This should not be difficult because most of the tests are untimed and should under normal circumstances be administered in small groups or individually. Some examples of reading readiness tests and illustrative items are shown in Figure 15–2.

Metropolitan Readiness Tests   Harcourt Brace Jovanovich, Inc., 1976. Grades K–1. Two Levels: I and II with Level I being recommended for children "judged to be at a relatively low level of skill development." Two forms (P and Q). Seven subtests in Level I: Auditory Memory, Rhyming, Letter Recognition, Visual Matching, School Language and Listening, Quantitative Language, and Copying (optional). Gives 6 subtest scores, a Visual Area, Language Area, and Total score. Nine subtests in Level II: Beginning Consonants, Sound-Letter Correspondence, Visual Matching, Finding Patterns, School Language, Listening, Quantitative Concepts, Quantitative Operations, and Copying (the latter three are optional). Gives 6 to 8 subtest scores, an Auditory Area, Visual Area, Language Area, Quantitative Area, Pre-Reading Skills Composite, and a Battery Composite score. Recommended there be a separate session for each subtest. Valuable features of the 1976 MRT are a Practice Test, and a Parent-Teacher Conference Report. Other features are large-city school system norms, provision for machine-scoring responses made on the *drawing*, and a Handbook of Skill Development Activities. Percentile ranks and stanines. Five *quality* levels for the Copying Test. Subtest scores, Area Scores, and Total Scores are also expressed in terms of three (Average, Low, and High) Performance Levels.

It should be readily evident that there is considerable variation among the various reading readiness tests with respect to the time required for administration, the number of scores obtained, the types of norms provided, and so forth. All, however, are designed to measure the skills the test authors deem important in reading and reading instruction.

Uses of Reading Readiness Tests   The primary use of the reading readiness test is to provide the teacher with basic information about the child's reading skills so that optimal learning conditions can be provided. On the basis of a reading readiness test, a classroom teacher can tailor his teaching program to best fit the needs of each pupil.[13] For example, one student may be deficient in his ability to recognize similarities and differences, whereas another may be having difficulty reading numbers. After ascertaining that the

---

[13] Because of the instability of test scores for very young children, the results should be interpreted cautiously.

deficiencies are not due to any physical factors, the teacher can institute remedial action where needed. In this illustration the test is used both as a prognostic device and as a criterion upon which the learning materials are organized and presented by the classroom teacher.

The results of reading readiness tests may also be used by school personnel when there are two or three first-grade classes, so that the pupils who are at about the same level can be grouped together for instructional purposes. It is much easier to teach groups that have similar abilities. Naturally, for homogeneous grouping, one should also consider other factors. But in the first grade, reading readiness may well be the most important.[14]

We would be remiss if we did not caution the prospective user of readiness test results to be very wary of their potential *misuse*—which, in the long run, might be more damaging than beneficial to pupils. As of now, the empirical evidence regarding the predictive validity of readiness test scores is very weak (Henderson & Long, 1970). Evidence has emerged of late on the role that test scores play in the academic expectancies of teachers toward pupils (Brophy & Good, 1970; Chaikin & Sigler, 1973; Long & Henderson, 1974; Rosenthal & Jacobson, 1968; Willis, 1973). The majority of these studies have shown that prior knowledge of pupils' test scores can have a marked influence on the teachers' expectancies (they may be realistic or biased) regarding their pupils' academic performance.

Because readiness test scores results appear to play such an important role in determining teacher expectancies, it is vital that *all* test users be thoroughly educated on the *limitations* of tests they are using or planning to use. And, as Long and Henderson (1974, p. 145) state, "If teachers are *overly* [italics added] influenced by relatively invalid tests [sic] scores, it might be better if children entering school were not tested at all."

Reading Tests

The ability to communicate by means of language is a fundamental necessity in today's society. Reading is one form of communication that must be developed in our pupils. If one were to look at the curriculum in the primary grades, it would be readily obvious that the development of communicative skills—reading, writing, and speaking—makes up a major portion of the curriculum. If one were to look at a survey battery, he would find at least one or more subtests for the assessment of a person's reading skills. The subtests may be classified in a variety of ways—reading comprehension, language arts, language skills—but regardless of the rubric used, they are essentially tests of the pupil's ability to read.

Because all survey batteries, regardless of grade level, have subtests to

[14] Intellectual ability is also important. However, many research studies have demonstrated the high correlation between reading and IQ. The IQ tests that are highly verbal in nature are especially highly correlated with reading readiness tests.

TEST 1: AUDITORY MEMORY

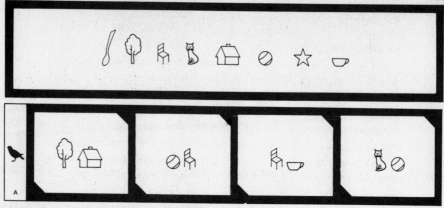

Look at the row of pictures at the top of the page (pointing to the top row). Let's name them together. SPOON, TREE, CHAIR, CAT, HOUSE, BALL, STAR, CUP. Now we all know what these pictures are.

This is what we're going to do. First, I'll tell you where to put your finger so you can find the right row. Then, you'll keep your finger there and close your eyes while I tell you what to mark.

A. Now put your finger on the little black BIRD. Close your eyes. Don't peek! Listen. CHAIR CUP. Open your eyes. Mark the right box.

You should have marked this box (pointing to the third box), because I said CHAIR CUP and this box has a CHAIR and then a CUP in it.

TEST 2: RHYMING

Listen to the words I say: LATE, DATE, GATE. Say each word with me. LATE, DATE, GATE.

Did you notice that all these words sound alike? Listen again: LATE, DATE, GATE. These words do not begin with the same sound, but they sound the same in the middle and at the end, so we say they RHYME.

I am going to say some more words. Tell me if they rhyme: BOOM, ROOM.

Pause for response.

Yes, BOOM and ROOM rhyme.

Tell me if these words rhyme: BIKE, BEAD.

Pause for response.

No, BIKE and BEAD do not rhyme.

A. Put your finger by the top row. The pictures are MILK, LEAF, TIE, BIKE. Listen to the word I say: LIKE. Mark the one that rhymes with LIKE, the one that rhymes with LIKE.

You should have marked the BIKE because BIKE rhymes with LIKE.

FIGURE 15–2 Types of items used on Reading Readiness Tests Sample items reproduced from the Metropolitan Readiness Tests. (Copyright © 1976 by Harcourt Brace Jovanovich. Reproduced by special permission of the publisher.)

STANDARDIZED EVALUATION PROCEDURES 490

TEST 3: LETTER RECOGNITION

P-1

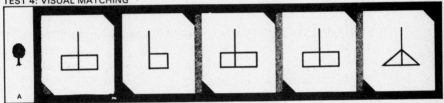

A. Put your finger on the little black SPOON at the beginning of the top row. Look at the letters in this row. Mark the S . . . the S.

You should have marked this (pointing to the fourth box), **the last letter in this row. That is the letter S.**

TEST 4: VISUAL MATCHING

P-1

A. Put your finger on the little black TREE. Look at what is in the red box. Then look over at the other shapes in the row. Find the one that is just like the one in the red box, and mark that box. Remember, the shape must be just the same in every way as the one you see in the red box. It must MATCH it.

You should have marked this box (pointing to the next-to-last box). **The shape in it is exactly like the one in the red box.**

TEST 5: SCHOOL LANGUAGE AND LISTENING

P-1

A. Put your finger on the little black BALL. Mark the picture that shows this: The duck is beside the flower . . . The duck is beside the flower.

You should have marked this picture (pointing to the last picture), **because it is the only picture that shows a duck beside a flower.**

TEST 6: QUANTITATIVE LANGUAGE

P-1

A. Put your finger on the little black HAND. Look at the rabbit in the red box. Now look over at the other rabbits. Mark the rabbit that is BIGGER THAN the rabbit in the red box . . . Mark the rabbit that is BIGGER THAN the rabbit in the red box.

You should have marked this rabbit (pointing to the next-to-last one) **because it is the only rabbit that is BIGGER THAN the rabbit in the red box.**

FIGURE 15–2 (*continued*)

measure the students' reading proficiency, one might well ask why it is necessary to have, and use, a separate reading test. Is it because the reading tests of the survey battery are invalid? Is it because they are unreliable? Not really. The major reasons for using separate tests for reading skills are: (1) Survey batteries may not be used until the second, third, or fourth grade, and it is vital that we identify students' reading skills proficiency as early as possible; (2) survey batteries are not so thorough in their coverage in any one area as are separate subject-matter (or skills) tests; and therefore (3) reading tests should be used if the scores from a survey battery indicate that the pupil is weak in the area.

All reading tests use essentially similar procedures for measuring the pupils' reading ability. Students are typically required to read a series of paragraphs and answer questions about them. Pupils are given items to see whether they are facile with words and sentences. Some tests may employ prose selections only, while others may use both prose and poetry to measure comprehension. Some of the tests are oral, whereas others are of the silent-reading type and can be administered in a group setting. Once again, regardless of the manner of assessment, reading tests all serve a common purpose—to see how well the individual can read. As we have mentioned earlier, the reading process is an extremely complex task and involves a variety of factors, some of which are continually interacting and cannot be isolated as distinct entities. No single test attempts to measure all these factors. Some of the factors, such as attitudes involved in reading or adult reading habits, are unlikely to be assessed by any test. Because there is some difference of opinion as to the skills deemed important in the reading process, we see different kinds of reading tests. This is not to say that one standardized reading test is more valid than another. The evaluation of any standardized reading (actually, any achievement) test depends upon the similarity of the user's and test constructor's objectives. The user alone must decide whether the objectives he deems important are measured by a test and how well his objectives are measured.

Q. Considering the high correlation between reading test scores and IQ scores, should teachers use a reading test? Isn't it a waste of time and money? Isn't it redundant?

A. No! In the primary grades at least, it has been shown that from a battery of reading, achievement, aptitude, and IQ tests, the *reading* test given to seven-year-olds did the *best* job of predicting eight-year-olds' oral reading performance (Henderson et al., 1973).[15]

---

[15] This should *not* be interperted as further justification for the banning of IQ tests from our schools. In fact, "performance IQ . . . is at least as effective a predictor of reading achievement for black boys as it is for any other group" (Henderson, Fay, Lindemann, & Clarkson, 1973, p. 354). And, even if intelligence and aptitude tests are not the most effective predictors of reading achievement, surely our schools are concerned with, and encounter diagnostic and curricular problems other than in reading. And in these other areas, IQ tests are the best predictor.

Many standardized reading tests are available. Some are good, some are bad. We will consider just two of the available reading tests to illustrate their format, technical features, and purpose.

Gates-MacGinitie Reading Tests[16]   Teachers College Press, 1965.[17] Replaces the familiar Gates Reading Tests. Seven separate tests for grades 1–12: Primary A (grade 1), Primary B (grade 2), Primary C (grade 3), each of which has two forms and provides scores in vocabulary and comprehension; Primary CS (grades 2.5–3) has three forms and provides scores in speed and accuracy; Survey D (grades 4–6) and Survey E (grades 7–9) each have three forms, and Survey F (grades 10–12) has two forms. All three surveys provide scores in speed and accuracy, vocabulary, and comprehension. Testing times varies from 40 to 50 minutes and the test can be administered in either one or two sessions.

The vocabulary test measures the child's ability to analyze or recognize isolated words. In the Primary A and B tests, this is done with pictures only; in the Primary C test, a combination of both pictures and words is used; and in the survey tests, words are used. A picture (or word) is presented and followed by four words (primary) or five words (survey). The pupil is required to recognize the correct word among the foils. This is a power test in the sense that the tasks become increasingly difficult, but it may also be a speed test, since many pupils (15 to 25 percent) do not finish in the allotted time.

The comprehension test measures the child's ability to read whole sentences and paragraphs with understanding. He is required not only to be able to read but also to understand what he has read and know how to follow written directions. The Primary A and B tests measure comprehension with 34 passages each; the Primary C test does this with 24 paragraphs. The passages are of increasing length and difficulty—easy at first and increasingly difficult as the test progresses. The survey tests measure the pupil's ability to read complete prose passages with understanding. In each of the 21 passages used, from two to three words are missing. The pupil is required to select from five words one word that is most appropriate for completing the statement so that the total passage is meaningful.

The speed and accuracy test of the Primary CS and survey tests are designed to measured how rapidly the student can read with understanding. The Primary CS test uses 32 short paragraphs, and the survey tests each use 36 short paragraphs. Time limits are 7, 5, 4, and 4 minutes for the Primary CS, Survey D, Survey E, and Survey F tests, respectively. In the allotted time, the pupil is to read the short paragraphs and answer the questions or complete the statements that follow by choosing the most correct word. This test

---

[16] Part of a comprehensive reading-testing program that provides a continuous series of reading tests from K to 12.

[17] Survey F was published in 1969.

is a speeded test because the authors contend that few students will be able to complete all paragraphs.

As is true in any test that attempts to span two or three grades, it is extremely difficult to control the difficulty of the items so that they are not too easy for the upper-level students or too difficult for the lower-level students. The Gates-MacGinitie tests are no exception, but they do show marked improvement over the older Gates Reading Tests.

Validity evidence as such is not presented. The authors do describe the population that was employed in the "tryout" of the test items and say that item analysis was used to determine which items were to be retained. However, neither descriptive data concerning the tryout sample nor information concerning the sources studied to develop items are provided.

Reliability estimates were made by the alternate-forms method as well as the split-halves procedure, and range from .67 to .94. In the main, the reliabilities of most of the subtests are above .80. The alternate-form reliabilities of the speed and accuracy test of Survey F are disappointingly low (.64–.81). The high correlation (.88) between the comprehension and vocabulary scores of Survey F strongly suggests that word-meaning skills are inherent in the comprehension test. Other intertest correlations are substantially lower than alternate-form reliabilities, which should provide for more meaningful interpretation of difference scores than is possible with earlier editions. Since some of the subtests have low reliability, notably the "speed number attempted," extreme caution must be used in interpreting subtest score differences.

The Gates-MacGinitie Reading Tests are attractively printed, easy to administer and score, and have norms that are more representative of American schoolchildren than those of the older Gates Reading Tests. Unfortunately, the norms and various tables provided are not accompanied by descriptive information concerning the population studied. The content appears to reflect current trends in the teaching of reading as well as to recognize that the experiential domain of today's student is much broader than it was a decade or two ago. The teacher's manual and technical supplement are complete, well organized, and easy to follow. The present edition is a marked improvement over earlier editions. Despite the criticism noted earlier, the tests are popular with teachers.

Iowa Silent Reading Tests (ISRT)   Harcourt Brace Jovanovich, Inc., 1973. Two forms (E and F) at each of three levels: Level 1 (grades 6–9 and high school students reading below grade level); Level 2 (grades 9–14); and Level 3 (academically accelerated high school students and college). Vocabulary, reading comprehension, reading power (V+RC) and speed of reading with comprehension are measured at all levels. In addition, Levels 1 and 2 measure use of reference materials and skimming and scanning for specific information. The ISRT differs from previous editions in that it uses novel approaches to assess those skills deemed important in reading. Major emphasis is placed on the measurement of the *application* of skills and knowledge rather than knowledge per se. Content and construct validity are emphasized. The standard errors of measurement and reliability estimates computed (alternate-form and K-R 20) appear to be adequate. Norms were developed on a stratified sample of about 78,000 students in grades 6–12. Raw scores can be expressed as standard scores, percentile ranks, and stanines. Norms for Levels 2 and 3 are differentiated according to post high school plans; that is, 4-year college, 2-year community or junior college, and no college. A Reading Efficiency Index (index of speed and accuracy) is claimed by the authors as "a score no other test offers. . . . [It] is a content-referenced score based on reading rate with comprehension." A separate Guide for Interpretation and Use is provided and it illustrates with examples how the classroom teacher can use the pupil profile for instructional purposes. This Guide also discusses various administrative decisions that can be made with the test results.

Other Single-Subject-Matter Tests

As mentioned earlier, there is a variety of single-subject-matter tests available. We could ask (as we did when discussing reading tests), "Why give a separate mathematics test when the battery we use contains a subtest in mathematics?" A survey test for special subject-matter area does not differ in principle from a battery subtest covering the same subject. Both are concerned with assessing the individual's present state of knowledge and contain much the same material. They do differ, however, in their degree or intensity of coverage. For example, an achievement test for arithmetic would contain more items and cover more aspects of arithmetic than would be possible in the battery's arithmetic subtest. Another advantage of the single-subject-matter test is that a particular school's objectives might be more in harmony with the objectives of a specific content test than with the subtest of a battery. There are other reasons that we should use single-subject-matter tests. One is to obtain more information about a pupil who has done poorly on the subtest of a battery. Another use is for guidance and counseling purposes. Finally, because high schools have less of a uniform curriculum than do elementary schools, conventional test batteries will not have subtests for unique subjects such as Latin, Spanish, or psychology. Also, single-subject-matter tests normally reflect curricular changes sooner than batteries do.

STANDARDIZED ACHIEVEMENT-TEST SURVEY BATTERIES

Because survey batteries lend themselves best to a level where there is a common core of subjects and objectives, we find the largest number of them at the primary and elementary levels, although there are survey batteries at all other levels.

When we examine the numerous survey batteries that have been published for the primary and elementary grades, we find more similarities than differences among them. These survey batteries contain subtests in spelling, language usage, reading knowledge, vocabulary, arithmetic reasoning, and arithmetic fundamentals. Survey batteries often provide a total score as well as separate subtest scores. They often provide separate norms (sex, grade, age) to enable the user to make various comparisons. They provide for the conversion of raw scores to standard scores to assist in test interpretation. The most common method of expressing test scores is in terms of grade equivalents,[18] although percentiles are frequently given. In the newer tests, stanines are usually reported.

We will now consider some of the survey batteries most frequently used in the elementary and secondary grades, beginning with a detailed review of the Stanford Achievement Test and followed by brief reviews of other commonly used survey achievement batteries. Although standardized achievement survey batteries are available for college, graduate, and professional school, these will not be considered here.

Critical Evaluation of the 1973 Stanford Achievement Test[19]

We have selected the Stanford for our detailed review because it is one of the most popular and useful standardized survey achievement test batteries used in our schools. This is not to be construed as signifying that the Stanford is the only good survey battery (others are available); or that it is perfect (that there are some limitations will be evident in the ensuing discussion). However, it has been selected because it represents one of the better test batteries for surveying school achievement from kindergarten to high school.

Grade Level and Content[20]

Table 15–3 presents the tests, scores, number of items, and administration time by grade level. For each of the levels except Primary I and TASK, there

[18] See Chapter 5 for a discussion of the limitations of grade-equivalent scores.

[19] The 1973 edition is published by Harcourt, Brace Jovanovich, Inc. There are eight different levels in the 1973 edition plus the Stanford Early School Achievement Test (SESAT) and TASK (Test of Academic Skills). SESAT has two levels: Level 1 (K.1–1.1) and Level 2 (1.1–1.8). Four tests in SESAT are common to both levels: environment, mathematics, letters and sounds, and aural comprehension. Level 2 has, in addition, word reading and sentence reading. Separate subtest and total score for each level (five and seven scores for Levels 1 and 2, respectively). One form. Requires five and seven sittings (90 and 140 minutes) for Levels 1 and 2, respectively. Reviews in Buros (1972) are quite favorable. With SESAT and TASK, the 1973 Stanford provides for an articulated measure of knowledge and skills in various content areas from grades K to 13.

[20] For a description of how the 1964 and 1973 editions differ, refer to the 1973 Administrator's Manual.

TABLE 15–3 List of Tests by Battery Level and Number of Items and Administration Time per Test for the 1973 Stanford Achievement Tests

COMPLETE BATTERY[a] TESTS BY LEVEL AND SCORES	Primary Level I Gr. 1.5–2.4 16 Pages		Primary Level II Gr. 2.5–3.4 24 Pages		Primary Level III Gr. 3.5–4.4 32 Pages		Intermed. Level I Gr. 4.5–5.4 32 Pages		Intermed. Level II Gr. 5.5–6.9 32 Pages		Advanced Level Gr. 7–9.5 32 Pages		Task Level I Gr. 9–10 16 Pages		Task Level II Gr. 11–13 16 Pages	
	Items	Time	Items	Time	Items	Time	Items	Time	Items	Time	Items	Time	Items	Time	Items	Time
Vocabulary	37	20	37	20	45	25	50	25	50	25	50	20	—	—	—	—
Reading Comprehension[b]	87	45	93	45	70	35	72	35	71	35	74	35	78	40	78	40
Word Study Skills	60	25	65	25	55	25	55	25	50	20	—	—	—	—	—	—
Mathematics Concepts	32	25	35	20	32	20	32	20	35	20	35	20	48	40	48	40
Mathematics Computation[c]	32	30	37	30	36	30	40	35	45	35	45	35	—	—	—	—
Mathematics Applications	—	—	28	20	28	25	40	35	40	35	40	35	—	—	—	—
Spelling[d]	30	20	43	25	47	15	50	15	60	20	60	20	—	—	—	—
Language	—	—	—	—	55	35	79	35	80	35	79	35	69	40	69	40
Social Science	—	—	27	20	44	25	60	30	54	30	60	30	—	—	—	—
Science	—	—	27	20	42	25	60	30	60	30	60	30	—	—	—	—
Listening Comprehension	26	25	50	35	50	35	50	35	50	35	—	—	—	—	—	—
Stanford Total[e]	304	190	442	260	504	295	588	320	595	320	503	260	195	120	195	120

[a] Basic Battery, Primary Level II through Intermediate, excludes Social Science, and Listening Comprehension tests. Basic Battery for Advanced excludes Social Science and Science. No Basic Battery for TASK.

[b] Reading, at Primary Levels I and II, is in two parts (Word Reading Comprehension), which may be administered separately.

[c] Mathematics Computation and Applications is a combined test at Primary Level I.

[d] Optional for Primary I.

[e] All levels except TASK report a Total Battery Score, Total Reading, Total Mathematics. All levels except Advanced and TASK report a Total Auditory Score.

[f] A college edition (Gr. 13) is scheduled for later publication.

are both Complete and Basic Skills batteries. The Complete and Basic batteries differ in that the latter do not have subtests in Social Science and Science, and (for Primary II and III) Listening Comprehension. There are two forms (A and B) for the Complete battery for each level. A Special Form C which will contain only the Reading and Mathematics tests (it is designed for special large programs) is scheduled for publication at a later date.

The Stanford Achievement Test at all grade levels is concerned with measuring the outcomes of a core curriculum—vocabulary, reading, comprehension, and arithmetic skills. The test items were prepared after consultation with subject-matter specialists and after a careful and thorough analysis of textbooks, word counts, and syllabi.

Word study and listening comprehension are measured at all levels except Advanced. Beginning with the Primary Level II, all batteries also measure spelling, science, and social studies. The measurement of language begins at Primary III.

Vocabulary is measured by a separate test and has a separate score at all levels except TASK, where it is incorporated with the English Test. In the elementary (K–junior high grades) levels, the teacher dictates 3 or 4 words and the pupil selects the one (of the 3 or 4 words given) that best completes a sentence read by the teacher. (The Vocabulary items, except for Advanced, are read by the examiner to give a measure of the pupil's verbal development independent of his reading ability.) The test words used were selected by sampling word counts in science, social studies, arts and crafts (for primary level batteries) plus words common to fiction, nonfiction, and reference books (intermediate levels and above). One-half of the items in the elementary batteries are content dependent (those encountered in school subjects, per se). The other half are general vocabulary found in the language arts. In other words, the vocabulary test is basically a measure of the verbal competency the child *brings to* school as well as those concepts *taught in* school. For this, the test can be diagnostically useful, especially in the lower grades.

Reading is measured at all levels. At the Primary I and II levels, the Reading test is actually two separate tests—Word Reading and Reading Comprehension—each with its own score. At the Primary III level and above, only Reading Comprehension is measured. A rather novel approach was used to test for Word Reading in the Primary I and II batteries: The pupil is presented with a picture followed by three sets of words, each set having *one* word related to the picture. The pupil selects the one word in each set that tells something about the picture. The words used (both the correct answer and distracters) were sampled from those generally taught in grades 1 and 2. Although some pupils could use phonics to arrive at the correct answer, Word Reading is *not* a phonics test. Since the words tested are in the average child's speaking and listening vocabulary, we have "essentially a measure of the ability to go from the printed to spoken word." In the Primary III, Intermediate, and Advanced Battery, Reading Comprehension is measured by having the pupil read a story or poem (the content is varied and the reading vocabulary is appropriate for the age level tested) and then answer questions based on the selections read. In the Intermediate and Advanced Battery, the selections range from 8 to 25 lines in length, and from 5 to 7 items are asked per selection. Phonics and vocabulary skills are de-emphasized, the major emphasis being on measuring the pupils' ability to "gather information from connected discourse." The ability of the student to make inferences, to comprehend the content, and to ascertain what *should* be inferred from the content is also measured. As expected, emphasis on the higher skills (e.g., drawing inferences, use of context for word and paragraph meaning) increases according to grade level tested.

A separate reading test is found in TASK. An ingenious approach is used to test for vocabulary. It resembles a matching exercise where words in one column are matched with words in another column that bear some relationship to the word being matched.

Word Study Skills tests are contained in all Primary and Intermediate batteries. At the Primary I level, it is actually a word recognition test. In the Primary II battery and above, the test has two parts: one to measure the pupils' knowledge of phonics, the other to measure the pupils' abilities in structural analysis. The test authors claim that the pupils' performance should not be influenced markedly by the size of their sight vocabulary and that the words are generally within the pupils' listening vocabulary.

The Mathematics Concepts test is found at all levels and is concerned with measuring meaning and understanding rather than with just carrying out numerical operations. For the Primary levels, the teacher reads the questions aloud to the pupils to minimize the influence of reading ability. Even at the upper levels, the language used is kept simple so as to focus on measuring knowledge of mathematics rather than on reading ability. Both the "new" and "old" mathematics curricula are reflected in the test. The pupils' ability to read graphs and charts is tested as early as the first grade.

The Mathematics Computation test is found at all levels and contains items to measure the pupils' knowledge of fundamental arithmetic processes —addition, subtraction, multiplication, and division—by both verbal problems and in the conventional manner such as $3 + 3 = ?$

The Mathematics Applications test is a separate test at all levels except Primary I, where it is part of the computation test. The tests rely heavily on verbal problems to test the pupils' knowledge of fundamental arithmetic processes and concepts. At the higher levels, especially the Advanced, the pupil is required "to identify a suitable solution strategy" or to convert a problem into a mathematical sentence. Many of the problems attempt to stress computational ability to solve problems that occur in life situations.

As one progresses from the primary to advanced level, there is more emphasis on the interpretation of graphed data, reading of charts and tables, use of maps and scales, and English and metric measures.

In TASK, mathematics computation, application, and concepts are measured by a single test designed "to measure general mathematical competence; it emphasizes arithmetical and numerical concepts, computation, and application with some minor emphasis on algebra, geometry, and measurement." There is little emphasis on the "new" math.

Spelling is tested at all levels, although it is optional at the Primary I level. With the exception of TASK, a separate spelling score is obtained. In the Primary I battery, the teacher reads the word to be spelled, both as a separate word and then again in a sentence context, and the pupil then writes out the word. However, we wonder whether the majority of first- and second-grade children have the ability to spell, no less to write. In the Primary II and III tests, the pupil selects the incorrectly spelled word contained in a set of four words. At the Intermediate and Advanced levels, a series of four phrases, each with a word underlined, is presented to the pupil. He then selects the incorrectly spelled word from those underlined. In TASK, spelling is part of the English test and consists of groups of four words. The pupil is asked to determine how many words are correctly spelled in each group. We are a little concerned with the fact that in only the Primary I level is the pupil required to write out the correct spelling, whereas at the other levels, he must only be able to recognize an incorrectly spelled word. Spelling is more than just recognition, and in written expression the individual must recall correct spelling rather than just recognize it.

With the exception of the Primary I and II batteries, language is tested at all levels, with separate subtests (*not* separate scores) for measuring the pupils' knowledge of usage (grammar), punctuation, capitalization, and sentence use. The only difference among the various batteries is the manner in which these skills and knowledge are tested. For example, in the Intermediate and Advanced batteries, usage and capitalization are measured by presenting a series of statements or groups of words which could be made into one or more complete sentences by correct punctuation or could not be made into a complete sentence(s) by correct punctuation. In TASK, this same skill is measured by three paragraphs that may contain a variety of errors. The pupil must decide whether there is an error in (1) grammar, (2) punctuation, (3) capitalization, or (4) no error. This testing approach differs from the conventional one such as that found in other achievement tests, where a set of items that are either correct or incorrect for a specific part of language such as punctuation or grammar is presented to the examinee. In the Intermedate and Advanced batteries and in TASK, there are separate sections to measure the pupils' knowledge of dictionary usage, word meaning, different types of reference books, literary concepts, knowledge of morphemes and grammatical concepts. It would appear that the section on dictionary usage and word meaning is more like a vocabulary test than an English test per se.

In TASK, the English test consists of five sections designed to measure the pupils' knowledge and effective use of the English language. The first section deals with the use of a dictionary and reference materials. The second section requires the student to identify errors, if any, in punctuation, grammar, and capitalization. The third section is predominantly a spelling test, the majority of errors being in phonics and word-building skills. The fourth section tests English expression by having four compound words or complex sentences from which the student selects the one that best expresses an idea. The final section consists of four jumbled sentences that the subject must arrange to present an idea clearly.

Two additional tests common to all the complete batteries except Primary I and TASK are the science and social studies tests. At the Primary II level the social studies test resembles, in part, a vocabulary test of social studies concepts but is independent of the pupils' reading ability since pictures are used for the foils and the items are read to the students by the examiner. Even at this level, the test measures critical thinking ability and map-reading skills. At all levels there are items on history, civics, sociology, anthropology, economics, and government. Although the lower levels have some vocabulary-type items to measure the pupil's knowledge of social studies concepts, at the Intermediate and Advanced levels more emphasis is placed on measuring knowledge as well as the pupil's ability to predict, infer, conclude, and reason by means of maps, charts, and graphs. At the Intermediate and Advanced levels the items reflect the modern curriculum, which stresses critical thinking and the interrelationship between content and structure of the social sciences. In fact, in the Advanced level, newer social studies concepts are tested, for example, the pupils' ability to relate knowledge of economics to the interpretation of maps, predicting future trends, and so forth. In the Intermediate II and Advanced levels, at least 50 percent of the items emphasize the measurement of the higher mental process. As in the science tests, at the Primary I and II levels pictures rather than words are used for the stimuli and foils. The types of items used measure the pupils' ability to read and interpret graphs, tables, maps, and globes.

The science tests are designed to measure the pupils' knowledge of, and ability to apply their knowledge of scientific concepts and principles, to make inferences and estimates, and to measure. There are items on the life sciences, chemistry, physics, conservation, and the scientific method. Pictorial materials only are used at the Primary level and in Primary I and II, the teacher reads the instructions. As one progresses from the lower to higher level, it is readily apparent that more attention is paid to the measurement of the higher mental processes. We would like to see still greater emphasis on testing the students' ability to draw conclusions based on experimental data.

Listening Comprehension (LC) is measured at all levels except Advanced and TASK. This is a new test in the Stanford series and is designed to "measure ability to comprehend spoken communication." The objectives measured by the LC test are similar to those assessed by the Reading test, but the skills used may differ. Collectively, the LC and Reading tests provide a global measure of the "comprehension" of communication. According to the test authors, the primary purposes of the LC test are (1) to evaluate the pupil's progress in listening comprehension, and (2) to use the test results to improve diagnosis of reading comprehension.

Listening Comprehension is measured by a technique whereby the teacher reads a short story or poem and then asks the pupils one or more questions based on the material read. In many instances the pupil is required to make an inference, and we question whether or not too much reliance is placed on the pupil's memory, especially for young children. Although there are some factual questions, there are also questions that require the pupil to use interpretive skills, to perceive relationships and concepts, and to see implied meaning. The LC test is definitely *not* a vocabulary test, and the selections used vary in content so they should be appealing to most pupils regardless of their interests. For example, in the Intermediate II battery, the content comes from the sciences, the social sciences, poetry, and current events. There are some instances, especially in the Primary III battery, where there may be more than one correct answer.

Figure 15–3 illustrates some of the types of items used in the Intermediate II battery. Although the subtests of the other levels have not been illustrated, the reader should now have a general knowledge of the types of items used. Only after examining and taking the test will the user be able to determine how well adapted the test will be to his purposes.

Administration

The Stanford Achievement Test can be administered by the classroom teacher without any formal training. The manuals accompanying each battery are well written, complete, and concise for both examiner and examinees. For the pupils, there are examples that are worked out as well as practice items that are attempted before the actual test is begun. If necessary, the examiner can and should give assistance on these practice items.

Scoring

Machine-scorable booklets are available for all levels. (The publisher recommends that MRC answer sheets *not* be used below grade 4.) The Primary batteries, in addition, can be hand-scored. For the Intermediate I through TASK, a variety of scoring (answer sheet) formats are available. The decision on which format to use often depends upon the output data desired from the publisher. The directions for scoring are clear and can be easily followed.

Types of Scores

Four types of scores (norms only for the first three) are used: grade equivalents, percentile ranks, stanines, and scaled scores. Scaled scores are a quasi-ratio scale of measurement and provide approximately equal units on a continuous scale. With them, it is possible to convert all the raw scores to a single common scale. Accordingly, with a single subtest area such as, say, Reading, scaled scores are comparable from grade to grade, battery to battery, and form to form. This permits the user to make meaningful comparisons of growth. Scaled scores are *not* comparable from one subtest area to another.

Norming

Much of the information on norming, especially the technical details, is reported in a Technical Data Report. Some of the more salient points, however, are covered in the Norms Booklet.

For the Primary through Advanced Levels, a stratified sample (109 school systems drawn from 43 states) provided over 275,000 pupils for the three standardization programs used. For all batteries except TASK, three decisions were made regarding the standardization: (1) There would be two major standardization programs; in May, to reflect near the end-of-year performance, and in October to reflect beginning-of-year performance. (In addition, the Primary I and II batteries were also standardized in February for a midyear standardization because it was felt that the rapid achievement growth during grades 1 and 2 would not be accurately reflected in an October-May testing.) (2) Since three preliminary forms were developed for all levels except TASK, it was decided to standardize all three forms simultaneously in both the spring and fall testings. (3) After specifying the stratification variables, it was decided that in all participating schools, every pupil in a sample of regular classes in at least eight consecutive grades would be included in the standardization sample in order to avoid the question of selection from grade to grade. After issuing invitations to school systems meeting the criteria established, the pupil sample selected was administered all three forms of the Stanford as well as the appropriate level of the Otis-Lennon Mental Ability Test (OLMAT). This provides the user with a means whereby the achievement test score can be compared with intelligence.

After data collection, weighting procedures were used to build individual grade level norms that were comparable in mental ability to the OLMAT norms groups. By this procedure a Stanford norm group is provided for each grade level with a normal IQ distribution, and a mean OLMAT deviation IQ where the mean is 100 and the standard deviation is 16.

TEST 1: Vocabulary

STEPS TO FOLLOW

  I. Listen to each sentence your teacher reads to you.

  II. Choose the word from those below that *best* completes each sentence.

  III. Look at the answer spaces at the right or on your answer sheet (if you have one).

  IV. Fill in the space which has the same number as the word you have chosen.

SAMPLE

The name of a winter month is —

A 1 April   3 January

     2 October   4 June

TEST 2: Reading Comprehension

STEPS TO FOLLOW

  I. Read each selection.

  II. Read the questions that follow the selection.

  III. Choose the *best* answer for each question.

  IV. Look at the answer spaces at the right or on your answer sheet (if you have one).

  V. Fill in the space which has the same number as the answer you have chosen.

SAMPLES

Joe is often quite tardy. This week, however, he has been on time every day.

A Joe is often —

  1 late   2 ill   3 tired   4 early A ● ② ③ ④

B This week he has been —

  5 worse   7 on time

  6 absent   8 late   B ⑤ ⑥ ● ⑧

TEST 4: Mathematics Concepts

STEPS TO FOLLOW

  I. Read each statement or question.

  II. Decide which answer is *best*.

  III. Look at the answer spaces at the right or on your answer sheet (if you have one).

  IV. Fill in the space which has the same letter as the letter beside your answer.

SAMPLE

A Which numeral has the greatest value?

  a seven   c eight

  b nine   d three   ⓐ ● ⓒ ⓓ

TEST 5: Mathematics Computation   Part A

STEPS TO FOLLOW

  I. Read each mathematical sentence.

  II. Decide which of these signs will make it true:

     > is greater than < is less than = is equal to

  III. Look at the answer spaces at the right or on your answer sheet (if you have one).

  IV. Fill in the space which has the same letter as the answer you have chosen.

SAMPLE

A   2 + 4 ● 4 + 2   A ⓐ ⓑ ●

Part B

STEPS TO FOLLOW

  I. Work each exercise.

  II. Look at the possible answers beside each problem and see if your answer is here.

  III. If it is, fill in the space at the right or on your answer sheet (if you have one) which has the same letter as your answer.

  IV. If your answer is *Not Here*, fill in the space which has the same letter as the letter beside NH.

SAMPLE

B   25   a 97

    + 73   b 88

           c 98

           d 89

           e NH B ⓐ ⓑ ● ⓓ ⓔ

TEST 6: Mathematics Applications

STEPS TO FOLLOW

  I. Solve each problem. Unless you are told otherwise, there is no sales tax.

  II. Look at the possible answers under the problem. Is your answer here?

  III. If it is, fill in the space at the right or on your answer sheet (if you have one) which has the same letter as your answer.

  IV. If your answer is *Not Here*, fill in the space which has the same letter as the letter beside NH.

SAMPLE

A Susan lost 2 beads. She now has 8 left. How many beads did Susan have at first?

  a 4   c 6

  b 12   d 10

       e NH A ⓐ ⓑ ⓒ ● ⓔ

FIGURE 15–3   Sample items reproduced from the Intermediate II battery of the Stanford Achievement Test. (Copyright © 1973 by Harcourt Brace Jovanovich, Inc. Reproduced by special permission of the publisher.)

TEST 7: Spelling Part A

STEPS TO FOLLOW (Questions 1-8)
I. Read each group of phrases. Look at the underlined word in each phrase. One of the underlined words is misspelled for the way it is used in the phrase.
II. Find the word that is *not* spelled correctly.
III. Look at the answer spaces at the right or on your answer sheet (if you have one).
IV. Fill in the space which has the same number as the word you have chosen.

SAMPLE:

A 1 <u>no</u> school today   3 a honey <u>be</u>
   2 <u>meet</u> at the bus   4 the two dogs

Part B

STEPS TO FOLLOW (Questions 9-60)
I. Read each group of words.
II. Find the misspelled word in each group.
III. Look at the answer spaces at the right or on your answer sheet (if you have one).
IV. Fill in the space which has the same number as the word you have chosen.

SAMPLE

B 5 cow   7 sky
  6 bagg   8 tell

TEST 8: Language Part A

STEPS TO FOLLOW (Questions 1-42)
I. Read each sentence.
II. Look at the four different ways in which you can fill in the blank.
III. Choose the best form to write in a school paper.
IV. Look at the answer spaces at the right or on your answer sheet (if you have one).
V. Fill in the space which has the same number as the answer you have chosen.

SAMPLES

A My teacher lives on ___
  1 Center street
  2 Center Stree
  3 center street.
  4 center Street.

A ① ● ③ ④

TEST 8: Language Part C

STEPS TO FOLLOW (Questions 51-70)
I. Read each group of words.
II. Fill in, in the spaces at the right or on your answer sheet (if you have one), the space for:
   1 if the group of words makes *ONE* complete sentence with the addition of a period or question mark
   2 if the group of words makes *TWO OR MORE* sentences without changing or omitting any words
   N if the group of words is *NOT* a complete sentence.

SAMPLE

C It was raining
  a 1   b N   c 2

C ● ⓑ ⓒ

TEST 9: Social Science

STEPS TO FOLLOW
I. Read each question.
II. Choose the *best* answer.
III. Look at the answer spaces at the right or on your answer sheet (if you have one).
IV. Fill in the space which has the same number as the answer you have chosen.

SAMPLE

A Which one of the following is a continent?
  1 England   3 Mexico
  2 Africa   4 Canada   A ① ● ③ ④

Figure 15-3   (*continued*)

For TASK there are separate norms for high school students by grade (8–12) and Junior/Community college freshmen. Although a preliminary standardization was conducted in the spring, the norms are based on an October testing of 46,961 students in grades 8–13 from 29 states. Norms were developed on the basis of only an October testing since previous research indicated that this would suffice.

Reliability

All reliability data are in the form of split-half reliability coefficients, Kuder-Richardson estimates, and standard errors of measurement. The 75 split-half coefficients reported for Form A of Primary I through Advanced range from .69 to .96 with all but four being above .85. The 75 Kuder-Richardson coefficients range from .67 to .96 with all but six being above 85. S_e's range from 2.0 to 4.0 raw score points. All of the lower coefficients are found in the Mathematics Concepts and Listening Comprehension Test of the Primary I battery and in the Social Sciences, Science, Vocabulary, and Mathematics Applications tests of the Primary II battery.

For TASK the split-halves and K-R 20 coefficients and standard errors of measurement are reported for each of the beginning of grades 8 through 12. Of the 60 coefficients reported for each form of Levels I and II, all are above .92. The 30 standard errors of measurement range from 2.5 to 3.4.

On the whole, the test reliabilities are quite high. We regret that the publisher did not report grade-score standard errors of measurement (raw score S_e's are published and scaled-score S_e's are available from the publisher).

Although the publishers have provided tables indicating the standard error of measurement for the various subtests, we feel that they have not fully explained how this statistic is to be interpreted.

Validity

Content validity was stressed during the construction of the Stanford Achievement Test. The authors state that a major goal was to make sure that the test content would be in harmony with present-day school objectives. and would measure what is actually being taught in today's schools. To achieve this, they made an extensive curricular study by (1) a thorough review of widely used textbooks in the various content areas, (2) a review of research in developmental and educational psychology concerning children's concepts, experiences, and vocabulary at successive age levels, and (3) a consultation with subject-matter specialists. In addition, item analysis data from the experimental editions (over 61,000 pupils were used in the tryout phase) guided the test constructors in their attempt to obtain higher validity.

A variety of editing procedures were employed in constructing the 1973 edition. All items were reviewed by subject-matter specialists, test construction experts, general editors, members of minority groups, and teachers.

Construct validity was also stressed in the development of the test. To be considered for final inclusion the items had to be passed by a larger proportion of pupils at the higher grade levels (this is both good and bad since we would expect a seventh-grader to know more than a sixth-grader, but forgetting can and does occur over time, especially information that is seldom used); the items had to correlate well with other editions of the Stanford as well as other achievement tests; and each subtest had to have high internal consistency.

The manual states that the test authors wanted to construct a battery that would measure the knowledge, skills, and understanding commonly considered important in our public schools. The test authors felt that recent, extensive curriculum research and the results of item analyses demonstrated the test's reflection of current instructional goals, materials, and methods. They also indicated that appropriate weight is given both to traditional objectives and to recent curriculum trends. On the whole the tests reflect some of "the significant changes that had occurred in the elementary grades" in the previous ten years. The major claim for validity is made on the basis of the description of content sampling. Perhaps the authors place too much emphasis upon the user's judgment, which, although commendable, is not entirely defensible. Also, if the test is to be used for more than assessment, it must demonstrate predictive validity.

Format

The tests and administrator's manual for each of the six levels are presented in 8½- by 11-inch booklets. The booklet covers at each level are of a different color. All printing is in black ink on white paper. The quality of paper, reproduction, and illustrations is excellent. With the exception of the TASK, the back page of each primary level test booklet and the front page of the Intermediate and Advanced booklets provide space for personal information, as well as a place for recording the number correct, scaled score, grade equivalent, percentile rank, and stanine for each subtest as well as the four types of total scores (auditory, reading, mathematics, and total battery). Included with each test packet are a record and a class analysis chart that provide the user with a cumulative picture of the pupils' test performance.

Interpretation and Use

In this section, our attention is focused on some of the strengths and deficiencies of the Stanford Achievement Test and how they relate to the ultimate value and use of the test scores in the making of valid and reliable educational decisions.

INSTRUCTIONAL USE   A major advantage of this battery is that it provides for a continuous measurement of skills, knowledge, and understanding in the fundamental or core curriculum subjects from grades 1.5 through 13. This continuous articulation of content readily permits the teacher or counselor (1) to identify persistent strengths or weaknesses and (2) to obtain a global concept of the pupil's growth in the various content areas. The user, after plotting the pupil's performance, will have a chart that "will permit ready identification of areas of strength and weakness, and the magnitude of the departure from typical performance in the various subjects."[21]

The test manual states that the Stanford Achievement Test measures what is being taught in our schools today and that appropriate attention is given to both the traditional and modern curricula. Teachers may use this test to ascertain whether their goals of instruction are compatible with those measured by the Stanford. However, the teacher must be cautious in his use of the Stanford as the sole criterion of what should be taught in his class.

Let us now consider a hypothetical pupil who has taken the Stanford. What information does the teacher have, and what can be done with that information to help the classroom teacher provide optimal instruction? First, the teacher can plot the various scores in the Pupil Information Box located on the front (or back) page of the test booklet. Then, she can plot the stanines and prepare a profile depicting the pupil's strengths and weaknesses. Let us assume that Billy has an IQ of 135 on the Otis-Lennon; stanines in the normal range (4–6) for reading, math concepts, math computation, math applications, spelling, listening comprehension, and the four total scores (battery, auditory, reading, and mathematics). Let us further assume that Billy evidences weakness in vocabulary, word study skills, sciences, and social science. Here are some clues: Billy is above average in ability, so the problem is not because of a lack of ability. Low scores on the Reading and Listening Comprehension tests suggest a lack of language competency and that Billy should be given added instruction in these areas. But in what specific areas? The teacher can refer to Billy's answer for each item and ascertain the objective(s) that is causing Billy's problems, that is, the items answered incorrectly. Now, if this substantiates the teacher's impressions gained by observation, she can then initiate remedial instruction accordingly, using either her own method or those suggested in the manual (each item is geared to a particular objective so it is possible to "zero in" on the problem).

Billy's weakness in science and social science may be a reflection of a

[21] Stanford Achievement Test, *Manual Part II, Norms Booklet Form A*, Advanced Battery, p. 12.

lack of understanding of verbal material as much as lack of knowledge in science or social science. However, if Billy had low science and social science scores but a very high vocabulary score, this would suggest that the problem is subject-matter–related. This procedure in essence should be followed when interpreting the results of any test score. The '73 Stanford is of additional value in that it provides the teacher with specific classroom instructional activities to be used, depending upon the problem(s) at hand.

With the Class Record, the teacher can plot the scores for all the pupils and obtain rather quickly a picture of the overall level of performance on the various subtests. In this way, the teacher can see whether there are very low scores on any of the subtests, which may suggest reteaching or making a more thorough individual analysis. And if she has some indicator of the average mental ability of the class, she can enter this into her equation for decision making.

The Stanine Analysis of Pupils in Class is one of the most useful devices for analyzing and interpreting pupil performance. After plotting the stanine values, the teacher can readily group the class performance in terms of the number of pupils (and who they are) who are in need of further instruction, the number performing at the average level, and the number of pupils doing well. The information provided also permits the teacher to (1) compare her pupils' performance with that of others in the same grade level, (2) see subject area strengths and weaknesses in comparison to national achievement, (3) identify individual pupils who might benefit from extra instruction, and (4) see the interrelationships among the various subtests.

There is no denying the fact that the Stanford is one of the most (if not the most) carefully constructed tests with respect to reflecting the curriculum in our public schools. This fact, however, does not negate the possibility that there are deficiencies in the test. Some of the specific criticisms of the 1973 Stanford that the user *must* consider in interpreting the pupils' scores are as follows:

1. There is too much reliance on memory in the Listening Comprehension tests, especially at the lower age levels. At the Intermediate II level, the student is read 15 prose passages and 1 poem ranging in length from 3 to 30 lines and asked 1 to 6 questions on each selection. Since many of the items call for drawing inferences, recognizing and remembering details, and perceiving concepts and relationships, we feel that this might be expecting too much from the average fourth- or fifth-grader.

2. There are items throughout the various batteries where there may be more than one correct or best answer.

3. Although the Mathematics test in TASK was specifically designed to measure general mathematical competence, there is a lack of emphasis on the "new" mathematics curriculum.

4. The authors are to be commended for their use of nonconventional

approaches. But at the same time, they may have introduced problems. For example, in the verbal problems testing for skill in division, it might have been easier for the pupil to understand the questions had they been presented in two sentences: the first one, a declarative statement; the second, the actual question.

5. A spelling test, we feel, should be one in which the pupil must recall and write the word rather than just be able to recognize whether a word is or is not correctly spelled. Recognition does not assure knowledge of how to spell; moreover, when one writes, he must recall rather than recognize.

6. At all levels, the directions accompanying the subtest to measure the pupil's knowledge of usage and capitalization are very confusing, especially those relating to the second type of error—"if the group of words makes two or more sentences without changing or omitting any words." How is the pupil to interpret this? What about those cases where no words are changed or omitted but, with proper *punctuation*, would make two or more sentences? How does the pupil answer such an item? The directions contained in the Teacher Administration Manual are much better and more lucid, and we recommend that in a future printing they be used.

7. For the Science tests, especially at the Intermediate Levels and above, we feel that there should be more emphasis on testing the pupil's ability to draw conclusions based on experimental results.

8. The Listening Comprehension test requires the examiner to read the various passages at a slow, deliberate speed. But what is slow for one teacher may be fast for another, and vice versa. It would have been much better had the authors specified the amount of time to be spent reading each passage. As it is now, variations in pupils' performance may well be a reflection between the differences in examiners' reading rates.

9. The Listening Comprehension Test at the Intermediate Levels requires a separate answer sheet. We would recommend that all responses be marked on the same answer sheet or in the test booklet so as to minimize the possibility of confusion among the pupils.

10. Although the norms provided are adequate and are based upon sound sampling techniques, it would have been very valuable, insofar as making interschool comparisons are concerned, to have access to at least geographical and even district or city norms. Although this need not be part of the material reported in either the manual or technical supplement, such data should be made available to interested users.

11. Although some evidence is given to support the degree of overlap among the tests, no interbattery correlation matrix is presented. Also, with regard to the equivalence of the various forms, there are no actual studies reported.

Many of these deficiencies can be readily corrected, and if these revisions were made, the Stanford Achievement Test would be more useful. They have been discussed primarily to caution the user in his application and interpretation of the Stanford scores. In order to validly appraise his curriculum, his method of teaching, and his pupils' strengths and weaknesses, the teacher should be cognizant of these and other deficiencies.

The Stanford is quite valid for evaluating pupil status and progress. For teachers who frequently like to obtain a cumulative index of their pupils' progress, the Stanford, with SESAT and TASK, provides a cumulative assessment of pupil knowledge with an articulated series of tests from grades K to 13.

Many instances arise when a teacher is interested in knowing whether a pupil is working at the level of his capacity. The Stanford, because it was standardized with the Otis-Lennon Mental Ability Test, provides for such information.

The Stanford, as well as other survey batteries, can be used to evaluate the relative strengths and weaknesses of pupils because of its extensive set of subscores. However, provision of many subtests invariably results in short tests (because of time factors), some of which may have relatively low reliabilities. Therefore, although we may get an individual profile, it is difficult to interpret, and it may result in gross remedial errors.

The *Teacher's Guide for Interpreting and Using Test Results* contains some helpful suggestions for the classroom teacher. After presenting a brief history of the Stanford series, there are sections describing how the 1973 edition differs from older ones and why; definitions of basic measurement terms; factors that can affect pupil performance; and examples of how to use the various class record and analysis charts. Most important, however, is the final section, which offers the teacher concrete suggestions not only on how to interpret a particular score, but also on what remedial instruction appears to be warranted.

GUIDANCE AND COUNSELING USE   The Stanford Achievement Test is valuable to the counselor because it (1) provides for a cumulative measurement, (2) provides for a ready identification of strengths and weaknesses because of the profile feature, and (3) permits a comparison of the pupil's achievement with his capacity. With test scores from the Stanford, the counselor can assist the student in making a more sound educational or vocational decision than if these data were not available. However, very cautious predictions should be made because the Stanford's predictive validity has not as yet been demonstrated.

ADMINISTRATIVE USES   Although results from the Stanford Achievement Test can be used for a multitude of administrative decisions, the more common ones are (1) student selection, classification, and placement, and (2) curriculum planning and evaluation.

Selection, classification, and placement. Although the Stanford Achievement Test results may be used to select, classify, or place students for particular programs or instructional purposes, the reader should be cognizant of the fact that scores at either extreme (high or low) may be very misleading and could conceivably result in misclassification. In actual practice we recommend that when either a very high or very low test score is obtained for a pupil, he should be given either the next higher or lower level battery in a retest situation so that a more valid estimate of his performance can be obtained. For example, assume that when Johnny was given the Primary II tests, he scored very high. If the teacher wishes to ascertain whether the first score is a relatively accurate picture of his performance, Johnny should be given the next higher level, the Intermediate I battery. Then, if he performs (scores) fairly well on the Intermediate I, the teacher can feel fairly confident that the high score obtained on the Primary II battery is valid.

Any decisions pertaining to the classification, selection, or placement of students must be made with caution and with as much supporting data as possible. The results of any standardized survey battery should be used as supplementary and not absolute information.

Curriculum planning and evaluation. Quite frequently public schools are criticized for not keeping up with changing social conditions. It is claimed that they are behind the times. Although we do not feel that the Stanford Achievement Test (nor any other standardized achievement test) should be the sole criterion for evaluating the school curriculum, standardized test results may be valuable in helping make such decisions. (Remember: A good standardized achievement test reflects the important objectives stressed throughout the country. If teachers and administrators do not subscribe to the test's objectives, they should *not* evaluate their curriculum with that test's scores.) The Stanford Achievement Test was meticulously constructed and standardized, and reflects the opinions of curriculum experts and teachers and syllabi throughout the country. However, the Stanford may not stress the application of knowledge as much as some other standardized tests or to the degree the teacher desires. And it may not measure some instructional objectives deemed important in a particular school (Remember: Validity is *specific*; not general.) Accordingly, the administrator using Stanford test scores should be guided in his decisions about curriculum revision.

The *Administrator's Guide for Interpretation* uses examples to show how the administrator can use test results for assistance in decision making at the building and district level. Discussion is also centered upon how the administrator can interpret test results to various audiences such as the school board, parents, and the community at large. In every instance a major point is based upon a particular profile, chart, or table. The authors are to be commended for presenting a logical argument of the cautions that must be observed before using test results to rate teachers and instructional programs.

OTHER AIDS   In addition to the *Norms Booklet* and the *Teacher's* and *Administrator's Handbooks* for each level previously discussed, a *Technical*

Data Report is available. The *Technical Data Report* contains a thorough discussion of the procedures and rationale underlying the construction of the 1973 edition. It also reports on the item tryout programs, the standardization programs, the scaling procedures and how scaled scores are to be interpreted, how the norms were developed, a more thorough discussion of standard errors of measurement than that contained in the *Norms Booklet*, reports of supplementary research, plans for future research, and a discussion on how the '73 Stanford can be used for criterion-referenced purposes and instructional improvement. A series of Research Reports are available on request.

Summary of the Stanford Achievement Test

Despite some minor criticisms of the Stanford noted earlier, we recommend it highly. The Stanford series were meticulously constructed and standardized. With SESAT and TASK they provide for continuous measurement with a series of articulated tests from grades K to 13. The various manuals contain many useful suggestions for the teacher, counselor, and administrator. The final decision, however, regarding the tests' validity must rest on the user's instructional objectives.

Some Brief Reviews

Iowa Tests of Basic Skills (ITBS)   Multilevel edition (Forms 5 and 6). Houghton Mifflin Company, 1971. Grades 3–8.[22] It consists of 11 separate tests—measuring skills in the five areas of vocabulary, reading comprehension, language skills, work-study skills, and mathematics skills[23]—and yields 15 scores, the majority of which are in reading and language arts. Two forms are available. The complete battery requires a working time of 279 minutes. It is a very thorough battery of tests designed to "provide for comprehensive and continuous measurement of growth in [skills which are] crucial to current day-to-day learning activities as well as to future educational development." Specific content areas such as science and social studies are not covered. An asset of multilevel tests is that, for most students, they circumvent base or ceiling effects. A liability is that stopping and beginning at different places in the test can be very troublesome and confusing for young children. Of the 84 reliability coefficients reported for the various subtests, only 6 are in the .70s; the others are in the .80s and .90s. The composite score reliabilities are all .98. Standard errors of measurement are reported for each subtest for each grade for raw scores and grade equivalents. Three types of converted scores, each with its own percentile rank and stanine, are available separately for each level and each subtest: grade equivalent (GE), age equivalent, and standard scores. The teacher's manual

---

[22] The primary battery (Levels 7 and 8) to be used for grades 1 and 2.
[23] A multilevel (grades 3–8/9) Modern Math supplement is available as a separate test.

contains grade-equivalent conversion tables separately for each level and subtest, and average grade equivalents for the total language, total work-study skills, total mathematics, and composite score. It also gives national percentile norms for grade equivalents for the beginning, middle, and end of school year. The provision of percentile norms for different times permits flexibility in the school testing program. Schools using the ITBS need not restrict themselves to a single testing period, nor do they have to depend on extrapolation. Special GE percentile norm tables are also provided for regional areas, Catholic schools, and large city schools. In addition, national percentile norms for age equivalents for age groups and national percentile norms for standard scores are also available. Teachers using the publisher's scoring service may select a variety of output data.

An added feature of the ITBS is that it has been standardized jointly with the Cognitive Abilities Test and the Tests of Academic Progress (an achievement test designed for use in grades 9–12). This permits the teacher to compare a pupil's achievement with that of pupils of similar academic aptitude for grades 3–12.

As were previous editions, the current ITBS has been carefully constructed. The 1971 ITBS was carefully normed on a representative sample. The multilevel edition is attractively packaged in a reusable, spiral-bound booklet. The illustrations used are clear and the type is easily read. To accommodate more "tailor-made" individualized testing, new reporting services were developed. To assist those teachers whose pupils are mostly "out-of-level," the tests were prepared and packaged by age rather than grade levels.

Notwithstanding the many admirable features of the 1971 ITBS, it has some limitations that the test user should consider when evaluating this battery. Specifically, these deficiencies are as follows:

1. The vocabulary test stresses only the knowledge of words, although it is purported to test basic skills.

2. The spelling test indicates only that the student may recognize an incorrectly spelled word given out of context, but does not necessarily indicate that he knows the correct spelling. For example, on one exercise the word "stor" is misspelled if we are spelling star, stir, or stove. For what word are we testing spelling knowledge?

3. The language-skills test places more emphasis on spelling, capitalization, and punctuation than on language usage.

4. Language usage is equally stressed at all age levels (9 to 14). We think that this skill is stressed differentially in the various grades and hence should be weighted differentially.

5. The work-study skills test may not be valid for those teachers who do not stress map reading as an instructional objective.

6. The map-reading test may prove to be a little frustrating for the younger pupils.

7. The arithmetic-skills test leans quite heavily on content, is highly verbal, and—depending on the mathematics program used in the school—may not be totally appropriate.

We recognize that in constructing any test, it is most difficult to specify objectives that are common to all schools and teachers. The intent of our discussion of the deficiencies is to focus the user's attention on some specifics. Only after a careful and thorough review of the test and manual should the user confirm our comments.

The test is accompanied by a manual that is thorough and informative, and contains many features that will assist the teacher in using test results to improve instruction. With the Pupil Profile Chart, the pupil's progress, strengths, and weaknesses can be ascertained quickly and easily. In summary, the ITBS is highly recommended if one wishes to test primarily basic skills.

Adult Basic Learning Examination (ABLE)   The Psychological Corporation, 1967–1971. Three levels (adults with achievement levels, grades 1–4, 5–8, 9–12). Two forms for each level. Designed for use with adults who have not completed eighth grade. Each level has six scores: vocabulary, reading, spelling, arithmetic (computation, problem solving, total). Testing time ranges from about 145 minutes to about 215 minutes. Only Level III (9–12) is timed. For Levels I and II, responses are marked directly in the test booklet; for Level III, a separate answer sheet is used. A short screening test is available to determine the appropriate level to administer the examinee. Cassettes are available for test administration.

Concurrent validity data are reported with subtests of the 1964 Stanford Achievement Tests as criterion variables. The reported coefficients are respectable.

Split-half reliabilities are reported separately for each level for three groups: a school group of children in grades 2–4 and 6–7; a Job Corps group for Levels 1 and 2; an adult group enrolled in basic education classes; and other adult groups, one of them being a prison population. Although the reliabilities are quite satisfactory (with the exception of the reading subtest), most of the tests appear to be overly difficult for optimum reliability. The easiest tests are the vocabulary and arithmetic problem solving.

Raw scores for Levels I and II are converted to grade-level scores, based upon the performance of 100 pupils in grades 2–7. For Level III percentile rank and stanine norms tables are available.[24] We agree with the test authors

---

[24] The publisher has available, upon request, distributions of scores as well as technical information for several different, well-defined adult reference groups.

that "the use with adults of grade norms based on children's performance does present some unique problems." A 20-year-old who has completed only the fourth grade is *not* the same as a 9-year-old who has completed fourth grade. Their experiential backgrounds differ markedly. The test authors wisely suggest developing local norms.

As in any product, ABLE has some limitations: (1) In the vocabulary subtest, undue emphasis is placed upon nouns (32/50 words in Level 1, Form A, are nouns); (2) the arithmetic computation tests are rather short; (3) the reading test, which requires the examinee to select a missing word, is not meaningful, nor does it measure reading comprehension. Adults do *not* do this kind of reading. For example, how many adults read for the purpose of selecting a word to fit a given context? Moreover, (4) no attention is paid to grammar, punctuation, and language-usage skills.

An accompanying handbook explains how the test results can be used and interpreted. The material is presented clearly and should be of practical value. It points out both the advantages and limitations of the tests.

As a survey battery designed for use with adults who have not completed eighth grade, the ABLE is a promising instrument.

Summary of Standardized Achievement Tests

Achievement tests run the gamut from readiness and diagnostic tests to prognostic content-oriented tests (be they single-subject-matter tests, single survey tests, or survey batteries), norm-referenced to criterion-referenced, and from preschool to graduate and professional school. All, however, regardless of their format, or types of knowledge and skills surveyed, or types of items used, are designed to give us an index of what the student knows at a particular point in time.

Readiness tests are normally restricted to reading, whereas diagnostic tests are confined primarily to reading and arithmetic. These tests are used most frequently in the primary grades, and hence the largest number of readiness and diagnostic tests are to be found in grades K–3. Readiness and diagnostic tests differ from the conventional standardized achievement (subject-matter content) tests in that they are in, or attempt to confine themselves to, a very limited area, in which they ascertain whether the pupil possesses those skills and knowledge to begin a reading program or learn the nature of the pupil's difficulties in, say, reading or arithmetic. The majority of these tests are similar in format, and therefore it is nearly impossible to recognize a test only from an inspection of just a few items. There are some differences, however, in the reading readiness tests that are published; these differences reflect the importance attached to certain facets deemed to be important in beginning to learn to read. For example, one test author might feel that it is essential for the beginning reader to be able to recognize similarities and differences in geometric shape. Another test author might feel that this skill is unimportant. Hence, if these authors were each to construct a reading readiness test, there would be a difference in the kinds of items employed. Diagnostic tests appear to have more similarity than readiness tests. Their major purpose is to help the teacher recognize the pupil's difficulties; therefore, diagnostic tests are constructed so that they permit the pupil to maximize the number of errors he can make. There may be a difference of opinion as to whether a pupil is ready to learn to read, but there is very little difference as to whether he exhibits tendencies of reversals or omissions when he is reading. It is also important to remember that no single readiness or diagnostic test can assess all the skills and knowledge needed by the pupil to learn effectively.

We have considered some of the more popular survey batteries used at the elementary and secondary levels as well as specific "tailor-made" criterion-referenced achievement tests such as the SCORE Program. (Such programs are increasing in popularity.) If the teacher desires to obtain a better picture of the pupil's knowledge, he is advised to select a standardized achievement test in that particular subject. Single or specific achievement tests are also valuable to the counselor. For example, if a student plans to become a doctor, it would be helpful to know how well he performs on specific biology and chemistry tests because these two areas are of vital importance in medicine (or at least in medical education).

Some of the survey batteries, such as the Stanford, provide for continuous measurement from kindergarten through high school, and even adult. Others, like the ITBS, span the upper elementary and junior high grades. Others are intended for grades 4 to 14 (Sequential Tests of Educational Progress), or for only high school students (Tests of Academic Progress). It should be readily obvious that a survey battery cannot adequately measure all or even most of the outcomes of every (or any) instructional program. However, all batteries attempt to provide measures of achievement in the core subjects by having tests of vocabulary, arithmetic, spelling, reading, and language. The various batteries provide separate subtest scores as well as a total score. Using normative data, the raw scores are transformed to some form of standard score to permit meaningful comparisons among the various subtests.

There are other differences among the various survey batteries. At the primary level (grades 1–3) the content is similar, although the format may differ from one battery to another. After the fourth or fifth grade, the contents of the various batteries differ markedly. Some batteries measure work-study skills; others do not. Some batteries may devote 15 percent of the test to measuring reading comprehension, while others will devote about 30 percent. Only the Stanford has the separate test of Listening Comprehension. The various batteries also differ in the number of subtests. For example, at the elementary level, the Stanford yields 6 to 11 scores, whereas the ITBS gives 15 separate scores. The ITBS and Stanford measure the fundamental skills of reading, mathematics, and language.

The types of scores provided by the various survey batteries are another point of difference. The ABLE presents only percentile norms, and the Stanford provides grade-equivalent scores, percentiles, and stanines.

Because of the nature of their construction, survey batteries should not be used to obtain a thorough estimate of a pupil's knowledge or skills in a specific area. Although a science or language art subscore can be obtained, this score will normally be influenced by the sample of tasks measured by that particular subtest.

Although the various batteries may differ slightly with respect to the fundamental educational goals emphasized, they all share common purposes: to help the student and teacher recognize strengths and weaknesses—the student in his learning, the teacher in his teaching.

USING ACHIEVEMENT-TEST RESULTS

The authors of many of the better standardized achievement tests and batteries suggest specific uses, and supplement their tests with valuable interpretive examples. At the same time, the ingenious classroom teacher may discover a use that is applicable only in his classroom. The remarks that follow should be thought of as only some suggested uses of standardized achievement tests.

The purpose of any standardized achievement test is to provide the user with information concerning an individual's knowledge or skills. However, gathering this information just for the sake of compiling data would be completely useless. The major purpose of gathering achievement-test data, or for that matter any kind of data, is to enable the user to make decisions—of selection and classification, for academic and vocational counseling, about the relative effectiveness of two or more methods of instruction—that are more valid than they would be if such data had not been employed to make the decision. Achievement-test results can be used to measure the outcomes of learning, to identify those pupils who are in need of remedial instruction, to identify those pupils who may lack certain fundamental skills (whether they be cognitive or psychomotor) needed before they can begin reading, to aid in the assignment of course grades, to facilitate learning by the pupils, and as a criterion in evaluating various instructional techniques (Tyler, 1958).

Although we will consider the use of standardized achievement tests under such headings as instructional uses, guidance uses, and administrative uses, the reader should be aware that this classification imposes rigidity in treatment and may result in the fallacious assumption that there is little, if any, overlap. Seldom is there a situation in which standardized achievement-test results serve only a single purpose. Because there will be strengths and weaknesses in *all* standardized achievement tests (for example, the content validity is good but predictive validity is poor; or the normative data are excellent but the test is too time consuming; or the test is valid but the scoring is too complex and requires an experienced examiner to administer and interpret), their limitations must be carefully considered and weighed against their virtues in test selection. In the final analysis, the good is taken with the bad, but we want to be certain that we choose a test with minimum limitations and maximum advantages.

Instructional Uses

Achievement-test results can be invaluable to the classroom teacher. For example, reading readiness test scores can assist the teacher in learning which of his pupils possess the skills and knowledge needed to begin the reading program. These test scores help the teacher group his pupils (tentatively, at least) for maximum instructional benefits. Students, who, on the basis of other evidence, demonstrate that they should be successful in reading or arithmetic but who are experiencing difficulty or score poorly on a subject-matter test, may benefit from the administration of a diagnostic test. The diagnostic test can aid the teacher in locating the nature of the difficulty. Diagnostic tests may also be used to identify those students who might benefit from additional remedial work. Diagnostic and readiness tests may be used as an initial screening device to be followed by a more thorough investigation if needed.

Single-subject-matter tests and survey batteries help the teacher ascertain the strengths and weaknesses of his class and thereby suggest modification of his instructional method or the reteaching of certain materials. Or, the teacher can reevaluate his goals if the data suggest this. He can evaluate the effectiveness of a specific teaching method by using achievement-test results.

Standardized achievement tests (excluding readiness and diagnostic tests) also play an important role with respect to standardizing grading. Quite frequently we hear that Miss Smith is an "easy grader" and that Mr. Jones is a "hard grader." Although standardized achievement tests should not be used to assign course grades, they can be used by both teachers to evaluate their grading practices. For example, when Miss Smith, the easy grader, compares the achievement of her pupils on standardized tests to that of other teachers' pupils and learns that her class achieves less well, she can then see that the high grades she assigned may be misleading. This does not imply, however, that standardized achievement-test results should be used as the only reference point in assigning course grades. They should be used to give the individual teacher some perspective. Many other factors must be considered before Miss Smith concludes that she is too easy in her grading. The standardized achievement test should be used as supplementary data upon which to build a valid estimate of the pupil's achievement and hence his final grade.

Achievement-test results can be used to help the teacher provide optimal learning conditions for every pupil. In order to do this, the teacher should know as much as possible about every student. Standardized achievement tests will provide some of this needed information. Test results will assist in the grouping of pupils for instructional purposes. They will also be extremely valuable in assisting the teacher to fit the curriculum to each child in a class. Some children should get enriching experiences; others may require remedial work. Cox and Sterrett (1970) present a simple model of how standardized achievement-test results can be scored so that the classroom teacher may make both criterion- and norm-referenced interpretations of the test scores. For example, Mr. Pedagogy may classify the test items in a particular standardized achievement test according to his instructional objectives. He could end up with three groups: one consisting of items that his pupils have studied and are expected to know; one of items that have not been studied, but which the pupils will be expected to know at a later time; and one of items that are not relevant. The test can then be administered and scored to yield three scores, such as: Ilene correctly answered 90 percent of the items she was expected to know, 45 percent of those not yet studied, and 5 percent of the remaining items. With this information for each pupil, Mr. Pedagogy would plan his instruction accordingly.

As mentioned earlier, commercial test publishers now provide reporting services (for a slight additional fee) that group students of similar abilities and offer the classroom teacher suggestions on the instructional strategy to be used with these groups; provide item analysis data; report the number of items answered correctly by each pupil; and the like. An example of this type of printout is presented in Figure 15–4.

With education moving more and more toward individualized instruction, and with the gearing of standardized achievement tests to textbooks becoming more common, the results of achievement tests can aid appreciably in fitting the curriculum to the child rather than the child to the curriculum. Criterion-referenced (or scored) standardized tests, if successfully developed, should permit the teacher to prescribe individual learning experiences appropriately.

Conventional standardized achievement-test results should *not* be used for individual diagnosis, but they can (and should) be used effectively as a springboard for the teacher to explore areas of pupils' strengths and/or weaknesses. (With the newer types of programs and standardized C-R tests such as SCORE, DMI/PRI/IET, Diagnosis; An Aid to Instruction, and so on, individual diagnosis is possible. But there aren't too many such tests available now.)

Criterion-referenced achievement tests can play a vital role in the instructional process. They can be used to ascertain the status of the student's knowledge, that is, his degree of mastery of specific objectives. They provide the teacher with valuable supplementary information that may be difficult or impossible to obtain with norm-referenced achievement tests, which are usually given only at the end of the year.

If tests are to be used for grouping purposes, and if only one testing period is available, we recommend that there be an early fall testing so that the results will be most beneficial to both pupils and teachers.

Occasionally, teachers will use the results of a standardized achievement test as the major criterion in determining the status of their pupils and will then plan their instructional program accordingly. This should never occur. Other factors need to be strongly considered. For example, how well do the test objectives meet those of the particular teacher? How reliable is a part score in a battery or, for that matter, how reliable are, say, the four or five items used to test the pupil's knowledge of simultaneous equations or atomic structure? Is the course structure centered on skills or on content, or on both? Because of these and other considerations, standardized achievement tests should not (1) be a major criterion in course planning or (2) be the focus of the course content to be taught by the teacher. With few exceptions, the common single-subject-matter test, readiness test, survey test, or survey battery should not be used for *individual* diagnostic purposes.

Guidance and Counseling Uses

Achievement tests can be important in assisting the classroom teacher, principal, school counselor, or clinical psychologist in vocational and educational guidance. In combination with other data, achievement test results can be used to help the student plan his future educational or vocational program. It should be remembered that achievement test data by themselves have limited meaning. They need to be augmented by other information—data about interests, aptitudes, and attitudes—to arrive at the best decision possible. An illustration may help clarify the situation.

Girder, a senior in high school, is interested in studying engineering. The school counselor has a variety of information about Girder. On the basis of a survey battery, Girder's strengths are in verbal skills and he is deficient in science and mathematics. His interest test scores suggest that he possesses interests shared by journalists. His scholastic aptitude score indicates that he is of average ability. The counselor should use all these data in helping Girder arrive at a decision concerning the appropriateness of an engineering major in college. The counselor should point out that marked improvement would be needed in science and mathematics in order to succeed in the engineering curriculum. Actually, what the counselor is doing here is making a tentative prediction of probable success based upon test data.

Achievement-test results are being used more frequently today in helping high school seniors select a college. With data from national testing

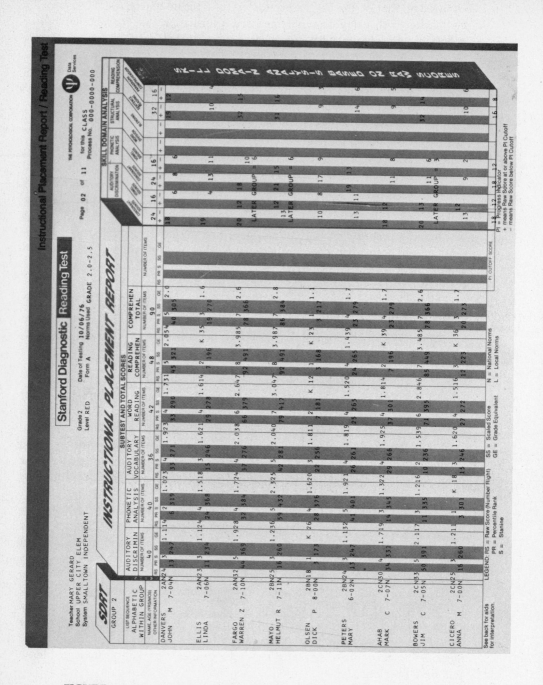

FIGURE 15-4(a) Instructional Placement Report/SDRT. (Copyright © 1976 by Harcourt Brace Jovanovich, Inc. Reproduced by special permission of the publisher.)

STANDARDIZED EVALUATION PROCEDURES 522

GROUP 2: DECODING

Pupils in this group have been placed in one of three subgroups: 2A—pupils with *general decoding* problems; 2B—pupils with *auditory discrimination* problems; and 2C—pupils with *phonetic analysis* problems. Since pupils in Group 2 are likely to have severe decoding problems, they will not be able to make steady progress in reading unless these problems are cleared up.

SUGGESTIONS

1 Start by developing pupils' sensitivity to similarities and differences among the sounds in words. This can best be accomplished through the use of listening games. Rhyming games are particularly helpful in the beginning stages. For example, you can ask pupils to provide the last word of a two-line rhyming jingle or to suggest words that rhyme. If you write down these rhyming words, you can use this technique to make the transition from auditory to visual skills.

2 Help pupils see how each letter contributes to the sounds within words and how one letter can change a word's sound or meaning. A good place to start is with word families, such as "at," "sat," "cat," "rat," etc.

3 Play word games and have pupils do exercises in which they choose words that differ from other words with respect to initial, middle, or final sounds. Pupils select objects or pictures of objects with names that begin or end like a given word.

4 In the beginning stages, have pupils decode words they already know. First, use words with sounds that present the least difficulty for pupils; then proceed to words containing more difficult sounds. The order to be followed is: consonant sounds represented by single consonant letters, consonant sounds represented by consonant clusters (blends), short vowel sounds, long vowel sounds, consonant sounds represented by digraphs, and other vowel sounds (diphthongs, consonant-controlled vowel sounds, etc.). Be sure to show pupils how the phonics principles they are learning apply to the reading situation.

5 Although the principles pertaining to structural analysis are not taught until the later grades and are not measured by the Red Level of SDRT, some preliminary work can be done with compound words and common suffixes in the primary grades. To introduce the concept of compound words, start out with auditory exercises; then go on to some visual ones. To teach common endings (*-ed*, *-s*, *-es*, and *-ing*), use words containing known root words, such as "going," "dresses," and "started."

6 For additional information on how to teach decoding skills, consult L. Burmeister's *Words—From Print to Meaning* (Addison-Wesley Publishing Co., 1975).

FIGURE 15–4(a)   *(continued)*

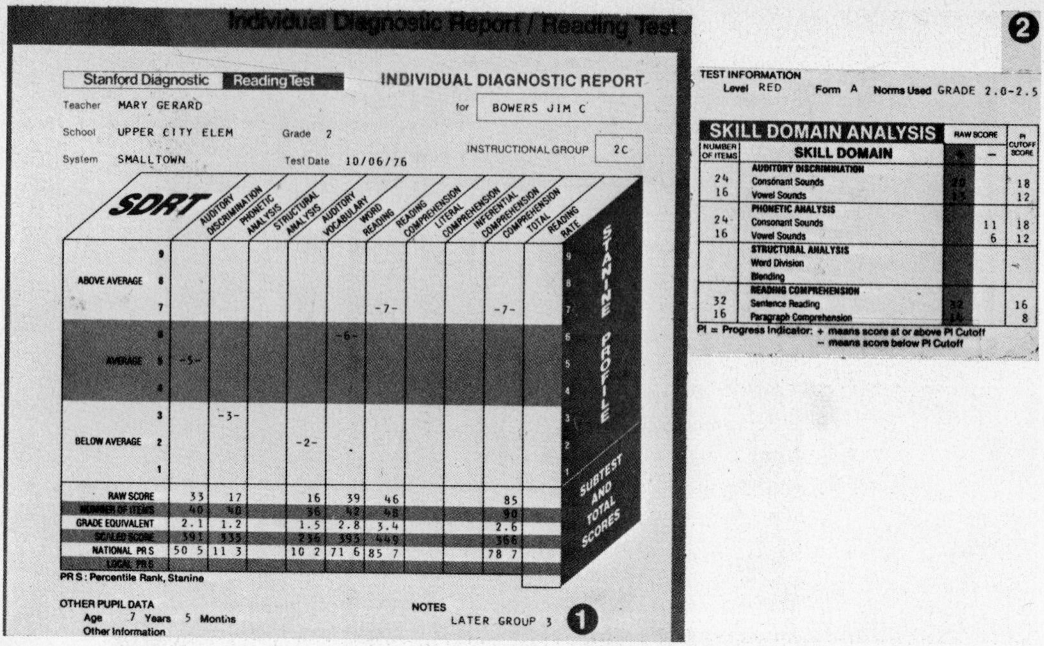

FIGURE 15–4(b)   Individual Diagnostic Reading Report. SDRT. (Copyright ©
1976 by Harcourt Brace Jovanovich, Inc. Reproduced by special permission of the
publisher.)

programs such as the ACT and CEEB (these will be discussed in greater detail
in Chapter 18), it is possible for high school counselors to relate standardized
achievement-test scores to college grades with fairly high validity. In fact,
some programs provide the student with an indication of his probable success at a particular college or university. If test results are used in this way,
the student may be guided to an institution where, because of less competition, he will be more successful and more likely to be graduated.

In conclusion, it must be remembered that achievement-test results are
not absolute measures and that success in vocational training, graduate, or
professional school is dependent upon a multitude of factors, only one of
which is prior achievement. Failure to consider these other vitally important
factors will result in poor guidance and counseling.

Administrative Uses

Selection, Classification, and Placement

There are many instances when achievement-test results are used to select
individuals for a particular training program or for a specific vocation. When
this is the case, the achievement test must demonstrate high predictive
validity.

STANDARDIZED EVALUATION PROCEDURES   524

Selection is more common in industry and higher education than it is in our elementary and secondary schools. For example, a life insurance company may select agents on the basis of an achievement test if it has been found that the test is a good predictor of sales volume. Likewise, a college may select its entering freshmen on the basis of a standardized achievement test if the test has been found to be a valid predictor.

More often today than before (because of people's greater mobility), administrators are confronted with determining where the transfer student should be placed. A fourth-grader from Los Angeles should not necessarily be placed in the fourth grade in Syracuse because the schools may not require equal levels of achievement. The results of a standardized achievement test can be used effectively to help the administrator evaluate the transfer student's past performance. This is especially true if the same test is used in both schools. If different tests are used and no comparisons are possible, the principal should administer the test used in his school.

The data presented in Table 15–4 are for a hypothetical 10-year-old transferring from an ungraded school in Los Angeles to a Syracuse city school in January. The pupil's test scores were obtained in the fall, when he entered the "fourth" grade. The norms in both schools are based on national norms.

What do we know about this pupil? We know that (1) he is below the average fourth-grader except in spelling, (2) he is more like Syracuse third-graders than fourth-graders, (3) he is more proficient in verbal skills than in arithmetic skills, and (4) if he is placed in the fourth grade, then he may experience a great deal of competition, even to the extent that he might become frustrated and develop a negative attitude toward school.

Of what help can the data in Table 15–4 be to a principal? Would he be

TABLE 15-4 Hypothetical Grade Score Equivalents on the Stanford Achievement Test, Primary I Battery

SUBTEST	Transfer Student's Grade Score Equivalent	Mean Grade Score Equivalent for Syracuse 3d-Graders	Mean Grade Score[a] Equivalent for Syracuse 4th-Graders
Word reading	3.2	3.5	4.2
Paragraph meaning	3.4	3.4	4.4
Vocabulary	3.4	3.7	4.8
Spelling	4.8	3.8	4.6
Word study skills	3.6	3.6	4.9
Arithmetic	2.5	3.5	4.4

[a] Norms in both schools based on fall testing.

likely to make a more valid educational decision with these data than without them? With data such as these, the principal would exercise extreme caution before automatically placing the pupil in the fourth grade because of his age. The principal could either place the pupil in the fourth grade and recognize that the teacher will have to spend extra time with the pupil; or the principal could place the pupil in the third grade and know that he may be out of place physiologically and psychologically. If the pupil is placed in the fourth grade, his teacher needs to understand that he may have difficulty at first, that remedial teaching will be in order, and that additional work will be needed before the pupil will absorb the material as readily as the average fourth-grader.

As was discussed earlier, test results can be of help in decision making. In this example, two kinds of decisions must be made: (1) where to place the pupil, and (2) how best to assist the individual after the first decision has been made.

Another example of how standardized achievement tests can aid the user is in the classification or placement of students in special courses or programs. The kind of classification possible will depend upon the type of test used and the physical facilities available in the school. For example, if a survey battery is used, a variety of information is provided. The results may suggest that a student take algebra in an average class, reading in a superior class, and social studies in a remedial class.

Comparing Test Scores

Although a variety of administrative decisions concerning selection, classification, and placement can be made on the basis of standardized achievement-test results, the examples discussed above pertain to the use of the *same* test. What kinds of decisions, if any, can be made with different survey battery or single-subject-matter test results? Can one compare a pupil's performance when two different tests are used? Can comparisons be made between scores obtained on the *same* subtest (content area) of *different* tests?

Comparing Scores on Different Tests

Let us assume that Allan, who moved from an ungraded school in Los Angeles to an ungraded school in Syracuse, took the Gates-MacGinitie Reading Test in Los Angeles in September. Let us assume further that the Stanford Reading Test is used in Syracuse. Can Allan's new teacher in Syracuse translate the scores from the Gates-MacGinitie to equivalent scores on the Stanford? Only if Allan took the tests *after* 1974 (that is when the U.S. Office of Education conducted the "Anchor Test Study," where eight different reading tests commonly used in grades 4–6 were calibrated on a common frame of reference). However, because tests are constantly undergoing revision, attempting to equate their scores so that they are comparable is just about worthless.

Comparing Scores on Similarly Named Subtests of Different Achievement Batteries

Although one might assume that the Mathematics Computation subtest in the Stanford measures the *same* knowledge and skills as the Mathematics Computation test in the Metropolitan (especially since they were developed and published by the same publisher), such an assumption may be wholly unwarranted. On the surface, it might appear that the same instructional objectives (knowledge and skills) are being measured. But only a careful examination of the test manual and test blueprint will provide the information necessary to judge the comparability of the two subtests. But even this is *not* sufficient to judge the similarity of the Mathematics Computation subtests from the two survey batteries. The test items might differ in difficulty and discrimination power. The norming population may be (and often is) different. The validity and reliability of the subtests may be dissimilar. Even though it has been shown that there is a high correlation between the *total* scores obtained on the Stanford and Metropolitan, it has also been shown that there is a low correlation between similarly named subtests in these two batteries (Goolsby, 1971). Only by carefully studying the subtests themselves as well as the respective test manuals can the user ascertain whether the subtests are similar.

Evaluation of Instruction and Teachers[25]

One of the misuses of standardized achievement tests is in making educational decisions (regarding the effectiveness of a teacher, of an instructional technique such as a film, of the school curriculum, or of a class or school) *solely* on the basis of standardized achievement-test results. Teacher effectiveness should not be determined solely on the basis of test results. It would be extremely difficult to compare Miss Smith and Miss Jones, both third-grade teachers in the same school, when we know that one classroom contains an overabundance of bright pupils and the other contains many slower pupils. Even assuming that the average ability of the two classes is comparable, how can we rate the teachers when Miss Smith, for example, feels certain skills are more easily learned at the end of the term while Miss Jones prefers to teach these skills at the beginning of the term, but we administer our tests in the middle of the term?

Achievement-test results, regardless of their nature, are measures that

[25] For a thorough discussion of accountability see Roueche and Herscher (1973) and Taylor and Cowley (1972).

depend upon past learning. In other words, if Miss Smith's sixth-graders are weak in certain arithmetic skills, it may be due to the fact that the essential components of this skill were not developed in an earlier grade. Hence, blaming Miss Smith because her pupils score below national norms would be utterly ridiculous. There is no doubt that teachers play an instrumental role in determining how well their pupils score on achievement tests. However, this is *not* analogous to the claim that achievement-test results *only* (be they norm- or criterion-referenced) be used to rate teachers.

When achievement-test results are used to rate teachers, they frequently instill fear into the teachers. This fear conceivably may result in a reduction of teacher effectiveness and in a tendency for "test teaching." Teaching for a test may encourage undue emphasis on cognitive development, the end result being a lack of concern for the social and emotional development of pupils.

We believe that standardized achievement-test results can and should (where deemed appropriate) be used to improve the instructional program. Further, we feel that test results should be used to help the teacher rather than to evaluate him. Such self-help can be of marked benefit to the teacher. He can see the strengths and weaknesses of his class (either as a whole or for the individual pupils) if he uses a survey battery. He can, by means of an item analysis, see what skills or facts have and have not been learned. He can, using national norms, make comparisons between his students and students in the same grade nationally. He can, with local norms, compare the status of his students with other students in the same school or in the same school system. He can compare the content of his course with the content deemed appropriate by experts.

In summary, although the results from standardized achievement tests are sometimes used as the *sole* criterion to evaluate teachers, we strongly oppose this practice—too many factors other than teaching competency can, and do, influence the test score a pupil receives. But we *do recommend* that standardized achievement-test scores be used *judiciously* as *one* of *many* variables in teacher evaluation.

Curriculum Evaluation

Achievement-test results may also be used as one of the criteria upon which to evaluate the curriculum. For example, 20 years ago it was common practice to delay the teaching of a foreign language until the student reached the seventh or eighth grade. However, it has been found that elementary school children are able to master a foreign language. It has also been demonstrated that with the same amount of training, elementary school pupils do as well on the foreign language achievement test as junior high school pupils. Findings such as these suggest that our curriculum must be flexible. Frequently, achievement-test results provide evidence needed to instigate curriculum revision.

The preceding example of the use of achievement-test results for studying the efficacy of introducing a foreign language in the primary grades is a somewhat simple one. There are instances, however, where the data upon which to base curriculum revision are not so clear-cut.

The profile depicted in Figure 15–5 is for the performance of third-graders in a particular school in contrast to the performance of third-graders in other schools in the same city. The profile is based upon data collected on the Iowa Test of Basic Skills, which was administered during the first week of classes. Following are some questions and suggested answers:

Q. What does the profile show?

A. Students in the third grade in "Walnut Street" School have an average scaled-score performance of about 35, in contrast with the mean scaled-score performance of all other third-graders of about 60. Also, the "Walnut Street" pupils appear to be more proficient in arithmetic skills than they are in either language or work-study skills.

Q. Are the "Walnut Street" pupils markedly better on one subtest than another? For example, are they better in arithmetic concepts than in reading graphs and tables?

A. It is true that these pupils received the highest and lowest scores on the arithmetic concepts and reading graphs and tables subtests, respectively. This does not mean, however, that they are necessarily better in one than in the other. Much is dependent upon the variability of the pupils and the subtest intercorrelations. (If you don't know why, go back to Chapter 5 and restudy the discussion of reliability of difference scores.)

Q. Should the principal change the instructional program at "Walnut Street" School?

A. For this, there is no definite answer. If the "Walnut Street" pupils come, in the main, from an impoverished environment, the decision made could be markedly different from that made if these pupils were to come from an average or above-average socioeconomic area. In the former, we would have an instance of a poor environment that may not permit pupils to experience verbal and language-type activities, at least the kind that are measured by this or any other standardized achievement test. If the pupils were above average in intelligence, the principal would have to consider the adequacy of the teachers, the motivation of the pupils, the validity of the test, and other factors before making a decision.

Some modification of the curriculum might be in order for the "Walnut Street" School. The kind of modification (namely, having more free reading, introducing pupils to the public library, or motivating the pupils to achieve at their maximum), however, would be dependent upon the many factors that influence learning. It is conceivable that the curriculum may not have to be modified. Rather, the manner in which the curriculum

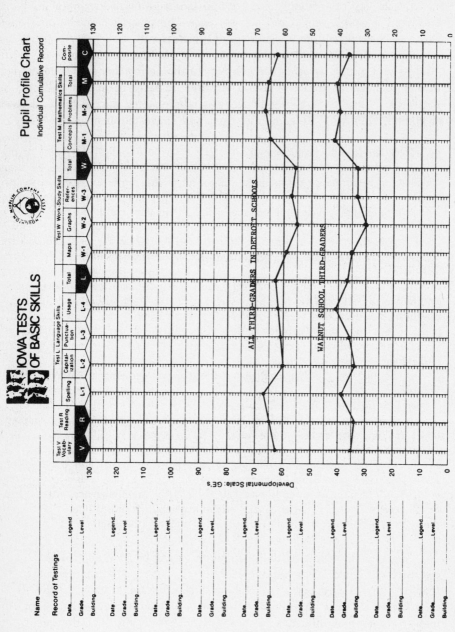

FIGURE 15–5 Hypothetical profile for third-graders in Walnut Street School and third-graders in all Detroit schools. (Reproduced with permission of Houghton Mifflin Company.)

is introduced may have to be altered. For example, if the test results at the end of the third grade showed that this discrepancy no longer existed, this would suggest that (1) the preparation of the "Walnut Street" pupils in the second grade was markedly different from that of the other third-graders when they were in the second grade, or (2) the "Walnut Street" third-grade teachers either taught for the test or were able to make up any deficiencies that existed.

An interesting feature of this hypothetical profile is the strange isomorphism between the "Walnut Street" School third-graders and all third-graders in the city. The peaks and valleys are nearly identical. Might this indicate something about the curriculum in all the schools? In other words, is it reasonable to expect that more attention might have to be paid to certain work-study skills? Not necessarily! From the profile, one is unable to determine the significance of the differences.

In conclusion, we must reemphasize that achievement-test scores, whether they be from standardized or teacher-made tests, must be interpreted with caution. Test scores can and do serve as a valuable supplementary criterion upon which to make more valid educational decisions. But they are supplementary and not absolute, and they are influenced by a myriad of factors.

Grading

In general, standardized achievement-test results should not be used to assign course grades. They may be used to assist the teacher in assigning the final course grade, provided the test reflects local objectives. As was pointed out earlier, standardized achievement tests are constructed so that they measure broad rather than specific outcomes of instruction. Also, the objectives of instruction may vary, not only from school to school but also from teacher to teacher. For these and other reasons, grades should typically be assigned on the basis of teacher-made tests. These tests, properly constructed, reflect the goals of the individual teacher to a much greater extent than do even the best standardized achievement tests.

In the preceding pages we have attempted to discuss some of the more common uses of achievement-test results. As we said before, we have not treated all the possible uses. We have neglected to consider using standardized achievement-test results for such purposes as (1) motivating pupils, and (2) demonstrating to the student what is expected of him. Hopefully, it will be evident that the use of standardized achievement tests is limited only by the resourcefulness and ingenuity of the classroom teacher and that achievement-test results should be used as a supplement to other evidence, to make sound educational decisions.

SUMMARY

The principal ideas, suggestions, and recommendations made in this chapter are summarized in the following statements:

1. Standardized and teacher-made achievement tests differ markedly in terms of their purpose, method of construction, sampling of content, and availability of norms (although both share the goal of appraisal of present knowledge).

2. The trend today in standardized achievement tests is away from measuring factual knowledge and toward emphasizing application and interpretation.

3. Teacher-made and standardized achievement tests complement each other. It is futile to argue that one is better than the other.

4. Standardized achievement tests may be classified as diagnostic, single-subject-matter, and survey batteries and as criterion- or norm-referenced. Single-subject-matter tests may be further subdivided into readiness and prognostic tests.

5. Standardized achievement tests differ little in terms of their construction and technical features. They do differ markedly in their purpose. To see whether a kindergarten child is ready for the first grade, a reading readiness test should be used. To obtain an indication of a pupil's strengths and weaknesses, a diagnostic test is recommended. To see whether a pupil is proficient in a subject-matter area such as history or physics, a single-subject-matter test should be used. To ascertain the strengths and weaknesses (actually plot a profile) of pupils in the various core subjects, one should use a survey battery.

6. Within the past few years, commercial test publishers and other firms have begun to pay more attention to producing criterion-referenced standardized achievement tests; very specific, prescriptive diagnostic tests; mastery tests; and "tailor-made" tests.

7. The factors to be considered by the user in selecting a standardized achievement test were illustrated by means of a critical review of the Stanford Achievement Test.

8. Standardized test publishers are paying more attention to providing the teacher with prescriptive suggestions on the basis of his pupils' achievement-test performance.

9. Standardized test publishers are providing a variety of output data (for a slight additional fee) to users. Various item analyses, grouping students of similar abilities with suggestions of instructional strategies to be used with these groups, and keying items to objectives and commonly used textbooks are some of the reporting services now available.

10. Various examples were given to suggest the different uses of standardized achievement-test results for instructional, guidance, and administrative uses.

CHAPTER SIXTEEN
Interest, Personality, and Attitude Inventories

Should Girder be encouraged to study engineering in college? What are Allan's interests? How can we explain why Beth, who scored at the 95th percentile on the WISC, only scored at the 25th percentile on the Stanford Achievement Test? Is Ilene really an aggressive and hostile child? Is Pearl unstrung? Are Ruth's concerns about peer acceptance atypical for an average 13-year-old? What are problem check lists? Should teachers interpret noncognitive inventories? Are there some noncognitive inventories that should be barred from the classroom? Does the information derived from interest, personality, and attitude inventories help educators make more valid decisions than could be made if such data were not used? These are some of the questions that are discussed in this chapter.

There are a variety of procedures by which an individual's behavior can be ascertained: rating scales, anecdotal records, other observational techniques, and standardized pencil-and-paper inventories. In this chapter we concern ourselves with standardized noncognitive inventories, since teacher-made attitude scales were discussed in Chapter 12. Observational techniques such as rating scales and anecdotal records are useful methods, especially for adults. They provide much valuable data, but they may not provide data as valid as that obtained from standardized tests. Standardized noncognitive tests are uniformly administered and, in general, objectively scored. Many of them also have valuable normative data that enable one to make valid comparisons between a pupil in one community and pupils throughout the country. With standardized noncognitive inventories, one can help ascertain whether Ilene is abnormally aggressive or whether Ruth's concerns about peer acceptance are natural.

At this point, one may counter that these questions could be answered by natural observation that would have an additional feature over a testing situation: People are more apt to display their true behavior in natural settings that are informal, unstructured, and nonthreatening. Teachers are able to observe their students in real-life situations. But, are their observations valid? Are teachers objective? Do they know what behavior is significant and what can be overlooked? Can teachers draw correct inferences from observed behavior? As imprecise as noncognitive tests may appear to be, they do provide us with valuable information about the pupil, information that the teacher cannot acquire through observation but which may be necessary to understand the pupil's behavior. There are some who argue that test scores should be used only to supplement teachers' observations. There are others who argue the converse. The important thing to remember is that both teachers' observations and test data provide information about the pupils' behavior, and both should be used.

After studying this chapter, the student should be able to—

1. Recognize the value to teachers of information about pupil interests, attitudes, and personality.

2. Understand that noncognitive measures are not so psychometrically elegant as cognitive measures.

3. Recognize the problems involved in measuring noncognitive characteristics—problems of definition, response set, faking, validity, reliability, and interpretation.

4. Recognize the three most commonly used procedures for constructing and keying noncognitive inventories—empirical, homogeneous, and logical.

5. Differentiate between attitudes and interests.

6. Discuss the major approaches used to measure interests.

7. Evaluate the more popular interest inventories in terms of their construction, grade level, content, administration, scoring, validity, reliability, and interpretability.

8. Recognize how interest-test results can be used for instructional and guidance purposes.

9. Appreciate the use of career-awareness inventories.

10. Understand the various ways in which personality can be assessed.

11. Recognize the limitations of personality inventories.

12. Evaluate attitude scales.

13. Appreciate the value of study-habits inventories.

INTRODUCTION

It is generally agreed that everyone concerned with the education of children must understand them in their totality in order that optimal learning conditions may be provided. This totality goes beyond academic skills and knowledge. A student's mental health has direct relevance to his ability to learn, his interest in learning, and his attitudes toward the value of an education. Quite frequently, learning difficulties are related to a student's personality (August, Rychlak & Felker, 1975; Goldfried & D'Zurilla, 1973; Rutkowski & Domino, 1975), and any attempt to correct the difficulty will be doomed to failure if one does not consider the student's total strengths and weaknesses in both the cognitive and noncognitive areas. Whether teachers realize it or not, they *are* influenced by their students' attitudes, values, interests, and general makeup. If a teacher knows that his students dislike history, he could (and hopefully would) employ a variety of techniques to motivate them—films, playacting, and humorous skits—to try to instill a positive attitude toward the value of studying history. If he knows that some students who are poor readers are interested in mechanics, he might use stories with a mechanical flavor in the reading program. Teachers can and do capitalize upon the interests and attitudes of their pupils. However, before one is able to apply knowledge, he must obtain it. Before teachers can use data about their pupils' interests, attitudes, values, and general personality makeup, they must obtain these data.

The classroom teacher and counselor should be able to interpret problem check lists with minimal training (although some ensuing actions may require some extensive training and experience). The counselor should be able to interpret the results of interest inventories without too much difficulty. No one, however, unless he has had considerable training and experience, should attempt to interpret measures that are designed to depict abnormality or maladjustment.

The classroom teacher, as a member of a professional team vitally concerned with both cognitive and noncognitive behavior, must, in order to be an effective team member, speak the language. Otherwise, he will not be able to communicate effectively with other team members—school psychologist, clinician, and counselor. In order to do so, he must know something about noncognitive tests—what they are, what they can and cannot do, the different kinds of noncognitive tests, and so forth—and about the behaviors that they measure.

By helping establish optimal, positive test-taking attitudes, teachers through their knowledge of noncognitive assessment can indirectly help the counselor to work with the students. Rapport is essential in any testing situation. But it may be more vital in noncognitive assessment, especially when the test is envisaged by the testee as threatening. Also, in noncognitive tests one can fake either good or bad, and the teacher can aid much in diminishing faking by establishing rapport. The pupil may be more likely to trust his teacher, with whom he is in daily contact, than he is to trust the counselor or clinician, whom he sees infrequently. The classroom teacher, especially the one that is trusted and accepted by his pupils, can aid the clinician by breaking the ice and helping the child accept the clinician as someone who is trying to help him.

In summary, knowledge about pupils' interests, personalities, and attitudes is important to educators to help them understand pupils better and to help them communicate effectively with other professionals. Knowledge about noncognitive tests (especially interest inventories) is important because they are (1) being used in our schools, especially in the secondary grades; (2) valid in providing us with some information about a student's vocational or avocational interests; (3) more objective than the informal observational approach; and (4) frequently used for research on learning. We must reiterate that, despite their limitations, standardized noncognitive tests can play an important role in education.

Before discussing the various procedures and tests available to measure noncognitive traits, their advantages and limitations, and their uses and misuses, we must consider some of the methodological problems associated with noncognitive tests: problems of definition, response set, faking, low validity and reliability, interpretation, and sex bias. To observe that the measurement of affect poses methodological problems not encountered in cognitive assessment is deceptively simple.

PROBLEMS OF MEASURING NONCOGNITIVE CHARACTERISTICS[1]

There are many unresolved problems in the assessment of noncognitive traits. Because noncognitive assessment (or for that matter, any assessment) involves the differences among individuals as well as changes in behavior

[1] For a thorough and thought-provoking discussion of the principles to be considered in the development and use of interest inventories (many of the principles, however, are pertinent to any noncognitive inventory), see Kuder (1970). See Fiske (1963) for an excellent discussion of the measurement problems involved in assessing noncognitive characteristics.

over time, validity and reliability are of vital importance. Holtzman (1964) discussed the problems involved in personality measurement (applicable to most noncognitive tests) and raised the following questions: (1) What do we mean by *personality*? (2) How much must we know about an individual before we are truly able to understand his personality? (3) How can one separate personality variance from method variance? (4) Can we ever hope to develop a theory of personality that is comprehensive, systematic, and closely linked with empirical data? It should be evident that until problems connected with definitions, response sets, validity and reliability, and faking are resolved, noncognitive assessment will be subject to much criticism.

Problems of Definition

Noncognitive tests, even more than aptitude or achievement tests, are confronted with the problem of definition. Allport (1963) considered at least 50 definitions of personality before he advanced his own. If 100 psychologists were asked to define *personality*, one might get 100 different definitions. This helps account for the inconclusive and often contradictory findings in noncognitive research. Frequently, different researchers arrived at different conclusions because they were studying different variables, even though the variables studied were all labeled the same—for example, *honesty* or *estheticism*. To some, the terms *attitudes*, *beliefs*, *values*, and *interests* are used synonymously and interchangeably. To others, there are definite demarcations. To still others, attitudes and values are considered one category, beliefs and opinions another, and interests still another. The concept of personality has multiple and complex meanings, the various definitions are at best crude, and the techniques for evaluation are sometimes lacking in scientific rigor. Yet we cannot give up our research or interest in the area of affective development. Grandiose and ethereal constructs such as honesty, beauty, truth, and virtue can be translated to behavioral terms. Once this is done, an attempt can be made to measure these behavioral traits.

Just as we must talk about a specific kind of validity (such as content or predictive) or reliability (stability or equivalence), so, when we discuss a personality trait such as authoritarianism, we must be specific and refer to it as, for example, the "F Scale's authoritarianism" or "Rokeach's authoritarianism." Until we are able to develop definitions for noncognitive constructs, we will be looking for a needle in a haystack without knowing what a needle looks like.

Problems of Response Set

All noncognitive tests are susceptible to response set, that is, the tendency of an individual to reply in a particular direction, almost independent of content.[2] An individual exhibiting response set will answer identical questions (but presented in different formats) differently. For example, he may be predisposed to select the neutral category if a disagree-agree continuum is used, or the "true" statement in true-false items, or he may guess on all items that he is unsure of. There are many types of response set: acquiescence, social desirability, guessing, and sacrificing accuracy for speed (or vice versa).

The response set that has been of most concern in noncognitive measurement is social desirability (Edwards, 1957b). This is the tendency for an individual to respond favorably to the items that he feels are socially accepted, such as, "People should be concerned with how their behavior affects others," or "There should be open-housing legislation enacted by Congress." Here, the subject may answer not on the basis of how he truly feels but on the basis of what he thinks is a socially acceptable or desirable answer.

The original goal in the study of response sets such as social desirability was to devise a means whereby their effects could be eliminated (as much as possible) as scaling artifacts. It appears that a controversy exists as to whether we can automatically assume the existence of response sets and, if they do exist, whether response sets should be measured or eliminated from noncognitive tests (Cronbach, 1946, 1950; Crowne & Marlowe, 1960; Jackson & Messick, 1962; Rorer, 1965). For example, the California F Scale consists of strongly worded opinions, most of which express a critical attitude toward human nature. Hence, any tendency to accept these statements may in itself be an indication of authoritarianism, and any attempt to eliminate acquiescence may eliminate or prevent measurement of this important behavioral trait (Gage et al., 1957). There is also some disagreement on whether response set is a general or specific factor (Morf & Jackson, 1972).

If, however, one decides it valuable, steps can be taken to try to control for response set. Cronbach (1950) found that response set is particularly prevalent on tests that (1) contain ambiguous items, (2) require the individual to respond on a disagree-agree continuum, and (3) lend themselves to responses in either a favorable or unfavorable direction. Various techniques (such as the forced-choice format, having an equal number of positively and negatively worded statements, or having more negative than positive statements)[3] have been used in an attempt to control response set. These techniques have not eliminated the problem completely.

People using personality, attitude, value, and interest tests must pay particular attention to the presence of response sets and must govern their conclusions and recommendations accordingly. More research is needed on response sets: What kinds of people are susceptible? What kinds of items

[2] Response sets may also be present in cognitive measures. However, in cognitive tests the response sets can be controlled more easily. For example, guessing can be controlled for in an achievement test through clear directions and correction formulas.

[3] Larkins and Shaver (1968) recommend having more negative statements than an equal number of positively and negatively worded statements.

lend themselves to this? Why are some tests affected while others are not? Can (or should) their influence be neutralized?

Faking

Faking can and does occur on cognitive as well as noncognitive tests, but it is more common on the latter. One psychologist aptly said, "As long as a subject has sufficient education to enable him to answer a personality inventory, however, he probably has the ability to alter his score appreciably in the desired direction (Anastasi, 1968, p. 456)." Although an individual can fake either good or bad on a noncognitive test, he can only fake bad (one can fake ignorance, not knowledge) on a cognitive test. The tendency to fake is a characteristic inherent in the individual rather than a test artifact (Kroger, 1974).

Although the examiner expects the subject to give valid information, the examiner does not always receive it. The subject comes to the test and will either be truthful or will lie, depending upon the purpose of the test and his perception of how the test results will be used.[4] Often responses may be rationalizations or unconscious modifications rather than deliberate lies. A candidate for college admission might try to fake good if inventory results might affect his chances for admission. Quite frequently, an individual is motivated to lie when he knows that his selection or consideration for a particular job depends upon the types of answers he gives on an interest or personality test. Hence, in his attempt to obtain the position, the subject will do everything possible to create the desired impression (Green, 1951; Wesman, 1952). A high school senior, because of his stereotypic impression of a surgeon's life (glamor and prestige), may try to convince his guidance counselor that he likes medicine, or may fake some interest tests to indicate that he has a liking for medicine.

Although the subject will most often try to present himself in a favorable light, there are instances when subjects fake their scores so that they will appear maladjusted or abnormal. A murderer may go out of his way to exhibit tendencies of maladjustment so that he will be judged insane and unfit to stand trial. The tendency to fake bad (that is, to obtain a bad or poor score) is more prevalent in testing convicts. Most of them may feel they have nothing to lose and everything to gain by demonstrating maladjustment.

Various procedures have been studied and are used to combat faking. One such procedure (perhaps the best) is to establish rapport with the subject and to convince him that in the long run he will be better off if he gives truthful responses. Another method is to attempt to disguise the purpose of the test. This does not always work, especially with intelligent subjects who

---

[4] Because of faking, it is very difficult in clinical psychotherapy to evaluate the effect of the treatment from test-taking behavioral changes.

may see through the disguise by the nature of the test items. However, in some instances it is possible to disguise the purpose of the test. For example, a researcher interested in studying honesty may prepare a list of book titles, some of which are fictitious. The student is asked to check those book titles he has read. On the surface, the test looks as though it is measuring reading interests, but it really is not. It is actually measuring honesty. If a student indicates that he has read a fictitious book, he is obviously lying. Disguising the purpose of a test can result in some ethical and practical problems, affect the image of psychologists and counselors, and destroy future attempts at establishing rapport.

Another approach to combat faking is to use the forced-choice technique. Here, two or more equally desirable or undesirable statements are presented together, such as

A.　I like to read good novels.
B.　I like to watch good movies.

The subject is required to choose one answer from the set. One of the answers, however, is a better indicator of the criterion being studied than is the other(s). The force-choice method, unfortunately, also has its defects. It requires more time to obtain an equal number of responses; it is sometimes resisted by examinees (and may result in negative attitudes toward future testing and/or the counseling interviews); and it may lower the reliability because the choice is more difficult to make.

Still another approach is the construction of scales to *detect* rather than *prevent* faking. Tests such as the Minnesota Multiphasic Personality Inventory (MMPI), the Edwards Personal Preference Schedule (EPPS), and the Kuder Occupational Interest Surveys have special subtests to detect the faker. Of the three, only the verification score (one of its four validity scales) of the MMPI is used to adjust the obtained score. The MMPI has two scale scores (L and F) to detect faking. Examples of these scale-score items[5] are:

L(ie) score—"At times I feel like swearing." An individual who responds False to items such as this is usually not honest in his self-appraisal. A high L score suggests that the test responses are invalid.
F score—"I have nightmares every few nights." An individual responding True to this type of item indicates that there may be something wrong with his responses. A high F score suggests carelessness or misunderstanding. F scores also tend to be high for subjects trying to fake bad.

In conclusion, whatever elaborate procedures are employed by the test to

[5] From the Minnesota Multiphasic Personality Inventory. Reproduced by permission. Copyright 1943 renewed 1970 by the University of Minnesota. Published by The Psychological Corporation, New York, N.Y. All rights reserved.

minimize distortion—whether it be by response set, faking, or cheating—we must realize that the subject will provide only the information that he is able and willing to report. People interpreting both cognitive and affective tests (more so the latter) must consider this.

Reliability and Validity

The reliability of noncognitive tests tends to be considerably lower than for cognitive tests of the same length. For example, in studying stability reliability, how a person behaves—that is, how he responds to an affective-type item—is governed, in part at least, by the momentary situation. For example, a person with liberal attitudes towards blacks, if interviewed a few hours after being attacked by blacks might respond in a bigoted fashion. Because of the susceptibility of affective items to the momentary situation, the reliabilities of some items might be very low. In addition, some of the more common procedures for studying reliability may be somewhat inappropriate when it comes to noncognitive tests. Because human behavior is vacillating rather than constant, reliability coefficients derived from test-retest methods (coefficient of stability) will tend to be spuriously low and misleading in judging the test's precision. Inconsistency in test responses may be either an important aspect of an individual's personality or a test artifact. The split-half, coefficient alpha, and Kuder-Richardson methods (measures of internal consistency) are most frequently used to study the reliability of noncognitive tests. When low reliabilities are found, careful attention must be paid to the interpretation of difference scores in a test profile because only marked differences may suggest true intraindividual differences.

It is difficult to ascertain the predictive validity of a noncognitive measure for two reasons: (1) We infer the existence of a behavioral trait on the basis of overt test responses. In other words, we assume that an individual who says on an attitude test that he is prejudiced toward blacks will exhibit this behavior in a real situation. In some instances, making inferences of overt behavior from personality questionnaires is valid, but because of faking and response set, sometimes they are not. (2) Adequate external-criterion data are often lacking.

The research conducted with noncognitive inventories has led to many attempts to improve their validity. Some of the approaches used are (1) using correction scores rather than discarding inventories that appear to be suspect, (2) disguising the purpose of the test,[6] (3) randomly assigning items throughout the test rather than presenting them in blocks, so that the traits being measured do not appear obvious to the examinee, (4) using verification scores

---

[6] Weiner (1948) suggested that this be used for subjects who are normal and exhibit social desirability. Obvious items work well for the maladjusted who are honest and seek help.

to reveal test-taking attitudes, and (5) selecting test items on the basis of empirical rather than a priori grounds. Although these and other approaches are used to improve the validity of personality tests, the evidence today indicates that noncognitive tests still do not approach the criterion-related validity of intellectual measures, mainly, perhaps, because of the problem of valid external-criterion data.

In summary, then, in noncognitive tests (1) validity and reliability are not so high as in ability tests, and (2) we are most concerned with construct validity and reliability expressed in terms of internal consistency or homogeneity of items. Rather than conclude that noncognitive test lack the desired degree of validity and reliability needed for making valid educational decisions, we should ask how much information we can get from the inventory and how it will help us. Another way to look at it would be in terms of a cost analysis. In the long run, does the use of noncognitive inventories reduce the incidence of costly error?

Problems of Interpretation

Noncognitive tests are really not tests in the sense that aptitude and achievement tests are, because there are not necessarily any right answers. Noncognitive tests are generally interpreted in relation to the traits held by "normal" ("average") people. Hence, a Canadian exhibiting modal, normal behavior in Canada could, if behaving the same way, appear abnormal in Peru, even though, according to his own subcultural modes, the Canadian is behaving in a normal fashion.

Another problem in the interpretation of noncognitive tests, especially attitude scales, reflects the kinds of responses permitted. Most attitude-scale responses provide for a neutral response. But what does a neutral response mean? Does it mean that the individual is really neutral, or does it mean that he is unwilling to commit himself? How does one interpret a neutral response? One way to circumvent the problem of neutral responses is to eliminate this type of response. But, if we do so, might we be eliminating the measurement of a true behavioral trait or might we end up with untrue measurement?

Also a problem in interpreting the results from affective inventories is that there may be intervening factors which affect how an individual responds to a particular personality inventory item (Kuncel, 1973).

Perhaps one of the more serious problems in interpreting noncognitive tests is that associated with ipsative forced-choice tests.

Assume anyone is given a forced-choice item such as

A.   I like to build model airplanes.
B.   I like to play bridge.
C.   I like to collect stamps.

where he is required to select the one statement in the triad that he likes most. Each of the three possible choices is keyed under a different subscale. Thus, if he picks "A," he may receive a point on the scientific scale. If he selects "B," he may receive a point on the sociability scale. If he chooses "C," he may receive a point on the clerical scale. The essential characteristic of such items is that when a person makes a choice in favor of one subscale (by choosing a particular item), he is at the same time rejecting the other subscales. A test composed of such items (where one is forced to make a choice) gives one an ipsative scale, and the scores are ipsative scores. Although multiple-choice cognitive tests also require the individual to make a choice, there is only one correct answer for everyone. Hence, problems associated with ipsative forced-choice tests are unique only to some noncognitive tests.

The essential characteristic of an ipsative scale is that the total score summing across all the subscales is the same for all persons. Ipsative scores do not reflect the intensity of the subject's feeling, and yet this is something that would be of extreme value in interpreting an individual's responses. For example, three boys purchase vanilla ice cream cones. Does this imply that they all like vanilla ice cream to the same degree? Not necessarily so. Or, if each of the three boys purchased a different flavor, does this signify that the boy who wanted and chose vanilla likes vanilla more than the boy who chose chocolate?

Ipsative scales permit only intraindividual comparisons. In an ipsative scale, every individual will probably have some high scores and some low scores (he could have all scores at the mean). He cannot have all his scores either high or low. Some psychometrists contend that the ipsative forced-choice technique parallels real life in that one is always forced to choose between activity A and activity B. For example, a child, when offered some ice cream, must choose, normally, between chocolate and vanilla. Others argue that this forced choice can sometimes induce frustration in the subject, especially when all the statements (choices) are equally desirable or undesirable.

Interpreting a forced-choice profile is very difficult. How does one interpret to a student the profile of an ipsative interest test with ten subscales? One cannot say that his interest in outdoor activities is higher than his interest in musical activities (even though he may have had a higher score on the outdoor scale) because the scores are not absolute. One cannot say that two persons who rank at the 90th percentile in terms of the national norm group have equal outdoor interests because the scores are ipsative.

Problems of Sex Bias

Although this issue has been discussed in other sections, we briefly reintroduce it inasmuch as much of the fervor on sex bias has been directed primarily towards interest measurement. In fact, Campbell—possibly because of pressure—revised the SVIB (Campbell, 1974) so that it avoided all sexual stereotypes. The issue at hand is not whether a test differentiates among individuals—be it blacks versus whites, males versus females, high socio-economic versus low socioeconomic—as long as it does so validly. In fact, the major purpose of a test, be it criterion- or norm-referenced, but particularly the latter, has as its major purpose one of differentiation. Just because research has shown that males tend to be more quantitative while females tend to be more verbal (Macoby & Jacklin, 1974; Strassberg-Rosenberg & Donlon, 1975), this is not prima facie evidence that the tests used are biased in favor of one sex over the other. We agree with Prediger and Hanson (1974), who contend that sex restrictiveness must be considered separately from sex bias since sex restrictiveness is an important characteristic of interest inventories and its presence does *not* connote sex bias. There are some psychologists who maintain that differences in interests between males and females are the result of *basic differences* in the interests between the sexes rather than sex bias per se (Noeth, Roth, & Prediger, 1975; Shaffer, 1976) or differences in aptitude (Cegelka, Omvig, & Larimore, 1974).

If the test is valid, it is supposed to point up any differences that are present between and/or among groups or individuals. But a test is biased if the item content is in terms of sexual stereotypes that affect the performance of males and females differentially or if a test is *deliberately* constructed so that male futures are separated from female futures invalidly.

Yes! Numerous commissions have been established (AMEG, 1973; Diamon, 1975a,b) and many reports and articles have been written (Harmon, 1973, 1974; Tanney, 1974; Tittle, 1973) on the sex bias in interest inventories. As of now, however, there is more rhetoric than record (Gottfredson, 1976). If anything, the hue and cry that has been raised may, in the long run, be more detrimental than good to the future vocational and educational guidance of women, and *may* be detrimental to interest measurement in general.

Construction and Keying

Constructing and keying (scoring) noncognitive tests also present problems. Because it is extremely difficult at times to distinguish between a particular technique used to construct and key a test, both operations will be considered together. Cognitive tests have only a single, accepted correct answer. Noncognitive tests, on the other hand, need not always be amenable to a "correct" answer. In a noncognitive test, especially one that has been empirically keyed, an item may be keyed one way as the "correct" answer for plumbers, but it may be incorrect for some other group. Three procedures are commonly used to construct and key noncognitive tests: empirical, homogeneous, and logical.

Empirical Construction

In the empirical or criterion method, one makes no assumption about the traits or characteristics of people in different groups but attempts to develop items that will discriminate men (or women) in one group from those in another group. Each item is evaluated in terms of its relationship to some criterion. The criterion, say for, a test of paranoia might be those patients in a mental institution who have been diagnosed as paranoiacs. The control group (or normals) could be those people who come to visit the paranoiacs. In a criterion-keyed interest inventory, a person's interests are compared with the interests held by people successful in various occupations (only those items that empirically differentiate among different groups are selected—the items are not selected on sheer faith as in logical keying).

Items used in the Strong-Campbell Interest Inventory, the Kuder Occupational Interest Survey, and the Minnesota Multiphasic Personality Inventory were empirically selected and keyed. Although the scoring is usually in terms of unitary weights, differential weights can be assigned in proportion to the difference in responses between the criterion groups.

One virtue of empirical construction (and keying) is that it is very difficult for the examinee to fake his responses. This is true because the examinee does not know how the criterion group responded to the various items.

Homogeneous Construction

The test constructor employing the homogeneous method first begins with a large number of items. Then, through factor analysis, clusters are identified, and the items are organized to fit the identified clusters. A psychometric characteristic of a homogeneous-keyed test is that the items of any one scale have high intracorrelations; that is, a common factor runs throughout that scale; the scale intercorrelations are relatively low (or they should be if more than one trait or cluster has been identified).

Logical Construction

In the logical method the items are selected and keyed on a logical or rational basis rather than on empirical grounds. The test constructor specifies the traits or skills or knowledge needed for the task and then prepares appropriate items. He then scores the items in accordance with his perception of the underlying psychological theory. For example, let us assume that one prepares an interest scale and has as one of his questions, "I like to read blueprints." Logically, one would expect that engineers would like to read blueprints, and if logical keying were used, one would assign a +1 on the engineering scale to those who responded affirmatively. It is conceivable, however, that engineers do not like to read blueprints. If empirical keying had been used to key the test and if it was found that engineers do not like this activity, then one would not assign an individual a +1 on the engineering scale to those who responded affirmatively to this item.

MEASUREMENT OF INTERESTS

As was previously mentioned, teachers must be concerned not only with *what* pupils learn but also with *how* and *why* they learn. People have a tendency to excel or at least to devote more effort and energy to the activities they like. In order for the classroom teacher to best capitalize on the likes and dislikes of his students, it is necessary that he know something of their interests. Interest inventories assist him in gaining this knowledge. In order for the counselor to aid the student in arriving at a decision in regard to his vocational and educational plans, he also must be cognizant of interest measurement.

Teachers should certainly strive to make their objectives (whether they be cognitive skills, factual knowledge, or wholesome attitudes and values) palatable and interesting to their students. The teacher of ninth-grade social studies might explore students' interests (or at least have the students think about their interests) as they are related to various occupations when he discusses the world of work. The high school teacher who knows that Bill is a poor reader may attempt to provide meaningful learning experiences by capitalizing upon Bill's interests and may assign Bill books that are related to his interests. The fifth-grade teacher working upon addition or subtraction skills may exploit students' interests insofar as the types of story problems used. The important thing to remember is that because pupil interests can influence how well they learn, teachers must be concerned with interest measurement.

Knowledge of an individual's interests provides a sound basis for educational and vocational guidance. Interest inventory results may help the classroom teacher understand why a bright pupil is performing poorly. They can be of assistance to the student, if only to make him think more about his future.

Attitudes versus Interests

Attitudes and interests are both concerned with likes and dislikes. Both can be related to preferences for activities, social institutions, or groups. Both involve personal feelings about something. It is this "something" that distinguishes attitudes from interests. An attitude is typically conceptualized as being a feeling toward an *object*, a *social institution*, or a *group*. An interest, on the other hand, is conceptualized as being a feeling toward an *activity*.

Attitude and interest inventories share many things in common. They are both highly susceptible to faking, require frank responses from the subject, and therefore are able to assess only the characteristics that the individual is able to, or wishes to, reveal.

Historical Development of Interest Inventories

The study of interests has received its greatest impetus from educational and vocational counseling. School and industrial psychologists share the common concern that the application of test results may permit better decisions to be made by (1) the individual selecting an occupation and (2) the firm selecting job applicants.

Interest inventories have progressed a great deal from the initial attempts of G. Stanley Hall in 1907 to develop a questionnaire to measure children's recreational interests. Although the measurement of interests was of concern prior to the 1920s, the first formal, scientific, and orderly approach to the study and measurement of interests began in 1919. In a graduate seminar on interests, conducted at the Carnegie Institute of Technology, students and professors developed items to distinguish between members of different occupations. Many inventories evolved from this seminar, the most notable being the Strong Vocational Interest Blank (SVIB). In constructing the original SVIB, two innovations to the measurement of interests were introduced: (1) The items dealt with a subject's likes and dislikes, and (2) the responses were empirically keyed for the different occupational groups. The SVIB was the beginning of "criterion keying." It was not until 1939 that another standardized interest inventory appeared. In that year, the Kuder Preference Record was published. It differed considerably from the SVIB in construction in that it employed homogeneous keying. Kuder and Strong employed markedly different techniques to develop their initial interest inventories. In both the revised edition of the SVIB and some of the revised editions of the Kuder, criterion keying was employed. Each author conceptualized interests, or at least the measurement of interests, differently. Strong employed the very specific occupation, whereas Kuder used the broad category, such as mechanical or scientific rather than engineer or architect.

In 1943 the Lee-Thorpe Occupational Interest Inventory (OII) was published. Whereas both the SVIB and the Kuder inventories employed empirical and statistical grounds for keying their tests, the OII employed a logical approach. In other words, the OII consists of items that demonstrate logical rather than empirical validity. Still another approach to the construction of interest inventories was used by Guilford and his colleagues. In 1948 Guilford's Interest Survey was published. Two unique features of this inventory were the use of factor analysis in the refinement of the various scales and separate scores for vocational and avocational interests. In 1959 the Geist Picture Inventory was published. It was designed to substitute for the highly verbal inventories. Little evidence has been presented to support the claim that a nonverbal interest inventory is as valid as a verbal interest inventory.

Prior to the advent of Guilford's Interest Survey, interest inventories were concerned only with vocational interests. Now, some attention is being paid to avocational interests. Initial standardized interest inventories were designed primarily for college-bound students. There are now inventories designed for use with students who will terminate their education after high school. The Minnesota Vocational Interest Inventory (MVII), published in 1965, is useful for high school students who are occupation bound rather than college bound. In 1969, the Ohio Vocational Interest Survey (OVIS), which, like the MVII, is based upon occupations described in the Dictionary of Occupational Titles (DOT) was published. In 1970 Super's Work Values Inventory (WVI) was published. The WVI is concerned with those factors (extrinsic and intrinsic) that motivate people to work. In the same year, Holland's Vocational Preference Inventory (VPI) was published. The VPI is somewhat of a radical departure from general interest inventories in that Holland conceptualizes interests and vocational choice as an expression of an individual's personality. As will be discussed later, the VPI consists of 11 scales—6 scales measure specific interests and relate them to learning environments; 5 scales yield information about the individual's personality. In 1971 Holland presented a hexagonal model depicting the relationship among the personality types. Holland's thesis and the VPI's validity have been supported by empirical research (Cole & Hanson, 1971; Elton & Rose, 1970; Folsom, 1973; Jacobs, 1972a; Johnson & Moore, 1973; Muchinsky & Hoyt, 1973; Rose & Elton, 1971; Wakefield & Doughtie, 1973).

Although not directly related to the measurement of interests per se, the field of vocational maturity measurement and career interest and planning programs has generated much interest in the past decade. In 1965 Crites constructed the Vocational Development Inventory, which was designed to measure "the dispositional factor in the construct of vocational maturity." In 1971 Super et al. developed the Career Development Inventory which "represents an overall measure of vocational maturity as defined by the individual scales." In 1971 Westbrook constructed the Cognitive Vocational Maturity Test designed to measure career knowledge and abilities in six areas of the cognitive domain of vocational maturity. All three scales differ markedly in item content and method of construction. (For an excellent comparison of these three scales, see Westbrook and Mastie, 1973).

Although interest inventories and the study of interest and career development has progressed in the past decade, much still remains to be done. We still need better theoretical foundations regarding the development of interests; need more knowledge about the relationship of interests to other aspects of human behavior, such as ability, intelligence, and personality,[7]

[7] Guilford and his co-workers believed that, in time, interest inventories may be used as personality tests. They suggested—and there is no reason to doubt this—that interests must be related to motives, aspirations, and need, that interests just do not develop in a vacuum. Recent work in career development lends support to Guilford's hypothesis (see Ginsberg, 1971; Holland, 1973; Super, 1972; Westbrook, 1974).

and need more evidence regarding the construct of interests. Fortunately, much research is being conducted in the area of interests, and some answers should be forthcoming in the near future. (See Holland, 1966, 1973.)

Types of Standardized Interest Inventories

An individual's interests (his likes and dislikes, his preferences and aversions) can be ascertained in a variety of ways. Super and Crites (1962, pp. 377–379) suggest four approaches that can be used to ascertain an individual's interests: (1) direct questioning, (2) direct observation, (3) tested interests, and (4) interest inventories. Measuring an individual's interests by means of interest inventories has proved to be the most fruitful, encouraging, and valid approach. This method is the only one discussed here. The interest inventory contains statements about various occupations and activities. These statements may be presented singly, in pairs, or in triads. The subject responds to each of the statements in terms of his preference for, or aversion to, the activity or occupation.

At least two dozen standardized interest inventories are commercially published, some of which are designed for vocational guidance only, others for educational guidance only, and others that can be used for both educational and vocational guidance. Some are designed for use with high school seniors, college students, and adults; others with junior high school children. Some are applicable only to students who intend to pursue a college education, whereas others are designed for adolescents not bound for college. Some are verbal; others, pictorial.

Some authors, like Strong (1966), developed interest inventories on the assumption that interests are not a unitary trait but a complex interaction of many traits. Other authors, like Kuder (1966), conceptualized interests as an assortment of unitary traits, and this is reflected in the homogeneity of each of Kuder's interest scales. Still other authors constructed their interest inventories on the basis of logical validity. In spite of the different construction approaches (criterion keying, homogeneous keying, and logical keying), all interest inventories share the common purpose of assessing an individual's preferences for various activities. Most interest inventories are based on some common assumptions regarding interests: (1) interests, rather than being innate, are learned as a result of the individual's being engaged in an activity; (2) interests tend to be relatively unstable for young children, but after about age 20, they tend to become stabilized, with little change occurring after age 25; (3) people in different occupations share similar likes and dislikes regarding activities; (4) interests vary in intensity from one person to another; and (5) interests motivate the individual to action.

Because of space limitations we must restrict our discussion of interest inventories to those that are most frequently used in our schools. Since we feel that it is useful for classroom teachers to be cognizant of the various interest inventories available, we have made a comparison of the more popular ones in terms of their construction, grade level and content, administration and scoring, validity, reliability, and ease of interpretation. The examples have been selected to illustrate certain principles of test construction.

Empirically Keyed Interest Inventories

Strong-Campbell Interest Inventory (SCII)   Stanford University Press, 1974. Fourteen-year-olds and over. Six General Occupational Themes (GOT). 23 Basic Interest Scales (BIS). 124 Occupational Scales (OS). 3 types of Administrative Indexes, and 2 Special Scales. Untimed but takes from 20 to 60 minutes to complete. One form.

Because of the severe criticism leveled at interest tests in general, and the Strong Vocational Interest Blank (SVIB) in particular, regarding the SVIB's sex bias (see Campbell, Chrichton, & Webber, 1974; Cole, 1973; Johannson & Harmon, 1972), the 1966 Form for Men and the 1969 Form for Women were replaced by a single form, the SCII. The SCII is essentially a neuterized version of the SVIB.

The SCII is suitable for older adolescents and adults considering higher-level professional or skilled occupations. The SCII contains 325 items which are grouped under such topics as (1) occupations, (2) school subjects, (3) activities, (4) amusements, (5) types of people, (6) preference between activities, and (7) your characteristics (a quasi-personality inventory requiring the respondent to rate his abilities and characteristics). The items are both vocational and avocational, the subject responding to most of the items (281) by means of a three-element key: like, dislike, or indifferent. Care was taken to select items that (1) were free from sexual stereotypes (e.g., stewardess), (2) were balanced in terms of favoring one sex over the other (actually, there are a few more items favoring females), and (3) were not influenced or dependent upon previous work experience but on activities that the average adolescent could be expected to know about or at least imagine.

Strong conceived an interest inventory as a group of items that discriminate people in specific occupations from a general group of similar-age subjects (but not in that occupation). To be included in Strong's criterion group (as a member of a specific occupation), the individual had to be between the ages of 25 and 55, employed in that occupation for at least 3 years, and have indicated a liking for his (her) work. For each of the items, the percentage of men (or women) responding "like, dislike, indifferent" was compared with the percentage of "men (or women)-in-general" responding in a similar manner.[8] The responses were then assigned weights ranging from +1 to −1. A person who receives a high score on the engineer scale, say, displays interests similar to engineers in the norming sample. This is not analogous to saying that the individual would like to be an engineer, or that he would be

[8] The *new* "in-general" sample (now called the General Reference Sample, or GRS) was not selected in as meticulous a fashion as the former reference groups.

successful as a professional engineer, or that he should study engineering in college. Rather, the test score indicates only the similarity of interests shared by the subject and the engineers selected in the norming sample.

The *General Occupational Themes* based on Holland's typology provides an organizing structure that aids the counselor in interpreting the Basic Interest Scales and Occupational Scales. Holland (1973) has developed an occupational-classification system that postulates that people can be categorized in terms of six types—realistic, investigative, artistic, social, enterprising, or conventional—such that each person is characterized by one, or some combination, of these types. Now, instead of talking to the student in terms of over 100 different occupations and/or clusters, the counselor can provide the counselee with a global picture of his occupational orientation. High scores on the GOT scales *suggest* the general kind of activities the person will enjoy, the type of occupational environment where one will be most comfortable, the kinds of activities one will be most willing to deal with, and the kinds of persons who will be found most appealing as co-workers. Research indicates that the themes possess adequate validity and short-term (30-day) stability.

The *Basic Interest Scales*, like the GOTs, aid the user in obtaining a better understanding of the Occupational Scales. Because of the heterogeneity of the occupational scales, the authors collected items into somewhat homogeneous subsets and refer to these subsets as BIS, such as Public Speaking, Office Practices, and Religious Activities. It was felt that the BIS would be more easily understood than the occupational scales and would reduce the need for endless revisions of the existing occupational scales. Since the BIS constitute a major focus in interpreting the SCII—they are to be inspected first because this is the "most important interpretive step" (Campbell, 1969, p. 22) —it is essential that more empirical evidence be presented to demonstrate the relationship between the BIS and the earlier SVIB occupational scales, as well as between BIS and the GOT.

The *Occupational Scales* are the most valid and reliable scales of the SCII and have been the bulwark of the Strong since it was first published in 1927. Because of societal changes, new occupations (e.g., women pilots, male nurses) have been added for both men and women (possibly favoring the females), the profile scores are organized into Holland's system, new "In-General" samples have been drawn, criteria for selecting and weighting the items for a specific occupation were modified from the earlier rules, and new norms were prepared. Of the 325 items in the SCII, only two are completely new; 180 items were common to both of the earlier booklets; 74 appeared only on the Men's form; and 69 appeared only on the Women's form. In the earlier editions, each sex had its own booklet and scoring keys. In the SCII, the counselor has the option of scoring the inventory on either the male scales, the female scales, or both, and interpreting the scores accordingly. The profile is organized such that scores on both same-sex and opposite-sex scales can be represented. In this way, all the scores are available but, at the same time, normative information appropriate for each sex is presented.

In addition to the GOT, BIS, and OS previously described, there are two Special (nonoccupational) scales: Academic Orientation (AOR) and Introversion-Extroversion (IE), and three types of administrative indices: Total Responses (TR), Infrequent Responses (IR), and like percentage, dislike percentage, and indifferent percentage (LP, DP, and IP).

The AOR replaces the former Academic Achievement scale and is a "measure of probable persistence in an academic setting" rather than a predictor of grades. The IE replaces the former Occupational Introversion-Extroversion scale. The IE scale provides useful clinical information and has been shown to discriminate successfully between people- and nonpeople-oriented occupations. The TR index indicates the total number of responses marked and is suggestive of action only if it is less than 310. The IR index is based on responses infrequently selected by the GRS. The purpose of the IR index is to identify those responses that may be incorrectly marked. Although a high score is suggestive that a problem exists, it does *not* indicate *why*. The LP, DP, and IP indices are used to detect errors which *might* be the result of incorrect scoring, a mismarked answer sheet, or misunderstood directions. On the other hand, they might be indicative of the subject's response style.

Reference is made to the validity and reliability of the various scales of the SCII in the manual. Since the bulk of the data are based on the SVIB, they are found in the *Handbook* (Campbell, 1971), which contains a cornucopia of information that should be *required* reading for every SCII user. (We would expect the *Handbook* to contain these data since much of the SCII is reflected in the older Strong scales.) On inspection, the items appear to have good face validity, and the reliability and criterion-related evidence presented are acceptable. The BIS have lower concurrent and predictive validity than the Occupational Scales, which have higher internal consistency but slightly lower consistency over time. The predictive validity of the SCII (which can be inferred from research with the SVIB) is equally good for very able black and white students. The SVIB did *not* demonstrate any racial bias (Borgen, 1972; Borgen & Harper, 1973).

Hand-scoring keys are not available for the SCII. Answer sheets can be scored only by agencies licensed by the publisher. Letter grades (in the earlier SVIB) to present summary statistics that were developed to help the layman understand scores on the Occupational Scales were found to be ineffectual and have been dropped. To assist the teacher, counselor, or student interpret the test scores, raw scores on the BIS and OS are converted to T scores. Also, a computer-generated, printed interpretive profile is provided (see Figure 16–1). In addition, the SCII profile has, for the BIS, bars printed to represent the middle-half or the GRS distribution; for each occupation, there is a shaded area to represent the "average" range (see Figure 16-2). These "bands" should aid in making decisions about the significance of an interest score.

STRONG VOCATIONAL INTEREST BLANK
STRONG-CAMPBELL INTEREST INVENTORY RESULTS FOR

SANDY SMITH

THE FOLLOWING STATISTICAL RESULTS HAVE BEEN COMPILED FROM YOUR ANSWERS
TO THIS INVENTORY.

THREE TYPES OF INFORMATION ARE PRESENTED-

1) YOUR SCORES ON 6 GENERAL OCCUPATIONAL THEMES. THESE GIVE
   SOME IDEA OF YOUR OVERALL OCCUPATIONAL OUTLOOK.

2) YOUR SCORES IN 23 BASIC INTEREST AREAS. THESE SHOW THE
   CONSISTENCY, OR LACK OF IT, OF YOUR INTERESTS IN EACH OF
   THESE SPECIFIC AREAS.

3) YOUR SCORES ON 124 OCCUPATIONAL SCALES. THESE TELL YOU
   HOW SIMILAR YOUR INTERESTS ARE TO THOSE OF EXPERIENCED WORKERS
   IN THE DESIGNATED OCCUPATIONS.

FIRST, A CAUTION. THERE IS NO MAGIC HERE. THIS REPORT WILL GIVE YOU
SOME SYSTEMATIC INFORMATION ABOUT YOURSELF BUT YOU SHOULD NOT EXPECT MIRACLES.
YOUR SCORES ARE BASED SIMPLY ON WHAT YOU SAID YOU LIKED OR DISLIKED.

MOST IMPORTANTLY---THIS TEST DOES NOT MEASURE YOUR ABILITIES-IT IS CONCERNED
ONLY WITH YOUR INTERESTS.

THE GENERAL OCCUPATIONAL THEMES

PSYCHOLOGICAL RESEARCH HAS SHOWN THAT OCCUPATIONS CAN BE GROUPED
INTO SIX GENERAL THEMES. ALTHOUGH THESE ARE CRUDE, THEY DO PROVIDE
USEFUL GUIDELINES. HERE IS AN ANALYSIS OF HOW YOUR INTERESTS
COMPARE WITH EACH OF THESE THEMES-

R-THEME- THIS TYPE IS RUGGED, ROBUST, PRACTICAL, STRONG, AND
         FREQUENTLY AGGRESSIVE IN OUTLOOK. THEY HAVE GOOD PHYSICAL SKILLS
         BUT SOMETIMES HAVE TROUBLE COMMUNICATING THEIR FEELINGS TO OTHERS.
         THEY LIKE TO WORK OUTDOORS AND WITH TOOLS, ESPECIALLY WITH LARGE POWERFUL
         MACHINES. THEY PREFER TO DEAL WITH THINGS RATHER THAN WITH IDEAS
         OR PEOPLE. THEY USUALLY HAVE CONVENTIONAL POLITICAL AND ECONOMIC
         OPINIONS, LIKE TO CREATE THINGS WITH THEIR HANDS, AND PREFER
         OCCUPATIONS SUCH AS MECHANIC, LABORATORY TECHNICIAN, SOME
         ENGINEERING SPECIALTIES, FARMER, OR POLICE OFFICER. THE TERM
         REALISTIC IS USED TO SUMMARIZE THIS PATTERN, THUS, R-THEME.

YOUR ANSWERS SHOW THAT FOR YOUR SEX YOU ARE LOW IN THESE
CHARACTERISTICS AS YOUR STANDARD SCORE WAS 35.

FIGURE 16-1   SVIB-SCII interpretive profile, generated and printed out by computer (first sheet only). (Reprinted from the Manual for the Strong-Campbell Interest Inventory, Form T325 of the STRONG VOCATIONAL INTEREST BLANK, SECOND EDITION, by David P. Campbell, with the permission of the publishers, Stanford University Press. Copyright © 1974, 1977, by the Board of Trustees of the Leland Stanford Junior University.)

INTEREST, PERSONALITY, AND ATTITUDE INVENTORIES

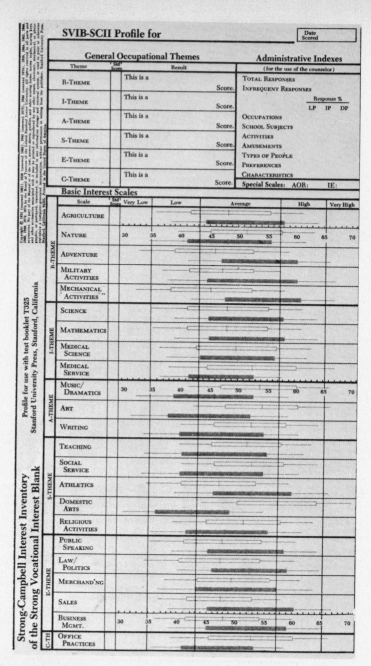

FIGURE 16–2 SCII Profile Sheet. (Reprinted from the Manual for the Strong-Campbell Interest Inventory, Form T325 of the STRONG VOCATIONAL INTEREST BLANK, SECOND EDITION, by David P. Campbell, with the permission of the publishers, Stanford University Press. Copyright © 1974, 1977, by the Board of Trustees of the Leland Stanford Junior University.)

Occupational Scales

Code	Scale	Sex Norm	Std Score / Profile	Code	Scale	Sex Norm	Std Score / Profile
RC	FARMER	m		AE	INT. DECORATOR	m	
RC	INSTRUM. ASSEMBL.	f		AE	ADVERTISING EXEC.	m	
RCE	VOC. AGRIC. TCHR.	m		A	LANGUAGE TEACHER	f	
REC	DIETITIAN	f		A	LIBRARIAN	f	
RES	POLICE OFFICER	m		A	LIBRARIAN	m	
RSE	HWY. PATROL OFF.	m		A	REPORTER	f	
RE	ARMY OFFICER	f		A	REPORTER	m	
RS	PHYS. ED. TEACHER	f		AS	ENGLISH TEACHER	f	
R	SKILLED CRAFTS	m		AS	ENGLISH TEACHER	m	
RI	FORESTER	m		SI	NURSE, REGISTERED	f	
RI	RAD. TECH. (X-RAY)	f		SIR	PHYS. THERAPIST	m	
RI	MERCH. MAR. OFF.	m		SRC	NURSE, LIC. PRACT.	f	
RI	NAVY OFFICER	m		S	SOCIAL WORKER	f	
RI	NURSE, REGISTERED	m		S	SOCIAL WORKER	m	
RI	VETERINARIAN	m	15 25 45 55	S	PRIEST	m	15 25 45 55
RIC	CARTOGRAPHER	m		S	DIR., CHRISTIAN ED.	f	
RIC	ARMY OFFICER	m		SE	YWCA STAFF	f	
RIE	AIR FORCE OFFICER	m		SIE	MINISTER	m	
RIA	OCCUP. THERAPIST	f		SEA	ELEM. TEACHER	m	
IR	ENGINEER	f		SC	ELEM. TEACHER	f	
IR	ENGINEER	m		SCE	SCH. SUPERINTEND.	m	
IR	CHEMIST	f		SCE	PUBLIC ADMINISTR.	m	
IR	PHYSICAL SCIENTIST	m		SCE	GUIDANCE COUNS.	f	
IR	MEDICAL TECH.	f		SER	RECREATION LEADER	f	
IR	PHARMACIST	f		SEC	RECREATION LEADER	m	
IR	DENTIST	f		SEC	GUIDANCE COUNS.	f	
IR	DENTIST	m	15 25 45 55	SEC	SOC. SCI. TEACHER	f	15 25 45 55
IR	DENTAL HYGIENIST	f		SEC	SOC. SCI. TEACHER	m	
IRS	PHYS. THERAPIST	f		SEC	PERSONNEL DIR.	m	
IRS	PHYSICIAN	m		ESC	DEPT. STORE MGR.	m	
IRS	MATH-SCI. TEACHER	m		ESC	HOME ECON. TCHR.	f	
ICR	MATH-SCI. TEACHER	f		ESA	FLIGHT ATTENDANT	f	
IC	DIETITIAN	f		ES	CH. OF COMM. EXEC.	m	
IRC	MEDICAL TECH.	m		ES	SALES MANAGER	m	
IRC	OPTOMETRIST	m		ES	LIFE INS. AGENT	m	
IRC	COMPUTER PROGR.	f		E	LIFE INS. AGENT	f	
IRC	COMPUTER PROGR.	m		E	LAWYER	f	
I	MATHEMATICIAN	f		E	LAWYER	m	
I	MATHEMATICIAN	m	15 25 45 55	EI	COMPUTER SALES	m	15 25 45 55
I	PHYSICIST	f		EI	INVESTM. FUND MGR.	m	
I	BIOLOGIST	m		EIC	PHARMACIST	m	
I	VETERINARIAN	f		EC	BUYER	f	
I	OPTOMETRIST	f		ECS	BUYER	m	
I	PHYSICIAN	f		ECS	CREDIT MANAGER	m	
I	SOCIAL SCIENTIST	m		ECS	FUNERAL DIRECTOR	m	
IA	COLLEGE PROFESSOR	f		ECR	REALTOR	m	
IA	COLLEGE PROFESSOR	m		ERC	AGRIBUSINESS MGR.	m	
IS	SPEECH PATHOL.	f		ERC	PURCHASING AGENT	m	
IS	SPEECH PATHOL.	m		ESR	CHIROPRACTOR	m	
IAS	PSYCHOLOGIST	f		CE	ACCOUNTANT	m	
IAS	PSYCHOLOGIST	m	15 25 45 55	CE	BANKER	f	15 25 45 55
IA	LANGUAGE INTERPR.	f		CE	BANKER	m	
ARI	ARCHITECT	m		CE	CREDIT MANAGER	f	
A	ADVERTISING EXEC.	f		CE	DEPT. STORE SALES	f	
A	ARTIST	f		CE	BUSINESS ED. TCHR.	f	
A	ARTIST	m		CES	BUSINESS ED. TCHR.	m	
A	ART TEACHER	f		CSE	EXEC. HOUSEKEEPER	f	
A	PHOTOGRAPHER	f		C	ACCOUNTANT	f	
A	MUSICIAN	f		C	SECRETARY	f	
A	MUSICIAN	m		CR	DENTAL ASSISTANT	f	
A	ENTERTAINER	f		CRI	NURSE, LIC. PRACT.	f	
AE	INT. DECORATOR	f		CRE	BEAUTICIAN	f	

Column headings for the profile bands: Very Dissimilar, Dissimilar, Ave, Similar, Very Similar.

In summary, the SCII contains the "best" from the last revisions of the SVIB. The SCII is about 20 percent shorter than the SVIB; items have been reworded so that the grammar and vocabulary are neutral; there is now only one form to be used for both men and women; sexual stereotypes have been removed; the distribution of items favoring one sex over the other has been roughly balanced; the scoring was altered so that both sexes can be scored on the same booklet; scores on the profile have been reorganized into Holland's occupational classification system; the number of occupations has been increased; there are new administrative indexes; greater emphasis is placed on the Basic Interest Scales; the profile sheet has been redesigned; and hand scoring is no longer possible. The SCII is characterized by careful construction with up-to-date, unambiguous, low reading-ability-needed items. Some questions or potential problems are as follows: (1) Will the fact that the printed standard score is based on the combined male-female sample, whereas the printed interpretive statement is based on the distribution of scores for the examiner's sex, result in confusion? (2) How much faith can one place in the reliability of the General Occupational Themes considering that very small samples were studied? (3) What effect, if any, does the sampling design used to develop new general-reference groups have on the validity of the Occupational Scales? (4) Do the code types aid in interpreting the profile? We are confident that the SCII author will address himself to such questions, and it is evident from the material contained in the manual that further research is already under way.

Minnesota Vocational Interest Inventory (MVII)   The Psychological Corporation, 1965. One form. Two editions. Untimed but takes about 45 minutes to administer. Twenty-one occupational scales and nine "homogeneous" scales (of highly intercorrelated items) similar to the BIS of the SVII. Designed for high school students who do not aspire to professional vocations. Reading level of the inventory is at about the ninth-grade level.

The MVII should find a useful purpose in counseling students who intend to go into skilled, nonprofessional occupations. It does not do as good a job separating different occupational groups as does the SCII, but this may be due to the nature of interests in skilled trades being less well defined. It suffers from an inadequate standardization and although published in 1965, it still has too few empirical studies to support any real claim for validity and reliability. What has been reported in the manual is respectable—we ask only that more respectability (in terms of "hard" data) be offered. The MVII does not appear to be as fakable as some of the other interest inventories. Even so, faking can occur, and, as is suggested in the manual, the MVII should not be used in employment selection programs. It is easy to administer and score; the quality and format are good; many counselors' suggestions are contained in the manual; and it can be used with ninth-graders, although one must recognize that the interest of young teenagers may still not be crystallized.

We have some serious reservations about the wisdom in providing the examinee with a profile sheet for self-interpretation of the MVII, even though the intent and scales are described with clarity and appropriate caution. Why should we sanction the opportunity for distortion? All in all, teachers and counselors in systems where the majority of students enter into skilled or semiskilled nonprofessional occupations should find the MVII an asset to their existing testing program.

Kuder Occupational Interest Survey (OIS), Form DD   Science Research Associates, Inc., 1964. Replaces Kuder Preference Record Occupational (Form D). Manual and interpretive leaflet revised in 1970. High school students and adults. One form. Untimed, but takes about 30 minutes to complete. Vocabulary level at about sixth grade. Thirty core scales.

Although Kuder contends that the OIS scores are related to vocational maturity, no evidence is presented to support this (Stahmann & Matheson, 1973).

The OIS has a verification key that can assist the counselor in ascertaining how honest and careful a subject was in responding to the inventory. Although such a score is of value and, from the data presented, this scale appears to be valid, approximately the same amount of space is devoted in the manual to this scale as is devoted to reliability or validity.

The OIS has been carefully constructed and has some features not found in other interest tests.[9] It contains an interpretive leaflet for the examinee that is well written. The manual is also well written and contains some useful suggestions for the counselor. The discussion on the development of the test and the description of the criterion groups is clear and should prove of value to the counselor who is considering the use of the OIS. A major disadvantage of the test is that it can be scored only by the publisher.

In comparison to the SCII, the Kuder DD has the following advantages: (1) scoring of college-major interests, (2) a broader range of occupations (more technical and trade level), and (3) scores for females on selected men's occupational and college-major scales. The major advantages of the SCII are that it shows evidence of predictive validity, has more reliability data, and is easier to interpret. Studies have shown congruent validity between the same and similarly named scales of the OIS and SCII (Johnson, 1971; Zytowski, 1972). However, although the SCII and OIS have some likenamed scales, under *no* circumstances should they be interpreted in the same way (Kuder, 1969; Lefkowitz, 1970), because they were designed for different purposes and measure a different domain of interests. O'Shea and Harrington (1971) go even further and say that both instruments should *not* be used with the same client since the results may only serve to confuse the undecided even

---

[9] For females, the scores for college majors are reported using data based on the male groups.

further. And, like the SCII but unlike other interest inventories, the same form is used for both men and women. The OIS also resembles the SCII somewhat, in that those occupations that present opportunities for either sex, for example, medicine, scores are reported using data based on the male groups.

Homogeneous Keyed Interest Inventories

Kuder General Interest Survey (GIS), Form E   Science Research Associates, Inc., 1964. Grades 6–12. One form. Untimed but takes about one hour to administer. Provides 11 scores.

The GIS is suitable for students in grades 6 to 12, and research is now under way to see whether it is valid for adults. Its reading level is sufficiently low to permit its use with high school students who have a limited vocabulary. The GIS consists of 552 statements that are grouped into 184 triads. The subject selects the statement or activity liked "most" and the one liked "least" in each of the triads. Kuder contended that the scoring is such that the GIS is not a purely ipsative scale, even though it is of a forced-choice format. Kuder (1966) offered some rational arguments concerning the nonipsative nature of the GIS, but we feel he has stretched the point in his argument. The GIS has been constructed with younger people in mind: (1) It has a vocabulary that is at the sixth-grade level, and (2) it attempts to avoid using occupational titles (the meanings associated with them are relatively unstable, especially for younger people). The GIS differs from the Kuder Occupational Interest Survey and the SVIB in that it expresses vocational preferences only as cluster areas rather than specific occupational choices. There are ten occupational scales: outdoor, mechanical, computational, scientific, persuasive, artistic, literary, musical, social service, and clerical. In addition, there is a verification scale. The number of items assigned to a particular scale varies from 16 in the musical scale to 70 in the persuasive scale. Because the scales do not contain an equal number of items, the raw scores not only *can* vary from individual to individual but also *do* vary from one scale to another. Although this may not confuse the trained counselor, it probably will confuse the student because the GIS can supposedly be self-administered, self-scored, and self-interpreted.

Over a decade after publication, we feel, is sufficient time for the author and publisher to have obtained and published validity data. Yet this has not been done. It is hoped, however, that when such data are forthcoming, they will be published in a supplementary manual. It is also hoped that the validity data for the GIS will be more inclusive than that for its predecessor (Kuder Form C), which is woefully inadequate with respect to specific occupational criterion data. Another form of validity is content or face validity. When one glances through the inventory, he is apt to notice that the activities referred to are biased in favor of middle-class American values. There are only a few items that relate to activities that the underprivileged could be expected to experience. This strongly suggests that the GIS not be used in poverty areas or in schools that have a major proportion of their pupils coming from a racial or economic ghetto. A third aspect of validity presented in the manual pertains to the intercorrelations among the eleven scales. Although homogeneous keying attempts to produce scales that have highly intracorrelated items but low intercorrelations (among the scales), we are unable to explain some of the obtained correlations. For example, should there be a substantial correlation between the musical and artistic interest scales? Even with an ipsative scale where one obtains low interest correlations, we would expect to find correlations higher than .02 or .03 between the musical and artistic scales. Inasmuch as the profile leaflet encourages self-interpretation, this dependence upon the relatedness (or unrelatedness) of the constructs measured can result in misuse and should be clarified.

The reliability estimates provided are in terms of stability data and Kuder-Richardson measures of internal consistency. The average test-retest (six-week-interval) correlations for boys and girls are .50 and .43, respectively. This would therefore severely limit the use of the GIS for making individual and possibly even group predictions for sixth- and seventh-graders. It would be of value to have data demonstrating whether the highest scores tend to remain high and the lowest scores tend to remain low. Such data are especially of significance in vocational and educational counseling.

The normative data are adequately presented in the manual. The descriptions of the sampling procedures used and the nature of the standardization sample are clear. The publishers exercised care in attempting to obtain a fairly representative sample although some of the geographical regions are slightly under- or overrepresented.

Raw scores are converted to percentiles, and these percentile scores are then used to prepare the test profile. This procedure does not eliminate the possibility that the reported score may be an inaccurate representation of the subject's interest. For example, an individual can obtain a high percentile score and still have little interest in the area, and vice versa, due to the ipsative nature of the scales.

A somewhat disturbing feature of the profile leaflet is the description of the various interest areas. Specific references are made to occupations or vocations, and these occupations are then grouped within a larger interest cluster. For example, in defining a persuasive interest the publishers say that most salesmen, personnel managers, and buyers have high persuasive interest. Yet no empirical evidence is presented in the manual to support such a claim. For this reason we feel that the user should exercise extreme caution in interpreting the test profile. We further suggest that because of possible misinterpretation of the profile leaflet (especially by younger pupils), the counselor or teacher does the actual interpretation.

In conclusion, we are pleased that an attempt has been made to try to measure the interests of younger people in the Kuder General Interest Survey. Our knowledge of the development and stability of interests is not complete, but this should not dissuade us from trying to measure them. Our interest, however, in the development of such an inventory should not make us sacrifice quality. From the data presented in the manual regarding the test's validity and reliability, it would appear that the test was published before sufficient and adequate predictive validity data were obtained. For the early high school years the GIS may be appropriate, but for older high school students who aspire to college the new SCII appears to be superior.

Vocational Preference Inventory (VPI)   Consulting Psychologists Press, 1970. One form. Can be used for persons 14 years of age and older. Self-administering. Untimed but takes from 15 to 30 minutes to complete. Yields 11 scores—6 of which (realistic, intellectual, social, conventional, enterprising, and artistic) measure specific interests and relate them to learning environments; and 5 of which (self-control, masculinity, status, infrequency, and acquiescence) yield information about the subject's personality.

The rationale underlying Holland's VPI is that our environment can be classified into six types of combinations and that humans can also be classified into one or a combination of these six types. Holland claims that people of a particular type seek out a compatible environment of that same type, thereby giving us a person-environment match. The goodness of the match between the person and his environment is dependent on a variety of factors.

The subject responds to each of the 160 occupational titles presented in terms of a "Yes" (interest in that occupation) or "No" (lack of interest in that occupation) format. The highest score represents a dominant personality type; the four highest scores yield a personality interest pattern.

The test-retest reliabilities are moderate to high (.62 to .98) but have been computed on very small samples.

Most of the validity studies cited by Holland (1973) are of the concurrent and predictive type and indicate that (1) the VPI scales measure essentially similar constructs to some of those assessed by the California Psychological Inventory, the MMPI, and the SCII; (2) the VPI scores differentiate between men and women, persons in different occupations, and normal and abnormal people; (3) students' self-descriptions are consistent with their scale scores; and (4) VPI scores are correlated with such things as supervisor's ratings, choice of vocation, choice of major field, and psychiatric versus nonpsychiatric patients. Although the validity studies are highly favorable (Lucy, 1976; McLaughlin & Tiedeman, 1974; Toenjes & Borgen, 1974), more research is needed (and no doubt will be conducted) on noncollege persons. (Much of Holland's original research was conducted with National Merit Scholars, a very bright group. It is conceivable that a more heterogeneous group might yield different results.)

Generally, the numerous validity studies lend support to Holland's hypothesis of the relationship between occupational preferences and personality as well as to the meaning of the scales (Cole & Hanson, 1971; Folsom, 1973). Two major limitations of the VPI are that (1) there appears to be a sex bias, with many of the occupational titles not being appropriate for women, and (2) the VPI, unlike the SCII or OIS, does *not* give the subject information on how his likes or dislikes compare with those of people in other occupations. Two additional limitations are that (1) there is some question whether the Acquiescence scale is valid (Jacobs, 1972), and (2) as already mentioned, the subjects Holland used in the development of his instrument were very homogeneous.

The manual is very good and outlines a clinical interpretation for each scale, presents a conceptual definition for each variable, and discusses some actual case studies.

The VPI is a very promising scale. It is based upon the hypothesis that an individual's choice of an occupation is an expression of his personality (that is, the subject "projects" himself into an occupational title, thereby making the VPI both a structured personality inventory as well as an occupational-interest inventory); personal stability, career satisfaction, or stable career pattern depends greatly on the "goodness of fit" between one's personality and the environment in which he works; each occupation has an environment characteristic of the people in it; and people in a particular vocation have similar personalities. These assumptions are testable, have been tested, and in general, support Holland's thesis.

Holland's theory (and hence the VPI) differs markedly from the conception of interests held by others such as Strong and Kuder. And, as Campbell (1974) states, "Holland's ideas have already had a substantial impact on research in the areas of vocational counseling, the measurement of interests, and occupational typology."

Logically Keyed Interest Inventories

Ohio Vocational Interest Survey (OVIS)   Harcourt Brace Jovanovich, Inc., 1969. Grades 8–12. One form. Untimed, but takes about 60 to 90 minutes to administer. Test authors prefer one extended sitting, although they say that two sittings are permissible. Yields 24 scores.

The OVIS is a popular, well-constructed, and well-standardized vocational interest inventory for use with high school students. The rationale underlying the development of the OVIS was based on the Dictionary of Occupational Titles' (DOT)[10] cubistic model of involvement of data, people, and things. The OVIS consists of three parts: (1) a student information questionnaire of six items—one requiring the student to indicate his first and

---

[10] Published by the United States Employment Service (USES); contains descriptions of virtually all occupations.

second choice from 27 job descriptions, one asking for his first and second choice of school subjects liked, one on the type of high school program enrolled in (or contemplated), two questions on future plans, and one item on the student's first and second choice of 23 high school business and vocational programs (for example, bookkeeping, appliance repair, drafting); (2) a local survey information section, in which opportunity is given the user to ask one to eight questions of local concern or interest; and (3) an interest inventory of 280 items.

The inventory portion of the OVIS consists of 280 items, based on the DOT, which are grouped into clusters of five to six items. Of the 280 items, 248 are scored jointly for males and females. The 280 items used were based on refinement of the 114 homogeneous areas of the DOT into 24 broad-interest categories (scales), with each scale being represented by 11 homogeneous items.[11] Of the 24 scales, 19 are common to both men and women, and 5 contain items differentiated by sex. To each item, the subject responds by means of a five-element key: would like the activity very much, would like, neutral, would dislike, and would dislike very much. The responses are weighted +5 to +1 respectively. Hence a subject's score on any one scale may vary from 11 to 55.

Although the DOT model has three levels for each of data, people, and things for a total of 27 cells, the OVIS has only 24 scales. The missing three scales have been purposefully omitted since the OVIS scales are based only on the real world of work and, in the *real* world, some jobs would never exist in a practical sense, although they could be portrayed theoretically.

Five of the cells are represented by two or more scales because it was found that to accurately describe the job groups represented, a combination of data-people-things, one would have to use two (or more) scales rather than one.

Extensive and detailed planning went into the development and standardization of the OVIS. The authors are to be commended for their painstaking efforts in developing and standardizing the OVIS. The authors state that the comments of users ". . . will be taken into account in future revisions of the instrument."

Although predictive and concurrent validity are the *sine qua non* of interest inventories, no such data are presented. Construct validity was illustrated and a mimeographed supplement from the publisher describes the scales in detail. However, if validity, as the manual states, is to be assessed by determining the extent to which realistic plans for the student's future are developed, then evidence *must* be presented to demonstrate this. We realize that longitudinal data are needed for some types of validity (especially to determine the long-range utility of the OVIS), but criterion-related validity

[11] The elaborate procedure used to select items and develop the scales is thoroughly described in the manual.

could and should have been presented before the test was published even if only on the experimental editions. The OVIS is not the only culprit. Many test publishers place their product on the market before satisfying the minimal standards adopted by the APA-AERA-NCME Committee on Test Standards (see American Psychological Association, 1974).

Reliability was ascertained by means of stability estimates (.72 to .84 for a sample of eighth-graders and .74 to .90 for a sample of tenth-graders) over an interval of two weeks. Lacking in the manual are internal-consistency estimates.

Normative data—including means, standard deviations, and scores at five different percentile points—are reported for each scale by sex, grade, and geographical region. Each student's raw scores, percentiles, stanines, and clarity indices (a clarity index on a given scale indicates the degree of consistency in responses to the 11 job activities on that scale) are available to the student in a personalized report folder. (As we commented for the MVII, we question the advisability of such an approach, especially for interest inventories.)

All in all, the OVIS may well be one of the best interest tests of the future, inasmuch as so much attention is placed upon entering occupations as depicted by the DOT. Most of the problems discussed—including lack of validity data—can be remedied. We are confident that they will be. The major question to which the test authors must address themselves surrounds the rationale and implementation of the data-people-things model of interests.

Lee-Thorpe Occupational Interest Inventory (OII)   Revised edition. California Test Bureau, 1956. One form. Two levels: intermediate (grades 7–adult) and advanced (grades 9–adult). Ten scores. Untimed, but takes about 45 minutes to administer.

The OII consists of 120 pairs of statements and has a forced-choice format. The authors began with definitions of occupations listed in the DOT and established six broad categories or fields of interest: personal-social, natural, mechanical, business, arts, and sciences. The ten scores that are obtained can be grouped into one of three categories: (1) fields of interest, (2) types of interests (verbal, manipulative, and computational), and (3) levels of interests. Within each of the six fields of interest, tasks were selected to represent the three levels of interest or responsibility (high, low, and medium). Validity and reliability data are lacking. The relationships found between field and type scores are misleading and are, to a large extent, an artifact of the inventory. The normative data provided are not only inadequate but also misleading. In general, the OII should be used only for research purposes until the authors can present empirical data to demonstrate the inventory's validity and reliability.

Work Values Inventory (WVI)   Houghton Mifflin Company, 1970. One form. Grades 7 and above. Fifteen value scores (e.g., creativity, altruism, independence). Untimed but takes about 10 to 15 minutes to complete. Super believes that interests are related to values and that we must be concerned with those factors that motivate people to work. The values measured are *extrinsic to* and *intrinsic in* work. The WVI contains 45 items (developed from job satisfaction research) to which the subject responds by means of a five-point scale. Content, construct, concurrent, and predictive validity were studied, but the empirical data presented are very sparse. No reliability data are given. Scores are expressed as percentiles. There are separate sex norms for grades 7–12. As of now, the WVI should *not* be used for individual counseling.

Comparisons among Selected Interest Inventories

There is very little difference, if any, among the various interest inventories with respect to their general purpose. All are concerned with an assessment of one's likes and dislikes for various occupations so that the examinee, with the help of a trained counselor, can make more valid decisions regarding future educational or vocational plans than if interest inventory data were not available. There are, however, some marked differences between the various standardized interest inventories with respect to their method of construction, scoring, ease of administration, and ease of interpretation. Also, they differ in the grade level at which they can be used. We will now consider briefly the inventories previously discussed. (Those interested in a very comprehensive treatment of the purpose, method of construction, technical features, and interpretations possible of the inventories discussed here, except the SCII, should see Zytowski, 1973.)

Method of Construction

The Strong-Campbell Interest Inventory (SCII), Minnesota Vocational Interest Inventory (MVII), and Kuder Occupational Interest Survey (OIS) employed criterion keying (contrasted groups). The SCII and MVII used as their criterion groups men-and-women-in-general, whereas the OIS compared men in one occupation with those in many other occupations. The Lee-Thorpe Occupational Interest Inventory (OII), the Work Values Inventory (WVI), and the Ohio Vocational Interest Survey (OVIS) employed logical keying. The Kuder General Interest Survey (GIS) and the Vocational Preference Inventory (VPI) used homogeneous keying.

Grade Level and Content

The SCII should not be used below junior high school. The OIS should not be used for students who are not at least juniors in high school. The MVII and VPI can be used for pupils in the ninth grade (about 15 or 16 years old).

The OVIS can be used with eighth-graders. The OII and WVI can be used for seventh-graders, but the results should be interpreted cautiously. The Kuder GIS can be used for bright sixth-graders.

With respect to content, there is very little difference, if any, between the Kuder OIS, and Strong inventories. They stress activities and interests related to professional occupations and vocations. These inventories, however, differ from the OII, OVIS and MVII, which are concerned more with non-professional occupations, especially the MVII. The OII items are more hetero-geneous than the SCII or Kuder items, and hence the OII may be more difficult to interpret. Because the OII and OVIS are based on the *Dictionary of Occupational Titles* (DOT), they may sample many activities with which the student has little knowledge or experience. The Kuder scales are the only ones that contain a verification key per se, although the SCII has six admin-istrative indices scores to detect examinee errors in responding.

The most marked difference is between the WVI and the other scales in that the WVI is concerned with measuring values, while the other inventories can be thought of as measuring interests per se. On the other hand, the VPI relates one's personality and the job environment to measured interests.

Administration and Scoring

All interest inventories are untimed, but they take about 10 to 90 minutes to administer. None requires any formal training for either administration or scoring. All are group-administered. Interest inventories are, in a sense, self-administering.

The eight inventories discussed here differ markedly in their ease of scoring. The OII, WVI, and GIS are relatively easy to score and can be either hand- or machine-scored. The SCII, OVIS, and the OIS are complex to score, and can be scored only by the publisher (SCII can be scored only by com-panies licensed by the publisher). The MVII and VPI are between the two extremes.

Validity and Reliability

The degree of confidence that the user can place in his interpretation is directly related to both validity and stability of the instrument(s) used. The amount of evidence supporting claims for validity and reliability differs among the interest inventories. If one were to conceptualize a continuum running from most to least empirical evidence in support of reliability and validity data, the results would be as depicted in Figure 16–3. Although the Kuder GIS does not have much data to lend support to its predictive validity, it does have a little more than the OII, WVI, or OVIS. It is understandable why OVIS, VPI, and WVI do not have too much predictive data—they are rela-tively new instruments. But at least the authors are cognizant of this and

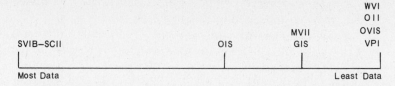

FIGURE 16–3   Empirical evidence for validity and reliability.

promise that predictive validity data will be forthcoming. Unfortunately this does not appear to be so insofar as the OII is concerned. The OII has been around for a long time, and the authors have failed to heed the criticisms leveled regarding the paucity of validity and reliability data.

Interpretation

One may think that the less complex an inventory the easier is its interpretation. This does not hold true, at least for interest inventories. All interest inventories are difficult to interpret properly. If they are to be used for more than exploratory purposes, they should be interpreted only by a trained counselor or psychologist. Of the eight inventories discussed earlier, the OII and the GIS convey more general (rather than specific) information and hence may be frustrating to some students. It is one thing to tell a student that he exhibits the interests shared by chemists or lawyers, but it is something else when you tell him that he has scientific interests. What are scientific interests? In using the SCII, the OIS, or the MVII, the counselor can be both specific (using the separate occupational scores) and general (using the cluster or area interest scores), but with the OII or the GIS, the counselor can be only general in his evaluation of the examinee's interests. Interpretations of WVI scores are a little different since the WVI, rather than measuring interests per se, describes the individual's value orientation, and the scores are interpreted in a clinical fashion. The VPI, although it gives an indication of the individual's likes and dislikes for various occupations, may be conceived as being rooted in personality theory to explain one's vocational preferences.

The SCII, OIS, and MVII are better for job orientation because the scores tell one what people in a specific vocation or profession (as well as people in broad areas such as scientific, mechanical, and business) like and dislike. Unlike the OII and the GIS, we do not have to infer an individual's interests from a general scale such as personal-social or computational. The OVIS and OII, because they were constructed according to the DOT, are more applicable to specific occupations than is the GIS.

With regard to interpretation, one must keep in mind that the Kuder tests and the MVII, because they are forced-choice inventories, are ipsative rather than normative scales. This means that the choice of one response automatically results in the rejection of the other(s). In other words, an ipsative scale results in a high score in one scale to be accompanied by a low score in another scale.

The OII and VPI may be more susceptible than the other scales to responses being made in terms of stereotypes that the examinee holds rather than in terms of interests per se. In addition, the OII, OVIS and MVII are not so applicable to higher-level professional occupations as is either the Kuder OIS or the SCII. In comparison to the MVII, the OVIS has broader application to the entering occupations described in the DOT.

Although similar labels, such as *scientific,* may be attached to scales in the various interest inventories, the counselor must be cautious in inferring that scales having the same designation are measuring exactly the same trait or characteristic. Just as one should not judge a book by its cover, the counselor should not interpret a scale by its name. The counselor must be thoroughly familiar with the test, the operational definitions of the terms used to describe the scale, and the theoretical orientation of the test constructor. All these cautions reinforce our position that, for other than exploratory information, the user be trained in terms of both formal course work and practical experience.

Users of the WVI have been cautioned by Super to avoid ascribing their own meanings to the scores. In interpreting the WVI, the user should look for patterns of scores. For example, a high independence score accompanied by high creativity and intellectual stimulation scores would suggest that the respondent's independence and intellectualism might lead to his pursuit of a research career. But, on the other hand, a high independence score coupled with a high variety and economic return scores would suggest that the respondent's independence is of a financial nature, which might lead to satisfaction for him in selling bonds or life insurance.

The OIS and the SCII are relatively unsatisfactory for people entering occupations that are below the professional-managerial level, even though there are many scales that are occupational in nature. Of the two tests, the OIS is more suitable for persons contemplating lower-level occupations. This is not to imply that Kuder and Strong believed the measurement of interests for skilled workers to be futile. Indeed, this was not the case. Strong (1966) went so far as to recommend some inventories to be used with individuals contemplating skilled, nonprofessional occupations. The nature of the research conducted in the development of the Strong and the OIS was such that the inventories are biased in favor of professional and managerial people. Use of either the SCII or the OIS for high school seniors who intend to enter the apprenticeship program of skilled craftsmen is strongly discouraged. In fact, using these inventories for these persons is a misuse (the MVII or OVIS would be appropriate here).

In conclusion, there are some similarities as well as marked differences among the various interest inventories. Although Strong and Kuder originally approached the measurement of interests differently, their tests are now very similar. Strong adopted the interest clusters advocated by Kuder, and Kuder adopted the specific interest areas used by Strong. Although criticisms can be leveled at any of the interest inventories, the deficiencies of the Strong and Kuder inventories are mild in comparison to the deficiencies of the OII. One reviewer of the OII went so far as to say that this is a good example of how efficient packaging and advertising can make a worthless test appear to be valid (Bordin, 1949).

Using Interest Inventory Results

As might be expected, the greatest utility of interest inventory results is for guidance and counseling—occupational, educational, and personal. Used appropriately, these tests' scores may help an individual crystallize his interests by having him think about his future plans or may clarify some misconceptions that he has about future occupational or vocational goals. It should be stressed here that it is not the test scores per se that help achieve this self-discovery. It is the professional interpretation made of the test scores. Those who interpret interest test scores must be thoroughly trained and familiar with interest inventories: their uses and misuses, their fallibility, and their general value in helping make sound educational and vocational decisions.

Before considering the various uses of interest inventory results by educators, we feel that it would be appropriate to summarize what we have learned about the nature of interests and interest inventories.

1. Interests tend to become progressively more stable with age (particularly after adolescence), but they are never permanently fixed. Although a broad area of interest, such as medicine, may not change, there can be a shift in one's interests regarding general practice versus specialization or regarding different specialties. Using interest inventory results to counsel students who are not yet juniors in high school into making specific vocational decisions is to be discouraged because interests are changeable at this age. Interest test scores can and should be used in discussions about various occupations and professions. Only the Strong has demonstrated empirically that its results are quite reliable (in terms of long-term stability) for individuals around 25 years of age.

2. Interest inventories are susceptible to response set and faking; some more so than others. The user should therefore interpret the results of interest inventories accordingly.

3. Interest inventory scores can be influenced by the ambiguity of the questions asked. For example, two people may respond to the item "Like to play bridge" in the same way but for different reasons. One individual may

answer "Like" because it affords him an opportunity to meet people and establish future contacts, even though he may dislike bridge. Another person might answer "Like" for different reasons. He may like bridge because of the challenge it offers; yet this person might not like people and may avoid them whenever possible. Responses to interest inventory items are relative rather than absolute indicators of likes and dislikes. It is of vital importance that interest inventories be carefully constructed so as to remove the influence of ambiguity as much as possible.

4. Interest inventories are verbal in nature. The examinee must be able to comprehend what is being asked of him. Although the reading levels of the interest inventories vary, nearly all assume that the examinee can read at least at the sixth-grade level. This therefore precludes the use of such inventories as the SCII, OIS, GIS, and OII for illiterates and students who have a reading deficiency. The verbal nature of these interest inventories also leaves open the possibility of misunderstanding or misinterpreting.

5. There is disagreement among interest inventory authors with respect to the kinds of items that are most valid. Kuder (1970) says that "activities" are more valid; Holland (1973) contends that "occupational titles" are more valid. Since interest inventory authors agree that vocational interests in occupations are sex-related (Campbell, 1974; Holland, 1973) and since we appear to be so concerned with sex stereotyping and bias, the kinds of items used can be significant. As of now, only one small study has been reported and the findings indicate that "activity" items are less susceptible to sex stereotyping than are "occupational titles" (Harmon & Conroe, 1976).

6. Interest inventories do not do very well in predicting job success, academic success, job satisfaction, or personality adjustment. There is no interest test on the market that will permit one to say that Johnny should become a doctor, lawyer, or carpenter. There is no interest inventory that will indicate whether or not Johnny will be happy or successful in vocations or occupations in which he has obtained high scores. This does not mean that interest inventories have no predictive validity. They do, but they are not so valid as cognitive measures. There is a slight relationship between interest inventory scores and academic success (correlations normally are about .39). And there is a slight relationship between interest scores and such things as job success and personality. This, however, should not necessarily be interpreted as evidence of a relationship that is of practical significance (even though it may be of statistical significance), nor should it be construed as a cause-and-effect relationship. In predicting job satisfaction, it should be remembered that many factors must be considered, of which interests are but one factor. The relationship between interest scores and job success is vague in part because of the problem of obtaining a valid measure of job success. Interest inventory scores may be related to various measures of job and/or academic success and satisfaction. However, the nature of the relationship is such that interest scores alone should never be used to pre-

dict future success or satisfaction. It is because the untrained user may make exaggerated statements about the probability or degree of success (or satisfaction) in a profession or vocation that we find interest inventories being severely and unduly criticized. Once again, we reiterate that in many instances the instrument is made the scapegoat.

7. Some empirically constructed interest inventories may be more susceptible to sex bias than those constructed by the homogeneous method (Cole, 1973; Johansson & Harmon, 1972).

Although persons may have a natural tendency to accent the negative and eliminate or forget the positive, we hope that this tendency is not exercised when interest inventories are concerned. When used properly, interest inventory results can provide valuable information for the teacher and counselor—information that is more valid than that obtained by nonstandardized approaches—so that they will better understand the pupils' cognitive and noncognitive behavior.

Guidance Purposes

After cognitive measures, interest inventory results play the greatest role in occupational and educational counseling. Interest inventory results are beneficial to both the counselor and the counselee. The counselor can use the results as an introduction to the interview. The interest test may be used as a gambit in situations where it is difficult to establish rapport. The counselor can use the test results to help open the way to discussing other problems such as academic difficulty, personal-social relationships, and the like. The counselee, on the other hand, has an opportunity to view himself as he described himself. He can look at his present plans and with the assistance of the counselor see whether his aspirations are realistic, confirm his feelings, and do some "reality testing." The counselee can use the test results as leads for further consideration. The counselee and counselor can use the test results to see whether the expressed interests are related or unrelated (whether they all fit into a pattern such as humanitarian or technical or whether they are distinct), whether the program that the counselee is intending to follow is compatible with his profile of interests and abilities, and whether the counselee's vocational or avocational goal will be realized by the program he is now following.

Interest-test results, if used cautiously, can help an individual find himself in terms of the activities he feels are important and interesting. Interest-test results should not be used for classroom selection purposes (though they may be useful for classification). They should not be used to tell Johnny that he should enter the field of engineering. They should not be used as a major criterion in occupational and educational counseling. High scores on an interest inventory are not analogous to saying that the individual has either the aptitude or potential for success in a particular vocation. The test scores provide only a relative index of the individual's likes and dislikes, and for some inventories it is possible to compare the student's interests with those of individuals who are successful in a vocation or profession. In actual practice, interest-inventory results should be used only for their valuable ancillary information. Other factors such as ability, aptitude, motivation, and the like must be considered. The total profile rather than just part of it must be considered so that as complete a picture as possible of the individual's interests can be obtained. Finally, we shouldn't argue whether *expressed* vocational interests are more valid than inventoried interests. Rather, we should consider *both* when counseling students.

Instructional Purposes

Although interest inventory results can be used for grouping students, they normally are not used for this purpose. In a somewhat indirect fashion, interest inventory results can be used by the classroom teacher to provide optimal learning conditions. Take, for example, the junior high school student who is a poor reader. Recognizing the limitations of interest inventory scores for junior high school students, the teacher who knows that Billy likes mechanics may attempt to motivate him to read more by suggesting books, magazines, or articles that are of mechanical content. Hence although the test score is not used as an instructional device per se, it is used to provide a learning experience that may be quite beneficial insofar as Billy's reading is concerned.

Interest inventories can be used as a learning device. For example, in the unit on "Work" in Social Studies, the teachers may have the students take an interest test. He can use this technique to get the students to think somewhat systematically about the relationships between personal interests and occupational choice. Any interest inventory used in a group fashion should be used for discussion purposes only. Hopefully, divergent thinking rather than convergent thinking will ensue.

Summary

Knowledge about an individual's interests can be of much value to the classroom teacher, or counselor (as a gambit for a discussion between the student and counselor regarding the student's vocational plans), and to the individual (they can help him give some considerations to professions and vocations that he might never have thought about).

The three techniques most frequently used to construct interest inventories are: logical-keying, homogeneous-keying, and criterion-keying. Although the two men most renowned for their work in the area of interest measurement, Strong and Kuder, employed different approaches in the initial development of their inventories, the revised editions of the Strong and Kuder are more similar than different. The interest patterns or clusters identified or at least designated by Kuder and Strong have, in the main, been confirmed by empirical research.

Despite the fact that interest inventories have certain limitations (fakable, susceptible to response set, may be answered on the basis of stereotypes, and may be difficult to interpret especially if they are ipsative forced-choice tests) they do have much value in occupational and educational counseling *if* and *when* used properly.

Some inventories, like the Kuder OIS and SCII, are designed for individuals who plan to attend college and aspire to managerial or professional roles. Other inventories, such as the MVII, are designed for students who plan to enter into apprenticeship programs after leaving high school.

More research is needed about the relationship among the scores of the various inventories. There have been many instances reported in the literature regarding discrepancies. Needless to say, research directed toward resolving such discrepancies will permit the counselor to make a more valid interpretation of the test profile.

Interest inventories have come a long way from Strong's initial attempts in the 1920s. They are not only becoming more refined but they are also beginning to emphasize or at least recognize the need for a theoretical position on the development of interests. They can assist the counselor in establishing rapport. They can help the student by giving him something to consider or reflect upon and by providing him with some ideas that he can develop more fully by reading and discussion. They can help the teacher organize meaningful learning experiences. All in all, they can help school personnel obtain a more complete picture of the individual by providing valuable data about his likes and dislikes. Such data are best obtained from standardized interest inventories.

CAREER AWARENESS AND DEVELOPMENT

It is becoming increasingly evident that an individual requires *more* than just an interest in, and possibly an aptitude or ability for, a particular vocation in order to be counseled for that vocation. Between 1958, when ETS published its Guidance Inquiry, and 1968 there was a void in the development and publication of standardized instruments to measure the various aspects of career development—cognitive, affective, and psychomotor—all of which are involved in the decision-making process engaged in by the counselor and counselee with regard to career choice. Since 1968, however, at least four major career-planning programs have been initiated; numerous articles have been written (see McClure & Buan, 1973, for a collection of essays) on career education; and six career-development/vocational-maturity standardized tests have been published: Readiness for Vocational Planning Test in 1968; Cognitive Vocational Maturity Test in 1970; Career Development Inventory in 1971; Self-Directed Search in 1971; Assessment of Career Development in 1972; Career Maturity Inventory in 1973; and Planning Career Goals in 1976. (See Super et al., 1972; Super & Crites, 1962; Westbrook & Parry-Hill, 1973.) Although all of these instruments are designed to measure those factors deemed important for career development, it is not surprising to find that they differ markedly in terms of the constructs measured (hence the traits measured and items used also differ). An analysis by Westbrook (1974) showed that the inventories differed (widely at times) in (1) their coverage of cognitive, affective, and psychomotor behaviors, and (2) their coverage of specific behaviors within a given component. These findings are different from, say, an analysis of reading readiness tests, no doubt because our state of knowledge of the reading process is at a more advanced level than that for career development or vocational maturity. (See Crites, 1974, for a discussion of the methodological issues in measuring career maturity.)

Career-Planning Programs

Within the past decade there has been increased concern by commercial test publishers about developing assessment batteries and programs that would aid both the student and counselor in vocational and educational planning. Two such programs are the Career Planning Program (CPP), sponsored by the American College Testing Program, and the College Guidance Program (CGP), conducted by Science Research Associates. There are many similarities between the two programs, the most striking one being that they are more than aptitude and achievement tests. They consider, in addition, such factors as interests, aspirations, career-related experiences, and work preferences. Both programs provide useful information for the student who knows his future plans as well as for the student who is undecided. In addition, the CPP sends information to the institution(s) selected by the student. We will now consider these two programs briefly.

College Guidance Program   Science Research Associates, 1972. The CGP is designed for eleventh-graders and consists of a College Planning Test (CPT) which resembles the SAT or ACT and provides a reading, verbal, mathematics, and composite score. The scores are expressed as standard scores and percentiles. The CPT takes about 2¼ hours to administer. An optional test is the Kuder Interest Survey, College Edition, which is similar to the Kuder OIS except that fewer occupational scores are reported.

The CGP has a *Counselor's Guide* and a *College Planning Notebook*.

The Guide has a very brief and technical (too technical, in fact, to be understood by the majority of high school counselors) discussion of the prediction of ACT-SAT scores from CPT scores.

The heart of the program, in our opinion, is the *Notebook*, which is thorough, well written, and easily comprehended by high school seniors. The student uses the information and the planning sheets to assist him in narrowing his choice of a college to three that are compatible with the student's expectations and where the probability of his being accepted is high.

Career Planning Program, Grades 8–12   Houghton Mifflin, 1974. The CPP is really two programs—an *assessment* component and a *career-guidance* component—in one. The CPP is a comprehensive package of aptitude and interest tests as well as career-related experiences designed to ". . . stimulate and facilitate self and career exploration, including the exploration of self in relation to career" in one articulated program. Besides the Vocational Interest Profile, Form A, and six ability scales, there is a Student Information Report (self-report measures of a potpourri of things such as job values, occupational preferences, certainty of occupational preferences, working condition preferences, educational plans, and self-rated abilities). Test-retest and internal consistency reliability estimates are reported, and they appear to be respectable. Construct and criterion-related validity were studied and reported. A variety of norms tables are presented in the *Handbook*.

The format is good. The CPP has a *Handbook* that discusses in clear fashion the development and use of the program, contains an annotated bibliography of career-guidance materials, and contains a complete lesson plan outline for a 9-unit "Mini Course in Career Planning."

The *Student Report* is well written and should be understood by nearly all students. It gives the student step-by-step suggestions on how to interpret the information and how to go about exploring suggested career options.

An adjunct of the CPP is the Assessment of Career Development for grades 8–12. On the basis of students' responses to 42 critical questions (the user can add up to 19 locally developed questions), a school can evaluate it's career development program and modify it, if necessary, to meet students' needs.

In summary, the CPP is a well-designed instrument program. The test's technical qualities are acceptable, although we regret that the publisher did *not* provide empirical data to permit one to evaluate the guidance component of the program. It serves both the student and the school: The former receives information that should be of assistance in career exploration and educational planning; the latter receives information on its student body that hopefully will be of value in the development or modification (as well as evaluation) of its career guidance program.

It should be recognized at the outset that neither the CPP nor the CGP is intended to replace the counselor. However, if the results are used judiciously, they should help the counselor deal more effectively with students in helping them make realistic, viable, and valid decisions regarding their future educational and vocational plans.

PERSONALITY ASSESSMENT

Personality characteristics are or should be of concern to classroom teachers. It is generally agreed that education must be concerned with attitudes, values, and interests to the same degree as it is concerned with the development of cognitive skills and knowledge. What values will accrue to society from individuals who can solve a quadratic equation or are able to detect the components of LSD, but who are hostile or aggressive? Education should be concerned with developing a well-rounded individual.

What Personality Is

Although a variety of definitions of personality have been posited, they all share the common theme that it subsumes the *total* individual—both his cognitive and noncognitive traits. We will, however, restrict our discussion of personality assessment to problem check lists, general adjustment inventories, and projective tests. We recognize that an individual's interests, his attitudes, and his opinions are an integral component of his general makeup (as are his cognitive traits).

We must emphasize that personality inventories, with possibly the exception of some problem check lists, should not be administered and interpreted by the classroom teacher. The assessment of an individual's behavior is dependent upon the synthesis of many particles of information. Valid synthesis should and can be undertaken only by persons trained in this area.

During the past decade or so, research on personality assessment has tended to focus less upon techniques and more upon the development of a theory of personality. No technique such as factor analysis will ever replace the need for formulating constructs on the basis of personality theory. An example of a personality test based upon theory is the Edwards Personal Preference Schedule (EPPS), which is based on Murray's needs theory. Today, emphasis in personality testing is directed toward the assessment of normal behavior.

Types of Standardized Personality Assessment Devices

Personality can be measured in a variety of ways. Three commonly used approaches to study personality are to see (1) what the individual says about himself (self-report inventories), (2) what others say about the individual (sociometric inventories), and (3) what the individual does in a particular kind of situation (observational techniques).

Another way in which personality tests can be classified is in terms of the method by which one's behavior is studied or of the manner in which the stimuli are presented. Stimuli can be presented as either *structured* or *unstructured*. The structured test consists of items or questions that can be interpreted in relatively the same way by all examinees (for example, "Do you daydream?"). The unstructured test (sometimes referred to as the projective test, although projective devices can be either completed unstructured or semistructured) consists of ambiguous pictures or ink blots to which the examinee responds according to his interpretation of the stimulus. In the structured test the subject projects his feelings when describing the ambiguous stimulus or completing the incomplete statement or word. Unstructured tests differ from structured tests in that they are usually not quantitatively scored, although they could be. Structured personality tests are objectively scored with predetermined keys.

Personality tests can further be classified in terms of their method of construction. As discussed earlier in the chapter, three common approaches used to construct personality tests are (1) criterion keying (used in the MMPI and the California Psychological Inventory), (2) factor analysis (used in the many Cattell personality tests), and (3) the logical approach (used in the Bernreuter Personality Inventory). In essence then, personality tests can be differentiated in terms of *how* they do what they do. However, it is essential that the reader be cognizant of *what* they do. That is, does the test attempt to isolate problems, or does it attempt to give an indication of possible adjustment?

In this chapter, we consider only the self-report inventories, recognizing that although other techniques provide valuable information, they are typically locally constructed rather than commercially standardized tests.

Structured Self-Report Inventories

Structured self-report inventories are the most common type of personality tests used in schools (and industry) today. They are a basic tool in the diagnosis of "illness," whether it be physical or mental. Just as the physician will ask what hurts you and where and when it started, the psychiatrist and clinician will ask you whether you have nightmares, a tendency to daydream, or similar questions. Over the years, the answers to these kinds of questions have been found to be more indicative of maladjustment than those to other questions that could be asked. When such questions are selected and put together in a list to be checked off by the examinee, it is a test or inventory. Self-report inventories can be classified into either problem check lists or general adjustment inventories. They can also be classified in terms of their method of construction: criterion groups, factor analysis, or the logical approach. All, however, are structured.

Problem Check Lists

Problem check lists are the most applicable personality measure in our public schools because of their limited demand upon formal training and experience for the examiner. In fact, one can go so far as to say that no formal training is required to administer and score a problem check list. Interpretation, on the other hand, demands training, sophistication, and experience. It is one thing to administer a check list and still another to interpret it. For example, let us assume that Peter indicates he has difficulty with his brothers and sisters. What can, should, or does one do? Naturally, the untrained teacher should obtain professional assistance in whatever action he undertakes. In fact, we strongly recommend that assistance in the interpretation of, and subsequent action to, a problem check list be obtained from a qualified counselor or clinician. Sibling rivalry in Peter's case may appear, on the surface, easy to deal with. However, it is usually more complex and may require professional assistance.

Problem check lists can be used by the classroom teacher to confirm some of his subjective impressions that he obtained by observation. For example, in Peter's case the teacher may have noticed that Peter is depressed or moody, whereas a few months earlier he was a happy child. Problem check lists can be used by the teacher (or counselor) to obtain a better understanding of the pupil—his problems, his behavior. It is quite conceivable that a pupil like Peter will suddenly begin doing poor, sloppy work. Possibly, from the results of a problem check list, the teacher will be able to learn that Peter's performance is because of something that is bothering him, rather than because of laziness. Problem check lists, especially when administered to the whole class, will make pupils less self-conscious and willing to reveal their problems. This is especially true if the teacher discusses the *general* findings. At no time should individual responses or pupils be identified and discussed. With discussion centering on general findings, the pupil is able to see that he is not atypical, that other pupils are also bothered or concerned about a variety of things. Problem check lists also serve as excellent screening devices for the counselor. On the basis of their results and an interview, the counselor may suggest more thorough treatment if needed.

It should be remembered that problem check lists are just that—they do not make any claims to measuring personality traits. In problem check lists, the individual checks only the statements that are applicable to him (and that he wishes to check) and that he is consciously aware of. Problem check lists have their greatest value in acting as a communication vehicle between the pupil and the counselor. The test results can help save the counselor much valuable time by indicating what the problem appears to be and can help establish rapport between the pupil and counselor.

Problem check lists are essentially concerned with such areas as family, peer relationships, finances, study skills, health, and relations with adults. Even so, they differ slightly in their format. In some, the pupil checks only the statements that he perceives as problems. In others, the pupil indicates the degree of severity: minor, moderate, severe. In still others, the pupil writes a statement about his problems.

Mooney Problem Check List　　The Psychological Corporation, 1950, revised edition. Untimed, but takes about 30 minutes. Has four levels: (1) Junior high school for grades 7 to 9, which yields seven scores (health and physical development; school; home and family; money, work, and future; boy-and-girl relations; relations to people in general; and self-centered concerns). (2) High school for grades 9 to 12, which yields 11 scores (health and physical development; finances, living conditions, employment; social and recreational activities; social-psychological relations; personal-psychological relations; courtship, sex, marriage; home and family; morals and religion; adjustment to school work; the future—vocational and educational curriculum; and teaching procedures). (3) College for grades 13 to 16, which yields the same scores as the high school form. (4) Adult, which measures problems in nine areas (health, economic security, self-improvement, personality, home and family, courtship, sex, religion, and occupation).

The items used were selected after a thorough analysis of written statements of problems by over 4000 students and through adults' statements of problems, a survey of the literature, and the author's counseling experience. Some examples[12] of the items used are:

> Have trouble with my teeth.
> Not living with my parents.
> Slow in reading.

For each of the levels, provision is made for the student to indicate whether he would like to discuss his problems with someone. In the high school and college forms the student can specify the person with whom he would like to discuss his problems.

The subject responds to each of the items only if he is worried or concerned. Because this is not a test in the usual sense, we find validity and reliability data lacking, although the manual does report a few studies. It would indeed be helpful if more data were provided. There are no

---

[12] Reproduced by permission from the Mooney Problem Check List. Copyright © 1950, The Psychological Corporation, New York, N.Y. All rights reserved.

normative data—the authors claim that local norms are more appropriate in a check list.

The Mooney, like other problem check lists, is designed to provide ancillary and supplementary information about the student. There are no right or wrong answers as such but only indicated problems or areas of concern. The authors make frequent cautions to the user regarding the instrument's interpretation and applicability. They are conservative when they say:

> At all times the counselor must keep in mind that the *Problem Check List* is not a test. It does not yield scores on traits or permit any direct statements about the adjustment status of the person who made the responses. Rather, the *Problem Check List* is a form of simple communication between the counselee and the counselor designed to accelerate the process of understanding the student and his real problems (*Mooney Problem Check List Manual*, 1950, p. 5).

SUMMARY OF PROBLEM CHECK LISTS   Problem check lists must be accepted at face value. They are composed of items that are intended to be representative of problems that people face in different areas such as home, family, school, and occupation. No claim is made that they measure personality characteristics, and, in fact, problem check list authors caution the user to avoid adopting this view. The responses only reflect the areas that the student is aware of and willing to discuss. The responses to problem check lists should not be considered as a test or subtest score. The teacher and counselor should use the responses as a guide for further exploration. If used in this way, problem check lists are quite valid and helpful.

Problem check lists are primarily used to identify individuals who are concerned with social and personal relationships. Another type of structured self-report inventory is the adjustment inventory. This type is concerned primarily with the identification of neuroticism and pathological deviation. In addition, there have been developed structured self-report inventories that are most concerned with the assessment of narrowly defined behavior characteristics such as sociability, masculinity-femininity, and introversion-extroversion. These latter inventories place major emphasis on the measurement of individual differences within the normal range of deviation. They will not be discussed here because of their limited educational value.

General Adjustment Inventories

It is not our intent to delve too deeply into the measurement of personality by means of general adjustment inventories. However, we do feel that educators should have at least a rudimentary knowledge of the different types as well as some awareness of their strengths and weaknesses.

The user must be very cautious in the interpretation of noncognitive test results. Problems of validity, reliability, language (ambiguity and/or interpretation made of such words as *usually* or *good*), faking, response set, scoring, and interpretation are such that they preclude the use of most personality inventories by the classroom teacher. Nevertheless, as discussed earlier in this chapter, the teacher must know something about the area of personality and personality assessment in order that he provides for optimal learning conditions. We feel that it is just as (if not more) valuable for the teacher and counselor to know what is bad about tests as it is for them to know what is good about tests. In addition, as we mentioned earlier, teachers and counselors must realize that they are still able to obtain more reliable and valid information about the noncognitive characteristics of their pupils with tests than they can by other means.

General adjustment inventories are of value because they (1) help establish rapport between counselor and counselee by having some basis upon which to begin an interview, (2) permit the examinee to express problems that are of relevance (or those which he thinks are of relevance or importance) to him, and (3) provide the counselor or clinician with more information about the individual so that a global picture of the individual is obtained.

Unstructured Inventories

Structured self-report inventories are not the only manner in which an individual's behavior can be measured. Another standardized approach to the assessment of personality is the one frequently used by the clinician: the unstructured or projective test. Whereas self-report structured inventories require the subject to describe himself, projective tests call upon the individual to interpret objects other than himself. These objects may be pictures, incomplete sentences, drawings, and the like. Anastasi (1968) classified projective techniques into five types: associative techniques (Rorschach Ink Blot Test), construction procedures (Thematic Apperception Test), completion tasks (Rotter Incomplete Sentence Test), ordering devices (Szondi Test), and expressive methods (Machover Draw-A-Person Test). In the latter, both product and process are evaluated. Projective tests may also be differentiated from self-report inventories in many other ways: (1) Projective tests normally present unstructured stimuli, whereas self-report inventories are predominantly structured.[13] (See Figure 16–4.) The unstructured task permits the individual to project his feelings, which reflect his needs, motives, and concerns. (2) Projective tests (because

---

[13] The difference between structured and unstructured stimuli depends upon the degree of agreement regarding the stimuli. If there is consensus that the object in Figure 16–4(a) is a cup or at least a receptacle to hold something, it would be termed a structured stimulus. If there is lack of agreement because of the ambiguity of the stimulus in Figure 16–4(b), it would be termed unstructured.

(a)   (b)

FIGURE 16-4   Structured and unstructured stimuli.

they are innocuous) are more resistant to faking and the influence of response set than are self-report inventories.[14] (3) Projective tests are interesting and novel and hence can easily be used with young children or with individuals who are afraid of a formal pencil-and-paper test. (4) Projective tests can be either verbal or nonverbal, but self-report inventories are verbal and hence are not applicable to illiterates and very young children. (5) Self-report inventories, at least most of them, can be objectively scored, but projective tests are very susceptible to the subjective feelings of the scorer, even when certain guidelines are used in the scoring. (6) Projective tests usually are based upon or reflect psychoanalytic theory such as that of Jung or Freud. (7) Projective tests (as do some nonprojective methods) normally utilize a global approach in the assessment of personality[15] and often go beyond personality syndromes per se and concern themselves with creativity and critical-thinking ability.

Projective tests and self-report inventories share many things in common: (1) They have relatively low validity and reliability; (2) they provide some of the information needed to obtain a better understanding of the individual; and (3) they can be administered either individually or in groups. Both structured and unstructured personality tests should be interpreted only by qualified persons. Because the administration, scoring, and interpretation of projective tests is complex and because of the formal training and experience needed to work with them, we will dispense with an evaluation of some of those commercially available.

Summary

Personality inventories (adjustment inventories) are not yet ready for general use in our schools and should not be part of the test battery that is normally and routinely administered in school testing programs. Even the best of them must be used with caution and only by trained and experienced clinicians. With the exception of the problem check lists one may go so far

---

[14] Even though a maladjusted person may attempt to fake his responses, it is quite conceivable that his faked responses will indicate that he is maladjusted.

[15] Color, movement, size, and so forth are frequently considered when interpreting a test protocol.

as to say that personality assessment should be barred from the classroom teacher. This does not imply, however, that personality assessment should be barred from the public school. In order to gather empirical data (data that have been lacking for personality tests in general and projective techniques in particular), it is necessary to administer tests to pupils. The test results, however, should be used primarily for counseling and research rather than for making instructional decisions. Until personality tests achieve the stature of our cognitive measures and of some of the interest scales, they should be handled with great caution.

ATTITUDE AND VALUE ASSESSMENT

In Chapter 12 we discussed at some length the value of, and need for, teachers being knowledgeable of their pupils' attitudes. To recapitulate, the essential points of our discussion in Chapter 12, as well as at the beginning of this chapter, were as follows:

1. Attitudes are predispositions to respond overtly to social objects.

2. A variety of definitions have been posited for attitudes, but all share a common theme that attitudes guide and direct an individual's behavior. For this reason, it is imperative for teachers to know something about attitudes, how they are formed, how they are changed, and how they relate to the teaching-learning process.

3. Attitude scales can be constructed in a variety of ways, the most common ones being the Thurstone, Likert, Guttman, and Semantic Differential.

4. Attitude scales are highly susceptible to faking, and therefore any interpretation of this type of self-report behavior should be made accordingly.

5. Attitude scales, like any affective instrument, are beset with a multitude of methodological problems that make their interpretation dubious.

6. Despite the variety of problems associated with affective measurement, despite the fact that the validity and reliability of attitude scales are lower than for cognitive measures, and despite the reluctance of many teachers to pay appropriate attention to affective instructional/learning objectives, attitude scales can often be used effectively by the classroom teacher to obtain a better understanding of his pupils. The results obtained from attitude scales can be useful in educational planning and evaluation. Acquisition of desirable attitudes is one of the major goals in our schools. Without knowledge of the prevailing attitudes of the pupil, class, or school, it would be difficult to plan accordingly.

Evaluation of Attitude Scales

The usefulness of any test or scale depends upon its reliability, validity, norms, and ease of administration, scoring, and interpretation. We now briefly summarize how these factors relate to attitude scales.

Reliability. Attitude scales, by and large, have reliabilities around .75. This is much less than those obtained for cognitive measures, and hence the results obtained from attitude scales should be used primarily for group guidance and discussion.

Validity. In general, attitude measures have less validity data available than do other noncognitive measures. This is in part because of the problems inherent in measuring attitudes and in part because many of the measures were constructed primarily for research purposes.

The correlations obtained between the scale scores and observed behavior are typically low. Nevertheless, knowledge of the disparities between expressed attitudes and actual behavior is useful in understanding and working with the individual.

Norms. In the majority of instances there are no norms accompanying standardized attitude scales. The user must be careful in his evaluation of a published test, especially one that has employed the Likert method. The interpretation of Likert scores is based upon the distribution of sample scores and therefore has meaning only by making comparisons to the norm group. Naturally, one can prepare local norms. Even if appropriate sampling techniques have been employed to select the standardization sample and even if the normative data are adequate, the fact that conditions affecting attitudes are so variable leads us to suggest that very recent norms be used. For example, American attitudes toward Japan were markedly different on December 6 and 8, 1941.

Administration, scoring and interpretation. In contrast to the projective tests considered in the previous section, attitude scales are easy to administer and score. They require no formal training and can be handled easily by the classroom teacher. The interpretation of attitude-test scores, on the other hand, is an entirely different matter. Because of psychometric problems, the user should be cautious in the interpretations he makes.

Assessment of Pupil Study Habits and Attitudes Toward School

As has been mentioned at various points in this text, the matter of how well a student does on an aptitude or achievement test is dependent upon factors other than basic ability or intelligence. Some of the factors that must be considered in assessing or appraising an individual's academic performance are (1) mental maturity, (2) motivation, (3) study habits, (4) study skills, and (5) attitudes toward the value of an education, teachers, school, and courses. The brightest student (speaking in terms of scholastic aptitude may be performing at a somewhat mediocre level. He may be getting C's and D's, whereas we would predict from a valid measure of his scholastic aptitude that he should be receiving A's and B's. On the other hand, the intellectually poorer student might be getting B's, although we would predict that he would obtain C's. Why the discrepancy between predicted achievement and realized achievement? No doubt, how the pupil studies and his attitudes toward education play a significant role in an explanation of such discrepancies.

We will now briefly consider two standardized study-habits and skills inventories.

Survey of Study Habits and Attitudes (SSHA)   The Psychological Corporation, 1965. Two forms: H (for grades 7–12) and C (for college students and high school seniors). Untimed, but majority of students complete the SSHA within 20 to 35 minutes. Seven scores (based upon four basic scales): delay avoidance (DA), work methods (WM), study habits (SH = DA + WM), teacher approval (TA), educational acceptance (EA), study attitudes (SA = TA + EA), and study orientation (SO = SH + SA or the total of the four basic scales).

The SSHA was designed (1) to identify the differences in study habits and attitudes between students who do well in their academic work and those who do poorly, (2) to assist students who might benefit from improved study habits (this improvement may come about as a result of counseling and/or instruction on how to study), and (3) to predict academic success for high school and college students. The SSHA consists of 100 items such as[16]

> Daydreaming distracts my attention from my lessons while I am studying (DA).
> My teachers criticize my written work for being poorly planned or hurriedly written (WM).
> My teachers make their subjects interesting and meaningful to me (TA).
> I feel that I would study harder if I were given more freedom to choose subjects that I like (EA).

which attempt to assess the "motivation for study and attitudes toward academic work" syndromes rather than just the mechanics of study. This perhaps is the most differentiating factor of the SSHA from other study-habit inventories. Subjects respond to each item by means of a five-element key ranging from Rarely (0–15 percent of the time) to Almost Always (86–100 percent of the time). In an attempt to control for response set, the "acceptable" (keyed) responses are randomly distributed at both ends of the continuum. The extreme positions are weighted twice that of the near-extreme positions. That is, if a negative item is keyed Rarely it is given a weight of 2; and a Sometimes response is given a weight of 1.

Both logical and empirical validity were stressed in test development.

---

[16] Reproduced by permission. Copyright © 1953, 1965, The Psychological Corporation, New York, N.Y. All rights reserved.

(For a discussion on predictive validity, see Goldfried and D'Zurilla, 1973). Items were chosen on the basis of interviews with students, and each item was empirically validated (correlations of the SSHA with grades, teacher's ratings, and aptitude scores) as to its applicability to the problem. For Form H (grades 7–12), student advice was obtained so that the language would be clear and meaningful to junior and senior high school students. The validity data presented in the test manual shows that the SSHA is independent of scholastic achievement and that there is an increase in the predictive efficiency of grades when the SSHA is used in combination with aptitude test scores. Internal consistency (.87–.89) and test-retest (.83–.88) reliability estimates are reported for Form C. Test-retest reliabilities for Form H vary from .93 to .95. It is unfortunate that these data are based on only Texas students, especially because the correlation data reported for Form C show differences between college students in Texas and those in other parts of the country. Percentile norms are reported separately for each of the seven scores. For Form H, norms are provided for grades 7 to 9 combined and grades 10 to 12 combined. The Form H norming sample appears to be heavily weighted in favor of students from Texas and the southwestern region of the country.

To aid in test interpretation, the percentile scores can be plotted on the diagnostic profile sheet (on the reverse side of the answer sheet); see Figure 16–5. The pupil's scores can then be compared with the performance of the norm group and his strengths and weaknesses identified. In addition, a separate counseling key is provided. This key enables the teacher or counselor to identify critical responses—those items that differentiate between high and low scholastic achievers. Still, the test authors recommend that the counselor and student make a detailed item-by-item analysis of the responses. It would have been desirable had the test authors presented more descriptive information on the development of this key.

In summary, the SSHA was well conceived in its development. It is easy for the pupil to understand and complete the inventory. It is easy to administer and score. It stresses the motivational and attitudinal aspects of study more than any other study-habits inventory.

Study Skills Test: McGraw-Hill Basic Skills System   McGraw-Hill, 1970. Two forms. Grades 11–14. Designed to measure what students have learned and retained after completing the "Study Skills" section of the Basic Skills System. Six scores: problem solving (15 items), underlining (10 items), library information (20 items), study skills information (20 items), total score; inventory of study habits and attitudes (49 items). The manual provides the user with little or no helpful information. The manual cautions the user against using the subtest scores, claiming they lack sufficient reliability. Because of technical flaws in the items themselves, lack of appropriate emphasis on such skills as studying for examinations, and the fact

DIAGNOSTIC PROFILE FOR SURVEY OF STUDY HABITS AND ATTITUDES

W. F. Brown and W. H. Holtzman

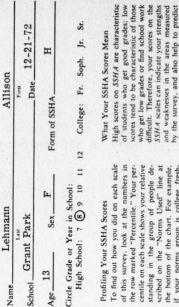

Name ___Lehmann___ ___Allison___
         Last   First
School ___Grant Park___ Date ___12-21-72___

Age ___13___ Sex ___F___ Form of SSHA ___H___

Circle Grade or Year in School:
High School: 7 ⑧ 9 10 11 12   College: Fr. Soph. Jr. Sr.

Profiling Your SSHA Scores

To find out how you did on each scale of this survey, look at the numbers in the row marked "Percentile." Your percentile on each scale shows your relative standing in the group of people described on the "Norms Used" line at the bottom of the chart. For example, if your norms group is college freshmen and your percentile on the TA scale is 45, it means that 45 per cent of the freshmen received lower scores than yours on the TA scale, while 55 per cent of them received higher scores. Thus, your percentile tells where you rank in comparison with others in your norms group.

You can complete your profile by making a heavy line across each column at the level which corresponds to your percentile rank on that scale. For example, if your percentile rank on the DA scale is 65, make a heavy line across the DA column halfway between 60 and 70. Draw a line corresponding to your percentile rank for all seven scales.

Then start at the horizontal line you have drawn and black in each column up to or down to the 50th percentile line. Since the 50th percentile line represents the score made by the middle student of your group, the vertical bars above that line on your profile show those scales on which you have scored higher than the middle student and the bars below that line show the scales on which you scored lower.

What Your SSHA Scores Mean

High scores on SSHA are characteristic of students who get good grades; low scores tend to be characteristic of those who get low grades or find school work difficult. Therefore, your scores on the SSHA scales can indicate your strengths and weaknesses in the areas measured by the survey, and also help to predict future academic achievement.

What the SSHA Measures

(DA) DELAY AVOIDANCE—your promptness in completing academic assignments, lack of procrastination, and freedom from wasteful delay and distraction.

(WM) WORK METHODS—your use of effective study procedures, efficiency in doing academic assignments, and how-to-study skills.

(TA) TEACHER APPROVAL—your opinions of teachers and their classroom behavior and methods.

(EA) EDUCATION ACCEPTANCE—your approval of educational objectives, practices, and requirements.

(SH) STUDY HABITS combines the scores on the DA and WM scales to provide a measure of academic behavior.

(SA) STUDY ATTITUDES combines the scores on the TA and EA scales to provide a measure of scholastic beliefs.

(SO) STUDY ORIENTATION combines the scores on the SH and SA scales to provide an overall measure of study habits and attitudes.

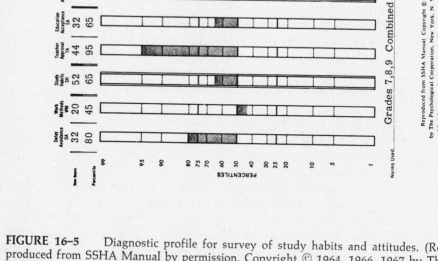

Grades 7, 8, 9 Combined

FIGURE 16–5   Diagnostic profile for survey of study habits and attitudes. (Reproduced from SSHA Manual by permission. Copyright © 1964, 1966, 1967 by The Psychological Corporation, New York, N.Y. All rights reserved.)

that the instrument is so restrictive, we strongly recommend that it not be used.

In conclusion, study-habit inventories have a place in the classroom and can be administered, scored, and interpreted by the classroom teacher. Although the majority of them stress the process of locating information, the Survey of Study Habits and Attitudes stresses attitudes and motivational aspects. Study-habit inventories, as with all self-report techniques, are dependent upon the respondent's honesty—they are only surveys of self-report. The essential question, "Do the results of a study-habit inventory in combination with previous GPA yield a higher cross-validated multiple R than do only previous GPA?" remains unanswered for most study-habit inventories.

SUMMARY

The principal ideas, suggestions, and recommendations of this chapter are summarized in the following statements:

1. Classroom teachers need to know about their pupils' attitudes, values, interests, and personality. This not only will give them a better understanding about the pupils' behavior (both cognitive and noncognitive), but also will permit them to communicate with other professionals such as the school diagnostician, psychologist, psychometrist, and psychiatrist.

2. The classroom teacher should be able to administer problem check lists, rating scales, observational schedules, and interest inventories, with no formal training needed. Problem check lists and rating scales can be interpreted by the classroom teacher. Interest inventories and personality tests should be interpreted only by specially trained personnel.

3. The major problems involved in measuring noncognitive characteristics are problems of (a) definition, (b) response set, (c) faking, (d) validity and reliability, and (e) interpretation.

4. Noncognitive assessment devices are not so psychometrically elegant as cognitive tests. Despite the limitation of noncognitive tools, they do provide useful information that often cannot be obtained by other means.

5. Three commonly used procedures used for keying and constructing noncognitive tests are empirical, homogeneous, and logical.

6. Attitudes and interests are both concerned with likes and dislikes. Whereas attitudes have groups and social situations as their referent objects, interests are related to activities.

7. The measurement of interests has progressed from the nonempirical approach used by Hall in his 1907 questionnaire to measure children's recreational interests to the more elegant, formal, scientific, and orderly

approaches exemplified by the work of Strong, Kuder, Super, Campbell, and Holland, to name a few.

8. Interest inventories were originally concerned with a person's vocation and were designed primarily for college-bound high school youth. Today's inventories measure avocational interests, can be used with junior high school students, and are not "geared" to college-bound students.

9. Earlier interest inventories have focused on the subject's likes and dislikes. Today more attention is being paid to other traits—motivation and personality—as they relate to interests.

10. More attention is now being paid to the study of vocational maturity and the development of inventories that will be useful in career development.

11. Although interest inventories differ in their content, their predictive validity, reliability, ease of scoring, and interpretation, they all share a common purpose of helping the user make better vocational and educational decisions. Despite the many similarities among interest inventories, there are nevertheless marked differences among them. The user must study the inventories carefully before adoption.

12. Interests become more stable with age, but they are never permanently fixed. Thus, interest inventory results obtained in junior high school or for elementary school children should be interpreted with extreme caution.

13. Interest inventories are *not* designed to predict job success, academic success, job satisfaction, or personality adjustment. They are designed to be helpful to the teacher or counselor in helping students make vocational and educational decisions based upon the similarity of their interests with persons successful in a particular vocation or avocation.

14. Interest inventory results can be helpful to the classroom teacher in terms of helping him develop teaching strategies that will be most relevant to his pupils' interests.

15. Within the past few years, much interest has been demonstrated in the study of career development and vocational maturity. Since 1968 at least six standardized tests related to these areas have been published and three large-scale career development programs initiated. Some of the tests are concerned with the subject's value orientation, some with personality, and some with motivation.

16. Personality inventories can be classified as either structured or unstructured, as well as in terms of their method of construction.

17. With the exception of problem check lists, personality measures should only be administered and interpreted by trained and experienced clinicians.

18. Problem check lists are essentially structured self-report inventories which provide the user with information the subject feels is of concern

or a cause of worry. Problem check lists have no right or wrong answers and are not intended to measure personality per se.

19. Personality inventories can assist us in identifying those persons who are in need of assistance and may help in ascertaining where or what their problems are. Despite their shortcomings, if used judiciously and if proper rapport is established and maintained, these inventories do permit the user to obtain a more complete understanding of the subject. They also provide the subject an opportunity to express and discuss his feelings.

20. Attitude scales are much less reliable and valid than are cognitive measures. They usually do not have norms. Although they can be administered by the classroom teacher, their interpretation is complex and questionable. Like many other affective measures, they provide the user with a better understanding of the individual, *provided* the subject has been truthful. Because there are so few standardized attitude inventories available for elementary and secondary school pupils, the teacher should be knowledgeable about the various techniques that can be used when constructing these inventories. There was a brief discussion of tests of study habits and attitudes.

21. Much research is presently under way to improve personality measurement instruments. Hopefully, we will see the personality tests of the future become more reliable, have better predictive validity, and be less complex to score and interpret.

EVALUATION: ITS DISCLOSURE AND THE PUBLIC

UNIT 5

PEANUTS.
featuring "Good ol' CharlieBrown"
by Schulz

Bleah!

A "C"?

A "C"? I GOT A "C" ON MY COAT-HANGER SCULPTURE?

HOW COULD ANYONE GET A "C" IN COAT-HANGER SCULPTURE?

MAY I ASK A QUESTION?

WAS I JUDGED ON THE PIECE OF SCULPTURE ITSELF? IF SO, IS IT NOT TRUE THAT TIME ALONE CAN JUDGE A WORK OF ART?

WAS I JUDGED ON WHAT I HAD LEARNED ABOUT THIS PROJECT? IF SO, THEN WERE NOT YOU, MY TEACHER, ALSO BEING JUDGED ON YOUR ABILITY TO TRANSMIT YOUR KNOWLEDGE TO ME? ARE YOU WILLING TO SHARE MY "C"?

PERHAPS I WAS BEING JUDGED ON THE QUALITY OF THE COAT HANGER ITSELF OUT OF WHICH MY CREATION WAS MADE...NOW, IS THIS ALSO NOT UNFAIR?

3-26

IF I WAS JUDGED ON MY EFFORT, THEN I WAS JUDGED UNFAIRLY FOR I TRIED AS HARD AS I COULD!

OR WAS I JUDGED ON MY TALENT? IF SO, IS IT RIGHT THAT I BE JUDGED ON A PART OF LIFE OVER WHICH I HAVE NO CONTROL?

AM I TO BE JUDGED BY THE QUALITY OF COAT HANGERS THAT ARE USED BY THE DRYCLEANING ESTABLISHMENT THAT RETURNS OUR GARMENTS? IS THAT NOT THE RESPONSIBILITY OF MY PARENTS? SHOULD THEY NOT SHARE MY "C"?

"THE SQUEAKY WHEEL GETS THE GREASE!"

CHAPTER SEVENTEEN
Marking and Reporting the Results of Measurement

Hopefully, all readers of this book are by now aware that measurement is an integral part of the teaching-learning process. Measurement (and evaluation) helps us determine what to teach and what procedures are most effective. Few, if any, professional educators doubt the wisdom of determining what students have learned, and how well. Not to do so would mean that we could never evaluate the job schools are doing or the progress students are making. However, how to record what students have learned and in what fashion are more debatable issues. It seems self-evident that some record keeping of student progress is necessary. Not all decisions that are dependent upon level of student achievement can be made at the time the achievement level is observed. Thus, the data should be recorded. Further, information regarding student progress needs to be systematically reported.

After completing this chapter the student should be able to—

1. Recognize the necessity for reporting schemes and discuss how reports can be useful for different groups of people.

2. Know that the major basis for a report is the degree to which a student has achieved the educational objectives of the school.

3. Discuss six different systems of reporting (marks, check lists, letters, conferences, self-evaluation, and contracts) and identify the advantages and disadvantages of each.

4. Discuss the considerations that must be taken into account when using single summary symbols.

5. Discuss who should receive information on standardized test results and how those data should be disseminated.

NECESSITY FOR REPORTING PROCEDURES: WHO NEEDS THEM

Many people make, or help the student make, decisions based in part upon how the student has done in school. A particular decision may depend upon highly specific information (for example, how well the student can type) or upon much more general data (for example, whether the student is a good writer). Thus, we obviously need a variety of reporting procedures. Before discussing these, we should take a look at who needs information and how these people use it.

Students

There has been an increased emphasis in education on the importance of *feedback* to students. Of course, there are two stages to this feedback: the *measurement* of the degree to which a student has reached the objectives and *communication* of this information to him. As mentioned in Chapter 11, feedback to students serves the purpose of guidance. Research and common sense tell us that it is difficult to improve unless we know how we are presently doing. If one wishes to become a better marksman, he should know how close his previous shots have come to the bull's-eye. Knowledge of results improves subsequent learning.

Students need information to guide them in their immediate decision making (Should I study more this weekend? Was the review session with Joe and Ted helpful enough to be repeated? Do I need to review the division of fractions?) and in their long-range plans (Should I go to medical school?). Formative evaluation (informing students of their progress during the instruction) is most helpful for the immediate decision making that students face. This kind of feedback, of course, would not require that the schools provide summary evaluations or that they keep permanent records of the achievement of the pupils. The daily interaction between teachers and students should result in the students' having fairly good knowledge about the quality of their achievements necessary for immediate decision making. Of course, this depends upon the teacher's skill in daily feedback. Effective feedback depends upon determining what a student needs to know to facilitate further learning, gathering accurate data, and presenting these data to the student in a fashion he will comprehend.

Although formative evaluation is perhaps most helpful to the student, summative (or terminal) evaluation of the kind provided at periodic marking periods also can assist him in his decision making—particularly in the formation of long-range plans. Pupils cannot easily combine all the daily feedback provided and obtain an overall summative picture of how they are doing. They need the insight teachers can provide. Thus, an overall summary is of value. As Feldmesser pointed out, it is not enough for a student in a biology course to know

> that his lab work was weak while his grasp of abstract concepts was strong, that he was high on understanding of cell structure but low on understanding of ecological relationships and middling on understanding of reproductive systems. He will want to know what it all adds up to—whether, all things considered, he did "well" or "poorly." . . . [The grade] helps a student decide whether . . . biology is a field in which further inputs of his resources are likely to be productive for him . . . . (Feldmesser, 1971, pp. 2, 3)

Besides guidance, a second possible purpose of reporting to students is to enhance motivation. The motivating dimension of feedback is more debatable than the guidance dimension. It is possible for feedback to either reduce or enhance motivation, and the same reporting scheme may have differential motivating impact on different students. Teachers should take this into account. Some students need friendly encouragement, some need mild chastising, others may need to be motivated through fear.

Nevertheless, many educators and students firmly believe that feedback (and recording grades) does have the effect of inducing students to apply themselves to learning things they would not otherwise learn (Katz et al., 1968; Sparks, 1969; Stallings & Lesslie, 1970). Some educators feel this is bad and that students should feel free to learn what they wish. Feldmesser addressed himself to this whole issue of motivation. He discussed whether motivation can come from feedback to the student alone or whether recording that information and using it for short-run decisions is necessary. We quote in part:

> . . . many students . . . deliberately decide, on what seem to them to be rational grounds, that the subject matter of a particular course, or particular parts of a course, are irrelevant to their needs and therefore *ought* not to be learned. We might say that that's their business; if they choose not to

learn, they will and should bear the consequences of their decision. I think that's a cop-out; it is shirking our educational duty, if not undermining our educational pretensions. The student, after all, is young, and his very presence in a course indicates that he knows relatively little about the field. Consequently, he *doesn't* necessarily know what will be relevant to his needs over the long run; and in any event, his needs and his interests change. His teachers claim to have more foresight than he does, particularly with respect to what will prove relevant in their fields (if they are unwilling to make that claim, they shouldn't be his teachers). Thus, they are entitled —I would say obliged—to exert some pressure on the student to get him to learn material whose importance he is not yet in a position to perceive. One effective and appropriate way of accomplishing that is to make it in the student's immediate self-interest to take his instructors' evaluations seriously, and that can be accomplished, in turn, by using those evaluations as the basis for short-run important decisions about the student—for example, decisions about his further study or about his employment. If, finally, that is to be done, the evaluations must be reported to some central agency which has the authority to make those decisions or to transmit the information to others who can. And this reporting function, as I have argued above, demands grades to carry it out. . . . If no one else cared what evaluations had been made of his work, why should the student care? If no one else based any important decisions on those evaluations, wouldn't the message to the student be that the evaluations were, in fact, not important? Why, then, should he allow them to influence his academic behavior? It is therefore apparent that grades give impetus to the feedback function of other evaluations. (Feldmesser, 1971, pp. 7, 8)

Regardless of the stand our readers may take on Feldmesser's opinion regarding grades, it seems obvious that whatever the method of reporting, all students should receive accurate reports of how they are doing. In discussing the educational implications of self-concept theory, LaBenne and Greene (1969) stressed that teachers must be honest with their pupils. They suggest that, unfortunately, when teachers talk to students they purposely distort the evidence and provide false praise for poor performance. They stated: ". . . the student is not fooled by this sham . . . confrontation with reality in an atmosphere of warmth and acceptance is imperative for an accurate view of self" (LaBenne & Greene, 1969, pp. 28–29).

Parents

Parents also need to know how their children are doing in school, and *good* reporting practices *should* result in improved relations between school and home. Unfortunately, many schools do not do an effective enough job in this respect. Parents often do not know what the school's objectives are, let alone whether or not their children are accomplishing those objectives.

Many parents would be willing to help their children in weak areas, but without knowledge of what those weak areas are, it is impossible to do so.

Since parents' opinions play a role in a child's educational and vocational planning, it behooves them to be as knowledgeable as possible in the area. Parents do not have daily contact with the school, so the quality of the formal periodic reporting scheme and frequent informal formative reports (graded test papers, assignments, and similar evidence) are very important.

Administrators, Counselors, and Teachers

Curriculum and instructional decisions should be based primarily on the quality of student outcomes. Administrators and counselors need to make decisions with regard to the proportion of "college prep" courses, whether new curricula innovations should be continued, whether Johnny should be placed in a special class, whether Susan should be encouraged to take trigonometry, and countless other decisions that are more rationally made with some knowledge of how the students are achieving.

Reporting also helps a teacher evaluate his own strengths and weaknesses. If students are doing well in some aspects of a course, but poorly in others, a teacher should examine his instructional procedures to formulate possible hypotheses as to why that is so. Teachers, unlike students, may not be so dependent upon a periodic reporting scheme for their feedback information, but the task of preparing a formal report may cause a teacher to look more carefully at student achievements than he might otherwise do. If a teacher needs to submit a report, he will probably feel some obligation to develop reasonable bases for it. He will wish to be able to defend it if questioned. Thus he will likely set up a better evaluation system, one that can provide more useful feedback to students, than if no formal report is required.

Prospective Employers

Many people may feel with some justification that how a student achieves should be private information between that student and the school. Although there is some legal basis for the nonrelease of data without student permission, the permission is typically granted. If Donna applied for a secretarial job after high school, it is reasonable to expect the prospective employer to ask school personnel what secretarial courses Donna took and how well she did in those courses. If Donna did not agree to let the school release such data, her application might be rejected. Certainly, if Sean applies for a government job requiring security clearance, a part of that clearance will involve a search of the school records. An engineering firm considering Girder as an applicant for a position will surely want to know about his technical competencies. To not have appropriate school records or to withhold them from employers would require that these employers greatly expand their own personnel departments and/or make poor selection and classification decisions.

College Admissions Officers

There is a growing debate about whether records of high school achievement should play a role in college admissions. It is generally recognized that, for most students, the best single predictor available is high school grades. (Contrary to beliefs of many people, there is considerable research evidence to suggest that aptitude tests are better predictors than high school grades for disadvantaged youth. See, for example, Thomas and Stanley, 1969.) This debate is not based primarily on the empirical question of whether high school achievement can predict college success. Rather, the debate seems to center on the philosophical question of whether anyone should be denied the right to a higher education. If colleges move toward admitting all graduates of high school on a "first come, first served" basis, then it is obvious that high school grades and all other data would become irrelevant for *selection* decisions. However, in such a case, they would become very important data to assist in *placement* decisions. Either way, records and reports of high school achievement are valuable to college personnel.

BASES FOR MARKING AND REPORTING

The phrase "bases for marking/reporting" can imply two quite different concepts: (1) what aspects or student *characteristics* we wish to report, and (2) what *kinds of data* we will use as evidence in making our report. Both bases for marking interact with methods used for marking and reporting. For example, if we are going to base our marks on affective objectives, we might use a different set of symbols for reporting than we would use for reporting on cognitive objectives. And if we are going to use standardized test scores as evidence for having achieved certain objectives, we might use a different scheme for reporting than if we are going to use classroom participation. Since we seldom want to report on only one basis, this leads to the conclusion that it may well be advantageous to use different schemes for reporting. This will be dealt with further in the next section. Here, we wish to discuss briefly what aspects we may wish to report and the kinds of data we might gather for the report.

The major factor that should be reported is the degree to which the student has achieved the educational objectives of the course. This could well be accompanied by data suggestive of reasons why the student achieved at that level as opposed to some higher or lower level. But, of course, all this is not as easy as it sounds. Schools may have many objectives—often too intangible and certainly too many to be reported on any reasonable report—and the task confronting educators is to choose which of those objectives are most crucial and should be reported. A common fault of many traditional "report cards" is that they are so inadequate with respect to their coverage of objectives. This relates to the problems encountered in measuring some objectives—particularly in the affective areas. But we wish to reiterate that if we hold certain affective objectives to be important, we should attempt to *measure* them and we should *report* the results of those attempts.

The data obtained through all the methods we have considered in this book are appropriate to consider in any thorough report. Informal tests, classroom observations, products, and standardized test results are all useful data in reporting pupil progress. Data suggestive of reasons as to the degree of objective attainment would include such things as ability level, attendance, effort, interest, and cooperation on the part of the pupil. (The last four may be objectives in their own right, but they are also related to the achievement of other objectives.)

MARKING AND REPORTING PROCEDURES FOR TEACHER-MADE INSTRUMENTS

We suggested in the preceding section that a variety of people have good reason for desiring information about student achievement and that there are different bases for marking. Thus, the schools may need to consider different reporting procedures for communicating adequately with all interested parties. Reporting schemes may also vary, depending on the grade level of the student. For example, a single summary mark may not be desirable for early elementary grades, whereas such a score may be almost mandatory for reporting high school students' achievement to colleges or college students' achievements to graduate schools (Hassler, 1969; Law School Admission Test Council, 1970).

Comparing different reporting procedures should not be on an either-or basis. It is certainly possible, and usually advantageous, to use several procedures simultaneously.

In this section we discuss a variety of marking and reporting procedures, and point out some advantages and disadvantages of each. We discuss marks, check lists, letters, conferences, self-evaluation, and contract grading. The most important requirements of any procedure are that (1) it be understood by those persons receiving the reports, and (2) the reports be based on the objectives the school is striving to reach.

Marks

By marks we refer to those systems that use summary symbols of some type. These symbols may be letters such as A, B, C, D, F or O, S, U; numbers such as 9 through 1; pass-fail; or almost any other set of symbols. Since these symbols as traditionally used convey an overall impression of the student's total performance in a subject-matter area, they are more useful in summative than in formative evaluation. Whether or not marks serve any useful function depends upon how a teacher decides which symbol to give a child and whether the meaning the teacher has for the symbol is the one interpreted by whomever it is reported to.

Several considerations must be taken into account when using symbols. One must decide if the grades should represent achievement or attitude. If the former, should it be achievement relative to an individual's own ability, relative to a set standard, or relative to peer performance? Should one mark on status or growth? What *set* of symbols should be used? What percent of the students should fail? How many different marks should be used? That is, how fine should the scale be?[1]

Achievement or Attitude (Effort)?

Most educators believe that if only a *single* mark is given, it should represent achievement in the subject matter rather than attitude or effort. There are several reasons for this: (1) Achievement is easier to measure accurately; attitudes can be faked. (2) Most people interpret scores as if they indicated degree of competency rather than degree of effort. (3) Students must learn to realize that real-life achievement is generally more important than effort or interest. (How hard surgeons or pilots try is not nearly so important as whether they do the job for which they are hired.)

Teachers are often tempted to let a single symbol represent some combination of achievement and attitude. This is poor practice because it makes the symbol impossible to interpret. There is no way to know how much of the symbol was due to each factor or in which of the two the student was deemed best. Teachers, however, should have the development of good attitudes as one of their objectives. It is important to evaluate the degree to which that objective is met and to report on it, in some fashion at least, to students and parents. If the student's general attitudes are to be reported via a single symbol, it should be a separate mark from the one that reports achievement level.[2] Many schools use symbols A to F to represent achievement level and 1 to 3 to represent general attitude. Thus, one student may get a B-1 and another student a B-3. This dual system communicates more effectively than reporting only on achievement or, worse yet, raising the first student's mark to an A and/or lowering the second student's mark to a C because of respectively good and poor attitudes. Actually, some sort of expanded report form such as a check list would be a much better system for reporting attitudes, since they are not likely to be unidimensional.

Achievement Relative to a Set Standard, a Norm Group, or One's Own Ability?

Historically, marks were dependent on a set "standard" or were criterion-referenced. A student had to achieve a 94 percent for an A, an 88 percent

---

[1] See Terwilliger (1971) for a more extended discussion of these considerations.

[2] This is analogous to the point we made about grading essay tests separately for spelling, punctuation, grammar, and other usage skills.

for a B, and so forth. As we pointed out before, the percent right on a test is as dependent on test characteristics as on student characteristics. Thus, there is simply no mathematical, psychological, or educational basis for such things as equating 94 percent or more with an A, and 69 percent or less with F.

Recognizing the fallacies of such set standards, some educators have chosen a norm-referenced system of assigning marks. Thus, a student's grade is dependent upon how others achieve. But there seems to be considerable reaction by teachers and students against such norm referencing. People mistakenly think it means "grading on the normal curve," and therefore also means failing 5 (or 7) percent and giving A's to 5 (or 7) percent of every class. Marking on a normative basis does *not* necessarily mean that each class will have a normal distribution of grades or that anyone will necessarily fail. It simply means that the symbol used indicates how a student achieved relative to other students.[3]

Certainly there are dangers of using a normative basis for assigning marks if the norm group is too small. No one who knows even the rudiments of sampling theory would suggest that all classes should have equal distributions of grades. This is particularly true when one considers that students are often not assigned to classes at random. But if all teachers would try to keep in mind the performance level of students in general, and grade on a normative basis, there would likely be more consistency in grading among teachers than if every teacher graded on the basis of his own arbitrary standards.

Actually, the debate between norms and standards is, in a sense, a false one. As Ebel (1972, p. 322) pointed out, sometimes those who argue for standards maintain that experienced teachers know what the standards should be and that inexperienced teachers can quickly learn them. But this means that "standards" are derived from observing students' performances, so they are actually norms!

Of course, if schools move to more mastery-learning approaches to instruction, educators should adopt criterion-referenced measurement as opposed to norm-referenced measurement so that the reporting system would be based on criteria, or standards (see Chapter 3). But, as opposed to the percentage-grade procedure, the teachers using the mastery-learning approach should have the same set of standards. Thus, the "grade" a student receives might well be a statement regarding his position in the sequence of materials. (For example, if Johnny has finished Unit III-A in Arithmetic, his grade is III-A.) Although this grade would be standard rather than norm-based, there is nothing to prevent the report from *also* including some normative data. (For example, about 85 percent of the students who have been in school 3 years have finished Unit II-C, 40 percent have completed III-A, and the top 15 percent have finished Unit IV-D.)

[3] Interestingly enough, we once heard a parent discussing marks at a school board meeting say that ". . . my children are different and I don't want them compared to anyone." We wondered how he knew they were different if he hadn't compared them to someone!

A criticism occasionally made of marking systems based on either a norm or a set standard is that such systems ignore individual differences. That is not true. Such systems explicitly *report* individual differences in achievement. Yet a question that often arises in education is whether one should hold different standards for students of different ability levels and let the set of symbols used in marking take on variable meaning for students of differing abilities. Of course, in one sense of the word, we should hold different standards. We should expect more from some students than from others. And we should report—at least in formative evaluations—whether a student is doing as well as we expect. This should certainly be communicated to students and parents in some fashion. But to give one student an "A" because his low achievement comes up to a level we would expect, considering his low level of ability, and to give another student a "B" because, although he is achieving very well, his work is not quite up to what we would expect, considering his ability level, would result in confusion. Any reporting of achievement relative to one's own ability should *not* be accomplished via a system that obscures information about actual level of achievement. Also, it should be pointed out that when one compares two fallible measures—level of achievement with level of aptitude—any "difference" between them is likely to be quite unreliable (see Chapter 5 on the reliability of difference scores). Thus, only reasonably large discrepancies should be noted.

In the story presented below, Chase effectively made a good point concerning marking on ability.

Mr. Grossbucket, manager of the Aces professional basketball team, is talking with Coach Fasbrake of West State U.

G: I need a new forward, who is your best man?

F: Well, Harry Short gets my highest rating!

G: But he's only 5 feet 2 inches, and weighs 205 pounds—what kind of a basketball player is that?

Achieved His Goal

F: Well, his goal in his three years of eligibility was to be able to run the length of the court without stopping to catch his breath. He reached this goal by the middle of his junior year, and then set a new goal of being able to dribble the ball without fumbling it while running the length of the court. As a senior, he has now achieved this goal. On the basis of his having done all that he set out to do, I have to give him the highest rating.

G: But what about Jim Long? He's 6 feet 7 inches, runs the hundred in 10 seconds, and has averaged 25 points and 18 rebounds a game. That looks pretty good to me!

F: Negative! Long is way down on the list. He has achieved almost no objective in his entire college playing career. He wanted to average 30 points to a game; he wanted to average 20 rebounds—he's reached neither of these goals. Furthermore, he plays the game just the way the coaching staff tells him it should be played. He has developed skills exactly as the coaches have described them to him. This tolerance for the we-shall-oversee-you attitude promoted by the coaches is clearly undesirable. He has to get a low rating.

G: But Long was picked on the All-Conference first team and received a number of nominations for All-American—how does this stack up with your rating?

F: Irrelevant! All-Conference and All-American selectors are applying criteria established by authorities on basketball. This is unimportant for judging Long's quality because Long didn't devise these criteria—authorities be damned.

G: Well, what about George Baachbord? He has scored on the average of 21 points per game. Would you rank him below Jim Long who averaged 25 points?

No Common Criterion

F: How can you compare two players on that kind of data? Long played because he wanted to acquire some old fashioned basketball skills; Baachbord played because it give him social status on the campus. How can you compare these two players—there's no relevant common criterion. Besides, if average points per game *were* a relevant criterion for comparison, how can you say one man does better than the other? There's so much error in shooting a basketball that you can't say a 25-point average is really higher than a 21-point average.

No, if you really want a good man for your pro team you'll pick Harry Short. He's the only one who has shown that he can do it all, just like he set out to do.

G: Thanks, I think I'll look elsewhere for help. (Chase, 1972)[4]

Status or Growth

Some instructors and students (even graduate students!) think grades would be fairer if based on the level of improvement (growth) a student makes rather than on the final level of achievement (status). Marking on the basis of growth has similar problems to marking on effort or in comparison to aptitude:

1. Growth is hard to measure. Change scores are notably unreliable. Regression effects result in an advantage to students with initially low scores. Students soon learn to fake ignorance on pretests, to present an illusion of great growth.
2. Most score interpretation is of status rather than growth.
3. In the long run, competence is more important than growth.

[4] Reprinted with permission of *The Chronicle of Higher Education*, May 8, 1972. Copyright © 1972 by Editorial Projects for Education, Inc.

Of course, no teacher should ignore growth, and there should be communication of that growth (as well as it can be measured) to students and parents. This is particularly true in elementary school. But reporting growth should not be a replacement for reporting status. *Growth is more valuable in formative evaluation, while status is more important in summative reports.*

What Symbols Should Be Used

Some school officials who are antagonistic toward the A–F set of symbols that connote level of achievement have adopted a different set of symbols (such as O, S, and N for outstanding, satisfactory, and more effort needed). Such sets of symbols are usually less clear to the students and parents than the traditional A–F. While it is true that some symbols connote level of achievement (measurement) and others connote the teacher's satisfaction with that level (evaluation), it is very hard for either students or parents to interpret the latter without knowing the former. It is relatively meaningless for a teacher to communicate his value judgment about the student's level of achievement without first conveying some information about that level.

We know of one school that replaced the traditional letter grades with the terms "consistent progress," "improvement shown," and "improvement needed." This supposedly allowed a teacher to "individualize" his report so that two students could receive the same "mark" even though they achieved at different levels—thus accounting for individual differences! Apart from the fact that giving the same mark for different levels of performance obscures rather than accounts for differences, the terms themselves are uninterpretable. As many teachers, parents, and students in the system pointed out, one could make consistent progress, show improvement, and need improvement simultaneously. Yet only one of the ratings was to be checked!

While we are in no way advocating the A–F set of symbols as opposed to other possible sets, it does seem important that the *rank order* of the symbols be interpretable and that they represent mutually exclusive categories. Far too often the complaints against grading have been "solved" by changing the set of symbols used. These changes have usually complicated the problems of interpretation. The use of symbols has both advantages and disadvantages. The particular symbols used are usually not that important unless they are changed—as in the case mentioned above—so as to become almost completely uninterpretable. In general, symbols should connote level of achievement, if that is what is being reported, and they should connote the teacher's affect regarding that level if that is what is to be reported.

Few Marks or Many

Many educators seem to feel that, since grades are unreliable, it is better to have only a few unique marks representing broad categories (such as honors, pass, fail) rather than using more specific categories (such as A+, A, A−, . . . D+, D, D−, F). This is a misconception. Ebel (1969b, 1972) showed mathematically that reduction in the number of marks leads to a decrease in the reliability of those marks. While one obviously cannot grade in finer categories than one can discriminate, it is not psychometrically advantageous to collapse reliable discriminations already made into broader categories. As Ebel indicated, any argument for fewer categories must be on the grounds of convenience and simplicity rather than on grounds of increasing reliability. Dressel and Nelson (1961) noted that the five-category scheme seems the most popular. Schemes that have departed either toward more or fewer categories tend to get modified back to a five-category system. Juola (1976) reports the results of a survey which suggests a trend in college grading to an increase in the number of grading categories.

The Pass–Fail System

In spite of the higher reliability of a multicategory system of reporting, there was a considerable move toward a more restrictive two-category (pass–fail) system in the late 1960s and early 1970s. The pass–fail system had been adopted, at least for a few courses, by about two-thirds of the American colleges and universities (Burwen, 1971). A few high schools were also adopting a modified form of the pass–fail (P–F) system (Pinchak & Breland, 1973). There has been considerable discussion in the literature about whether this is good or bad. Warren (1970, p. 1) reported that, of the almost 200 papers related to grading that were published between 1965 and 1970, about one-fourth were concerned with the *form* of grades—usually whether a two-category system should replace the more usual five-category system.

The most commonly claimed justification for the P–F plan is that it encourages students to take courses they would otherwise not take because of a fear of lowering their grade-point average (GPA). Other stated purposes are that such a system reduces student anxiety, gives students greater control over the allocation of study time, and shifts students' efforts from grade-getting to learning. (See, for example, Benson, 1969; Feldmesser, 1969; Milton, 1967; Quann, 1970.)

Questionnaires and empirical studies on the results of the P–F system suggest that—

1. Roughly 75 to 85 percent of the students who elect to take a course with pass–fail would have taken the course anyway (Karlins, 1969; Morishima & Micek, 1970). Warren (1975, p. 3) makes an even stronger statement: "the evidence is now overwhelming that pass–fail grading does *not* induce students to take courses they would have avoided under a traditional grading system for fear of depressing their grade-point average."

2. Students report that they feel less anxious in P–F courses (Cromer, 1969; Karlins, 1969; Melville & Stamm, 1967).

3. Students do use the P–F option to reduce study time in that area and concentrate on other courses (Feldmesser, 1969; Freeman, 1969; Karlins, 1969; Milton, 1967; and Morishima & Micek, 1970).

4. The motivation to learn in a pass–fail course is about the same or *less* for 85 percent of the respondents in one study (Hales, Bain & Rand, 1971).

5. Students do not perform as well in P–F courses as in regular courses (Karlins, 1969; Stallings & Smock, 1971).

Whether these studies in general support or refute the advantages of a P–F system is debatable. The major goal of schooling is to induce learning, and since the evidence suggests that students neither learn nor feel as motivated to learn in P–F courses, we might consider the evidence as negative. Since excellence is not recognized or rewarded, there is no external motivation to do more than just get by. Indeed, 31 percent of the respondents in one survey admitted that in a P–F course, they attempt to earn a grade just high enough to pass (Hales et al., 1971). On the other hand, we do wish to encourage students to explore different areas—and a *few* more probably do if we offer a P–F option. Also, if students *reallocate* their study time and learn less in the P–F courses, they may be learning more in their other courses.

Considering the total set of findings regarding P–F systems, some educators believe that there is more to be gained than lost in initiating a *partial* P–F system. This could be initiated at any point in junior or senior high school. A school probably should not allow a pupil to take more than 10 to 15 percent of his course work under such a plan for the following reasons:

1. It appears that study effort may be reduced.

2. A two-category system of reporting is less reliable and certainly less informative. It reduces the data available to a student or others for decision making. This is upsetting to many who have to make decisions about further study (Dale, 1969; Hassler, 1969; Law School Admission Test Council, 1970; Rossmann, 1970).

3. A P–F system does not allow for compensation. We might decide, for example, that if a medical student received a C-average, he should graduate. D's in some subjects could be counterbalanced by B's in others. However, if one went to a pass–fail system and defined a score equivalent to "C" as passing, excellence in some areas could not compensate for minimal performance (D's) in others. If "D" is defined as passing, standards have been lowered from the original scheme.

Those schools adopting a partial P–F option may wish to consider a slight deviation of this scheme and use a Pass–No-Record grade. Using this procedure, no record at all would be entered on the transcript in the event of a no-pass. Some faculty object to this because the no-pass would not count in the GPA and a student could continue going to school indefinitely until he finally accumulated enough credits to graduate. But this would not be necessarily bad. As Warren remarked: "The basic argument is whether students taking courses in which they can fail without penalty would constitute an inefficient use of the institution's resources. No one knows" (Warren, 1970, p. 19).

To Fail or Not to Fail

As Mouly indicated, a distinction on whether to pass or fail must be made between what he termed the public school and professional school philosophy.

> In a professional school, e.g., the medical school, grades serve to protect society from professional incompetence. In teacher training, the college sets certain standards of attainment, and, for the protection of the children who might be harmed by having an incompetent teacher, fails any prospective teacher unable to meet these standards. Here grades are a screening device and the welfare of society takes precedence over that of the individual aspiring to professional status. In the public school, on the other hand, the primary purpose . . . is to determine the student's status as a prerequisite for planning his further growth. Presumably, then, a student would be failed only when his teacher is convinced that his growth can be promoted more effectively in his present grade than in the next. (Mouly, 1968, pp. 436–437)

If the guideline is not to fail a person unless it is in the best interests of that person, then we should fail very few students. Research shows quite conclusively that repeating a grade, or even a specific course, seldom results in improved performance (Goodlad, 1952). What is called automatic or social promotion is reasonably common. This *may* be best for the students in elementary and secondary schools. It does mean, however, that employers should not interpret the possession of a high school diploma as indicative of any minimum level of knowledge. Rather, it should be interpreted as saying, "the holder of this diploma attended school twelve years." Interestingly, a Gallup poll conducted in 1974 indicated that the policy of automatic promotion finds little support throughout the nation. Only 7 percent of adults and 10 percent of high school juniors and seniors support this idea (Gallup, 1974). A 1976 poll shows that 65 percent of adults are in favor of requiring all students to pass a standard nationwide examination in order to receive a high school diploma. This is up from 50 percent in 1958 (Gallup, 1976). If this trend in public opinion continues, and if public opinion impacts educational practices, the day may come when possession of a high school diploma does indicate some knowledge.

A recent concern of many is the degree to which the public school philosophy of not failing anyone should be adopted at the college level. Studies of grading practices at various universities throughout the country show quite conclusively that the probability of failing out has decreased in recent years.

Juola (1971) presented data showing that, for one large midwestern university, 22 percent of the freshmen with ability scores in the *lowest 10 percent* had GPAs of 2.0 or higher in 1961 (the minimum level for graduation), while 70 percent of a comparable set of 1970 freshmen obtained such grades. As he stated: "The trend is clear. We are rapidly approaching the stage where minimal academic requirements for the university . . . will be non-existent." This is especially true for those colleges that give university credits for remedial courses in reading and arithmetic.

The tendency to grade on the public school philosophy is even more prevalent in colleges of education. Weiss and Rasmussen (1960), in a survey of grading practices in six large midwestern state universities, found that education professors are more generous in marking than instructors in other areas. Whether this is a good or bad finding can be debated. It depends on the philosophy one holds. But as Weiss and Rasmussen suggested, if education is perceived as an easy field, many may enter that field motivated more by fear of other disciplines than by a desire to teach. Further, "Educators must realize that they are preparing their students to enter a profession. Certainly not everyone should be allowed to become a teacher, just as not everyone should be permitted to become a doctor or a lawyer" (Weiss & Rasmussen, 1960, p. 149).

Grade Inflation

The increase in pass–no-credit courses, the adoption of the public school philosophy of failing no one (or very few) and a general relaxing of academic standards in colleges has contributed to grade inflation. Juola (1974) reported a nationwide study indicating that the grade-point average of college students had risen an average of .404 from 1960 to 1973, with the greatest rate of increase occurring since 1968. At Yale, 46 percent of the senior class graduated with honors ("Too Many A's," 1974). At Harvard, 82 percent of all seniors graduated cum laude and half graduated with honors (Will, 1976). A Dartmouth College report indicated that 41.1 percent of all grades received by graduating seniors in their spring semester were A's (Pressley, 1976). Many academicians and the general public have become concerned about this. Some feel the very integrity of academic institutions is being threatened. Perhaps because of this concern, there is some evidence that the period of grade inflation is over, and possibly is even being reversed. In a follow-up to his 1974 study Juola (1976) reports a decrease of grades by .022 between 1974 and 1975. Juola suggests that a force that appears to be operating in combating grade inflation is the fear that the meaningfulness of inflated grades has deteriorated. As he points out, inflated grades provide inaccurate feedback, which may represent intellectual dishonesty. We hope his latest survey is accurate in suggesting that grade inflation has ended and that colleges are attempting to make grades more intellectually honest and meaningful.

© 1973 United Feature Syndicate, Inc.

Disadvantages of Marks

Before listing some disadvantages and advantages of marks, we remind the reader that we are not comparing the different reporting systems on an either-or basis. The use of summary symbols in no way precludes the use of other methods.

The most often mentioned disadvantages of using a single symbol to represent the degree to which a student has achieved certain objectives are as follows (see Anderson, 1966, and Ebel, 1974).

1. Marks are inaccurate measures of competence and are not used in a comparable way from school to school, or even instructor to instructor. To one teacher, B may be average, while to another C− may be average. One teacher may mark on effort; another, on results. One may fail 30 percent of the class; another, none. These types of inconsistencies are very harmful and destroy the interpretability of such marking schemes.

2. Marks are not related to the important objectives of the school.

3. Marks are inadequate in communicating between the home and school.

4. Marks produce side effects detrimental to the welfare of the child. The side effects usually mentioned are:

    a. the debilitating impact of failure;

    b. excess competitiveness;

c. cheating;

d. a distortion of educational values, which makes marks rather than learning the important criterion of success.

These objections need not necessarily apply to marks, nor are they unique to the symbol system. Both (1) and (2) above are often relevant criticisms of existing practices, but the symbol system does not force these disadvantages. Marks *should* be comparable and *could* be made more comparable, at least within a single school district; they *could* and *should* be related to important objectives. They will always be somewhat inaccurate, but no more so than any other system of recording evaluations. Objection (3) is true. However, the implication of recognizing that truth could just as well be to *supplement* the marks with additional means of communication rather than to eliminate marks. Every other single system is inadequate also. Most parents are in favor of marks and do *not* want them eliminated. Objection (4a) may be true. Certainly, many social psychologists have gathered data that they maintain support that claim. But it is really an irrelevant criticism of symbols. None of the symbols needs to represent failure in the sense of not receiving credit for the course. And failure, however defined, could be reported via any system. One does not need to use *symbols* to communicate inadequate performance. And if inadequate performance unduly affects self-concept, let us remember that it is the inadequate performance that is the problem, not the reporting of it. Objections (4b) through (4d) are made with little solid evidence to support them. If they are true, however, it is due to an overemphasis on reporting rather than to any inherent limitation of the method of reporting by symbols rather than by letters, check lists, or conferences.

Advantages of Marks

Some of the advantages of marks are as follows:

1. Marks are the least time consuming and most efficient method of reporting.

2. Symbols can be converted to numbers. Thus, GPAs (and high school ranks) can be computed. These GPAs are useful in many types of selection, placement, and classification decisions. They are the best single predictor of success in future schooling. If an organization needs to make many decisions, an actuarial approach using GPA as one of the input variables is much more efficient and results in a greater number of accurate decisions than would result if clinical decisions were made on the basis of letters of recommendation.

3. Marks relate not only to one's chances to obtain good grades in future courses; they also relate somewhat to achievements beyond school. This relationship is not often very high for a number of reasons. Nevertheless, Tilton

(1951), for example, reported that the highest tenth in college marks had three times as many people elected to the National Academy of Sciences as the other nine-tenths combined!

4. A mark serves as an overall summary index, and students want and need to know how they did on the whole—all things considered—as well as how they did on each separate subobjective. A national assessment citizenship question (National Assessment of Educational Progress, 1970a) showed, perhaps surprisingly, that students *want* to receive these overall summary reports.

Assigning Marks

If single summary marks are to be recorded and reported, two other factors need to be considered: (1) How does one combine (weight) the various data to arrive at a single index, and (2) how can the meaning of the symbols be made more comparable across teachers?

COMBINING DATA   Given data from a variety of sources such as class discussion, daily homework, major reports, quizzes, and final examinations, a teacher must combine or weight these data to end up with a single index. There is certainly no consensus as to which type of data should receive the greatest emphasis. Some educators feel that any measurement obtained for formative evaluation purposes should not be weighted in determining a final summary index. Others point out that not to use such data and to use only a final exam would result in a less reliable (and probably less valid) summary mark. The only general guidelines we can offer is that weightings should reflect both the relative importance of the specific educational objectives and the reliability and validity of the data. This is certainly partly a subjective determination. Whether one feels that class discussions or final examinations measure the most relevant objectives depends on the subject matter, the objectives, the type of class discussions, and the type of final. In general, the final test score will be the most reliable single measure. Whatever subjective decision a teacher makes about weightings, the students should be informed at the beginning of the course concerning what these weights are. (This serves the same purposes as informing a student about the weights in a table of specifications. See Chapter 7.)

When finally combining data, one more point must be kept in mind—the differences in variability of the original scores affect the weights. Consider the following example. Suppose we wish the midterm to count one-fourth, the class project to count one-fourth, and the final to count one-half. Suppose Mary got the highest grade in class on the midterm and the lowest on the final, while John did just the opposite. Assume further that they both did the same on the class project. Now, if the final is twice as important in determining the summary mark, it seems John should receive the highest combined score. But what if the range of scores on the midterm is from 25 to

58 and the range on the final is from 32 to 40? If both received 40 on the project they would have the following scores:

	Mary	John
Project	$1 \times 40 = 40$	$1 \times 40 = 40$
Midterm	$1 \times 58 = 58$	$1 \times 25 = 25$
Final	$2 \times 32 = \underline{64}$	$2 \times 40 = \underline{80}$
	162	145

In this example the midterm is actually more important in determining the final score than the final test, even though the final test was "weighted" twice as much! This is, of course, due to the unequal variability of the midterm and final exam score distributions. A procedure that avoids this problem is to transform all scores into standard scores (such as z or T) so as to mathematically equate the variances of the sets of scores prior to weighting and combining.

MAKING MARKS COMPARABLE   As we have mentioned, one of the limitations of marks is that they are not comparable from school to school or teacher to teacher. Even within a school building, where every teacher uses the same set of symbols supposedly defined the same way, we find large disparities. For example, in an A–F system some teachers will continue to use "C" as average, whereas others will interpret anything less than "B" as indicative of inadequate performance, or perhaps mark so that everyone who achieves the minimum level of mastery receives an "A"! Such disparities are frustrating to the students and cause confusion for anyone attempting to decipher what a "B" really means.

There are several steps a school can take to help assure comparability. One is to make sure that teachers in the system understand both the meaning the school attaches to the symbols and the importance of the commonality of meaning across teachers. Thus, if a school is using symbols such as O, S, and U (outstanding, satisfactory, and unsatisfactory) these terms must be defined by the school. If a school is using an absolute system, it should make clear just what level of performance is necessary for an "O" grade. If the school is using a relative marking system, it should make clear what percentage of students can really be outstanding. Also, when using the relative system the school will need to provide each teacher with some information about how his class compares with the total school population. This should help prevent the unfairness of an average student's receiving a high grade because he is in a poor class or a good student's receiving an average grade because he is in an outstanding class.

Suppose that a high school is using a five-point A–F set of marks that are to connote relative levels of performance. Suppose further that the school has defined an A to mean that the student is in the top 15 percent, a B to mean the student is in the next 25 percent, a C to mean the next 40 percent, and the bottom 20 percent receiving D's (except for those few students who are perceived likely to profit from an F). If this is the school's adopted and published meaning of the marks, then every teacher should use the same meaning even though some may prefer different definitions. But some teachers may have more gifted students. And it is not true that each teacher should assign 15 percent A's and so on. What each teacher needs is some information about how his students compare to the total set of students in the school. One solution is for the school to tell each teacher the number (or percentage) of students he has that fall in the top 15 percent and in other levels of the total school. Either previous GPA or a scholastic aptitude test could be used for this purpose. Suppose Mr. Atom, the chemistry teacher, has 30 students. Seven of these are in the top 15 percent of the school on a scholastic aptitude test, 15 are in the next 25 percent, 8 are in the next 40 percent, and none are in the bottom 20 percent. This means his grade distribution should be *roughly* as follows:

$$
\begin{array}{rl}
A - & 7 \\
B - & 15 \\
C - & 8
\end{array}
$$

His grades should be higher than average because he has a higher-than-average group of students. Now, Mr. Atom should not be forced to follow this distribution *exactly*. Possibly one or two students should receive D's or (even F's). And perhaps he has nine (or only five) students who deserve A's. The point is that he has been given some rough guidelines as to how his grade distribution should look, and these guidelines should be given very serious consideration. If a teacher simply *refuses* to adopt the grading system of the school, we believe that the school has the right to alter that teacher's mark.

Check Lists and Rating Scales

Perhaps the major limitation of a single mark is that it does not provide enough specific information to be helpful in diagnosing a student's strengths and weaknesses. The feedback to the pupil, his parents, and other teachers is just too limited for them to plan diagnostic or remedial help. One solution is to provide more detailed check lists or rating scales. These rating scales or check lists should include the major cognitive (or psychomotor) objectives for each subject-matter area. Check lists or rating scales on the affective objectives should also be developed. These affective scales may be common across all subject-matter areas.

Subject-matter rating scales appropriate to early elementary school pupils are shown in Figure 17–1. Major objectives are listed, and the teacher is to

READING	O	S	U	NB	SCIENCE	O	S	U	NB
1. Hears differences in sounds					1. Understands scientific concepts				
2. Sees differences in shapes, words and letters					2. Experiments to find answers				
3. Reads orally with accuracy and expression					3. Values and uses science in everyday life				
4. Reads with understanding					SOCIAL STUDIES				
5. Uses word-attack skills					1. Shows understanding of his world				
6. Reads for enjoyment					2. Participates in group activities				
ENGLISH/ LANGUAGE					3. Shows interest in everyday events				
1. Expresses ideas well in writing					4. Uses globes and maps				
2. Expresses ideas well in speaking					5. Uses reference materials				
3. Listens with understanding					MUSIC				
HANDWRITING					1. Participates in music class				
1. Forms letters and numbers correctly					2. Sings in tune				
2. Writes legibly and neatly					3. Reads music				
SPELLING					4. Enjoys listening to music				
1. Spells correctly the assigned lists of words					ART				
2. Spells correctly in written work					1. Enjoys art activities				
3. Uses dictionary					2. Uses tools purposefully				
MATHEMATICS					3. Uses own ideas				
1. Understands basic concepts					HEALTH AND PHYSICAL EDUCATION				
2. Knows mathematical processes					1. Observes good health habits				
3. Reasons well in problems					2. Participates in games				
					3. Skillful in games				

O = Outstanding, S = Satisfactory, U = Unsatisfactory, NB = No basis for judgment

FIGURE 17–1   Rating scales for various subjects.

mark an O, S, U, or NB column for each objective. Examples of rating scales in the work habits and social areas are shown in Figure 17–2.

If a school wishes to use more specific and detailed rating scales than that provided in Figure 17–1, it may be necessary to use a different set of objectives for each grade level. This would be commendable in a graded school, but hard to do in a nongraded school. If general instructional objectives have been written out for each course, these could serve as the basis for a check list or rating scale. For example, the objectives listed at the beginning of each chapter in this book could be used for a course in measurement. The teacher could check each one according to whether the objective had been achieved, or he could rate the degree to which the objectives had been achieved on a three- (or five) point scale.

Figure 17–3 shows a more detailed report for just one area—mathematics. A school system using this detailed a report for each subject matter is indeed providing the reader with a great deal of information. Such a report requires that a teacher keep an accurate record of just what it is each child can do. Teachers, of course, should do this anyway, but many would not do so unless it was necessitated by such a report. One inadequately researched question is how detailed a report can be without overwhelming the reader with information overload. A report as detailed as the example in Figure 17–3 for each subject matter provides a lot of information. If a parent has three or four children in elementary school, that parent will have to devote considerable time and effort to reading the reports, let alone knowing what they mean as to how, in general, the children are doing in school.

If rating scales are to be useful, it is absolutely mandatory that they

	O	S	U	NB
Work Habits				
1. Listens carefully				
2. Follows directions				
3. Uses time wisely				
4. Works independently				
5. Works well with others				
6. Takes pride in work				
Social Habits				
1. Is courteous and considerate				
2. Respects authority				
3. Respects personal and others' property				
4. Assumes responsibility for his own actions				
5. Plays well with others				
6. Uses self-control				

O = Outstanding, S = Satisfactory, U = Unsatisfactory, NB = No basis for judgment

FIGURE 17–2   Rating scales for work and social habits.

Code

☐ **Does Not Apply** — has not been introduced or has been previously mastered.

☒ **Working On** — has been introduced, but progress has not been evaluated.

■ **Doing Well** — has been evaluated, and progress is satisfactory.

◩ **Needs Attention** — has been evaluated and progress is unsatisfactory.

INSTRUCTIONAL MATH LEVEL

_____ _____ _____

NUMBER—NUMERATION

☐☐☐ Works with sets _____, _____, _____.
☐☐☐ Counts numbers to _____, _____, _____.
☐☐☐ Recognizes numbers to _____, _____, _____.
☐☐☐ Writes numbers _____, _____, _____.
☐☐☐ Counts by 2's, 5's, 10's to _____, _____, _____.
☐☐☐ Identifies place value _____, _____, _____.
☐☐☐ Uses place value _____, _____, _____.
☐☐☐ Uses ordinal terms (first, second, third, etc.) _____, _____, _____.

USES SYMBOLS

☐☐☐ Orders using >,< . _____, _____.
☐☐☐ Operations +, −, x, = _____, _____, _____.

ADDITION

☐☐☐ Understands the process of addition _____,_____,_____.
☐☐☐ Knows addition facts _____, _____, _____.
☐☐☐ Adds numbers _____, _____, _____.
☐☐☐ Applies addition to problem solving _____,_____ , _____.
☐☐☐ Rounds factors and estimates products _____, _____, _____.

SUBTRACTION

☐☐☐ Understands the process of subtraction _____, _____, _____.
☐☐☐ Subtracts numbers _____, _____, _____.
☐☐☐ Applies subtraction to problem solving _____, _____, _____.
☐☐☐ Rounds addends and estimates differences _____, _____, _____.

MULTIPLICATION

☐☐☐ Understands the process of multiplication _____, _____, _____.
☐☐☐ Knows multiplication facts _____, _____, _____.
☐☐☐ Multiplies numbers _____, _____, _____.
☐☐☐ Applies multiplication to problem solving _____, _____, _____.
☐☐☐ Rounds factors and estimates products _____, _____, _____.

FIGURE 17-3 Sample report in mathematics.

FRACTIONS

☐ ☐ ☐ Understands the concept of fractions ——, ——, ——.
☐ ☐ ☐ Identifies fractional symbols ——, ——, ——.
☐ ☐ ☐ Reads fractional symbols ——, ——, ——.
☐ ☐ ☐ Writes fractional symbols ——, ——, ——.
☐ ☐ ☐ Recognizes equivalent fractions ——, ——, ——.
☐ ☐ ☐ Puts fractions into order ——, ——, ——.
☐ ☐ ☐ Identifies factors of whole numbers ——, ——, ——.
☐ ☐ ☐ Identifies multiples of whole numbers ——, ——, ——.
☐ ☐ ☐ Adds fractions ——, ——, ——.
☐ ☐ ☐ Subtracts fractions ——, ——, ——.
☐ ☐ ☐ Multiplies fractions ——, ——, ——.
☐ ☐ ☐ Applies fractions to problem solving ——, ——, ——.

MEASUREMENT

			(Non-Standard)	(Standard)

☐ ☐ ☐ Finds length using ——, ——, —— ‖ ——, ——, ——.
☐ ☐ ☐ Finds area using ——, ——, —— ‖ ——, ——, ——.
☐ ☐ ☐ Finds volume (capacity) using ——, ——, —— ‖ ——, ——, ——.
☐ ☐ ☐ Finds weight (mass) using ——, ——, —— ‖ ——, ——, ——.

☐ ☐ ☐ Identifies money ——, ——, ——.
☐ ☐ ☐ Makes change ——, ——, ——.
☐ ☐ ☐ Uses clock to tell time ——, ——, ——.
☐ ☐ ☐ Uses calendar to tell time ——, ——, ——.
☐ ☐ ☐ Reads temperature using a thermometer ——, ——, ——.

GEOMETRY

☐ ☐ ☐ Recognizes shapes. ——, ——, ——.
☐ ☐ ☐ Introduced to geometric terminology ——, ——, ——.

COMMENTS: _____

_____

_____

_____

FIGURE 17–3   (continued)

accurately reflect the school's objectives and that teachers gather sufficient data (through observations, tests, and other means) so that ratings can be completed accurately. Using rating scales such as those shown in Figures 17–1, 17–2, or 17–3 *in conjunction with* a summary symbol that gives some relative information as to progress toward the school's objectives can provide a very meaningful report.

Letters (Narrative Reports)

Letters can be used to report school progress to parents, prospective employers, and college admissions officers. They are used in a repetitive systematic fashion only with parents. An advantage of a letter is that it can emphasize many different aspects of a child's school experiences. Physical, social, and emotional development along with subject-matter achievement can be reported. A major limitation is that letters are very time consuming if done adequately. Although not an inherent disadvantage of the method, most letters tend to become very monotonous, stereotyped, and minimally informative. One must keep in mind the distinction between saying something to you and *telling* you something. Letters often *say* a lot. They often don't *tell* you a lot! The following letter would not be too atypical.

> Johnny is a very likeable child. He appears to be adjusting well to school and his emotional development is proceeding at a normal rate. He seems to enjoy his classes and is achieving satisfactory progress in all his subjects.

In order to write a good letter, a teacher must have not only adequate time, but also a good grasp of the objectives. While we are certainly not suggesting that a teacher can assign correct symbols without having established some objectives, the lack of objectives may be less noticeable under such a system. Any vagueness in objectives *will* probably be noticeable in a letter. An example of a reasonably good letter follows:

Dear Mr. and Mrs. Smith:

Johnny is a very likeable child. He is friendly and outgoing with his fellow classmates. He has two classmates who are quite close friends and he gets along well with the other students. This observation is in agreement with the results of a questionnaire given to the students this fall.

Johnny appears to like school as well as the average fourth-grade boy. He is polite and attentive during discussion periods and works well independently during study time. He does have a slight tendency to "goof off" when working in small groups, but I interpret this more as being due to his vivacious manner than due to any dislike or disinterest in the task.

Although Johnny did not show up on our routine school physical as having any disabilities, I have noticed him frowning and/or squinting while reading. You might wish to have his eyes examined.

Johnny is progressing satisfactorily in all subject-matter content. He is at or above grade level on all the subtests of Iowa Test of Basic Skills, with the exception of spelling, where he is just slightly below average. He did particularly well in the arithmetic portions of the test. If you wish more complete details on what the Iowa Test of Basic Skills measures or how well Johnny did on it, please feel free to stop in and see me.

Johnny is presently reading at a level comparable to the average fifth-grader. He is in the second from the top reading group in my class. He should be particularly commended for this, for as you know, he was reading slightly below average last year. He tells me that he read a lot last summer, and this activity apparently was very helpful.

Johnny did an outstanding job on his social studies project. His talk on Korea and the display map he built were very well received by his classmates. Johnny also seemed to enjoy and learn from the reports of his classmates.

In summary, Johnny is getting along very well in school. His social-emotional development is above average. He likes others and they like him. He has a favorable attitude toward schoolwork and is learning the types of things expected of fourth-graders. If you wish to discuss any aspect of Johnny's progress, please feel free to make an appointment.

Sincerely,
Mrs. Angela Brown

Conferences

Conferences are certainly a good idea in theory. Misunderstandings and mis-communications between home and school would be much less frequent if parents and educators were to meet face to face so that all communication need not be written. Unfortunately, the beneficial results of actual conferences are not so great as they should be. There are several reasons for this.

1. Typically there are two conferences per year. The first is often scheduled too soon—before the teacher really knows the child. The second one is scheduled too late to do much good.
2. Teachers do not prepare well enough for conferences.
3. Parents may not take the time necessary to have a conference with all five or six of their child's teachers.
4. Some parents do not show up at all.
5. Parents and teachers are often defensive.
6. The conferences are often too short.
7. The excessive time necessary for adequate preparation and conducting of conferences may keep a teacher from performing other important tasks.

The task of holding a successful, meaningful dialogue with a parent about his or her child is not an easy one. A teacher needs considerable preparation for such a task. Many schools hold workshops to help teachers improve their skills in this area. Helpful guidelines to such conferences are given below (Romano, 1959):

1. Establish a friendly atmosphere free from interruption.
2. Be positive—begin and end the conference by enumerating favorable points.
3. Be truthful, yet tactful.
4. Be constructive in all suggestions to pupils and parents.
5. Help parents to achieve better understanding of their child as an individual.
6. Respect parents' and children's information as confidential.
7. Remain poised throughout the conference.
8. Be a good listener; let parents talk.
9. Observe professional ethics at all times.
10. Help parents find their own solutions to a problem.
11. Keep vocabulary simple; explain new terminology.
12. If you take notes during the conference, review them with parents.
13. Invite parents to visit and participate in school functions.
14. Base your judgments on all available facts and on actual situations.
15. Offer more than one possible solution to a problem.

Self-Evaluation

An aspect of evaluation that is being emphasized more and more is the value of student self-evaluation. Self-evaluation is obviously important if one is to be involved in self-directed learning. And self-directed learning is essential both in school and after the student leaves school. Unfortunately, research does not indicate clearly how teachers can improve students' abilities in self-evaluation (Russell, 1953; Sawin, 1969, pp. 194ff). Sawin (1969, pp. 196–197) suggested, however, that the following objectives should be considered:

1. The student comprehends the fallacy of generalizing on the basis of a single instance.
2. The student is able to recognize when evidence is or is not relevant to the evaluation that he wishes to make.
3. The student understands that his own beliefs about what he can and cannot do may be inaccurate and that it often is necessary to get evidence obtained independently by outside observers.
4. The student comprehends the necessity of obtaining evidence on varied aspects of the ability or characteristics he wishes to evaluate.
5. The student comprehends the importance of focus and is able to achieve it in evaluating himself.
6. The student is able to make simple content analyses of his own work.

Sawin suggested that we should help students learn what kinds of characteristics they can evaluate and when it is wise to attempt self-evaluation. He made the following specific suggestions for helping students attain the objectives listed above (Sawin, 169, pp. 198–199):

1. Set a good example in the practice of evaluation and self-evaluation.
2. Maintain a classroom atmosphere that encourages self-evaluation.
3. Conduct classroom activities in such a way that student efforts toward self-evaluation result in satisfying experiences.
4. Encourage self-evaluation, but do not try to force it.
5. Give the student opportunities to practice the evaluation skills you want him to develop.
6. Work at joint evaluation with students.
7. Discourage the student from trying to evaluate too many things at a time.
8. Have students maintain written records of certain goals and their progress toward them.
9. Have class discussions for clarifying important goals and criteria for self-evaluation.
10. Have programmed textbooks, teaching machines, and exercises with answers available for supplementary use.

Self-evaluations should *not* be used as a replacement for the marking and reporting done by the teachers. Students are not always very accurate in self-evaluations, and such a procedure could penalize the honest student and reward the dishonest one. However, there would be nothing wrong with allowing a student to fill out a report, both to be sent home and filed in the school's cumulative record, regarding his perception of progress toward the educational objectives.

Contract Grading

Contract grading is where the student and teacher agree at the beginning of the course on the amount and quality of work necessary for a given grade. This may involve self-evaluation of the quality on the part of the student, but more likely that judgment is made by the teacher. Nevertheless, the participation by the student in establishing the original contract should minimize later complaints about the unfairness of a course grade. Of course, in setting contracts, a teacher still needs to be concerned about comparability of grades. An A (if letter grades are used) should still represent outstanding achievement if that is the school-wide meaning of an A.

DISSEMINATION, RECORDING, AND INTERPRETING STANDARDIZED TEST RESULTS

If standardized test results are to be used effectively, they must (1) be made available (and interpreted) as quickly as possible to the users, and (2) be recorded and filed in a fashion that facilitates their use. How test results are disseminated and recorded will vary from school to school because school facilities differ. However, for each test, the school personnel must decide (1) to whom the test results should be distributed, and (2) a method of disseminating information that will be efficient and yet ensure correct and adequate communication.

Dissemination

We take as a given that properly interpreted results should be disseminated to the pupils who have taken standardized tests. In this section we will discuss who else should be told of the test results.

The public correctly has two somewhat conflicting concerns regarding the dissemination of test information. They are concerned with how the schools are doing and feel that the schools should release data so that the public can judge the school's performance. (This is the accountability issue and is discussed further in Chapter 18.) Parents also want to know how their own particular children are doing in school and what some reasons might be for whatever performance level is reached. Thus, there is a general feeling that data should be released. On the other hand, the public correctly is concerned about schools releasing information to the wrong people. Thus, schools have to tread carefully between releasing information to those who should have it and withholding it from those who shouldn't. Various guidelines have been written on the topic of releasing information. One of the best guidelines is by the Russell Sage Foundation (1970).

Those guidelines advocate five major principles for the collection of pupil records. First, there should be informed consent for the collection of data. Second, pupil data should be classified into categories according to potential sensitivity, and these categories should be treated differently in terms of access. Third, all data kept should be verified for accuracy. Fourth, parents and pupils should have access to the data. Fifth, no agency or persons other than the parent or school personnel who deal directly with the child concerned should have access to pupil data without parental or pupil permission.

A legal guideline, "Family Educational Rights and Privacy Act of 1974" (Section 438 of Public Law 93–380), was passed by Congress and became effective in November, 1974. It prohibits giving federal funds to any educational institution

> . . . which has a policy of denying, or which effectively prevents, the parents of students attending any school of such agency, or attending such institution of higher education, community college, school, preschool, or other educational institution, the right to inspect and review any and all official records, files, and data directly related to their children, including all material that is incorporated into each student's cumulative record folder, and intended for school use or to be available to parties outside the school or

school system, and specifically including, but not necessarily limited to, identifying data, academic work completed, level of achievement (grades, standardized achievement test scores), attendance data, scores on standardized intelligence, aptitude, and psychological tests, interest inventory results, health data, family background information, teacher or counselor rating and observations, and verified reports of serious or recurrent behavior patterns. Where such records or data include information on more than one student the parents of any student shall be entitled to receive, or be informed of, that part of such record or data as pertains to their child. Each recipient shall establish appropriate procedures for the granting of a request by parents for access to their child's school records within a reasonable period of time, but in no case more than forty-five days after the request has been made.

Parents shall have an opportunity for hearing to challenge the content of their child's school records, to insure that the records are not inaccurate, misleading, or otherwise in violation of the privacy or other rights of students, and to provide an opportunity for the correction or deletion of any such inaccurate, misleading, or otherwise inappropriate data contained therein. (Public Law 93–380, Sec. 513, p. 89.)

The law not only specifies that parents (or students over 18) will have access to records, it also specifies a policy on the releasing of personal records. In general the policy states that no personal records should be released without written parental (or student over 18) consent except to certain authorities such as school officials or state educational authorities.

There is considerable concern about the interpretation and consequences of this act. Portions of it are vague, and clarifying amendments will need to be added. Although most educators would support the intent behind the act, there is less unanimity in the prediction of its consequences. For example, what effect, if any, will this law have on letters of recommendations? Or suppose a high school senior has received below-average scores on several standardized aptitude and achievement tests throughout his school career. He (or his parents) may challenge the accuracy of those scores and request they be deleted. Even though the school believes the records to be accurate they may delete them rather than go through litigation. Now, what inferences would prospective employers and college admissions officers make regarding the quality of the missing data? Wouldn't it be reasonable to infer the removed data were negative? Would that benefit the student? Although many questions remain unanswered, school personnel who help develop policy regarding the release of school data should study both the Russell Sage Foundation guidelines and Public Law 93–380.

Aptitude and Achievement Test Data

We do not regard results of aptitude or achievement tests as private information between the test taker and some other single individual such as the school psychologist. We take the position that the results of all achievement and aptitude tests should be disseminated to all professional staff members in the school, the individuals who were tested, and the parents of those individuals. In fact, parents have a legal right to the test information contained in the official school record (Pub. Law 93–380 Sec. 513). This right may not apply for students over 18 unless the student gives his permission to release the data to his parents.

Goslin (1967, pp. 19, 77, 92) presented public school principals with a variety of reasons for using standardized tests, and found the reasons that received the highest vote of importance all involved dissemination of test-result information to pupils and parents. He also found that over 60 percent of the public secondary school students and parents of elementary school children sampled felt that intelligence-test information should be routinely reported to them. In contrast to this desire, Goslin found that approximately half the teachers in his sample had never given a pupil even a general idea of his intelligence, although nearly all teachers felt they ought to have free access to such information about their students. Goslin used this type of evidence to conclude that there is a "need for a clear statement of policy regarding the dissemination of test scores and information resulting from test scores, both by teachers and other school personnel" (Goslin, 1967, p 26). We certainly concur with that statement. Such a clear statement of policy should come from the local school district, and not from textbook writers. The policy should be dependent upon such school characteristics as student-counselor ratio, measurement competencies of the teachers, and whether or not in-service training is available for measurement-naïve teachers. The important point is that some *professional* interpretation of aptitude- and achievement-test scores should be made available to every parent and child.

Aptitude- and achievement-test scores should also be made available to other school systems (primary, secondary, or college) where the student intends to enroll. It is probably advisable to receive consent from parents (or students, if over 18) before such a release, but we would not deem it absolutely essential. The school should *not* release the aptitude- or achievement-test scores of a pupil to any other person or agency (such as a prospective employer, a physician, or psychiatrist) without written permission.

A practice that is becoming increasingly common is for schools to release group achievement test results to the press. The demands for accountability data and the increased number of state-supported testing programs have served as incentives to this procedure. We have no objection to this general release of data as long as some accompanying explanatory and cautionary interpretative exposition accompanies the data. The release should *not* identify particular students' scores or the average score of any single class.

Interest Inventory Data

Interest inventory results should, in general, be made available (that is, recorded where all would have access to it) to professional staff, students, and parents, but active dissemination and discussion of the information need only be done with the students. Naturally, any interested parent should be able to receive professional interpretation of his child's interest-test scores. Teachers should know what kind of interest-inventory information is available and where it can be obtained. They should be strongly urged to avail themselves of this information and to use it, much as they would other data in the cumulative record, to aid in the full understanding of each individual child. No interest inventory data should be released to other agencies without the written consent of the student or parent.

Personality Inventory Data

As a matter of normal routine, personality and attitude inventory results should not be made available to anyone except the student without his explicit permission. One way to minimize faking is to alleviate anxiety about who will have access to the test results and about how they will be used. If a counselor or school psychologist wishes to obtain an accurate measure from a student, he may well emphasize the confidential nature of the information. If confidentiality is promised or even implied, it should not be broken. Oftentimes, however, the professional who gathered the information will deem it beneficial for the student to share the information with others, such as parents or teachers. If so, he should obtain the student's permission to release the data. It should be pointed out that whether counselors or school psychologists legally enjoy privileged communications, as do physicians or attorneys, is debatable. Recall that Public Law 93–380 specifies that parents have the right to "inspect and review any and all official records, files, and data directly related to their children . . ." (p. 89). These could also be subpoenaed. Counselors might argue, however, that their records (including personality-test scores) are not a part of the official school records.

Recording

The recording of the test results not considered private information can be accomplished by trained clerks. Even these results, however, are *not* in the public domain, and the clerks should be cautioned to treat the results as confidential. Test results are generally stored in pupils' cumulative folders. In the future they will no doubt be placed in computer storage. In either case, one must somehow ensure that the information is readily available for those who should have access to it and not available to those who should not have access to it. These two goals are hard to reach simultaneously. Test results must be kept under lock and key, but teachers should have easy access to them and be encouraged to use them. Of course, some teachers are not knowledgeable enough to use test results correctly. This places us somewhat in an ethical dilemma when we suggest that aptitude-, achievement-, and interest-test results be made available to all the professional staff. However, it is really the teachers' ethical responsibility to know how to use most, if not all, of the scores in the areas mentioned. If not, they should surely recognize their limitations in the area and not use the information without obtaining guidance.

All data on file should be reviewed periodically to determine their present usefulness and accuracy. Aptitude- and achievement-test data should probably be retained throughout secondary school for most pupils. (The achievement data may be stored even after graduation.) However, there are occasions where a test score is of doubtful validity or almost assuredly far from correct. These scores should be deleted from the record. (For example, if a student is obviously very ill while taking an exam, the test results should certainly not be made a part of the record.) Interest-inventory scores are not likely to be useful for more than three or four years. There is no reason to retain such scores on a pupil's record once he has graduated (except perhaps in a very secure file for research purposes). As we have mentioned, personality inventory data should not be a regular part of the pupil's records. Anecdotal data should be reviewed annually and discarded when no longer of use.

Interpreting Test Information to Others

Just as the parent and pupil have a right to certain kinds of test information, the school has the responsibility to communicate this information so that it will be understood correctly. This means that raw test-score information would probably not be disseminated. The major aspects to be communicated are (1) what information the test score gives us, (2) the precision of this information, and (3) how the information can be used appropriately.

Many times confusion exists as to what information the test score provides. This may be due to one of two reasons: (1) The type of score (that is, percentile, stanine, and so on) may not be understood, and (2) the construct being measured may not be understood. These problems can be overcome, but the educator needs to be sufficiently aware of the possible confusion that can take place in a parent's or pupil's mind. Confusion concerning the type of score may result from mistaking percentiles for percentages, while a misunderstanding of a construct may be the result of confusing aptitude with interest. Even administrators, counselors, and teachers do this! If a professional can make such a mistake, it reinforces our belief that we must be very careful in interpreting to others what the test is measuring.

The precision of the test information is another important aspect of test interpretation. What needs to be interpreted is an accurate impression of test score accuracy. This, of course, varies from test to test. There has been much concern in the past about laymen not being aware of the imprecision of tests. The attempt by some to differentiate between scores only one point apart illustrates insensitivity to the concept of errors of measurement. One should guard against this danger of overinterpretation. Although teachers or counselors cannot teach a parent or student about the theoretical concepts of reliability or standard error of measurement, they certainly can and should communicate the general idea. A good way to do this is through band interpretation. Presenting a range of values encompassing $\pm 1S_e$ from the observed score as indicating where the individual would probably score if he retook the test, usually gets across the point of imprecision. The idea of band interpretation is most often accomplished using percentile bands, although raw score or z or T score bands could be used. Percentile bands are reported for the better-constructed tests. If not reported, they can be easily computed for any test that reports percentiles and a standard error of measurement. One simply looks up the percentiles that correspond to $X \pm 1\ S_e$. One can be about 68 percent confident that a person's true percentile will be within this range. A possible misinterpretation of percentile bands is that a person unsophisticated in this type of score may think that the percentile corresponding to a person's observed score is halfway between the two percentile band end points. (Or, as mentioned earlier, it is possible to confuse percentiles and percentages.) Because percentiles are rectangularly distributed and observed scores are typically distributed in a fairly normal fashion, this will not be the case—except when a person's observed score is equal to the mean of the distribution. Thus, if percentile bands are used, the percentile for the observed score should be given along with the two end percentiles.

Although many people overinterpret small differences in scores, it is also true that other people place too little faith in test results and underinterpret score differences. This has probably become even more true because of the recent criticisms of testing that have received so much space in the press. In particular, students who score poorly on tests have a tendency to discount the results. Although a teacher or counselor should not argue with a parent or student over the accuracy of a test score, the precision of a test should not be underplayed. There has been much talk recently about the importance of a good self-concept. This is fine, but there is no evidence to suggest that a person who has an inaccurately high self-concept will make better decisions than a person who perceives himself accurately. A good decision, by definition, is dependent upon an accurate self-concept, not a good self-concept.

It is possible that people will understand what characteristic has been measured and how accurately it has been measured without understanding how this information is useful to them. For example, for an individual to know that he is at about the 80th percentile on a test that measures creativity may not be particularly useful to him. It is up to the test interpreter to help the individual understand how that information is related to the decisions he must make.

Although not ideal, it is probably acceptable to present interpretations of achievement- and aptitude-test results to groups of teachers. Parents and students who are somewhat less sophisticated with regard to test interpretation should receive more individualized interpretations.

Some schools routinely send home the results of standardized achievement tests accompanied by short brochures (prepared by the publishers of the tests or the local school) that describe the test and explain the meaning of the scores in terms parents can understand. We have mixed feelings about such a practice. The advantage is that it ensures broad dissemination of information. A possible disadvantage is that the information will be either incompletely understood or misunderstood. Another approach is to announce in a school paper or through direct mailings to parents that the results are available and a counselor or homeroom teacher will explain the information if the parents wish to visit the school.[5] Another possibility is to explain routinely the scores at one of the regularly held parent-teacher conferences.

The interpretation of interest inventories is best done individually, although group interpretations of some interest inventories are appropriate. If the purpose of the interest inventory is primarily to start the student thinking about how his interests relate to his educational plans and the world of work, then group interpretation is appropriate. If the interest-inventory data are to be used to assist the individual in an educational or vocational decision, then individual interpretation of the data in a counseling situation is necessary.

Any interpretation of personality-inventory results should be done in an individual interview by qualified personnel. Problems inherent in personality measurement lead us to strongly recommend that the results of such inventories be discussed only in general terms.

Any sharing of information between parents (or students) and teachers (or counselors) regarding test score results is subject to misinterpretation. The following guidelines should be useful in minimizing the problems (Lien, 1976, p. 297–300).

1. Make sure that both you and the person to whom you are interpreting the test results have a clear, immediate goal in mind which will serve as a reason for the interpretation.
2. Never discuss the implication of the scores in terms of absolute answers (e.g., this score shows you won't get through college).
3. Try to concentrate on increasing understanding rather than posing as an expert. Use simple nontechnical terms whenever possible.
4. Remember that understanding and acceptance are two different concepts.
5. Never compare one student with another particular student.

Much more could be said concerning specific techniques of test interpretation (see Ricks, 1959). Separate courses should be taken in counseling techniques of test interpretation beyond an introductory course. The main point to be made here is that, in any interpretation of test data, *the focus*

---

[5] This forcefully illustrates the importance of classroom teachers being knowledgeable about the interpretation of test scores.

should always be on the student, not on the test score. For a further discussion of test interpretations, see Goldman (1971).

CRITERIA FOR A MARKING-REPORTING SYSTEM

The following criteria should be helpful to educators who wish to evaluate their own marking and reporting system.

1. Is the system based on a clear statement of educational objectives?
2. Is the system understood both by those making the reports and those to whom they are sent?
3. Does the system desirably affect the students' learning?
4. Is the system detailed enough to be diagnostic and yet compact enough to be operational?
5. Does the system involve *two*-way communication between home and school?
6. Does the system promote desirable public relations?
7. Is the system reasonably economical in terms of teacher time?

Any single method of reporting may not achieve all these criteria. We recommend a combination of procedures to be most effective. Which procedures depend on the school's objectives, the grade level of the student, and the recipient of the reports.

SUMMARY

The major ideas, conclusions, and implications of this chapter are summarized in the following statements:

1. Measurement and evaluation are necessary for wise educational decision making. Since all decisions are not made at the time of measurement, it is necessary to keep a record of student progress.
2. Since many people make, or help the student make, decisions based upon school achievement, we need to consider what reporting procedures can best communicate the student's achievements.
3. Students, parents, administrators, teachers, prospective employers, and college admissions officers all need information from the school to assist them in decision making.
4. Students need feedback information to guide them in their decision making. They primarily should receive such information through daily interaction with their teachers, but formal periodic reports can also assist in student decision making.
5. Many educators and students believe that recording of grades motivates students to learn things they would not otherwise learn.
6. There exist a variety of reporting procedures such as marks, check lists,

letters, and conferences. Each has advantages and limitations. A school may use different schemes at different grade levels as well as use different schemes for the same grade level for reporting to different people.

7. The most important requirements of any marking-reporting procedure are that (1) those using it understand the system, and (2) the reports are based on the objectives the school is striving to teach.

8. Marks refer to those systems that use summary symbols of some type.

9. If only a *single* symbol is assigned, it should represent achievement in the subject matter (not attitude) and status rather than growth.

10. In traditional classroom situations, marks should be based on a normative interpretation. In mastery-learning approaches to instruction, marks should be criterion-referenced.

11. Decreasing the number of categories in a marking system will decrease the reliability of the marks.

12. The partial pass-fail system of marking is probably a beneficial educational procedure. A complete pass-fail system likely would be deleterious.

13. The major faults of grading are not inherent faults of the marking system, but are due to teachers not using the system correctly.

14. Procedures should be applied that help make marks more comparable across teachers.

15. The major limitation of a single summary mark is that it does not provide enough specific information to be helpful in diagnosing a student's strengths and weaknesses.

16. Check lists or rating scales can provide more detailed information, which may help in diagnostic or remedial planning.

17. Letters are occasionally used in reporting. Their main advantage is that they can report on many different aspects of a child's school experiences. Their major limitation is that, if done correctly, they are very time consuming.

18. If a teacher prepares properly, conferences can be a very effective method of presentation.

19. Aptitude- and achievement-test data should be disseminated to all professional staff members in the school, the individuals who were tested, and the parents of those individuals. They should be released to other schools where the individual intends to enroll. They should not be released to any other person or agency without written permission.

20. Interest-inventory data should be made available to professional staff, students, and parents, but active dissemination and discussion of the data need only be done with students.

21. Results from personality inventories should not be made available to anyone except the student without his explicit permission.

22. In interpreting test information to others, we must clarify (1) what information the test score gives us, (2) the precision of this information, and (3) how the information can be used appropriately.

CHAPTER EIGHTEEN
Accountability and Evaluation Programs

Educators have long been known to latch onto certain terms or battle cries. Bandwagons are easy to jump on, and each new bandwagon purports to carry us over the problems of education. A popular term today is accountability. It is too soon to pass judgment on what this concept has done or will do in education. We view it in a cautious but positive light. However, there are some severe pitfalls and limitations of the concept if one views it as an all-pervasive good.

In this chapter we talk about some philosophical and measurement concerns related to accountability and some approaches to and possible consequences of accountability. Next we discuss the related field of program evluation and two types of internal evaluation programs: standardized testing programs and evaluation programs for individualized instruction. Both types of programs can provide limited accountability data, though neither one was implemented as a response to the demand for accountability. Finally, we discuss three kinds of external evaluation programs: college selection and placement programs, the National Assessment of Education Progress, and state assessment programs. The last two are outgrowths of the demand for accountability.

After studying this chapter, the student should be able to—

1. Define accountability.
2. Recognize the reasons for the popularity of the accountability concept.
3. Recognize the philosophical concerns related to accountability.
4. Understand the measurement problems of accountability programs.
5. Judge various accountability programs with respect to their philosophical and measurement limitations.
6. Understand the distinctions between and similarities of program and student evaluation.
7. Recognize that program evaluation is not so rigorous in an experimental research sense as one might ideally hope.
8. Understand the dangers of evaluation bias.
9. Understand the importance of attending to unintended outcomes in program evaluation.
10. Differentiate between formative and summative evaluation.
11. Appreciate the necessity for cooperative planning in setting up a testing program.
12. Understand the various steps necessary in planning and administering a testing program.
13. Propose and defend a standardized testing program.
14. Recognize the various evaluation needs in individualized instruction.
15. Differentiate between internal and external evaluation programs.
16. Understand the functions of college selection and placement programs.
17. Know the basic purposes and procedures of the National Assessment of Educational Progress.
18. Recognize some priorities, trends, and problems of state assessment programs.

ACCOUNTABILITY

The 1970s have been referred to as the decade of accountability in education. The concept of accountability has indeed become a major controversial topic of discussion. Accountability means different things to different people, and it has been defined in a myriad of ways (Barro, 1970; Bell, 1971; Cunningham, 1971; Gooler, 1971; Lessinger, 1970a,b; Lindman, 1971; Locke, 1971; Porter, 1971; Saretsky, 1973). A typical definition of accountability would include *setting* correct goals, *evaluating* their degree of achievement (we discuss program evaluation in the next section) and at what *price, presenting and interpreting* this information to the public, and *accepting responsibility* for any results that are perceived inadequate. A few users of the term would evidently allow educators to attempt to explain why all failures may not be their fault. In the abstract, accountability is basically the process of justifying costs by presenting the positive effects derived from expenditures. Perhaps in the concrete it boils down to (1) who gets hanged when things go wrong and (2) who does the hanging? (Browder, 1971, p. 19).

Reactions to accountability among educators have been mixed. It has been said that any new idea passes through the following stages: (1) indignant rejection, (2) reasoned objection, (3) qualified opposition, (4) tentative acceptance, (5) qualified endorsement, (6) judicious modification, (7) cautious adoption, (8) impassioned espousal, (9) proud parenthood, and (10) dogmatic propagation. As Browder, Atkins, and Kaya (1973, p. vi) suggest with respect to accountability, some legislators, school boards, and commercial hucksters short-circuited the evolutionary sequence and reached a point of impassioned espousal rapidly. Many others are still at the point of indignant rejection.

The president of the American Federation of Teachers suggested that from the teacher's point of view, the concept of accountability is to be feared (Shanker, 1971). The December 1972 NEA position statement with respect to accountability expresses the concern that accountability has become "a political Shibboleth, a code word that communicates coercion and control under the mask of concerned and responsible leadership" (National Education Association, 1972). It suggests that the only relevant accountability question is why teachers don't possess the authority and decision-making power to perform their professional tasks.

But in spite of the two major teacher organizations' warnings about accountability, many still view it as being "a powerful catalyst in achieving that basic reform so sorely needed in the school system" (Lessinger, 1970b, p. 339).

What does all this have to do with the contents of a textbook in measurement? Simply this: Accountability depends upon good measurement and the correct uses of that measurement data. As accountability procedures are implemented, educators and prospective educators who are readers of this book should be alerted to the various philosophical and measurement aspects inherent in such programs in order to maximize their values and minimize their dangers. We, and probably most educators, are in favor of the abstract principle of accountability. But it is impossible to say in the abstract whether accountability is a blessing or burden, a miracle or mirage, a milestone or millstone, and potential problems arise when we try to move from the abstract to the specific. What are some of the philosophical and measurement concerns educators should be alert to, and what are some of the potential approaches to and consequences of accountability?

Philosophical Concerns

Basically the philosophical concerns center around who is accountable and for what they are accountable. We are not suggesting that we have the answers to these questions, but we can present some different dimensions that pertain to the questions.

Who Is Accountable?

There is certainly no current agreement about who is presently being held accountable in education or who should be. Deterline (1971, p. 16) said that educators operate so that "all failures and ineffective aspects of our instruction are slyly laid on the students, in the form of a grade or rating, [and] we never really have to face the facts of our own incompetence in the field of instruction." He suggests that students are held accountable if they do not learn—in spite of any failures, deficiencies, and incompetence in our teaching—and he welcomes educational accountability as a countervailing force.

Campbell argued that Deterline is guilty of fighting yesterday's wars instead of today's.

> There was a time when teachers were scarcely held accountable for their shortcomings as instructors, but this has not been the state of affairs I have noted in my 20 years in education. Rather, there has been a drumfire of extramural criticism and intramural breast-beating rising to the present crescendo. Through every possible medium, including his professional journals, the teacher receives the same message: "You are a failure. You are incompetent at best and probably insensitive, unimaginative, lazy, and cruel as well." His grade is a straight F/U.
>
> By contrast, "failure" for students is like the death penalty—still legal, but seldom applied. (Campbell, 1971, p. 176)

In the 1971 Gallup survey of public attitudes toward education, the following question was asked: "When some children do poorly in school, some people place the blame on the children, some on the children's home life, some on the school, and some on the teachers. Of course, all of these things share the blame, but where would you place the chief blame?" Of those interviewed, 54 percent placed the chief blame on the children's home life, 14 percent named children, 8 percent teachers, and 6 percent the schools. When the same question was put to high school juniors and seniors, 51 percent blamed the children (themselves), 25 percent said home life, 11 percent teachers, and 5 percent said the school. Interestingly, when professional educators (members of Phi Delta Kappa) were asked this question, almost one-fifth (19 percent) said the school was the chief reason for student's poor performance. This is more than three times as high as the public's 6 percent response and almost four times as high as the pupil's 5 percent response!

Whether or not it has, it does seem to us that the pendulum can swing too far toward holding educators accountable for lack of pupil learning in spite of any failures, deficiencies, and incompetence in the students and/or parents. The definition of teaching for many educational critics has changed from an activity *intended* to induce learning to an activity that *does* induce learning. Although it seems condescending to assume that students have no responsibility for their own learning, most writers on educational account-ability do not mention students' (or parents') accountability. Yet, "substitut-ing the teacher . . . for the pupil as the *only* accountable party is an example of reactionary thinking" (Campbell, 1971, p. 177). Educators *alone* cannot be held accountable for a product when they have virtually no control over their resources or raw material.

> When students are regarded as "products" of the school, it is implied that the school is a factory and should be fully accountable for the behavior of its products. Yet, without the power to select its raw material and reject defective products, the school cannot guarantee its product. (Lindman, 1971, p. B-4)

The foregoing paragraph is not meant to let educators off the hook. Just because educators are not accountable for everything does not mean they are not accountable for anything. But we need to be somewhat moderate in any approach to accountability. We have to recognize that "Each participant [including students and teachers] in the educational process should be held responsible only for those educational outcomes that he can affect by his actions or decisions and only to the extent that he can affect them" (Barro, 1970, p. 199).

Educators, then, should be held accountable for some aspects of chil-dren's learning, but there is no easy way to discern which portions are under their control; accountability programs must keep this in mind. The "who is accountable" question cannot at present be answered, and until (and if) it is answered, we must remember that the purpose of accountability programs should not be punitive in nature, but rather should be accepted as a means of quality control. We should not use educators as the whipping boys of society.

Accountable for What?

Perhaps even more difficult than the question of who should be held account-able is the question of "accountable for what?" The simpleminded answer is that we should be held accountable for the pupils' attainments of our educa-tional objectives. But although there is a consensus about many desired out-comes, there still remain diverse goals or objectives held by our educational systems. Some people maintain "good citizenship" or "healthy self-concepts" are more important than reading skills. Others assert just the opposite. This difference of opinion causes considerable difficulty when it comes to institut-ing accountability. And since we can measure some objectives more readily than others, there may be a tendency for accountability programs to focus narrowly on these easily measured objectives. We will discuss this further in the section on measurement problems related to accountability.

There are differences of opinion not only about what the outcome objectives should be, but also what the *distribution* of these results should be. Downs (1968) discussed four diverse goals regarding distribution:

1. The *minimum-citizenship (level) goal:* All students should be brought up to some basic *minimum* level of proficiency.

2. The *maximum-system-output-goal:* The total capabilities of all students considered as a group (perhaps best measured by their total resulting productivity) should be made as large as possible.

3. The *equal-opportunity (really equal-outcome) goal: All* students emerging from the system (say, upon high school graduation) should have approximately the same capabilities for entering into the postschooling portion of their lives.[1]

4. The *maximum-individual-advancement goal:* Each student should be given as much development of his individual potential as possible.

As Downs pointed out,

> . . . pursuing each of the above goals exclusively, without regard to the others, would result in very different allocations of publicly-supplied educational inputs. At one extreme, the equal-opportunity goal would require a heavy concentration of resources among the poorest and most culturally-deprived students. They would receive much higher inputs than children from higher-income and more advantaged homes . . . In contrast . . . the maximum system output goal would concentrate publicly-supplied inputs on the best qualified students. This would result in the greatest total gain in technical proficiency per dollar invested (Downs, 1968, pp. 16, 17).

It seems to us that people advocating accountability are, *in general,* operating as if their goal were the *minimum citizenship* mentioned (see Lessinger, 1971; Porter, 1971). However, this is not completely clear, since often the stated minimum goal is to bring everyone up to average! This is, in effect, the equal-opportunity (read "outcome") goal. (Many educators seem to be unaware that, by definition, half of the pupils will always fall below the median unless all score at the same point. We are continually amazed that so many people operate as if they are not aware of this basic fact. For example, Lessinger (1970a, p. 220) spoke of the right of every child to read at his

---

[1] This would coincide with the definition Coleman et al. (1966) gave to equal opportunity as the equality of outcome.

grade level. See the definition of grade equivalents in Chapter 6 if you cannot see what is wrong with his statement.)

We should not leave this topic before stating that the fourth goal regarding distribution of outcomes is idealistic and can never be achieved as long as resources—goods, services, time, energy, and money—are limited. We simply cannot do as much as possible for each child, and educators should quit acting as if it were feasible (for example, when discussing how we will account for individual differences).

Other writers (Dyer, 1970b; Harmes, 1971; Lindman, 1971; Shanker, 1971; and Tye, 1971) approach "accountability for what" in a different way. Dyer, for example, emphasized:

> . . . that staff members are to be held accountable for keeping themselves informed about the diverse needs of their pupils and for doing the best they can to meet those needs. In light of what we know about the teaching-learning process, this is the most we may reasonably expect. To hold teachers, or anybody else, accountable for some sort of "guaranteed pupil performance" is likely to do more harm than good in the lives of children (Dyer, 1970, p. 206).

Thus, Dyer discussed a *process* accountability rather than a *product* accountability. This seems more in agreement with the definition of teaching, which states that the *intent* of teaching is to induce learning.

Harmes (1971, p. 52), in talking about Performance Contracts, made much the same point. However, he expanded it by saying:

> Perhaps, losing faith in the ability of educators to select, implement and operate the best programs, school boards are beginning to see product output-performance as their *only* recourse for securing the best programs for their clients, the public (Harmes, 1971, p. 56).

We are strong advocates of the position that the role of educators is to facilitate certain types of student learning. We believe that educators need to measure student outcomes in order to make wise educational decisions. But this position is not analogous to blaming teachers for any specified lack of pupil performance. Whether one wishes to say they are *accountable* for pupil outcomes depends in part on how one wants to define accountability and in part upon philosophical/political considerations. We are inclined to agree with the position taken by Dyer, but most proselytes of accountability preach as though educators are accountable for specified pupil performances.

Thus there are considerable differences of opinion on the *what* issues. Whether we should assess basic cognitive skills or affective objectives, what the ideal distribution of educational results is, and whether we should have process or product assessment are the three we have briefly discussed.

Measurement Concerns

The measurement problems in accountability are very difficult to surmount. We do not intend to discuss all these problems in detail. Rather, we wish to introduce the reader to a few key concerns. As a professional educator you almost invariably will be subject to some accountability programs, and therefore you should be alert to some of the more pressing measurement problems involved. You may wish to refer back to the problems of obtaining reliable gain measures as discussed in Chapter 5. As mentioned there, many accountability programs try to use such gain measures in their assessment. (See Wrightstone, Hogan, & Abbott, 1972, for a further treatment of the measurement problems.)

Establishing Causal Relations

The determination of causal relationships is directly related to the philosophical issue of *who* is to be held accountable. The abstract answer is that one should be held responsible only for those outcomes he can affect. Concrete details of how to determine that are at best incomplete. But even if we determine that a teacher can and should affect reading skills, how can we determine that a student who reads well does so because of the teacher's efforts?

Specialists in educational measurement and evaluation have historically concentrated their efforts on determining *what is*, rather than *who is responsible* or *accountable* for what is. Many problems still exist in the first determination, such as measuring in the affective domain. However, by comparison, we can do a fairly accurate job of measuring what is. What we cannot do very well is to establish causal relationships between these outcomes and various input and process variables. To do this requires something more than measurement; it requires a research design. Barro (1970) and Dyer (1970b) have established two of the best accountability models, but both models are oversimplified. They present the case in which objectives are uniform across all learners, as opposed to the more realistic case of objectives that are variable across learners, classes, schools, and systems. Yet, as oversimplified as the models are in theory, they are probably too complicated to work in practice (Lennon, 1971). Nevertheless, Barro, Dyer, and Lennon would all assert that we must attempt to develop accountability programs.

Dyer (1970b, p. 207) referred to four groups of variables that must be taken into account in any thorough accountability research design:

1. *Input variables*, or the characteristics of the *pupils* as they *enter* a particular phase of schooling—their health, level of achievement, self-concept, aspirations, and other considerations.

2. *Surrounding conditions* within which the school operates, including the home, community, and school conditions.

3. The *educational process*.

4. *Output variables*, or the characteristics of the pupils as they emerge from a particular phase of schooling.

Dyer very emphatically stressed the importance of taking these variables into account:

> . . . a meaningful and equitable accounting of school effectiveness is possible only under two stringent conditions: (1) it must rest on at least two measures of pupil performance with a sufficient interval between them—probably not less than two years—to permit the school to have an effect on pupil learning which is large enough to be observable; and (2) any output measure of pupil performance must be read in light of the level of pupil input and also in light of the conditions in which the school has been forced to operate . . . this point cannot be too strongly stressed. To compromise with this basic principle would wreck the entire enterprise (Dyer, 1970, p. 211).

However, it is difficult to take the first three variables into account, and many accountability programs will not be likely to do so. Thus there is a danger that schools (and teachers) in those districts where surrounding conditions are poor will be unduly chastised for low outputs. This problem is accentuated during this period in our society when some vociferous critics of education hold the naive belief that the school can and should be held accountable for overcoming poor input and negative surrounding variables. Yet research such as the report from Coleman et al. (1966) shows quite clearly that a large proportion of the variance in performance levels is accounted for by out-of-school variables, such as pupils' socioeconomic status and home environments.

Validity

Just as the measurement problem of establishing causal relations is related to the philosophical issue of who is to be held accountable, the measurement problem of validity is related to the "what is to be assessed" issue. Because "basic skill" areas are very important as well as the easiest areas to assess, many accountability programs focus only on these areas. Since the school's objectives are ordinarily much broader than attainment of basic skills alone, the assessment tools may have inadequate content validity. Although poor content validity is always deplorable, it is particularly troublesome when the results of an assessment device are used to hold the schools accountable.

Such questions as whether the performances observed on an assessment instrument are indeed the school's goals or only indicants of the school's goals, and under what circumstances teaching for the test is a harmful educational practice deserve careful consideration. Whenever the performance tested is only a sample (or indicant) of our objectives, teaching directly for the test (that is, teaching for those specific questions on the test) is inappropriate. If a test indeed covers accepted objectives, it is appropriate to teach for the general topics covered by the test. But when the objectives covered on the test are much more narrow in focus than the objectives of the school, it would be inappropriate to stress only the general objectives covered by the test, and to do so could seriously alter the overall substance of the educational product.

Approaches to and Consequences of Accountability

Since educational accountability is defined in so many different ways, there are many different approaches to it. Remember that the concept of accountability usually includes setting correct goals in terms of student outcomes (often with community help), evaluating whether these goals have been achieved (through either external or internal approaches) and at what price, divulging this information to the public, and accepting responsibility for inadequacies in performance. Operationalizing a construct as complicated as this is more of a building process than simply adopting some complete and adequate accountability program.

Accountability will force schools to do a better job of specifying and evaluating objectives. There will be an increased focus on the relationship between outcomes, input, and process variables. Schools will work toward adopting better management techniques and fiscal controls. There will be more concerted efforts to keep the public informed of educational objectives, expenses, processes, and results. All this seems commendable.

Various evaluation programs are discussed in the next three sections of this chapter. Some of these programs were in existence long before the recent use of the term *accountability*. Others have been undertaken largely in response to the accountability issue.

PROGRAM EVALUATION

Whether or not educators wish to use the term "accountability," they are invariably involved in curriculum and instructional decision making. And to make these decisions, *program evaluations* are necessary. The recognition of the importance of such evaluations has increased tremendously in the past decade. The basic distinction between program and student evaluation is related to the decisions that are to be made. If we wish to make a decision about an individual, such as when we ask whether Susan should take advanced algebra or how she did in first-year French, we are concerned with student evaluation. When we wonder whether nongraded classrooms like those operating in elementary school A should be effected in school B, we are concerned with program evaluation. Whether French should be taught in fourth grade or a programmed text used in ninth-grade algebra are program decisions. The decision of whether to continue any experimental program (such as using the Initial Teaching Alphabet) requires program evaluation.

Thus program evaluation is considerably broader than student evaluation. Student evaluation involves the determination of whether a student is making appropriate progress toward stated goals. Students' progress toward goals is but one dimension of program evaluation—though probably the most important.

In program evaluation we are concerned with such things as why the student goals were, or were not, achieved; the evaluation of the goals (objectives) themselves; the need to be particularly alert to unintended outcomes; the impact the curriculum has on persons other than the students; obtaining measures of cost effectiveness; and formative as well as summative evaluation.

Although school personnel have always made implicit evaluations of their curriculum (that is, they have made decisions about their curriculum), current school personnel are ill equipped to handle the more formal, explicit aspects of program evaluation. Typically, they have had no training in the area. They are unsure of what the term encompasses, how program evaluation differs from student evaluation, and what procedures are appropriate.

We will not attempt in this introductory book to cover all aspects of program evaluation. It is a reasonably complex topic, and to become an expert in it would require knowledge in statistics, research design, and educational philosophy, as well as extensive reading in the area of program evaluation per se. Every school district should have a program evaluation expert. However, this book intends only to introduce our readers to this growing and important field of program evaluation in the hope that some will continue their education in this area. (See Payne, 1974, pp. 9 and 10, and Worthen, 1975, pp. 14–16, for lists of the required skills or competencies of evaluation experts.) In addition, all educators—from teachers to administrators—should be cognizant of the dimensions and importance of this field. Good program evaluation requires the cooperation of many people. Educators will be better able and more willing to assist if they have at least some exposure to the topic.

Models of Evaluation

Several specific models of program evaluations exist (see Cronbach, 1963; Dick, 1968; Metfessel & Michael, 1967; Provus, 1971; Scriven, 1967, 1973, 1975; Stake, 1967a,b, 1975; Stufflebeam et al., 1971; Tyler et al., 1967; Wittrock & Wiley, 1970) and many examples of major evaluation projects are available in the literature (see, for example, Alkin et al., 1974; Grobman, 1968; Welch & Walberg, 1972). Worthen and Sanders (1973) give an excellent overview of many of the models and we refer those readers who wish to learn more about the various models to that reference. Wolf (1969) has written an interesting satire on evaluation describing some of the far too frequent but inappropriate applications of evaluation "models." There is the "cosmetic method" which involves taking a cursory look at a program and deciding it looks good. One uses the "cardiac method" when empirical data turn out wrong. The cardiac method allows one to dismiss the data and believe in his heart that the new program is a good one! Hopefully these "models" will be be used less frequently in the future.

Evaluation versus Research

In evaluating the causal effects of curriculum (or instructional procedures), one needs to be concerned with the activities that preceded (and inferentially produced) the outcomes. There is some disagreement about how rigorous one's "research design" need be—or whether, indeed, program evaluation should be classified as research—but the inference is usually made that certain student outcomes are the causal result of the teaching-learning activities that preceded them (see Guba, 1969, and Stanley, 1969).

Program evaluation often cannot be as rigorous as one might wish. If one wishes to view it as research, it probably comes closest to what Corey (1953) called action research or what Cronbach and Suppes (1969) called decision-oriented research.

Politics, Evaluation, and Evaluation Bias

One major impetus for increased evaluation came from the various governmental funding agencies. It follows that much evaluation takes place in a political context. As Weiss points out:

> The programs with which the evaluator deals are not neutral, antiseptic, laboratory-type entities. They emerged from the rough and tumble of political support, opposition, and bargaining. Attached to them are the reputations of legislative sponsors, the careers of administrators, the jobs of program staff, and the expectations of clients (Weiss, 1973, p. 38).

Further, many evaluation results indicate that programs dealing with social and educational problems fail to accomplish their goals. Since program founders and administrators as well as many evaluators are uncomfortable when negative or inconclusive evaluation findings are used to justify an end to spending on social or educational programs we must recognize the ever present danger of evaluation bias. Scriven (1975) has written about the problem of evaluation bias and its control. One major step in attempting to reduce bias is to use an external, independent evaluator. These are two separate points. An external evaluator is not necessarily independent.

> Suppose you do hire an outside firm for evaluating a project, a firm whose headquarters are in a distant state. This *looks* like real independence. But ask yourself what the reward system is for that firm. It isn't any more rewarding for them if your project is successful or not, *per se*—and that's why you value their opinion, why they appear independent. But look a little deeper, or *longer*. What is rewarding to them *over the years*? Success

is their business, which of course requires a continued flow of contracts. Since such firms are very well aware of the power of the grapevine in getting further clients, they are often well aware that an evaluation which shows the client in a good light is much more conducive to later contracts than a critical evaluation. The reverse side of this coin was brought home to me when communicating with a network of evaluators on a USOE grant. I heard more than one sad tale of "blackballing" an evaluator who gave a deservedly critical evaluation. In short, the "independence" of an external evaluator can be seriously compromised by the constraints of business success (Scriven, 1975, p. 17).

One way to help combat the problem of bias for internal and external (but not independent) evaluations is through employing what Scriven termed Meta-Evaluation—the evaluation of evaluations or evaluators. If evaluators knew they and their reports were subject to evaluation, this should do much to minimize the bias of their reports! (See Stufflebeam, 1974, for more on Meta-Evaluation.)

Evaluating Program Goals

As we mentioned before, program evaluation is broader than evaluating the degree to which—and reasons why—we have achieved certain outcomes. It also involves determining whether the stated goals are appropriate. As Scriven (1967, p. 52) pointed out, "it is obvious that if the goals aren't worth achieving then it is uninteresting how well they are achieved."

Because new curricula (or instructional procedures) have somewhat different goals from those of the old curricula, comparing the efficacy of different curricula is difficult. Existing standardized achievement tests, for example, which are generally considered to be quite adequate measures of particular kinds of student achievement, may not be sufficient for comparing two different curricula. According to Scriven:

> The result of attempts to evaluate recent new curricula has been remarkably uniform; comparing students taking the old curriculum with students taking the new one, it usually appears that students using the new curriculum do rather better on the examinations designed for that curriculum and rather worse on those designed for the old curriculum, while students using the old curriculum perform in the opposite way (Scriven, 1967, p. 62).

This is, of course, not surprising, but it does illustrate the importance of evaluating the goals in deciding whether to stick to the newer curricula. As discussed in Chapter 2, the evaluation of the goals must take into account their realism and relevance. The needs of the learner as well as the community and society as a whole must be considered.

Unintended Outcomes

In evaluating a program we must be particularly alert to the side effects or the unintended outcomes for students. As Dyer (1967, p. 20) emphasized, "Evaluating the side effects of an educational program may be even more important than evaluating its intended effects." A student may learn more arithmetic under a new program, but may also develop a hatred toward it. A student may become a better convergent thinker, but a poorer divergent thinker. As we discussed in Chapter 2, teachers should be alert to measuring these unintended outcomes. For example, in Project PLAN (Flanagan, 1971) the teachers were requested to report critical incidents that they believed resulted from use of the PLAN system. This is one way to assist the teachers in evaluating unintended outcomes.

Other program side effects would be the effects on teachers, effects on students not in that particular program or curriculum, and effects on parents and taxpayers. Is a teacher's knowledge updated with a new curriculum? Does the teacher suffer from more fatigue? Has he become more enthusiastic about teaching? Scriven (1967, p. 77), for example, pointed out that some programmed texts have left teachers feeling less significant. Are other teachers in the system forced to teach less attractive courses or increase their work load as a result of the new curriculum program? Is there jealousy, or are these other teachers stimulated through contact with the teachers in the new program? Do students who are not in the new program feel discriminated against? Are there positive side effects such as improved library facilities or an improved teacher/pupil ratio? How does the community at large react to the new program? The controversy on sex education in the schools is a good example to illustrate the importance of considering public attitudes.

Cost

In evaluating a program one must certainly also consider cost factors. As Alkin (1970, p. 221) stated:

> The only time an individual can safely disregard cost is when he finds himself in the happy situation of having unlimited resources—not only in terms of material goods and services but also in terms of time and energy. To be in a situation in which costs can be disregarded is certainly not the reality of today.

Formative and Summative Program Evaluation

One final topic that should be discussed is the distinction between formative and summative evaluation (Scriven, 1967). The gathering of data during the time the program is being developed for the purpose of guiding the developmental process is formative evaluation. Making an overall assessment or decision with regard to the program is a summative evaluation. New curricular innovations are not born fully developed, nor are they ever perfected. A person who is continually evaluating his program will find many things that can be changed for the better during the operation of the program. Most educators would feel it unprofessional not to make these improvements, even though they may upset the "research design." However, these formative evaluations—accompanied by shifts in the program's operations—can hinder the process of making causal inferences about outcomes from processes.

Summary of Program Evaluation

As can be seen, there are a multitude of factors to consider in program evaluation. Various models have been developed that emphasize different evaluation tasks. Although evaluation is not identical to research, we often still wish to make causal inferences. Politics play a role in evaluation, and this may lead to evaluation bias. Evaluation goes beyond the measurement of student outcome data and includes evaluating goals, unintended outcomes, and cost effectiveness.

Often we cannot easily obtain measurements of all the factors that have the important properties of reliability, validity, and objectivity. However, if enough different types of data are obtained, the quality of any single set of data becomes somewhat less important. Also, in program evaluation we are not using data to make decisions about a single individual, and therefore the data need not have such high reliability and validity. Of course, in program evaluation, one should obtain the highest quality of data possible, but since the quality will not always be uniformly high, we are suggesting that it is important to obtain a wide variety of data.

INTERNAL EVALUATION PROGRAMS

Internal testing/evaluation programs are those over which the local school district has full control. The school selects the instruments, determines the scheduling, administers the tests, and determines what to do with the results. We discuss two topics in this section: standardized testing programs and testing programs used in individualized instruction programs.

Standardized Testing Programs

The selection, interpretation, and dissemination of results of different kinds of tests have been discussed previously in some detail. Now we discuss who should plan, direct, and administer the program; steps in planning the total program; some administrative decisions to make and details to attend to. We then give an example of a typical school testing program.

Who Should Be Involved?

A good school testing program should be a cooperative venture from the planning stage through the recording, interpretation, and dissemination of the results. Teachers, administrators, counselors, and, to some extent, parents and students, all need to understand the program and to realize that it is designed for the benefit of all groups. Without cooperative involvement the program cannot achieve its full potential. If the original program planning is conducted by only a single individual or special-interest group, the rest of the professional staff, the parents, and the students cannot necessarily be expected to endorse and adopt the program with enthusiasm.

Cooperative planning should lead not only to more enthusiastic test use, but also to a better and more complete program. Teachers, counselors, administrators, parents, and students have overlapping yet somewhat unique needs to be met from testing programs. The unique needs of each group may not be well known to others. For example, the instructional decisions of teachers require somewhat different data from those needed for curricular decisions made by administrators. If a member of each group does not have an opportunity to assist in the planning of a program, that program will more than likely be incomplete. Thus a committee representing all interest groups should actively participate in the planning of a testing program.

Though it is extremely important that many subgroups be represented in the planning so that a variety of viewpoints is obtained, competent planning is of more importance than cooperative planning, and the final decisions should be the responsibility of the professional staff. Although parents and students are unlikely to bring professional expertise to program planning, their involvement will promote better community understanding of the what and why of testing programs. Specific decisions (for example, which achievement battery should be used) should be left to the school staff. The actual administration of the program should be made the responsibility of only a single professional person. This individual should be one who (1) is well trained in tests and measurements and is dedicated to the philosophy of measurement (that is, that test results do aid in decision-making processes); (2) can communicate and cooperate with the various interest groups in the school; and (3) has at least a little tolerance for, and expertise in, administrative duties, since the total program from planning to ordering tests, administering tests, seeing to the scoring, analysis, recording, and appropriate distribution and interpretation of results does require administrative "know-how." This role is typically filled by a counselor who has special interest and training in testing. Since directing a testing program is a time-consuming task, the director should be given released time from other duties.

Steps in Planning the Program

Several steps are necessary in planning a good testing program. The first and probably the most important step is that the planning committee specify as clearly as possible the purposes of the testing program for their school. As has been repeatedly emphasized, different tests serve different purposes. Without some purposes in mind the committee would be hard put even to designate areas the program should cover, let alone select the best instruments. Although schools will surely have some different purposes, there are many commonalities. Most schools will expect their testing programs to serve some instruction, guidance, and administrative purposes. Hopefully, all schools will also use their testing programs for research purposes, although it may be that no test would be selected solely for its research uses (except, of course, when the research has been funded by an external agency!).

Second, after thorough consideration has been given to what a testing program should accomplish, the committee must consider the practical aspects of the testing program. There are always unfortunate limitations such as lack of money and too few or inadequately trained personnel. Once priorities have been set, the committee is ready to make some decisions about what specific tests should be given; the when, how, and who of administration, scoring, and analysis; the system of record keeping; and the methods of distributing and interpreting results. Table 18–1 provides a sample check list for the committee and/or administrator to follow in a testing program.

Administrative Decisions and Details

We have no desire to irritate our readers by condescendingly spelling out the detailed specifics in administering a testing program. We do want to emphasize, though, that even small details are important. Many a testing session has been less than ideal because someone overlooked a detail. Sufficient tests, answer sheets, and pencils should be available. An administrator's test manual is necessary. There does need to be sufficient time for the test. Adequate seating space must be provided. A watch or clock is frequently needed. It often is necessary to have proctors. And secretaries do need to be given directions about what to do with those little gummed labels with numbers on them that are returned from the scoring service! Two topics that deserve some additional discussion are the scheduling of the tests and preparing the faculty and students for the testing.

SCHEDULING THE TESTS   There are many views on the question of the time at which tests should be administered. Some feel that all tests should be administered in the morning, when individuals are physically and mentally at their peak. Some feel that tests should never be given on Mondays or Fridays. Some feel that tests should be administered at the same time of the year that the tests were given to the standardization sample, while others feel that interpolations or extrapolations of the norm data can be made validly to correct for differing time conditions.

In general, time of day and day of the week are not too important. It would probably be best not to give the test right after lunch or right before

TABLE 18-1   A Check List of Factors Affecting the Sucess of a Testing Program

	CHECK
1. Purposes of the program:	
Clearly defined	_____
Understood by parties involved	_____
2. Choice of tests:	
Valid	_____
Reliable	_____
Appropriate difficulty level	_____
Adequate norms	_____
Easy to administer and score	_____
Economical	_____
Best available for purpose	_____
3. Administration and scoring:	
Administrators well trained	_____
All necessary information provided	_____
Scorers adequately instructed	_____
Scoring carefully checked	_____
4. Physical conditions:	
Sufficient space	_____
Sufficient time	_____
Conveniently scheduled	_____
5. Utilization of test results:	
Definite plans for use of results	_____
Provision for giving teachers all necessary help in using scores	_____
Provision for systematic follow-up on use of results	_____
6. System of records:	
Necessary for purpose	_____
Sufficient for purpose	_____
Convenient form for use	_____
7. Personnel:	
Adequately trained for the purpose	_____
8. Affiliated research:	
Full advantage taken of results	_____
Provision for special studies, analyses, or other work	_____

SOURCE: From R. T. Lennon, "Planning a Testing Program," Test Service Bulletin No. 55, issued by Harcourt Brace Jovanovich, Inc., New York. Reproduced by special permission of the publisher.

a pep rally for the homecoming game, but no valid evidence suggests that some days or times of day are particularly bad. However, it is important in achievement testing to try to administer the test at the same time of year as when the norming was done. Assume that the normative data for a test were gathered in October. The norm group's seventh-graders might have a mean raw score of 85; the eighth-graders, a mean raw score of 125. Can one predict from these data what a mean raw score for the norm group's seventh-graders would have been had they been tested in June (nine months after the norm group was actually tested)? Some test companies would answer affirmatively and provide interpolated norms depicting this mean to be 115 (three-fourths the distance between 85 and 125). However, in some subjects it might well be that at the end of the year, seventh-graders perform better than beginning eighth-graders because the latter forget during the summer months. This illustrates one of the dangers of attempting to use the interpolated norms of test companies—norms that are arrived at mathematically rather than empirically. For this reason it is best to administer achievement tests at the same time of year as the actual norm data were gathered. Another possibility is to choose a test that has norms gathered during the time of year you wish to test.

Suppose one must make a choice between two equally valid achievement tests. They differ only insofar as the time normative data were gathered—fall and spring. Which test should be used? This is indeed an important point to consider. If the data are to be used to assist the teacher during the regular school year, it might be advisable to test in the fall. Adams suggested five basic advantages of testing in the fall:

> (1) It permits the teacher to obtain a complete test record for each student. When students have been tested the preceding spring, pickup testing is necessary for new entrants. (2) The data are up-to-date. During a long vacation, many students lose in varying degrees their proficiency in certain skills; on the other hand some students have gained in reading achievement through their summer reading. Others may have gained in skill subjects through attendance at summer school or through special tutoring. (3) Fall testing places the emphasis on the analysis of student needs, rather than the evaluation of teaching. (4) More time is available for the administration and scoring of tests and the analysis of results. End-of-year pressures can result in tests being filed away without being used. (5) Up-to-date test results can be used as a basis for grouping students for differentiated work or special corrective instruction. Moreover, scores on survey tests serve as a starting point for the use of supplementary diagnostic methods to determine specific retraining needs. (Adams, 1964, p. 499)

Thus, in fall testing, we use the results as input data. Spring testing is more useful as accountability outcome data. We can use it for such purposes as determining the school's standing in comparison to other schools in the district, state, or nation; in making future curriculum and instructional decisions;

as research data in determining teaching effectiveness; and in helping determine which students are in need of summer instruction. All in all, the time of testing will depend, in large part, upon the uses to which the data will be put.

In addition to scheduling the time of testing, someone has to schedule the place of testing. Test administrators often neglect to ensure that pupils take the test under similar physical testing conditions. In other words, they sometimes neglect to consider the seating arrangements, the ventilation, the heat, the lighting, and other physical conditions.

There is no doubt that an individual's test score can be somewhat influenced by the physical conditions under which the test is taken. All individuals should take the test under conditions that duplicate as closely as possible the conditions that existed when the test was standardized. (One usually assumes these conditions to have been optimal.) Even though reliability formulas are typically not used to estimate the error variance due to differing physical conditions, this does not imply that the errors are nonexistent, nor does it detract from the fact that we are obligated to provide testees with optimal testing conditions.

After decisions have been made as to when and where the tests are to be given, exact schedules should be given to all professional educators in the school so that they will not plan other activities (such as field trips) for the same time. Of course this requires two-way cooperation. The test director should not schedule tests to conflict with other scheduled activities (such as the pep rally for homecoming).

PREPARING FACULTY AND STUDENTS   Each year teachers and other school personnel should have a brief in-service workshop describing various aspects of the testing program. Suggested topics for this program would include—

1.   Why the school gives standardized tests.
2.   A brief description of each test—what it measures and its intended purpose.
3.   How test results can assist the classroom teacher.
4.   How to administer standardized tests.

The first and third topics often are inadequately covered in these workshops. Yet they are important. Teachers sometimes resent the amount of instructional time lost to standardized test administration. If the teachers could see how the data were to be used, they might be less resentful of tests and the time necessary to administer them properly.

The last topic (how to administer standardized tests) is important because teachers, in all likelihood, will serve as test administrators. We feel that, for most group tests, the ordinary classroom teacher is capable of administering the test without any formal or specialized training beyond an in-service workshop. What must be stressed is that it is essential that the directions in the test manual be followed exactly (Yamamoto and Dizney, 1965). For example, if test A has three subparts and the manual states that part 1 is to be given first, then the administrator must administer part 1 first even though he feels that it would be better to administer the test in a different order. Should the test administrator deviate from the directions given, the norms provided will be misleading.

Occasionally the instructions to the students concerning guessing are vague. Because it is not always made clear, test administrators frequently are asked whether there is a penalty imposed for guessing. If the test administrator knows how the test is to be scored (that is, whether or not a guessing formula will be applied), but the directions read to the students are vague, it is necessary that any questions students raise related to the use of guessing formulas be answered without giving additional information. This could be done, for example, by the administrator's saying something like "The directions suggest that . . ." and then rereading the directions. Any direct answer providing more information than the original directions would destroy the test makers' attempt to establish a certain mental set without providing specific instructions.

Students also need to be prepared for taking standardized tests. Individuals usually perform better at any endeavor, including test taking, if they approach that experience with a positive attitude. And yet test administrators frequently fail to establish a positive mental attitude in the individuals being tested. Research on the general mental attitude and motivation of individuals and the correlation of these traits with test performance is inconclusive. However, we do know that test anxiety affects optimum performance. It is the task of the administrator to prepare the student emotionally for the test. Students should be motivated to do their best, but should not be made unduly anxious. If students are made aware of the benefits they will derive from accurate test results, this should do much toward setting the proper emotional climate.

Besides the motivating factor, there are other characteristics of students that may affect their test performance but are not related to what the test is attempting to measure. All individuals have certain personality characteristics that govern their test-taking behavior.

Students also vary in their degree of test-wiseness or in their ability to pick up cues from the format of the test item or from the format of the test. To equate for this variable, it would be best to attempt to have all students at approximately the same level of test-taking sophistication. Books such as those written by Millman and Pauk (1969) and Juola (1968) are useful in teaching students some test-taking skills. For those of you interested in reviewing more literature on the topic of test-taking skills, we refer you to Moore (1971), and Slakter, Koehler, and Hampton (1970) as good places to start.

A Typical School Testing Program

As mentioned, testing programs can and should vary, depending upon such characteristics as the size of the school, the characteristics of the student body, and the number and quality of the pupil personnel workers. Nevertheless, surveys of school testing programs show a great many similarities.

One might conceptualize a typical testing program (to be routinely administered to all students) as illustrated in Table 18–2. This typical program is not necessarily the best pattern for all schools. Other tests such as individual intelligence tests, special aptitude and achievement tests, diagnostic tests, and various types of interest, value, attitude, and personality inventories should be available for use with individual students.

The specific tests chosen depend upon the characteristics and needs of each school district, but we strongly recommend that the *same* achievement battery be used at the designated grade levels to provide some continuity. Naturally, if the content validity of a specific test used at the lower grades is inappropriate in a higher grade, use of an alternate achievement battery is warranted. Also, it is helpful if schools use scholastic aptitude tests that have been normed on the same population as the achievement battery. This will permit the user to meaningfully compare scores on the two types of tests.

Because various states have different testing requirements, programs may differ from the one given so as to follow those regulations. We have mixed feeling regarding these external state regulations. They do serve a useful purpose by forcing schools to maintain minimum testing programs. On the other hand, external regulations always mean a certain amount of rigidity, and there is the danger of being forced to administer tests that the schools will not use, either because they have no objectives relevant to those tests or because they are inadequately staffed to use the results correctly. It may also

---

TABLE 18-2 A Typical School Testing Program

GRADE	KIND OF TEST
K	Reading readiness test
2 or 3	Scholastic aptitude test
4	Achievement battery
5	Achievement battery
5	Scholastic aptitude test
6	Achievement battery
7	Achievement battery
8	Multifactor aptitude test
10	Achievement battery
9, 10, 11 or 12	Interest inventory

lead to duplication of testing. Some schools overtest. Perhaps this is due to external funds made available to the schools that follow certain prescriptions.

A more recent phenomenon related to state-imposed requirements for certain standardized tests is for states actually to administer their own testing programs. We will discuss this further under external evaluation programs. One potential result of state testing programs is that some schools may feel they no longer need internal testing programs. This is not true. Many state programs are quite limited. Even if they expand considerably in future years, they are not likely to replace the need for local schools to administer those unique tests that are necessary for local decision making. Just as there can be too much overlap between local and state programs, there also can be such a concern with overlap that valuable local testing programs are overcurtailed.

If all schools would adopt the position that a test not be given unless the results are to be used, there would be less testing. *However, what is needed in most schools is probably not less testing but better use of the tests now being given.* Nevertheless, there is overlap in many existing testing programs. For example, schools will occasionally administer both the DAT and a general intelligence test in the same grade, even though research shows fairly conclusively that the VR + NA score of the DAT correlates very well with scores from most group intelligence tests. Some aptitude and achievement tests are so highly correlated that we may well question whether both need be given. Any unnecessary duplication of testing or administration of tests whose results remain unused should be eliminated. This is a waste of valuable time and materials, and results in a negative attitude toward testing by all involved—pupils, teachers, parents, and taxpayers.

Evaluation for Individualized Instruction

Psychologists and educators have long recognized individual differences and the implications of these differences for instruction. Yet it is only recently that much of an impetus has really been given to setting up formal individualized instruction programs.

Regardless of the particular type of individualized instruction program, a teacher's job ideally involves undertaking (or assisting the pupil in undertaking) several basic tasks (Heathers, 1971):

1. Deciding on and specifying in behavioral terminology the desired objectives;

2. Assessing the extent to which the student already has mastered the objectives;

3. Assessing the student's learning characteristics (or learning styles) to determine the best media for achieving the objectives;

4. Using the assessment data mentioned in 2 and 3 above to develop a specific plan with the student;

5. Monitoring the pupil's progress, assessing his mastery of the tasks, and determining whether the student is ready to select further tasks.

As can be seen, an individualized program demands considerable evaluative skills on the part of a teacher. Determining and specifying objectives, measuring present student inputs (including both levels of achievement on the objectives and data on learning styles), and continually monitoring the progress of each of 25 to 40 pupils in order to guide the subsequent learning tasks are demanding jobs. The fact that evaluation is so necessary and yet so demanding for a truly individualized instruction program accounts for the attention given to it in many recently developed programs.

Although most individualized instruction programs are still at a developmental stage, some are quite thoroughly developed and their testing procedures are well standardized and, in some cases, commercially available (e.g., Individually Prescribed Instruction, Project PLAN). To give you a better understanding of the amount of evaluation necessary in individualized programs, we will discuss briefly the evaluation portion of the Individually Prescribed Instruction Program (IPI).

The pupil evaluation in IPI involves four types of instruments: placement tests, pretests, curriculum-embedded tests, and posttests.

Placement tests are administered at the beginning of the school year and provide a general profile of pupil performance over many units of work. These placement tests have been constructed for each level of the curriculum, and would be similar to general standardized achievement tests except that they are suited to the particular objectives of the IPI curriculum. Interpretation is criterion- rather than norm-referenced. A pupil is considered to have achieved proficiency on any unit in which he scores 80 percent or better. This criterion level is admitted to be arbitrary (Lindvall & Cox, 1970, p. 17) and serves only as a guideline for a teacher's decision.

The *pretests* are an extension of the placement tests for each specific unit in the curriculum. The items on a unit pretest measure achievement on the knowledge or skill in that unit. There are more items per skill on the pretests than on the placement tests, and therefore they can be more *diagnostic* in determining pupil strengths and weaknesses. If the pupil achieves proficiency (85 percent or above) in *every skill* on the pretest, he is given the pretest for the next unit. If not, he is assigned work in those skills where he scored below 85 percent. Thus, a student may be asked to study only one or two skills within a unit.

These pretests indicate only where a pupil is deficient, not which instructional procedures would be best. Ideally, other data such as measures of general scholastic aptitude, reading level, interests, and learning styles would help determine which method would be utilized in the instructional process. The IPI program has not yet developed very far along these lines.

A *curriculum-embedded test* (CET) is composed of two parts. The first is a short test, used in monitoring the pupil's progress toward a particular objective. The second part of the CET measures the student's performance on the very next objective. In a sense, it is a very short pretest designed to help assess the transfer and generalizability of skill from one objective to another.

Unit posttests are also given to monitor pupil progress. These posttests are usually alternate forms of the pretests and help to determine whether the student is ready for the next unit of work. The criterion for proficiency is the same as on the pretests—85 percent or better on each skill.

Concluding Statement

Individualized instruction is increasing in American education. Although there is considerable variation in programs designed for this purpose, they all demand that increased attention be paid to the evaluation aspects. All programs should require extensive pretesting to determine the entry behavior of an individual, both with respect to subject-matter achievement and styles of learning. There should be frequent testing or monitoring of a pupil's progress while in a program, and a posttest to determine final achievement. In most cases the achievement tests are criterion-referenced, since in individualized instruction the intent is to compare a pupil's level of achievement to a specified set of objectives, *not* to a norm group. Data gathered on styles of learning may well be norm referenced. Most programs place great emphasis on detailed objectives and frequent feedback to students regarding their progress. Computer facilities are often used to assist in collecting, analyzing, storing, and disseminating test information. Usually, decision rules are established to assist in using the test data.

Many of the evaluative techniques *needed* for individualized instruction are also *useful* in group instruction. Objectives should be specified, there should be frequent monitoring and feedback regarding pupils' progress, a posttest should be given, and computers could be used to assist in instruction, testing, and record keeping. Pretesting would also be useful in group instruction for grouping purposes. Usually, however, in group instruction we would want to norm-reference the results of the posttests, although (as we pointed out in Chapter 3) every norm-referenced test score is also related to objectives.

EXTERNAL TESTING PROGRAMS

By *external testing programs* we mean those that are administered under the control of agencies other than the school. These programs often are administered in the school, by school personnel, but the school is not officially in charge. We will discuss three such types of programs: college selection and placement programs, the National Assessment of Educational Progress, and state assessment programs.

College Selection and Placement Programs

Before discussing the specifics of two college testing programs, let us discuss briefly the general concept of using tests for college selection and placement. Many colleges have limited resources and cannot admit everyone who applies. In general, college admission officers have felt that their job was to admit those who have the greatest probability of success. The criterion for judging success has typically been grades in college. It has been shown time and time again that high school grades are the best single predictor of college grades, that scholastic aptitude tests are the second best predictors, and that the two predictors combined in a multiple regression equation give a significantly better prediction than either one alone. The average correlation between high school performance and first year college grades is around .50 and .55. When scholastic aptitude tests are added as a predictor, the multiple correlation is raised from .05 to .10 points (Astin, 1971; Hills, 1964). Research suggests that biographical data, interviews, references, personality variables, and work samples have seldom added any practical precision to the prediction process (Hills, 1971, p. 694). In summary, research clearly shows that if one wishes to admit students on the basis of predicted success in college, scholastic aptitude tests are useful.

Within the past decade there have been some severe critics of college admission procedures. Some of these critics feel that it is the right of every high school graduate to attend regardless of his chances of success. They argue for an open admissions policy. The desirability of this policy is debated, but much of the debate is purely academic, since some colleges simply do not have the money to admit all who wish to attempt college and others have routinely admitted all high school graduates. Other critics argue for admissions decisions based on a quota system. In either case, testing for college entrance would still be useful. Under an open admissions policy one would need tests to assist in placement decisions (and, of course, the facilities to adapt treatments to student needs). (In the absence of open admission policies, placement decisions need to be made in addition to selection decisions.) Under a quota system, one would still probably want to select, within each subgroup, those who are most likely to succeed. Thus selection tests are useful. Existing aptitude tests predict about as well within one subgroup as another (see the section in Chapter 19 on fairness of tests to minority groups for a fuller discussion of this point).

The two major organizations in this country that provide college selection and placement programs are the College Entrance Examination Board

(CEEB) and the American College Testing Program (ACT). About one-third of each year's crop of high school seniors takes the CEEB Scholastic Aptitude Test (SAT) and about one-third takes the ACT test. These two tests are not taken by exactly the same third, but many students do take both batteries. The reason for a student's taking both tests is that different colleges have different requirements, so unless a student knows for sure what college he will be attending, he ends up being forced to take more than one test. There has been some concern from school personnel (Joint Committee on Testing, 1962) about the overlap and the amount of student time and money these tests consume. The SAT and ACT tests do overlap somewhat, and many persons have wondered whether the tests could not be equated statistically so that only one of these tests need be taken and the score on it converted into equivalent scores on the other test. The problems of equating tests have been discussed considerably in the literature (Angoff, 1964; Lindquist, 1964), and the consensus of the psychometric experts is that such tests cannot be equated completely because they measure, in part, different constructs. Nevertheless, transformation tables have been built allowing conversions of scores on one test to the other (for example, Astin, 1971). Since the two tests are highly correlated, and since tests are never used as the sole criterion, it seems that some flexibility by colleges regarding which test was taken is justifiable.

College Entrance Examination Board

The College Entrance Examination Board (CEEB) is "an association of schools and colleges that concerns itself primarily with the movement of students into college. The chief purpose of the College Board is to increase access to that movement and to make it more equitable and efficient" (*Report of the Commission on Tests*, 1970, p. 11). The operational phases of the CEEB are conducted by Educational Testing Service (ETS). Although the CEEB's services are not restricted to college entrance examinations, it is best known for three such exams: The Preliminary Scholastic Aptitude Test (PSAT), the Scholastic Aptitude Test (SAT), and a series of Achievement Tests.

The PSAT is basically a shortened (1 hour and 40 minutes) version of the SAT. Until 1971 it was given to juniors primarily as a guidance instrument to aid the students. Now it has replaced the National Merit Scholarship Qualifying Test (NMSQT) and is referred to as the PSAT/NMSQT. The PSAT/NMSQT reports two scores, verbal and mathematical. The scores range from 20 to 80.

The SAT is a 3-hour objective test. It is considered a test of ability, not of factual knowledge. Verbal, mathematics, and English scores are provided. In addition, separate scores on the reading comprehension and vocabulary subtests of the verbal test are reported. Scores range from 200 to 800.

The CEEB Achievement Tests are a series of 1-hour tests. These tests are in a variety of subject-matter areas such as American history and social studies, biology, chemistry, physics, English composition, two levels of mathematics, and several foreign languages. Like the SAT, scores range from 200 to 800.

Many colleges require that applicants take the SAT and three of the achievement tests. Some colleges request specific achievement tests; others allow prospective students to choose among them.

Besides the admission tests already mentioned, the CEEB offers many other services. One such service is the Advanced Placement Program (APP). The APP is based on the belief that many students can complete college-level courses while still in high school. The program provides outlines of college-level courses and administers and grades 3-hour exams based on these courses. As of 1977 the APP offered exams in 13 subject-matter areas. College policies vary widely on the awarding of credit for passing grades. Some give credit, some give advanced placement but not credit for the basic course, and a few give neither placement nor credit.

Another service is the College Level Examination Program (CLEP). CLEP is a program that allows colleges to grant credit by examination, and nearly 1800 colleges use this service. The CLEP exams are of three types: General Examinations, which measure achievement in English composition, mathematics, natural sciences, humanities, and social sciences–history; Subject Examinations in 44 (at present) undergraduate subjects; and Brief Tests, which are shorter versions of the subject exams and are used not to give individuals credit but to evaluate groups of students.

Other services that CEEB provides are the Comparative Guidance and Placement Program, the College Scholarship Service, the Student Descriptive Questionnaire, and the College Locater Service. Some of these services have been added as a response to recommendations from the *Report of the Commission on Tests* (1970). This Commission, after reviewing criticism of current tests and their use, concluded that the CEEB should broaden its scope. The Commission felt that the three functions the CEEB should serve were distributive, educative, and credentialing functions. We are gratified to see the CEEB respond so positively to the recommendations.

ACT Assessment Program

The American College Testing Program (ACT) is an independent, non-profit corporation. The ACT Assessment Program, previously called the ACT Test Battery, is the major service of ACT. The main purposes of the Assessment Program (1973, p. 1) are to—

- Help students present themselves as persons with special patterns of educational abilities and needs

- provide estimates of a student's academic and out-of-class abilities

- provide interest inventory results to help students select college majors

- provide colleges with student admissions/enrollment data

- provide colleges with information about students' high school records

- provide students with information about their college choices

- provide dependable and comparable information for precollege counseling in high schools and for on-campus educational guidance

- provide information useful in granting scholarships, loans, and other kinds of financial assistance

- help colleges place freshmen in appropriate class sections in introductory courses in English, mathematics, social studies, and natural sciences

- help colleges identify students who would profit from special programs such as honors, remedial, and independent study

- help colleges estimate whether a student should be considered for advanced placement and further examination

- help colleges examine and improve their educational programs

The ACT Assessment instrument consists of four tests, a Student Profile Section, and an Interest Inventory. The tests—in English, mathematics, social studies, and natural sciences—are designed to "assess general educational development and the ability to perform college-level work" (American College Testing Program, 1973, p. 1). Scores range from 1 to 36, with 20 being the median score of college-bound, first-semester high school seniors. (Standard deviations range from 5 to 7.) The Student Profile Section asks for the information that a college typically requests on its application form, such as high school grades, vocational choice, and educational major. The ACT Interest Inventory provides six scores: Social Service, Business Contact, Business Detail, Technical, Science, and Creative Arts.

In the fall of 1976 ACT launched a new national program called the Proficiency Examination Program (PEP). This new ACT-PEP includes 47 college-level proficiency examinations in a variety of subjects. The tests are designed to certify a student's level of knowledge in specific courses and, like the CLEP exams, may be used by colleges as a basis for awarding college credit.

In addition to the Assessment Program and the Proficiency Examination Program, ACT provides a Student Needs Analysis Service, an Educational Opportunity Service, a Career Planning Program, and the Assessment of Career Development.

Declining Admission Test Scores

From about 1962 to 1975 there was a decline in the scores of students taking both the SAT and ACT. For example, in the 1962–1963 academic year the mean score on the verbal portion of the SAT was 478 and on the mathematics portion 502. In 1974–1975 the means were 437 and 473, respectively. These are drops of 41 and 29 points, respectively. The ACT scores have shown a similar decline. There has been considerable publicity and public reaction regarding these declines. The College Board in cooperation with ETS set up a 16-member panel to assess possible causes in the decline. Speculations about the possible explanations for these declines have been many and varied, but basically fall into four broad categories: (1) the psychometric qualities of the test, (2) the nature of the population being tested, (3) the nature of secondary education, and (4) the conditions of society. At the time of this writing we cannot draw any definite conclusions about the reasons for the decline—but one result of the decline, whether warranted or not, is far more public outcry about the quality of secondary schools and a stronger "back to basics" push.

National Assessment of Educational Progress

The National Assessment of Educational Progress (NAEP) is the most extensive assessment project ever initiated in the United States. NAEP was, in part, an outgrowth of the general demand for accountability in education. The concept of a national assessment program probably began as far back as 1867 with the establishment of the USOE. One of the charges then given the commissioners was to determine the progress of education. In 1964 people such as James Allen, John Gardner, Francis Keppel, and Ralph Tyler decided that such a charge had been neglected too long, and through aid from the Carnegie Corporation they originated what has since become known as the NAEP.

The basic purpose of the NAEP is to "gather data which will help answer the question, how much good is the expenditure of so much money doing, in terms of what Americans know and can do?" (National Assessment on Educational Progress, 1969). The data collected are not amenable to providing accountability in the sense of establishing cause-and-effect relationships or attaching blame. The data give an accounting in the sense that pupil outcome data are disseminated to educators and the general public. Baseline, census-like data are made available on the attainments of young Americans on certain specified objectives, and evidence concerning progress in attaining those objectives is periodically reported.

Areas Assessed

Knowledge, skills, and attitudes were assessed in ten subject-matter areas —art, career and occupational development, citizenship, literature, mathematics, music, reading, science, social studies, and writing. Periodically these areas are reassessed and reports are written reporting any changes which have taken place between the testings. Current plans call for a combination of citizenship and social studies into one area. Art, music, and literature also will be combined into one area.

By using approximately 50 percent of the same exercises (those used the first time) the second time an area is assessed, progress can be assessed. (Roughly 50 percent of the exercises in each area are made public after the first assessment and accordingly cannot be reused.)

Except for the reading exercises, all group-administered packages are presented on tape to standardize procedures and to facilitate understanding for youngsters with poor reading ability. Some packages at each age level are individually administered.

Reporting

Reporting is by separate exercises as well as by small subsets that measure the same objectives and/or produce similar results. National p values (The proportion getting the correct answer) and group differences from the national p value are reported for each of the approximately 50 percent released as well as the 50 percent unreleased exercises. Relevant comparisons are made across the categories of age, geographic region, type of community, sex, socio-educational status, and race.[2] Periodically, highlights of the data are released via press reports, and outcome dissemination occurs at all major professional educational association meetings. Following the reassessment cycle on the same subject-matter area, data on the increase or decline in performance are reported.

Value and Future of the NAEP

The value and future of national assessment are closely intertwined. Many benefits have already come from the national assessment plan. More and more people have become aware of the need to try harder in evaluating our educational product. Many research studies of the methods of exercise administration and results of item format change have brought new knowledge to the measurement field. The inexorable relationship between objectives and valid evaluation has been re-emphasized.

Whether the potentials will be realized is another matter. Some learning will be necessary if we are to profit fully from the data. We are sure that someone somewhere will misuse the data. We are also sure that many people will use the data as guides for making sound but unpopular decisions. In both cases, someone will wish to make the data the scapegoat, which will be unfortunate.

---

[2] Complete publications on the outcomes of the assessment are available from the Superintendent of Documents, U.S. Government Printing Office, Washington, D.C.

State Assessment Programs

The demands for accountability have had considerable impact at the state level. Many states have conducted statewide testing programs for years, but they now find these programs too narrowly conceived to answer accountability questions. A 1973 survey indicated that every state in the nation was either operating some kind of assessment program or preparing to do so (*State Educational Assessment Programs*, 1973). To describe any of these programs in detail would be superfluous. Most programs are new and in a state of flux, changing almost daily. Nevertheless, it does seem worthwhile to discuss briefly some priorities, trends, and problems of these state programs. (See *State Educational Assessment Programs*, 1973, for a more thorough discussion.)

Priorities

Dyer (1970a, p. 558) suggested several priorities of statewide evaluation programs as follows (listed in order of importance):

1. The evaluation program should provide basic information for helping every student in the state assess his own progress through the educational systems of the state, so that he can become increasingly mature in understanding himself, his educational needs, and his future possibilities.
2. It should provide the teachers and administrators in every school system with basic information for assessing the effectiveness of all the principal phases of their educational programs in sufficient detail to indicate the specific steps required for continually strengthening those programs.
3. It should provide the state education authority with basic information needed for allocating state funds and professional services in a manner best calculated to equalize educational opportunities for all children in all school systems of the state.
4. It should provide research agencies at both the state and local levels with data for generating and testing hypotheses concerning the improvement of all aspects of the educational process.
5. It should provide every school system with strong incentives to experiment, under controlled conditions, with new and promising educational programs, materials, devices, and organizational arrangements.
6. It should periodically provide the state legislature and the general public with readily interpretable information concerning the progress of the state system of education as a whole and of each local system.

Dyer is appropriately concerned that taxpayer demands for accountability may result in hurried, ill-conceived efforts that may well do more harm than good.

Trends

Probably the major trend is the involvement of both professional educators and lay citizens in the development of statewide educational goals. This is a time-consuming task and complete agreement on goals will probably never be reached, but input from both groups is desirable.

A second major trend is to increase the statewide testing programs as a step toward developing broader assessment plans. Most of these programs continue to test only in the basic skill areas, but a few have increased their breadth of coverage.

A third, very recent trend is for legislators to pass bills requiring students to pass minimum competency tests as a requirement for the issuance of a high school diploma. There currently is considerable appropriate concern about whether such legislation will have positive or negative results. As Pipho (1976, p. 3) has stated:

> The future of the movement could on the one hand lead toward a general improvement of education for all students or—in a positive sense—return the schools to a screening role for society that was evident 50 years ago.

Problems

Three major problems emerging from state assessment programs are (1) confusion and conflict about goals, (2) the handling of sensitive data, and (3) the use of assessment data in allocating state funds (*State Educational Assessment Program*, 1971). The problem of goal conflict becomes of great concern if state allocation of funds is tied to pupil performance.

The problem of sensitive data is twofold: (1) gathering of data such as a student's ethnic, economic, and social backgrounds; and (2) releasing test-score information to the public. Some kinds of questions are often considered an invasion of privacy and may be found offensive by the public. The NAEP program recognized this and had lay panels check questions for offensiveness (Berdie, 1971). State assessment programs have not always been so cautious, and some programs have been criticized for containing such questions on home characteristics, even though the data were gathered anonymously. This is discouraging because accountability programs do need input on home conditions. Perhaps as the public becomes more knowledgeable with respect to the uses of such data, their concerns about invasion of privacy will decrease.

The releasing of test-score information to the public, which would allow comparisons between schools, is very threatening to school administrators. They fear the data will be misinterpreted and invidious comparisons will be made. On the other hand, it is argued by many that the public has a right to know how their schools are doing. Whichever way one feels, it probably is unrealistic to assume that statewide assessment information on school districts will be withheld.

The way to use assessment data in allocating state funds is probably the most serious problem resulting from state assessment programs. Few people would probably want to take the abstract position that better allocation decisions can be made without data on student performances than with it. But when it comes down to actually making such decisions, many differences are observed. Should school districts that have demonstrated competence be reinforced for their previous good job by receiving more money— or should they be punished by receiving less? Should school districts where children do not perform well be rewarded or punished with more or less funds? If we reward failure by allocating more money to the school districts where performance is lowest, then are we suggesting that it is folly to be successful? Should educators intentionally overspeed test administrations so that their district will look poor? These are agonizing questions. Answers will be more dependent upon one's philosophy than any empirical evidence on what is best for the country. Which one of the four different goals a person holds regarding the distribution of achievement, discussed in the first section of this chapter, will affect his preference for one allocation procedure over another.

In spite of the many problems and concerns of statewide assessment programs, there is little doubt that they are increasing both in number and scope, and that states will be using the data in their educational decision making. The proper stance of educators should not be to accept these programs uncritically as a panacea for education. They certainly are not that. Neither should educators reject the concept of state programs and engage in hand wringing over their existence. Educators must work with the public and the politicians to make the assessments as valid and helpful as possible.

SUMMARY

The following statements summarize the major points of this chapter.

1. Accountability in education means different things to different people. However, the term usually encompasses setting correct goals, evaluating whether they have been achieved and at what price, releasing this information to the public, and accepting responsibility for any results that are perceived inadequate.
2. Each participant in the educational process should be held responsible only for those educational outcomes that he can affect.
3. There is a tendency for accountability programs to focus on those objectives that are more easily measured.

4. There are differences of opinion regarding what the distribution of educational outcomes should be.

5. In general, it seems that most people advocating accountability operate as if their goal is to bring all students up to some minimum level.

6. A good accountability program would assess input variables, surrounding conditions, and the educational process as well as the output variables, and attempt to establish causal relations between the first three and the latter. This is an extremely difficult task.

7. In program evaluation one would hope to be able to make inferences about what conditions lead to certain outcomes.

8. The politics of program evaluation are a potential cause of evaluation bias.

9. Program evaluation involves evaluating goal appropriateness as well as outcome achievement.

10. In program evaluation we must be alert to the side effects or unintended outcomes.

11. Formative evaluation is the gathering of data during the time a program is being developed, for the purpose of guiding that developmental process.

12. Summative evaluation is the process of making an overall assessment or decision about the program.

13. A good school testing program should be a cooperative venture involving teachers, administrators, counselors, students, and parents.

14. Whether one should administer standardized tests in the fall or spring depends upon the uses to which the data will be put. Fall testing is more useful if one wants input data. Spring testing is more useful in providing outcome data.

15. Both faculty and students need to be prepared for the administration of standardized tests.

16. More evaluation is necessary in a program of individualized instruction than in traditional instruction procedures.

17. All individualized instruction programs require extensive pretesting to determine the entry behavior of an individual, both with respect to subject-matter achievement and styles of learning. There should be frequent testing or monitoring of a pupil's progress and a posttest to determine final achievement.

18. There is considerable empirical evidence that college selection and placement programs assist in individual and institutional decision making.

19. The College Entrance Examinations Board (CEEB) is best known for three exams: the Preliminary Scholastic Aptitude Test (PSAT), the Scholastic Aptitude Test (SAT), and a series of Achievement Tests. Both the PSAT and the SAT provide verbal and mathematical scores.

20. The CEEB also offers other services such as the Advanced Placement

Program, the College Level Examination Program, the Comparative Guidance and Placement Program, the College Scholarship Service, the Student Descriptive Questionnaire, and the College Locator Service.

21. The ACT Assessment Program consists of four tests and a student questionnaire. The four tests are in English, mathematics, social studies, and natural sciences.

22. The basic purpose of the National Assessment of Educational Progress (NAEP) is to provide data on the attainments of young Americans on certain specified objectives.

23. The demands for accountability have resulted in an increased number of state assessment programs.

24. The way to use assessment data in allocating state funds is probably the most controversial aspect of state assessment programs.

CHAPTER NINETEEN
Public Concerns about and Future Trends in Evaluation

Many topics that could be classified as issues or trends have already been discussed in this text. *Issues* would include such topics as

1. What objectives should schools hold?
2. Need they be stated in behavioral terms?
3. Should norm- or criterion-referenced tests predominate?
4. What is the definition and structure of intelligence ?
5. What is the etiology of intellectual differences?
6. How stable are intelligence test scores?
7. Do we have, or should we develop, culture-fair tests?
8. How should we mark and report pupil progress?
9. Is accountability a good concept, and if so, how should we set up accountability programs?

Current *trends* discussed have included (1) behavioral objectives (a fairly old trend); (2) criterion-referenced tests; (3) expanded report forms; (4) program evaluation; (5) state and national assessment programs; and (6) testing for individualized instruction programs.

In this final chapter we wish to discuss three public concerns about measurement and evaluation. (By public we mean all non–measurement specialists. This would include teachers, counselors, and administrators as well as the lay public.) We do not mean to suggest that the public has been unconcerned about some of the previously discussed topics. They have been concerned about some issues (for example, methods of marking), but been largely unaware of other issues. We will also briefly mention some of the more recent and predicted future trends and give some appropriate references for those who wish to read more about these topics. After studying this chapter the student should be able to—

1. Recognize several public concerns about testing.
2. Differentiate between the relevant and irrelevant aspects of these concerns.
3. Discuss the concept of "cultural fairness."
4. Understand the research findings with respect to using scholastic aptitude tests for minority students.
5. Recognize some recent and predicted future trends in evaluation.

PUBLIC CONCERNS ABOUT MEASUREMENT AND EVALUATION

With an increase in testing in schools, industry, and government, it is natural and appropriate for the public to show interest in, and concern for, this enterprise. What started as a spark of concern was fanned in the early 1960s into a burning flame by writers who criticized tests in what has come to be typical journalistic exposé fashion (Black, 1963; Gross, 1962; Hoffmann, 1962). The phrase "antitest revolt" has often been used to express public concern. The "public" here most assuredly includes some educators. The editors of the *National Elementary Principal* and *Today's Education* have recently solicited manuscripts from educators known to be hostile toward standardized testing. Most of the criticism is directed at scholastic aptitude tests but since the push for accountability some educators are also fearful that the results of standardized achievement tests will be used "against" teachers. Although the critics raise a few valid concerns, in general they also fail to understand much about the field of measurement and the result is that their criticisms are frequently invalid. As Page (1976) points out, measurement is a technical field, and one cannot understand it, let alone criticize it intelligently, without some mastery of the content. In terms of technical competence many of the critics are analogous to the "flat earthers" who attacked the heliocentric theory.

Even though the validity of the criticisms expressed in the numerous books and articles is probably inversely proportional to the public acclaim they have received, all of these criticisms have been of value—if for no other reason than for forcing psychometricians to defend themselves against the sometimes unjust criticisms. Psychometricians, of course, share legitimate concerns of the public and are attempting to improve all aspects of their profession.

The most important concerns voiced revolve around the ethics of test use and the possible dire consequences of testing.

The public asks or should ask questions such as the following:

1. Who is qualified to administer and interpret tests?
2. What kinds of tests should be given?
3. How should test results be used?
4. Who should have access to test results?
5. Are tests fair?
6. Are our children being overtested?
7. Are our children being undertested?

The answers to questions like these are not independent of each other. For example, the kinds of tests that should be given depend upon the qualifications of the user and upon the proposed uses of the tests. Since public concern encompasses so many specific yet interrelated aspects of testing, it is difficult to present the topic completely in any tightly organized fashion. Therefore we have chosen to discuss three issues that seem of most concern to the public: (1) the use (or misuse) of test scores for making decisions about individuals, (2) the invasion-of-privacy issue, and (3) the fairness of tests to minority groups. Needless to say, these issues are neither mutually exclusive nor exhaustive.

The Use (or Misuse) of Test Scores

Public concern with the correct use of test scores has focused mainly on using standardized tests. We are not suggesting by this statement that data gathered from classroom evaluation procedures cannot be misused also. They can, but in general the public is unaware or unconcerned about teacher misuse of data from nonstandardized tests. The consequences of misusing tests can be quite severe and examples are legion. Using test scores to label or categorize instead of to assist in understanding a person is one accusation mentioned very frequently. The important point is that misusing tests is prevalent. This does not lead us to the conclusion that testing is bad; rather it makes us aware that we must concentrate our energies toward the goal of educating people on the correct use of test results. Most of the problems related to test misuse bear upon the overgeneralizations made by users rather than because the tests per se are invalid. Most test constructors display integrity and professional honesty in stipulating how these tests can be used. However, an educator is not being professionally honest when he uses a test he is not qualified to use.

Many people criticize the faulty decisions made through the misuse of test information. Fewer people realize that a far more costly misuse of tests is not to use them at all. Too many critics evaluate tests against nonexistent ideal predictors (Anastasi, 1968). Even if only a few better decisions were made with the help of test information than would have been made without that information, the long-term benefits would likely outweigh the initial costs of testing.

There is no question that tests predict imperfectly. So do all other prediction procedures. Does this make the test invalid? As Flaugher (1974, p. 13) states there is considerable misunderstanding among laymen about the concept of validity. "To a layman, a test is not valid if he knows, or knows of, someone who was turned away from an opportunity on the basis of test scores, but who somehow circumvented the barriers, went on, and succeeded. Any procedure that turns away someone who would have succeeded is in these terms, invalid." Laymen seem more willing to argue against tests in general because of a *specific example* of misuse than they do, for example, against aspirins in general because of some specific misuse. As Barclay has noted, one critic stated that his article criticizing testing "was occasioned by a desultory contact with *some* child who took *some* test at *some* time in *some* place and was not rated too bright in mathematics. Nevertheless, this particular individual went to *some* college *somewhere* and *somehow* succeeded, all of which proves beyond the shadow of a doubt . . . that *all* testing in *all* places and on *all* levels is similar to the cephalic index of the phrenologist!" (Barclay, 1968, p. 4)

Probably the concern with imperfect test validity would be less if tests were not seen as gatekeepers to better education and a better way of life. Tests are frequently designed to measure differences among individuals and this information may be used to help make decisions about the allocation of limited resources or opportunities. But, as we discussed in Chapter 18, the allocation of limited resources is not always to those who score high on tests. Compensatory education programs are obvious exceptions. Who deserves limited resources and what should be done about individual differences are *policy* questions. Tests simply provide information about what differences exist. It is not appropriate to call a test *unfair* (or invalid) because data from it are used to help allocate resources in a manner that runs opposite to our personal philosophies. Whether one wished to say the test was *misused* is somewhat of a semantic issue. If one believed admission to a college that had limited enrollment should be based on predicted academic success, and if test scores increased the predictive accuracy (they do), and if the admission offices use the test scores *correctly* in a regression equation (or set of regression equations—differentiated on ethnicity, sex, or whatever other demographic variable would increase predictive efficiency) to help predict success, then we would argue that the test was not unfair nor were the test data misused in any *measurement* sense. One can debate the correctness of the philosophy to limit enrollment based on predicted success, but *that* argument is independent of and of a different order than whether the test data are useful given the philosophical stance. But the above comments are surely not to suggest that tests cannot be misused.

Correct test use involves all aspects of testing, from selection to interpretation. But we wish to stress again that if test information is used correctly, it is impossible to make (in the long run) poorer decisions by using this additional information. Thus, if the public desired accurate decision making, their concern should not be whether tests should be used, but whether tests are used properly. Users of tests have an ethical responsibility to be qualified to administer, score, and interpret tests properly. Unfortunately, there are many test users who do not assume this responsibility. A pertinent question is *who* should stipulate users' qualifications. Is it the responsibility of the test publishers to be sure unqualified users do not obtain copies of tests? Should a professional organization such as the American Psychological Association set up standards? Should states have certification requirements?[1] Should a federal agency exert control? Any suggested answer to this question would probably raise as much controversy as one that decided who should assume responsibility for our safety while we ride in automobiles. The APA does have a set of ethical standards that covers test publication and test interpretation, but they cannot police nonmembers (see *Ethical Standards of Psychologists*, 1953). There are also some test publishers, not guided solely by the profit motive, who distribute only to those users who appear qualified. Whether or not we can ever arrive at a consensus on how to control the qualifications of test users, the problem is a legitimate one. It is an ethical issue with which we must somehow deal.

Ethical issues of testing, however, go far beyond the qualifications of the user. Such questions as to whom should test scores be released and what kinds of questions do we have the right to ask are also relevant.

The Invasion-of-Privacy Issue

Assume you are a counselor in a school system working with a disturbed youngster. You believe that additional information about the youngster will

[1] Although many states have certification requirements for psychologists, this doesn't really control for access to, and potential misuse of, test data.

enable you to deal with him more effectively. Do you have the right to ask him to answer "true" or "false" to such questions[2] as the following?

1. I have never been in trouble because of my sex behavior.
2. I have never indulged in any unusual sex practices.
3. I believe there is a Devil and a Hell in afterlife.
4. I have had some very unusual religious experiences.
5. There is something wrong with my sex organs.

These are examples of some of the more personal questions taken from the Minnesota Multiphasic Personality Inventory (MMPI). Criticism has been forthcoming from many people who are concerned that questions such as these are an invasion of privacy. Why should we tell anyone whether or not we have ever indulged in any unusual sex practices? Some people have even suggested that the very asking of such questions is harmful to the person taking the test. Irate citizens have been known to burn answer sheets from tests containing such questions (Nettler, 1959). Under the spur of a Congressional investigation, the Peace Corps and the United States Civil Service Commission have eliminated many such questions. The Peace Corps also decided to give trainees the right to refuse to take the MMPI and now requires destruction of the answer sheets and of any written evaluation of test scores.

Suppose you wish to gather some data regarding a pupil's home background. Can you ask questions such as the following?

1. How much education does your father have?
2. What does your father do for a living?
3. Do you have a set of encyclopedias at home?

Questions such as these have often been asked in an attempt to gain some information about an individual's socioeconomic status. Any accountability program that wishes to take into account such variables as home conditions needs to gather such data. But, again, many people object to such questions as being an invasion of privacy.

What really is the invasion-of-privacy issue? What is the fuss all about? It, of course, varies from person to person. Some people actually find it distasteful and degrading to read personal questions. They certainly would not want their daughters to read such "dirty" questions! The knowledge that some people feel this way suggests something to us about their psychological makeup. Their objections, however, are probably not valid objections to the asking of such questions. There is no known evidence to suggest that the

[2] From the Minnesota Multiphasic Personality Inventory. Reproduced by permission. Copyright 1943, renewed 1970 by the University of Minnesota. Published by the Psychological Corporation, New York, N.Y. All rights reserved.

reading of such questions makes a person more neurotic, more psychotic, or less moral.

Other people object on different grounds. Some are concerned not about having to read or answer such questions, but rather about how the answers will be used. This gets us into such problems as scorers' qualifications, their ethics, and storage of test information. What if the answer sheets to such tests as the MMPI are kept and filed? Who, then, will have access to these files? An ethical and knowledgeable user would never reveal to a third party an answer to a specific question. Seldom would he even interpret such an answer to the client himself. He would, instead, look at the patterns of responses as recorded on the profile sheet. But what about others who may have (or at some later date obtain) access to the files? Could not, for example, a lot of political hay be made by reporting a candidate's answers to the questions cited above! The merits of permanently storing data are that (1) we will have more information available to help make decisions about individual people, and (2) we will be able to improve our tests and learn more about people in general by doing follow-up research. The dangers center around who does (or may in the future) have access to the stored information. Will clerks have access to the data? Can it be subpoenaed? The public concern about what information is kept on file and who has access to it are very real and important concerns, but these should be recognized as issues separate from the question of whether we have a right originally to ask personal questions.

Beside the matter of confidentially, there is the issue of freedom versus coercion in responding to items. Some students may object to answering some questions, but feel they must comply because school authorities ask them to do so. Further, school authorities may never even tell students why the data are being gathered or how it will be used. Data are often gathered from individuals in early elementary school, who may not be aware of the importance of the data. The American Psychological Association's (1970, p. 266) position statement on psychological assessment and public policy asserts that—

> The right of an individual to decline to be assessed or to refuse to answer questions he considers improper or impertinent has never been and should not be questioned. This right should be pointed out to the examinee in the context of information about the confidentiality of the results.

School people, in general, have not been very alert to the kinds of questions or type of wording that the public will find offensive. Investigations such as those conducted by NAEP (Berdie, 1971) should alert educators to potential problem areas. Questions on such topics as family finances, relationships between children and parents, religion, minority groups, and sexual practices are likely to be considered either offensive or an invasion of privacy. One state even prohibited NAEP from asking a cognitive question regarding the menstrual cycle.

Although this is primarily a book for educators, let us move briefly from the educational setting to the government and private employment setting. In making a personnel decision about a person, does an employer have a right to pry into his personality? If an employer is going to invest time and money in training a person, won't he want a stable person with good work habits who can get along with his fellow workers?

Most psychologists would argue yes. As Hathaway (1964) pointed out, once you decide, for example, that a Peace Corps worker should not be maladjusted, then how will you find this out? If, for reasons of privacy, investigation of personal items is prevented, is not this analogous to the prudery that would not permit medical doctors to examine the body? It is our contention that this analogy holds, and our conclusion is that qualified psychologists should have the right to ask personal questions if the questions are pertinent. (We should not have to strip before the receptionist, only before the medical doctor, and we would object to having a medical doctor examine our body if the examination were irrelevant.) The problem is that laymen have a hard time judging the relevancy of what a professional does. How do we know whether or not it is relevant for a medical doctor to check our blood pressure and perform a urinalysis? How do we know whether or not it is relevant for a psychologist to ask us if we love our mother? If tests are not relevant, they are invasions of privacy. If they are relevant, they are not invasions of privacy.

Commentators on the invasion-of-privacy topic should stick to the important issues, that is, the relevancy of the information gathered, qualifications of the gatherer, immediate use to which information is put, and what is done about the storage of such information. They would, thus, find that they share the same concerns as professional psychologists. Some people carry their worries about invasion of privacy to the extreme. If we really were never allowed to find out anything about another person, then we would not even be allowed to give classroom achievement tests to find out how much the student has learned! (See Supplement, *Journal of Educational Measurement*, 1967, for a series of position papers on the invasion-of-privacy issue.)

Fairness of Tests to Minority Groups

We have discussed two topics related to this section in Chapter 14: the etiology of intellectual differences and culture-fair tests. This section is more directed to the concerns of the fair use of tests with minorities. It would be nice to believe that every logically thinking person in the United States is against unfairness of any sort. The question to be discussed is certainly not whether we should be fair but rather what is meant by fairness? What practices are and are not fair? Do tests discriminate against the disadvantaged? What is and is not discrimination? According to Webster (1965) "to discriminate" can be defined as either (1) "to make a distinction; to use good judgment," or (2) "to make a difference in treatment or favor on a basis other than individual merit."

Tests can and do help us make distinctions. Tests are often used to identify differences within and among individuals and within and among groups or classes of people. That is a major purpose of testing. If there were no differences in test scores (that is, if tests did not discriminate), they would be worthless.

Is it possible for tests to discriminate in an unfair sense (that is, using the second definition of discrimination)? Suppose that a company uses a selection tests on which it can be shown that blacks typically do less well than whites. Is the test unfair for revealing this difference? Many would say so. The test is certainly discriminating under the first definition, but is it unfair discrimination? To be sure, we could use test results to help us unfairly discriminate. For example, we could require that blacks receive higher scores in order to be hired (or vice versa, as some advocate). This would be discrimination of the second type. This, however, would be an example of unfair use of test results rather than the use of an unfair test.

Even if we do set up this kind of differential standard, is the test still unfair just because blacks, on the average, do poorer? This depends on the degree to which the test is relevant (or valid) for selecting prospective employees. If, indeed, there is a reasonable correlation between job success and test scores, it would seem to many that selection on the basis of test scores is a wise decision and not unfair, even though members of some subcultures do better than members of other subcultures.

If, however, a test does tend to discriminate (differentiate) between races or other subcultures, and if the differential scores are not related to what we are predicting (such as on-the-job success), then the test is unfair. This could occur for many reasons. For example, the test may demand knowledge that is dependent upon having been raised in a certain cultural environment, whereas the criterion may not depend upon this knowledge. Or, perhaps some subgroups do not do so well on tests, not because they do not know the material, but because they lack test-taking skills. This lack of test-taking skills may well not affect performance on the criterion at all. Thus, it can be seen that the question of test fairness is really one of test validity. A test may differentiate blacks from whites and be fair (valid) for some purposes and not for others. *Differentiation alone is not what makes a test unfair.*

Even a distinction based on validity is an oversimplification in determining whether a test is fair or unfair. Cleary offered the following, more precise, definition:

A test is biased for members of a subgroup of the population if, in the prediction of a criterion for which the test was designed, consistent nonzero errors of prediction are made for members of the subgroup. In other words, the test is biased if the criterion score predicted from the common regression line is consistently too high or too low for members of the subgroup. With this definition of bias, there may be a connotation of "unfair," particularly if the use of the test produces a prediction that is too low. (Cleary, 1968, p. 115)

Even this precise definition is an incomplete guideline. Hunter and Schmidt (1976) define three mutually incompatible ethical positions in regard to the fair and unbiased use of tests and present five *statistical* definitions of test bias and show how they are related to the three ethical positions. The three ethical positions are (1) unqualified individualism, (2) qualified individualism and (3) quotas. The *unqualified individualism* position in employment would be to give the job to the *person* best qualified to serve. Under this position it would be *un*ethical not to use whatever information increases the predictive validity of performance even if such information is sex or ethnic group membership. The *unqualified individualist* interprets "discriminate" to mean *treat unfairly,* and to refuse to recognize a difference between groups would result in *unfair* treatment. The *qualified individualist* believes it is *unethical* to use information about race, sex, and so on, even if it were scientifically valid to do so. "The qualified individualist interprets the word discriminate to mean *treat differently*" (p. 1054). The quota position is that the ethical position is to give every well-defined group (e.g., black, white; male, female; Protestant, Catholic, Jew) its "fair share" of desirable positions. "The person who endorses quotas interprets *discriminate* to mean *select a higher proportion of persons from one group than from the other group*" (Hunter & Schmidt, 1976, p. 1054).

The Cleary definition given above would be an example of unqualified individualism, and it turns out that under her definition unreliable tests are biased against whites and in favor of blacks. Thorndike (1971a) and Darlington (1971) have argued for different approaches, which Hunter and Schmidt show to be forms of quota setting. Darlington suggested that the term "cultural fairness" be replaced with the term "cultural optimality," which would include a subjective policy-level decision on the relative importance of two goals: maximizing test validity and minimizing test discrimination.

The whole Spring 1976 issue of the *Journal of Educational Measurement* is devoted to the topic of bias in selection. Peterson and Novick (1976) in a detailed evaluation of the existing models for culture-fair selection ultimately conclude that "the concepts of culture fairness and group parity are neither useful nor tenable . . . The problem, we think, should be reconceptualized as a problem in maximizing expected utility." Since this is a continuing debate, let us leave the models and discuss the uses in a more general fashion in employment and educational decisions.

In Employment

The whole issue of the cultural fairness of tests has been raised both with respect to educational decisions and employment decisions. We will discuss first the employment aspect of cultural fairness. The Supreme Court (*Gripps* v. *Duke Power Co.*, 1971) ruled that an employer is prohibited "from requiring a high school education or passing a standardized intelligence test as a condition of employment in or transfer to jobs when (a) neither standard is shown to be significantly related to successful job performance, (b) both requirements operate to disqualify Negroes at a substantially higher rate than white applicants, and (c) the jobs in question formerly have been filled only by white employees as part of a longstanding practice of giving preference to whites."

The ruling went on to state that—

> the Act proscribes not only overt discrimination but also practices that are fair in form, but discriminatory in operation. . . . If an employment practice which operates to exclude Negroes cannot be shown to be related to job performance, the practice is prohibited.
>
> . . . Nothing in the Act precludes the use of testing or measuring procedures; obviously they are useful. What Congress has forbidden is giving these devices and mechanisms controlling force unless they are demonstrably a reasonable measure of job performance. Congress has not commanded that the less qualified be preferred over the better qualified simply because of minority origins. Far from disparaging job qualifications as such, Congress has made such qualifications the controlling factor, so that race, religion, nationality, and sex become irrelevant. What Congress has commanded is that any tests used must measure the person for the job and not the person in the abstract.

The American Psychological Association praised this decision. Little, the APA executive officer, stated that "The court's decision is fully consistent with the APA's ethical standards which prohibit the misuse or misinterpretation of test results by psychologists" (*APA Monitor*, 1971).

While there is no doubt that the quotes given above are reasonable, the Court ruling does present some problems. If "significantly related" is interpreted as statistical significance, then what should be the α level? If it means practical significance, how is this to be determined? The *Federal Register* (1970) contained a chapter on Equal Employment, with a part prescribing guidelines on employee-selection procedures. These guidelines were useful, but were just what the heading implies—guidelines. They did not spell out exact requirements. In 1973, in an attempt to improve the guidelines and the coordination across federal agencies, the Equal Employment Opportunity Coordinating Council (EEOCC) (consisting of representatives of the Equal Employment Opportunity Commission, the U.S. Department of

Justice, the U.S. Civil Service Commission, the U.S. Department of Labor, and the U.S. Commission on Civil Rights) attempted to draw up a uniform set of guidelines. After four years of effort the Departments of Justice and Labor and the Civil Service Commission joined in issuing the Federal Executive Agency Guidelines on Employee Selection Procedures (Federal Executive Agency, 1976). The new guidelines better represent professionally accepted standards for determining validity than the original EEOC guidelines. But, as with its predecessor, the new guidelines are just guidelines. It is only through repeated, time-consuming, and costly court tests that employers will fully understand what is expected of them in terms of validity evidence. Some courts will probably be reasonable with respect to validity evidence; others, unreasonable. And how readers of this book define reasonable evidence will vary, depending upon their perceptions of the whole issue.

The problem of fair employment is made even more complicated by the fact that a test may predict success in job *training* but not in job performance. And the lack of relationship between test scores and job performance may be due to inadequate criterion measures. Nevertheless, the Supreme Court ruling should reduce the misuse of tests. As the ruling makes clear, those best qualified to do a job should be selected, regardless of race, religion, nationality, or sex.

In Education

With respect to cultural fairness of tests in educational uses, the major concern seems to be in using tests as screening devices. When achievement tests are used as measures of *outcomes* of education, few people question their applicability to minority groups. In fact, results on achievement tests have been used as evidence that schools are doing a poor job of educating minority children. But when either achievement or aptitude tests are used as predictors of future success (and therefore as screening devices), the applicability of the tests is often questioned.

As mentioned in Chapter 14, a few well-meaning psychologists have sought to devise culture-fair intelligence tests. Such tests have attempted to ask only those items that do not differentiate among groups coming from different cultures. The advocates of such procedures argue that this gives them a test that is independent of environmental influences and as close as possible is a measure of innate ability. In general, these tests have not been well accepted by most psychologists. It is very doubtful whether we could ever devise a paper-and-pencil test to measure innate ability (whatever that is). Certainly, scores on present tests are influenced by environmental factors. There is no debate about that. But, does that make them unfair? Clifford, a black educator, said:

To disparage testing programs for revealing the inequities which still exist in the social, the economic, the educational, and the cultural domains of American life is as erroneous as it would be for residents of Bismarck, North Dakota, to condemn the use of thermometers as biased, when, as this is being written, the temperature of Bismarck is $-11°F$ and in Miami, Florida it is $83°$ (Clifford & Fishman, 1963, p. 27).

Ausubel stated the case as follows:

> The intelligence test . . . proposes to measure functional capacity rather than to account for it. If the culturally deprived child scores low on an intelligence test because of the inadequacy of his environment, it is not the test which is unfair but the social order which permits him to develop under such conditions.
>
> By the same token we would not say that the tuberculin test is unfair or invalid (a) because the lower-class child really does not have any greater genic susceptibility to tuberculosis but happens to live in an environment that predisposes him to this disease, and (b) because it measures exposure to a particular disease which happens to be related to lower social class status rather than to one which is not so related. In terms of operational functional capacity, an intelligence test is no less fair or valid because a low score is reflective of cultural deprivation than because it is reflective of low genic endowment. Furthermore, to argue that test scores are valid is not to claim that they are necessarily immutable irrespective of future environmental conditions, or to defend those aspects of the social system that give rise to the culturally deprived environment (Ausubel, 1963).

It should be pointed out that both Clifford's and Ausubel's statements are based on the assumption that whoever interprets the intelligence-test scores will realize that they are *not* direct measures of genetic capacity and that they are influenced by environmental conditions. Although the test is not unfair, it would be an unfair use of a test score to interpret it as irrefutable evidence of only genetic capacity.

Most psychologists take the position that "culture-fair" tests would be less useful (valid) predictors of educational achievement than present aptitude and achievement tests. If a person's previous environment is related to school success, then using a test that masks out environmental differences will likely result in a loss of some predictive power.

Actually, considerable research has been done on the predictability (or fairness) of scholastic aptitude tests for minority students. The studies do not show that tests are biased (using Cleary's definition given earlier) against students with culturally disadvantaged backgrounds (Cleary, 1968; Hills, 1964; Hills & Gladney, 1966; Hills, Klock, & Lewis, 1963; Kallingal, 1971; Munday, 1965; Pfeifer & Sedlacek, 1971; Stanley & Porter, 1967; Temp, 1971). In fact, several studies suggest that the test scores overpredict the performance of blacks in college (Cleary, 1968; Kallingal, 1971; Pfeifer & Sedlacek, 1971; Temp, 1971). Findley and Bryan (1971) found much the same thing in reviewing the research on different tests used in the elementary grades. This overprediction would be a test bias in one sense of the word, but certainly not unfair to the minority groups. Thomas and Stanley (1969) clearly showed that scholastic aptitude tests are better than high school grades for predicting college grades of black students. This is the reverse of findings for white students. Stanley (1971a), in a thorough review of predicting college success of the educationally disadvantaged, urged a reversal of the current trend of waiving test scores in admitting disadvantaged applicants. He feels that the more disadvantaged an applicant, the more objective information one needs about him.

Using Moderator Variables

The moderator approach to studying validity is one that has considerable merit in ameliorating the problems associated with potential test bias. Using this approach, separate validities may be obtained for different subgroups (for example, black and white) in the same situation. This is done by using separate correlation coefficients (and regression equations) for the two groups. Thus, each person is compared with others within his own subgroup. Some of the studies using the moderator variable approach show an increase in predictive power (Kallingal, 1971; Kirkpatrick et al., 1968; Pfeifer & Sedlacek, 1971). Of course one would *not* use a moderator approach under the *qualified individualist* ethical position mentioned earlier.

Summary

In summary, tests should not be considered unfair just because they discriminate. That is what tests are supposed to do. Tests, however, can be invalid and therefore unfair, or people can give unfair interpretations of the results (whether the tests were valid or invalid).

Although there would be important exceptions that should be investigated, the effect of using objective measures such as test data is to make social class barriers more permeable.

Tests cannot see whether a youngster is black or white, rich or poor. Making decisions on the basis of objective measures is really more fair than making them on the affective feelings (positive or negative) we have toward different subcultures.

Conclusion on Public Concern about Evaluation

It is good that people feel free to voice their concerns. There are many legitimate concerns about evaluation. Many of the concerns, however, have not been relevant. If there are problems associated with test accuracy (there are), and if the misuse of tests has sometimes led to unfortunate consequences (it has), the appropriate procedures is to *correct the problems, not to stop testing*. We maintain that in many instances the issues of concern to the public such as invasion of privacy and unfair tests are problems associated with test use rather than with the psychometric properties of the tests. Psychologists are in part to blame for this misuse. They have an obligation to inform the public as to how tests should be used and as to how they are being used. However, much of the negative affect of the public toward tests is precisely because tests are used as they should be, to help make decisions. These decisions are not always pleasant to the people involved. Since tests help make decisions, they have been attacked. Unfortunately, there are some individuals who assume that by doing away with tests we could *avoid making decisions*. That is not the case. Decisions must be made! Information helps us make decisions. Tests provide information. As professionals we must ensure that valid tests are used for making appropriate decisions. We must not, and cannot, be intimidated by irresponsible critics of the testing movement.

FUTURE TRENDS IN EVALUATION

We have discussed such trends as program evaluation, state and national assessment programs, criterion-referenced tests, testing for individualized instruction programs, expanded reporting forms, and pass-fail grading. Future trends are harder to discuss. It is always harder to predict. Even with tests carefully designed to help predict specific future behavior, we often cannot make accurate predictions. Yet the authors of this text—without the aid of specific test results!—are audacious enough to make some tentative predictions concerning educational testing.

Content of Standardized Achievement Tests

The rapid expansion of knowledge in subject-matter areas and improved instructional methods have resulted in considerable curricular revisions. In the past, the content of standardized achievement tests has lagged behind curricular change. Although some published tests have provided impetus for curricular change (this is not necessarily bad, because test authors are generally subject-matter experts), in general the test-publishing industry has followed rather than led in this endeavor. We noted in Chapter 15 that standardized achievement tests are moving away from questions based on factual recall and turning toward those designed to measure understanding and application. This trend will continue as tests are revised in accordance with curricular changes. In spite of real efforts to update tests, we feel a realistic prediction is that test content will continue to lag behind curricular content.

This is unavoidable if the curriculum is to determine test content, rather than vice versa. It takes a considerable length of time to publish a good test, and the curriculum is, and should be, dynamic rather than static.

Within the past few years commercial test publishers and other firms have begun to produce standardized achievement tests that can be both norm- and criterion-referenced. Some have produced survey tests that are to be followed by prescriptive diagnostic tests. These kinds of tests are useful in formative evaluation. We expect to see the trend to criterion-referenced test interpretation continuing, but hopefully the limitations as well as the strengths of such interpretations will be understood in the future and we can get past the "fad" stage educators seem always to go through. We also expect to see an increase in the use of test publishing firms to serve as contractors to school systems—building achievement tests to fit the specific objectives of a particular school.

Computer-Aided Testing

Anyone who has read the technical manuals accompanying the better standardized tests realizes that computers already play a large role in the educational-testing enterprise. Computers are used in the development of tests by aiding in the processes of norming, deriving types of scores, computing item analyses, estimating reliability and validity, and in a host of other tasks. Computers are also used in the process of scoring and the reporting of results. For example, the Psychological Corporation scoring service will report the following information to each school that has taken the Stanford Achievement Tests.

1. An *individual record* for each pupil showing the number right, number possible, scaled score, local and/or national percentile rank, grade equivalent, and national stanine.

2. A *class summary*, which reports the mean number right, mean scaled score, mean grade equivalent, and the number and percent of pupils in each national stanine.

3. A *building summary*, reporting the above information *plus* a school building stanine.

4. A distributions and administrators' report for each building and the total district. This shows the total distribution of scores in terms of grade equivalents or scaled scores, national percentile points (10th, 25th, 50th, 75th, 90th) in terms of grade equivalents, mean score, standard deviations, and stanine summary. It also graphically displays a quartile profile showing the national percentile rank for the local 25th, 50th, and 75th percentiles.

5. A total item analysis for each item. This report groups an item under its corresponding instructional objective; gives the number and percent right

for the class, school, and system; the percent right in the national sample; and how each student responded.

6. Several other reports are also available—for example, a stanine bivariate distribution showing the proportions of students working at, above, or below where expected based on the Otis-Lennon (or Stanford Total Auditory).

Although this is an incomplete list of available reports, it should serve to illustrate the considerable use of computers by testing companies in reporting useful information to the schools.

Perhaps most important is the expected increase in the use of computers within the school itself. An exciting area of research that may well have a significant and lasting impact is in using computers to administer tests (Green, 1970; Lord, 1970b). This automated approach not only would free professional staff time for other duties, but also would eliminate administrator variability as a source of error in test scores, thus improving test reliability.

Use of computer administration will also facilitate test selection and the use of sequential testing. Computers could easily be programmed to present items of appropriate difficulty for an individual, as judged by that individual's responses to previous items, thus providing "tailor-made," "flexilevel," "adaptive," or "response-contingent" tests. A tailored test is typically built so that if an examinee answers an item correctly, he is administered the next hardest unanswered item (as judged by a difficulty index for group data). If an examinee misses an item, he is then administered an easier item, usually the most difficult of all the unanswered items that are easier than the one just missed. Lord (1970b, 1971b) found that for summative evaluation, tailored tests were no better than a conventional test for those individuals near the middle of the ability range for which the test is designed. However, for high- or low-scoring subjects, the tailored test is considerably more efficient. Green (1970) found that for tests used in certain instructional decision-making situations (formative evaluation), tailor-made tests are more efficient. See Weiss (1976) and Wood (1973) for thorough reviews of this topic.

The use of computers in the school should facilitate teaching-testing cooperation. The immediate storage, analysis, and printout of a student's examination results would help the teacher plan instructional processes. Using computer facilities in conjunction with expanded item banks (see Popham, 1970a) will allow teachers to do more instructional testing without taking an inordinate amount of their time in preparing, administering, and scoring tests.

Using computers to report and interpret test scores to pupils is also an area receiving increasing attention. Sharf (1971), for example, described a method of utilizing the computer to report the results of the Women's SVIB,

Super (1970) edited a book in computer-assisted counseling, and Chick (1970) discussed the use of computers in career information. A study by Mathews (1973), comparing a traditional test report (national and local percentiles, and grade-equivalents for the various subtests, summary scores, and a composite score) with a locally prepared computer-generated narrative report, indicated that classroom teachers rated the narrative format superior on 15 of 18 comparisons. If these findings can be substantiated by further research, we can expect an increase in computer-generated narrative reports by the major text publishers.

Affective-Domain Testing

Psychometrists vary in their opinions concerning the future of testing in the affective domain. Ebel, writing in 1963, hopefully predicted "less demand for paper and pencil tests of poorly defined personality traits such as motivation, creativity, leadership, adjustment, etc." (Ebel, 1963). Siegel, on the other hand, stated that we should "look for a relative de-emphasis of IQ testing and measurement in the cognitive area . . . we will see a heavier emphasis on tests designed to assess creativity and noncognitive factors" (Siegel, 1963).

There is no doubt that, in the past, tests of the noncognitive factors have been of poorer psychometric quality than their counterparts in the cognitive domain.

Although the authors of this text do predict increased testing in the affective domain, we are not in favor of this unless testing is done with better tests and/or unless better measures of the criterion behavior are developed. We are in agreement with Ebel that, hopefully, there will be less demand for test of *poorly defined* personality traits. However, we are optimistic concerning the possibilities of improving the tests in this area. The important task of improving the constructional definitions is not solely or even primarily the job of psychometricians. It is the task of all psychologists. Whether or not tests of noncognitive variables will ever be really successful as selection instruments is debatable because the problem of faking will always exist to some degree.

Career Development Testing Programs

One area where we expect to see a continued increase in testing is in career development. Some of the tests in this area are probably more properly thought of as cognitive tests since they tap such areas as knowledge of occupations. Other newer tests in the area are similar to the interest inventories that have been on the market for decades.

Aptitude Testing

There is still considerable controversy among psychologists over the meaning of terms like *aptitude, capacity, intelligence,* or *creativity.* Although current trends can be described, it is somewhat more risky to make predictions concerning future trends. However, there seems little doubt but that the multi-aptitude model of the structure of intelligence will continue to gain in popularity.

The attempt to measure creativity will consume much research energy. The prediction by Siegel quoted earlier mentions an emphasis on creativity testing. He has certainly been correct in his prognosis thus far, and we predict the trend to continue.

With the interest in such areas as Project Head Start there has been increased attention to assessing the aptitudes of preschool youngsters. This interest will probably continue, resulting in a goodly number of inadequate tests being published and purchased.

State Legislation on Testing

The 1970s have marked the onset of a trend toward the establishment of new criteria for the awarding of high school diplomas. Many states have laws, or at least bills introduced, that set as a graduation requirement the passing of a competency exam. These bills (laws) have the potential for both great positive and negative educational results. Whether more positive or negative results will be realized is problematic. At the time of this writing, one of the best documents addressing this whole issue of equivalency examinations is one by Fremer et al. (1976). We refer interested readers to that document. It discusses the purposes of competency assessment, political issues, administrative issues, social issues, and economic issues as well as technical measurement issues. Measurement experts have been concerned that many legislators introducing and/or voting for such bills have not consulted with measurement experts nor indeed do they have much understanding of the complex measurement issues involved. It is probably fair to say that at the present time we are more concerned about, than happy with, the trend to pass state laws mandating the passing of tests for high school diplomas.

Quality versus Quantity

It is the authors' hope, if not their prediction, that the years ahead will bring a reduction in the number of tests designed to test the same constructs. There are far too many tests of poor quality on the market. The fact that Buros (1972) lists 1157 tests, many of them scathingly criticized, is indicative of the extent of this problem. We would much prefer to see fewer tests, all of higher quality.

Buros obviously feels the same way. In the preface to *The Sixth Mental Measurements Yearbook* he wrote:

> When I initiated this test reviewing service in 1938, I was confident that frankly critical reviews by competent specialists representing a wide variety of viewpoints would make it unprofitable to publish tests of unknown or questionable validity. Now, 27 years and five *Mental Measurements Yearbooks* later, I realize that I was too optimistic. . . . Despite unfavorable reviews in the MMY's, the publication and use of inadequately validated tests seem to be keeping pace with the population explosion (Buros, 1965, pp. xxiii–xxiv).

Probably the only way for our hope to materialize is for consumers to stop purchasing inadequate tests. This, of course, cannot happen unless consumers are capable of making good judgments. This leads to our last prediction.

Consumer Competence

Smith stated that "educational measurement is not in the control of test authors or publishers. It is in the hands of test users . . ." (Smith, 1963). One of Anderson's eight "dreams and expectations" for educational testing was "increased sophistication on the part of test users" (Anderson, 1963).

It is the truthfulness of Smith's statement that makes Anderson's dream so important. Tests can be important and useful tools. Used correctly by competent personnel, tests will continue to play an increasingly important role in educational institutions. Tests used incorrectly by incompetent, unprofessional staffs may do more harm than good. In the past there have been far too many instances of incorrect use of tests by school personnel. Hagen and Lindberg, writing in 1963, made 16 recommendations concerning staff competency in testing. Three recommendations (Hagen & Lindberg, 1963) that pertain directly to classroom-teacher competency are as follows:

> *Recommendation 12.* In order to discharge their functions in the testing program effectively, the classroom teachers must have a basic understanding of the evaluative process and the place of the testing program in the total evaluation of the students and the educational program.
> *Recommendation 13.* Classroom teachers should know the general types of tests available and be aware of their uses, strengths, and limitations.
> *Recommendation 14.* Classroom teachers should be able to combine available test data with other records and to interpret them as they relate to individual children in their classes.

Unfortunately, neither these recommendations pertaining to classroom teacher competencies nor the recommendations they make concerning other professional staff competencies have been realized in many schools. *It is our hopeful prediction that professional educators' competencies in test use will increase to an acceptably high level.* If not, tests will continue to be misused in educational institutions.

It would be helpful if teachers' unions would join us in our goal to increase the competence of educators in test use. This approach would be far more beneficial to education than the negative stances toward measurement frequently taken by union leaders during the past decade.

SUMMARY

The major ideas, conclusions, and implications of this chapter are summarized in the following statements:

1. The public has concerns about measurement and evaluation in education. Some of these concerns are rational and relevant; others are irrational and irrelevant.
2. Tests have certainly been misused. Most of the problems related to test misuse bear upon overgeneralizations made by users.
3. Many people criticize tests because their use has sometimes led to faulty decisions. What they fail to realize is that even more decisions would be faulty in the absence of test data.
4. Whether tests invade one's privacy depends upon the relevancy of the information gathered, the qualifications of the gatherers, the use to which the information is put, and the confidentiality of the data.
5. A major purpose of tests is to differentiate (discriminate) among people. Differentiation alone does not make a test unfair.
6. There are a variety of definitions of test bias. Some are complementary, others are contradictory.
7. A recent Supreme Court ruling states that "if an employment practice which operates to exclude Negroes cannot be shown to be related to job performance, the practice is prohibited."
8. The major educational concern related to cultural fairness is the use of tests as screening or prediction devices. Few people suggest that achievement tests measuring the outcomes of education are unfair.
9. Culture-fair tests would likely be less valid predictors of educational achievement than present aptitude and achievement tests.
10. Research seems to show quite conclusively that scholastic aptitude tests are *not* biased against students with culturally disadvantaged backgrounds under the most common definitions of test bias.
11. Several future trends in evaluation were predicted. These include (a) changes in the content of standardized achievement tests away from measures of facts and toward measures of understanding and application, (b) an increased use of computers in giving tests and storing and reporting test data, (c) improvement in affective domain measurement, (d) more testing in the area of career development, (e) an increase in state legislative requirements for certain types of competence on the part of test users.

APPENDIX   A

Selective List of Test Publishers

American College Testing Prgroam, P. O. Box 168, Iowa City, Iowa, 52240

American Guidance Service, Inc., Publishers' Building, Circle Pines, Minnesota, 55014

Australian Council for Educational Research, Frederick St., Hawthorn E.2, Victoria, Australia

Bobbs-Merrill Company, Inc., 4300 West 62nd Street, Indianapolis, Indiana, 46268

Bureau of Educational Research and Service, University of Iowa, Iowa City, Iowa, 52240

California Test Bureau/McGraw-Hill, Del Monte Research Park, Monterey, California, 93940

Committee on Diagnostic Reading Tests, Inc., Mountain Home, North Carolina, 28758

Consulting Psychologists Press, Inc., 577 College Avenue, Palo Alto, California, 94306

Cooperative Tests and Services, Educational Testing Service, Princeton, New Jersey, 08540

Educational and Industrial Testing Service, P. O. Box 7234, San Diego, California, 92107

Educational Test Bureau, Division of American Guidance Service, Inc., 720 Washington Avenue, S.E., Minneapolis, Minnesota, 55414

Educational Testing Service, Princeton, New Jersey, 08540

Guidance Centre, Ontario College of Education, University of Toronto, 1000 Yonge Street, Toronto 289, Ontario, Canada

Houghton Mifflin Company, 110 Tremont Street, Boston, Massachusetts, 02107

Institute for Personality and Ability Testing, 1602 Coronado Drive, Champaign, Illinois, 61822

Lyons and Carnahan, 407 East 25th Street, Chicago, Illinois, 60616

Personnel Press, Inc., 20 Nassau Street, Princeton, New Jersey, 08540

The Psychological Corporation, 304 East 45th Street, New York, New York 10017

Psychometric Affiliates, Box 3167, Munster, Indiana, 46321

Public Personnel Association, 1313 East 60th Street, Chicago, Illinois, 60637

Scholastic Testing Service, Inc., 480 Meyer Road, Bensenville, Illinois, 60106

Science Research Associates, Inc., 259 East Erie Street, Chicago, Illinois, 60611

Stanford University Press, Stanford, California, 94305

Stoelting Co., 424 North Homan Avenue, Chicago, Illinois, 60624

Teachers College Press, Teachers College, Columbia University, New York, New York, 10027

University of London Press, Ltd., St. Paul's House, Warwick Square, London E.C.4, England

Western Psychological Services, 12031 Wilshire Blvd., Los Angeles, California, 90025

APPENDIX B

A Glossary of Measurement Terms[1]

BLYTHE C. MITCHELL, *Consultant, Test Department*

This glossary of terms used in educational and psychological measurement is primarily for persons with limited training in measurement, rather than for the specialist. The terms defined are the more common or basic ones such as occur in test manuals and educational journals. In the definitions, certain technicalities and niceties of usage have been sacrificed for the sake of brevity and, it is hoped, clarity.

The definitions are based on the usage of the various terms as given in the current textbooks in educational and psychological measurement and statistics, and in certain specialized dictionaries. Where there is not complete uniformity among writers in the measurement field with respect to the meaning of a term, either these variations are noted or the definition offered is the one that the writer judges to represent the "best" usage.

academic aptitude. The combination of native and acquired abilities that are needed for school learning; likelihood of success in mastering academic work, as estimated from measures of the necessary abilities. (Also called *scholastic aptitude, school learning ability, academic potential.*)

achievement test. A test that measures the extent to which a person has "achieved" something, acquired certain information, or mastered certain skills—usually as a result of planned instruction or training.

age norms. Originally, values representing typical or average performance for persons of various *age* groups; most current usage refers to sets of complete score interpretive data for appropriate successive age groups. Such norms are generally used in the interpretation of mental ability test scores.

alternate-form reliability. The closeness of correspondence, or correlation, between results on alternate (i.e., equivalent or parallel) forms of a test; thus, a measure of the extent to which the two forms are consistent or reliable in measuring whatever they do measure. The time interval between the two testings must be relatively short so that the examinees themselves are unchanged in the ability being measured. See

[1] Issued by the Test Department, Harcourt Brace Jovanovich, Inc., as *Test Service Notebook No. 13.* Reprinted with permission.

690

anecdotal record. A written description of an incident in an individual's behavior that is reported objectively and is considered significant for the understanding of the individual.

aptitude. A combination of abilities and other characteristics, whether native or acquired, that are indicative of an individual's ability to learn or to develop proficiency in some particular area if appropriate education or training is provided. Aptitude tests include those of general academic ability (commonly called mental ability or intelligence tests); those of special abilities, such as verbal, numerical, mechanical, or musical; tests assessing "readiness" for learning; and prognostic tests, which measure both ability and previous learning, and are used to predict future performance—usually in a specific field, such as foreign language, shorthand, or nursing.

Some would define "aptitude" in a more comprehensive sense. Thus, "musical aptitude" would refer to the combination not only of physical and mental characteristics but also of motivational factors, interest, and conceivably other characteristics, which are conducive to acquiring proficiency in the musical field.

arithmetic mean. A kind of average usually referred to as the *mean*. It is obtained by dividing the sum of a set of scores by their number.

average. A general term applied to the various measures of central tendency. The three most widely used averages are the arithmetic mean (mean), the median, and the mode. When the term "average" is used without designation as to type, the most likely assumption is that it is the *arithmetic mean*.

battery. A group of several tests standardized on the same sample population so that results on the several tests are comparable. (Sometimes loosely applied to any group of tests administered together, even though not standardized on the same subjects.) The most common test batteries are those of school achievement, which include subtests in the separate learning areas.

bivariate chart (bivariate distribution). A diagram in which a tally mark is made to show the scores of one individual on *two variables*. The intersection of lines determined by the horizontal and vertical scales form cells in which the tallies are placed. Such a plot provides frequencies for the two distributions, and portrays the relation between the two variables as a basis for computation of the product-moment correlation coefficient.

ceiling. The upper limit of ability that can be measured by a test. When an individual makes a score which is at or near the highest possible score, it is said that the test has too low a "ceiling" for him; he should be given a higher level of the test.

central tendency. A measure of central tendency provides a single most typical score as representative of a group of scores; the "trend" of a group of measures as indicated by some type of average, usually the *mean* or the *median*.

coefficient of correlation. A measure of the degree of relationship or "going-togetherness" between two sets of measures for the same group of individuals. The correlation coefficient most frequently used in test development and educational research is that known as the Pearson or *product-moment r*. Unless otherwise specified, "correlation" usually refers to this coefficient, but *rank*, *biserial*, *tetrachoric*, and other methods are used in special situations. Correlation coefficients range from .00, denoting a complete absence of relation, to +1.00, and to −1.00, indicating perfect positive or perfect negative correspondence, respectively. See CORRELATION.

composite score. A score which combines several scores, usually by addition; often different weights are applied to the contributing scores to increase or decrease their importance in the composite. Most commonly, such scores are used for *predictive* purposes and the several weights are derived through multiple regression procedures.

concurrent validity. See VALIDITY (2).

construct validity. See VALIDITY (3).

content validity. See VALIDITY (1).

correction for guessing (correction for chance). A reduction in score for wrong answers, sometimes applied in scoring true-false or multiple-choice questions. Such scoring formulas ($R-W$ for tests with 2-option response, $R-\frac{1}{2}W$ for 3 options, $R-\frac{1}{3}W$ for 4, etc.) are intended to discourage guessing and to yield more accurate rankings for examinees in terms of their true knowledge. They are used much less today than in the early days of testing.

correlation. Relationship or "going-togetherness" between two sets of scores or measures; tendency of one score to vary concomitantly with the other, as the tendency of students of high IQ to be above average in reading ability. The existence of a strong relationship—i.e., a high correlation—between two variables does not necessarily indicate that one has any causal influence on the other. See COEFFICIENT OF CORRELATION.

criterion. A standard by which a test may be judged or evaluated; a set of scores, ratings, etc., that a test is designed to measure, to predict, or to correlate with. See VALIDITY.

criterion-referenced (content-referenced) test. Terms often used to describe tests designed to provide information on the specific knowledge or skills possessed by a student. Such tests usually cover relatively small units of content and are closely related to instruction. Their scores have meaning in terms of *what* the student knows or can do, rather than in their relation to the scores made by some external reference group.

criterion-related validity. See VALIDITY (2).

culture-fair test. So-called culture-fair tests attempt to provide an equal opportunity for success by persons of all cultures and life experiences. Their content must therefore be limited to that which is equally common to all cultures, or to material that is entirely unfamiliar and novel for all persons whatever their cultural background. See CULTURE-FREE TEST.

culture-free test. A test that is free of the impact of all cultural experiences; therefore, a measure reflecting only hereditary abilities. Since culture permeates all of man's environmental contacts, the construction of such a test would seem to be an impossibility. Cultural "bias" is not eliminated by the use of nonlanguage or so-called performance tests, although it may be reduced in some instances. In terms of most of the purposes for which tests are used, the validity (value) of a "culture-free" test is questioned; a test designed to be equally applicable to all cultures may be of little or no practical value in any.

curricular validity. See VALIDITY (2).

decile. Any one of the nine points (scores) that divide a distribution into ten parts, each containing one-tenth of all the scores or cases; every tenth percentile. The first decile is the 10th percentile, the eighth decile the 80th percentile etc,

deviation. The amount by which a score differs from some reference value, such as the mean, the norm, or the score on some other test.

deviation IQ (DIQ). An age-based index of general mental ability. It is based upon the difference or deviation between a person's score and the typical or average score for persons of his chronological age. Deviation IQs from most current scholastic aptitude measures are standard scores with a mean of 100 and a standard deviation of 16 for each defined age group.

diagnostic test. A test used to "diagnose" or analyze; that is, to locate an individual's specific areas of weakness or strength, to determine the nature of his weaknesses or deficiencies, and, wherever possible, to suggest their cause. Such a test yields measures of the components of subparts of some larger body of information or skill. Diagnostic achievement tests are most commonly prepared for the skill subjects.

difficulty value. An index which indicates the percent of some specified group, such as students of a given age or grade, who answer a test item correctly.

discriminating power. The ability of a test item to differentiate between persons possessing much or little of some trait.

discrimination index. An index which indicates the *discriminating power* of a test item. The most commonly used index is derived from the number passing the item in the highest 27 percent of the group (on total score) and the number passing in the lowest 27 percent.

distractor. Any incorrect choice (option) in a test item.

distribution (frequency distribution). A tabulation of the scores (or other attributes) of a group of individuals to show the number (frequency) of each score, or of those within the range of each interval.

equivalent form. Any of two or more forms of a test that are closely parallel with respect to the nature of the content and the number and difficulty of the items included, and that will yield very similar average scores and measures of variability for a given group. (Also referred to as *alternate, comparable*, or *parallel* form.)

error of measurement. See STANDARD ERROR OF MEASUREMENT.

expectancy table ("expected" achievement). A term with two common usages, related but with some difference:

(1) A table or other device for showing the relation between scores on a predictive test and some related outcome. The outcome, or criterion status, for individuals at each level of predictive score may be expressed as (a) an average on the outcome variable, (b) the percent of cases at successive levels, or (c) the probability of reaching given performance levels. Such tables are commonly used in making predictions of educational or job success.

(2) A table or chart providing for an interpretation of a student's obtained score on an achievement test with the score which would be "expected" for those at his grade level and with his level of scholastic aptitude. Such "expectancies" are based upon actual data from administration of the specified achievement and scholastic aptitude tests to the same student population. The term "anticipated" is also used to denote achievement as differentiated by level of "intellectual status."

extrapolation. In general, any process of estimating values of a variable beyond the range of available data. As applied to test norms, the process of extending a norm line into grade or age levels not tested in the standardization program, in order to permit interpretation of extreme scores. Since this extension is usually done graphically, considerable judgment is involved. Extrapolated values are thus to some extent arbitrary; for this and other reasons, they have limited meaning.

f. A symbol denoting the *frequency* of a given score or of the scores within an interval grouping.

face validity. See VALIDITY (1).

factor. In mental measurement, a hypothetical trait, ability, or component of ability that underlies and influences performance on two or more tests and hence causes scores on the tests to be correlated. The term "factor" strictly refers to a theoretical variable, derived by a process of *factor analysis* from a table of intercorrelations among tests. However, it is also used to denote the psychological interpretation given to the variable—i.e., the mental trait assumed to be represented by the variable, as verbal ability, numerical ability, etc.

factor analysis. Any of several methods of analyzing the intercorrelations among a set of variables such as test scores. Factor analysis attempts to account for the interrelationships in terms of some underlying "factors," preferably fewer in number than the original variables, and it reveals how much of the variation in each of the original measures arises from, or is associated with, each of the hypothetical factors. Factor analysis has contributed to an understanding of the organization or components of intelligence, aptitudes, and personality; and it has pointed the way to the development of "purer" tests of the several components.

forced-choice item. Broadly, any multiple-choice item in which the examinee is *required* to select one or more of the given choices. The term is most often used to denote a special type of multiple-choice item employed in personality tests in which the options are (1) of equal "preference value," i.e., chosen equally often by a typical group, and are (2) such that one of the options discriminates between persons high and low on the factor that this option measures, while the other options measure other factors. Thus, in the *Gordon Personal Profile*, each of four options represents one of the four personality traits measured by the *Profile*, and the examinee must select both the option which describes him *most* and the one which describes him *least*.

frequency distribution. See DISTRIBUTION.

g. Denotes *general* intellectual ability; one dimensional measure of "mind," as described by the British psychologist Spearman. A test of "*g*" serves as a general-purpose test of mental ability.

grade equivalent (GE). The grade level for which a given score is the real or estimated average. Grade-equivalent interpretation, most appropriate for elementary level achievement tests, expresses obtained scores in terms of *grade* and *month of grade*, assuming a 10-month school year (e.g., 5.7). Since such tests are usually standardized at only one (or two) points(s) within each grade, grade equivalents between points for which there are data-based scores must be "estimated" by *interpolation*. See EXTRAPOLATION, INTERPOLATION.

grade norms. Norms based upon the performance of pupils of given grade placement. See GRADE EQUIVALENT, NORMS, PERCENTILE RANK, STANINE.

group test. A test that may be administered to a number of individuals at the same time by one examiner.

individual test. A test that can be administered to only one person at a time, because of the nature of the test and/or the maturity level of the examinees.

intelligence quotient (IQ). Originally, an index of brightness expressed as the ratio of a person's mental age to his chronological age, MA/CA, multiplied by 100 to eliminate the decimal. (More precisely—and particularly for adult ages, at which mental growth is assumed to have ceased—the ratio of mental age to the mental age normal for chronological age.) This quotient IQ has been gradually replaced by the deviation IQ concept.

It is sometimes desired to give additional meaning to IQs by the use of verbal descriptions for the ranges in which they fall. Since the IQ scale is a continuous one, there can be no inflexible line of demarcation between such successive category labels as very superior, superior, above average, average, below average, etc.; any verbal classification system is therefore an arbitrary one. There appears to be, however, rather common use of the term *average* or *normal* to describe IQs from 90-109 inclusive.

An IQ is more definitely "interpreted" by noting the normal percent of IQs within a range which includes the IQ, and/or by indicating its percentile rank or stanine in the total national norming sample. Column 2 of Table 1 shows the normal distribution of IQs for M=100 and S.D.=16, showing percentages within successive 10-point intervals. (For IQs whose S.D. is greater than 16, the percentages for the extreme IQ ranges will be larger, and those for IQs near the mean will be smaller, than those shown in the table.) Table 1 indicates that 47 percent, approximately one-half of "all" persons, have IQs in the 20-point range of 90 through 109; an IQ of 140 or above would be considered as extremely high, since fewer than one percent (0.6) of the total population reach this level, and fewer than one percent have IQs below 60. From the cumulative percents given in Column 3, it is noted that 3.1 percent have IQs below 70, usually considered the mentally retarded category. This column may be used to indicate the percentile rank (PR) of certain IQs. Thus an IQ of 119 has a PR of 89, since 89.4 percent of IQs are 119 or below; an IQ of 79 has a PR of 10.6, or 11. See DEVIATION IQ, MENTAL AGE.

internal consistency. Degree of relationship among the items of a test; consistency in content sampling. See SPLIT-HALF RELIABILITY.

interpolation. In general, any process of estimating intermediate values between two known points. As applied to test norms, it refers to the procedure used in assigning interpretive values (e.g., grade equivalents) to scores between the successive average scores actually obtained in the standardization process. Also, in reading norm tables it is necessary at times to interpolate to obtain a norm value for a score between two scores given in the table; e.g., in the table shown here, a percentile rank of 83 (from

TABLE 1 Normal Distribution of IQs with Mean of 100 and Standard Deviation of 16

(1) IQ Range	(2) Percent of Persons	(3) Cumulative Percent
140 and above	0.6	100.0
130-139	2.5	99.4
120-129	7.5	96.9
110-119	16.0	89.4
100-109	23.4	73.4
90- 99	23.4 46.8	50.0
80- 89	16.0	26.6
70- 79	7.5	10.6
60- 69	2.5	3.1
Below 60	0.6	0.6
Total	100.0	

81 + ⅓ of 6) would be assigned, by *interpolation*, to a score of 46; a score of 50 would correspond to a percentile rank of 94 (obtained as 87 + ⅔ of 10).

Score	Percentile Rank
51	97
48	87
45	81

inventory. A questionnaire or check list, usually in the form of a self-report, designed to elicit nonintellective information about an individual. Not tests in the usual sense, inventories are most often concerned with personality traits, interests, attitudes, problems, motivation, etc. See PERSONALITY TEST.

inventory test. An achievement test that attempts to cover rather thoroughly some relatively small unit of specific instruction or training. An inventory test, as the name suggests, is in the nature of a "stock-taking" of an individual's knowledge or skill, and is often administered prior to instruction.

item. A single question or exercise in a test.

item analysis. The process of evaluating single test items in respect to certain characteristics. It usually involves determining the difficulty value and the discriminating power of the item, and often its correlation with some external criterion.

Kuder-Richardson formula(s). Formulas for estimating the reliability of a test that are based on *interitem consistency* and require only a single administration of the test. The one most used, formula 20, requires information based on the number of items in the test, the standard deviation of the total score, and the proportion of examinees passing each item. The Kuder-Richardson formulas are not appropriate for use with speeded tests.

mastery test. A test designed to determine whether a pupil has mastered a given unit of instruction or a single knowledge or skill; a test giving information on *what* a pupil knows, rather than on how his performance relates to that of some norm-reference group. Such tests are used in computer-assisted instruction, where their results are referred to as content- or criterion-referenced information.

mean (M). See ARITHMETIC MEAN.

median (Md). The middle score in a distribution or set of ranked scores; the point (score) that divides the group into two equal parts; the 50th percentile. Half of the scores are below the median and half above it, except when the median itself is one of the obtained scores.

mental age (MA). The age for which a given score on a mental ability test is average or normal. If the average score made by an unselected group of children 6 years, 10 months of age is 55, then a child making a score of 55 is said to have a mental age of 6–10. Since the mental age unit shrinks with increasing (chronological) age, MAs do not have a uniform interpretation throughout all ages. They are therefore most appropriately used at the early age levels where mental growth is relatively rapid.

modal-age norms. Achievement test norms that are based on the performance of pupils of normal age for their respective grades. Norms derived from such age restricted groups are free from the distorting influence of the scores of underage and overage pupils.

mode. The score or value that occurs most frequently in a distribution.

multiple-choice item. A test item in which the examinee's task is to choose the correct or best answer from several given answers or options.

N. The symbol commonly used to represent the number of cases in a group.

non-language test. See NONVERBAL TEST.

nonverbal test. A test that does not require the use of words in the item or in the response to it. (Oral directions may be included in the formulation of the task.) A test cannot, however, be classified as nonverbal simply because it does not require reading on the part of the examinee. The use of nonverbal tasks cannot completely eliminate the effect of culture.

norm line. A smooth curve drawn to best fit (1) the plotted mean or median scores of successive age or grade groups, or (2) the successive percentile points for a single group.

normal distribution. A distribution of scores or measures that in graphic form has a distinctive bell-shaped appearance. Figures 1 and 2 show graphs of such a distribution, known as a *normal, normal probability*, or *Gaussian curve*. (Difference in shape is due to the different variability of the two distributions.) In such a normal distribution, scores or measures are distributed symmetrically about the mean, with as many cases up to various distances above the mean as down to equal distances below it. Cases are concentrated near the mean and decrease in frequency, according to a precise mathematical equation, the farther one departs from the mean. *Mean* and *median are identical.* The assumption that mental and psychological characteristics are distributed normally has been very useful in test development work.

norms. Statistics that supply a frame of reference by which meaning may be given to obtain test scores. Norms are based upon the actual performance of pupils of various grades or ages in the standardization group for the test. Since they represent average or typical performance, they should not be regarded as standards or as universally desirable levels of attainment. The most common types of norms are deviation IQ, percentile rank, grade equivalent, and stanine. Reference groups are usually those of specified age or grade.

objective test. A test made up of items for which correct responses may be set up in advance; scores are unaffected by the opinion or judgment of the scorer. Objective keys provide for scoring by clerks or by machine. Such a test is contrasted with a "subjective" test, such as the usual essay examination, to which different persons may assign different scores, ratings, or grades.

omnibus test. A test (1) in which items measuring a variety of mental operations are all combined into a single sequence rather than being grouped together by type of operation, and (2) from which only a single score is derived, rather than separate scores for each operation or function. Omnibus tests make for simplicity of administration, since one set of directions and one overall time limit usually suffice. The Elementary, Intermediate, and Advanced tests in the *Otis-Lennon Mental Ability Test* series are omnibus-type tests, as contrasted with the *Kuhlmann-Anderson Measure of Academic Potential*, in which the items measuring similar operations occur together, each with its own set of directions. In a *spiral-omnibus* test, the easiest items of each type are presented first, followed by the same succession of item types at a higher difficulty level, and so on in a rising spiral.

percentile (P). A point (score) in a distribution at or below which fall the percent of cases indicated by the percentile. Thus a score coinciding with the 35th percentile

(P_{35}) is regarded as equaling or surpassing that of 35 percent of the persons in the group, and such that 65 percent of the performances exceed this score. "Percentile" has nothing to do with the percent of correct answers an examinee makes on a test.

percentile band. An interpretation of a test score which takes account of the measurement error that is involved. The range of such bands, most useful in portraying significant differences in battery profiles, is usually from one standard error of measurement below the obtained score to one standard error of measurement above it.

percentile rank (PR). The expression of an obtained test score in terms of its position within a group of 100 scores; the percentile rank of a score is the percent of scores equal to or lower than the given score in its own or in some external reference group.

performance test. A test involving some motor or manual response on the examinee's part, generally a manipulation of concrete equipment or materials. Usually *not* a paper-and-pencil test.

(1) A "performance" test of mental ability is one in which the role of language is excluded or minimized, and ability is assessed by what the examinee *does* rather than by what he says (or writes). Mazes, form boards, picture completion, and other types of items may be used. Examples include certain *Stanford-Binet* tasks, the Performance Scale of *Wechsler Intelligence Scale for Children, Arthur Point Scale of Performance Tests, Raven's Progressive Matrices.*

(2) "Performance" tests include measures of mechanical or manipulative ability where the task itself coincides with the objective of the measurement, as in the *Bennett Hand-Tool Dexterity Test.*

(3) The term "performance" is also used to denote a test that is actually a *work-sample*; in this sense it may include paper-and-pencil tests, as, for example, a test in bookkeeping, in shorthand, or in proofreading, where no materials other than paper and pencil may be required, and where the test response is identical with the behavior about which information is desired. *SRA Typing Skills* is such a test.

The use of the term "performance" to describe a type of test is not very precise, and there are certain "gray areas." Perhaps one should think of "performance" tests as those on which the obtained differences among individuals may *not* be ascribed to differences in ability to use verbal symbols.

personality test. A test intended to measure one or more of the nonintellective aspects of an individual's mental or psychological make-up; an instrument designed to obtain information on the affective characteristics of an individual—emotional, motivational, attitudinal, etc.—as distinguished from his abilities. Personality tests include (1) the so-called *personality* and *adjustment inventories* (e.g., *Bernreuter Personality Inventory, Bell Adjustment Inventory, Edwards Personal Preference Schedule*), which seek to measure a person's status on such traits as dominance, sociability, introversion, etc., by means of self-descriptive responses to a series of questions; (2) *rating scales*, which call for rating, by one's self or another, the extent to which a subject possesses certain traits; and (3) *opinion or attitude inventories* (e.g., *Allport-Vernon-Lindzey Study of Values, Minnesota Teacher Attitude Inventory*). Some writers also classify interest, problem, and belief inventories as personality tests (e.g., *Kuder Preference Record, Mooney Problem Check List*). See PROJECTIVE TECHNIQUE.

power test. A test intended to measure level of performance unaffected by speed of response; hence one in which there is either no time limit or a very generous one. Items are usually arranged in order of increasing difficulty.

practice effect. The influence of previous experience with a test on a later administration of the same or a similar test; usually an increased familiarity with the directions, kinds of questions, etc. Practice effect is greatest when the interval between testings is short, when the content of the two tests is identical or very similar, and when the initial test-taking represents a relatively novel experience for the subjects.

predictive validity. See VALIDITY (2).

product-moment coefficient (r). Also known as the Pearson *r*. See COEFFICIENT OF CORRELATION.

profile. A graphic representation of the results on several tests, for either an individual or a group, when the results have been expressed in some uniform or comparable terms (standard scores, percentile ranks, grade equivalents, etc.). The profile method of presentation permits identification of areas of strength or weakness.

prognosis (prognostic) test. A test used to predict future success in a specific subject or field, as the *Pimsleur Language Aptitude Battery*.

projective technique (projective method). A method of personality study in which the subject responds as he chooses to a series of ambiguous stimuli such as ink blots, pictures, unfinished sentences, etc. It is assumed that under this free-response condition the subject "projects" manifestations of personality characteristics and organization that can, by suitable methods, be scored and interpreted to yield a description of his basic personality structure. The *Rorschach* (ink blot) *Technique,* the *Murray Thematic Apperception Test* and the *Machover Draw-a-Person Test* are commonly used projective methods.

quartile. One of three points that divide the cases in a distribution into four equal groups. The lower quartile (Q_1), or 25th percentile, sets off the lowest fourth of the group; the middle quartile (Q_2) is the same as the 50th percentile, or median, and divides the second fourth of cases from the third; and the third quartile (Q_3), or 75th percentile, sets off the top fourth.

r. See COEFFICIENT OF CORRELATION.

random sample. A sample of the members of some total population drawn in such a way that every member of the population has an equal chance of being included —that is, in a way that precludes the operation of bias or "selection." The purpose in using a sample free of bias is, of course, the requirement that the cases used be representative of the total population if findings for the sample are to be generalized to that population. In a *stratified* random sample, the drawing of cases is controlled in such a way that those chosen are "representative" also of specified subgroups of the total population. See REPRESENTATIVE SAMPLE.

range. For some specified group, the difference between the highest and the lowest obtained score on a test; thus a very rough measure of spread or variability, since it is based upon only two extreme scores. Range is also used in reference to the possible spread of measurement a test provides, which in most instances is the number of items in the test.

raw score. The first quantitative result obtained in scoring a test. Usually the number of right answers, number right minus some fraction of number wrong, time required for performance, number of errors, or similar direct, unconverted, uninterpreted measure.

readiness test. A test that measures the extent to which an individual has achieved a degree of maturity or acquired certain skills or information needed for successfully undertaking some new learning activity. Thus a *reading readiness* test indicates whether a child has reached a developmental stage where he may profitably begin formal reading instruction. *Readiness* tests are classified as *prognostic* tests.

recall item. A type of item that requires the examinee to supply the correct answer from his own memory or recollection, as contrasted with a *recognition item*, in which he need only identify the correct answer.

Columbus discovered America in the year _____

is a *recall* (or *completion*) item. See RECOGNITION ITEM.

recognition item. An item which requires the examinee to recognize or select the correct answer from among two or more given answers (options).

Columbus discovered America in

   (a) *1425*   (b) *1492*   (c) *1520*   (d) *1546*

is a *recognition* item.

regression effect. Tendency of a predicted score to be nearer to the mean of its distribution than the score from which it is predicted is to its mean. Because of the effects of regression, students making extremely high or extremely low scores on a test tend to make less extreme scores, i.e., closer to the mean, on a second administration of the same test or on some predicted measure.

reliability. The extent to which a test is consistent in measuring whatever it does measure; dependability, stability, trustworthiness, relative freedom from errors of measurement. Reliability is usually expressed by some form of *reliability coefficient* or by the *standard error of measurement* derived from it.

reliability coefficient. The coefficient of correlation between two forms of a test, between scores on two administrations of the same test, or between halves of a test, properly corrected. The three measure somewhat different aspects of reliability, but all are properly spoken of as reliability coefficients. See ALTERNATE-FORM RELIABILITY, SPLIT-HALF RELIABILITY COEFFICIENT, TEST-RETEST RELIABILITY COEFFICIENT, KUDER-RICHARDSON FORMULA(S).

representative sample. A sample that corresponds to or matches the population of which it is a sample with respect to characteristics important for the purposes under investigation. In an achievement test norm sample, such significant aspects might be the proportion of cases of each sex, from various types of schools, different geographical areas, the several socioeconomic levels, etc.

scholastic aptitude. See ACADEMIC APTITUDE.

skewed distribution. A distribution that departs from symmetry or balance around the mean, i.e., from normality. Scores pile up at one end and trail off at the other.

Spearman-Brown formula. A formula giving the relationship between the reliability of a test and its length. The formula permits estimation of the reliability of a test lengthened or shortened by any multiple, from the known reliability of a given test. Its most common application is the estimation of reliability of an entire test from the correlation between its two halves. See SPLIT-HALF RELIABILITY COEFFICIENT.

split-half reliability coefficient. A coefficient of reliability obtained by correlating scores on one half of a test with scores on the other half, and applying the Spearman-Brown formula to adjust for the doubled length of the total test. Generally, but not necessarily, the two halves consist of the odd-numbered and the even-numbered items. Split-half reliability coefficients are sometimes referred to as measures of the *internal consistency* of a test; they involve content sampling only, not stability over time. This type of reliability coefficient is inappropriate for tests in which speed is an important component.

standard deviation (S.D.). A measure of the variability or dispersion of a distribution of scores. The more the scores cluster around the mean, the smaller the standard deviation. For a normal distribution, approximately two thirds (68.3 percent) of the scores are within the range from one S.D. below the mean to one S.D. above the mean. Computation of the S.D. is based upon the square of the deviation of each score from the mean. The S.D. is sometimes called "sigma" and is represented by the symbol σ. (See Figure 1.)

standard error (S.E.). A statistic providing an estimate of the possible magnitude of "error" present in some obtained measure, whether (1) an *individual* score or (2) some *group* measure, as a mean or a correlation coefficient.

(1) standard error of measurement (S.E. Meas.): As applied to a single obtained score, the amount by which the score may differ from the hypothetical true score due to errors of measurement. The larger the S.E. Meas., the less reliable the score. The S.E. Meas. is an amount such that in about two-thirds of the cases the obtained score would not differ by more than one S.E. Meas. from the true score. (Theoretically, then, it can be said that the chances are 2:1 that the actual score is within a band extending from *true score minus 1 S.E. Meas.* to *true score plus 1 S.E. Meas.;* but since the true score can never be known, actual practice must reverse the true-obtained relation for an interpretation.) Other probabilities are noted under (2) below. See TRUE SCORE.

(2) standard error: When applied to group averages, standard deviations, correlation coefficients, etc., the S.E. provides an estimate of the "error" which may be involved. The group's size and the S.D. are the factors on which these standard

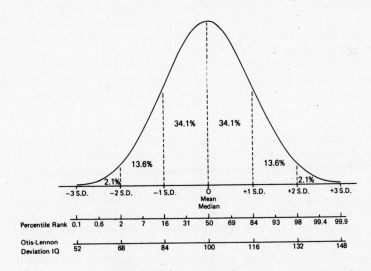

FIGURE 1   Normal curve, showing relations among standard deviation distance from mean, area (percentage of cases) between these points, percentile rank, and IQ from tests with an S.D. of 19.

errors are based. The same probability interpretation as for S.E. Meas. is made for the S.E.s of group measures, i.e., 2:1 (2 out of 3) for the 1 S.E. range, 19:1 (95 out of 100) for a 2 S.E. range, 99:1 (99 out of 100) for a 2.6 S.E. range.

standard score. A general term referring to any of a variety of "transformed" scores, in terms of which raw scores may be expressed for reasons of convenience, comparability, ease of interpretation, etc. The simplest type of standard score, known as a z-score, is an expression of the *deviation* of a score from the mean score of the group *in relation to* the standard deviation of the scores of the group. Thus

$$\text{standard score } (z) = \frac{\text{raw score } (X) - \text{mean } (M)}{\text{standard deviation } (S.D.)}$$

Adjustments may be made in this ratio so that a system of standard scores having any desired mean and standard deviation may be set up. The use of such standard scores does not affect the relative standing of the individuals in the group or change the shape of the original distribution. T-scores have a M of 50 and an S.D. of 10. Deviation IQs are standard scores with a M of 100 and some chosen S.D., most often 16; thus a raw score that is 1 S.D. above the M of its distribution would convert to a standard score (deviation IQ) of $100 + 16 = 116$. (See Figure 1.)

Standard scores are useful in expressing the raw scores of two forms of a test in comparable terms in instances where tryouts have shown that the two forms are not identical in difficulty; also, successive levels of a test may be linked to form a continuous standard-score scale, making across-battery comparisons possible.

standardized test (standard test). A test designed to provide a systematic sample of individual performance, administered according to prescribed directions, scored in conformance with definite rules, and interpreted in reference to certain normative information. Some would further restrict the usage of the term "standardized" to those tests for which the items have been chosen on the basis of experimental evaluation, and for which data on reliability and validity are provided. Others would add "commercially published" and/or "for general use."

stanine. One of the steps in a nine-point scale of standard scores. The stanine (short for *standard-nine*) scale has values from 1 to 9, with a mean of 5 and a standard deviation of 2. Each stanine (except 1 and 9) is ½ S.D. in width, with the middle (average) stanine of 5 extending from ¼ S.D. below to ¼ S.D. above the mean. (See Figure 2.)

survey test. A test that measures general achievement in a given area, usually with the connotation that the test is intended to assess group status, rather than to yield precise measures of individual performance.

t. A critical ratio expressing the relationship of some measure (mean, correlation coefficient, difference, etc.) to its standard error. The size of this ratio is an indication of the significance of the measure. If *t* is as large as 1.96, significance at the .05 level is indicated; if as large as 2.58, at the .01 level. These levels indicate 95 or 99 chances out of 100, respectively.

taxonomy. An embodiment of the principles of classification; a survey, usually in outline form, such as a presentation of the objectives of education.

test-retest reliability coefficient. A type of reliability coefficient obtained by administering the same test a second time, after a short interval, and correlating the two sets of scores. "Same test" was originally understood to mean identical content, i.e.,

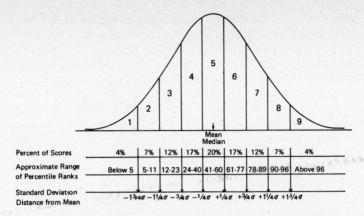

Percent of Scores	4%	7%	12%	17%	20%	17%	12%	7%	4%
Approximate Range of Percentile Ranks	Below 5	5-11	12-23	24-40	41-60	61-77	78-89	90-96	Above 96

Standard Deviation Distance from Mean
$-1\frac{3}{4}\sigma$ $-1\frac{1}{4}\sigma$ $-\frac{3}{4}\sigma$ $-\frac{1}{4}\sigma$ $+\frac{1}{4}\sigma$ $+\frac{3}{4}\sigma$ $+1\frac{1}{4}\sigma$ $+1\frac{3}{4}\sigma$

FIGURE 2   Stanines and the normal curve. Each stanine (except 1 and 9) is one half S.D. in width.

the same form; currently, however, the term "test-retest" is also used to describe the administration of different forms of the same test, in which case this reliability co-efficient becomes the same as the alternate-form coefficient. In either case (1) fluctuations over time and in testing situation, and (2) any effect of the first test upon the second are involved. When the time interval between the two testings is considerable, as several months, a test-retest reliability coefficient reflects not only the consistency of measurement provided by the test, but also the stability of the examinee trait being measured.

true score. A score entirely free of error; hence, a hypothetical value that can never be obtained by testing, which always involves some measurement error. A "true" score may be thought of as the average score from an infinite number of measurements from the same or exactly equivalent tests, assuming no practice effect or change in the examinee during the testings. The standard deviation of this infinite number of "samplings" is known as the *standard error of measurement.*

validity. The extent to which a test does the job for which it is used. This definition is more satisfactory than the traditional "extent to which a test measures what it is supposed to measure," since the validity of a test is always specific to the purposes for which the test is used. The term "validity," then, has different connotations for various types of tests and, thus, a different kind of validity evidence is appropriate for each.

(1) content, curricular validity. For achievement tests, validity is the extent to which the *content* of the test represents a balanced and adequate sampling of the outcomes (knowledge, skills, etc.) of the course or instructional program it is intended to cover. It is best evidenced by a comparison of the test content with courses of study, instructional materials, and statements of educational goals; and often by analysis of the processes required in making correct responses to the items. *Face validity,* referring to an observation of what a test appears to measure is a non-technical type of evidence; apparent relevancy is, however, quite desirable.

(2) criterion-related validity. The extent to which scores on the test are in agreement with (*concurrent validity*) or predict (*predictive validity*) some given

criterion measure. Predictive validity refers to the accuracy with which an aptitude, prognostic, or readiness test indicates future learning success in some area, as evidenced by correlations between scores on the test and future criterion measures of such success (e.g., the relation of score on an academic aptitude test administered in high school to grade point average over four years of college). In concurrent validity, no significant time interval elapses between administration of the test being validated and of the criterion measure. Such validity might be evidenced by *concurrent* measures of academic ability and of achievement, by the relation of a new test to one generally accepted as or known to be valid, or by the correlation between scores on a test and criteria measures which are valid but are less objective and more time-consuming to obtain than a test score would be.

(3) construct validity. The extent to which a test measures some relatively abstract psychological trait or construct; applicable in evaluating the validity of tests that have been constructed on the basis of an analysis (often factor analysis) of the nature of the trait and its manifestations. Tests of personality, verbal ability, mechanical aptitude, critical thinking, etc., are validated in terms of their construct and the relation of their scores to pertinent external data.

variability. The spread or dispersion of test scores, best indicated by their standard deviation.

variance. For a distribution, the average of the squared deviations from the mean; thus the square of the standard deviation.

References

Abu-Sayf, F. K. 1975. "Relative Effectiveness of the Conventional Formula Score," *Journal of Educational Research, 69*, 160–162.

Academic Council. 1969. *Code of Teaching Responsibilities.* East Lansing: Michigan State University.

Adams, G. S. 1964. *Measurement and Evaluation in Education, Psychology, and Guidance.* New York: Holt, Rinehart and Winston.

Adkins, D. C., and G. F. Kuder. 1940. "The Relation of Primary Abilities to Activity Preference," *Psychometrika, 5*, 251–262.

Ahlgren, A. 1969. "Reliability, Predictability, and Personality Bias of Confidence-Weighted Scores." Paper presented at the Annual Meeting of the American Educational Research Association, Los Angeles, Calif.

Ahmann, J. S. and M. D. Glock. 1971. *Evaluating Pupil Growth* (4th de.). Boston: Allyn and Bacon.

Aleamoni, L. M. 1974. *Typical Faculty Concern about Student Evaluation of Instruction.* Invited address presented at the Israel Institute of Technology, Haifa, Israel.

Alker, H. A., J. A. Carlson, and M. C. Hermann. 1967. "Multiple-Choice Questions and Student Characteristics." *Educational Testing Service Research Bulletin,* November.

Alkin, M. 1970. "Evaluating Net Cost-Effectiveness of Instructional Programs." In M. C. Wittrock and D. E. Wiley, *The Evaluation of Instruction: Issues and Problems.* New York: Holt, Rinehart and Winston.

Alkin, M. C., et al. 1974. *Evaluation and Decision Making: The Title VII Experience.* CSE Monograph Series In Evaluation, No. 4. Los Angeles: UCLA Center for the Study of Evaluation.

Allport, G. W. 1963. *Pattern and Growth in Personality.* New York: Holt, Rinehart and Winston.

AMEG, 1973. "AMEG Commission Report on Sex Bias in Measurement," *Measurement and Evaluation in Guidance, 6*, 171–177.

American College Testing Program. 1973. *Using ACT on the Campus.* Iowa City, Iowa: American College Testing Program.

American Psychological Association, 1970. "Psychological Assessment and Public Policy," *American Psychologist, 25*, 264–266.

American Psychological Association. 1974. *Standards for Educational and Psychological Tests and Manuals.* Washington, D.C.: American Psychological Association.

Ammons, M. 1964. "An Empirical Study of Progress and Product in Curriculum Development," *Journal of Educational Research, 27*, 451–457.

Anastasi, A. 1961. *Psychological Testing* (2d ed.). New York: Macmillan.

Anastasi, A. 1968. *Psychological Testing* (3d ed.). New York: Macmillan.

Anastasi, A. 1973. *Common Fallacies about Heredity, Environment, and Human Behavior,* ACT Research Report No. 51. Iowa City, Iowa: American College Testing Program, May.

Anastasi, A. 1976. *Psychological Testing* (4th ed.). New York: Macmillan.

Anderson, R. C., R. M. Kulhary, and T. Andre. 1971. "Feedback Procedures in Programmed Instruction," *Journal of Educational Psychology, 62*, 148–156.

Anderson, R. H. 1966. "The Importance and Purposes of Reporting," *National Elementary School Principal, 45*, 6–11.

Anderson, S. A. 1963. In Robert H. Bauernfeind, *Building a School Testing Program.* Boston: Houghton Mifflin, p. 302.

Angoff, W. H. 1964. "Technical Problems of Obtaining Equivalent Scores on Tests," *Journal of Educational Measurement, 1*, 11–13.

Angoff, W. H. 1971. "Scales, Norms, and Equivalent Scores." In R. L. Thorndike (ed.), *Educational Measurement* (2d ed.). Washington, D.C.: American Council on Education.

APA Monitor. 1971. Washington, D.C.: American Psychological Association, 2(4), 1.

Archer, S. H., and R. Pipert. 1962. "Don't Change the Answer!" *The Clearing House, 37,* 39–41.

Astin, A. W. 1962. "Productivity of Undergraduate Institutions," *Science, 136,* 129–135.

Astin, A. W. 1963a. "Differential College Effects on the Motivation of Talented Students to Obtain the Ph.D.," *Journal of Educational Psychology, 54,* 63–71.

Astin, A. W. 1963b. "Undergraduate Institutions and the Production of Scientists," *Science, 141,* 334–338.

Astin, A. W. 1971. *Predicting Academic Performance in College.* New York: Free Press.

Astin, A. W., and R. J. Panos. 1971. "The Evaluation of Educational Programs." In R. L. Thorndike (ed.), *Educational Measurement* (2d ed.). Washington, D.C.: American Council on Education.

August, G. J., J. F. Rychlak, and D. W. Felker. 1975. "Affective Assessment, Self-Concept, and the Verbal Learning Styles of Fifth-Grade Children," *Journal of Educational Psychology, 67,* 801–806.

Ausubel, D. P. 1963. "The Influence of Experience on the Development of Intelligence." Paper presented at the Conference on Productive Thinking in Education sponsored by the NEA Project on the Academically Talented Student, Washington, D.C.

Ausubel, D. P. 1968. *Educational Psychology: A Cognitive View.* New York: Holt, Rinehart and Winston.

Baker, F. B. 1971a. "Automation of Test Scoring, Administration, and Analysis." In R. L. Thorndike (ed.), *Educational Measurement.* Washington, D.C.: American Council on Education, pp. 202–236.

Baker, F. B. 1971b. "Computer Based Instructional Management Systems: A First Look," *Review of Educational Research, 41,* 51–70.

Baker, F. B. 1977. "Advances in Item Analysis," *Review of Educational Research, 47,* 151–178.

Bandura, A. 1969. *Principles of Behavior Modification.* New York: Holt, Rinehart and Winston.

Barcley, J. R. 1968. *Controversial Issues in Testing,* Guidance Monograph Series III. Boston: Houghton Mifflin.

Barro, S. M. 1970. "An Approach to Developing Accountability Measures for the Public Schools," *Phi Delta Kappan, 52,* 196–205.

Barsell, R. B., and J. Magoon. 1972. "The Persistence of First Impressions in Course and Instructor Evaluations." Paper presented at the Annual Meeting of the American Educational Research Association, Chicago, Ill.

Barzun, J. 1947. *Teacher in America.* Boston: Little, Brown.

Bauer, D. H. 1971. "The Effect of Test Instructions, Test Anxiety, Defensiveness, and Confidence in Judgment on Guessing Behavior in Multiple-Choice Situations," *Psychology in the Schools, 8,* 201–215.

Bauer, D. H. 1973. "Error Sources in Aptitude and Achievement Test Scores: A Review and Recommendation," *Measurement and Evaluation in Guidance, 6,* 28–34.

Bauernfeind, R. H. 1963. *Building a School Testing Program.* Boston: Houghton Mifflin, pp. 296–318.

Bayley, N. 1949. "Consistency and Variability in the Growth of Intelligence from Birth to Eighteen Years," *Journal of Genetic Psychology, 75,* 165–196.

Bayley, N. 1955. "On the Growth of Intelligence," *American Psychologist, 10,* 805–818.

Bayluk, R. J. 1974. "The Effects of Choice Weights and Item Weights on the Reliability and Predictive Validity of Reading Tests." Paper presented at the Annual Meeting of the National Council on Measurement in Education, Chicago, Ill.

Beck, M. D. 1974. "Achievement Test Reliability as a Function of Pupil-Response Procedures," *Journal of Educational Measurement, 11,* 109–114.

Beggs, D., E. Lewis, and R. Mayor. 1972. "The Effects of Various Techniques of Interpreting Test Results on Teacher Perception and Pupil Achievement," *Measurement and Evaluation in Guidance, 5,* 290–297.

Bell, T. 1971. "The Means and Ends of Accountability." *Proceedings of the Conferences on Educational Accountability.* Princeton, N.J.: Educational Testing Service.

Bennett, G. K., H. G. Seashore, and A. G. Wesman. 1951. *Counseling from Profile—A Casebook for the Differential Aptitude Tests.* New York: The Psychological Corporation.

Bennett, G. K., H. G. Seashore, and A. G. Wesman. 1963. *Differential Aptitude Tests.* New York: The Psychological Corporation.

Benson, W. W. 1969. "Graduate Grading Ssytems." Paper ED-036-262 presented at the Council of Graduate Schools in the United States, Washington, D.C.

Berdie, F. S. 1971. "What Test Questions Are Likely to Offend the General Public," *Journal of Educational Measurement, 8,* 2, 87–94.

Bereiter, C. E. 1963. "Some Persistent Dilemmas in the Measurement of Change." In C. W. Harris (ed.), *Problems in Measuring Change.* Madison: University of Wisconsin Press, pp. 3–20.

Bernhardson, C. H. 1967. "Comparison of the Three-Decision and Conventional Multiple-Choice Tests," *Psychological Reports, 20,* 695–698.

Biehler, R. F. 1971. *Psychology Applied to Teaching.* Boston: Houghton Mifflin.

Biggs, J. B. 1971. "Study Behavior and Performance in Objective and Essay Formats." Paper presented at the Annual Meeting of the American Educational Research Association, New York, N.Y.

Bills, R. E. 1975. *A System for Assessing Affectivity.* University, Ala.: University of Alabama Press.

Binet, A., and V. Henri, 1896. "Le Psychologie Individuell," *Année Psychologique, 2,* 411–465.

Binet, A., and Tr. Simon. 1905. "Methodes Nouvelles pour le Diagnostic du Niveau Intellectual des Anormaux," *Année Psychologique, 11,* 191–244.

Binet, A., and Tr. Simon. 1916, *The Development of Intelligence in Children.* Vineland N.J.: Training School Publication No. 11, p. 192.

Black, H. 1963. *They Shall Not Pass.* New York: Morrow.

Block, J. H. (ed.). 1971. *Mastery Learning: Theory and Practice.* New York: Holt, Rinehart and Winston.

Block, J. H. (ed.). 1974. *Schools, Society, and Mastery Learning.* New York: Holt, Rinehart and Winston.

Block, N. J. and G. Dworkin. 1974a. "I.Q.: Heritability and Inequality—Part 1," *Philosophy and Public Affairs,* Summer, 3(4), 331–409.

Block, N. J., and G. Dworkin. 1974b. "I.Q.: Heritability and Inequality—Part 2," *Philosophy and Public Affairs,* 4(1), 40–99.

Bloom, B. S. (ed.). 1956. *Taxonomy of Educational Objectives, Handbook I: The Cognitive Domain.* New York: McKay.

Bloom, B. S. 1964. *Stability and Change in Human Characteristics.* New York: Wiley, pp. 52–94.

Bloom, B. S. 1968. "Learning for Mastery," *Evaluation Comment,* UCLA, CSEIP, May, *1,* 2.

Bloom, B. S. 1971a. "Individual Differences in School Achievement: A Vanishing Point?" *Education at Chicago.* Chicago: Department and Graduate School of Education, University of Chicago, Winter, pp. 4–14.

Bloom, B. S. 1971b. "Mastery Learning and Its Implications for Curriculum Development." In E. W. Eisner (ed.), *Confronting Curriculum Reform.* Boston: Little, Brown.

Bloom, B. S. 1974. "Time and Learning," *American Psychologist, 29(9),* 682–688.

Bloom, B. S., J. Hastings, and G. F. Madaus. 1971. *Handbook on Formative and Summative Evaluation of Student Learning.* New York: McGraw-Hill.

Blumberg, H. H., C. B. De Soto, and J. L. Kuethe. 1966. "Evaluation of Rating Scale Formats," *Personnel Psychology, 19*, 243–260.

Board C., and D. R. Whitney. 1972. "The Effect of Poor Item Writing Practices on Test Difficulty, Reliability, and Validity." *Journal of Educational Measurement, 9*, 225–233.

Boggs, D. H., and J. R. Simon. 1968. "Differential Effect of Noise on Tasks of Varying Complexity," *Journal of Applied Psychology, 52*, 148–153.

Bordin, E. S. 1949. "Review of the OII." In O. K. Buros (ed.), *The Third Mental Measurement Yearbook*. New Brunswick, N.J.: Rutgers University Press.

Borgen, F. H. 1972. "Predicting Career Choices of Able College Men from Occupational and Basic Interest Scales of the Strong Vocational Interest Blank," *Journal of Counseling Psychology, 19*, 202–211.

Borgen, F. H., and G. T. Harper. 1973. "Predictive Validity for Measured Vocational Interests with Black and White College Men." *Measurement and Evaluation in Guidance, 6*, 19–27.

Borich, G. D., and D. Malitz. 1975. "Convergent and Discriminant Validation of Three Classroom Observation Systems: A Proposed Model," *Journal of Educational Psychology, 67*, 426–431.

Bormuth, John R. 1970. *On the Theory of Achievement Test Items*. Chicago: University of Chicago Press.

Bornstein, H., and K. Chamberlin. 1970. "An Investigation of the Effects of 'Verbal-Overload' on Achievement Tests," *American Educational Research Journal, 7*, 597–604.

Boynton, M. 1950. "Inclusion of 'None of These' Makes Spelling Items More Difficult," *Educational and Psychological Measurement, 10*, 431–432.

Bracht, G. H. 1969. *The Relationship of Treatment Tasks, Personological Variables and Dependent Variables to Aptitude-Treatment Interaction*. Boulder: Laboratory of Educational Research, University of Colorado.

Brandenburg, D. C., and D. R. Whitney. "Matched-Pairs True-False Scoring: Effect on Reliability and Validity," *Journal of Educational Measurement, 9*, 297–302.

Brennan, R. L., and L. M. Stolurow. 1971. "An Elementary Decision Process for the Formative Evaluation of an Instructional System." Paper presented at the Annual Meeting of the American Educational Research Association, New York, N.Y.

Brogden, H. E., and E. K. Taylor. 1950. "The Theory and Classification of Criterion Bias," *Educational and Psychological Measurement, 10*, 159–186.

Brophy, J. E., C. L. Coulter, W. J. Crawford, C. M. Evertson, and C. E. King. 1975. "Classroom Observation Scales: Stability Across Time and Context and Relationships With Student Learning Gains," *Journal of Educational Psychology, 67*, 873–881.

Brophy, J. E., and T. L. Good. 1970. "Teachers Communications of Differential Expectations for Children's Classroom Performance," *Journal of Educational Psychology, 61*, 365–374.

Browder, L. H., Jr. 1971. *Emerging Patterns of Administrative Accountability*. Berkeley, Calif.: McCutchan Publishing Corporation.

Browder, L. H., Jr. 1975. *Who's Afraid of Educational Accountability?* Denver: Cooperative Accountability Project.

Browder, L. H., Jr., W. A. Atkins, and E. Kaya. 1973. *Developing an Educationally Accountable Program*. Berkeley, Calif.: McCutchan Publishing Corporation.

Brown, F. G. 1970. *Principles of Educational and Psychological Testing*. Hinsdale, Ill.: Dryden.

Brown, F. G. *Principles of Educational and Psychological Testing*. (2d ed.). New York: Holt, Rinehart and Winston, 1976.

Burns, R. W. 1972. *New Approaches to Behavioral Objectives*. Dubuque, Iowa: William C. Brown Company.

Buros, O. K. (ed.). 1938. *The 1938 Mental Measurements Yearbook*. New Brunswick, N.J.: Rutgers University Press.

Buros, O. K. (ed.). 1941. *The Nineteen-Forty Mental Measurements Yearbook*. New Brunswick, N.J.: Rutgers University Press.

Buros, O. K. (ed.). 1949. *The Third Mental Measurements Yearkbook*. New Brunswick, N.J.: Rutgers University Press.

Buros, O. K. (ed.). 1953. *The Fourth Mental Measurements Yearbook*. Highland Park, N.J.: Gryphon Press.

Buros, O. K. (ed.). 1959. *The Fifth Mental Measurements Yearbook*. Highland Park, N.J.: Gryphon Press.

Buros, O. K. (ed.). 1965. *The Sixth Mental Measurements Yearbook*. Highland Park, N.J.: Gryphon Press.

Buros, O. K. (ed.). 1972. *The Seventh Mental Measurements Yearbook*. Highland Park, N.J.: Gryphon Press.

Buros, O. K. (ed.). 1974. *Tests in Print: II*. Highland Park, N.J.: Gryphon Press.

Burt, C. 1955. "The Evidence for the Concept of Intelligence," *British Journal of Educational Psychology*, 25, 158–177.

Burt, C. 1958. "The Inheritance of Mental Ability," *American Psychologist*, 13, 1–15.

Burt, C. 1966. "The Genetic Determination of Differences in Intelligence: A Study of Monozygotic Twins Reared Together and Apart," *British Journal of Psychology*, 57, 137–153.

Burt, C. 1972. "Inheritance of General Intelligence," *American Psychologist*, 27, 175–190.

Burwen, L. S. 1971. "Current Practices: A National Survey." Paper presented at the Annual Meeting of the American Educational Research Association, New York, N.Y.

Butcher, H. J. 1968. *Human Intelligence: Its Nature and Assessment*. New York: Harper & Row.

Calandra, A. 1964. "The Barometer Story," in *Current Science Teacher*, Jan 6, 14.

Callenbach, C. 1973. "The Effects of Instruction and Practice in Content-Independent Test-Taking Techniques upon the Standardized Reading Test Scores of Selected Second-Grade Students," *Journal of Educational Measurement*, 10, 25–30.

Campbell, D. P. 1969. *Strong Vocational Interest Blanks Manual—1969 Supplement*. Stanford, Calif.: Stanford University Press.

Campbell, D. P. 1971. *Handbook for the Strong Vocational Interest Blank*. Stanford, Calif.: Stanford University Press.

Campbell, D. P. 1974. *Manual for the SCII*. Stanford, Calif.: Stanford University Press.

Campbell, D. P., J. I. Chrichton, and P. Webber. 1974. "A New Edition of the SVIB: The Strong-Campbell Interest Inventory," *Measurement and Evaluation in Guidance*, 7, 92–94.

Campbell, D. T. 1950. "The Indirect Assessment of Social Attitudes," *Psychological Bulletin*, 47, 31.

Campbell, D. T., and J. C. Stanley. 1963. *Experimental and Quasi-Experimental Designs for Research*. Chicago: Rand McNally.

Campbell, R. E. 1971. "Accountability and Stone Soup," *Phi Delta Kappan*, 53, 176–178.

Carroll, J. B. 1963. "A Model of School Learning," *Teachers College Record*, 64, 723–733.

Carroll, J. B. 1971. "Problems of Measurement Related to the Concept of Learning for Mastery." In J. H. Block (ed.), *Mastery Learning: Theory and Practice*. New York: Holt, Rinehart and Winston, p. 152.

Carroll, L. 1916. *Alice's Adventures in Wonderland*. Chicago: Rand McNally.

Carter, H. C. 1969. Measurement of Attitudes toward School," *California Journal of Research*, 20, 186–192.

Cartwright, G. F., and J. L. Derevensky. 1975. "An Attitudinal Study of Computer-Assisted Testing as a Learning Method." Paper presented at the Annual Meeting of the American Educational Research Association, Washington, D.C.

Carver, R. P. 1974. "Two Dimensions of Tests: Psychometric and Edumetric," *American Psychologist*, 29, 512–518.

Cashen, V. M., and G. C. Ramseyer, 1969. "The Use of Separate Answer Sheets by Primary School Children," *Journal of Educational Measurement*, 6, 155–158.

Cattell, J. McK. 1890. "Mental Tests and Measurements," *Mind*, 15, 373–381.

Cattell, R. B. 1963. "Theory of Fluid and Crystallized Intelligence: A Critical Experiment," *Journal of Educational Psychology*, 54, 1–22.

Cattell, R. B. 1971. *Abilities: Their Structure, Growth, and Action*. Boston: Houghton Mifflin.

Cattell, R. B., and A. K. S. Cattell. 1973. *Handbook for the Individual or Group Culture-Fair Intelligence Test*. Champaign, Ill.: Institute for Personality and Ability Testing.

Cegelka, P. T., C. Omvig, and D. L. Larimore, 1974. "Effects of Attitude and Sex on Vocational Interests," *Measurement and Evaluation in Guidance*, 7, 106–111.

Chadwick, E. B. 1864. "Statistics of Educational Results," *The Museum, A Quarterly Magazine of Education, Literature, and Science*, 3, 480–484.

Chaikin, A. L., and E. Sigler, 1973. "Non-verbal Mediators of Teacher Expectancy Effects." Paper presented at the Eastern Psychological Association Annual Meeting, Washington, D.C.

Chase, C. I. 1964. "Relative Length of Options and Response Set in Multiple-Choice Items." *Journal of Educational Measurement*, 1, 38. (Abstract)

Chase, C. I. 1972. "Mad on Measurement? Tell it to Grossbucket," *The Chronicle of Higher Education*, May 8, p. 9.

Chick, J. M. 1970. "Innovations in the Use of Career Information." In the *Guidance Monograph Series IV: Career Information and Development*. Boston: Houghton Mifflin.

Clairborn, W. L. 1969. "Expectancy Effects in the Classroom: A Failure to Replicate," *Journal of Educational Psychology*, 60, 377–383.

Clark, C. A. 1962. "Should Students Change Answers on Objective Tests?" *Chicago Schools Journal*, 43, 382–385.

Clark, C. A. 1968. "The Use of Separate Answer Sheets in Testing Slow-Learning Pupils," *Journal of Educational Measurement*, 5, 61–64.

Clark, K. E. 1957. *Vocational Interests of Non-professional Men*. Minneapolis: University of Minnesota Press.

Claus, C. K. 1968. "Verbs and Imperative Sentences as a Basis for Stating Educational Objectives." Paper given at meeting of the National Council on Measurement in Education, Chicago, Ill.

Cleary, T. A. 1968. "Test Bias: Prediction of Grades of Negro and White Students in Integrated Colleges, *Journal of Educational Measurement*, 5, 115–124.

Cleary, T. A., L. G. Humphreys, A. S. Kendrick, and A. Wesman, 1975. "Educational Uses of Tests with Disadvantaged Students," *American Psychologist*, 30, 15–41.

Clifford, P. I., and J. A. Fishman, 1963. "The Impact of Testing Programs on College Preparation and Attendance." *The Impact and Improvement of School Testing Programs*. Yearbook LXII, Part II, NSSE. p. 87.

Coffman, W. E. 1971. "Essay Examinations." In R. L. Thorndike (ed.), *Educational Measurement*. Washington, D.C.: American Council on Education.

Coffman, W. E., and D. A. Kurfman, 1968. "A Comparison of Two Methods of Reading Essay Examinations," *American Educational Research Journal*, 5, 99–107.

Cole, N. S. 1973. "On Measuring the Vocational Interests of Women," *Journal of Counseling Psychology*, 20, 105–112.

Cole, N. S., and G. R. Hanson. 1971. "An Analysis of the Structure of Vocational Interests," *Journal of Counseling Psychology*, 18, 478–487.

Coleman, J. S., et al. 1966. *Equality of Educational Opportunity*, Washington, D.C.: U.S. Department of Health, Education and Welfare, Office of Education.

College Entrance Examination Board, 1966. *Annual Report of the College Board, 1965–66*. New York: College Entrance Examination Board.

Collet, L. S. 1971. "Elimination Scoring: An Empirical Evaluation," *Journal of Educational Measurement, 8,* 209–214.

Combs, A. W. 1967. "Humanizing Education: The Person in the Process." In R. R. Leeper (ed.), *Humanizing Education: The Person in the Process.* Washington, D.C.: Association for Supervision and Curriculum Development, pp. 73–88.

Commission on the Reorganization of Secondary Education. 1918. *The Seven Cardinal Principles of Secondary Education.* Washington, D.C.: Bureau of Education, Government Printing Office.

Committee on Concepts and Values. 1957. *A Guide to Content in the Social Studies.* Washington, D.C.: National Council for the Social Studies.

Cook, D. L. 1955. "An Investigation of Three Aspects of Free-Response and Choice-Type Tests at the College Level," *Dissertation Abstracts, 15,* 1351.

Cooley, W. W. 1971. "Techniques for Considering Multiple Measurements." In Robert L. Thorndike (ed.), *Educational Measurement* (2d ed.). Washington, D.C.: American Council on Education.

Coombs, C. H. 1964. *A Theory of Data.* New York: Wiley.

Corey, S. M. 1953. *Action Research to Improve School Practices.* New York: Teachers College, Columbia University.

Costin, F. 1970. "The Optimum Number of Alternatives in Multiple-Choice Achievement Tests: Some Empirical Evidence for a Mathematical Proof," *Educational and Psychological Measurement, 30,* 353–358.

Cox, R. C. 1964. "An Empirical Investigation of the Effect of Item Selection Techniques on Achievement Test Construction." Unpublished doctoral dissertation. East Lansing: Michigan State University.

Cox, R. C., and B. G. Sterrett, 1970. "A Model for Increasing the Meaning of Test Scores," *Journal of Educational Measurement, 7,* 227–228.

Cox, R. C., and J. S. Vargas. 1966, "A Comparison of Item Selection Techniques for Norm-Referenced and Criterion-Referenced Tests." Paper presented at the Annual Meeting of the National Council on Measurement in Education, Chicago, Ill.

Crehan, K. D. 1974. "Item Analysis for Teacher-Made Mastery Tests," *Journal of Educational Measurement, 11,* 255–262.

Crehan, K. D., R. A. Koehler, and M. J. Slakter. 1974. "Longitudinal Studies of Test Wiseness," *Journal of Educational Measurement, 11,* 209–212.

Crites, J. O. 1965. "Measurement of Vocational Maturity in Adolescence: I. Attitude Test of the Vocational Development Inventory," *Psychological Monographs, 72,* No. 55.

Crites, J. O. 1974. "Methodological Issues in the Measurement of Career Maturity," *Measurement and Evaluation in Guidance, 6,* 200–209.

Crockenberg, S. B. 1972. "Creativity Tests: A Boon or Boondazzle for Education," *Review of Educational Research, 42,* 27–46.

Crocker, L. M., and J. Benson, 1976. "A Comparison of Guessing, Risk-Taking, and Achievement under Norm-Referenced and Criterion-Referenced Testing Conditions." Paper given at the Annual Meeting of the National Council on Measurement in Education, San Francisco, Calif.

Crockett, L. M. 1974. "Observational Ratings For Evaluating Student Performance: Is Construct Validity Necessary?" Paper presented at the Annual Meeting of the National Council on Measurement in Education, Chicago, Ill.

Cromer, W. 1969. An Empirical Investigation of Student Attitudes toward the Pass–Fail Grading System at Wellesley College." Paper presented at a meeting of the Eastern Psychological Association, Philadelphia, Pa.

Cronbach, L. J. 1942. "Studies of Acquiescence as a Factor in the True-False Test," *Journal of Educational Psychology, 33,* 401–415.

Cronbach, L. J. 1946. "Response Sets and Test Validity," *Educational and Psychological Measurement, 6,* 475–494.

Cronbach, L. J. 1950. "Further Evidence on Response Sets and Test Design," *Educational and Psychological Measurement, 10,* 3–31.

Cronbach, L. J. 1951. "Coefficient Alpha and the Internal Structure of Tests," *Psychometrika, 16,* 297–334.

Cronbach, L. J. 1963. "Course Improvement through Evaluation," *Teacher's College Record, 64,* 672–683.

Cronbach, L. J. 1969. "Heredity, Environment, and Educational Policy," *Harvard Educational Review, 39,* 338–347.

Cronbach, L. J. 1970a. *Essentials of Psychological Testing* (3d ed.). New York: Harper & Row.

Cronbach, L. J. 1970b. "Review of Bormuth's *On the Theory of Achievement Test Items,*" *Psychometrika, 35,* 509–511.

Cronbach, L. J. 1971a. "Comments on Mastery Learning and Its Implications for Curriculum Development." In Elliot W. Eisner (ed.), *Confronting Curriculum Reform.* Boston: Little, Brown, pp. 49–55.

Cronbach, L. J. 1971b. "Test Validation." In R. L. Thorndike (ed.), *Educational Measurement* (2d ed.). Washington, D.C.: American Council on Education.

Cronbach, L. J. 1972. "Review of the Analysis of Learning Potential." In O. K. Buros (ed.), *The Seventh Mental Measurements Yearbook.* Highland Park, N.J.: Gryphon Press.

Cronbach, L. J. 1975. "Five Decades of Public Controversy over Public Testing," *American Psychologist, 30,* 1–14.

Cronbach, L. J., and L. Furby. 1970. "How We Should Measure 'Change'—or Should We?" *Psychological Bulletin, 74,* 1, 68–80.

Cronbach, L. J., and G. C. Gleser. 1965. *Psychological Tests and Personnel Decisions* (2d ed.). Urbana, Ill.: University of Illinois Press.

Cronbach, L. J., G. C. Gleser, H. Nanda, and N. Rajaratnam. 1972. *The Dependability of Behavioral Measurements: Multifacet Studies of Generalizability.* New York: Wiley.

Cronbach, L. J., and P. E. Meehl. 1955. "Construct Validity in Psychological Tests," *Psychological Bulletin, 52,* 281–302.

Cronbach, L. J., and R. E. Snow. 1969. *Final Report: Individual Differences in Learning Ability as a Function of Instructional Variables.* Stanford, Calif.: School of Education, Stanford University.

Cronbach, L. J., and P. Suppes (eds.). 1969. *Research for Tomorrow's Schools: Disciplined Inquiry for Education.* New York: Macmillan.

Cronbach, L. J., and W. G. Warrington. 1952. "Efficiency of Multiple-Choice Tests as a Function of Spread of Item Difficulties," *Psychometrika, 17,* 127–147.

Cronin, J., et al. 1975. "Race, Class, and Intelligence: A Critical Look at the I.Q. Controversy," *International Journal of Mental Health, 3*(4), 46–132.

Crowne, D. P., and D. Marlowe. 1960. "A New Scale of Social Desirability Independent of Psychopathology," *Journal of Consulting Psychology, 24,* 349–354.

Cunningham, L. L. 1971. "Our Accountability Problems." In L. H. Browder, Jr. (ed.). *Emerging Patterns of Administrator Accountability.* Berkeley, Calif.: McCutchan Publishing Corporation.

Cureton, E. E. 1966a. "The Correction for Guessing," *Journal of Experimental Education, 34,* 44–47.

Cureton, E. E. 1966b. "Simplified Formulas for Item Analysis," *Journal of Educational Measurement, 3,* 187–189.

D'Agostino, R. B., and E. F. Cureton, 1975. "The 27 Percent Rule Revisited," *Educational and Psychological Measurement, 35,* 47–50.

Dahl, T. A. 1973. "Test Review of the Boehm Test of Basic Concepts," *Measurement and Evaluation in Guidance, 6,* 63–65.

Dale, W. 1969. "Concerning Grading and Other Forms of Student Evaluation." Paper

ED-036-260 presented at the Council of Graduate Schools in the United States, Washington, D.C.

Dallis, G. T. 1970. "The Effect of Precise Objectives upon Student Achievement in Health Education," *Journal of Experimental Education, 39*, 20–23.

Darlington, R. B. 1971. "Another Look at 'Cultural Fairness,'" *Journal of Educational Measurement, 8*, 71–82.

DAT Manual (4th ed.). 1966. New York: The Psychological Corporation.

Davis, F. B. 1959. "Estimation and Use of Scoring Weights for Each Choice in Multiple-Choice Test Items," *Educational and Psychological Measurement, 19*, 307–314.

Davis, F. B. 1964. *Educational Measurements and Their Interpretation.* Belmont, Calif.: Wadsworth.

DeCecco, J. P. 1968. *The Psychology of Learning and Instruction: Educational Psychology.* Englewood Cliffs, N.J.: Prentice-Hall.

Derr, R. L. 1973. *A Taxonomy of Social Purposes of Public Schools.* New York: McKay.

Deterline, W. A. 1971. "Applied Accountability," *Educational Technology, 11*, 15–20.

DeVoto, B. 1952. "The Third Floor," *Harper's*, March.

Diamond, E. E. 1975a. "Guidelines For the Assessment of Sex Bias and Sex Fairness," *Measurement and Evaluation in Guidance, 8*, 7–11.

Diamond, E. E. (ed.), 1975b. *Issues of Sex Bias and Sex Fairness in Career Interest Measurement.* Washington, D.C.: U. S. Government Printing Office.

Diamond, J. J., and W. J. Evans, 1972. "An Investigation of the Cognitive Correlates of Test Wiseness," *Journal of Educational Measurement, 9*, 145–150.

Diamond, J. J., and W. J. Evans, 1973. "The Correction for Guessing." *Review of Educational Research, 43*, 181–192.

Dick, W. 1968. "A Methodology for the Formative Evaluation of Instructional Materials," *Journal of Educational Measurement, 5*, 99–102.

Diederich, P. B. 1967. "Cooperative Preparation and Rating of Essay Tests," *English Journal, 56*, 573–584.

Diederich, P. B. 1970. "Review of Bormuth's *On the Theory of Achievement Test Items*," *Educational and Psychological Measurement, 13*, 1003–1005.

Dionne, J. L. 1969. Paper presented at the American Personnel and Guidance Association Annual Meeting, New Orleans, La.

Donlon, T. F. 1975. "An Optimizing Weight for Wrong Scores." Paper presented at the Annual Meeting of the Northeast Educational Research Association, Provincetown, Mass.

Douglass, H. R., and M. Tallmadge. 1934. "How University Students Prepare for New Types of Examinations," *School and Society, 39*, 318–320.

Downey, R. G. 1974. *Associative Evaluations: Nominations Versus Ratings,* Technical Paper No. 253. Arlington, Va.: Army Research Institute for Behavioral and Social Sciences.

Downie, N. M., and R. W. Heath, 1970. *Basic Statistical Methods* (3d ed.). New York: Harper & Row.

Downs, A. 1968. "Competition and Community Schools." Mimeograph.

Doyle, K. O., Jr. 1975. *Student Evaluation of Instruction.* Lexington, Mass.: Heath.

Dressel, P. L. 1954. "Evaluation as Instruction," *Proceedings of the 1953 Invitational Conference on Testing Problems.* Princeton, N.J.: Educational Testing Service, pp. 23–24.

Dressel, P. L., and C. H. Nelson, 1961. "Testing and Grading Policies." In P. L. Dressel et al. (eds.), *Evaluation in Higher Education.* Boston: Houghton Mifflin.

DuBois, P. H. 1970. *A History of Psychological Testing.* Boston: Allyn and Bacon.

DuCette, J., and S. Wolk. 1972. "Test Performance and the Use of Optional Questions," *Journal of Experimental Education, 40*(3), 21–24.

Dudycha, A. L., and J. B. Carpenter, 1973. "Effects of Item Writing Format on Item Discrimination and Difficulty," *Journal of Applied Psychology, 58*, 116–121.

Dunn, T. F., and L. G. Goldstein, 1959. "Test Difficulty, Validity, and Reliability as Functions of Selective Multiple-Choice Item Construction Principles," *Educational and Psychological Measurement, 19,* 171–179.

Durnan, J., and J. M. Scandura. 1973. "An Algorithmic Approach to Assessing Behavior Potential: Comparison with Item Forms and Hierarchial Technologies," *Journal of Educational Psychology, 65,* 262–272.

Durost, W. N. 1961. *The Characteristics, Use, and Computation of Stanines,* Test Services Notebook No. 23. New York: Harcourt.

Dyck, W., and G. Plancke-Schuyten. 1976. "Manipulations with Multiple-Choice Tests: A Probability Function of a Total Testscore V," *Educational and Psychological Measurement, 36,* 259–262.

Dyer, H. S. 1967. "The Discovery and Development of Educational Goals." *Proceedings of the 1966 Invitational Conference on Testing Problems.* Princeton, N.J.: Educational Testing Service, pp. 12–29.

Dyer, H. S. 1970a. "Statewide Evaluation—What Are the Priorities?" *Phi Delta Kappan, 51,* 558–559.

Dyer, H. S. 1970b. "Toward Objective Criteria of Professional Accountability in the Schools of New York City," *Phi Delta Kappan, 52,* 206–211.

Ebel, R. L. 1951. "Writing the Test Item." In E. F. Linquist (ed.), *Educational Measurement.* Washington, D.C.: American Council on Education.

Ebel, R. L. 1953. In Robert H. Bauernfeind, *Building a School Testing Program.* Boston: Houghton Mifflin, p. 315.

Ebel, R. L. 1961. "Must All Tests Be Valid?" *American Psychologist, 15,* 640–647.

Ebel, R. L. 1962. "Content Standard Test Scores," *Educational and Psychological Measurement, 22,* 15–25.

Ebel, R. L. 1965a. "Confidence Weighting and Test Reliability," *Journal of Educational Measurements, 2,* 49–57.

Ebel, R. L. 1965b. *Measuring Educational Achievement.* Englewood Cliffs, N.J.: Prentice-Hall.

Ebel, R. L. 1968. "Blind Guessing on Objective Achievement Tests," *Journal of Educational Measurement, 5,* 321–325.

Ebel, R. L. 1969a. "The Relation Between Curricula and Achievement Testing." Mimeograph, Michigan State University.

Ebel, R. L. 1969b. "Relation of Scale Fineness to Grade Accuracy," *Journal of Educational Measurement, 6,* 217–221.

Ebel, R. L. 1970. "The Case for True-False Items," *School Review, 78,* 373–389.

Ebel, R. L. 1972. *Essentials of Educational Measurement.* Englewood Cliffs, N.J.: Prentice-Hall.

Ebel, R. L. 1974. "Shall We Get Rid of Grades?" *Measurement in Education, 5*(4), 1–5.

Ebel, R. L. 1975a. "Can Teachers Write Good True-False Test Items?" *Journal of Educational Measurement, 12,* 31–35.

Ebel, R. L. 1975b. "Prediction? Validation? Construct Validity?" Mimeograph.

Ebel, R. L., and D. Damrin. 1960. "Tests and Examinations." In C. W. Harris (ed.), *Encyclopedia of Educational Research* (3d ed.). New York: Macmillan, pp. 1502–1517.

Echternacht, G. J. 1976. "Reliability and Validity of Item Option Weighting Schemes," *Educational and Psychological Measurement, 36,* 301–309.

Echternacht, G. J., R. F. Boldt, and W. S. Sellman. 1972. "Personality Influences on Confidence Test Scores," *Journal of Educational Measurement, 9,* 235–241.

Eckland, B. K. 1967. Genetics and Sociology: A Reconsideration. *American Sociological Review, 32,* 173–194.

Educational Testing Service. 1960. *Short-Cut Statistics for Teacher-Made Tests.* Princeton, N.J.: Educational Testing Service.

Edwards, A. L. 1957a. *The Social Desirability Variable in Personality Assessment and Research.* New York: Holt, Rinehart and Winston.

Edwards, A. L. 1957b. *Techniques of Attitude Scale Construction.* New York: Appleton.

Edwards, A. L. 1970. *The Measurement of Personality Traits by Scales and Inventories.* New York: Holt, Rinehart and Winston.

Eells, W. C. 1930. "Reliability of Repeated Essay Grading of Essay Type Questions," *Journal of Educational Psychology, 31*, 48–52.

Eisner, E. W. 1969. "Instructional and Expressure Educational Objectives: Their Formulation and Use in Curriculum." In W. J. Popham et al., *Instructional Objectives.* Chicago: Rand McNally, pp. 1–18.

Elton, C. F., and H. A. Rose. 1970. "Male Occupational Constancy and Change: Its Prediction According to Holland's Theory," *Journal of Counseling Psychology Monographs, 17* (No. 6, Part 2).

Engelhart, M. D. 1965. "A Comparison of Several Item-Discrimination Indices," *Journal of Educational Measurement, 2*, 69–76.

Engelmann, S., and T. Englemann. 1968. *Give Your Child a Superior Mind.* New York: Simon and Schuster.

Erlenmeyer-Kimling, L., and L. F. Jarvik. 1963. "Genetics and Intelligence: A Review," *Science, 142*, December, 1477–1479.

Ethical Standards of Psychologists. 1953. Washington, D.C.: The American Psychological Association.

Ethical Standards for Psychologists. 1973. Washington, D.C.: The American Psychological Association.

Evans, F. R., and L. W. Pike. 1973. "The Effects of Instruction for Three Mathematics Item Formats," *Journal of Educational Measurement, 10*, 257–272.

Evans, J. W. 1974. "Evaluating Education Programs—Are We Getting Anywhere?" *Educational Researcher, 3*(8), 7–12.

Eysenck, H. J. 1971. *The IQ Argument.* Freeport, N.Y.: The Library Press.

Falls, J. D. 1928. "Research in Secondary Education," *Kentucky School Journal, 6*, 42–46.

Federal Executive Agency. 1976. "Guidelines on Employee Selection Procedures," *Federal Register, 41*(227), Nov. 23.

Federal Register, 1970. *35,* 149.

Feldmesser, R. A. 1969. *The Option: Analysis of an Educational Innovation,* Hanover, N.H.: Dartmouth College.

Feldmesser, R. A. 1971. "The Positive Function of Grades." Paper presented at the Annual Meeting of the American Educational Research Association, New York, N.Y.

Feldt, L. A. 1967. "Reliability of Differences between Scores," *American Educational Research Journal, 4*, 139–145.

Festinger, L. 1947. "The Treatment of Qualitative Data by Scale Analysis," *Psychological Bulletin, 44,* 149–161.

Findley, W. G. 1974. "Ability Grouping." Chapter 3 in G. R. Gredler (ed.), *Ethical and Legal Factors in the Practice of School Psychology.* Harrisburg, Pa.: Pennsylvania State Department of Education.

Findley, W. G., and M. M. Bryan. 1971. *Ability Grouping: 1970 Status, Impact and Alternatives.* Athens, Ga.: Center for Educational Improvement, University of Georgia.

Finley, C. J., and F. S. Berdie. 1970. *The National Assessment Approach to Exercise Development.* Denver: National Assessment of Educational Progress.

Fishbein, M. (ed.). 1967. *Attitude Theory and Measurement.* New York: Wiley.

Fiske, D. W. 1963. "Problems in Measuring Personality." In J. A. Wepman and R. W. Heine (eds.), *Concepts of Personality.* London: Aldine, pp. 449–473.

Fiske, E. B. 1976. "New Test Developed to Replace I.Q." *The New York Times,* February 18, p. 28.

Flanagan, J. C. 1971. "The Plan System for Individualizing Education," *Measurement in Education, 2*(2), January, 1–8.

Flanagan, J. C., and D. Russ-Eft. 1975. *An Empirical Study to Aid in Formulating Educational Goals.* Palo Alto, Calif.: American Institutes for Research.

Flanagan, J. C., W. M. Shanner, and R. Mager. 1971. *Behavioral Objectives: A Guide for Individualizing Learning.* New York: Westinghouse Learning Press.

Flaugher, R. L. 1970. *Testing Practices, Minority Groups and Higher Education: A Review and Discussion of the Research,* Research Bulletin 70-41. Princeton, N.J.: Educational Testing Service.

Flaugher, R. L. 1974. "Some Points of Confusion in Discussing the Testing of Black Students." Chapter 2 in L. P. Miller, *The Testing of Black Students.* Englewood Cliffs, N.J.: Prentice-Hall.

Fleming, E., and R. G. Anttonen. 1971. "Teacher Expectancy or My Fair Lady," *American Educational Research Journal, 8,* 241–252.

Follman, J., A. J. Lowe, and W. Miller. 1971. "Graphics Variables and Reliability and Level of Essay Grades," *American Educational Research Journal, 8,* 365–373.

Folsom, C. H. 1973. "Effects of Mental Abilities on Obtained Intercorrelations among VPI Scales," *Measurement and Evaluation in Guidance, 6,* 74–81.

Foote, R., and C. Belinsky. 1972. "It Pays to Switch?: Consequences of Changing Answers on Multiple-Choice Examinations," *Psychological Reports, 31,* 667–673.

Fraenkel, J. R. 1969. "Value Education in the Social Studies," *Phi Delta Kappan, 50,* 457–461.

Freeman, F. S. 1962. *Theory and Practice of Psychological Testing* (3d ed.). New York: Holt, Rinehart and Winston.

Freeman, J. T. 1969. *A Summary Progress Report on an Experimental Study of a Pass/No Report Grading System.* San Bernardino, Calif.: California State College at San Bernardino.

Fremer, J., et al. 1976. *Graduating Early. The Question of an Equivalency Examination for Florida High School Students.* Princeton, N.J.: Educational Testing Service.

French, J. M. 1965. "Schools of Thought in Judging Excellence of English Themes." In A. Anastasi (ed.), *Testing Problems in Perspective.* Washington, D.C.: American Council on Education.

French, J. W., and W. B. Michael. 1966. *Standards for Educational and Psychological Tests and Manuals,* Washintgon, D.C.: American Psychological Association.

French, J. W., et al. 1957. *Behavioral Goals of General Education in High School.* New York: Russell Sage.

Fricke, B. G. 1975. *Grading, Testing, Standards, and All That.* Ann Arbor: Evaluation and Examinations Office, University of Michigan.

Frisbie, D. 1971. "Comparative Reliabilities and Validities of True-False and Multiple-Choice Tests." Unpublished Ph.D. dissertation. Michigan State University, East Lansing, Mich.

Frisbie, D. A. 1974. "The Effect of Item Format on Reliability and Validity: A Study of Multiple-Choice and True False Achievement Tests." *Educational and Psychological Measurement, 34,* 885–892.

Fruchter, B. 1954. *Introduction to Factor Analysis.* Princeton, N.J.: Van Nostrand.

Furst, E. J. 1958. *Constructing Evaluation Instruments.* New York: McKay.

Futcher, W. G. A. 1973. "Test Performance and the Use of Optional Questions." *Journal of Experimental Education, 41*(4), 23–25.

Gaffney, R. F., and T. O. Maguire. 1971. "Use of Optically Scored Test Answer Sheets with Young Children," *Journal of Educational Measurement, 8,* 103–106.

Gage, N. L. 1972. "I.Q. Heritability, Race Differences, and Educational Research," *Phi Delta Kappan, 53,* 308–312.

Gage, N. L., et al. 1957. "The Psychological Meaning of Acquiescence Set for Authoritarianism," *Journal of Abnormal and Social Psychology, 55,* 98–103.

Gagné, R. M. 1965. "Educational Objectives and Human Performance." In J. D. Krumboltz (ed.), *Learning and the Educational Process.* Chicago: Rand McNally, pp. 1–24.

Gagné, R. M. 1970. *The Conditions of Learning.* New York: Holt, Rinehart and Winston.

Gaines, W. G., and E. A. Jongsma. 1974. "The Effect of Training in Test-Taking Skills on the Achievement Scores of Fifth Grade Pupils." Paper presented at the Annual Meeting of the National Council on Education, Chicago, Ill.

Gall, M. 1967. "They Learn More Than You Teach Them," *Grade Teacher Magazine*, April.

Gallagher, P. D., and L. R. Gay. 1976. "The Comparative Effectiveness of Tests versus Written Exercises in a Competency-Based Research Course." Paper presented at the Annual Meeting of the American Educational Research Association, San Francisco, Calif.

Gallup, G. H. 1971. "The Third Annual Survey of the Public's Attitudes toward the Public Schools," *Phi Delta Kappan, 53*, 33–48.

Gallup, G. H. 1974. "Sixth Annual Gallup Poll of Public's Attitudes Toward Education," *Phi Delta Kappan, 56*, 20–32.

Gallup, G. H. 1976. "Eighth Annual Gallup Poll of the Public's Attitudes toward the Public Schools, *Phi Delta Kappan, 58*, 187–201.

Garren, J. A. 1976. "Using Passage-Dependency in Constructing a Criterion-Referenced Reading Test." Paper presented at the Annual Meeting of the National Council on Measurement in Education. San Francisco, Calif.

Gates, A. I. 1947. *The Improvement of Reading: A Program of Diagnostic and Remedial Methods* (3d ed.). New York: Macmillan.

Gaynor, J., and J. Millham. 1976. "Student Performance and Evaluation under Variant Teaching and Testing Methods in a Large Lecture Course," *Journal of Educational Psychology, 66*, 312–317.

Gerberich, J. R. 1956. *Specimen Objective Test Items: A Guide to Achievement Test Construction.* New York: McKay.

Getzels, J. W. 1960. "Non-IQ Intellectual and Other Factors in College Admission." In K. E. Anderson, (ed.), *The Coming Crisis in the Selection of Students for College Entrance.* Washington, D.C.: American Educational Research Association.

Getzels, J. W., and P. W. Jackson. 1962. *Creativity and Intelligence.* New York: Wiley.

Ghiselli, E. E. 1966. *The Validity of Occupational Aptitude Tests.* New York: Wiley.

Gibb, B. G. 1964. "Test Wiseness as a Secondary Cue Response." Unpublished Ph.D. dissertation. Ann Arbor: University Microfilms, No. 64–7643.

Gideonse, H. D. 1969. "Behavioral Objectives: Continuing the Dialogue," *Science Teacher, 36*, January, 51–54.

Gilman, D. A., and P. Ferry. 1972. "Increasing Test Reliability through Self-Scoring Procedures." *Journal of Educational Measurement, 9*, 205–207.

Ginsberg, E. 1971. *Career Guidance: Who Needs It, Who Provides It, Who Can Improve It.* New York: McGraw-Hill.

Gladstone, R. 1975. "Where Is Fashion Leading Us?" *American Psychologist, 30*, 604–605.

Glaser, R. 1968. "Adapting the Elementary School Curriculum to Individual Performance," *Proceedings of the 1967 Invitational Conference on Testing Problems.* Princeton, N.J.: Educational Testing Service.

Glaser, R. 1973. "Individuals and Learning: The New Aptitudes." In M. C. Wittrock (ed.), *Changing Education.* Englewood Cliffs, N.J.: Prentice-Hall.

Glaser, R., and A. J. Nitko. 1971. "Measurement in Learning and Instruction." In R. L. Thorndike (ed.), *Educational Measurement* (2d ed.). Washington, D.C.; American Council on Education.

Glass, G. V. 1975. "A Paradox about Excellence of Schools and the People in Them," *Educational Researcher, 4*(3), 9–12.

Glass, G. V., and D. E. Wiley. 1964. "Formula Scoring and Test Reliability," *Journal of Educational Measurement, 1*, 43–47.

Goddard, H. H. 1946. "What Is Intelligence?" *Journal of Social Psychology, 24*, 68.

Godshalk, F. I., F. Swineford, and W. Coffman. 1966. *The Measurement of Writing Ability.* New York: College Entrance Examination Board.

Goldfried, D. M., and T. D'Zurilla. 1973. "Prediction of Academic Competence by Means of the Survey of Study Habits and Attitudes," *Journal of Educational Psychology, 64,* 116–122.

Goldman, L. 1971. *Using Tests in Counseling* (2d ed.). New York: Appleton.

Goodlad, J. I. 1952. "Research and Theory Regarding Promotion and Nonpromotion," *Elementary School Journal.* November, *53,* 150–155.

Gooler, D. D. 1971. "Some Uneasy Inquiries into Accountability." In L. M. Lessinger and R. W. Tyler (eds.), *Accountability in Education.* Worthington, Ohio: C. A. Jones.

Goolsby, T. M. 1971. "Appropriateness of Subtests in Achievement Test Selection," *Educational and Psychological Measurement, 31,* 967–972.

Gorow, F. F. 1966. *Better Classroom Testing.* San Francisco, Calif.: Chandler.

Gorth, W. P. (Organizer). 1969. "Comprehensive Achievement Monitoring." Symposium presented at the Annual Meeting of the American Educational Research Association, Los Angeles, Calif., February.

Gorth, W. P., A. Grayson, L. Popejoy, and T. Stroud. 1969. "A Tape-Based Data Bank from Educational Research or Instructional Testing Using Longitudinal Item Sampling," *Educational and Psychological Measurement, 29,* 175–177.

Goslin, D. A. 1967. *Teachers and Testing.* New York: Russell Sage, 1967.

Gosling, G. W. H. 1966. *Marking English Compositions.* Victoria, Australia: Australian Council for Educational Research.

Gottesman, I. I. 1968. "Biogenetics of Race and Class." In M. Deutsch, I. Katz, and A. R. Jensen (eds.), *Social Class, Race, and Psychological Development.* New York: Holt, Rinehart and Winston, pp. 11–51.

Gottfredson, G. D. 1976. "A Note on Sexist Wording in Interest Measurement," *Measurement and Evaluation in Guidance, 8,* 221–223.

Green, B. F., Jr. 1970. "Comments on Tailored Testing." In Wayne H. Holtzman (ed.), *Computer Assisted Instruction, Testing, and Guidance.* New York: Harper & Row.

Green, D. R. (ed.). 1974. *The Aptitude-Achievement Distinction.* Monterey, Calif.: CTB/McGraw-Hill.

Green, R. F. 1951. "Does a Selection Situation Induce Testees to Bias Their Answers on Interest and Temperament Test?" *Educational and Psychological Measurement, 11,* 501–515.

Greenwood, G. E., C. M. Bridges, Jr., W. B. Ware, and J. E. McLean. 1974. "Student Evaluation of College Teaching Behaviors," *Journal of Educational Measurement, 11,* 141–143.

Grier, J. B. 1975. "The Number of Alternatives for Optimum Test Reliability." *Journal of Educational Measurement, 12,* 109–113.

Griggs v. *Duke Power Co.* 1971. Supreme Court of the United States.

Grobman, H. 1968. *Evaluation Activities of Curriculum Projects,* AERA Monograph Series on Curriculum Evaluation, No. 2. Skokie, Ill.: Rand McNally.

Gronlund, N. E. 1959. *Sociometry in the Classroom.* New York: Harper & Row.

Gronlund, N. E. 1970. *Stating Behavioral Objectives for Classroom Instruction.* New York: Macmillan.

Gronlund, N. E. 1973. *Preparing Criterion-Referenced Tests for Classroom Instruction.* New York: Macmillan.

Gronlund, N. E. 1976. *Measurement and Evaluation in Teaching* (3rd ed.). New York: Macmillan.

Gross, M. L. 1962. *The Brain Watchers.* New York: Random House.

Grosswald, J. 1973. "The CRT vs. NRT Syndrome—A New Large City Plague," *Measurement News,* Official Newsletter of the National Council on Measurement in Education, April, *16,* 2, 4.

Guba, E. G. 1969. "Significant Differences," *Educational Research, 20*(3), 4.

Guilford, J. P. 1954. *Psychometric Methods* (2d ed.). New York: McGraw-Hill.

Guilford, J. P. 1959. "Three Faces of Intellect," *American Psychologist, 14,* 469–479.

Guilford, J. P. 1967. *The Nature of Human Intelligence.* New York: McGraw-Hill.

Guilford, J. P. 1969. *Intelligence, Creativity and Their Educational Implications.* San Diego: Educational and Industrial Testing Service.

Gulliksen, H. 1945. "The Relation of Item Difficulty and Inter-Item Correlation to Test Variance and Reliability," *Psychometrika, 10,* 79–91.

Hagen, E., and L. Lindberg. 1963. "Staff Competence in Testing." *The Impact and Improvement of School Testing Programs.* Yearbook 62, Part II. NSSE, p. 249.

Hakstian, A. R. 1971. "The Effects of the Type of Examination Anticipated on Test Preparation and Performance," *Journal of Educational Research, 65,* 319–324.

Hakstian, A. R., and W. Kansup. 1975. "A Comparison of Several Methods of Assessing Partial Knowledge in Multiple-Choice Tests: II. Testing Procedures," *Journal of Educational Measurement, 12,* 231–240.

Hales, L. W. 1972. "Methods of Obtaining Item Discrimination for Item Selection and Selected Test Characteristics: A Comparative Study," *Educational and Psychological Measurement, 34,* 929–938.

Hales, L. W., P. T. Bain, and L. P. Rand. 1971. "An Investigation of Some Aspects of the Pass–Fail Grading System." Mimeograph.

Hales, L. W., and E. Tokar. 1975. "The Effect of Quality of Preceding Responses on the Grades Assigned to Subsequent Responses to an Essay Question." *Journal of Educational Measurement, 12,* 115–117.

Hamalainen, A. E. 1943. "An Appraisal of Anecdotal Records," *Contributions to Education,* No. 891. New York: Teachers College, Columbia University.

Hambleton, R. K., and R. Novick. 1973. "Towards an Integration of Theory and Method for Criterion-Referenced Tests," *Journal of Educational Measurement, 10,* 159–170.

Hambleton, R. K., D. M. Roberts, and R. E. Traub. 1970. "A Comparison of the Reliability and Validity of Two Methods for Assessing Partial Knowledge on a Multiple-Choice Test," *Journal of Educational Measurement, 7,* 75–82.

Hambleton, R. K., and R. E. Traub. 1974. "The Effects of Item Order on Test Performance and Stress," *Journal of Experimental Education, 43,* 40–46.

Hanna, G. 1975. "Incremental Reliability and Validity of Multiple-Choice Tests with an Answer-until-Correct Procedure." *Journal of Educational Measurement, 12,* 175–178.

Hansen, R. 1971. "The Influence of Variables Other than Knowledge on Probabilistic Tests," *Journal of Educational Measurement, 8,* 9–14.

Harmes, H. M. 1971. "Specifying Objectives for Performance Contracts," *Educational Technology, 11,* 52–56.

Harmon, H. 1960. *Modern Factor Analysis.* Chicago: University of Chicago Press.

Harmon, L. W. 1973. "Sexual Bias in Interest Measurement," *Measurement and Evaluation in Guidance, 5,* 496–501.

Harmon, L. W. 1974. "Technical Aspects: Problems of Scale Development, Norms, Item Differences by Sex, and the Rate of Change in Occupational Group Characteristics." Paper presented at the National Institute of Education Workshop on Sex Bias and Sex Fairness in Career Interest Inventories, Arlington, Va.

Harmon, L. W., and F. L. Conroe. 1976. "Sex Stereotyping in Interest Items: Occupational Titles Versus Activities," *Measurement and Evaluation in Guidance, 8,* 215–220.

Harris, C. W. (ed.). 1963. *Problems in Measuring Change.* Madison: University of Wisconsin Press.

Harris, C. W. et al. (eds.). 1974. *Problems in Criterion-Referenced Measurement,* CSE Monograph Series in Evaluation, No. 3. Center for the Study of Evaluation, University of California, Los Angeles.

Harris, M. L., and D. M. Stewart. 1971. "Application of Classical Strategies to Criterion-Referenced Test Construction: An Example." Paper presented at the Annual Meeting of the American Educational Research Association, New York, N.Y.

Harris, R. J. 1967. *How to Improve Reading Ability: A Guide to Developmental and Remedial Methods* (4th ed.). New York: McKay, 1971.

Harrison, G. V. 1967. In J. A. R. Wilson (ed.), *The Instructional Value of Presenting Explicit versus Vague Objectives*. California Educational Research Studies, University of California, Santa Barbara.

Harrow, A. J. 1972. *A Taxonomy of the Psychomotor Domain*. New York: McKay.

Harvard Educational Review. 1969. *Environment, Heredity, and Intelligence*, Reprint Series No. 2.

Hassler, W. W. 1969. "Results of Pass–Fail Questionnaire Sent to Graduate School Deans." Report No. HE-001-388. Indiana, Pa.: Indiana University of Pennsylvania.

Hathaway, S. R. 1964. "MMPI: Professional Use by Professional People," *American Psychologist, 19,* 204–210.

Havighurst, R. J., and B. C. Neugarten. 1975. *Society and Education* (4th ed.). Boston: Allyn and Bacon.

Hays, W. A. 1973. *Statistics for Psychologists* (2d ed.). New York: Holt, Rinehart and Winston.

Hayward, P. 1967. "A Comparison of Test Performance on Three Answer Sheet Formats." *Educational and Psychological Measurement, 27,* 997–1004.

Heathers, G. 1971. "A Definition of Individualized Education." Paper presented at the 1971 Annual Meeting of the American Educational Research Association, New York, N.Y.

Hedges, W. D. 1964. "How to Construct a Good Multiple-Choice Test." *Testing Today*, No. 8. Boston: Houghton Mifflin.

Hedges, W. D. 1966. *Testing and Evaluation for the Sciences in the Secondary School*. Belmont, Calif.: Wadsworth.

Heil, L. M., et al. 1946. "Measurement of Understanding in Science." In *The Measurement of Understanding*, 45th Yearbook, National Society for the Study of Education, Part I. Chicago: University of Chicago Press.

Helmstadter, G. C. 1974. *A Comparison of Bayesian and Traditional Indices of Test Item Performance*. Paper presented at the Annual Meeting of the National Council on Measurement in Education, Chicago, Ill.

Henderson, E. H., and B. H. Long. 1970. "Predictors of Success in Beginning Reading among Negroes and Whites." In Figural, J. A. (ed.), *Reading Goals for the Disadvantaged*. Newark, Del.: International Reading Association, pp. 30–42.

Henderson, N. B., W. H. Fay, S. J. Lindemann, and Q. D. Clarkson. "Will the IQ Test Ban Decrease the Effectiveness of Reading Prediction?" *Journal of Educational Psychology. 65,* 345–355.

Henry, N. B. (ed.). 1946. *The Measurement of Understanding*, 45th Yearbook, National Society for the Study of Education. Chicago: University of Chicago Press.

Henrysson, S. 1971. "Gathering, Analyzing, and Using Data on Test Items." In R. L. Thorndike (ed.), *Educational Measurement*. Washington, D. C.: American Council on Education.

Herbert, J., and C. Attridge. 1975. "A Guide for Developers and Users of Observation Systems and Manuals," *American Educational Research Journal, 12,* 1–20.

Herrnstein, R. J. 1971. "I.Q.," *Atlantic Monthly*, September, 43–64.

Herrnstein, R. J. 1973. *I.Q. in the Meritocracy*. Boston: Little, Brown.

Heyns, R., and R. Lippitt. 1954. "Systematic Observational Techniques." In G. Lindzey (ed.), *Handbook of Social Psychology*, vol. I. Cambridge, Mass.: Addison-Wesley.

Hills, J. R. 1964. "Prediction of College Grades for All Public Colleges of a State," *Journal of Educational Measurement, 1,* 155–159.

Hills, J. R. 1971. "Use of Measurement in Selection and Placement." In Robert L. Thorndike, *Educational Measurement* (2d ed.). Washington, D.C.: American Council on Education.

Hills, J. R., and M. B. Gladney. 1966. "Predicting Grades from Below Chance Test Scores," *Research Bulletin 3-66, Office of Testing and Guidance*. Atlanta: Board of Regents of the University System of Georgia.

Hills, J. R., J. C. Klock, and S. Lewis. 1963. *Freshman Norms for the University System of Georgia, 1961–1962.* Atlanta: Office of Testing and Guidance, Regents of the University System of Georgia.

Hively, W., II, H. L. Patterson, and S. H. Page. 1968. "A 'Universe-Defined' System of Arithmetic Achievement Test," *Journal of Educational Measurement, 5,* 275–290.

Hoffman, R. J. 1975. "The Concept of Efficiency in Item Analysis," *Educational and Psychological Measurement, 35,* 621–640.

Hoffmann, B. 1962. *The Tyranny of Testing.* New York: Crowell-Collier-Macmillan.

Holen, M. C., and R. C. Newhouse. 1976. "Large versus Small Group Administration of Selected Attitude, Self-Concept, and Locus-of-Control Scales," *Measurement and Evaluation in Guidance, 8,* 255–257.

Holland, J. L. 1957. "Undergraduate Origins of American Scientists," *Science, 126,* 433–437.

Holland, J. L. 1966. *The Psychology of Vocational Choice.* Waltham, Mass: Blaisdell.

Holland, J. L. 1973. *Making Vocational Choices: A Theory of Careers.* Englewood Cliffs, N.J.: Prentice-Hall.

Holland, J. L., and G. D. Gottfredson. 1976. "Sex Difference, Item Revisions, Validity, and the Self-Directed Search," *Measurement and Evaluation in Guidance, 8,* 224–228.

Holmes, R. A., J. J. Michael, and W. B. Michael. 1974. "The Comparative Validities of Three Scoring Systems Applied to an Objective Achievement Examination in Chemistry," *Educational and Psychological Measurement, 34,* 387–390.

Holtzman, W. H. 1964. "Recurring Dilemmas in Personality Assessment," *Journal of Projective Techniques and Personality Assessment, 28,* 144–150.

Honzik, M. P., J. W. Macfarlane, and L. Allen. 1948. "The Stability of Mental Test Performance between Two and Eighteen Years," *Journal of Experimental Education, 17,* 309–324.

Hopkins, K. D., and G. H. Bracht. 1975. "Ten-Year Stability of Verbal and Nonverbal IQ Scores," *American Educational Research Journal, 12(4),* 469–477.

Hopkins, K. D., A. R. Hakstian, and B. R. Hopkins. 1973. "Validity and Reliability Consequences of Confidence Weighting," *Educational and Psychological Measurement, 33,* 135–141.

Hopkins, K. D., and B. R. Hopkins. 1964. "Intra-individual and Inter-individual Positional Preference Response Styles in Ability Tests," *Educational and Psychological Measurement, 24,* 801–805.

Horrocks, J. E., and T. I. Schoonover. 1968. *Measurement for Teachers.* Columbus, Ohio: Merrill.

Horst, P. 1966. *Psychological Measurement and Prediction.* Belmont, Calif.: Wadsworth.

Houston, J. P. 1976. "Amount and Loci of Classroom Answer Copying, Spaced Seating, and Alternate Test Forms," *Journal of Educational Psychology, 68,* 729–735.

Hovland, C. I., and M. Sherif. 1952. "Judgmental Phenomena and Scales of Attitude Measurement: Item Displacement in Thurstone Scales," *Journal of Abnormal and Social Psychology, 47,* 822–832.

Hoyt, C. J. 1941. "Test Reliability Estimated by Analysis of Variance," *Psychometrika, 6,* 153–160.

Hritz, R. J., J. Drugo, and S. S. Jacobs. 1970. "Test Directions and Student Personality." Paper presented at the Annual Meeting of the American Educational Research Association, Minneapolis, Minn., March.

Huck, S., and W. Bounds. 1972. "Essay Grades: An Interaction between Graders' Handwriting Clarity and Neatness of Examination Papers." *American Educational Research Journal, 9,* 279–283.

Huck, S., and N. D. Bowers. 1972. "Item Difficulty Level and Sequence Effects in Multiple-Choice Achievement Tests," *Journal of Educational Measurement, 9,* 105–111.

Huck, S., and J. D. Long. 1972. "The Effect of Behavioral Objectives on Student Achievement." Paper presented at the American Educational Research Association Meeting, Chicago, Ill.

Hudson, L. 1966. *Contrary Imaginations.* New York: Schocken Books.

Hughes, H. H., and W. E. Trimble. 1965. "The Use of Complex Alternatives in Multiple-Choice Items," *Educational and Psychological Measurement, 25,* 117–126.

Humphreys, L. G. 1967. "Critique of Cattell, 'Theory of Fluid and Crystallized Intelligence —A Critical Experiment,'" *Journal of Educational Psychology, 58,* 129–136.

Hunt, J. McV. 1961. *Intelligence and Experience.* New York: Ronald.

Hunter, J. E., and F. L. Schmidt. 1976. "Critical Analysis of the Statistical and Ethical Implications of Various Definitions of Test Bias." *Psychological Bulletin, 83*(6), 1053–1071.

Huynh, H. 1976. "On Consistency of Decisions in Criterion-Referenced Testing," *Journal of Educational Measurement, 13,* 253–264.

Ingle, R. B., and G. De Amico. 1969. "The Effect of Physical Conditions of the Test Room on Standardized Achievement Test Scores," *Journal of Educational Measurement, 6,* 237–204.

Ivens, S. H. 1970. *An Investigation of Items Analysis, Reliability and Validity in Relation to Criterion-Referenced Tests.* Unpublished doctoral dissertation.

Jackson, D. N., and S. Messick. 1962. "Response Styles and the Assessment of Psychopathology." In S. Messick and J. Ross (eds.), *Measurement in Personality and Cognition.* New York: Wiley.

Jackson, R. 1970. "Developing Criterion-Referenced Tests," *ERIC Clearinghouse on Tests, Measurement, and Evaluation,* June.

Jacobs, P. I., and S. Kulkarni. 1966. "A Test of Some Assumptions Underlying Programmed Instruction," *Psychological Reports, 18,* 103–110.

Jacobs, S. S. 1971. "Correlates of Unwanted Confidence in Response to Objective Test Items," *Journal of Educational Measurement, 1,* 15–20.

Jacobs, S. S. 1972a. "A Validity Study of the Acquiescence Scale of the Holland Vocational Preference Inventory," *Educational and Psychological Measurement, 32,* 477–480.

Jacobs, S. S. 1972b. "Answer Changing on Objective Tests: Some Implications For Test Validity," *Educational and Psychological Measurement, 32,* 1039–1044.

Jacobs, S. S. 1975. "Behavior on Objective Tests under Theoretically Adequate, Inadequate, and Unspecified Scoring Rules," *Journal of Educational Measurement, 12,* 19–30.

Jaeger, R. M. 1975. "The National Test-Equating Study in Reading (The Anchor Test Study), *NCME Measurement in Education, 4*(4), 1–8.

Jaeger, R. M., and T. D. Freijo. 1975. "Race and Sex as Concomitants of Composite Halo in Teachers' Evaluative Rating of Pupils," *Journal of Educational Psychology, 67,* 226–237.

Jarrett, R. F. 1948. "The Extra-Chance Nature of Changes in Students' Responses to Objective Test Items," *Journal of General Psychology, 38,* 243–250.

Jarvik, L. F., C. Eisdorfer, and J. E. Blum (eds.). 1973. *Intellectual Functioning in Adults: Psychological and Biological Influences.* New York: Springer.

Jastrow, J. 1901. "Some Currents and Undercurrents in Psychology," *Psychological Review, 8,* 1–26.

Jenkins, J. R., R. B. Bausell, and J. A. Magoon. 1972. "Selection of Prose Material for Testing," *Journal of Educational Measurement, 9,* 97–103.

Jenkins, J. R., and S. L. Deno. 1971. "Assessing Knowledge of Concepts and Principles," *Journal of Educational Measurement, 8,* 95–102.

Jenks, C. 1972. *Inequality: A Reassessment of the Effect of Family and Schooling in America,* New York: Harper & Row.

Jennings, H. J. 1948. *Sociometry and Group Relations.* Washington, D.C.: American Council on Education.

Jensen, A. R. 1968a. "Patterns of Mental Ability and Socioeconomic Status." *Proceedings of the National Academy of Sciences of the United States of America, 60,* 1330–1337.

Jensen, A. R. 1968b. "Social Class, Race, and Genetics: Implications for Education," *American Educational Research Journal, 5,* 1–42.

Jensen, A. R. 1969a. "How Much Can We Boost IQ and Scholastic Achievement?" *Harvard Educational Review, 39*, 1–123.

Jensen, A. R. 1969b. "Reducing the Heredity-Environment Uncertainty." *Environment, Heredity, and Intelligence,* Reprint Series No. 2. *Harvard Educational Review.*

Jensen, A. R. 1970a. "Hierarchical Theories of Mental Ability." In B. Dockrell (ed.), *On Intelligence.* Toronto, Canada: Ontario Institute for Studies in Education.

Jensen, A. R. 1970b. "IQ's of Identical Twins Reared Apart," *Behavioral Genetics, 2,* 133–146.

Jensen, A. R. 1972. "Review of the Analysis of Learning Potential." In O. K. Buros (ed.), *The Seventh Mental Measurements Yearbook.* Highland Park, N.J.: Gryphon Press.

Jensen, A. R. 1973a. *Educability and Group Difference.* New York: Harper & Row.

Jensen, A. R. 1973b. *Genetics and Education.* New York: Harper & Row.

Jensen, A. R. 1973c. "Let's Understand Skodal and Skeels, Finally," *Educational Psychologist, 10*(1), 30–35.

Jensen, A. R. 1975. "The Meaning of Heritability in the Behavioral Sciences," *Educational Psychologist, 11* (3), 171–183.

Jensen, A. R. 1976. "IQ Tests Are Not Culturally Biased for Blacks and Whites," *Phi Delta Kappan, 57,* 676.

Jessell, J. C., and W. L. Sullins. 1975. "The Effect of Keyed Response Sequencing of Multiple Choice Items on Performance and Reliability," *Journal of Educational Measurement, 12,* 45–48.

Johansson, C. B., and L. W. Harmon. 1972. "Strong Vocational Interest Blank: One Form or Two?" *Journal of Counseling Psychology, 19,* 404–410.

Johnson, D. M., and J. C. Moore. 1973. "An Investigation of Holland's Theory of Vocational Psychology," *Measurement and Evaluation in Guidance, 5,* 488–495.

Johnson, R. W. 1971. "Congruence of Strong and Kuder Interest Profiles," *Journal of Consulting Psychology, 18,* 450–455.

Joint Committee on Testing of the American Association of School Administrators. 1962. *Testing, Testing, Testing.* Washington, D.C.: National Education Association.

Jones, P. D., and G. G. Kaufman. 1975. "The Existence and Effects of Specific Determiners in Tests." Paper presented at the Annual Meeting of the American Psychological Association, New Orleans, La., 1974.

Jongsma, E. A., and E. Warshauer. 1975. *The Effects of Instruction on Test-Taking Skills upon Student Performance on Standardized Achievement Tests,* Final Report. Baton Rouge: Louisiana State University.

Jose, J., and J. Cody. 1971. "Teacher Pupil Interaction as It Relates to Attempted Changes in Teacher Expectancy of Academic Ability and Achievement," *American Educational Research Journal, 8,* 39–50.

Journal of Educational Measurement. 1976. *13,* Spring issue.

Juola, A. E. 1968. *Examination Skills and Techniques.* Lincoln, Neb.: Cliff's Notes, Inc.

Juola, A. E. 1971. *Academic Success by Ability Levels over the Past Ten Years,* OES Research Report No. 2. Office of Evaluation Services, Michigan State University, East Lansing, Mich.

Juola, A. E. 1974. "Grade Inflation (1960–1973): A Preliminary Report." Unpublished monograph, Michigan State University, East Lansing, Mich.

Juola, A. E. 1976. "Grade Inflation 1975—Is It Over?" Unpublished monograph, Michigan State University, East Lansing, Mich.

Kalisch, S. J., Jr. 1974. *The Comparison of Two Tailored Testing Models and the Effects of the Models' Variables on Actual Loss.* Unpublished Ph. D. dissertation. Florida State University, Tallahassee, Fla.

Kallingal, A. 1971. "The Prediction of Grades for Black and White Students at Michigan State University," *Journal of Educational Measurement, 8,* 263–266.

Kamin, L. J. 1974. *The Science and Politics of IQ.* Potomac, Md.: Erlbaum.

Kansup, W., and A. R. Hakstian. 1975. "Comparison of Several Methods of Assessing Partial Knowledge in Multiple-Choice Tests: I. Scoring Procedures," *Journal of Educational Measurement, 12*, 219–230.

Karlins, M. 1969. "Academic Attitudes and Performance as a Function of Differential Grading Systems: An Evaluation of Princeton's Pass-Fail System," *Journal of Experimental Education, 37*, 38–50.

Katz, J., et al. 1968. *No Time for Youth: Growth and Constraint in College Students.* San Francisco: Jossey-Bass.

Katz, M., and L. Norris. 1972. "The Contribution of Academic Interest Measures to the Differential Prediction of Marks," *Journal of Educational Measurement, 9*, 1–11.

Katz, M., L. Norris, and G. Halpern. 1970. *The Measurement of Academic Interests. Part I: Characteristics of the Academic Interest Measures,* College Board Research and Development Report 70–71, No. 4. Princeton, N.J.: Educational Testing Service.

Kaufman, R. A. 1971. "Accountability, a System Approach and the Quantitative Improvement of Education—An Attempted Integration," *Educational Technology*, January, *11*, 21–26.

Kearney, N. C. 1953. *Elementary School Objectives.* New York: Russell Sage.

Kelley, T. L. 1939. "The Selection of Upper and Lower Groups for the Validation of Test Items," *Journal of Educational Psychology, 30*, 17–24.

Kerlinger, F. N. 1967. *Foundations of Behavioral Research.* New York: Holt, Rinehart and Winston.

Kibler, R. J., L. L. Barker, and David T. Miles. 1970. *Behavioral Objectives and Instruction.* Boston: Allyn and Bacon.

Kippel, G. M. 1975. "Information Feedback, Need Achievement and Retention," *Journal of Educational Research, 68*, 256–261.

Kirkpatrick, J. J., et al. 1968. *Testing and Fair Employment.* New York: New York University Press.

Klein, S. P. 1971. "Choosing Needs for Needs Assessment." In Stephen P. Klein et al., *Procedures for Needs-Assessment Evaluation: A Symposium.* Los Angeles: Center for the Study of Evaluation Report No. 67, May, pp. 1–9.

Klein, S. P., and J. P. Kosecoff. 1975. *Determining How Well a Test Measures Your Objectives,* Report No. 94. Los Angeles: Center for the Study of Evaluation.

Klosner, N. C., and E. K. Gellman. 1973. "The Effect of Item Arrangement on Classroom Test Performance," *Educational and Psychological Measurement, 33*, 413–418.

Knapp, T. R. 1968. *The Choices Study.* Unpublished report. Exploratory Committee on Assessing the Progress of Education.

Knight, S. S. (n.d.) *Systematic Judgment of Children's Drawings.* Denver: National Assessment of Educational Progress.

Kocher, A. T. 1974. "An Empirical Investigation of the Stability and Accuracy of Flexilevel Tests." Paper presented at the Annual Meeting of the National Council on Measurement in Education, Chicago, Ill.

Koehler, R. A. 1971. "A Comparison of the Validities of Conventional Choice Testing and Various Confidence Marking Procedures," *Journal of Educational Measurement, 8*, 297–304.

Kogan, N., and M. A. Wallach. 1967. "Risk-Taking as a Function of the Situation, the Person, and the Group." In G. Mandler et al., *New Directions in Psychology III.* New York: Holt, Rinehart and Winston.

Kowalski, R. P., B. S. Ranthawan, and D. Hunt. 1974. "Immediate Feedback: Its Effects on Achievement and Stress on High Anxious and Low Anxious First Year Chemistry Students." Paper presented at the Annual Meeting of the National Council on Measurement in Education, Chicago, Ill.

Krathwohl, D.R., B. S. Bloom, and B. Masia. 1964. *Taxonomy of Educational Objectives, Handbook II: The Affective Domain.* New York: McKay.

Krathwohl, D. R., and Payne, D. A. 1971. "Defining and Assessing Educational Objectives." Chapter 2 in R. L. Thorndike (ed.), *Educational Measurement* (2d ed.). Washington: American Council on Education.

Krech, D., et al. 1962. *Individual in Society*, New York: McGraw-Hill, p. 177.

Kriewall, T. W. 1969. *Applications of Information Theory and Acceptance Sampling Principles to the Management of Mathematics Instruction.* Unpublished doctoral dissertion. University of Wisconsin, Madison, Wis.

Kroger, R. O. 1974. "Faking in Interest Measurement: A Social-Psychological Perspective," *Measurement and Evaluation in Guidance*, 7, 130–134.

Kuder, G. F. 1969. "A Note on the Comparability of Occupational Scores from Different Interest Inventories," *Measurement and Evaluation in Guidance*, 2, 94–100.

Kuder, G. F. 1970. "Some Principles of Interest Measurement," *Educational and Psychological Measurement*, 30, 205–226.

Kuncel, R. B. 1973. "Response Processes and Relative Location of Subject and Item," *Educational and Psychological Measurement*, 33, 545–563.

LaBenne, W. D., and B. I. Greene. 1969. *Educational Implications of Self-Concept Theory.* Pacific Palisades, Calif.: Goodyear.

Lange, A., I. J. Lehmann, and W. A. Mehrens. 1967. "Using Item Analysis to Improve Tests," *Journal of Educational Measurement*, 4, 65–68.

Larkins, A. G., and J. P. Shaver. 1968. *Comparison of Yes-No, Matched Pairs, and All-No Scoring of a First-Grade Economics Achievement Test*, ERIC Report No. ED 029701. Logan: Utah State University.

Law School Admission Test Council. 1970. *Statement on Pass–Fail Grading Systems*, Report No. HE-001-881. Oct. 27.

Lee, B. N., and M. D. Merrill. 1972. *Writing Complete Affective Objectives: A Short Course.* Belmont, Calif.: Wadsworth.

Lefkowitz, D. 1970. "Comparison of the Strong Vocational Interest Blank and the Kuder Occupational Interest Survey Scoring Procedures," *Journal of Counseling Psychology*, 17, 357–363.

Lehmann, I. J. 1974. "Evaluating Instruction." In W. Gephart and R. B. Ingle (eds.), *Evaluation of Instruction.* Bloomington, Ind.: Phi Delta Kappa.

Lennon, R. T. 1956. "Assumptions Underlying the Use of Content Validity," *Educational and Psychological Measurement*, 16, 294–304.

Lennon, R. T. 1971. "Accountability and Performance Contracting." Invited address to the American Educational Research Association.

Lessinger, L. M. 1970a. "Engineering Accountability for Results in Public Education," *Phi Delta Kappan*, 52(4), 217–225.

Lessinger, L. M. 1970b. "The Powerful Notions of Accountability in Education," *Journal of Secondary Education*, 45(8), 339–347.

Lessinger, L. M. 1971. "Accountability for Results: A Basic Challenge for America's Schools." In Leon M. Lessinger and Ralph W. Tyler (eds.), *Accountability in Education.* Worthington, Ohio: Charles A. Jones.

Lewis, J. 1974. "A Study of the Validity of the Metropolitan Readiness Tests," *Educational and Psychological Measurement*, 34, 415–416.

Lewis, J. 1975. "The Relationship between Academic Aptitude and Occupational Success for a Sample of University Graduates," *Educational and Psychological Measurement*, 35, 465–466.

Lien, A. J. 1971. *Measurement and Evaluation of Learning: A Handbook for Teachers* (2d ed.). Dubuque, Iowa: William C. Brown.

Lien, A. J. 1976. *Measurement and Evaluation of Learning*, Dubuque, Iowa: William C. Brown.

Likert, R. A. 1932. "A Technique for the Measurement of Attitudes," *Archives of Psychology*, No. 140.

Lindgren, H. C. 1967. *Educational Psychology in the Classroom.* New York: Wiley.

Lindman, E. L. 1971. "The Means and Ends of Accountability." *Proceedings of the Conference on Accountability.* Princeton, N.J.: Educational Testing Service.

Lindquist, E. F. 1951. "Preliminary Considerations in Objective Test Construction." In E. F. Lindquist (ed.), *Educational Measurement.* Washington: American Council on Education, pp. 119–158.

Lindquist, E. F. 1964. "Equating Scores on Non-parallel Tests," *Journal of Educational Measurement, 1,* 5–9.

Lindvall, C. M. (ed.). 1964. *Defining Educational Objectives.* Pittsburgh: University of Pittsburgh Press.

Lindvall, C. M., and J. O. Bolvin. 1967. "Programmed Instruction in the Schools: An Application of Programmed Principles in Individually Prescribed Instruction." In P. Lange (ed.), *Programmed Instruction.* 66th Yearbook, Part II. Chicago: National Society for the Study of Education.

Lindvall, C. M., and R. C. Cox. 1970. *The IPI Evaluation Program.* AERA Monograph Series on Curriculum Evaluation, No. 5. Skokie, Ill.: Rand McNally.

Little, E. B. 1962. "Overcorrection for Guessing in Multiple-Choice Scoring," *Journal of Educational Research, 55,* 245–252.

Livingston, S. A. 1970. *The Reliability of Criterion-Referenced Measures,* Report No. 73. Baltimore: The Center for the Study of Social Organization of Schools, Johns Hopkins University.

Livingston, S. A. 1972. "Criterion-Referenced Applications of Classical Test Theory," *Journal of Educational Measurement, 9,* 13–26.

Livingston, S. A. 1973. "'Verbal Overload' and Achievement Tests: A Replication," *American Educational Research Journal, 10,* 155–162.

Locke, R. W. 1971. "Accountability Yes, Performance Contracting Maybe." *Proceedings of the Conferences on Educational Accountability.* Princeton, N.J.: Educational Testing Service.

Lockheed-Katz, M. (n.d.). *Sex Bias in Educational Testing: A Sociologist's Perspective,* Research Memorandum 74-13. Princeton, N.J.: Educational Testing Service.

Loehlin, J. C., et al. 1975. *Race Differences in Intelligence.* San Francisco: Freeman.

Long, B. H., and E. H. Henderson. 1974. "Certain Determinants of Academic Expectancies among Southern and Non-southern Teachers," *American Educational Research Journal, 11,* 137–147.

Lord, F. M. 1952. "The Relationship of the Reliability of Multiple-Choice Tests to the Distribution of Item Difficulties," *Psychometrika, 18,* 181–194.

Lord, F. M. 1957. "Do Tests of the Same Length Have the Same Standard Error of Measurement?" *Educational and Psychological Measurement, 17,* 510–521.

Lord, F. M. 1963. "Formula Scoring and Validity," *Educational and Psychological Measurement, 23,* 663–672.

Lord, F. M. 1964. "The Effects of Random Guessing on Test Validity," *Educational and Psychological Measurement, 24,* 745–747.

Lord, F. M. 1970a. "The Self-Scoring Flexilevel Test," *Research Bulletin 68-38.* Princeton. N.J.: Educational Testing Service.

Lord, F. M. 1970b. "Some Test Theory for Tailored Testing." In W. H. Holtzman (ed.), *Computer Assisted Instruction, Testing, and Guidance.* New York: Harper & Row.

Lord, F. M. 1971a. The Self-Scoring Flexilevel Test," *Journal of Educational Measurement, 8,* 147–151.

Lord, F. M. 1971b. "A Theoretical Study of the Measurement Effectiveness of Flexilevel Tests," *Educational and Psychological Measurement, 31,* 4, 805–814.

Lowe, M. L., and C. C. Crawford. 1929. "First Impressions versus Second Thought in True-False Tests," *Journal of Educational Psychology, 20,* 192–195.

Lucy, W. T. 1976. "The Stability of Holland's Personality Types over Time," *Journal of College Student Personnel, 17,* 76–79.

Lyman, H. B. 1971. *Test Scores and What They Mean* (2d ed.). Englewood Cliffs, N.J.: Prentice-Hall.

Lynch, D. O., and B. C. Smith. 1972. "To Change or Not to Change Item Responses When Taking Tests: Empirical Evidence for Test Takers." Paper presented at the Annual Meeting of the American Educational Research Association, Chicago, Ill., April.

Lynch, D. O., and B. C. Smith. 1975. "Item Response Changes: Effects on Test Scores," *Measurement and Evaluation in Guidance, 7,* 220–224.

Macoby, E. E., and C. N. Jacklin. 1974. "The Psychology of Sex Differences." Paper presented at the Annual Meeting of the American Educational Research Association, Chicago, Ill., April.

Mager, F. 1962. *Preparing Objectives for Programmed Instruction.* Palo Alto: Fearon.

Mager, R. P. 1968. *Developing Attitudes toward Learning.* Palo Alto, Calif.: Fearon.

Maguire, T. O. 1972. "Semantic Differential Methodology for the Structuring of Attitudes," *American Educational Research Journal, 10,* 295–306.

Majors, G. W., and J. J. Michael. 1975. "The Relationship of Achievement on a Teacher-Made Mathematics Test of Computational Skills to Two Ways of Recording Answers and to Two Workspace Arrangements," *Educational and Psychological Measurement, 35,* 1005–1009.

Manuel, H. 1956. *Taking a Test.* New York: Harcourt Brace Jovanovich.

Marcus, A. 1963. "The Effect of Correct Response Location on the Difficulty Level of Multiple-Choice Questions," *Journal of Applied Psychology, 47,* 48–51.

Marshall, J. C. 1967. "Composition Errors and Essay Examination Grades Reexamined," *American Educational Research Journal, 4,* 375–386.

Marso, R. N. 1969. "Test Difficulty and Student Achievement," *American Educational Research Journal, 6,* 621–632.

Marso, R. N. 1970. "Test Item Arrangement, Testing Time, and Performance," *Journal of Educational Measurement, 7,* 113–118.

Martin, R. B., and K. Srikameswaran. 1974. "Correlation between Frequent Testing and Student Performance," *Journal of Chemical Education, 51,* 485–486.

Martin, W. H. 1976. "Maximizing Information from Free Response Exercises in Mathematics." Paper presented at the Annual Meeting of the National Council on Measurement in Education, San Francisco, Calif., 1975.

Masters, J. R. 1974. "The Relationship between Number of Response Categories and Reliability of Likert-Type Questionnaires," *Journal of Educational Measurement, 11,* 49–55.

Mathews, W. M. 1973. "Narrative Format Testing Reports and Traditional Testing Reports: A Comparative Study," *Journal of Educational Measurement, 10,* 171–178.

Mayhew, L. B. 1958. "And in Attitudes." In P. L. Dressel (ed.), *Evaluation in the Basic College at Michigan State University.* New York: Harper & Row.

Mayor, M. 1973. "Higher Education for All: The Case of Open Admissions," *Commentary,* February, p. 47.

McAshan, H. H. 1970. *Writing Behavioral Objectives: A New Approach.* New York: Harper & Row.

McAshan, H. H. 1974. *The Goals Approach to Performance Objectives.* Philadelphia: Saunders.

McCall, R. B., M. I. Appelbaum, and P. S. Hogarty. 1973. "Developmental changes in mental performance," *Monographs of the Society of Research in Child Development, 38* (3, Serial No. 150).

McCall, R. B., P. S. Hogarty, and N. Hurlburt. 1972. "Transitions in Infant Sensorimotor Development and the Prediction of Childhood IQ." *American Psychologist, 27,* 728–748.

McClure, L., and Buan, C. (eds.). 1973. *Essays on Career Education.* Portland, Ore. Northwest Regional Educational Laboratory.

McColly, W. 1970. "What Does Educational Research Say about the Judging of Writing Ability?" *Journal of Educational Research, 64,* 148–156.

McGaw, B., J. L. Wardrop, and M. A. Bunda. 1972. "Classroom Observation Schemes: Where Are the Errors?" *American Educational Research Journal, 9,* 13–27.

McKee, L. E. 1967. "Third Grade Students Learn to Use Machine-Scored Answer Sheets," *The School Counselor, 15,* 52–53.

McKinney, J. D., J. Mason, K. Peterson, and M. Clifford. 1975. "Relationship between Classroom Behavior and Academic Achievement," *Journal of Educational Psychology, 67,* 198–203.

McLaughlin, D. H., and D. V. Tiedeman. 1974. "Eleven-Year Stability and Change as Reflected in Project Talent Data through the Flanagan, Holland, and Roe Occupational Classification Systems," *Journal of Vocational Behavior, 5,* 177–196.

McMorris, R., and L. Gregory. 1976. "Item Response Changes and Cognitive Styles." Paper presented at the Annual Meeting of the National Council on Measurement in Education, San Francisco, Calif., April.

McNemar, Q. 1964. "Lost: Our Intelligence? Why?" *American Psychologist, 19,* 871–882.

Medley, D. M., and H. E. Mitzel. 1963. "Measuring Classroom Behavior by Systematic Observation." In N. L. Gage (ed.), *Handbook of Research on Teaching.* Skokie, Ill.: Rand McNally.

Meehl, P. E., and A. Rosen. 1955. "Antecedent Probability and the Efficiency of Psychometric Signs, Patterns, or Cutting Scores," *Psychological Bulletin, 52,* 194–216.

Mehrens, W. A. 1970. "Scientific Test Construction—Pure and Sterile," *Contemporary Psychology, 15,* 666–667.

Melville, G. L., and E. Stamm. 1967. *The Pass-Fail System and the Change in the Accounting of Grades on Comprehensive Examinations at Knox College,* Report ED-014-788. Galesburg, Ill.: Office of Institutional Research, Knox College.

Menges, R. J. 1973. "The New Reporters: Students Rate Instruction." In C. R. Pace (ed.), *New Directions in Higher Education: Evaluating Learning and Teaching.* San Francisco: Jossey-Bass, pp. 59–75.

Mercer, J. 1977. *SOMPA, System of Multicultural Pluralistic Assessment.* New York: The Psychological Corporation.

Merwin, J. C. 1973. "Educational Measurement of What Characteristics of Whom (or What), by Whom and Why?" *Journal of Educational Measurement,* Spring, *10,* 1–6.

Metfessel, N., and W. B. Michael. 1967. "A Paradigm Involving Multiple Criterion Measures for the Evaluation of the Effectiveness of School Programs," *Educational and Psychological Measurement, 27,* 931–943.

Metfessel, W. S., W. B. Michael, and D. A. Kirsner. 1969. "Instrumentation of Bloom's and Krathwohl's Taxonomies for the Writing of Behavioral Objectives," *Psychology in the Schools, 6,* 227–231.

Meyer, G. 1935. "An Experimental Study of the Old and New Types of Examinations: II. Methods of Study," *Journal of Educational Psychology, 26,* 30–40.

Micheels, W. J., and M. Ray Karnes. 1950. *Measuring Educational Achievement.* New York: McGraw-Hill.

Michigan Department of Education. 1970. *Objectives and Procedures of the Michigan Educational Assessment Porgram: 1970-71,* Assessment Report No. 7, December.

Miklich, D. P., and G. Gordon. 1968. "Test-Taking Carefulness versus Acquiescence Response Set on True-False Items." *Educational and Psychological Measurement, 28,* 545–548.

Miles, J. 1973. "Eliminating the Guessing Factor in the Multiple-Choice Test," *Educational and Psychological Measurement, 33,* 637–651.

Millman, J. 1972. *Tables for Determining Number of Items Needed on Domain-Referenced*

Tests and Number of Students to be Tested, Technical Paper No. 5. Los Angeles, Calif.: Instructional Objectives Exchange.

Millman, J. 1973. "Passing Scores and Test Lengths for Domain-Referenced Measures," *Review of Educational Research*, 43, 205–216.

Millman, J. 1974. "Criterion-Referenced Measurement." Chapter 6 in W. J. Popham (ed.), *Evaluation in Education: Current Applications*. Berkeley, Calif.: McCutchan Publishing Company.

Millman, J., C. H. Bishop, and R. L. Ebel. 1965. "An Analysis of Test Wiseness," *Educational and Psychological Measurement*, 25, 707–726.

Millman, J., and W. Pauk. 1969. *How To Take Tests*. New York: McGraw-Hill.

Milton, O. 1967. "Teaching-Learning Issues," No. 5. Knoxville: Learning Resources Center, University of Tennessee.

Monroe, W. S., and R. E. Carter. 1923. "The Use of Different Types of Thought Questions in Secondary Schools and Their Relative Difficulty for Students." Urbana: University of Illinois Bulletin 20, No. 34.

Mooney Problem Check List Manual. 1950. New York: The Psychological Corporation.

Moore, J. C. 1971. "Test Wiseness and Analogy Test Performance," *Measurement and Evaluation in Guidance*, 3, 198–202.

Moore, R. 1960. "Separate Answer Sheets for Primary Grades." In *17th Yearbook*. Ames, Iowa: National Council on Measurements Used in Education, 53–55.

Moreno, J. L. 1934. *Who Shall Survive?* Washington, D.C.: Nervous and Mental Disease Publishing Company.

Morf, M. E., and D. N. Jackson. 1972. "An Analysis of Two Response Styles: True Responding and Item Endorsement," *Educational and Psychological Measurement*, 32, 329–353.

Morishima, J. K., and S. S. Micek. 1970. "Pass–Fail Evaluation: Phase II. Questionnaire Analysis." Seattle: Office of Institutional Educational Research, University of Washington.

Morrison, H. C. 1926. *The Practice of Teaching in the Secondary School*. Chicago: University of Chicago Press.

Morse, J. A., and M. H. Tillman. 1972. "Effects on Achievement of Possession of Behavioral Objectives and Training Concerning Their Use." Paper presented at the American Educational Research Association Meeting. Chicago, Ill.

Mosier, C. I. 1947. "A Critical Examination of the Concepts of Face Validity," *Educational and Psychological Measurement*, 7, 191–205.

Mosier, C. I., M. C. Myers, and H. G. Price. 1945. "Suggestions for the Construction of Multiple-Choice Test Items," *Educational and Psychological Measurement*, 5, 261–271.

Mouly, G. J. 1968. *Psychology for Effective Teaching*. New York: Holt, Rinehart and Winston.

Mowsesian, R., and M. R. Heyer. 1973. "The Effect of Music as a Distraction on Test-Taking Performance," *Measurement and Evaluation in Guidance*, 6, 104–110.

Muchinsky, P. M., and D. P. Hoyt. 1973. "Academic Grades as a Predictor of Occupational Success among Engineering Graduates," *Measurement and Evaluation in Guidance*, 6, 93–103.

Mueller, D. J. 1975. "An Assessment of the Effectiveness of Complex Alternatives in Multiple-Choice Achievement Test Items," *Educational and Psychological Measurement*, 35, 135–141.

Mueller, D. J., and A. Schwedel. 1975. "Some Correlates of Net Gain Resultant From Changing Answers on Objective Achievement Test Items," *Journal of Educational Measurement*, 12, 251–254.

Mueller, D. J., and V. Wasser. 1977. "Implications of Changing Answers on Objective Test Items," *Journal of Educational Measurement*, 14, 9–14.

Muller, D., E. Calhoun, and R. Orling. 1972. "Test Reliability as a Function of Answer

Sheet Mode," *Journal of Educational Measurement, 9*, 321–324.

Mullis, I. V. S. 1976. "The Primary Trait System for Scoring Writing Tasks." Paper presented at the Annual Meeting of the National Council on Measurement in Education, San Francisco, Calif.

Multiple Choice Questions: A Close Look. 1963. Princeton, N.J.: Educational Testing Service.

Munday, L. 1965. "Predicting College Grades in Predominantly Negro Colleges," *Journal of Educational Measurement, 2*, 157–160.

Munley, P. H., B. R. Pretz, and D. H. Mills. 1973. "Female College Students' Scores on the Men's and Women's Strong Vocational Interest Blanks," *Journal of Counseling Psychology, 30*, 285–289.

National Assessment of Educational Progress. 1969. *Questions and Answers about National Assessment of Educational Progress.* Denver: NAEF, p. 1.

National Assessment of Educational Progress. 1970a. *Citizenship: National Results,* Partial Report No. 2. Denver: NAEP.

National Assessment of Educational Progress. 1970b. *Writing: National Results.* Report 3, 1969–1970. Denver: NAEP.

National Assessment of Educational Progress. 1972a. *Citizenship Objectives for the 1974–75 Assessment.* Denver: NAEP.

National Assessment of Educational Progress. 1972b. *Objectives in Ten Subject Matter Areas.* Denver: NAEP.

National Education Association. 1967. "Reports to Parents," *NEA Research Bulletin, 45*, 51–53.

National Education Association. 1970. *Marking and Reporting Pupil Progress,* Research Summary 1970-S1. Washington, D.C.: NEA.

National Education Associtaion. 1972. *Accountability.* Washington, D.C.: NEA.

Neill, J. A., and D. N. Jackson. 1976. "Minimum Redundancy in Item Analysis," *Educational and Psychological Measurement, 36*, 123–134.

Nelson, C. H. 1958. *Let's Build Quality into Our Science Tests.* Washington, D.C.: National Science Teachers Association.

Nettler, G. 1959. "Test Burning in Texas," *American Psychologist, 14*, 682–683.

Nichols, R. C. 1975. "Book Review of Jensen, A. R.: *Educability and Group Differences,*" *American Education Research Journal, 12*, 357–360..

Niedermeyer, F. C., and H. J. Sullivan. 1972. "Differential Effects of Individual and Group Testing Strategies in an Objectives-Based Instructional Program," *Journal of Educational Measurement, 9*, 199–204.

Nilsson, I., and I. Wedman. 1974. *On Test-Wiseness and Some Related Constructs,* Educational Reports No. 7. Umea, Sweden: Umea University.

Noeth, R., J. Roth, and D. Prediger. 1975. "Student Career Development: Where Do We Stand?" *Vocational Guidance Quarterly, 23*, 210–219.

Noll, V. H., and D. P. Scannell. 1972. *Introduction to Educational Measurement* (3d ed.). Boston: Houghton Mifflin.

Norris, L., and M. Katz. 1970. *The Measurement of Academic Interests. Part II: The Predictive Validities of Academic Interest Measures,* College Board Research and Development Report 70–71. Princeton, N.J.: Educational Testing Service.

Novick, M. R. 1973. *New Statistical Techniques to Evaluate Criterion-Referenced Tests Used in Individually Prescribed Instruction,* Final Report, Project 2-0067. Iowa City, Iowa: The American College Testing Program.

Novick, M. R., and C. Lewis. 1973. *Prescribing Test Length for Criterion Referenced Measurement,* ACT Technical Bulletin No. 18. Iowa City, Iowa: The American College Testing Program.

Nunnally, J. 1967. *Psychometric Theory.* New York: McGraw-Hill.

Oakland, T., and E. Weilert. 1971. *The Effects of Test-Wiseness Materials on Standardized*

Test Performance of Pre-School Disadvantaged Children. Paper presented at the Annual Meeting of the American Educational Research Association, New York, N.Y.

O'Bryan, K. G., and R. S. MacArthur. 1969. "Reversibility, Intelligence, and Creativity in Nine-Year-Old Boys," *Child Development, 40,* 33–45.

Olson, H. D., and R. S. Barickowski. 1974. "Test Item Arrangement and Adaptation Level." Paper presented at the Annual Meeting of the National Council on Measurement in Education, Chicago, Ill.

On Bias in Selection. 1976. Special issue of the *Journal of Educational Measurement, 13*(1).

O'Neill, J. 1975. "The Effect of Visual Format upon Test Performance of Spanish-Speaking Children." Paper presented at the Annual Meeting of the American Psychological Association, Chicago, Ill.

Oosterhoff, A. C. 1976. "Similarity of Various Discrimination Indices," *Journal of Educational Measurement, 13,* 145–150.

Oosterhoff, A. C., and D. R. Glassnapp. 1974. "Comparative Reliabilities and Difficulties of the Multiple-Choice and True-False Formats," *Journal of Experimental Education, 42,* 62–64.

Osburn, H. G. 1968. "Item Sampling for Achievement Testing," *Educational and Psychological Measurement, 28,* 95–104.

Osgood, C. E., G. J. Suci, and P. H. Tannenbaum. 1957. *The Measurement of Meaning.* Urbana: University of Illinois Press, 1957.

O'Shea, J. F., and T. F. Harrington. 1971. "Using the Strong Vocational Interest Blank and the Kuder Occupational Interest Survey, Form DD, with the Same Clients," *Journal of Counseling Psychology, 18,* 44–50.

Osterhouse, R. A. 1975. "Classroom Anxiety and the Examination Performance of Test-Anxious Students," *Journal of Educational Research, 68,* 247–250.

Overall, J. A., and J. A. Woodward. 1975. "Unreliability of Difference Scores: A Paradox for Measurement of Change," *Psychological Bulletin, 82,* 85–86.

Owens, R. E., G. S. Hanna, and F. L. Coppedge. 1970. "Comparison of Multiple-Choice Tests Using Different Types of Distracter Selection Techniques," *Journal of Educational Measurement, 7,* 87–90.

Page, E. B. 1966. "The Imminence of Grading Essays by Computer," *Phi Delta Kappan, 47,* 238–243.

Page, E. B. 1967. "Grading Essays by Computer; Progress Report," *Proceedings of the 1966 Invitational Conference on Testing Problems.* Princeton, N.J.: Educational Testing Service, pp. 87–100.

Page, E. B. (Chairman of Computer Analysis of Student Writing). 1972. "Progress in Style and Content." Symposium presented at the Annual Meeting of the American Educational Research Association, Chicago, Ill.

Page, E. B. 1974. "Top-Down Trees of Educational Values." *Educational and Psychological Measurement, 34,* 573–584.

Page, E. B. 1976. "Nader v. E.T.S." Letters column, *APA Monitor* 7(12), 2–3.

Parnell, D. 1973. In *Elementary and Secondary Education Amendments of 1973: Hearings before the General Subcommittee on Education of the Committee on Education and Labor, House of Representatives, Ninety-third Congress, First Session.* (On H.R. 16, H.R. 69, H.R. 5163, and H.R. 5823.) Part 3 and Appendix.

Pascale, P. J. 1974. "Changing Initial Answers on Multiple-Choice Achievement Tests," *Measurement and Evaluation in Guidance, 6,* 236–238.

Patnaik, D., and R. E. Traub. 1973. "Differential Weighting by Judged Degree of Correctness," *Journal of Educational Measurement, 10,* 281–286.

Payne, D. A. 1968. *The Specification and Measurement of Learning Outcomes.* Waltham, Mass.: Blaisdell.

Payne, D. A. (ed.). 1974. *Curriculum Evaluation.* Lexington, Mass.: Heath.

Peale, N. V. 1952. *The Power of Positive Thinking.* Englewood Cliffs, N.J.: Prentice-Hall.

Peddiwell, J. A. 1939. *The Saber-Tooth Curriculum*. New York: McGraw-Hill.

Perry, W. G., Jr. 1963. "Examsmanship and the Liberal Arts." In *Examining in Harvard College*.

Peterson, N. S., and M. R. Novick. 1976. "An Evaluation of Some Models for Culture-Fair Selection," *Journal of Educational Measurement, 13*, 3–30.

Peterson, C. C., and J. L. Peterson. 1976. "Linguistic Determinants of the Difficulty of True-False Test Items." *Educational and Psychological Measurement, 36*, 161–164.

Pettie, A. A., and A. C. Oosterhoff. 1976. "Indices of Item Adequacy for Individually Administered Mastery Tests." Paper presented at the Annual Meeting of the National Council on Measurement in Education, San Francisco, Calif.

Pettigrew, T. A. 1964. *Profile of the Negro American*. Princeton, N.J.: Van Nostrand.

Pfeifer, C. M., Jr., and W. E. Sedlacek. 1971. "The Validity of Academic Predictors for Black and White Students at a Predominantly White University," *Journal of Educational Measurement, 8*, 253–262.

Phillips, D. L. 1976. "Applications to Free Response Items from Career and Occupational Development." Paper presented at the Annual Meeting of the National Council on Measurement in Education, San Francisco, Calif., 1975.

Pinard, A., and E. Sharp. 1972. "IQ and Point of View," *Psychology Today*, June 1972, *6*(1), June, 65–68, 90.

Pinchak, B. M., and H. M. Breland. 1973. *Grading Practices in American High Schools*, Research Bulletin 73–45. Princeton, N.J.: Educational Testing Service.

Pines, M. 1969. "Why Some Three-Year-Olds Get A's—and Some C's," *New York Times Magazine*, July 6, 4–17.

Pipho, C. 1976. Quoted from "States Tackle Complex, Hot Issue," *National Assessment of Educational Progress Newsletter*. Denver: Education Commission of the States, *IX*, June, 3.

Planisek, S. L., and R. J. Planisek. 1972. "A Description of Fifteen Test Statistics Based upon Optically Scanned Instructor-Made Multiple-Choice Tests at Kent State University." Paper presented at the Annual Meeting of the National Council on Measurement in Education, Chicago, Ill.

Popham, W. J. 1969. "Objectives and Instruction." In W. J. Popham et al., *Instructional Objectives*. Skokie, Ill.: Rand McNally, pp. 32–52.

Popham, W. J. 1970a. "The Instructional Objectives Exchange: New Support for Criterion-Referenced Instruction," *Phi Delta Kappan, 52*, 174–175.

Popham, W. J. 1970b. "The Instructional Objectives Exchange: Progress and Prospects." Paper presented at the Annual Meeting of the American Educational Research Association, Minneapolis, Minn.

Popham, W. J. 1972. *Criterion-Referenced Measurement*. Englewood Cliffs, N.J.: Educational Technology Publications.

Popham, W. J. 1975. *Educational Evaluation*. Englewood Cliffs, N.J.: Prentice-Hall.

Popham, W. J., and T. R. Husek. 1969. "Implications of Criterion-Referenced Measurement," *Journal of Educational Measurement, 6*, 1–10.

Porter, J. W. 1971. "The Future of Accountability." In *Proceedings of the Conferences on Educational Accountability*. Princeton, N.J.: Educational Testing Service.

Powell, J. C., and A. C. Isbister. 1974. "A Comparison between Right and Wrong Answers on a Multiple-Choice Test," *Educational and Psychological Measurement, 34*, 499–509.

Prediger, D. J. 1971. *Converting Test Data to Counseling Information*. ACT Research Report No. 44. Iowa City, Iowa: The American College Testing Program.

Prediger, D. J., and G. R. Hanson. 1974. "The Distinction between Sex Restrictiveness and Sex Bias in Interest Inventories," *Measurement and Evaluation in Guidance, 7*, 96–104.

The President's Commission on Higher Education. 1947. *Higher Education for American Democracy*, vol. I, *Establishing the Goals*. Washington, D.C.: Government Printing Office.

Pressley, M. M. 1976. "Inflation Hits the Campuses," *Wall Street Journal*, Jan. 21.

Provus, M. 1971. *Discrepancy Evaluation for Educational Program Improvement and Assessment*. Berkeley, Calif.: McCutchan Publishing Corporation.

Psychological Corporation. 1976. *Catalog of Educational Tests and Services*. New York: The Psychological Corporation.

Public Law 93-380. 1974. August 21.

Pugh, R. C., and J. J. Brunza. 1975. "Effects of Confidence Weighted Scoring System on Measures of Test Reliability and Validity," *Educational and Psychological Measurement, 35*, 73–78.

Pyrczak, F. 1974. "Passage Dependency Items Designed to Measure the Ability to Identify the Main Ideas of Paragraphs: Implications for Validity," *Educational and Psychological Measurement, 34*, 343–348.

Pyrczak, F. 1976. "Context-Dependence of Items Designed to Measure the Ability to Derive the Meanings of Words from Their Context." Paper presented at the Annual Meeting of the National Council on Measurement in Education. San Francisco, Calif.

Quann, C. J. 1970. "Pass–Fail Grading: What Are the Trends?" Paper presented at the meeting of the American Association of Collegiate Registrars and Admissions Officers, New Orleans, La.

Quana, C. J. 1974. "Pass–Fail Grading—An Unsuccess Story," *College and University*, Spring, 230–235.

Quereshi, M. Y. 1974. "Performance on Multiple-Choice Tests and Penalty for Guessing," *Journal of Experimental Education, 42*, 74–77.

Raffeld, P. 1975. "The Effects of Guttman Weights," *Journal of Educational Measurement, 12*, 179–185.

Rakow, E. A. 1974. "Item Statistics: Are They Sufficiently Stable across Small Samples to Reject Defective Test Items?" Paper presented at the Annual Meetiing of the National Council on Measurement in Education, Chicago, Ill.

Ramos, R. A., and J. Stern. 1973. "Item Behavior Associated with Changes in the Number of Alternatives in Multiple-Choice Items," *Journal of Educational Mesaurement, 10*, 305–310.

Ramseyer, G. C., and V. M. Cashen. 1971. "The Effect of Practice Sessions on the Use of Separate Answer Sheets by First and Second Graders," *Journal of Educational Measurement, 8*, 177–182.

Rapaport, S., M. Gill, and R. Shafer. 1946. *Diagnostic Psychological Testing*, vol. II. Chicago: Year Book Medical Publishers.

Reckase, M. D. 1975. "The Effect of Item Choice on Ability Estimation When Using a Simple Logistic Tailored Testing Model." Paper presented at the Annual Meeting of the American Educational Research Association, Washington, D.C.

Reile, P. J., and L. J. Briggs. 1952. "Should Students Change Their Initial Answers on Objective Tests?: More Evidence Regarding an Old Problem," *Journal of Educational Psychology, 43*, 110–115.

Reiling, E., and R. Taylor. 1972. "A New Approach to the Problem of Changing Initial Responses to Multiple-Choice Questions," *Journal of Educational Measurement, 9*, 67–70.

Reilly, R. R. 1975. "Empirical Option Weighting with a Correction for Guessing," *Educational and Psychological Measurement, 35*, 613–619.

Remmers, H. H. 1954. *Introduction to Opinion and Attitude Measurement*. New York: Harper & Row.

Remmers, H. H., N. L. Gage, and J. F. Rummel. 1965. *A Practical Introduction to Measurement and Evaluation* (2d ed.). New York: Harper & Row.

Report of the Commission on Tests: I. Righting the Balance. 1970. New York: College Entrance Examination Board.

Resnick, L. B. (ed.). 1976. *The Nature of Intelligence*. Hillsdale, N.J.: Lawrence Erlbaum Associates.

Reynolds, C., and N. Cobean. 1976. "Constructing an Edumetric Test." Paper presented at the Annual Meeting of the National Council on Measurement in Education, San Francisco, Calif.

Ricks, J. H. 1959. *On Telling Parents about Test Results*, Test Service Bulletin No. 54. New York: The Psychological Corporation.

Romano, L. 1959. "The Parent-Teacher Conference," *National Education Association Journal*, 48, 21–22.

Rorer, L. G. 1965. "The Great Response-Style Myth," *Psychological Bulletin*, 62, 129–156.

Rose, H. A., and C. F. Elton. 1971. "Sex and Occupational Choice," *Journal of Counseling Psychology*, 18, 456–461.

Rosenthal, R., and L. Jacobson. 1968. *Pygmalion in the Classroom*. New York: Holt, Rinehart and Winston.

Ross, C. C., and J. C. Stanley. 1954. *Measurement in Today's Schools* (3d ed.). Englewood Cliffs, N.J.: Prentice-Hall.

Rossman, J. E. 1970. "Graduate School Attitudes to S-U Grades," *Educational Record*, 51, Summer, 310–313.

Roueche, J. E., and Herscher, B. R., 1973. *Toward Instructional Accountability: A Practical Guide to Educational Change*. Palo Alto, Calif.: Westinghouse Learning Press.

Rowley, G. L. 1974. "Which Examinees Are Most Favored by the Use of Multiple-Choice Tests?" *Journal of Educational Measurement*, 11, 15–23.

Rowley, G. L., and R. Traub. 1977. "Formula Scoring, Number-Right Scoring, and Test Taking Strategy," *Journal of Educational Measurement*, 14, 15–22.

Rubin, R. A. 1974. "Preschool Application of the Metropolitan Readiness Tests: Validity, Reliability, and Preschool Norms," *Educational and Psychological Measurement*, 34, 417–422.

Rulon, P. J., D. V. Tiedeman, M. M. Tatsuoka, and C. R. Langmuir. 1967. *Multivariate Statistics for Personnel Classification*. New York: Wiley.

Russell, D. H. 1953. "What Does Research Say about Self-Evaluation?" *Journal of Educational Research*, 46, 561–573.

Russell Sage Foundation. 1970. *Guidelines for the Collection, Maintenance & Dissemination of Pupil Records*. New York: Russell Sage.

Rutkowski, K., and G. Domino. 1975. "Interrelationship of Study Skills and Personality Variables in College Students," *Journal of Educational Psychology*, 67, 784–789.

Ryan, J. A. 1968. "Teacher Judgments of Test-Item Properties," *Journal of Educational Measurement*, 5, 301–306.

Ryan, J. P., and D. W. Hamm. 1976. "Practical Procedures for Increasing Reliability of Classroom Tests by Using the Rasch Model." Paper presented at the Annual Meeting of the National Council on Measurement in Education, San Francisco, Calif.

Sabers, D. L., and L. S. Feldt. 1968. "An Empirical Study of the Effect of the Correction for Chance Success on the Reliability and Validity of an Aptitude Test," *Journal of Educational Measurement*, 5, 251–258.

Samuda, R. J. 1975. *Psychological Testing of American Minorities*. New York: Dodd, Mead.

Sarason, H., K. Hill, and P. Zimbardo. 1964. "A Longitudinal Study of the Relation of Test Anxiety to Performance on Intelligence and Achievement Tests," *Monographs of the Society for Research in Child Development*, 29(7), Serial no. 98.

Saretsky, G. 1973. "The Strangely Significant Case of Peter Doe," *Phi Delta Kappan*, 54, 589–592.

Sassenrath, J. M. 1975. "Theory and Results on Feedback and Retention," *Journal of Educational Psychology*, 67, 894–899.

Sawin, E. I. 1969. *Evaluation and the Work of the Teacher*. Belmont, Calif.: Wadsworth.

Sax, G., and L. S. Collet. 1968. "The Effects of Differing Instructions and Guessing Formulas on Reliability and Validity," *Educational and Psychological Measurement*, 28, 1127–1136.

Sax, G., and T. R. Cromack. 1966. "The Effects of Various Forms of Item Arrangements on Test Performance," *Journal of Educational Measurement*, 3, 309–311.

Sax, G., and M. Reade. 1964. "Achievement as a Function of Test Difficulty Level," *American Educational Research Journal*, 1, 22–25.

Scannell, D. P., and J. C. Marshall. 1966. "Effect of Selected Composition Errors on Grades Assigned to Essay Examinations," *American Educational Research Journal*, 3, 125–130.

Schittjer, C. J., and C. M. Cartledge. 1976. "Item Analysis Programs: A Comparative Investigation of Performance," *Educational and Psychological Measurement*, 36, 183–187.

Schmeiser, C. B., and D. R. Whitney. 1975. "Effect of Two Selected Item-Writing Practices on Test Difficulty, Discrimination, and Reliability," *Journal of Experimental Education*, 43, 30–34.

Schoenfeldt, L. F. 1968. "An Empirical Comparison of Various Procedures for Estimating Heritability." Paper presented at the Annual Meeting of the American Psychological Association.

Schutz, R. E. 1971. "The Role of Measurement in Education: Servant, Soulmate, Stoolpigeon, Statesman, Scapegoat, All of the Above, and/or None of the Above," *Journal of Educational Measurement*, 8, 141–146.

Schwartz, A. A., and D. Tiedeman. 1957. *Evaluating Student Progress in the Secondary School*. New York: McKay.

Schwartz, J. 1955. *Pictorial Test Items in the Ground Equipment Maintenance (304) Career Field Ladder*, Evaluation Report 5515. 2200th Test Squadron, Mitchell Air Force Base, N.Y.

Scott, W. A. 1968. "Attitude Measurement." In G. Lindzey (ed.), *Handbook of Social Psychology*, Volume II. Reading, Mass.: Addison-Wesley.

Scriven, M. 1967. "The Methodology of Evaluation." In Ralph Tyler et al., *Perspectives of Curriculum Evaluation*. AERA Monograph Series on Curriculum Evaluation, No. 1. Skokie, Ill.: Rand McNally, pp. 39–83.

Scriven, M. 1973. "Goal-Free Evaluation." In E. House (ed.), *School Evaluation: The Politics and Process*. Berkeley, Calif.: McCutchan Publishing Corporation, pp. 319–328.

Scriven, M. 1975. *Evaluation Bias and Its Control*, Occasional Paper No. 4. Kalamazoo, Mich.: Evaluation Center, College of Education, Western Michigan University.

Seashore, H. 1959. Quoted in *Newsweek*, July 20, p. 93.

Sechrest, L. 1963. "Incremental Validity: A Recommendation," *Educational and Psychological Measurement*, 23, 153–158.

Servey, R. E. 1966. "The Effects of the Situation on the Quality of Children's Writing." Unpublished Ph.D. dissertation. University of Southern California, Los Angeles, Calif.

Severy, L. J. 1974. *Procedures and Issues in the Measurement of Attitudes*, TM Report 30. Princeton, N.J.: ERIC Clearinghouse on Tests, Measurement, and Evaluation.

Shaffer, M. 1976. "The Use of Item-Favorability Data as Evidence of Sex Bias in Interest Inventories." Paper presented at the Annual Meeting of the National Council on Measurement in Education, San Francisco, Calif.

Shanker, A. 1971. "Possible Effects on Instructional Programs." *Proceedings of the Conference on Educational Accountability*. Princeton, N.J.: Educational Testing Service, pp. F1-F11.

Shannon, G. A. 1975. "The Construction of Matching Tests: An Empirical Statement." Paper presented at the Annual Meeting of the National Council on Measurement in Education, Washington, D.C.

Shapiro, A. H. 1975. "Heat, Ethnic Differences, and Creativity in the Negev Desert," *Journal of Educational Psychology*, 67, 183–187.

Sharf, R. S. 1971. "A Computer-based Report for the Strong Vocational Interest Blank for Women," *Measurement and Evaluation in Guidance*, 4, 9–17.

Shaw, M. E. 1973. *A Theory of Attitudes*. Unpublished manuscript. University of Florida, Gainesville.

Shaw, M. E., and J. M. Wright. 1967. *Scales for the Measurement of Attitudes.* New York: McGraw-Hill.

Sheldon, W. H., et al. 1940. *The Varieties of Human Physique.* New York: Harper & Row.

Sheriffs, A. C., and D. S. Boomer. 1954. "Who Is Penalized by the Penalty for Guessing?" *Journal of Educational Psychology,* 45, 81–90.

Sherman, S. W. 1976. "Multiple-Choice Test Bias Uncovered By Use of An 'I Don't Know' Alternative." Paper presented at the Annual Meeting of the American Educational Research Association, San Francisco, Calif.

Shimuzu, T. 1965. "The Assumption of the Equal Probability of Chance Success," *Journal of Psychology,* 36, 295–301.

Shockley, W. 1971. "Models, Mathematics, and the Moral Obligation to Diagnose the Origin of Negro I.Q. Deficits," *Review of Educational Research,* 41, 369–377.

Shockley, W. 1972. "Dysgenics, Geneticity, Raciology: Challenges to the Intellectual Responsibility of Educators," *Phi Delta Kappan,* 53, 297–307.

Sieber, S. D., and D. E. Wilder. 1967. "Teaching Styles: Parental Preference and Professional Role Definitions," *Sociology of Education,* 40, Fall, 302–315.

Siegel, L. 1963. In R. H. Bauernfeind, *Building a School Testing Program.* Boston: Houghton Mifflin, p. 306.

Simpson, E. J. 1966. "The Classification of Educational Objectives: Psychomotor Domain," *Illinois Teacher of Home Economics,* 10(4), 110–144.

Sims, V. M. 1931. "The Objectivity, Validity, and Reliability of an Essay Examination Graded by Rating," *Journal of Educational Research,* 24, 216–223.

Sirontnik, K., and R. Wellington. 1974. "Scrambling Content in Achievement Testing: An Application of Multiple-Matrix Sampling in Experimental Design," *Journal of Educational Measurement,* 11, 179–188.

Slakter, M. J. 1968a. "The Penalty for Not Guessing," *Journal of Educational Measurement,* 5, 141–144.

Slakter, M. J. 1968b. "The Effect of Guessing Strategy on Objective Test Scores," *Journal of Educational Measurement,* 5, 217–221.

Slakter, M. J. 1970. "Learning Test-Wiseness by Programmed Texts," *Journal of Educational Measurement,* 7, 247–253.

Slakter, M. J., D. D. Crehan, and R. A. Koehler. 1975. "Longitudinal Studies of Risk-Taking on Objective Examinations," *Educational and Psychological Measurement,* 35, 97–105.

Slakter, M. J., R. A. Koehler, and S. H. Hampton. 1970. "Grade Level, Sex, and Selected Aspects of Test Wiseness," *Journal of Educational Measurement,* 7, 119–122.

Slakter, M. J., R. A. Koehler, S. H. Hampton, and R. I. Grennell. 1971. "Sex, Grade Level, and Risk-Taking on Objective Examinations," *Journal of Experimental Education,* 39, 65–68.

Smith, A., and J. C. Moore. 1976. "The Effects of Changing Answers on Scores of Non-Sophisticated Test Takers," *Measurement and Evaluation in Guidance,* 8, 252–254.

Smith, A. E. 1963. In R. H. Bauernfeind, *Building a School Testing Program.* Boston: Houghton Mifflin, p. 308.

Smith, R. B. 1968. "An Empirical Examination of the Assumptions Underlying the Taxonomy of Educational Objectives: Cognitive Domain," *Journal of Educational Measurement,* 5, 125–128.

Smith, R. B. 1970. "An Empirical Investigation of Complexity and Process in Multiple-Choice Items," *Journal of Educational Measurement,* 7, 33–42.

Sockloff, A. L., and A. C. Papacostas. 1975. "Uniformity of Faculty Attitude," *Journal of Educational Measurement,* 12, 281–293.

Solomon, R. J. 1965. "Improving the Essay Test in the Social Studies." In H. Berg (ed.), *Evaluation in Social Studies, 35th Yearbook.* Washington, D.C.: National Council for the Social Studies, chap. 7.

Sorotnik , F., E. S. Fleming, and R. G. Anttonen. 1974. "Teacher Knowledge of Standardized Test Information and Its Effect on Pupil IQ and Achievement," *Journal of Experimental Education, 43,* 79–85.

Sparks, D. S. 1969. "Grading and Student Evaluation." Paper ED-036-261, presented at the Council of Graduate Schools in the United States, Washington, D.C.

Spearman, C. 1927. *The Abilities of Man.* New York: Macmillan.

Stahmann, R. F., and G. F. Matheson. 1973. "The Kuder as a Measure of Vocational Maturity," *Educational and Psychological Measurement, 33,* 477–479.

Stake, R. E. 1967a. "Countenance of Educational Evaluation," *Teachers College Record, 68,* 523–540.

Stake, R. E. 1967b. "Toward a Technology for the Evaluation of Educational Programs." In R. Tyler et al., *Perspectives of Curriculum Evaluation,* AERA Monograph Series on Curriculum Evaluation, No. 1. Chicago: Rand McNally, pp. 1–12.

Stake, R. E. 1975. *Program Evaluation, Particularly Responsive Evaluation,* Occasional Paper No. 5. Kalamazoo, Mich.: Evaluation Center, College of Education, Western Michigan University.

Stake, R. E., and T. Denny. 1969. "Needed Concepts and Techniques for Studying More Fully the Potential for Evaluation." In R. W. Tyler (ed.), *Educational Evaluation: New Roles, New Media. 68th Yearbook,* National Society for the Study of Education. Chicago: University of Chicago Press, pp. 370–390.

Stake, R. E., F. B. Womer, and J. R. Hills. 1966. "The Answer Sheet Purchaser's Dilemma," *Journal of Educational Measurement, 3,* 269–276.

Stallings, W. M., and E. K. Lesslie. 1970. "Student Attitudes toward Grades and Grading," *Improved College and University Teaching, 18,* Winter, 66–68.

Stallings, W. M., and H. R. Smock. 1971. "The Pass–Fail Grading Option at a State University: A Five Semester Evaluation," *Journal of Educational Measurement, 8,* 153–160.

Stalnaker, J. M. 1936. "A Study of Optional Questions on Examinations," *School and Society, 44,* 829–832.

Stalnaker, J. M. 1938. "Weighting Questions in the Essay Type Examination," *Journal of Educational Psychology, 29,* 481–490.

Stalnaker, J. M. 1951. "The Essay Type of Examination." In E. F. Lindquist (ed.), *Educational Measurement.* Washington, D.C.: American Council on Education, pp. 495–530.

Stanley, J. C. 1960. "Review of the Stanford-Binet," *Personnel Guidance Journal, 39,* 226–227.

Stanley, J. C. 1964. *Measurement in Today's Schools* (4th ed.). Englewood Cliffs, N.J.: Prentice-Hall.

Stanley, J. C. 1969. "Reactions to the March Article on Significant Differences," *Educational Researcher, 20*(5), 8–9.

Stanley, J. C. 1971a. "Predicting College Success of the Educationally Disadvantaged," *Science, 171,* February 19, 640–647.

Stanley, J. C. 1971b. "Reliability." In R. L. Thorndike (ed.), *Educational Measurement* (2d ed.). Washington, D.C.: American Council on Education.

Stanley, J. C., and A. C. Porter. 1967. "Correlation of Scholastic Aptitude Test Scores with College Grades for Negroes versus Whites," *Journal of Educational Measurement. 1967, 4,* 199–218.

Stanley, J. C., and M. D. Wang. 1970. "Weighting Test Items and Test Item Options, an Overview of the Analytical and Empirical Literature," *Educational and Psychological Measurement, 30,* 21–35.

Starch, D., and E. C. Elliott. 1912. "Reliability of Grading High School Work in English," *School Review, 20,* 442–457.

Starch, D., and E. C. Elliott. 1913a. "Reliability of Grading High School Work in Mathematics," *School Review, 21,* 254–259.

Starch, D., and E. C. Elliott. 1913b. "Reliability of Grading High School Work in History Studies," *School Review, 21,* 676–681.

State Educational Assessment Programs. 1973. Princeton, N.J.: Educational Testing Service.

Stevens, S. S. 1946. "On the Theory of Scales of Measurement," *Science, 103,* 677–680.

Stoddard, G. D. 1943. *The Meaning of Intelligence.* New York: Macmillan.

Storey, A. G. 1966. "Review of Evidence for the Case against the True-False Item," *Journal of Educational Research, 59,* 282–285.

Stott, L. H., and R. S. Ball. 1965. "Infant and Preschool Mental Tests: Review and Evaluation," *Monographs of Social Research in Child Development, 30*(3), 151.

Strassberg-Rosenberg, B., and T. F. Donlon. 1975. "Content Influences on Sex Differences in Performance on Aptitude Tests." Paper presented at the Annual Meeting of the National Council on Measurement in Education, Washington, D.C.

Strong, E. K. 1966. *Vocational Interest Blank for Men.* Stanford, Calif.: Stanford University Press.

Stroud, J. B. 1946. *Psychology in Education.* New York: McKay.

Stufflebeam, D. L. 1974. *Meta-Evaluation,* Occasional Paper No. 3. Kalamazoo, Mich.: Evaluation Center, College of Education, Western Michigan University.

Stufflebeam, D. L., et al. 1971. *Educational Evaluation and Decision Making.* Bloomington, Ind.: Phi Delta Kappa, 1971.

Sturgis, P. T. 1973. "Information Delay and Retention: Effect of Information in Feedback and Tests," *Journal of Educational Psychology, 63,* 32–43.

Subkoviak, M. J. 1976. "Estimating Reliability from a Single Administration of a Mastery Test," *Journal of Educational Measurement, 13,* 265–276.

Summers, G. F. (ed.). 1970. *Attitude Measurement.* Skokie, Ill.: Rand McNally.

Super, D. E. (ed.). 1970. *Computer-Assisted Counseling.* New York: Columbia University, Teachers College.

Super, D. E. 1972. "The Future of Vocational Development Theory." In J. M. Whitely, (ed.), *Perspectives in Vocational Development.* Washington, D.C.: American Personnel and Guidance Association.

Super, D. E., M. J. Bohn, D. J. Forrest, J. P. Jordaan, R. H. Lindeman, and A. A. Thompson. 1972. *Career Development Inventory.* New York: Columbia University, Teachers College.

Super, D. E., and J. O. Crites. 1962. *Appraising Vocational Fitness by Means of Psychological Tests* (rev. ed.). New York: Harper & Row.

Supplement, *Journal of Educational Measurement,* 1967, 4(1), 1–31.

Surber, J. R., and R. C. Anderson. 1975. "Delay-Retention Effect in Natural Classroom Settings," *Journal of Educational Psychology, 67,* 170–173.

Swaminathan, H., R. K. Hambleton, and J. Algina. 1974. "Reliability of Criterion-Referenced Tests: A Decision Theoretic Formulation," *Journal of Educational Measurement, 11,* 263–267.

Swaminathan, H., R. K. Hambleton, and J. Algina. 1975. "A Bayesian Decision-Theoretic Procedure for Use with Criterion-Referenced Tests," *Journal of Educational Measurement, 12,* 87–98.

Sweigert, R. L. 1968a. "Need Assessment—The First Step toward Deliberate Rather than Impulsive Response to Problems." California State Dept. of Education.

Swineford, F. 1956. *Test Analysis of CEEB Tests of Developed Ability.* Princeton, N.J.: Educational Testing Service.

Swineford, F., and P. M. Miller. 1953. "Effects of Directions Regarding Guessing on Item Statistics of a Multiple-Choice Vocabulary Test," *Journal of Educational Psychology, 44,* 129–139.

Tannenbaum, A. J. 1965. "Review of the Culture-Fair Intelligence Tests." In O. K. Buros (ed.), *The Sixth Mental Measurements Yearbook.* Highland Park, N.J.: Gryphon Press.

Tanney, M. F. 1974. "Face Validity of Interest Measures: Sex Role Stereotyping." Paper presented at the National Institute of Education Workshop on Sex Bias and Sex Fairness in Career Interest Inventories, Arlington, Va.

Taylor, P. A., and D. M. Cowley. 1972. *Readings in Curriculum Evaluation.* Dubuque, Iowa: William C. Brown.

Teachers Opinion Poll. 1974. *Today's Education,* 63(2), 4.

Temp, G. 1971. "Validity of the SAT for Blacks and Whites in Thirteen Integrated Institutions," *Journal of Educational Measurement, 8,* 245–252.

Terman, L. M. 1916. *The Measurement of Intelligence.* Boston: Houghton Mifflin.

Terman, L. M., and M. A. Merrill. 1937. *Measuring Intelligence.* Boston: Houghton Mifflin.

Terman, L. M., and M. A. Merrill. 1960. *Stanford-Binet Intelligence Scale: Manual for the Third Revision,* Form L-M. Boston: Houghton Mifflin.

Terry, P. W. 1933. "How Students Review for Essay and Objective Tests," *Elementary School Journal, 33,* 592–603.

Terwilliger, J. S. 1971. *Assigning Grades to Students.* Glenview, Ill.: Scott, Foresman.

Thomas, C. L., and J. C. Stanley. 1969. "Effectiveness of High School Grades for Predicting College Grades of Black Students: A Review and Discussion," *Journal of Educational Measurement, 6,* 203–216.

Thorndike, R. L. 1971a. "Concepts of Cultural Fairness," *Journal of Educational Measurement, 8,* 63–70.

Thorndike, R. L. 1971b. "Reproducing the Test." In R. L. Thorndike (ed.), *Educational Measurement.* Washington, D.C.: American Council on Education.

Thorndike, R. L. (ed.). 1971c. *Educational Measurement.* Washington, D.C.: American Council on Education.

Thorndike, R. L. 1975. "Mr. Binet's Test 70 Years Later," *Educational Researcher,* 4(5), 3–7.

Thorndike, R. L., and E. Hagen. 1977. *Measurement and Evaluation in Psychology and Education* (4th ed.). New York: Wiley.

Thurstone, L. L. 1933. *The Theory of Multiple Factors.* Privately published.

Thurstone, L. L., and E. J. Chave. 1929. *The Measurement of Attitude.* Chicago: University of Chicago Press.

Tilton, J. W. 1951. *Educational Psychology of Learning.* New York: Macmillan.

Tinkelman, S. N. 1971. "Planning the Objective Test." In R. L. Thorndike (ed.), *Educational Measurement.* Washington, D.C.: American Council on Education.

Tinkelman, S. L. 1975. *Improving the Classroom Test: A Manual of Test Construction Procedures for the Classroom Teacher.* Albany: New York State Department of Education.

Tinsley, H. E. A., and D. J. Weiss. 1975. "Interrater Reliability and Agreement of Subjective Judgments," *Journal of Counseling Psychology, 22,* 358–376.

Tittle, C. K. 1973. "Minimizing Sex Bias in Interest Measurement through the Context of Testing and Interpretive Materials." Paper presented at the Annual Meeting of the American Personnel and Guidance Association, New Orleans, La.

Tittle, C. K. 1974. "Sex Bias in Educational Measurement: Fact or Fiction," *Measurement and Evaluation in Guidance, 6,* 219–227.

Toenjes, C. M., and F. H. Borgen. 1974. "Validity Generalization of Holland's Hexagonal Model," *Measurement and Evaluation in Guidance, 7,* 79–85.

"Too Many A's." 1974. *Time,* November 11, p. 206.

Torgerson, T. L., and G. S. Adams. 1954. *Measurement and Evaluation,* Hinsdale, Ill.: Dryden.

Torrance, E. P. 1962. *Guiding Creative Talent.* Englewood Cliffs, N.J.: Prentice-Hall.

Torrance, E. P. 1965. *Reward Creative Behavior.* Englewood Cliffs, N.J.: Prentice-Hall.

Towle, N. J., and P. F. Merrill. 1975. "Effects of Anxiety Type and Item-Difficulty Sequencing on Mathematics Test Performance," *Journal of Educational Measurement, 12,* 241–250.

Traub, R. E., and C. W. Fisher. (n.d.) *On the Equivalence of Constructed-Response and Multiple-Choice Tests.* Toronto, Canada: Ontario Institute for Studies in Education.

Traub, R. E., and R. K. Hambleton. 1972. "The Effect of Scoring Instructions and Degree of Speededness on the Validity and Reliability of Multiple-Choice Tests," *Educational and Psychological Measurement, 32,* 737–758.

Traub, R. E., R. K. Hambleton, and B. Singh. 1969. "Effects of Promised Reward and Threatened Penalty on Performance on a Multiple-Choice Vocabulary Test," *Educational and Psychological Measurement, 29,* 847–861.

Travers, R. M. W. 1955. *Educational Measurement.* New York: Macmillan.

Traxler, A. E. 1951. "Administering and Scoring the Objective Test." In E. F. Lindquist (ed.), *Educational Measurement.* Washington, D.C.: American Council on Education.

Trent, J. W., and A. M. Cohen. 1973. "Research on Teaching in Higher Education." In R. M. W. Travers (ed.), *Second Handbook of Research on Teaching.* Chicago: Rand McNally, 997–1071.

Trentham, L. L. 1975. "The Effect of Distractions on Sixth Grade Students in a Testing Situation," *Journal of Educational Measurement, 12,* 13–17.

Tuinman, J. J. 1974. "Determining the Passage Dependence of Comprehension Questions in Five Major Tests," *Reading Research Quarterly, 9,* 206–223.

Tversky, A. 1964. "On the Optimal Number of Alternatives of a Choice Point," *Journal of Mathematical Psychology, 1,* 386–391.

Tye, K. A. 1971. "Educational Accountability in an Era of Change." In L. H. Browder, Jr. (ed.), *Emerging Patterns of Administrative Accountability.* Berkeley, Calif.: McCutchan Publishing Corporation.

Tyler, L. E. 1976. "The Intelligence We Test." Chapter 2 in L. B. Resnick (ed.), *The Nature of Intelligence,* Hillsdale, N.J.: Lawrence Erlbaum Associates.

Tyler, R. W. 1933. "Tests in Biology," *School Science and Mathematics, 33.*

Tyler, R. W. 1950. *Basic Principles of Curriculum and Instruction.* Chicago: University of Chicago Press.

Tyler, R. W. 1958. "The Education of Teachers: A Major Responsibility of Colleges and Universities," *The Educational Record, 39,* 253–261.

Tyler, R. W. et al. 1967. *Perspectives of Curriculum Evaluation,* AERA Monograph Series on Curriculum Evaluation, No. 1. Skokie, Ill.: Rand McNally.

The Use of Multifactor Tests in Guidance. 1957. A reprint series from *Personnel Guidance Journal.* Washington, D.C.: American Personnel and Guidance Association.

Vallance, T. R. 1947. "Comparison of Essay and Objective Examinations as Learning Experiences," *Journal of Educational Research, 41,* 279–288.

Van Der Kamp, L. J. 1973. "Thurstone Revisited: Multidimensional Similarity Sealing of Attitude toward the Church," *Educational and Psychological Measurement, 33,* 577–586.

Van De Kamp, L. J., and G. D. Mellenbergh. 1976. "Agreement between Raters." *Educational and Psychological Measurement, 36,* 311–317.

Vargas, J. S. 1972. *Writing Worthwhile Behavioral Objectives.* New York: Harper & Row.

Vernon, P. E. 1961. *The Structure of Human Abilities* (2d ed.). London: Methuen.

Vernon, P. E. 1964. "Creativity and Intelligence," *Journal of Educational Research, 6,* 163–169.

Vernon, P. E., and G. D. Millican. 1954. "A Further Study of the Reliability of English Essays," *British Journal of Statistical Psychology, 7,* 64–74.

Wagner, E. E., and T. O. Hoover. 1974. "The Effect of Serial Position on Ranking Error," *Educational and Psychological Measurement, 34,* 289–293.

Wakefield, J. A., and E. B. Doughtie. 1973. "Personality Types and the VPI," *Journal of Consulting Psychology, 20,* 513–518.

Waks, L. J. 1969. "Philosophy, Education, and the Doomsday Threat," *Review of Educational Research, 39,* 607–622.

Wallach, M. A., and N. Kogan. 1965. *Modes of Thinking in Young Children,* New York: Holt, Rinehart and Winston.

Walter, L. J. 1970. "COMBAT: A System Now in Operation." Paper presented at the Annual Meeting of the National Council on Measurement in Education, Minneapolis, Minn.

Warren, J. R. 1970. "College Grading Practices: An Overview." Princeton, N.J.: Educational Testing Service.

Warren, J. R. 1975. *The Continuing Controversy over Grades*, TM Report 51, ERIC Clearinghouse on Tests, Measurement, and Evaluation. Princeton, N.J.: Educational Testing Service.

Warrington, W. G. 1973. "Student Evaluation of Instruction at Michigan State University." In A. L. Sockloff (ed.), *Proceedings: Faculty Effectiveness as Evaluated by Students*. Philadelphia: Measurement and Research Center, Temple University.

Washburne, C. W. 1922. "Educational Measurements as a Key to Individualizing Instruction and Promotions," *Journal of Educational Research*, 5, 195–206.

Washington, W. N., and R. R. Godfrey. 1974. "The Effectiveness of Illustrated Items." *Journal of Educational Measurement*, 11, 121–124.

Wason, P. 1961. "Response to Affirmative and Negative Binary Statements," *British Journal of Psychology*, 52, 133–142.

Waters, B. K. 1975. *Empirical Investigation of the Stratadative Testing Model for the Measurement of Human Ability*. Williams AFB, Ariz.: Air Force Human Resources Laboratory.

Waters, C. W., and L. K. Waters. 1976. "Validity and Likability Ratings for Three Scoring Instructions for a Multiple-Choice Vocabulary Test," *Educational and Psychological Measurement*, 31, 935–938.

Waters, L. K. 1967. "Effects of Perceived Scoring Formula on Some Aspects of Test Performance," *Educational and Psychological Measurement*, 27, 1005–1010.

Webb, E. J., et al. 1966. *Unobtrusive Measures: Nonreactive Research in the Social Sciences*. Skokie, Ill.: Rand McNally.

Webb, S. C. 1955. "Scaling of Attitudes by the Method of Equal-Appearing Intervals," *Journal of Social Psychology*, 42, 215–239.

Webster's Seventh New Collegiate Dictionary. 1965. Springfield, Mass.: Merriam.

Wechsler, D. 1944. *The Measurement of Adult Intelligence*. Baltimore: Williams & Wilkins, p. 3.

Wechsler, D. 1955. *Wechsler Adult Intelligence Scale, Manual*. New York: The Psychological Corporation.

Wechsler, D. 1958. *The Measurement and Appraisal of Adult Intelligence* (4th ed.). Baltimore: Williams & Wilkins.

Weidemann, C. C. 1933. "Written Examination Procedures," *Phi Delta Kappan*, 16, October.

Weiner, B., and A. Kukla. 1970. "An Attributional Analysis of Achievement Motivation," *Journal of Personality and Social Psychology*, 15, 1–20.

Weiner, B., and P. Potepan. 1970. "Personality Characteristics of Superior and Failing College Students," *Journal of Educational Psychology*, 61, 144–151.

Weiner, D. N. 1948. "Subtle and Obvious Keys for the Minnesota Multiphasic Personality Inventory," *Journal of Consulting Psychology*, 12, 164–170.

Weiss, C. H. 1973. "Where Politics and Evaluation Research Meet." *Evaluation*, 1(3), 37–45.

Weiss, D. J. 1976. *Computerized Ability Testing 1972–1975*, Final Report of Project NR150-343, NOO 14-67-A-0113-0029. Minneapolis: University of Minnesota.

Weiss, R. M., and G. R. Rasmussen. 1960. "Grading Practices in Undergraduate Education Courses," *Journal of Higher Education*, 31, 143–149.

Welch, W. W., and H. J. Walberg. 1972. "A National Experiment in Curriculum Evaluation," *American Educational Research Journal*, 9, 373-384.

Werts, C. E., K. G. Joreskog, and R. L. Linn. 1976. "Analyzing Ratings with Correlated

Intrajudge Measurement Errors," *Educational and Psychological Measurement, 36,* 319–328.

Wesman, A. G. 1952. "Faking Personality Test Scores in a Simulated Employment Situation," *Journal of Applied Psychology, 36,* 112–113.

Wesman, A. G. 1971. "Writing the Test Item." In R. L. Thorndike (ed.), *Educational Measurement.* Washington, D.C.: American Council on Education.

Wesman, A. G., and G. K. Bennett. 1946. "The Use of 'None of These' as an Option in Test Construction," *Journal of Educational Psychology, 37,* 541–549.

Westbrook, B. W. 1974. "Content Analysis of Six Career Development Tests," *Educational and Psychological Measurement, 7,* 172–180.

Westbrook, B. W., and M. M. Mastie. 1973. "The Measurement of Vocational Maturity: A Beginning to Know About," *Measurement and Evaluation in Guidance, 6,* 8–16.

Westbrook, B. W., and J. W. J. Parry-Hill. 1973. "The Measurement of Cognitive Vocational Maturity," *Journal of Vocational Behavior, 3*(3).

Wexley, K. N., and C. L. Thornton. 1972. "Effect of Verbal Feedback of Test Results Upon Learning," *Journal of Educational Research, 66,* 119–121.

Whalen, T. E. 1971. "The Analysis of Essays by Computer: A Simulation of Teacher Ratings." Paper presented at the Annual Meeting of the American Educational Research Association, Chicago, Ill.

Whitely, S. E., and R. V. Dawis. 1976. "The Influence of Test Context on Item Difficulty," *Educational and Psychological Measurement, 36,* 329–337.

Wicker, W. A. 1969. "Attitudes Versus Actions: The Relationship of Verbal and Overt Behavioral Responses to Attitude Objects," *Journal of Social Issues, 25,* 41–78.

Wilbur, P. H. 1965. "Positional Response Set in the Multiple-Choice Examination." Unpublished Ph.D. dissertation. University of Southern California, Los Angeles, Calif.

Wilhelms, F. T. (ed.). 1967. *Evaluation as Feedback and Guide.* Washington, D.C.: Association for Supervision and Curriculum Development, 1967.

Will, G. F. 1976. "D is for Dodo," *Newsweek,* February 9, p. 84.

Willis, S. L. 1973. "Formations of Teachers' Expectations of Students' Academic Performance, *Dissertation Abstracts,* May.

Williams, B. G., and R. L. Ebel. 1957. "The Effect of Varying the Number of Alternatives per Item on Multiple-Choice Vocabulary Test Items." In *Fourteenth Yearbook of the National Council on Measurements Used in Education.* Princeton, N.J.: NCMUE, pp. 122–125.

Williams, R. L. 1974. "Stimulus/Response: Scientific Racism and IQ—The Silent Mugging of the Black Community," *Psychology Today, 7,* 12, 32, 34, 37–38, 41, 101.

Williamson, M. L., and K. D. Hopkins. 1967. "The Use of 'None of These' versus Homogeneous Alternatives on Multiple-Choice Tests: Experimental Reliability and Validity Comparisons," *Journal of Educational Measurement, 4,* 53–58.

Wissler, C. 1961. "The Correlation of Mental and Physical Tests." In J. J. Jenkins and D. G. Paterson (eds.), *Studies in Individual Differences.* New York: Appleton, p. 43.

Wittrock, M. C. 1970. "The Evaluation of Instruction: Cause-and-Effect Relations in Naturalistic Data." In M. C. Wittrock and D. E. Willey, *The Evaluation of Instruction: Issues and Problems.* New York: Holt, Rinehart and Winston.

Wittrock, M. C., and D. E. Wiley. 1970. *The Evaluation of Instruction: Issues and Problems.* New York: Holt, Rinehart and Winston.

Wolf, R. 1969. "A Model for Curriculum Evaluation," *Psychology in the Schools, 6,* 107–108.

Wood, D. A. 1960. *Test Construction.* Columbus, Ohio: Merrill.

Wood, R. 1973. "Response-Contingent Testing," *Review of Educational Research, 43, 4,* 529–544.

Wood, R. 1976. "Inhibiting Blind Guessing: The Effect of Instructions," *Journal of Educational Measurement, 13,* 297–308.

Woodfin, M. J. 1966. *The Written Expression of Third Grade Children under Differing Time Limits.* Unpublished Ph.D. dissertation. University of Southern California, Los Angeles, Calif.

Woodfin, M. J. 1972. "Correlations among Certain Variables and the Quality of the Written Expression of Third Grade Children under Structured and Non-Structured Teaching Situations," *Educational and Psychological Measurement, 32,* 1099–1102.

Woodley, K. K. 1975. "Test-Wiseness: A Cognitive Function." Paper presented at the Annual Meeting of the National Council on Measurement in Education, Washington, D.C.

Woodson, M. I. C. E. 1974. "The Issue of Item and Test Variance for Criterion-Referenced Tests," *Journal of Educational Measurement, 11,* 63–64.

Worthen, B. R. 1975. "Competencies for Educational Research and Evaluation," *Educational Researcher, 4*(1), 13–16.

Worthen, B., and J. R. Sanders. 1973. *Educational Evaluation: Theory and Practice.* Worthington, Ohio: Charles R. Jones Publishing Company.

Wrightstone, J. W., T. P. Hogan, and M. M. Abbott. 1972. "Accountability in Education and Associated Measurement Problems." *Test Service Notebook 33.* New York: Harcourt Brace Jovanovich.

Yamamoto, K., and H. F. Dizney. 1965. "Effects of Three Sets of Test Instructions on Scores on an Intelligence Scale," *Educational and Psychological Measurement, 25,* 87–94.

Yarborough, B. H., C. C. Raper, and M. M. Clark. 1976. "A Study of the Validity of the Use of Visual-Motor Tests as Indicators of Pupil Readiness for Reading." Paper presented at the Annual Meeting of the National Council on Measurement in Education, San Francisco, Calif.

Yelon, S. L., and R. O. Scott. 1970. *A Strategy for Writing Objectives.* Dubuque, Iowa: Kendall/Hunt.

Young, D. 1962. "Examining Essays for Eleven-plus Classification," *British Journal of Educational Psychology, 32,* 267–274.

Zern, D. 1967. "Effects of Variations in Question Phrasing on True-False Answers by Grade School Children," *Psychological Reports, 20,* 527–533.

Zimbardo, P., and E. B. Ebbesen. 1970. *Influencing Attitudes and Changing Behavior.* Reading, Mass.: Addison-Wesley.

Zytowski, D. G. 1972. "Equivalence of the Kuder Occupational Survey and the Strong Vocational Interest Blank Revisited," *Journal of Applied Psychology, 56,* 184–185.

Zytowski, D. G. (ed.). 1973. *Contemporary Approaches to Interest Measurement.* Minneapolis: University of Minnesota Press.

Index of Names

Index of Subjects